HMH SOCIAL STUDIES

WORLD HISTORY

Teacher's Guide

Educational Advisory Panel

The following educators provided ongoing review during the development of prototypes and key elements of this program.

Jose Colon
Berkeley High School
Berkeley, California

Bethany Copeland
Peach County High School
Fort Valley, Georgia

Darrel Dexter
Egyptian Community Unit School
Tamms, Illinois

Charles Dietz
Burnett Middle School
San Jose, California

John Hogan
Brevard High School
Brevard, North Carolina

Jeffrey Kaufman
Aspirations Diploma Plus High School
Brooklyn, New York

Beth E. Kuhlman
Queens Metropolitan High School
Forest Hills, New York

Beatrice Nudelman
Aptakisic Junior High School
Buffalo Grove, Illinois

Kyle Race
Greene High School
Greene, New York

Gretchen Ritter Varela
Northville High School
Northville, Michigan

Sharon Shirley
Branford High School
Branford, Connecticut

Yvette Snopkowski
Davis Junior High School
Sterling Heights, Michigan

La-Shanda West
Cutler Bay Senior High School
Cutler Bay, Florida

Printed in the U.S.A.

ISBN 978-0-544-91591-6

2 3 4 5 6 7 8 9 10 0877 25 24 23 22 21 20 19 18 17

4500665783 B C D E F G

Table of Contents

Table of Contents

Module 30
The Colonies Become New Nations 1920–2005

Module 31
Struggles for Democracy 1945–Present

Table of Contents

Module 32
Global Interdependence 1960–2015

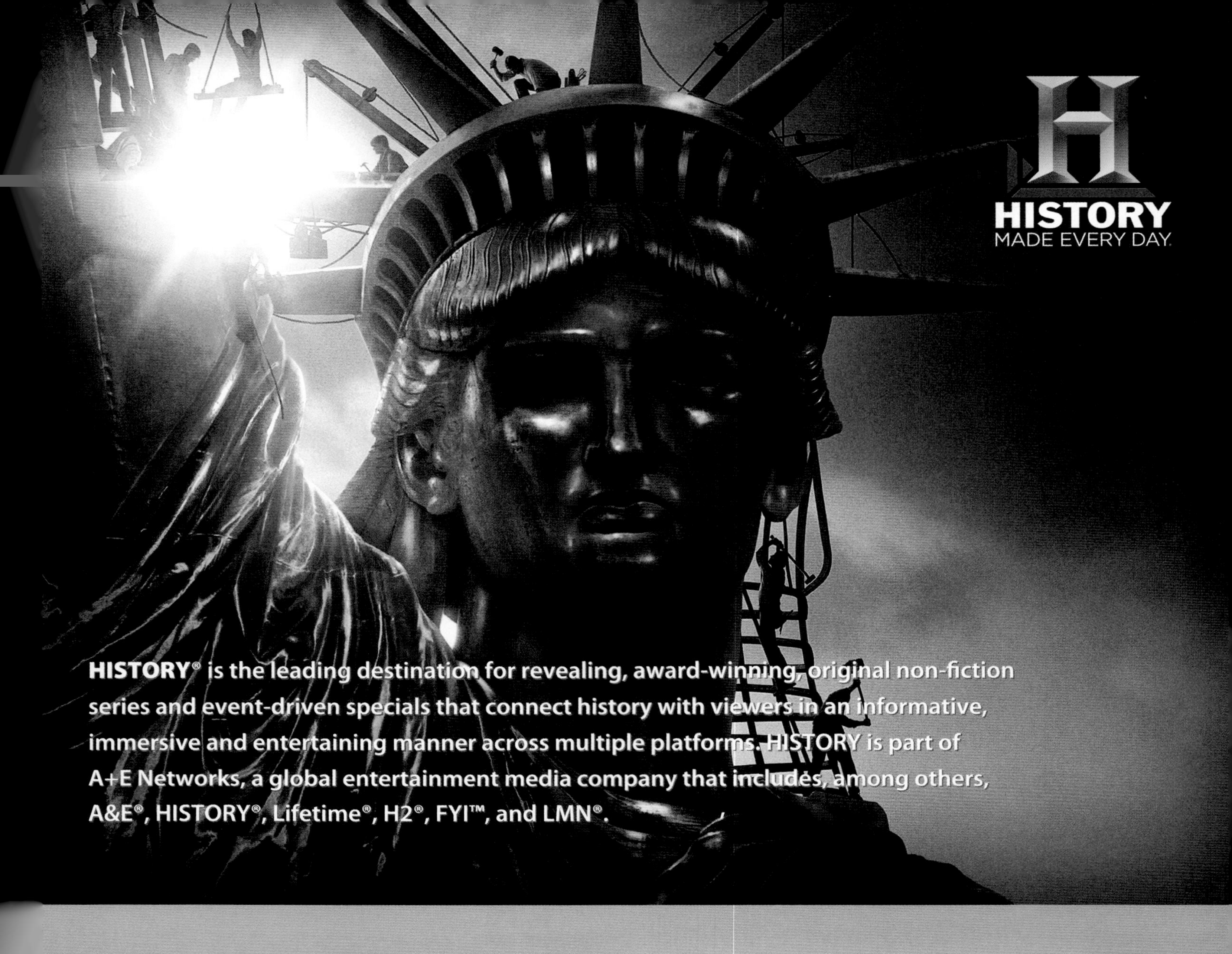

HISTORY programming greatly appeals to educators and young people who are drawn into the visual stories our documentaries tell. Our Education Department has a long-standing record in providing teachers and students with curriculum resources that bring the past to life in the classroom. Our content covers a diverse variety of subjects, including American and world history, government, economics, the natural and applied sciences, arts, literature and the humanities, health and guidance, and even pop culture.

The HISTORY website, located at **www.history.com**, is the definitive historical online source that delivers entertaining and informative content featuring broadband video, interactive timelines, maps, games, podcasts and more.

"We strive to engage, inspire and encourage the love of learning..."

Since its founding in 1995, HISTORY has demonstrated a commitment to providing the highest quality resources for educators. We develop multimedia resources for K–12 schools, two- and four-year colleges, government agencies, and other organizations by drawing on the award-winning documentary programming of A&E Television Networks. We strive to engage, inspire and encourage the love of learning by connecting with students in an informative and compelling manner. To help achieve this goal, we have formed a partnership with Houghton Mifflin Harcourt.

The Idea Book for Educators

Classroom resources that bring the past to life

Live webcasts

HISTORY Take a Veteran to School Day

In addition to premium video-based resources, **HISTORY** has extensive offerings for teachers, parents, and students to use in the classroom and in their in-home educational activities, including:

- ***The Idea Book for Educators*** is a biannual teacher's magazine, featuring guides and info on the latest happenings in history education to help keep teachers on the cutting edge.
- **HISTORY Classroom (www.history.com/classroom)** is an interactive website that serves as a portal for history educators nationwide. Streaming videos on topics ranging from the Roman aqueducts to the civil rights movement connect with classroom curricula.
- **HISTORY email newsletters** feature updates and supplements to our award-winning programming relevant to the classroom with links to teaching guides and video clips on a variety of topics, special offers, and more.
- **Live webcasts** are featured each year as schools tune in via streaming video.
- **HISTORY Take a Veteran to School Day** connects veterans with young people in our schools and communities nationwide.

In addition to **Houghton Mifflin Harcourt**, our partners include the *Library of Congress*, the *Smithsonian Institution, National History Day, The Gilder Lehrman Institute of American History*, the Organization of American Historians, and many more. HISTORY video is also featured in museums throughout America and in over 70 other historic sites worldwide.

Keeping the **Story** in History

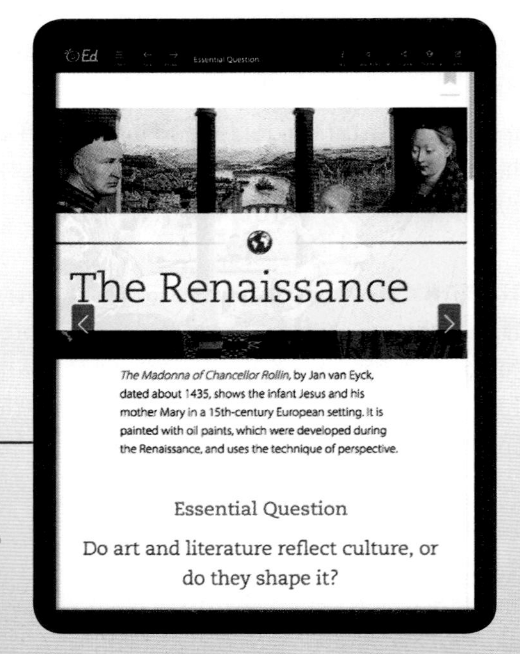

Houghton Mifflin Harcourt delivers a powerful and personal narrative to captivate students' curiosity and help them connect their learning to their lives and interests.

Essential Questions begin every Module in *HMH Social Studies World History* to help spark students' curiosity about the content.

HISTORY® Videos, introduced in Module openers, embedded within the narrative, and highlighted in Multimedia Connections, bring the content to life through primary source footage, dramatic storytelling, and expert testimonials.

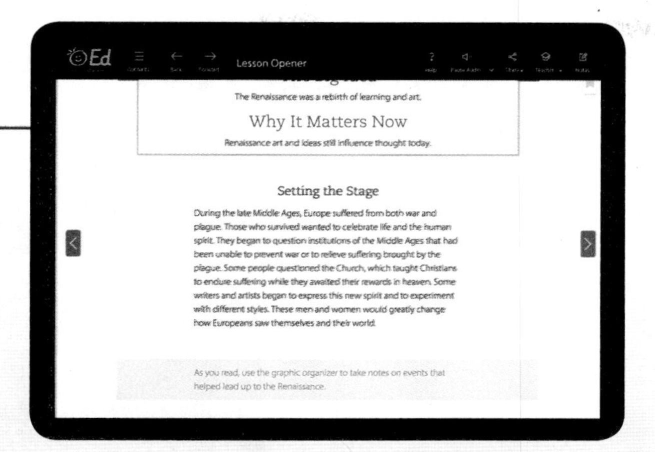

Setting the Stage Lesson introductions place lesson content in a broader historical context.

Interactive Features, Maps, and Games, at point of instruction in the Online Student Edition, provide quick entertaining activities and assessments that present important content in a fun way.

HMH Current Events gives students regularly updated articles organized by disciplinary themes on today's news of the day and offers access to safe, trustworthy news sources for further exploration and research. Combined with a subscription to Channel One News, the HMH Current Events site offers unparalleled access to the latest world developments tailored for students, helping them to connect what they learn in history class to the world around them.

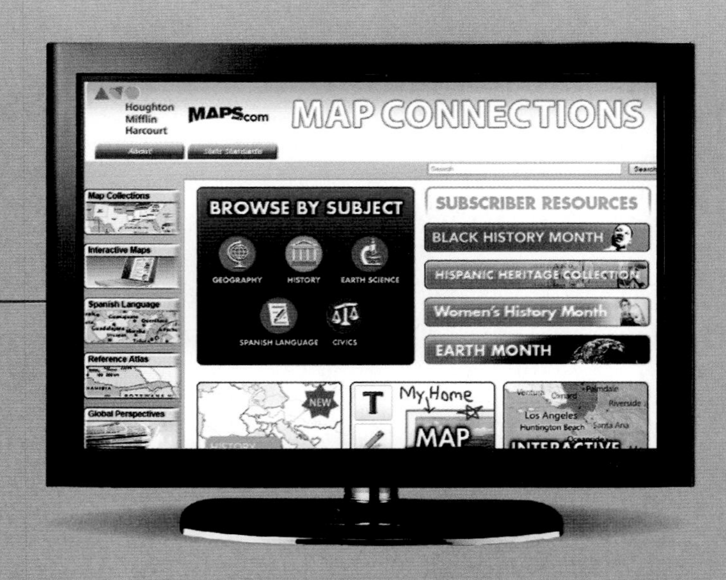

Map Connections, provided through a partnership with Maps.com, offers a wealth of resources, such as interactive maps, games, and data, to support geography instruction and using geography to tell the story of history.

image credits: *computer monitor* ©Yahia Loukkal/Fotolia; *Smart phone* ©Pixsooz/Alamy

Supporting **Inquiry** and **Active Learning**

HMH Social Studies offers the tools and support necessary to challenge students to approach history through active inquiry.

Online Student Edition

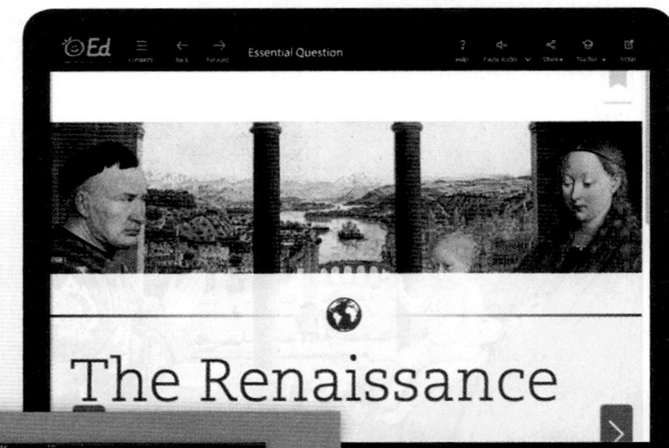

Essential Question Preview

Do art and literature reflect culture, or do they shape it?
Have students consider the Essential Question and capture their initial responses.

Essential Questions open every Module in *HMH Social Studies World History* to help students kick off the inquiry process by modeling the development of key questions. The **Teacher's Guide** provides support to help students create and answer supporting questions to driving their understanding of the Big Idea and Why it Matters Now for every Lesson.

Teacher's Guide

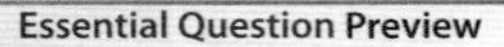

Essential Question Preview

Do art and literature reflect culture, or do they shape it?
Have students consider the Essential Question and capture their initial responses.

Explore the Essential Question

- Explore with students the difference between art and literature reflecting culture versus shaping it.
- Describe to students ways that art and literature reflect culture, using current examples of both to begin a discussion. For example, display images of street art and ask students how it reflects or shapes culture.

Help students plan inquiries and develop their own supporting questions such as

What new ideas and values led to the Renaissance?

How did humanism play a key role in the artistic achievements of the Renaissance?

You may want to assign students to write a short essay in response to the Essential Question when they complete the module. Encourage students to use their notes and responses to inform their essays.

Explore the Online Video

ANALYZE VIDEOS

Da Vinci's World
Invite students to watch the video to learn about the transformation of the world in which Leonardo da Vinci lived: Florence, Italy.

History What is the name of the family that restored Florence? *the Medici family*

Module 14

The Renaissance

Essential Question
Do art and literature reflect culture, or do they shape it?

About the Painting: *The Madonna of Chancellor Rollin*, painted by Jan van Eyck in about 1435, shows the infant Jesus and his mother Mary in a 15th-century European setting. It is painted with oil paints, which were developed during the Renaissance, and uses the technique of perspective.

Explore ONLINE!
VIDEOS, including...
- Da Vinci's World
- Da Vinci and the Code He Lived By

- Document Based Investigations
- Graphic Organizers
- Interactive Games
- Image Compare: Perspective
- Image with Hotspots: Printing Press

In this module you will learn how European society was revitalized as classical art and ideas were embraced and improved upon.

What You Will Learn ...

536 Module 14

Lesson 1 Big Idea
The Renaissance was a rebirth of learning and art.
Why It Matters Now
Renaissance art and ideas still influence thought today.

Lesson 2 Big Idea
The Italian Renaissance was a rediscovery of learning that produced many great works of art and literature.
Why It Matters Now
Renaissance art and literature still influence modern thought and modern art.

Lesson 3 Big Idea
In the 1400s, the ideas of the Italian Renaissance began to spread to northern Europe.
Why It Matters Now
Renaissance ideas such as the importance of the individual are an important part of modern thought.

Lesson 4 Big Idea
The Renaissance was a period of striking achievements in many areas.
Why It Matters Now
The achiev... writers, scie... affect peop...

536 Module 14

Lesson 2 Big Idea

The Italian Renaissance was a rediscovery of learning that produced many great works of art and literature.

Why It Matters Now
Renaissance art and literature still influence modern thought and modern art.

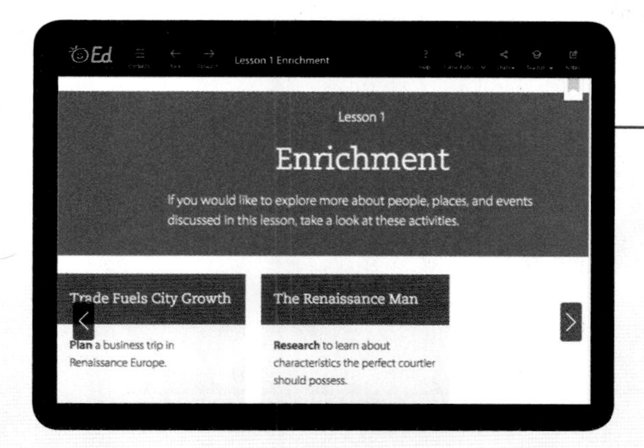

Enrichment Activities close every Lesson giving students an opportunity to explore additional topics in depth to deepen their understanding of the content studied and apply it actively in their community.

Document-Based Investigations build throughout every Module featuring documents in each Lesson with practice and short answers. In the Module Review, a unified Document-Based Investigation asks students to re-examine the featured documents and to draw upon the entire set of documents to demonstrate their understanding of the Module's main concepts through a presentation or essay.

Lesson DBI

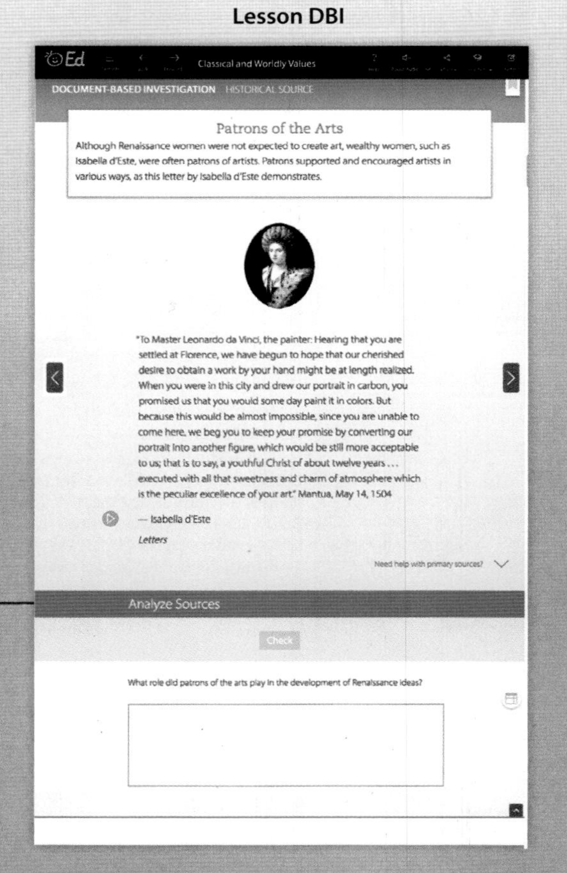

Module Review DBI

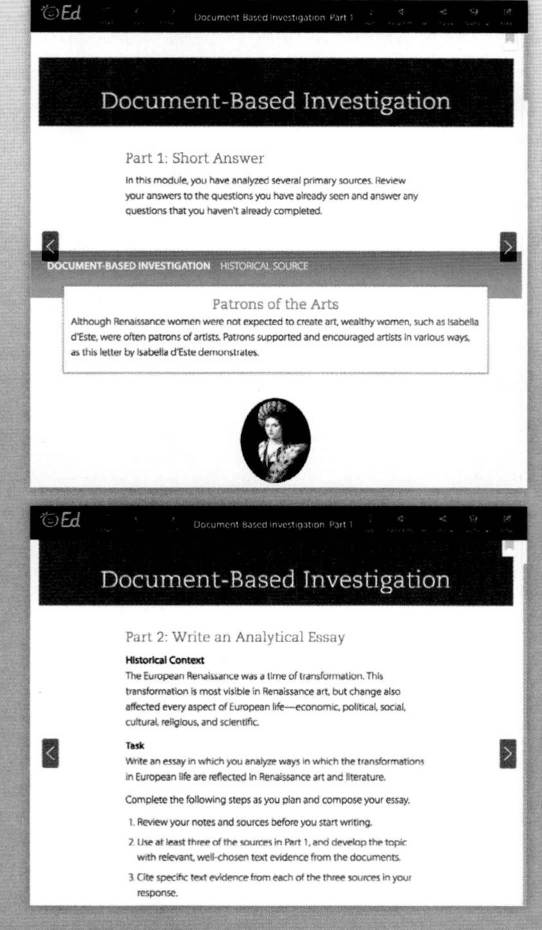

Skills Support links analyzing visuals, sources, writing, and other tasks accompany activities at point of use to help students tackle these challenging and critical social studies skills.

Program Highlights

Providing **Choice** and Supporting **Learning Needs**

HMH Social Studies World History *presents material and activities in a variety of ways to allow students and teachers to choose the path that works best for them. Differentiated instruction and assessments with built-in feedback provide support for all students.*

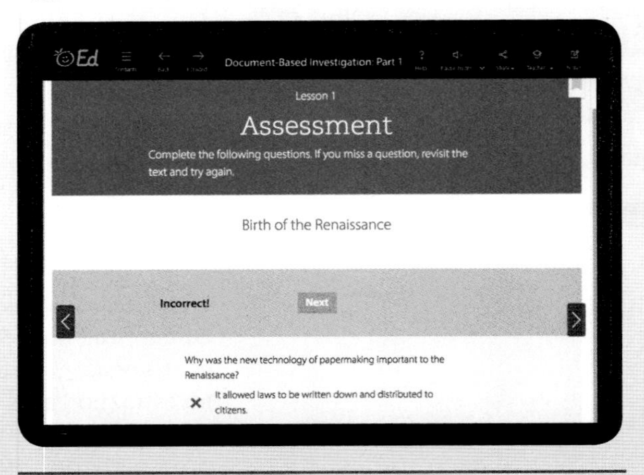

Lesson-Level Assessments serve to inform instruction rather than simply assign grades to students. If a student misses a question, the system gives them the option to pause, review instructional material, and then go back to their work. Teachers can further guide this process through reports on their students' performance, tied to standards and curriculum, to provide personalized intervention.

Differentiated Instruction Activities in the Teacher's Guide offer further options for varying lessons to meet the needs of every student.

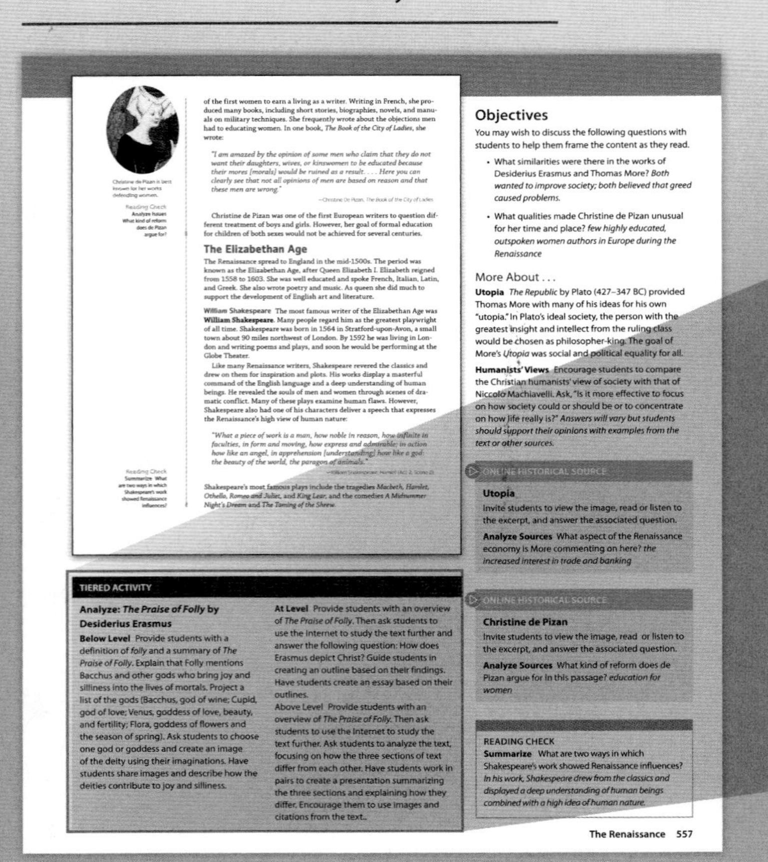

TIERED ACTIVITY

Analyze: *The Praise of Folly* by Desiderius Erasmus

Below Level Provide students with a definition of *folly* and a summary of *The Praise of Folly*. Explain that Folly mentions Bacchus and other gods who bring joy and silliness into the lives of mortals. Project a list of the gods (Bacchus, god of wine; Cupid, god of love; Venus, goddess of love, beauty, and fertility; Flora, goddess of flowers and the season of spring). Ask students to choose one god or goddess and create an image of the deity using their imaginations. Have students share images and describe how the deities contribute to joy and silliness.

At Level Provide students with an overview of *The Praise of Folly*. Then ask students to use the Internet to study the text further and answer the following question: How does Erasmus depict Christ? Guide students in creating an outline based on their findings. Have students create an essay based on their outlines.

Above Level Provide students with an overview of *The Praise of Folly*. Then ask students to use the Internet to study the text further. Ask students to analyze the text, focusing on how the three sections of text differ from each other. Have students work in pairs to create a presentation summarizing the three sections and explaining how they differ. Encourage them to use images and citations from the text..

Enrichment Activities at the end of every lesson provide avenues for students to stretch their curiosities and explore select topics in greater depth than called for by the standards.

Name ______________________ Class______________________ Date__________

The Renaissance

Lesson 1

Birth of the Renaissance

Key Terms and People

Renaissance period of rebirth of art and learning in Europe lasting from about 1300 to 1600

humanism focus on human potential and achievements

secular concerned with worldly rather than spiritual matters

patron person who financially supported artists

Before You Read

In the last lesson, you read about the development of the Incan Empire.

In this lesson, you will learn about the beginnings of the Renaissance.

As You Read

Use a chart to describe the cause-and-effect relationships that led to the birth of the Renaissance.

A TIME OF CHANGE

***What* factors led to the birth of the Renaissance?**

The years 1300 to 1600 saw a rebirth of learning and culture in Europe called the **Renaissance**. This rebirth involved an explosion of creativity in art, architecture, and writing. The Renaissance had its roots in an effort to bring back the culture of classical Greece and Rome. However, new ideas and values also developed and gained influence.

The Renaissance grew out of important changes in society, economics, learning, and politics. First, famine and disease caused Europe's population to become much smaller. With fewer people to feed, the general standard of living was higher. People were also becoming better educated. Second, an increase of trade led to the growth of a middle class made up of merchants, bankers, and tradespeople. People in the middle class had extra money to spend on luxuries. Third, Europeans also regained access to learning from classical times. Greek texts, which had been preserved by Byzantine and Islamic scholars, became more available. This spread of classical knowledge was helped along by the introduction of new technologies. Papermaking, for example, helped make possible the development of printing. The ability to create and store books led to the growth of libraries and the spread of knowledge. Finally, a long period of almost constant warfare was brought to a close. Peace returned to much of the continent

Guided Reading Workbook Lesson Summary

Note-Taking Support exists throughout the program:

- Within the **Modular Online Edition,** students can complete and save a graphic organizer for every Lesson.
- In print, the **Guided Reading Workbook** provides lesson summaries and note-taking templates that serve as scaffolds for learning.
- The **Spanish/English Guided Reading Workbook** supports students who are more proficient in Spanish with lesson summaries and note-taking templates in side-by-side Spanish and English language versions.

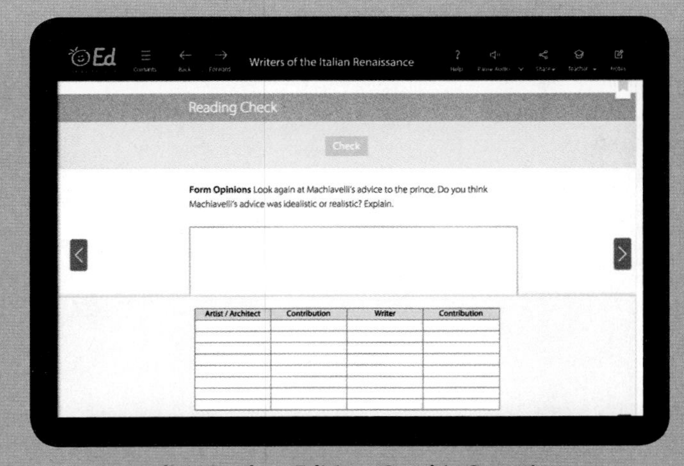

Online Student Edition: Graphic Organizer

image credit: *Smart phone* ©Pixsooz/Alamy

Giving the **Freedom** **To Teach** Your Way

Designed for flexibility, HMH Social Studies World History *provides resources in a variety of formats to allow you to easily address content in the manner that best fits students' needs and your instructional style.*

The **Teacher's Guide** serves as the starting point for teachers to blend their instruction how they see fit, with as much print and digital as they choose, and tying all of the program's pieces, such as the printed Student Edition and fully digital Modular Online Edition, together.

Lesson 1 Planner

Birth of the Renaissance

Video

Visuals

Maps, Graphs, and Charts

LESSON 1

Big Idea

The Renaissance was a rebirth of learning and art.

Extend and Enrich

Historical Sources

Assessment

- Islamic Cultural Influences in Spain

- **Map:** Europe, 1500

- **Biography:** Lorenzo de Medici
- Trade Fuels City Growth
- The Renaissance Man

- **Document-Based Investigation:** Patrons of the Arts
- Renaissance Man

- Key Terms Review
- Reading Check
- Graphic Organizer Activity
- Lesson Assessment

537a Module 14, Lesson 1

Built for maximum compatibility, *HMH Social Studies World History* provides digital resources with options to support various levels of connectivity and devices. The Modular Online Edition resides on a responsive platform enabling it to function across operating systems and devices. **The HMH Player App** allows students and teacher to download material, work offline, and re-sync with the system upon reconnecting.

Program Highlights

Flexible Assessment options appear at the Lesson, Module, and Benchmark levels. *HMH Social Studies World History* includes a robust writing strand to allow students to demonstrate their learning through a variety of essay types, such as informative and argumentative. Online assessments offer quizzes and tests that are scored automatically.

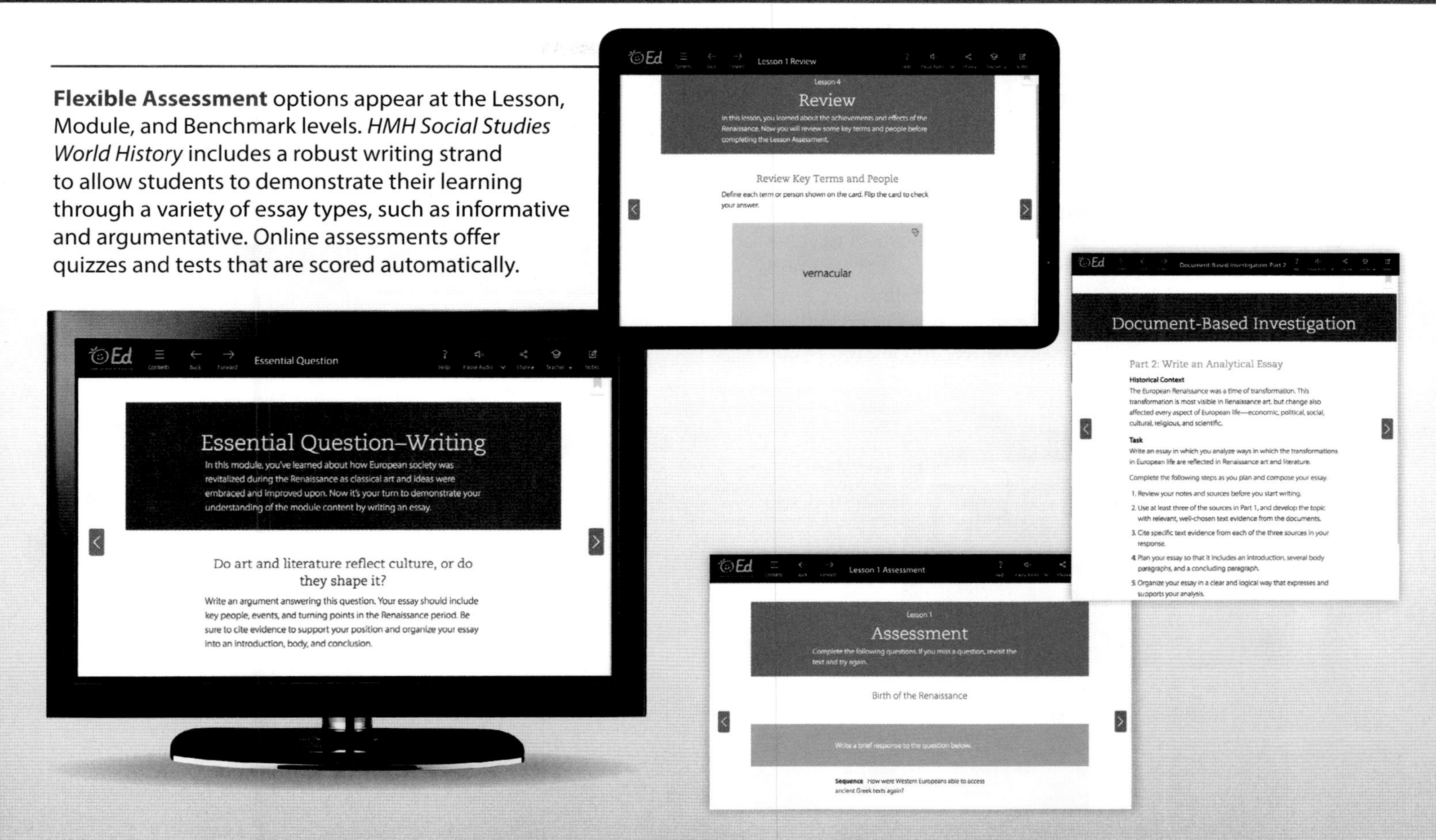

Flexible Arrangement with *HMH Social Studies World History's* modular format allows schools to purchase exactly the content that they want. While the material can always be bought with its full, pre-set table of contents, customers now also have the option to order individual Modules to build and sequence a program that follows their exact curriculum.

image credit: *computer monitor* ©Yahia Loukkal/Fotolia

Content Structure

In HMH Social Studies World History, *the structure of content is shared in digital and print. This enables seamless navigation and content synchronization whether digital, print, or both are used.*

Modules are the broadest content category and cover historical eras, seminal events, and/or essential Social Studies concepts and themes. Each Module opens with an Essential Question to spark student interest and provide connections between content and context. Rich imagery, HISTORY© videos, and timelines are also used to engage students. These elements are reinforced in the Module Review through essays and activities, and are followed by Module Assessments that gauge understanding.

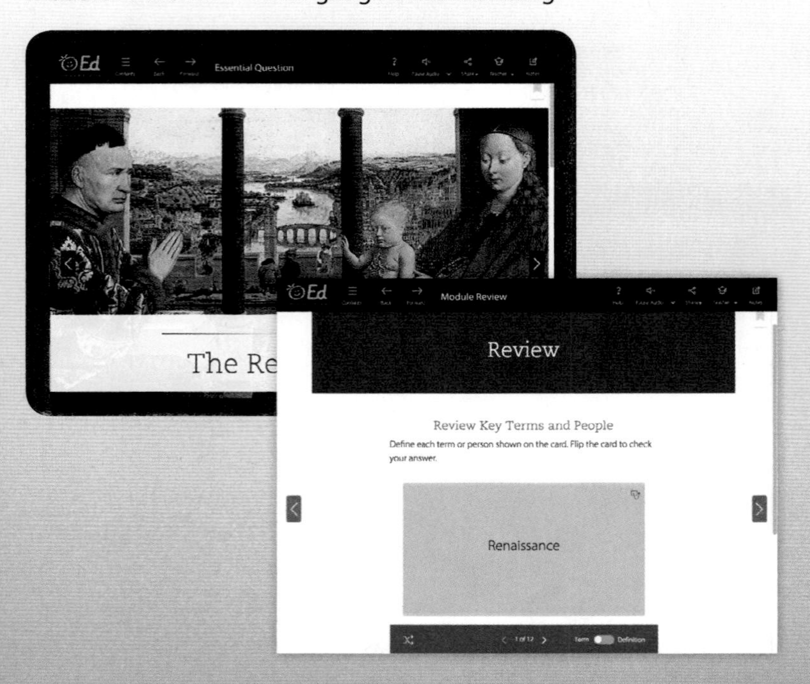

Lessons present Module content in focused, manageable divisions based on subtopics and/or contributing events. Each Lesson opens with a Big Idea, encapsulating the primary point of the Lesson. *Setting the Stage* places lesson content in a broader historical context. Key Terms and People are presented throughout Lessons, and graphic organizers and flipcards in Lesson Reviews prepare students for Lesson Assessments.

Segments organize Lesson content into discrete sections and are the smallest content category. Each segment ends with a Reading Check question to check comprehension.

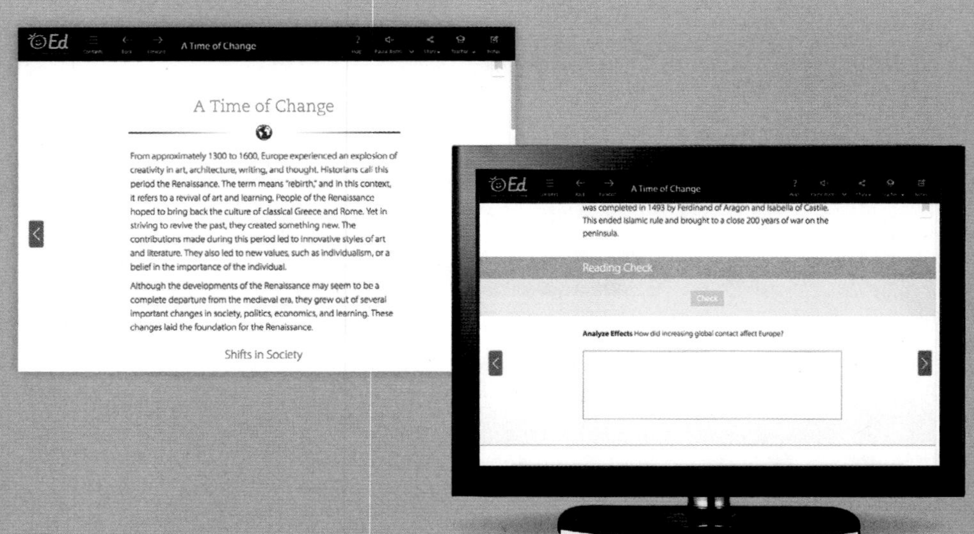

image credit: *computer monitor* ©Yahia Loukkal/Fotolia

Teacher's Guide

Content alignment allows instructors to use the print Teacher's Guide to steer instruction whether students are using digital, print, or both.

Lesson Planner

Module Planner

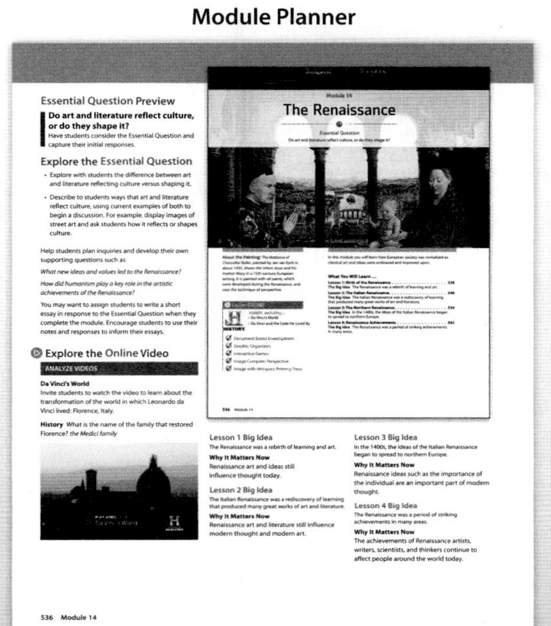

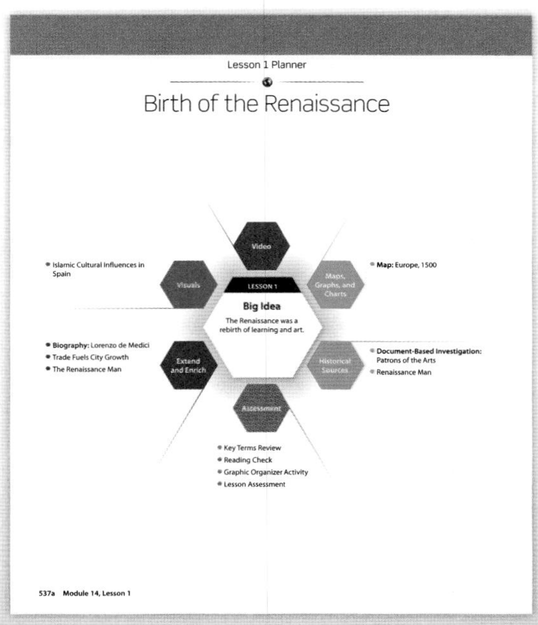

Planning is simplified through clean, at-a-glance planners detailing elements of Modules and Lessons. Color-coding visually identifies print-only components and organizes Module, Lesson, and Segment content.

Lesson Highlights

Module Highlights

Module and Lesson Highlights provide overviews of integral Module and Lesson elements. Features detailing overarching Module themes, skills instruction, whole class collaborative activities, and review tools including flipcards, graphic organizers, sequencing activities, and more are included.

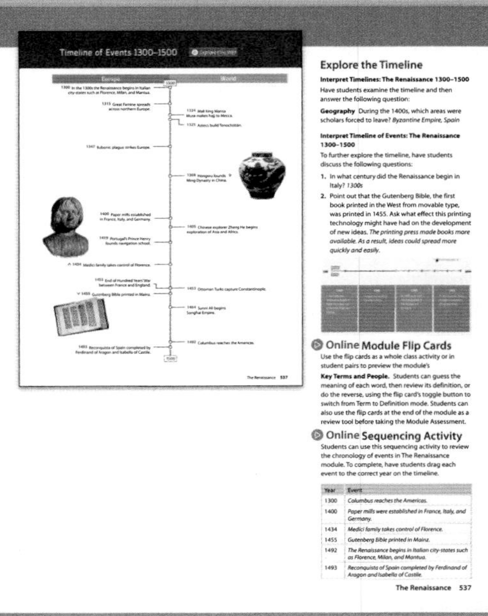

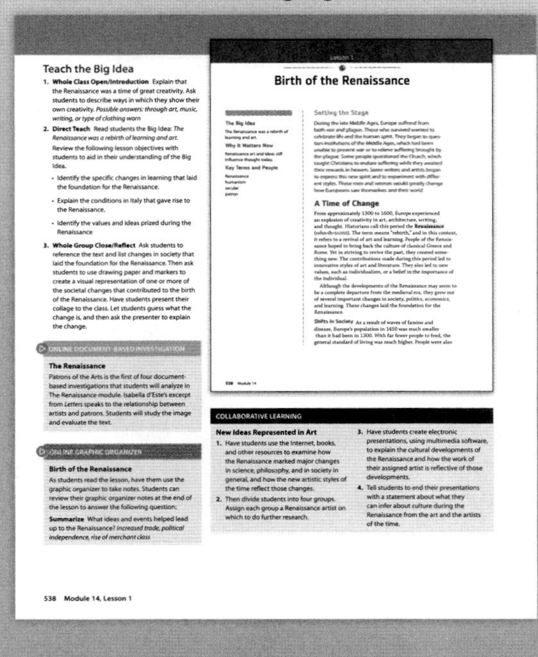

Instruction is presented at point of use for ease of navigation and discovery. Content extension, differentiated activities, instructor scaffolding, questions, answers, suggestions on engaging students, help with program features and more are all presented in sequence with student materials. The Teacher's Guide bridges student digital and print editions, providing seamless instruction for both environments.

Teacher's Guide: Core Instruction

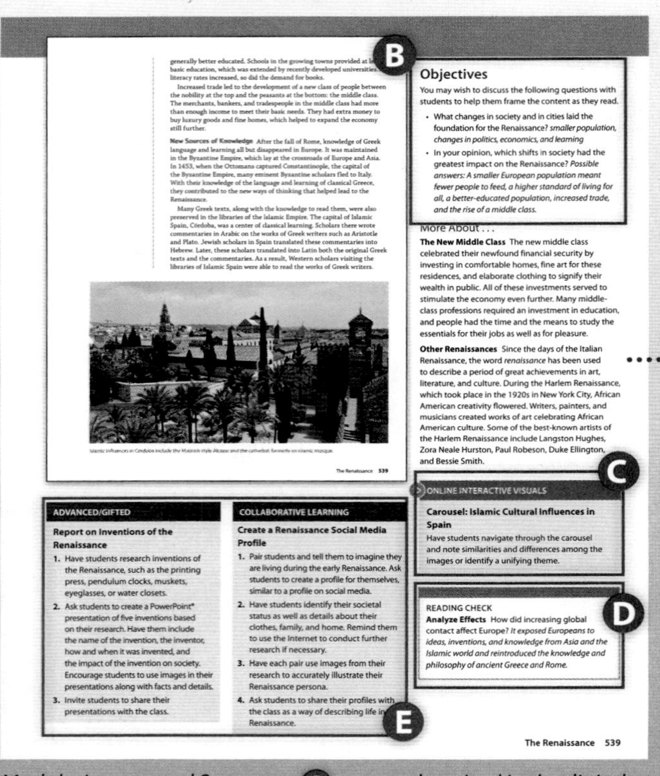

Module, Lesson, and Segments **A** *are synchronized in the digital and print student editions, so core instruction unpacking Big Ideas* **B** *serves both environments. Instruction for elements including visuals, maps, graphs, and Document-Based Investigations* **C** *is provided in the Teacher's Guide, and all elements are identified as digital, print, or shared. Assessment items and answers* **D** *are presented at point of use, and differentiated individual and whole-class activities* **E** *are provided throughout.*

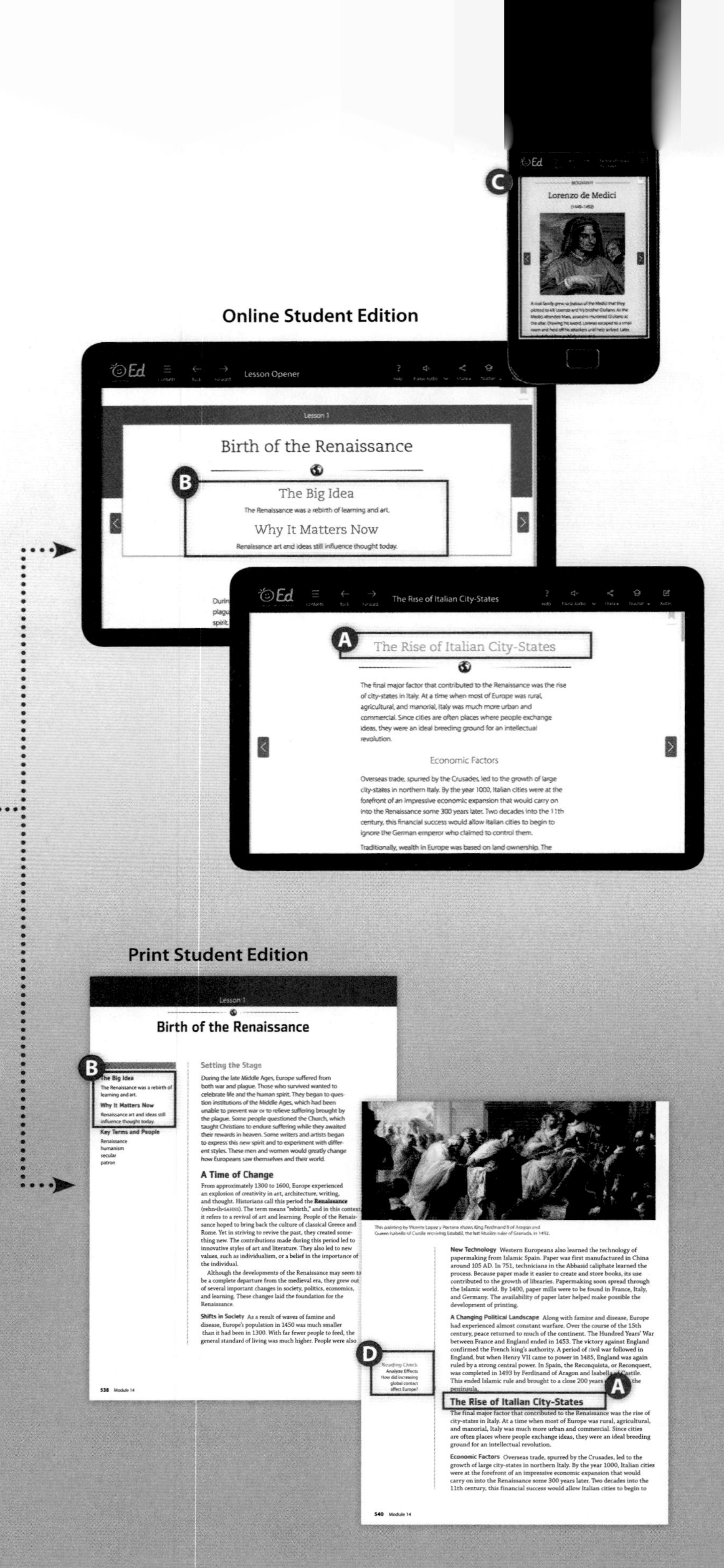

image credit: *Smart phone* ©Pixsooz/Alamy

Teacher eBook and Resources

HMH Social Studies World History instruction can also be accessed in a digital-only environment. Additional resources provide even more options and tools for instructors.

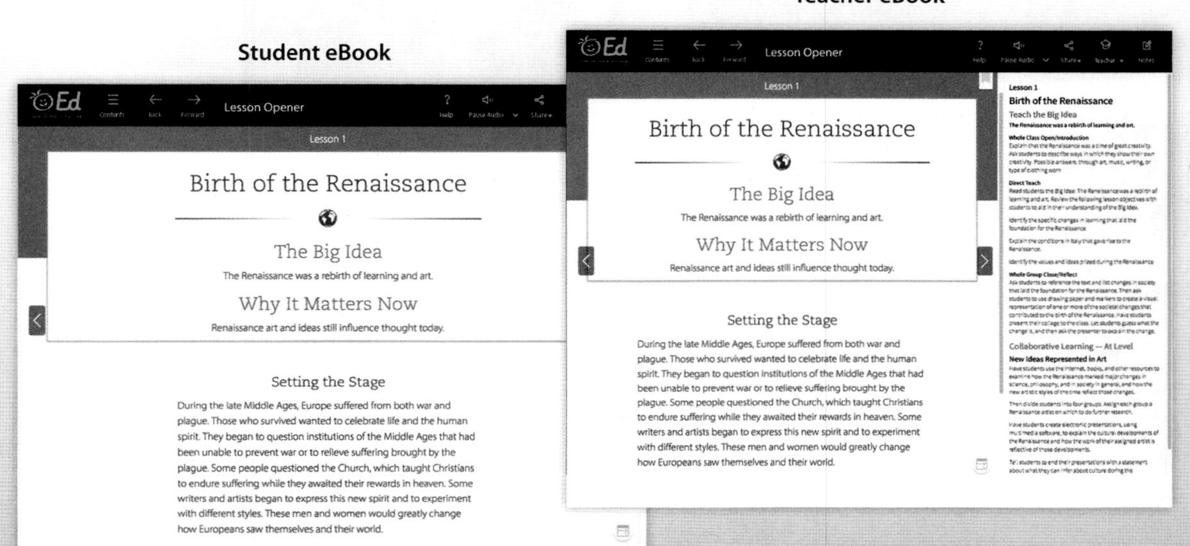

The Teacher eBook presents the same instructional content as the print Teacher's Guide, but is focused solely on digital content. In addition to core instruction provided in the print Teacher's Guide, links to completed graphic organizers, rubrics, and other resources are provided in the Teacher eBook overlay.

Resources beyond the Teacher's Guide and Teacher eBook include presentations, skills instruction, online assessments, rubrics, activities, and more. These resources supplement instruction, provide additional channels for differentiation, and aid in planning and delivery.

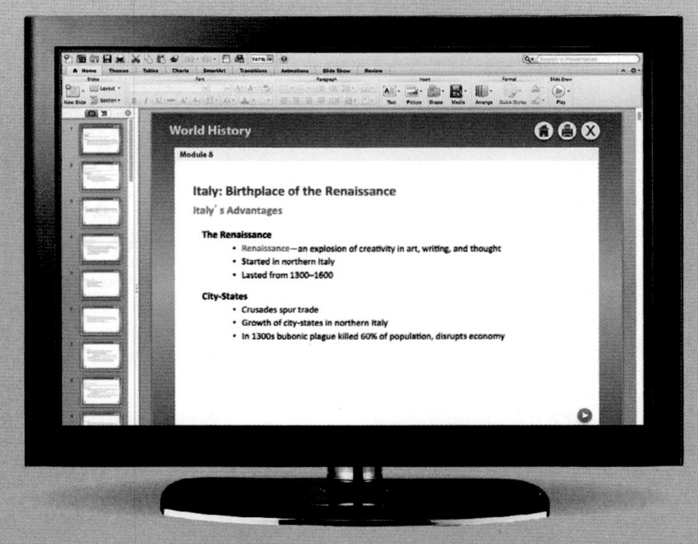

image credit: *computer monitor* ©Yahia Loukkal/Fotolia

HMH Social Studies World History
Dashboard

Designed for today's digital natives, ***HMH Social Studies*** offers you and your students a robust, intuitive online experience.

Your personalized Teacher Dashboard is organized into four main sections:

1. **Discover**—Quickly access content and search program resources
2. **Assignments**—Create assignments and track progress of assignments
3. **Data & Reports**—Monitor students' daily progress
4. **HMH Drive**—Personalize your experience and upload your own content

Houghton Mifflin Harcourt® is **changing** the way students **experience** social studies.

By delivering an immersive experience through compelling narratives enriched with media, we're connecting students to history through experiences that are energizing, inspiring, and memorable activities. The following pages highlight some digital tools and instructional support that will help students approach history through active inquiry so they can connect to the past while becoming active and informed citizens for the future.

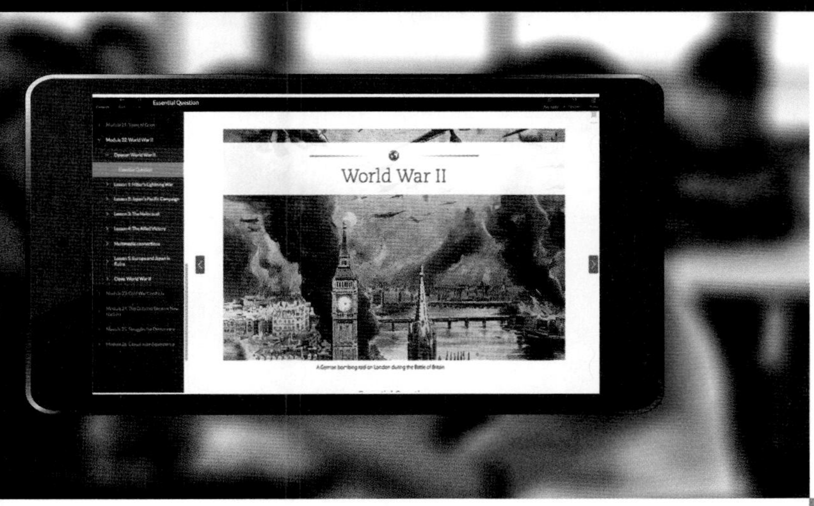

The Student eBook is the primary learning portal.

More than just the digital version of a textbook, the Student eBook serves as the primary learning portal for students. The narrative is supported by a wealth of multimedia and learning resources to bring history to life and give your students the tools they need to succeed.

Bringing Content to Life

HISTORY® videos and Multimedia Connections bring content to life through primary source footage, dramatic storytelling, and expert testimonials.

In-Depth Understanding

Close Read Screencasts model an analytical conversation about primary sources.

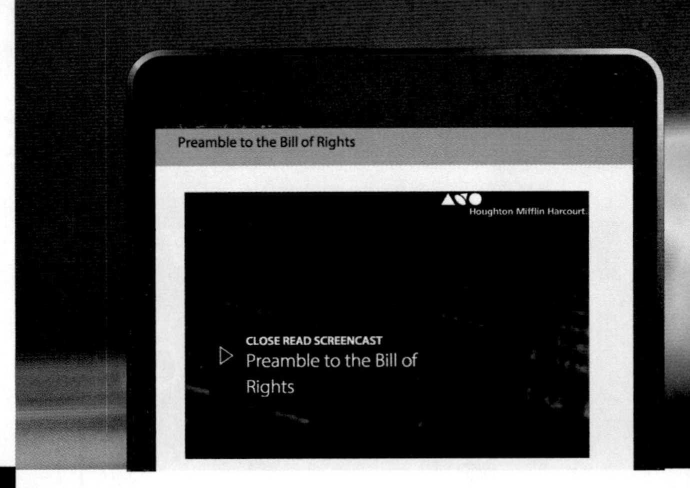

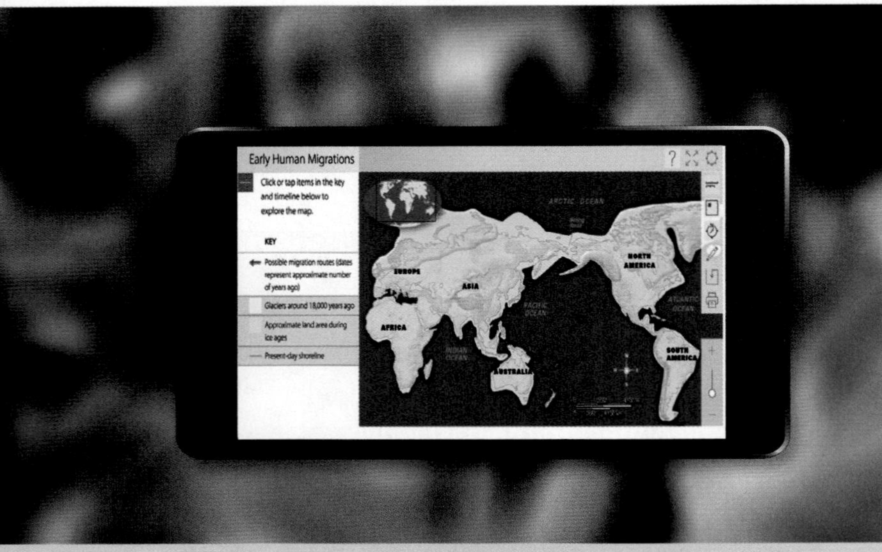

Content in a Fun Way

Interactive Features, **Maps**, and **Games** provide quick, entertaining activities and assessments that present important content in a fun way.

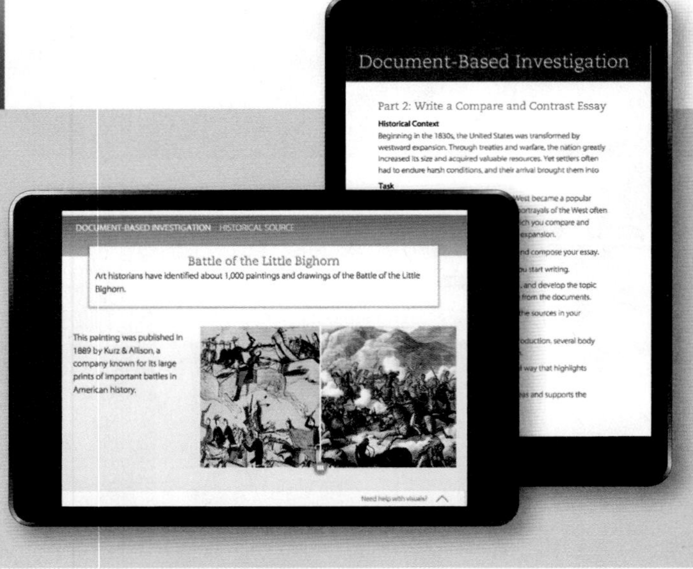

Investigate Like a Historian

Document-Based Investigations in every lesson build to end-of-module DBI performance tasks so students can examine and assess primary sources as historians do.

Full-Text Audio Support

Students can listen while they read.

Skills Support

Point-of-use support is just a click away, providing instruction on critical reading and social studies skills.

Personalized Annotations

Notes encourages students to take notes while they read and allows them to customize their notes to their preferences. Students can easily access their notes to review later as they prepare for exams.

Interactive Lesson Graphic Organizers

Graphic organizers help students process, summarize, and keep track of their learning for end-of-module performance tasks.

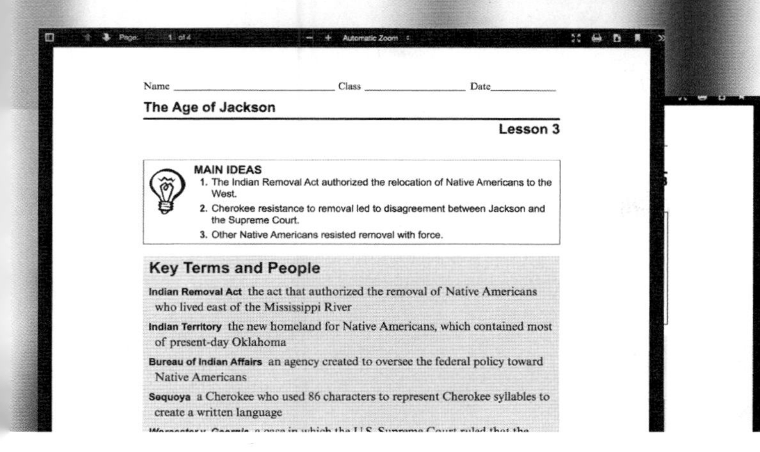
Name _______________ Class _______________ Date_______________

The Age of Jackson

Lesson 3

MAIN IDEAS
1. The Indian Removal Act authorized the relocation of Native Americans to the West.
2. Cherokee resistance to removal led to disagreement between Jackson and the Supreme Court.
3. Other Native Americans resisted removal with force.

Key Terms and People

Indian Removal Act the act that authorized the removal of Native Americans who lived east of the Mississippi River

Indian Territory the new homeland for Native Americans, which contained most of present-day Oklahoma

Bureau of Indian Affairs an agency created to oversee the federal policy toward Native Americans

Sequoya a Cherokee who used 86 characters to represent Cherokee syllables to create a written language

The **Guided Reading Workbook** and **Spanish/ English Guided Reading Workbook** offer students lesson summaries with vocabulary, reading, and note-taking support.

Map Connections connects students with history and geography through interactive maps, games, and data.

Current Events features trustworthy articles from today's news that connect what students learn in class to the world around them.

No Wi-Fi®? No problem!

With the **HMH Player®** app, **connect** to content and resources by downloading when online and accessing when offline.

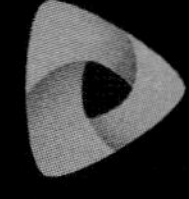

HMHPLAYER® also allows you to:

Collaborate

Open a Collaborative Classroom Session to use dynamic presentation tools, conduct informal polling, or instant message directly with students.

Communicate

Quickly access real-time reporting to monitor progress and identify areas for improvement.

Customize

Create custom lessons, upload your own content, or link to external resources to target particular skills and topics.

Essential Question Preview

Why did the Allies win World War II?
Have students consider the Essential Question and capture their initial responses.

Explore the Essential Question

- Tell students that World War II began with a series of stunning victories for the Axis powers.
- Explain why the Allied nations entered into the war and what they hoped to accomplish.

Help students plan inquiries and develop their own supporting questions such as:

What role did the United States play in World War II?

How did civilians help the war effort?

You may want to assign students to write a short essay in response to the Essential Question when they complete this module. Encourage students to use their notes and responses to inform their essays.

Explore the Online Video

ANALYZE VIDEOS

Battleground
Invite students to watch the video to see an overview of soldiers' lives during World War II.

History What feeling do you get about the soldiers fighting in World War II from the video? *that fighting in a war is a dirty, difficult, and scary ordeal*

Module 28

World War II

Essential Question
Why did the Allies win World War II?

About the Illustration: A German bombing raid on London during the Battle of Britain.

Explore ONLINE!

VIDEOS, including...
- A Global Battleground
- The Bataan Death March
- The Holocaust

- Document Based Investigations
- Graphic Organizers
- Interactive Games
- Image Compare: Jewish Resistance
- Carousel: The Atomic Bomb

In this module you will learn that, during World War II, the Allied forces defeated the Axis powers, the Jewish people suffered through the Holocaust, and Europe and Japan were left devastated.

What You Will Learn ...

Lesson 1 Big Idea

Using the sudden mass attack called the blitzkrieg, Germany overran much of Europe and North Africa.

Why It Matters Now
Hitler's actions set off World War II. The results of the war still affect the politics and economics of today's world.

Lesson 2 Big Idea

Japan attacked Pearl Harbor in Hawaii and brought the United States into World War II.

Why It Matters Now
World War II established the United States as a leading player in international affairs.

Lesson 3 Big Idea

During the Holocaust, Hitler's Nazis killed six million Jews and five million other "non-Aryans."

Why It Matters Now
The violence against Jews during the Holocaust led to the founding of Israel after World War II.

Lesson 4 Big Idea

Led by the United States, Great Britain, and the Soviet Union, the Allies scored key victories and won the war.

Why It Matters Now
The Allies' victory in World War II set up conditions for both the Cold War and today's post-Cold War world.

Timeline of Events 1939–1945

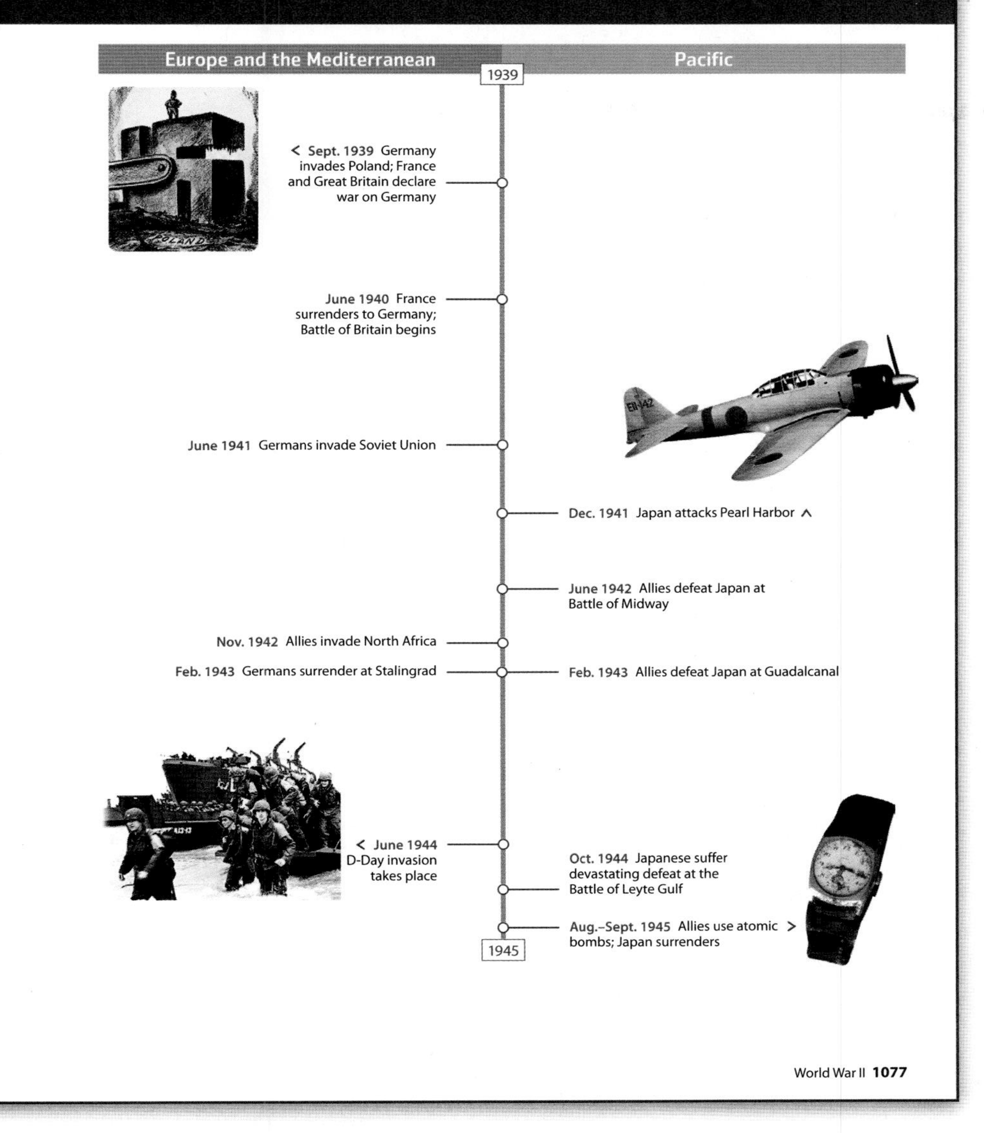

Lesson 5 Big Idea

World War II cost millions of human lives and billions of dollars in damages. It left Europe and Japan in ruins.

Why It Matters Now

The United States survived World War II undamaged, allowing it to become a world leader.

Explore the Timeline

Interpret Timelines: World War II, 1939–1945

Have students examine the timeline and then answer the following question:

History In each theater of war, how did the war progress for the Axis nations of Japan and Germany? *successful attacks and invasions from 1939–1941; devastating defeats and surrender from 1942–45*

Interpret Timeline of Events: Timeline of Events 1939–1945

To further explore the timeline, have students discuss the following questions:

1. The United States and the Soviet Union joined the Allies in 1941. What happened to each of these countries in that year? *Each was attacked by a member of the Axis.*
2. Why was February 1943 a bad month for the Axis powers? *The Germans and the Japanese each suffered a major defeat.*

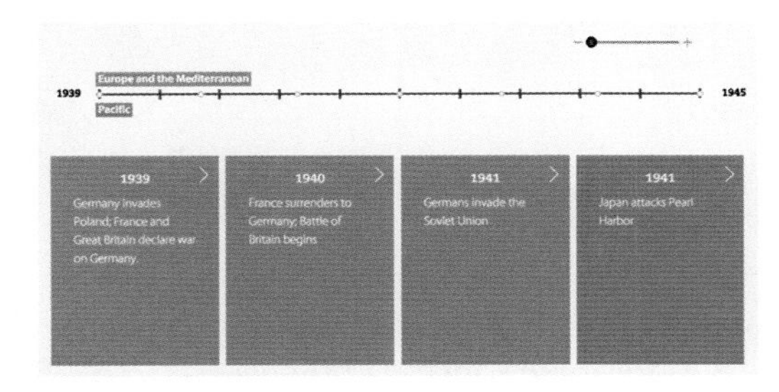

Online Module Flip Cards

Use the flip cards as a whole class activity or in student pairs to preview the module's Key Terms and People. Students can guess the meaning of each word, then review its definition, or do the reverse, using the flip card's toggle button to switch from Term to Definition mode. Students can also use the flip cards at the end of the module as a review tool before taking the Module Assessment.

Online Sequencing Activity

Students can use this sequencing activity to review the chronology of events in the World War II Module. To complete, have students drag each event to the correct year on the timeline.

Year	Event
1939	*Germany invades Poland; France and Great Britain declare war on Germany*
1940	*France surrenders to Germany; Battle of Britain begins*
1942	*Allies defeat Japan at Battle of Midway*
1944	*D-Day invasion takes place*
1945	*Germany surrenders; Allies use atomic bomb; Japan surrenders*

Lesson 1 Planner

Hitler's Lightning War

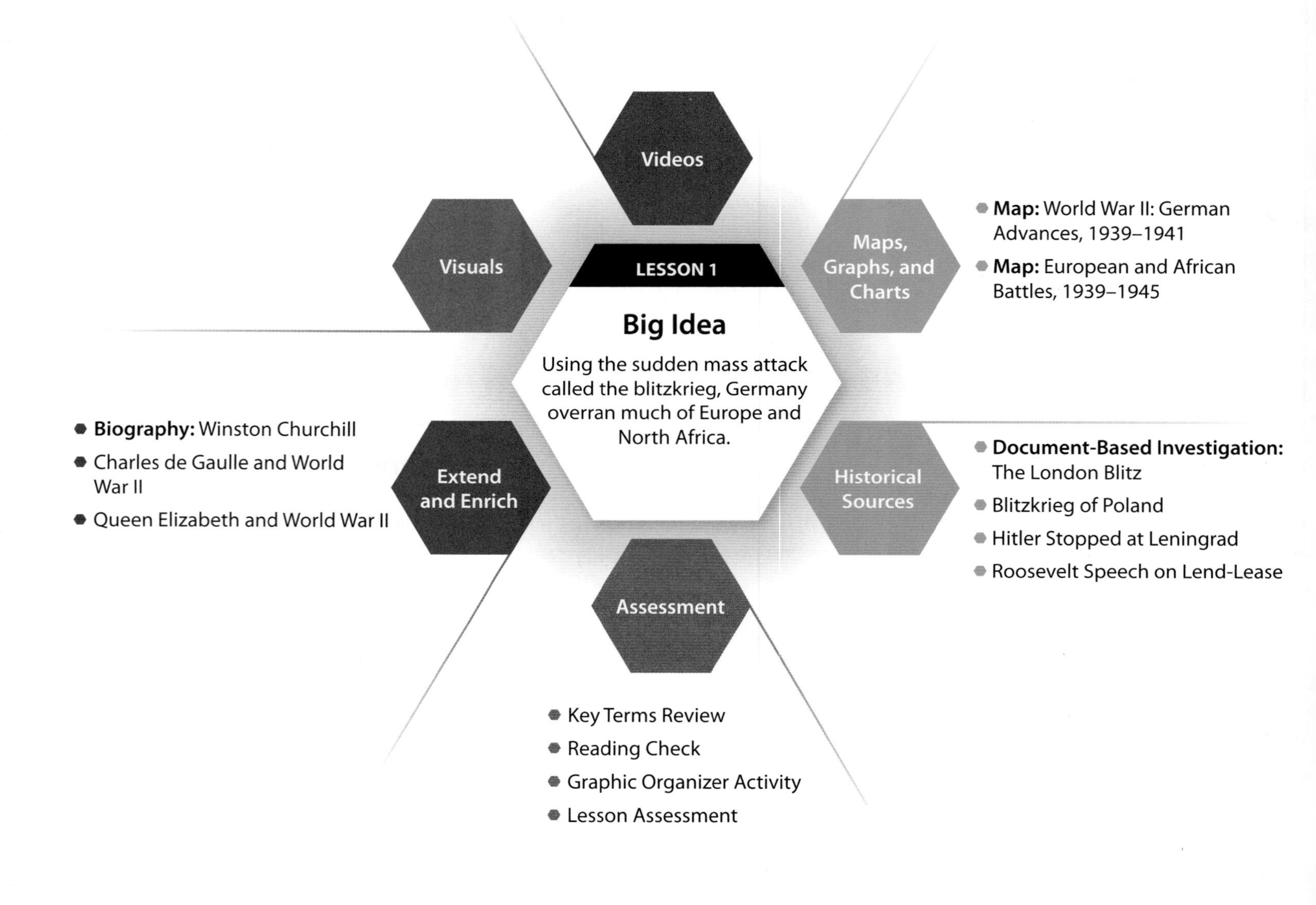

Maps, Graphs, and Charts

- **Map:** World War II: German Advances, 1939–1941
- **Map:** European and African Battles, 1939–1945

Extend and Enrich

- **Biography:** Winston Churchill
- Charles de Gaulle and World War II
- Queen Elizabeth and World War II

Historical Sources

- **Document-Based Investigation:** The London Blitz
- Blitzkrieg of Poland
- Hitler Stopped at Leningrad
- Roosevelt Speech on Lend-Lease

Assessment

- Key Terms Review
- Reading Check
- Graphic Organizer Activity
- Lesson Assessment

Online Lesson 1 Enrichment Activities

Charles de Gaulle and World War II

Biography Students read about Charles de Gaulle and his role in French military affairs before and during World War II. Then they explain a major irony of de Gaulle's military career leading up to World War II. They do this by exploring how de Gaulle's military background contributed to his credibility politically.

Queen Elizabeth and World War II

Biography Students read about England's Queen Elizabeth and her symbolic importance during World War II's Battle of Britain. Then they imagine that they live in London during World War II and the Battle of Britain's London Blitz. Using information from the biography, they write a letter to Queen Elizabeth expressing their appreciation for her presence in London and the concern she showed for citizens of the city during that time.

Teach the Big Idea

1. **Whole Class Open/Introduction** The Nazis attacked rapidly with massive force. Discuss whether recent wars have involved the use of this technique. *Air assaults early in the second Gulf War were designed to produce "shock and awe" in the Iraqi ranks.*
2. **Direct Teach** Read students the Big Idea: *Using the sudden mass attack called the blitzkrieg, Germany overran much of Europe and North Africa.* Review the following lesson objectives with students to aid in their understanding of the Big Idea.
   - Summarize the events that led to war.
   - Describe the fall of France.
   - Describe the Battle of Britain.
   - Explain the conflicts in the Mediterranean and on the Eastern Front.
   - Describe U.S. aid to the Allies.
3. **Whole Group Close/Reflect** Have students use their own words to write a summary of what they have read about German aggression in Europe.

Lesson 1

Hitler's Lightning War

The Big Idea
Using the sudden mass attack called the blitzkrieg, Germany overran much of Europe and North Africa.

Why It Matters Now
Hitler's actions set off World War II. The results of the war still affect the politics and economics of today's world.

Key Terms and People
nonaggression pact
blitzkrieg
Charles de Gaulle
Winston Churchill
Battle of Britain
Erwin Rommel
Atlantic Charter

Setting the Stage
During the 1930s, Hitler played on the hopes and fears of the Western democracies, and acted on his promise to restore Germany to greatness and expand its territory. Each time the Nazi dictator grabbed new territory, he would declare an end to his demands. Peace seemed guaranteed—until Hitler moved again. Germany's expansionism and Britain and France's policy of appeasement were on a crash course toward war. After his moves into the Rhineland, Austria, and Czechoslovakia, Hitler turned his eyes to Poland. After World War I, the Allies had cut out the Polish Corridor from German territory to give Poland access to the sea. In 1939, Hitler demanded that the Polish Corridor be returned to Germany.

Germany Sparks a New War in Europe
In August of 1939, Soviet dictator Joseph Stalin signed a ten-year **nonaggression pact** with Hitler. After being excluded from the Munich Conference, Stalin was not eager to join with the West. Also, Hitler had promised him territory. In a secret part of the pact, Germany and the Soviet Union agreed to divide Poland between them. They also agreed that the USSR could take over Finland and the Baltic countries of Lithuania, Latvia, and Estonia. It was an unlikely alliance between the fascist and communist leaders of two traditionally enemy countries, and it shocked Britain and France, who had been discussing an alliance with Stalin. His pact with Hitler indicated that war with Germany was inevitable.

Germany's Lightning Attack
After the nonaggression pact with the Soviets was revealed, Hitler quickly moved ahead with plans to conquer Poland. His surprise attack took place at dawn on September 1, 1939. German tanks and troop

German soldiers invading Poland, September 1939

1078 Module 28

ONLINE DOCUMENT-BASED INVESTIGATION

World War II

The London Blitz is the first of five historical sources that students will analyze in the World War II module. German aerial bombing during the London Blitz destroyed huge areas of the city and killed tens of thousands of people, but the British people refused to surrender. Have students read the text and explore the image.

ONLINE GRAPHIC ORGANIZER

Hitler's Lightning War

As students read the lesson, have them use the graphic organizer to take notes. Students can review their graphic organizer notes at the end of the lesson to answer the following question:

Analyze Events Which events might be considered turning points for the Allies before the United States joined the war effort? *the first blitzkrieg in Poland; Allies rescued at Dunkirk; Hitler calling off attack of Britain; U.S. Lend-Lease Act*

Turning Points for the Allies

Event		Effect
	→	
Event		Effect
	→	
Event		Effect
	→	
Event		Effect
	→	

COLLABORATIVE LEARNING

Compile World War II Encyclopedia Entries

1. Tell students that they will work in groups to write encyclopedia articles. Have students brainstorm possible topics about specific people, places, and events during the period from 1938–1941.
2. Organize the class into groups, and have each group select two of the topics listed.
3. Then have students begin work on their encyclopedia entries. Encourage students to ensure that everyone has an important responsibility. Specialized tasks might include conducting research, writing articles, and drawing illustrations.
4. Request that students put their entries into as final a form as time allows.
5. Have groups exchange articles, review each other's entries, and provide feedback.

COLLABORATIVE LEARNING

The Soviet Factor

1. Organize the class into four groups to represent the military high commands of Germany, Great Britain, France, and Poland. Have each group discuss what course a war in Europe might take and how the Soviet Union might be a factor.
2. Have each group draft a memorandum detailing a recommended plan of action for its national leaders.

trucks rumbled across the Polish border. At the same time, German aircraft and artillery began a merciless bombing of Poland's capital, Warsaw.

France and Great Britain declared war on Germany on September 3. But Poland fell some time before those nations could make any military response. After his victory, Hitler annexed the western half of Poland. That region had a large German population.

The German invasion of Poland was the first test of Germany's newest military strategy—the **blitzkrieg** (BLIHTS•kreeg), or "lightning war." The massive rearmament and conscription programs that Hitler began in the mid-1930s had produced thousands of state-of-the-art fighter and bomber planes, tanks, and a greatly expanded infantry force. The blitzkrieg involved using air strikes, fast tanks, and artillery, followed by soldiers sped into battle on trucks, to take enemy defenders by surprise and quickly overwhelm them. It was a mobile assault quite advanced from the limited air power and slower tanks available in World War I. In the case of Poland, the strategy worked.

The Soviets Make Their Move On September 17, Stalin sent Soviet troops to occupy the eastern half of Poland. Stalin then moved to annex countries to the north of Poland. Lithuania, Latvia, and Estonia fell without a struggle, but Finland resisted. In November, Stalin sent nearly one million Soviet troops into Finland. The Soviets expected to win a quick victory, so they were not prepared for winter fighting. This was a crucial mistake.

The Finns were outnumbered and outgunned, but they fiercely defended their country. In the freezing winter weather, soldiers on skis swiftly attacked Soviet positions. In contrast, the Soviets struggled to make progress through the deep snow. The Soviets suffered heavy losses, but they finally won through sheer force of numbers. By March 1940, Stalin had forced the Finns to accept his surrender terms.

The Phony War After they declared war on Germany, the French and British had mobilized their armies. They stationed their troops along the Maginot (MAZH•uh•noh) Line, a system of fortifications along France's border with Germany. There they waited for the Germans to attack—but nothing happened. With little to do, the bored Allied soldiers stared eastward toward the enemy. Equally bored, German soldiers stared back from their Siegfried Line a few miles away. Germans jokingly called it the *sitzkrieg*, or "sitting war." Some newspapers referred to it simply as "the phony war."

Suddenly, on April 9, 1940, the calm ended. Hitler launched a surprise invasion of Denmark and Norway. In just four hours after the attack, Denmark fell. Two months later, Norway surrendered as well. The Germans then began to build bases along the Norwegian and Danish coasts from which they could launch strikes on Great Britain.

Reading Check
Analyze Motives
What were Stalin's goals in Europe at the beginning of World War II?

Objectives

You may wish to discuss the following questions with students to help them frame the content as they read.

- How did the blitzkrieg get its name? *from the German words for "lightning war"*
- How did mechanization make the blitzkrieg possible? *allowed tanks and aircraft quick movement*
- How did the reaction of Great Britain and France to the invasion of Poland differ from reactions to previous German expansion? *When Germany invaded Poland, Great Britain and France declared war on Germany. Previously they stood by, allowing Hitler to have his way.*

More About . . .

English Roots of Nazi Geopolitics Hitler's plan for German expansion owed much to theories of geopolitics,or the relationship between land and foreign policy. In the early 1900s, English geopolitician Sir Halford Mackinder argued that a nation's power depended on its control of large areas of land. Mackinder believed the most important area was Eurasia and Africa, a vast connected landmass that he called the World Island. Whoever controlled the central regions of Eurasia that included Germany and Russia could control the rest of the World Island as well. His ideas received little attention in Great Britain before World War II, but they were used in Germany to support the Nazis' geopolitical ideas.

Each plan should include two alternatives—one that assumes the Soviet Union will continue to cooperate with Germany and another that assumes that the Soviet Union will enter the war on the side of the Allies.

3. Have volunteers from each group present their plans of action to the class.
4. Guide the class in a discussion of each group's plan.

ADVANCED/GIFTED

Recognize the Value of War Technology

1. Discuss historical examples of new technology that gave a country a military advantage over its rivals. For example, in the 800s BC the Assyrians had better iron weapons than their rivals, in the 1300s the Ottoman Turks started using cannons, and in the early 1900s the British pioneered the use of the tank.
2. Divide students into four groups to research one of the following technologies: radar, jet propulsion, decoding devices, rockets.
3. Ask groups to trace the development, use, and effectiveness of each technology and then present reports to the class.
4. Encourage students to discuss whether each technology had an impact on the outcome of a war and whether it affected the ethics of war.

ONLINE LESSON FLIP CARDS

Review Key Terms and People

Students can use the flip cards in the Lesson Review at any time to review the lesson's key terms and people: *nonaggression pact, blitzkrieg, Charles de Gaulle, Winston Churchill, Battle of Britain, Erwin Rommel,* and *Atlantic Charter.*

ONLINE HISTORICAL SOURCES

Blitzkrieg of Poland

Invite students to view the image and answer the associated question.

Analyze Sources How did German blitzkrieg tactics rely on new military technology? *The development of new tanks and airplanes made blitzkrieg tactics effective.*

READING CHECK
Analyze Motives What were Stalin's goals in Europe at the beginning of World War II? *Stalin aimed at expanding the Soviet Union's territory and power, while keeping his country out of the war.*

Objectives

You may wish to discuss the following questions with students to help them frame the content as they read.

- How did the retreat at Dunkirk affect Britain's ability to fight Hitler? *saved troops to fight later*
- Do you think that de Gaulle's speech applied to the British who had evacuated at Dunkirk? *Yes—He resented any refusal to fight Hitler. No—He was speaking only to the French.*

More About . . .

Charles de Gaulle At 6 feet 4 inches, de Gaulle was an imposing figure, and his manner was often arrogant. "I am France," he declared. De Gaulle's arrogance irritated Allied leaders, but he prevailed. When France was liberated, his resistance movement was recognized as the legitimate government of France.

The Maginot Line After World War I, the French spent millions of francs building a defensive structure known as the Maginot Line. It consisted of a vast series of underground bunkers and fortresses, which were connected by underground tunnels and underground railways. This system could be used to defend the entire border with Germany against attack. What the builders did not anticipate, however, was that the Germans would overrun the Netherlands and Belgium and invade France through them. The Maginot Line proved virtually useless against the German attack in 1940.

ONLINE INTERACTIVE MAPS

World War II: German Advances, 1939–1941

Have students explore the map using the interactive features and answer the associated questions.

Movement Which of the following European countries did Germany invade in 1939? *Poland*

In print edition, see map of same title.

1. **Region** Which countries did Germany invade? *France, Belgium, the Netherlands, Denmark, Norway, Czechoslovakia, Austria, Hungary, Yugoslavia, Albania, Greece, Bulgaria, Romania, Poland, Lithuania, Latvia, Estonia, Finland, the Soviet Union*
2. **Location** In what way was Germany's geographic location an advantage when it was on the offensive in the war? *It was centrally located in Europe and could attack in all directions.*

Interpret Maps

1. **Region** Which countries did Germany invade?
2. **Location** In what way was Germany's geographic location an advantage when it was on the offensive in the war?

The Fall of France

In May of 1940, Hitler began a dramatic sweep through the Netherlands, Belgium, and Luxembourg. This was part of a strategy to strike at France. Keeping the Allies' attention on those countries, Hitler then sent an even larger force of tanks and troops south to slice through the Ardennes (ahr•DEHN). This was a heavily wooded area in northern France, Luxembourg, and Belgium. The Allies considered the forest, hills, and poor roads of the Ardennes a hindrance to the heavily armored Nazi offensive, and so it was lightly defended. German forces moved steadily through the forest, and fought their way around the Maginot Line. From there, they moved across France and reached the country's northern coast in ten days.

1080 Module 28

ENGLISH LANGUAGE LEARNERS

Report on the Rescue of Dunkirk

1. Divide students into small groups. Have each group reread the text entitled "Rescue at Dunkirk." Write definitions or synonyms for difficult words on the board. *outnumbered = having too many enemies; civilian = not part of an army, navy, or air force; armada = a large group of warships*
2. Have groups write a radio or newspaper report that describes the events at Dunkirk. Encourage students to use strong verbs and descriptive language. Have a member of each group report aloud to the class.
3. Discuss why Dunkirk is considered an example of bravery. *People who weren't soldiers risked death to rescue threatened troops.*

Rescue at Dunkirk After reaching the French coast, the German forces swung north again and joined with German troops in Belgium. By the end of May 1940, the Germans had trapped the Allied forces around the northern French city of Lille (leel). Outnumbered, outgunned, and pounded from the air, the Allies retreated to the beaches of Dunkirk, a French port city near the Belgian border. They were trapped with their backs to the sea.

In one of the most heroic acts of the war, Great Britain set out to rescue the army. It sent a fleet of about 850 ships across the English Channel to Dunkirk. Along with Royal Navy ships, civilian craft—yachts, lifeboats, motorboats, paddle steamers, and fishing boats—joined the rescue effort. From May 26 to June 4, this amateur armada, under heavy fire from German bombers, sailed back and forth from Britain to Dunkirk. The boats carried some 338,000 battle-weary soldiers to safety.

France Falls Following Dunkirk, resistance in France began to crumble. By June 14, the Germans had taken Paris. Accepting the inevitable, French leaders surrendered on June 22, 1940. The Germans took control of the northern part of the country. They left the southern part to a puppet government headed by Marshal Philippe Pétain (pay•TAN), a French hero from World War I. The headquarters of this government was in the city of Vichy (VEESH•ee).

After France fell, **Charles de Gaulle** (duh-GOHL), a French general, set up a government-in-exile in London. He committed all his energy to reconquering France. In a radio broadcast from England, de Gaulle called on the people of France to join him in resisting the Germans:

> *"It is the bounden [obligatory] duty of all Frenchmen who still bear arms to continue the struggle. For them to lay down their arms, to evacuate any position of military importance, or agree to hand over any part of French territory, however small, to enemy control would be a crime against our country."*
>
> —General Charles De Gaulle, quoted in *Charles de Gaulle: A Biography*

Reading Check
Analyze Effects How was Hitler's attack through the Ardennes forest a bold strike and an early turning point in the war?

De Gaulle went on to organize the Free French military forces that battled the Nazis until France was liberated in 1944.

The Battle of Britain

With the fall of France, Great Britain stood alone against the Nazis. **Winston Churchill**, the new British prime minister, had already declared that his nation would never give in. In a rousing speech, he proclaimed, "We shall fight on the beaches, we shall fight on the landing grounds, we shall fight in the fields and in the streets . . . we shall never surrender." Hitler now turned his mind to an invasion of Great Britain. His plan was first to knock out the Royal Air Force (RAF) and then to land more than 250,000 soldiers on England's shores. In the summer of 1940, the Luftwaffe (Looft•VAHF•uh), Germany's air force, began bombing Great Britain. At first, the Germans targeted British airfields and aircraft

Vocabulary
Luftwaffe the German word for "air weapon"

Objectives

You may wish to discuss the following questions with students to help them frame the content as they read.

- How might the German attacks on Britain have strengthened Britain's resistance? *Attacks on cities inspired the British to fight.*
- How did Hitler's attack on France differ from his attack on Britain? *He used tanks and troops to invade France, but he used aircraft to attack Britain.*

More About . . .

Blackouts During the Blitz, Londoners were subject to blackout restrictions and had to cover their windows at night with black material. Streetlights were not lit, and drivers were not permitted to turn on their headlights. These precautions were taken to make it harder for German bombers to find their target.

Saving Children As early as September 1939, fearing potential air attacks, British authorities prepared to evacuate children from London. Thousands of children relocated from the city to temporary homes in the countryside beyond the reach of German bombers. Although relocating children separated families, it saved many lives as Germans persistently bombed London during the Blitz.

Tip for Struggling Readers *Enigma*, the name of the German code, means "a statement, situation, or person that is baffling," like a puzzle or a mystery.

READING CHECK
Analyze Effects How was Hitler's attack through the Ardennes Forest a bold strike and an early turning point in the war? *It was a surprise attack through difficult terrain, and it led to the fall of France.*

COLLABORATIVE LEARNING

The Blitz

1. Have small groups conduct outside research on the London Blitz.
2. Have each group write a short scene from a play or film about the London Blitz. Scripts should provide roles for each group member. Students can focus on the Blitz from the point of view of Royal Air Force pilots, London civilians, or German pilots.
3. Have groups present their scenes as reader's theater.

BIOGRAPHY

Winston Churchill

Have students read the biography of Winston Churchill, who voiced opposition to the policy of appeasement and later led Great Britain through World War II as its prime minister.

ONLINE DOCUMENT-BASED INVESTIGATION

The London Blitz

German aerial bombing during the London Blitz destroyed huge areas of the city and killed tens of thousands of people, but the British people refused to surrender. Have students explore the image and answer the associated question.

Analyze Sources What aspects of total war were evidenced in the Battle of Britain? *Germany's relentless aerial bombardment of London and the great destruction there; the mobilizing efforts of Great Britain's government and citizens to resist the attack, and the civilian casualties incurred by Great Britain*

DOCUMENT-BASED INVESTIGATION HISTORICAL SOURCE

The London Blitz

During the aerial bombing of London beginning in September, 1940, the German goal was to terrorize the British people so that they would lose the will to fight. The London Blitz destroyed huge areas of the city and killed tens of thousands of people, but the British people refused to surrender. In this photo, a London bus is submerged in a bomb crater after a German air raid.

READING CHECK

Analyze Effects Why was the outcome of the Battle of Britain important for the Allies? *They learned that Hitler's attacks could be stopped and turned back.*

BIOGRAPHY

Winston Churchill
(1874–1965)

Possibly the most powerful weapon the British had as they stood alone against Hitler's Germany was the nation's prime minister—Winston Churchill. "Big Winnie," Londoners boasted, "was the lad for us."

Although Churchill had a speech defect as a youngster, he grew to become one of the greatest orators of all time. He used all his gifts as a speaker to rally the people behind the effort to crush Germany. In one famous speech he promised that Britain would

". . . wage war, by sea, land and air, with all our might and with all the strength that God can give us . . . against a monstrous tyranny."

factories. Then, on September 7, 1940, they began focusing on the cities, especially London, to break British morale. Despite the destruction and loss of life, the British did not waver. The RAF, although badly outnumbered, began to hit back hard. Two technological devices helped turn the tide in the RAF's favor. One was an electronic tracking system known as radar. Developed in the late 1930s, radar could tell the number, speed, and direction of incoming warplanes. The other device was a German code-making machine named Enigma. A complete Enigma machine had been smuggled into Great Britain in the late 1930s. Enigma enabled the British to decode German secret messages. With information gathered by these devices, RAF fliers could quickly launch attacks on the enemy. To avoid the RAF's attacks, the Germans gave up daylight raids in October 1940 in favor of night bombing. At sunset, the wail of sirens filled the air as Londoners flocked to the subways, which served as air-raid shelters. Some rode out the bombing raids at home in smaller air-raid shelters or basements. This **Battle of Britain** continued until May 10, 1941. Stunned by British resistance, Hitler decided to call off his attacks. Instead, he focused on the Mediterranean and Eastern Europe. The Battle of Britain taught the Allies a crucial lesson. Hitler's attacks could be blocked.

Reading Check
Analyze Effects Why was the outcome of the Battle of Britain important for the Allies?

A London bus is submerged in a bomb crater after a German air raid.

1082 Module 28

MAKE INFERENCES

Discuss the Battle of Britain

1. Review the skill of making inferences with students.
2. Use these questions to initiate a discussion of the Battle of Britain: What factors helped Britain resist German attacks? *Churchill's inspiration, radar, breaking German code, fought in homeland* What was Great Britain's strategic importance to the Germans? *could help them protect the rest of Western Europe* What was Great Britain's strategic importance to the Allies? *could provide a base to stage an Allied attack on Europe's mainland*
3. Have students write a paragraph explaining why both the Allies and the Axis were so determined to win the Battle of Britain.

The Mediterranean and the Eastern Front

The stubborn resistance of the British in the Battle of Britain caused a shift in Hitler's strategy in Europe. He decided to deal with Great Britain later. He then turned his attention east to the Mediterranean area and the Balkans—and to the ultimate prize, the Soviet Union.

Axis Forces Attack North Africa Germany's first objective in the Mediterranean region was North Africa, mainly because of Hitler's partner, Mussolini. Despite its alliance with Germany, Italy had remained neutral at the beginning of the war. With Hitler's conquest of France, however, Mussolini knew he had to take action. After declaring war on France and Great Britain, Mussolini moved into France.

Mussolini took his next step in North Africa in September 1940. While the Battle of Britain was raging, he ordered his army to attack British-controlled Egypt. Egypt's Suez Canal was key to reaching the oil fields of the Middle East from the Mediterranean, so it was a crucial colonial interest for both the Allies and Axis powers. Within a week, Italian troops had pushed 60 miles inside Egypt, forcing British units back. Then both sides dug in and waited.

Vocabulary
Middle East
region that includes the countries of Southwest Asia and northeast Africa

Britain Strikes Back Finally, in December, the British forces—including troops from its colony, India, and Commonwealth nations Canada, Australia, New Zealand, and South Africa—struck back. The result was a disaster for the Italians. By February 1941, the British had swept 500 miles across North Africa and had taken 130,000 Italian prisoners. Hitler had to step in to save his Axis partner. To reinforce the Italians, Hitler sent a crack German tank force, the Afrika Korps, under the command of General **Erwin Rommel**. In late March 1941, Rommel's Afrika Korps attacked. Caught by surprise, British forces retreated east to Tobruk, Libya.

After fierce fighting for Tobruk, the British began to drive Rommel back. By mid-January 1942, Rommel had retreated to where he had started. By June 1942, the tide of battle turned again. Rommel regrouped, pushed the British back across the desert, and seized Tobruk—a shattering loss for the Allies. Rommel's successes in North Africa earned him the nickname "Desert Fox."

The War in the Balkans While Rommel campaigned in North Africa, other German generals were active in the Balkans. Hitler had begun planning to attack his ally, the Soviet Union, as early as the summer of 1940. The Balkan countries of southeastern Europe were the key to Hitler's plan. Hitler wanted to build bases there for the attack on the Soviet Union. He also wanted to make sure that the British did not interfere.

To prepare for his invasion, Hitler moved to expand his influence in the Balkans. By early 1941, through the threat of force, he had persuaded Bulgaria, Romania, and Hungary to join the Axis powers. Yugoslavia and Greece, which had pro-British governments, resisted. In early April 1941, Hitler invaded both countries. Yugoslavia fell in 11 days. Greece surrendered in 17. In Athens, the Nazis celebrated their victory by raising swastikas on the Acropolis.

Objectives

You may wish to discuss the following question with students to help them frame the content as they read.

- How long had the German-Soviet pact existed when Hitler began planning to invade his ally? *less than one year*

More About . . .

Erwin Rommel The German general proved to be a fierce enemy of Allied troops. Even so, few military experts cast doubt on Erwin Rommel's military skills. He is remembered for employing the element of surprise and for using both keen offensive and defensive strategies. Though despised by citizens of Allied countries, Rommel was extremely popular with German citizens. That's why Rommel was often called "the People's Marshall" in addition to his more-familiar "Desert Fox" nickname.

The Siege of Leningrad During the siege, composer Dmitri Shostakovich not only worked on his Seventh, or "Leningrad," Symphony, but also broadcast appeals to the people to resist the invaders. He said that he would always see Leningrad as the beautiful city it had been. Authorities moved Shostakovich to a safer city, where he finished the symphony. The score was put on microfilm and flown out of the Soviet Union to the West. Years later, the composer wrote that the work was not about the German siege of the city but about the suffering of Leningrad under the terrible Stalinist purges of the 1930s.

STRUGGLING READERS

Chart the War on the Eastern Front

1. Explain that one event often leads to another. Continue by saying that the first event is a cause of the second.
2. Have student pairs create a flow chart that traces events leading to the siege of Moscow.
3. Have students display their charts in the classroom.

SUMMARIZE EVENTS

Below Level Have student pairs research Yugoslavia's stand against Germany and make a flow chart showing the sequence of events that led to the nation's defeat.

At Level Have students find out more about Bulgaria, Yugoslavia, and Greece during World War II and make an illustrated poster comparing the fates of the three nations.

Above Level Have students research the Mediterranean and the Eastern Front. Then ask them to sketch a map of the regions, identifying the location of eight to ten events. Next they should add several sentences that describe each event. Encourage creativity in organizing their maps.

ONLINE HISTORICAL SOURCES

Hitler Stopped at Leningrad

Invite students to view the image and answer the associated question.

Analyze Sources What factors helped the Soviet army and citizens resist the Germans amidst the horrific circumstances at Leningrad? *The Soviets were defending one of their own cities and were able to reinforce the army with fresh soldiers.*

HISTORICAL SOURCE

Hitler Stopped at Leningrad

The German invasion of the Soviet Union in the summer of 1941 was a success. Eventually, however, the Soviets began to recover from the huge number of casualties they had suffered in the early fighting. They survived the German onslaught at Leningrad, and for the first time began to fight back. In this photo, Russian soldiers prepare to attack German lines outside Leningrad.

ONLINE INTERACTIVE MAPS

European and African Battles, 1939–1945

Have students explore the map using the interactive features and answer the associated question.

Place Which country were the Axis powers only able to wrest partial control of from the Allies? *Egypt*

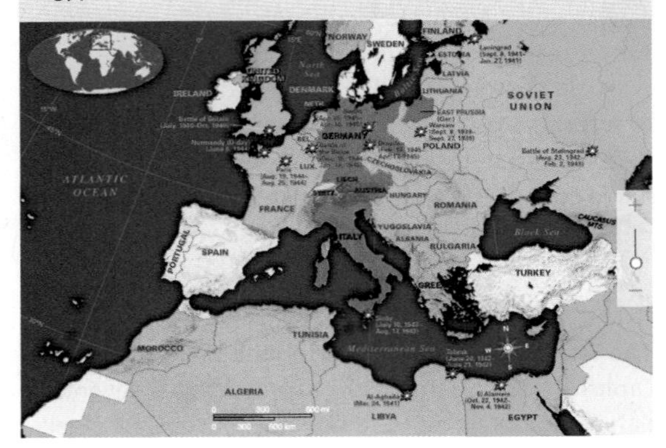

ONLINE HISTORICAL SOURCES

Roosevelt Speech on Lend-Lease

Invite students to read the speech and answer the associated question.

Analyze Sources Why do you think some American citizens and members of Congress opposed the Lend-Lease Act? *Isolationism was still the preferred policy of many, and the Lend-Lease Act appeared to bring the United States a step closer to war.*

HISTORICAL SOURCE

Roosevelt Speech on Lend-Lease

President Franklin Roosevelt delivered this speech the week that the Lend-Lease Act was passed by Congress in March, 1941. At the time only the British were still resisting the Nazis. Roosevelt felt it was urgent that the United States act as an "arsenal of democracy" by providing the Allies with much-needed war materials.

"We believe firmly that when our production output is in full swing, the democracies of the world will be able to prove that dictatorships cannot win.

But, now, now, the time element is of supreme importance. Every plane, every other instrument of war, old and new, every instrument that we can spare now, we will send overseas because that is the common sense of strategy.

The great task of this day, the deep duty that rests upon each and every one of us is to move products from the assembly lines of our factories to the battle lines of democracy—Now!"

—President Franklin Delano Roosevelt

Russian soldiers prepare to attack German lines outside Leningrad.

Hitler Invades the Soviet Union With the Balkans firmly in control, Hitler could move ahead with Operation Barbarossa, his plan to invade the Soviet Union. Early in the morning of June 22, 1941, the roar of German tanks and aircraft announced the beginning of the invasion. The Soviet Union was not prepared for this attack. Although it had the largest army in the world, its troops were neither well equipped nor well trained.

The invasion rolled on week after week until the Germans had pushed 500 miles inside the Soviet Union. As the Soviet troops retreated, they burned and destroyed everything in the enemy's path. The Russians had used this scorched-earth strategy against Napoleon.

On September 8, German forces put Leningrad under siege. By early November, the city was completely cut off from the rest of the Soviet Union. To force a surrender, Hitler was ready to starve the city's more than 2.5 million inhabitants. German bombs destroyed warehouses where food was stored. Desperately hungry, people began eating cattle and horse feed, as well as cats and dogs and, finally, crows and rats. Nearly one million people died in Leningrad during the winter of 1941–1942. Yet the city refused to fall.

Impatient with the progress in Leningrad, Hitler looked to Moscow, the capital and heart of the Soviet Union. A Nazi drive on the capital began on October 2, 1941. By December, the Germans had advanced to the outskirts of Moscow. Soviet General Georgi Zhukov (ZHOO•kuhf) counterattacked. As temperatures fell, the Germans, in summer uniforms, retreated. Ignoring Napoleon's winter defeat 130 years before, Hitler sent his generals a stunning order: "No retreat!" German troops dug in about 125 miles west of Moscow. They held the line against the Soviets until March 1943. Hitler's advance on the Soviet Union gained nothing but cost the Germans 500,000 lives.

Reading Check
Make Inferences What does the fact that German armies were not prepared for the Russian winter indicate about Hitler's expectations for the Soviet campaign?

READING CHECK

Make Inferences What does the fact that German armies were not prepared for the Russian winter indicate about Hitler's expectations for the Soviet campaign? *Hitler expected a quick victory in the Soviet Union and did not think that his army would still be in combat by the time winter set in.*

The United States Aids Its Allies

Most Americans felt that the United States should not get involved in the war. Between 1935 and 1937, Congress passed a series of Neutrality Acts. The laws made it illegal to sell arms or lend money to nations at war. But President Roosevelt knew that if the Allies fell, the United States would be drawn into the war. In September 1939, he asked Congress to allow the Allies to buy American arms. The Allies would pay cash and then carry the goods on their own ships.

Under the Lend-Lease Act, passed in March 1941, the president could lend or lease arms and other supplies to any country vital to the United States. By the summer of 1941, the U.S. Navy was escorting British ships carrying U.S. arms. In response, Hitler ordered his submarines to sink any cargo ships they met.

Although the United States had not yet entered the war, Roosevelt and Churchill met secretly and issued a joint declaration called the **Atlantic Charter**, which outlined their purpose for the war. It stated that they sought no territorial gain in the war, and it upheld the principles of free trade among nations and the right of people to choose their own government.

On September 4, a German U-boat fired on a U.S. destroyer in the Atlantic. In response, Roosevelt ordered navy commanders to shoot German submarines on sight. The United States was now involved in an undeclared naval war with Hitler. To almost everyone's surprise, however, the attack that actually drew the United States into the war did not come from Germany. It came from Japan.

Reading Check
Find Main Ideas Why did President Franklin Roosevelt want to offer help to the Allies?

Lesson 1 Assessment

1. **Organize Information** Which of the listed events might be considered a turning point for the Allies? Why?

Cause	Effect
First blitzkrieg	
Allies stranded at Dunkirk	
Lend-Lease Act	

2. **Key Terms and People** For each key term or person in the lesson, write a sentence explaining its significance.
3. **Compare and Contrast** Review the events that led directly to World War I. Then compare and contrast them with the events that led directly to World War II.
4. **Synthesize** What do you think is meant by the statement that Winston Churchill was possibly Britain's most powerful weapon against Hitler's Germany?
5. **Make Inferences** What factors do you think a country's leaders consider when deciding whether to surrender or fight?
6. **Compare** In what ways were the consequences of Hitler's decisions on the Eastern Front similar to those of Napoleon when he invaded Russia?

Objectives

You may wish to discuss the following questions with students to help them frame the content as they read.

- Under what conditions do you think the United States should remain neutral when other countries are fighting? Possible answer: *when the conflict does not threaten the United States*
- Do you think Germany was justified in attacking cargo ships? *Yes—The ships carried arms for killing Germans. No—The United States was neutral.*
- How did the United States help the Allies before actually entering the war? *lent or leased arms and other supplies, signed the Atlantic Charter, and took part in an undeclared naval war with Hitler*

More About . . .

Lend-Lease Act Soon after signing the act, Congress made use of its terms by sending billions of dollars' worth of aid to Britain, Nationalists in China, the Soviet Union, and more than 25 other countries. The aid came in a variety of forms such as tanks, airplanes, trucks, and food. The borrowing nations were not required to directly pay for the items they received. A number of Americans objected to the act because it indicated that the United States was no longer neutral and removed from the war. In promoting the Lend-Lease Act, President Roosevelt referred to the United States as the "Arsenal of Democracy."

READING CHECK
Find Main Ideas Why did President Franklin Roosevelt want to offer help to the Allies? *He feared an Allied defeat would pull the United States into the war.*

ADVANCED/GIFTED

Create a Lend-Lease Act

1. Have students form small groups. Inform them that they are members of the Senate during the time of World War II.
2. Ask group members to work together to create their own Lend-Lease bill to be submitted for a vote. Their act should describe terms of the act, including what will be offered, who can authorize the exchange of goods, who is eligible to receive goods, how much will be spent, and other items they feel are important to include.
3. Tell group members to write up their bill in the form of numbered points.
4. Then have groups find a copy of the actual Lend-Lease Bill and compare and contrast it to their bill.

Print Assessment

1. **Organize Information** Which of the listed events might be considered a turning point for the Allies? Why? *Possible answer: Blitzkrieg—Fall of Poland. Dunkirk—338,000 soldiers saved. Lend-Lease—War goods to Allies. Turning point—Battle of Britain showed that Hitler could be halted.*
2. **Key Terms and People** For each key term or person in the lesson, write a sentence explaining its significance. *Explanations of the lesson's key terms can be found on the following pages: nonaggression pact, p. 1078; blitzkrieg, p. 1079; Charles de Gaulle, p. 1081; Winston Churchill, p. 1081; Battle of Britain, p. 1082; Erwin Rommel, p. 1083; Atlantic Charter, p. 1085*

(continued)

Print Assessment *(continued)*

3. **Compare and Contrast:** Review the events that led directly to World War I. Then compare and contrast them with the events that led directly to World War II. *Possible answer: The assassination by a Serbian of Austria's Archduke Ferdinand led directly to World War I. Germany's blitzkrieg invasion of Poland was the immediate event that sparked World War II. Both were acts of violence that led to declarations of war. Hitler's actions were a more deliberate provocation.*
4. **Synthesize** What do you think is meant by the statement that Winston Churchill possibly was Britain's most powerful weapon against Hitler's Germany? *His powerful speeches boosted the morale of the British people.*
5. **Make Inferences** What factors do you think a country's leaders consider when deciding whether to surrender or fight? *Possible answer: the country's ability to fight, its willingness to accept casualties, the costs of foreign control*
6. **Compare** In what ways were the consequences of Hitler's decisions on the Eastern Front similar to those of Napoleon when he invaded Russia? *Both underestimated the defending army and the dangers of a Russian winter, ending in disaster for the invading troops.*

Online Assessment

1. Which of the following is a reason that Stalin signed the nonaggression pact with Hitler?
   - ○ Britain wanted to join forces with Hitler.
   - ○ Poland had declared war on the Soviet Union.
   - ○ Stalin wanted to bring communism into Germany.
   - ● The West had excluded Stalin from the Munich Conference.

   Alternate Question *Select the answer choice from the drop-down list to complete the sentence correctly.* Stalin agreed to sign a nonaggression pact with Hitler because Hitler promised to give *territory* to Stalin. Stalin also was not eager to join forces with the West because he felt slighted during the Munich Conference.

2. Why did the Allies need to be rescued at Dunkirk?
   - ○ The Nazis had invaded Poland.
   - ○ The Nazis had taken over Paris.
   - ○ The Nazis had resorted to blitzkrieg.
   - ● The Nazis had backed them to the sea.

   Alternate Question *Select the answer choice from the drop-down list to complete the sentence correctly.* The Allied forces were trying to escape from the Nazis in May 1940. They found themselves in *Dunkirk* with their backs to the sea.

3. What did Hitler plan to do first in his attack against Great Britain?
   - ○ destroy London
   - ○ send in ground troops
   - ● disable the Royal Air Force
   - ○ surround the island nation with warships

   Alternate Question *Select the answer choice from the drop-down list to complete the sentence correctly.* Hitler's plan of attack on Great Britain was to first *immobilize the Royal Air Force* and then invade the country.

4. Why did Hitler decide to temporarily turn his attention away from Great Britain in late 1940?
   - ○ The Italians wanted to take over France.
   - ○ The Americans had promised to help the British.
   - ● The British had put up too much of a resistance.
   - ○ The Soviets had betrayed him on the eastern border.

   Alternate Question *Select the answer choice from the drop-down list to complete the sentence correctly.* In late 1940 Hitler decided to refocus his strategy and move toward the *Mediterranean* and away from Great Britain because the British were more difficult to conquer than Hitler had anticipated.

5. What event placed the United States in an unofficial war with Hitler?
   - ○ The United States passed the Neutrality Acts.
   - ○ British ships carried supplies from the United States.
   - ● A German U-boat fired on a U.S. destroyer in the Atlantic.
   - ○ The United States agreed to the Atlantic Charter with Great Britain.

   Alternate Question *Select the answer choice from the drop-down list to complete the sentence correctly.* The United States began an unofficial war with Hitler when *a German U-boat fired on a U.S. destroyer* and Roosevelt responded by ordering the U.S. Navy to shoot German submarines on sight.

6. **Compare and Contrast** What was the blitzkrieg, and how was it different from the warfare of World War I?

   Possible answer: The blitzkrieg was "lightning war." This type of warfare included air strikes, fast tanks, and artillery followed by massive attacks with infantry forces. This was meant to take enemy forces by surprise and quickly overwhelm them. This was very advanced compared to the warfare of World War I. The air power was limited in that war and the tanks were much slower.

7. **Elaborate** What led Charles de Gaulle to set up a government in exile in London, and how did he govern?

   Possible answer: The Nazis had taken Paris in June 1940. French leaders surrendered, and the Nazis took control of the northern part of the country and set up a puppet government in Vichy. Charles de Gaulle was a French general and had escaped to Britain. He committed all of his energy to reconquering France. He gave radio addresses from London to the French people. He organized the Free French military forces that battled the Nazis until France was finally liberated in 1944.

8. **Cause and Effect** What were the effects of radar and Enigma on the success of the Royal Air Force (RAF) in its fight against the Nazis?

   Possible answer: Radar allowed the RAF to know the number, speed, and direction of incoming warplanes. Enigma was a German code-making machine. One had been smuggled into Great Britain in the late 1930s. The Nazis didn't realize that the British had it. With it, the British were able to decode many of the Nazis' secret messages and know their plans ahead of time. Both of these technologies allowed the RAF to take an offensive position and also properly defend themselves when the Nazis struck.

9. **Elaborate** Why was the Suez Canal an important area for both the Allies and the Axis powers?

   Possible answer: Both sides needed petroleum to fuel their war equipment. The Suez Canal was a key access point to the Middle East. Whoever controlled the canal had access to the valuable oil reserves that were found in that region.

10. **Make Judgments** Why was the Lend-Lease Act of 1941 an important victory for the Allied forces in Europe?

    Possible answer: The Lend-Lease Act allowed Roosevelt to lend or lease arms to any country vital to the United States. Great Britain desperately needed help from the United States, but laws passed in the 1930s forbade the United States from getting involved in another conflict. The Lend-Lease Act allowed Great Britain to obtain the supplies and weaponry that it needed. According to the Act, the goods had to be transported on British ships, but the U.S. Navy could act as an escort to ensure that the ships arrived back to Europe safely.

Lesson 2 Planner

Japan's Pacific Campaign

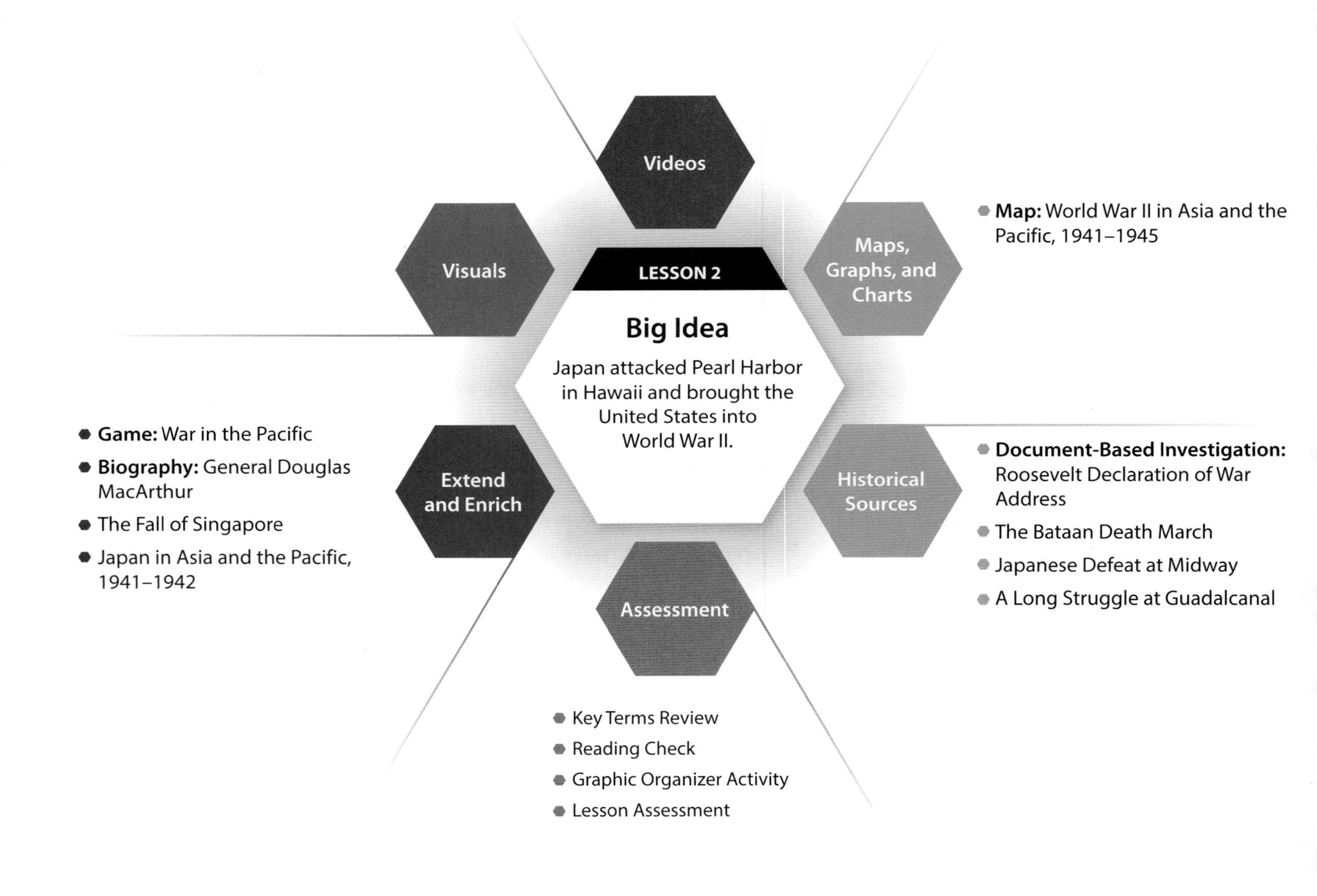

- **Map:** World War II in Asia and the Pacific, 1941–1945

- **Game:** War in the Pacific
- **Biography:** General Douglas MacArthur
- The Fall of Singapore
- Japan in Asia and the Pacific, 1941–1942

- **Document-Based Investigation:** Roosevelt Declaration of War Address
- The Bataan Death March
- Japanese Defeat at Midway
- A Long Struggle at Guadalcanal

- Key Terms Review
- Reading Check
- Graphic Organizer Activity
- Lesson Assessment

Online Lesson 2 Enrichment Activities

The Fall of Singapore

Article Students read how the Japanese captured the strategic island of Singapore from the British in early 1942. Then they take on the persona of Winston Churchill, having just learned about the Japanese advance through the Malayan jungle toward the Johore Strait and Singapore. They write a memorandum to the general in charge of the British forces explaining their view of the situation.

Japan in Asia and the Pacific, 1941–1942

Writing Activity Students Imagine that they are foreign diplomats living in Asia during World War II. Then they write journal entries describing the Japanese advance across Asia and the Pacific during 1941 and 1942.

Teach the Big Idea

1. **Whole Class Open/Introduction** Discuss how countries justify starting wars. Consider whether surprise attacks are ever completely unforeseen.
2. **Direct Teach** Read students the Big Idea: *Japan attacked Pearl Harbor in Hawaii and brought the United States into World War II.* Review the following lesson objectives with students to aid in their understanding of the Big Idea.
   - Explain how Japanese expansionism led to war with the Allies in Asia.
   - Describe Japan's early battle successes.
   - Explain how the Allies were able to stop Japanese expansion.
   - Summarize Allied battle strategy.
3. **Whole Group Close/Reflect** Have students write a cause-and-effect paragraph about the conflict between Japan and the Allies over control of the Pacific.

ONLINE DOCUMENT-BASED INVESTIGATION

World War II

Roosevelt Declaration of War Address is the second of five historical sources that students will analyze in the World War II module. A day after the Japanese attack at Pearl Harbor, President Franklin Roosevelt addressed Congress to request a declaration of war against Japan and its allies. Students can read the introductory text as well as the quotation itself.

DOCUMENT-BASED INVESTIGATION HISTORICAL SOURCE

Roosevelt Declaration of War Address

A day after the Japanese attack at Pearl Harbor, President Franklin Roosevelt addressed Congress requesting a declaration of war against Japan and its allies.

ONLINE GRAPHIC ORGANIZER

Japan's Pacific Campaign

As students read the lesson, have them use the graphic organizer to take notes. Students can review their graphic organizer notes at the end of the lesson to answer the following question:

Analyze Effects Which of the events noted in your graphic organizer was most significant in turning the tide of the war in the Pacific against the Japanese? Why? *The Battle of Midway, because the Allies were able to break Japanese codes and destroy a significant part of the Japanese fleet.*

Lesson 2

Japan's Pacific Campaign

The Big Idea
Japan attacked Pearl Harbor in Hawaii and brought the United States into World War II.

Why It Matters Now
World War II established the United States as a leading player in international affairs.

Key Terms and People
Isoroku Yamamoto
Pearl Harbor
Battle of Midway
Douglas MacArthur
Battle of Guadalcanal

Setting the Stage

Like Hitler, Japan's military leaders also had dreams of empire. Japan's expansion had begun in 1931. That year, Japanese troops took over Manchuria in northeastern China. Six years later, Japanese armies swept into the heartland of China. They expected quick victory. Chinese resistance, however, caused the war to drag on. This placed a strain on Japan's economy. To increase their resources, Japanese leaders looked toward the rich European colonies of Southeast Asia, signaling a confrontation with the West.

Surprise Attack on Pearl Harbor

By October 1940, Americans had cracked one of the codes that the Japanese used in sending secret messages. Therefore, they were well aware of Japanese plans for Southeast Asia. If Japan conquered European colonies there, it could also threaten the American-controlled Philippine Islands and Guam. To stop the Japanese advance, the U.S. government sent aid to strengthen Chinese resistance. And when the Japanese overran French Indochina—Vietnam, Cambodia, and Laos—in July 1941, Roosevelt cut off oil shipments to Japan.

Despite an oil shortage, the Japanese continued their conquests. They hoped to catch the European colonial powers and the United States by surprise. So they planned massive attacks on British and Dutch colonies in Southeast Asia and on American outposts in the Pacific—at the same time. Admiral **Isoroku Yamamoto** (ih•soh•ROO•koo-yah•muh•MOH•toh), Japan's greatest naval strategist, also called for an attack on the U.S. fleet in Hawaii. It was, he said, "a dagger pointed at [Japan's] throat" and must be destroyed.

1086 Module 28

COLLABORATIVE LEARNING

Plan a "War in the Pacific" Exhibit

1. Divide the class into groups. Ask members of each group to imagine that they are on a committee to plan a "War in the Pacific" exhibit for a local museum.
2. Ask students to begin by choosing a committee head and a note taker. They may also want to divide the roles of text researcher, visual researcher, audio researcher, and sketch artist among themselves.
3. Have students brainstorm ideas and conduct outside research according to their fields of expertise.
4. Then have students create a diagram of what their exhibit will look like along with a one-page written overview.
5. Ask students to share their plans with the class.

The *U.S.S. West Virginia* is engulfed by flames after taking a direct hit during the Japanese attack on Pearl Harbor.

Day of Infamy Early in the morning of December 7, 1941, American sailors at **Pearl Harbor** in Hawaii awoke to the roar of explosives. A Japanese attack was under way. U.S. military leaders had known from a coded Japanese message that an attack might come. But they did not know when or where it would occur. Within two hours, the Japanese had sunk or damaged 19 ships, including 8 battleships, moored in Pearl Harbor. More than 2,300 Americans were killed—with over 1,100 wounded. News of the attack stunned the American people. The next day, President Roosevelt addressed Congress, which quickly accepted his request for a declaration of war on Japan and its allies.

> *"Yesterday, December 7th, 1941—a date which will live in infamy—the United States of America was suddenly and deliberately attacked by naval and air forces of the Empire of Japan. . . . As Commander in Chief of the Army and Navy, I have directed that all measures be taken for our defense. But always will we remember the character of the onslaught against us. . . . I believe that I interpret the will of the Congress and of the people when I assert that we will not only defend ourselves to the uttermost, but will make it very certain that this form of treachery shall never again endanger us."*
>
> —President Franklin Delano Roosevelt, *Address to Congress, Dec. 8, 1941*

World War II 1087

Objectives

You may wish to discuss the following questions with students to help them frame the content as they read.

- Why did American leaders ban oil sales to Japan? *in response to the Japanese invasion of French Indochina*
- How did Yamamoto justify a preemptive strike on the United States? How might American actions have justified his concern? *He argued that the United States had threatened Japan. Roosevelt had cut off oil shipments.*
- What indicates that Japan's attack on Pearl Harbor was part of a larger strategy? *also planned attacks on British and Dutch holdings*

More About . . .

USS *Arizona* Memorial The surprise Japanese attack on Pearl Harbor sunk America's naval fleet, including the USS *Arizona*. This ship and the many sailors who lost their lives are not forgotten, however. Today the USS *Arizona* Memorial stands directly above the sunken ship. Visitors can board a boat to the museum. There they can look down to view the wreckage of the long-lost ship.

ONLINE DOCUMENT-BASED INVESTIGATION

Roosevelt Declaration of War Address

A day after the Japanese attack at Pearl Harbor, President Franklin Roosevelt addressed Congress to request a declaration of war against Japan and its allies. Students can read the introductory text as well as the quotation itself.

Analyze Sources What aspect of total war does Roosevelt suggest when he says " . . . defend ourselves to the uttermost . . ."? *using the complete resources of the United States to mobilize for war and defend the country*

ONLINE LESSON FLIP CARDS

Review Key Terms and People

Students can use the flip cards in the Lesson Review at any time to review the lesson's key terms and people: *Isoroku Yamamoto, Pearl Harbor, Battle of Midway, Douglas MacArthur,* and *Battle of Guadalcanal.*

ENGLISH LEARNING

You Are There at Pearl Harbor

1. Have students form small groups to discuss what it would have been like to be at Pearl Harbor during the attack.
2. Tell students to imagine that they have just survived the attack. First, have students talk about what they heard. Follow this with what they saw. Continue with what they may have smelled, tasted, or touched.
3. Have students write a descriptive paragraph describing the event.

LINK TO LANGUAGE ARTS

Attack on Pearl Harbor Newspaper Article

1. Ask students to use the Internet to research more about the attack on Pearl Harbor. Encourage students to take notes of important events that took place right before the attack, during it, and immediately after it.
2. Tell students to imagine that they are newspaper reporters in Hawaii at the time of the attacks. Their task is to write an unbiased account of the attack.
3. Once students have completed a rough draft, have them exchange articles with a partner, who will offer constructive criticism. Have students address the criticism and prepare a final version.

Objectives

You may wish to discuss the following questions with students to help them frame the content as they read.

- What can you infer about the attitude of many Asians toward colonization from the effort by the Japanese to win their support? *European and American colonial rulers were unpopular.*
- Summarize the fighting in the Pacific between December 1941 and April 1942. *Possible answer: Japan had a series of victories, some easy and some hard fought.*

More About . . .

Corregidor Known as The Rock, the island fortress of Corregidor in Manila Bay was the last U.S. position in the Philippines to surrender. For a month after the fall of Bataan, 13,000 American and Filipino troops held out in a concrete cave called Malinta Tunnel. Bombarded night and day by Japanese guns and suffering from hunger and exhaustion, the defenders finally surrendered on May 6 when Japanese troops swarmed over the rock. The last message sent from Corregidor said that soldiers broke down crying, having to give up their fight. The commander, Lieutenant General Jonathan Wainwright, and other survivors joined the Bataan Death March.

READING CHECK
Analyze Causes and Effects What were the causes and effects of Japan's attack on the United States? *Causes—Japan's military expansion and aggression; alliance with Germany and Italy; response to America's ban on the sale of oil; Effects—The United States declared war on Japan.*

READING CHECK
Find Main Ideas How did the Japanese often treat the native people of East Asia and their prisoners of war in territory they conquered? *They often treated native people and their prisoners of war with cruelty and contempt.*

Reading Check
Analyze Causes and Effects What were the causes and effects of Japan's attack on the United States?

Almost at the same time as the Pearl Harbor attack, the Japanese launched bombing raids on the British colony of Hong Kong and American-controlled Guam and Wake Island. (See the map World War II in Asia and the Pacific, 1941–1945.) They also landed an invasion force in Thailand. The Japanese drive for a Pacific empire was under way.

Japanese Victories

Lightly defended, Guam and Wake Island quickly fell to Japanese forces. The Japanese then turned their attention to the Philippines, controlled by the United States with several military bases there. In January 1942, they marched into the Philippine capital of Manila. American and Filipino forces took up a defensive position on the Bataan (buh•TAN) Peninsula on the northwestern edge of Manila Bay. At the same time, the Philippine government moved to the island of Corregidor just to the south of Bataan. After about three months of tough fighting, the Japanese took the Bataan Peninsula in April. Corregidor fell the following month.

The Japanese also continued their strikes against British possessions in Asia. After seizing Hong Kong, they invaded Malaya from the sea and overland from Thailand. By February 1942, the Japanese had reached Singapore, strategically located at the southern tip of the Malay Peninsula. After a fierce pounding, the colony surrendered. Within a month, the Japanese had conquered the resource-rich Dutch East Indies (now Indonesia), including the islands of Java, Sumatra, Borneo, and Celebes (SEHL•uh•beez). These British and Dutch colonies in Southeast Asia held much-needed oil, rubber, and other raw materials needed to defend Japan's expansion. The Japanese also moved westward, taking Burma. From there, they planned to launch a strike against India, the largest of Great Britain's colonies.

By the time Burma fell, Japan had taken control of more than 1 million square miles of Asian land. About 150 million people lived in this vast area. Before these conquests, the Japanese had tried to win the support of Asians with the anticolonialist idea of "East Asia for the Asiatics." After victory, however, the Japanese quickly made it clear that they had come as conquerors. They often treated the people of their new colonies with extreme cruelty.

Reading Check
Find Main Ideas How did the Japanese often treat the native people of East Asia and their prisoners of war in territory they conquered?

However, the Japanese reserved the most brutal treatment for Allied prisoners of war. The Japanese considered it dishonorable to surrender, and they had contempt for the prisoners of war in their charge. On the Bataan Death March—a forced march of more than 50 miles up the peninsula—the Japanese subjected their captives to terrible cruelties. 500 Americans and approximately 2,500 Filipino prisoners died on the march. Thousands more later perished at the inhumane prison camp. Of the approximately 76,000 prisoners who started the Bataan Death March, only 54,000 survived.

STRUGGLING READERS

Causes and Effects of Japanese Victories

1. Review with students the identify causes and effects skill.
2. Tell students that you will ask them cause-and-effect questions about each paragraph in the segment "Japanese Victories." After you ask each question, they are to reread the related paragraph to help them find the answer.
3. Pose the following questions, one at a time:

Paragraph 1: Why did Guam and Wake Island fall quickly? *They were lightly defended.* What was the effect of the conquest of Guam and Wake Island? *The Japanese turned their attention to the Philippines.*

Paragraph 2: What effect did the capture of Java, Sumatra, Borneo, and Celebes have on the Japanese? *They gained much-needed raw materials that would help them expand.*

Paragraph 3: What effect did the Japanese conquests have on the conquered people? *They received harsh treatment.*

Paragraph 4: What caused the Japanese to treat Allied prisoners of war so harshly? *The Japanese considered it dishonorable to surrender.*

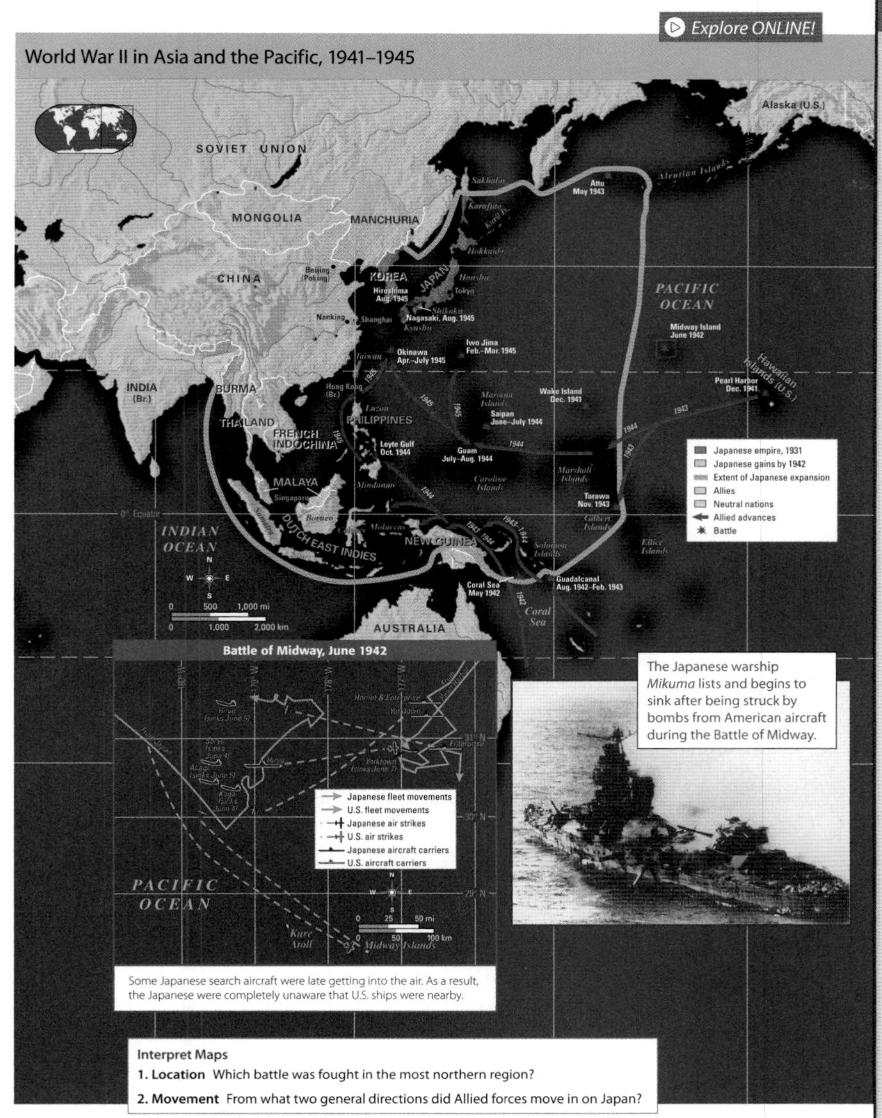

ONLINE HISTORICAL SOURCES

The Bataan Death March

Have students watch the video individually or as a class. You may wish to use the associated question as a discussion prompt.

Analyze Sources What were two factors that contributed to the Japan soldiers' inhumane treatment of the prisoners of war on the Bataan Death March? *The Japanese did not follow the Geneva Convention standards for treatment of prisoners of war, and they had no respect for soldiers who surrendered.*

HISTORICAL SOURCE

The Bataan Death March

American and Filipino forces were overrun when the Japanese invaded the Philippines in early 1942. Those who survived were forced by the Japanese to take the Bataan Death March, an arduous 60-mile trek under barbarous conditions. Japanese treatment of the prisoners on the march was later judged a war crime.

ONLINE INTERACTIVE MAPS

World War II in Asia and the Pacific, 1941–1945

Have students explore the map using the interactive features and answer the associated questions.

Movement From what two general directions in the Pacific did Allied forces move in on Japan? *east and south*

In print edition, see map of same title.

1. **Location** Which battle was fought in the most northern region? *Attu Island in May 1943*
2. **Movement** From what two general directions did Allied forces move in on Japan? *east and south*

Objectives

You may wish to discuss the following questions with students to help them frame the content as they read.

- What did the Battle of the Coral Sea imply about the importance of air power in the Pacific? *It was important: it even determined naval battles.*
- How did Midway show the value of military intelligence? *Breaking a Japanese code aided the victory.*

More About . . .

Chester Nimitz Unlike many military leaders who garnered fame during World War II, Chester Nimitz was known for his easy-going personality. He spoke softly and proved to be a role model for those he commanded. Nimitz was a gifted leader and filled positions under him wisely. Team building was one of his specialties. He is remembered most for demonstrating his military and leadership skills rather than boasting of them. After the war ended, Nimitz became Chief of Naval Operations.

GAME

War in the Pacific

Have students play the game to test their knowledge of facts about the war in the Pacific.

ONLINE HISTORICAL SOURCES

Japanese Defeat at Midway

Invite students to view the image and answer the associated question.

Analyze Sources What advantage did the U.S. military have that helped overcome the Japanese forces in the Battle of Midway? *Americans had broken the secret Japanese code used to transmit messages and knew the date and location of the planned attack.*

READING CHECK

Analyze Motives Why might the Americans send their entire Pacific Fleet to defend Midway Island? *Midway was located just west of Hawaii, so the Americans would want to keep the Japanese away from this important American territory.*

The Allies Strike Back

After a string of victories, the Japanese seemed unbeatable. Nonetheless, the Allies—mainly Americans and Australians—were anxious to strike back in the Pacific. The United States in particular wanted revenge for Pearl Harbor. In April 1942, a squadron of 16 B-25 bombers under the command of Lieutenant Colonel James H. Doolittle bombed Tokyo and several other Japanese cities. The bombs did little damage. The raid, however, made an important psychological point to both Americans and Japanese: Japan was vulnerable to attack.

The Allies Turn the Tide Doolittle's raid on Japan raised American morale and shook the confidence of some in Japan. As one Japanese citizen noted, "We started to doubt that we were invincible." In addition, some Japanese worried that defending and controlling a vast empire had caused them to spread their resources too thin.

Vocabulary
invincible unable to be overcome by force

Slowly, the Allies began to turn the tide of war. Early in May 1942, an American fleet with Australian support intercepted a Japanese strike force headed for Port Moresby in New Guinea. This city housed a critical Allied air base. Control of the air base would put the Japanese in easy striking distance of Australia.

In the battle that followed—the Battle of the Coral Sea—both sides used a new kind of naval warfare. The opposing ships did not fire a single shot. In fact, they often could not see one another. Instead, airplanes taking off from huge aircraft carriers attacked the ships. The Allies suffered more losses in ships and troops than did the Japanese. However, the Battle of the Coral Sea was something of a victory, for the Allies had stopped Japan's southward advance.

The Battle of Midway Japan next targeted Midway Island, some 1,500 miles west of Hawaii, the location of a key American airfield. Thanks to Allied code breakers, Admiral Chester Nimitz, commander in chief of the U.S. Pacific Fleet, knew that a huge Japanese force was heading toward Midway. Admiral Yamamoto himself was in command of the Japanese fleet. He hoped that the attack on Midway would draw the whole of the U.S. Pacific Fleet from Pearl Harbor to defend the island.

On June 4, with American forces hidden beyond the horizon, Nimitz allowed the Japanese to begin their assault on the island. As the first Japanese planes got into the air, American planes swooped in to attack the Japanese fleet. Many Japanese planes were still on the decks of the aircraft carriers. The strategy was a success. American pilots destroyed 332 Japanese planes, all four aircraft carriers, and one support ship. Yamamoto ordered his crippled fleet to withdraw. By June 7, 1942, the battle was over. The **Battle of Midway** turned the tide of war in the Pacific. (See the map World War II in Asia and the Pacific, 1941–1945.)

Reading Check
Analyze Motives Why might the Americans send their entire Pacific Fleet to defend Midway Island?

MAKE A PRESENTATION

Report on the War in the Pacific

1. Divide students into groups. Discuss with the class the segment "The Allies Strike Back." Gauge which topics students might like to learn more about.
2. List the topics students are interested in on the board. Examples: Doolittle's raid, Battle of the Coral Sea, Battle of Midway, Admiral Chester Nimitz, Admiral Yamamoto, and War in the Pacific National Historical Park
3. Have students research their topic and prepare an oral presentation. Students should include a visual.

An Allied Offensive

U.S. Marines storm ashore at Guadalcanal.

With morale high after their victory at Midway, the Allies took the offensive. The war in the Pacific involved vast distances. Japanese troops had dug in on hundreds of islands across the ocean. General **Douglas MacArthur**, the commander of the Allied land forces in the Pacific, developed a plan to handle this problem.

MacArthur believed that storming each island would be a long, costly effort. Instead, he wanted to "island-hop" past Japanese strongholds. His strategy was to capture weaker Japanese-controlled islands, then use these bases to seize islands closer to Japan. In the process, the Allies would cut off supply lines needed to keep the Japanese navy afloat.

MacArthur's first target soon presented itself. U.S. military leaders had learned that the Japanese were building a huge air base on the island of Guadalcanal in the Solomon Islands. The Allies had to strike fast before the base was completed and became another Japanese stronghold. At dawn on August 7, 1942, several thousand U.S. Marines, with Australian support, landed on Guadalcanal and the neighboring island of Tulagi.

BIOGRAPHY

General Douglas MacArthur
(1880–1964)

Douglas MacArthur's qualities as a leader and a fighting soldier emerged in France during World War I. Showing incredible dash and courage on the battlefield, he received several decorations for bravery. And he won promotion from the rank of major to brigadier general.

After serving in several positions in the United States, MacArthur received a posting to the Philippines in 1935. He remained there until shortly before the islands fell in 1941. But he left very reluctantly. In a message to the troops who remained behind, he vowed, "I shall return." As you will read later, MacArthur kept his promise.

Objectives

You may wish to discuss the following questions with students to help them frame the content as they read.

- What were potential disadvantages of the "island-hop" plan? *Possible answer: difficult to supply faraway troops*
- Do you think the Allies progressed quickly against the Japanese? *Yes—The Allies covered vast distances and hundreds of islands. No—Allied success took years of bloodshed.*

More About . . .

Douglas MacArthur The military leader had been posted in the Philippines from 1935–1941. He was forced to leave when the Philippines fell to the Japanese. MacArthur promised the Filipino people that he would be back. His declaration "I shall return" was memorable because it was short, personal, and confident. Flamboyant and self-assured, MacArthur skillfully publicized himself, which is partly why Generals George Marshall and Dwight Eisenhower did not like him.

Battle of Guadalcanal The Allies' first important offensive action proved to be a success. In fact, it is considered to be a turning point in the war in the Pacific. The Allies gained a strategic location within the Solomon Islands. Control of Guadalcanal meant that Australia was safe from Japanese attack. In addition, the Allies had gained a base in the South Pacific. The Allied victory at Guadalcanal bolstered the spirits of soldiers stationed in the Pacific. They had stopped the Japanese advance.

MAKE A MODEL

Understand Island Hopping

1. Read students the second paragraph in this segment. Students should reread the paragraph to themselves.
2. Tell students that it might be easier to understand the term *island-hop* by making a model.
3. Have students make a model of a string of islands using a chess set. They should place the pieces of one color across the board, with the powerful pieces spread out. Discuss how MacArthur planned to leave the strong pieces in place and attack the weaker ones at first. Ask for a volunteer to demonstrate this plan.

ADVANCED/GIFTED

Evaluate General Douglas MacArthur's Legacy

1. Ask students to find out more about General Douglas MacArthur's military career and write a detailed resumé for the famed general.
2. Then tell students to think about what they have learned about MacArthur's career and his strengths and weaknesses. Have them write an overall evaluation of MacArthur's skill as a leader.

BIOGRAPHY

General Douglas MacArthur

Have students read the biography of General Douglas MacArthur, the American general who commanded U. S. troops in the southwest Pacific during World War II and administered Japan after the war ended.

ONLINE HISTORICAL SOURCES

A Long Struggle at Guadalcanal

Invite students to view the image and answer the associated question.

Analyze Sources What did the Battle of Guadalcanal reveal about the Japanese fighters? *that they were an implacable foe, not likely to accept defeat or surrender*

HISTORICAL SOURCE

A Long Struggle at Guadalcanal

Guadalcanal was the first major Allied offensive in the Pacific. After the U.S. Marines launched a surprise attack in August 1942, they were able to capture and hold the air

READING CHECK

Identify Problems If the vast distances of the Pacific caused problems for the Allies, how might they have also caused military problems for the Japanese? *Supplying their outposts and keeping the Allies out of thousands of square miles of ocean would be problems for the Japanese.*

Print Assessment

1. **Organize Information** Which event was most important in turning the tide of the war in the Pacific against the Japanese? Why? *Possible answer: Attack on Pearl Harbor—The United States enters the war. Attack on Tokyo—Japan shows vulnerability. Battle of Midway—Strong Allied victory. Battle of Guadalcanal—Long and bloody struggle. Turning point—Midway severely damaged the Japanese navy.*
2. **Key Terms and People** For each key term or person in the lesson, write a sentence explaining its significance. *Explanations of the lesson's key terms can be found on the following pages: Isoroku Yamamoto, p. 1086; Pearl Harbor, p. 1087; Battle of Midway, p. 1090; Douglas MacArthur, p. 1091; Battle of Guadalcanal, p. 1092*
3. **Evaluate** Did Admiral Yamamoto make a wise decision in bombing Pearl Harbor? Why or why not? *Unwise—It drew Americans away from Europe to become a determined enemy of Japan. Wise—It weakened a likely foe.*
4. **Analyze Motives** Why do you think the Japanese changed their approach from trying to win the support of the colonized peoples to acting as conquerors? *Possible answer: no longer needed local support after conquest*
5. **Identify Problems** What problems did Japan face in building an empire in the Pacific? *Possible answer: controlling a vast empire, opposition from colonial interests, fear of vulnerability at home*

The marines had little trouble seizing Guadalcanal's airfield. But the battle for control of the island turned into a savage struggle as both sides poured in fresh troops. In February 1943, after six months of fighting on land and at sea, the **Battle of Guadalcanal** finally ended. After losing more than 24,000 of a force of 36,000 soldiers, the Japanese abandoned what they came to call "the Island of Death."

To American war correspondent Ralph Martin and the U.S. soldiers who fought there, Guadalcanal was simply "hell":

> *"Hell was red furry spiders as big as your fist, . . . enormous rats and bats everywhere, and rivers with waiting crocodiles. Hell was the sour, foul smell of the squishy jungle, humidity that rotted a body within hours. . . . Hell was an enemy . . . so fanatic that it used its own dead as booby traps."*
>
> —Ralph G. Martin, *The GI War*

Reading Check
Identify Problems If the vast distances of the Pacific caused problems for the Allies, how might they have caused military problems for the Japanese also?

As Japan worked to establish a new order in Southeast Asia and the Pacific, the Nazis moved ahead with Hitler's design for a new order in Europe. This design included plans for dealing with those Hitler considered unfit for the Third Reich. You will learn about these plans in the next lesson.

Lesson 2 Assessment

1. **Organize Information** Which event was most important in turning the tide of the war in the Pacific against the Japanese? Why?

Event	Effect

2. **Key Terms and People** For each key term or person in the lesson, write a sentence explaining its significance.
3. **Evaluate** Did Admiral Yamamoto make a wise decision in bombing Pearl Harbor? Why or why not?
4. **Analyze Motives** Why do you think the Japanese changed their approach from trying to win the support of the colonized peoples to acting as conquerors?
5. **Identify Problems** What problems did Japan face in building an empire in the Pacific?

Online Assessment

1. Which of the following is a way that the United States tried to stop Japan's aggression in the Pacific?
   - ● The United States cut off oil shipments to Japan.
   - ○ The United States sent its entire naval fleet to the Philippines.
   - ○ The United States broke the Japanese code used to send secret messages.
   - ○ The United States planned attacks on British and Dutch colonies in the Pacific region.

   Alternate Question *Select the answer choice from the drop-down list to complete the sentence correctly.* The United States wanted to stop Japan's aggression in the Pacific. One way it did so was to *send aid to China*.

2. What is one reason that the Japanese wanted to conquer the Dutch East Indies?
   - ● The area was rich in natural resources.
   - ○ The area was a gateway to the South Pacific.
   - ○ The area was home to many native Japanese.
   - ○ The area was the home of the British naval fleet.

   Alternate Question *Select the answer choice from the drop-down list to complete the sentence correctly.* The Japanese invaded the *Dutch East Indies* in March 1942, which was helpful to the Japanese war effort because this area was rich in natural resources.

3. How was the Battle of the Coral Sea a different type of naval warfare?
   - ● Airplanes from aircraft carriers attacked the ships.
   - ○ Submarines sent nuclear bombs toward the battleships.
   - ○ Land-to-sea missiles were sent from faraway shores to strike the ships.
   - ○ Radar on submarines was used to detect where the ships at sea were located.

   Alternate Question *Select the answer choice from the drop-down list to complete the sentence correctly.* The Battle of the Coral Sea was particularly significant because it was the first battle in which both sides used *airplanes* to attack each other.

4. Why did the Allied forces need to act quickly in their attack on Guadalcanal?
   - ○ The Japanese were establishing industries there.
   - ● The Japanese were building a huge air base there.
   - ○ The Japanese were starting to set up colonies there.
   - ○ The Japanese were holding Allied prisoners of war there.

   Alternate Question *Select the answer choice from the drop-down list to complete the sentence correctly.* *Guadalcanal* was an important target for the Allied forces because the Japanese were building a huge airbase there.

5. **Make Judgments** Why was the bombing of Pearl Harbor a significant moment in U.S. history?

   Possible answer: The bombing of Pearl Harbor was a surprise attack. Within just two hours, the Japanese had sunk or damaged 19 ships, 8 of which were huge battleships. In the attack, 2,300 Americans were killed and 1,100 were wounded. The American people were stunned and outraged. The next day when Roosevelt addressed Congress, the members unanimously voted to declare war on Japan and its allies. Just 28 hours after the attack, the United States had entered World War II. So, the event was significant not only for the amount of lives lost, but also because it was the driving force to get the United States into the war.

6. **Make Judgments** What did Japanese treatment of conquered countries and Allied prisoners of war illustrate about the Japanese military at that time?

   Possible answer: The Japanese treated the conquered people and the Allied prisoners of war with great cruelty. For example, more than 20,000 soldiers died because of their treatment in the Philippines on the Bataan Death March. This showed that they had little regard for human life. They believed that they were conquerors, so they could treat the conquered people however they wanted. They also believed that it was a disgrace to surrender, so the Allied soldiers who were prisoners of war were treated with severe contempt.

7. **Elaborate** Why was the Battle of Midway a turning point in the war in the Pacific, and what caused this particular outcome for this battle?

   Possible answer: The Battle of Midway was considered a turning point in the war in the Pacific. The United States completely crippled the Japanese fleet—destroying 332 planes, all 4 aircraft carriers, and 1 support ship. The United States was able to achieve this outcome because of the strategy outlined by Admiral Chester A. Nimitz, who had advanced knowledge of the Japanese attack because the Japanese code for its secret messages had been broken.

8. **Elaborate** What was MacArthur's strategy in the Pacific after the success at Midway?

   Possible answer: MacArthur didn't think that storming each island controlled by the Japanese would be effective. He decided to "island-hop" past Japanese strongholds and capture weaker Japanese-controlled islands. Then the Allied forces could use those islands to cut off supply lines to the Japanese.

Lesson 3 Planner

The Holocaust

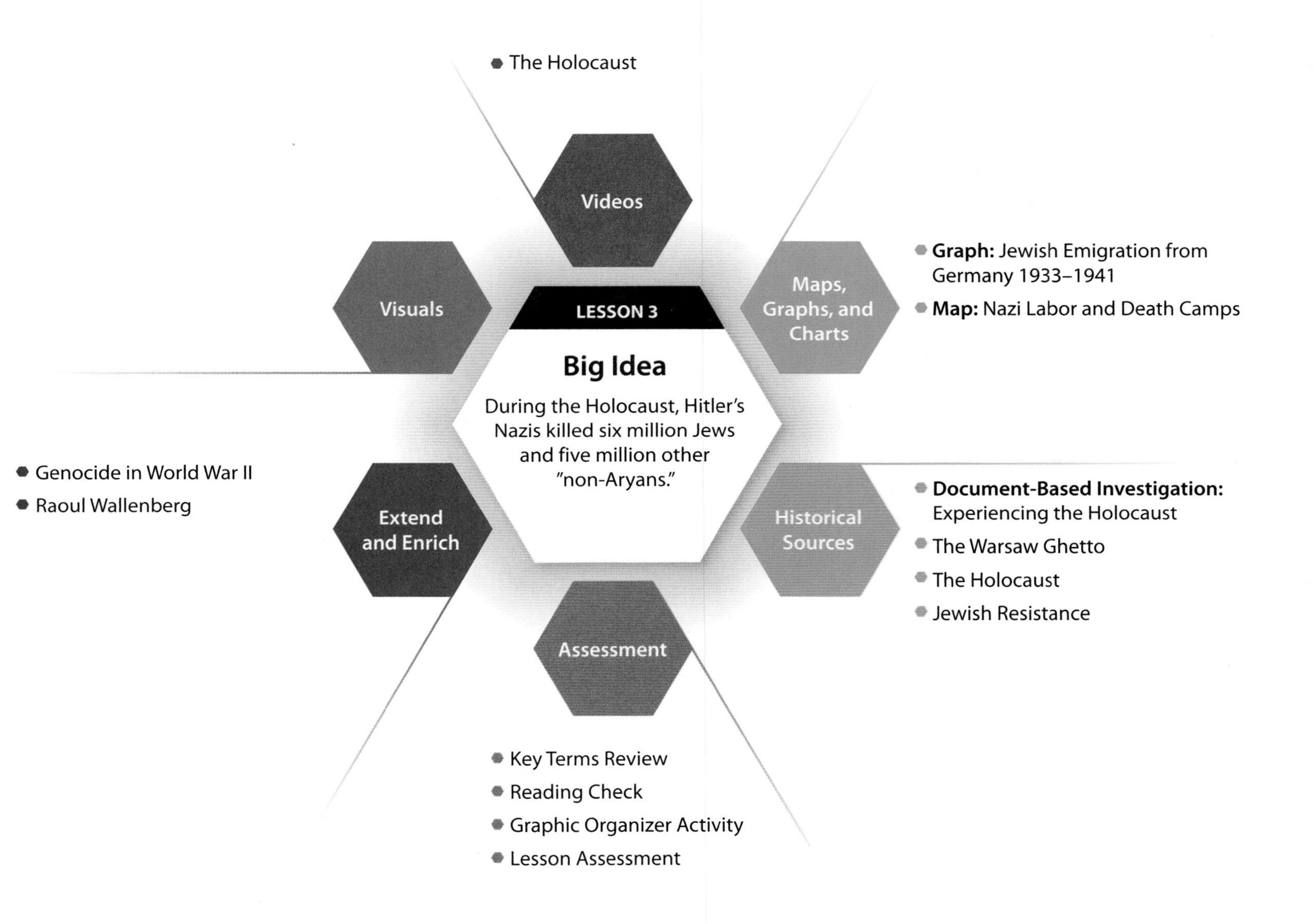

Online Lesson 3 Enrichment Activities

Genocide in World War II

Memoir Students read how Jacob Wiernik, an inmate at the Treblinka death camp in Poland, described being compelled to help build new gas chambers for the camp. The new chambers could hold as many as 3,800 victims; the old ones held only 600. Next they find information from newspaper articles and websites on instances of genocide and ethnic cleansing in the last 20 years. Use the information to create an annotated map titled "Genocide in the Late 20th Century."

Raoul Wallenberg

Biography Students read about Swedish diplomat Raoul Wallenberg's heroic efforts to save Jewish lives in Hungary during World War II. Then they write a speech for the occasion of this special honor.

Lesson 3

The Holocaust

The Big Idea

During the Holocaust, Hitler's Nazis killed six million Jews and five million other "non-Aryans."

Why It Matters Now

The violence against Jews during the Holocaust led to the founding of Israel after World War II.

Key Terms and People

Aryan
Holocaust
Kristallnacht
ghetto
Final Solution
genocide

Setting the Stage

As part of their vision for Europe, the Nazis proposed a new racial order. They proclaimed that the Germanic peoples, or **Aryans**, were a "master race." (This was a misuse of the term *Aryan*. The term actually refers to the Indo-European peoples who began to migrate into the Indian subcontinent around 1500 BC.) The Nazis claimed that all non-Aryan peoples, particularly Jewish people, were inferior. This racist message would eventually lead to the **Holocaust**, the systematic mass slaughter of Jews. In addition, the Nazis murdered millions of other people they deemed inferior.

The Holocaust Begins

To gain support for his racist ideas, Hitler knowingly tapped into a hatred for Jews that had deep roots in European history. Anti-Semitism, a hostility toward or prejudice against Jews, had existed in Christian Europe since the Middle Ages. For generations, many Germans, along with other Europeans, had targeted Jews as the cause of their failures. Some Germans even blamed Jews for their country's defeat in World War I and for its economic problems after that war.

In time, Hitler made the targeting of Jews a government policy. The Nuremberg Laws, passed in 1935, deprived Jews of their rights to German citizenship and forbade marriages between Jews and non-Jews. Laws passed later also limited the kinds of work that Jews could do.

"Night of Broken Glass" Worse was yet to come. Early in November 1938, 17-year-old Herschel Grynszpan (GRIHN•shpahn), a Jewish youth from Germany, was visiting an uncle in Paris. While Grynszpan was there, he received a postcard. It said that after living in Germany for 27 years, his father had been deported to Poland. On November 7, wishing to avenge his father's deportation, Grynszpan shot a German diplomat living in Paris.

Teach the Big Idea

1. **Whole Class Open/Introduction** Ask students what they know about the Holocaust. Note that the Nazis focused on Jews but viewed many groups as inferior.
2. **Direct Teach** Read students the Big Idea: *During the Holocaust, Hitler's Nazis killed six million Jews and five million other "non-Aryans."* Review the following lesson objectives with students to aid in their understanding of the Big Idea.
   - Trace the course of the persecution of Jews by the Nazis.
   - Describe the results of the "Final Solution."
3. **Whole Group Close/Reflect** Have each student write several paragraphs about whether the Holocaust, or something similar to it, could happen today.

ONLINE DOCUMENT-BASED INVESTIGATION

World War II

Experiencing the Holocaust is the third of five historical sources that students will analyze in the World War II module. Elie Wiesel, a Jew who was nearly 15 years old when he entered Auschwitz, wrote of the nightmare he experienced at the Auschwitz and Buchenwald concentration camps in 1944–1945. Have students read the quotation by Elie Wiesel.

ONLINE LESSON FLIP CARDS

Review Key Terms and People

Students can use the flip cards in the Lesson Review at any time to review the lesson's key terms and people: *Aryan, Holocaust, Kristallnacht, ghetto, "Final Solution,"* and *genocide.*

ONLINE GRAPHIC ORGANIZER

The Holocaust

As students read the lesson, have them use the graphic organizer to take notes. Students can review their graphic organizer notes at the end of the lesson to answer the following question:

Make Inferences How do you think Hitler ensured that his Nazi soldiers executed his actions of the "Final Solution"? *Years of relentless propaganda demonizing the Jews caused many to believe Hitler's claim that Jews were a grave threat to the state. Others may have feared that disobedience would result in loss of their own lives.*

Objectives

You may wish to discuss the following questions with students to help them frame the content as they read.

- What was the immediate pretext for Kristallnacht, and what were its underlying causes? *Pretext—A Jewish youth shot a German. Underlying causes—Many Europeans blamed Jews for social and political problems and shared Nazi anti-Semitic attitudes.*
- How did anti-Semitism outside of Germany contribute to the problems of Jews in Germany? *Countries refused to accept Jewish refugees.*

More About . . .

The United States Holocaust Memorial Museum

Visitors to Washington, DC, can learn about the tragic events faced by the Jewish people at Hitler's hand. Doors at the United States Holocaust Memorial Museum open daily as a memorial to the millions of lives lost. In the main exhibition, visitors move from floor to floor, studying artifacts and photographs, viewing films, and reading the words of those who survived the Holocaust and those who lost their lives during this terrifying event.

ONLINE INTERACTIVE GRAPHS

Jewish Emigration from Germany 1933–1941

Have students explore the graph and answer the associated question.

Interpret Graphs In what year did the fewest number of Jews emigrate from Germany? *1941*

ONLINE HISTORICAL SOURCES

The Warsaw Ghetto

Invite students to view the image and answer the associated question.

Analyze Sources What was Hitler's motive in creating ghettos in countries he conquered? *He wanted to separate the Jews from the rest of the population under conditions in which they would suffer and die.*

READING CHECK

Find Main Idea What steps did Hitler take to rid Germany of Jews? *He tried to force them to emigrate. When this plan failed, he ordered all Jews moved into ghettos, where he hoped they would die of starvation or disease.*

When Nazi leaders heard the news, they used this pretext to launch a violent attack on the Jewish community. On November 9, Nazi storm troopers attacked Jewish homes, businesses, and synagogues across Germany and Austria and murdered close to 100 Jews. Using the practice of ethnic cleansing, they rounded up 30,000 Jews and sent them to concentration camps, where many died. An American in Leipzig wrote, "Jewish shop windows by the hundreds were systematically . . . smashed. . . . The main streets of the city were a positive litter of shattered plate glass." The night of November 9 became known as ***Kristallnacht*** (krih•STAHL•nahkt), or "Night of Broken Glass." A 14-year-old boy described his memory of that awful night:

> *"All the things for which my parents had worked for eighteen long years were destroyed in less than ten minutes. Piles of valuable glasses, expensive furniture, linens—in short, everything was destroyed. . . . The Nazis left us, yelling, "Don't try to leave this house! We'll soon be back again and take you to a concentration camp to be shot."*
>
> —M. I. Libau, quoted in *Never to Forget: The Jews of the Holocaust*

Kristallnacht marked a major step-up in the Nazi policy of Jewish persecution. The future for Jews in Germany looked truly grim.

A Flood of Refugees After *Kristallnacht*, some Jews realized that violence against them was bound to increase. By the end of 1939, a number of German Jews had fled to other countries. Many, however, remained in Germany. Later, Hitler's forces conquered territories in which millions more Jews lived.

At first, Hitler favored emigration as a solution to what he called "the Jewish problem." Getting other countries to continue admitting Germany's Jews became an issue, however. After admitting tens of thousands of Jewish refugees, such countries as France, Britain, and the United States abruptly closed their doors to further immigration. Germany's foreign minister observed, "We all want to get rid of our Jews. The difficulty is that no country wishes to receive them."

After 1941, all Jews in German-controlled areas had to wear a yellow Star of David patch.

Isolating the Jews When Hitler found that he could not get rid of Jews through emigration, he put another plan into effect. He ordered Jews in all countries under his control to be moved to designated cities. In those cities, the Nazis herded the Jews into dismal, overcrowded **ghettos**, or segregated Jewish areas. The Nazis then sealed off the ghettos with barbed wire and stone walls. They hoped that the Jews inside would starve to death or die from disease.

Even under these horrible conditions, the Jews hung on. Some, particularly the Jews in Warsaw, Poland, formed resistance organizations within the ghettos. They also struggled to keep their traditions. Ghetto theaters produced plays and concerts. Teachers taught lessons in secret schools. Scholars kept records so that one day people would find out the truth.

Reading Check
Find Main Ideas What steps did Hitler take to rid Germany of Jews?

ANALYZE PRIMARY SOURCES

Read Like a Historian

1. Guide the class in a discussion of Hitler's anti-Semitism. How did he go about blaming his victims? Why would they have felt a sense of helplessness?
2. Have students find primary sources written by concentration camp survivors.
3. Have each student choose one primary source and write a short essay introducing it.
4. Have volunteers read their essays to the class, and encourage class discussion.

ENGLISH LANGUAGE LEARNERS

Identify Main Idea and Details

1. Review with students the identify main idea and details skill. Remind students that the first sentence of a paragraph often states the main idea. Continue by saying that sometimes the main idea can be located elsewhere in the paragraph.
2. Work with students to identify the main idea of the first paragraph of the segment "The Holocaust Begins." Then ask them to state specific details related to the main idea.
3. Use the same process for the next two paragraphs. Then have students work through the rest of the paragraphs in the segment independently.

The "Final Solution"

Hitler soon grew impatient and decided to take more direct action. His plan was called the **Final Solution**. It was actually a program of **genocide**, the systematic murder of an entire people.

Hitler believed that his plan of conquest depended on the purity of the Aryan race. He had adopted the view of late 19th-century European anti-Semites that Jews constituted not only a separate religion, but a separate race, one intent on polluting Aryan blood. To protect racial purity, the Nazis had to eliminate other races, nationalities, or groups they viewed as inferior—as "subhumans." These included the Roma (gypsies), who were regarded as nomadic outsiders of mixed race, as well as Poles, Russians, homosexuals, the insane, the disabled, and the incurably ill. But the Nazis focused especially on the Jews.

The Mass Killings Begin As Nazi troops swept across Eastern Europe and the Soviet Union, the mass killings began. Units from the SS (Hitler's elite security force) moved from town to town to hunt down Jews. The SS and their collaborators rounded up men, women, children, and even babies and took them to isolated spots. They then shot their prisoners in pits that became the prisoners' graves.

German soldiers round up Jews in the Warsaw ghetto.

Objectives

You may wish to discuss the following questions with students to help them frame the content as they read.

- Why did Hitler begin mass killings of Jews? *He did not think starvation and disease were killing them fast enough.*
- What was the difference between a concentration camp and an extermination camp? *Concentration camps were slave-labor prisons. Extermination camps were for mass murder.*
- What is the theme of the quotation from Elie Wiesel? *He will never forget those who died in the Holocaust*

More About . . .

Anne Frank Anne Frank was a young Jewish girl who lived in Germany when Hitler came to power. Anne and her family soon fled to the Netherlands. After war erupted, German troops began rounding up Jews in the Netherlands, and the Franks were forced to hide above Anne's father's office. Anne kept a diary of her family's two years in hiding. In 1944 the Nazi secret police discovered the Franks and sent them to a concentration camp. Anne was eventually transferred to the Bergen-Belsen camp, where she died of disease in March 1945. Just a few weeks later, the camp was liberated by Allied troops. Anne's diary was published following the war. It has since been translated into more than 50 languages.

Nazi Medicine German doctors used Jews for medical experiments that often resulted in great suffering or death. For example, doctors infected prisoners with typhus and other diseases to see how long they could survive. To practice surgery, student doctors would operate on prisoners without anesthesia. Many of these experiments had no medical value.

COLLABORATIVE LEARNING

Take Action Against Genocide

1. Organize students into groups of four or five. Tell them that it is 1942 and they have just heard about Hitler's widespread killing of Jews in Europe.
2. Have each group develop a campaign to convince the U.S. government to take action to save European Jews. Campaigns may include letters to editors or elected officials, speeches, posters, or other materials they think would help convince people to stop Hitler's widespread killing of Jews.
3. Have each group present its campaign to the rest of the class.
4. Lead the class in a discussion of the campaign materials created by students.

ONLINE ANALYZE VIDEOS

The Holocaust

HISTORY

Have students watch the video individually or as a class. You may wish to use the associated question as a discussion prompt.

Analyze Videos Describe Nazi anti-Semitic policies in the 1930s before the outbreak of war. *Jews were segregated, denied citizenship, and had limited rights to work and own property.*

World War II 1095

ONLINE INTERACTIVE MAPS

Nazi Labor and Death Camps

Have students explore the map using the interactive features and answer the associated question.

Place In which country were most death camps located? *Poland*

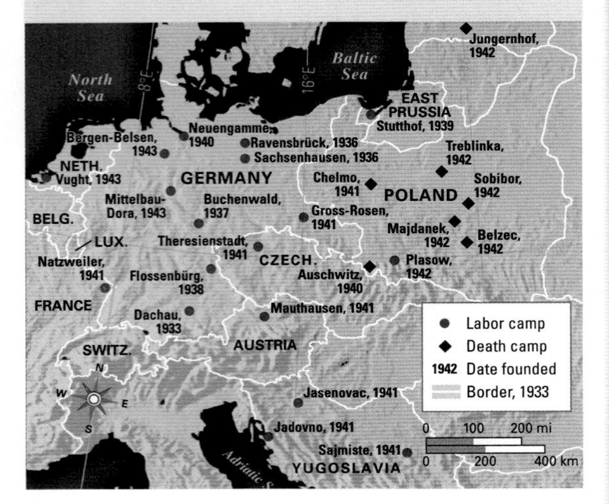

Jews in communities not reached by the killing squads were rounded up and taken to concentration camps, or slave-labor prisons. These camps were located mainly in Germany and Poland. Hitler hoped that the horrible conditions in the camps would speed the total elimination of the Jews.

The prisoners worked seven days a week as slaves for the SS or for German businesses. Guards severely beat or killed their prisoners for not working fast enough. With meals of thin soup, a scrap of bread, and potato peelings, most prisoners lost 50 pounds in the first few months. Hunger was so intense, recalled one survivor, "that if a bit of soup spilled over, prisoners would . . . dig their spoons into the mud and stuff the mess in their mouths."

The Final Stage Hitler's war on the Jews turned toward the Final Solution in 1942. The Nazis built extermination camps equipped with huge gas chambers that could kill as many as 6,000 human beings in a day.

When prisoners arrived at Auschwitz (OUSH•vihts), the largest of the extermination camps, they paraded before a committee of SS doctors. With a wave of the hand, these doctors separated the strong—mostly men—from the weak—mostly women, young children, the elderly, and the sick. Those labeled as weak would die that day. They were told to undress for a shower and then led into a chamber with fake showerheads. After the doors were closed, cyanide gas poured from the showerheads or holes in the ceiling. All inside were killed in a matter of minutes. Later, the Nazis installed crematoriums, or ovens, to burn the bodies.

Interpret Maps

1. **Location** In which country were most death camps located?

ADVANCED/GIFTED

Report on Examples of Genocide

1. Remind students that *genocide* means the systematic killing of a group of people. Tell the class that, although the word was first used in connection with Hitler's "Final Solution," genocide has taken place throughout history.
2. Have students conduct independent research to identify places in the world where genocide has taken place. *Cambodia, Rwanda, Iraq, Armenia, Bosnia, Sri Lanka, Guatemala, East Timor, Sudan (Darfur)*
3. Then tell students to choose one of the examples of genocide and write a report about its causes, its effects, and how (or if) it stopped.
4. Group students into discussion groups, ensuring that different examples of genocide are represented in each group. Have students orally present their reports to the group.
5. Encourage group members to discuss similarities and differences between the examples and to make several generalizations about genocide

History in Depth

Jewish Resistance

Even in the extermination camps, Jews rose up and fought against the Nazis. At Treblinka in August 1943, and at Sobibor in October 1943, small groups of Jews revolted. They killed guards, stormed the camp armories, stole guns and grenades, and then broke out. In both uprisings, about 300 prisoners escaped. Most were killed soon after. Of those who survived, many joined up with partisan groups and continued to fight until the end of the war.

Late in 1944, prisoners at Auschwitz revolted, too. Like the escapees at Treblinka and Sobibor, most were caught and killed. Young women like Ella Gartner and Roza Robota made the Auschwitz uprising possible. Gartner smuggled gunpowder into the camp from the munitions factory where she worked. Robota helped organize resistance in the camp. Gartner and Robota were executed on January 6, 1945. Less than a month later, Auschwitz was liberated.

Ella Gartner

Roza Robota

Critical Thinking

Form Generalizations What do you think Gartner, Robota, and other Jews who revolted had in common?

ONLINE HISTORICAL SOURCES

Jewish Resistance

Have students explore and compare the images using the interactive slider.

Analyze Sources What do you think Gartner, Robota, and other Jews who revolted had in common? *a desire to resist their oppressors at all costs*

In print edition, see History in Depth: Jewish Resistance.

Form Generalizations What do you think Gartner, Robota, and other Jews who revolted had in common? *a desire to resist their oppressors at all costs*

HISTORICAL SOURCE

Jewish Resistance

Even in the extermination camps, Jews rose up and fought against the Nazis. Late in 1944, prisoners at Auschwitz revolted. Young women like Ella Gartner and Roza Robota made the uprising possible. Gartner smuggled gunpowder into the camp from the munitions factory where she worked. Robota helped organize resistance in the camp. After prisoners blew up a crematorium, Gartner and Robota were tortured, then executed on January 6, 1945. Less than a month later, Auschwitz was liberated.

STRUGGLING READERS

A Chronology of the Holocaust

1. Explain to students that creating a timeline can be an effective way of taking notes.
2. Pair a struggling reader with a more proficient reader. Have pairs review the content of this lesson and create a timeline that summarizes major events in students' own words.
3. Encourage students to use their timelines to help them review the material before a quiz or test.

Jews Murdered Under Nazi Rule*			
	Original Jewish Population	Jews Murdered	Percent Surviving
Poland	3,300,000	2,800,000	15%
Soviet Union (area occupied by Germans)	2,100,000	1,500,000	29%
Hungary	404,000	200,000	49%
Romania	850,000	425,000	50%
Germany/Austria	270,000	210,000	22%

*Estimates

Source: Hannah Vogt, *The Burden of Guilt*

Response from the Allies Reports of the deportation and mass executions of Jews reached Allied leaders as early as 1942. The Allies officially condemned the Nazi's extermination of Jews in Europe and promised punishment, but it is not clear that they truly believed or understood the full ramifications of the Final Solution. In 1944, the War Refugee Board was created in the U.S., and this helped rescue some 200,000 European Jews. No military action, however, was undertaken to disrupt the transport and murder of Jews during the war.

The Survivors Some six million European Jews died in the extermination camps and in Nazi massacres. Fewer than four million survived. Some escaped the horrors of the extermination camps with help from non-Jewish people. These rescuers, at great risk to their own lives, hid Jews in their homes or helped them escape to neutral countries.

The Roma of Europe were also exterminated in the Nazi death camps. It is estimated that 25% of the one million Roma in Europe did not survive the Holocaust. Millions of others – including Poles, Slavs, homosexuals, and the disabled – died in the camps.

Those who survived the camps were changed forever by what they had experienced. Elie Wiesel, a Jew who was nearly 15 years old when he entered Auschwitz, wrote:

> *"Never shall I forget the small faces of the children whose bodies I saw transformed into smoke under a silent sky. Never shall I forget those flames that consumed my faith forever. . . . Never shall I forget those moments that murdered my God and my soul and turned my dreams to ashes. . . . Never."*
>
> —Elie Wiesel, quoted in *Night*

Reading Check
Analyze Effects How was the Final Solution a natural outcome of Nazi racial theory?

Lesson 3 Assessment

1. **Organize Information** What Nazi actions were part of the Final Solution?

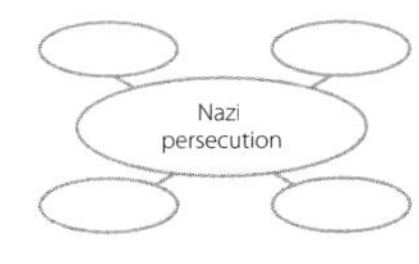

2. **Key Terms and People** For each key term or person in the lesson, write a sentence explaining its significance.
3. **Analyze Motives** Why might people want to blame a minority group for most of their country's problems?
4. **Draw Conclusions** Why do you think the Allies did not respond to the forced removal, or ethnic cleansing, and genocide of Jews in countries under Nazi control?
5. **Make Inferences** Why do you think German people were bystanders, and went along with the Nazi policy of persecution of the Jews?
6. **Identify Effects** What impact did the Holocaust have on the Jewish and Roma population of Europe?

READING CHECK

Analyze Effects How was the "Final Solution" a natural outcome of Nazi racial theory? *The Nazis believed that the To remain a superior race, the Aryans had to remain pure. Therefore, all the inferior races, especially the Jews, had to be eliminated.*

ONLINE DOCUMENT-BASED INVESTIGATION

Experiencing the Holocaust

Elie Wiesel wrote of the nightmare he experienced at the Auschwitz and Buchenwald concentration camps. Students can click on the audio button beneath the historical source to hear the excerpt read aloud.

Analyze Sources What aspect of Hitler's total war did Wiesel experience? *Part of Hitler's war strategy was the systematic extermination of the Jewish people in territory conquered.*

DOCUMENT-BASED INVESTIGATION HISTORICAL SOURCE

Experiencing the Holocaust

Elie Wiesel, a Jew, nearly 15 years old when he entered Auschwitz, wrote of the nightmare he experienced at the Auschwitz and Buchenwald concentration camps in 1944–1945.

Print Assessment

1. **Organize Information** What Nazi actions were part of the "Final Solution"? *Possible answer: Nuremberg Laws, Kristallnacht, ghettos, concentration camps. Students might mention other actions related to the "Final Solution"—program designed to kill Jews by starving, shooting, or gassing them, or by working them to death.*
2. **Key Terms and People** For each key term or person in the lesson, write a sentence explaining its significance. *Explanations of the lesson's key terms can be found on the following pages: Aryan, p. 1093; Holocaust, p. 1093; Kristallnacht, p. 1094; ghetto, p. 1094; Final Solution, p. 1095; genocide, p. 1095*
3. **Analyze Motives** Why might people want to blame a minority group for most of their country's problems? *Possible answer: Blaming a minority takes responsibility away from a country and its leaders.*

(continued)

Print Assessment *(continued)*

4. **Draw Conclusions** Why do you think the Allies did not respond to the forced removal, or ethnic cleansing, and genocide of Jews in countries under Nazi control? *Possible answer: They did not fully believe the reports, or were militarily unwilling to stop the movement of Jews to concentration camps. Some leaders may have been indifferent to the plight of the Jews.*
5. **Make Inferences** Why do you think German people were bystanders and went along with the Nazi policy of persecution of the Jews? *Possible answer: out of fear, out of agreement with Nazi policy, or out of indifference*
6. **Identify Effects** What impact did the Holocaust have on the Jewish and Roma population of Europe? *It reduced the Jewish population by about two-thirds and left the survivors devastated. It reduced the Roma population by one-quarter.*

Online Assessment

1. What was Hitler's first plan to rid Germany of its Jewish population?
   - ○ He wanted to isolate the Jews in ghettos.
   - ● He wanted the Jews to immigrate to other places.
   - ○ He wanted to destroy Jewish shops and businesses.
   - ○ He wanted the Jews to be exterminated in concentration camps.

   Alternate Question *Select the answer choice from the drop-down list to complete the sentence correctly.*
   At first, Hitler wanted to force the Jews of Germany to *immigrate to other nations*, but then he had to resort to other more diabolical measures when that plan didn't work out as he wanted.

2. What was the key element of the "Final Solution"?
   - ● The Nazis built gas chambers in the extermination camps.
   - ○ The Nazis forced the Jews to work seven days a week as slaves.
   - ○ The Nazis reduced the food supply of the Jews in the labor camps
   - ○ The Nazis forced the men and women to be separated from each other.

   Alternate Question *Select the answer choice from the drop-down list to complete the sentence correctly.*
   The Nazis built *gas chambers* in camps such as Auschwitz so they could institute Hitler's plans for the "Final Solution."

3. **Make Inferences** What was Kristallnacht, and how was the idea of retaliation used by the Nazi leaders in this event?

   Possible answer: Kristallnacht is translated to mean "night of broken glass." It was called this because the Nazi leaders ordered that Jewish shops, businesses, and synagogues throughout Germany and Austria be destroyed. The streets were filled with shattered plate glass from thousands of windows. Approximately 100 Jews were killed, and 30,000 were rounded up and sent to concentration camps. Kristallnacht was in response to the death of a German diplomat in Paris. This man was killed by a Jew who was upset that his family had been deported to Poland. The Nazi leaders launched a violent attack on the Jewish community in response to this event, blaming all Jews for the action of one.

4. **Make Inferences** What was the most likely reason that Allied leaders did not completely believe or understand the full ramifications of the "Final Solution" when they first heard about it?

   Possible answer: The "Final Solution," or the mass extermination of the Jews, was so barbaric and so unbelievable that many people simply didn't believe that it could really be happening. Allied leaders most likely thought that the reports and the intelligence they had on the matter were overexaggerated. After all, nothing like that had ever happened in modern history, so it was likely way beyond anything they could ever imagine happening.

ADDITIONAL LESSON CONTENT

COLLABORATIVE LEARNING

Plan a Holocaust Film

1. If possible, show students a scene from a movie about the Holocaust, such as *Schindler's List, Life Is Beautiful, The Pianist, The Diary of Anne Frank,* or *The Boy in the Striped Pajamas.* Select a scene that is both moving and relevant to the topic of the Holocaust but is not too graphic or disturbing.
2. Have students form groups to plan their own film about the Holocaust.
3. Ask students to hold a brainstorming session where they decide on the plot, setting, characters, theme, and tone of the movie.
4. Next, request that students think about a scene in the film and work together to write it out.
5. Have groups present their scenes as reader's theater.

Lesson 4 Planner

The Allied Victory

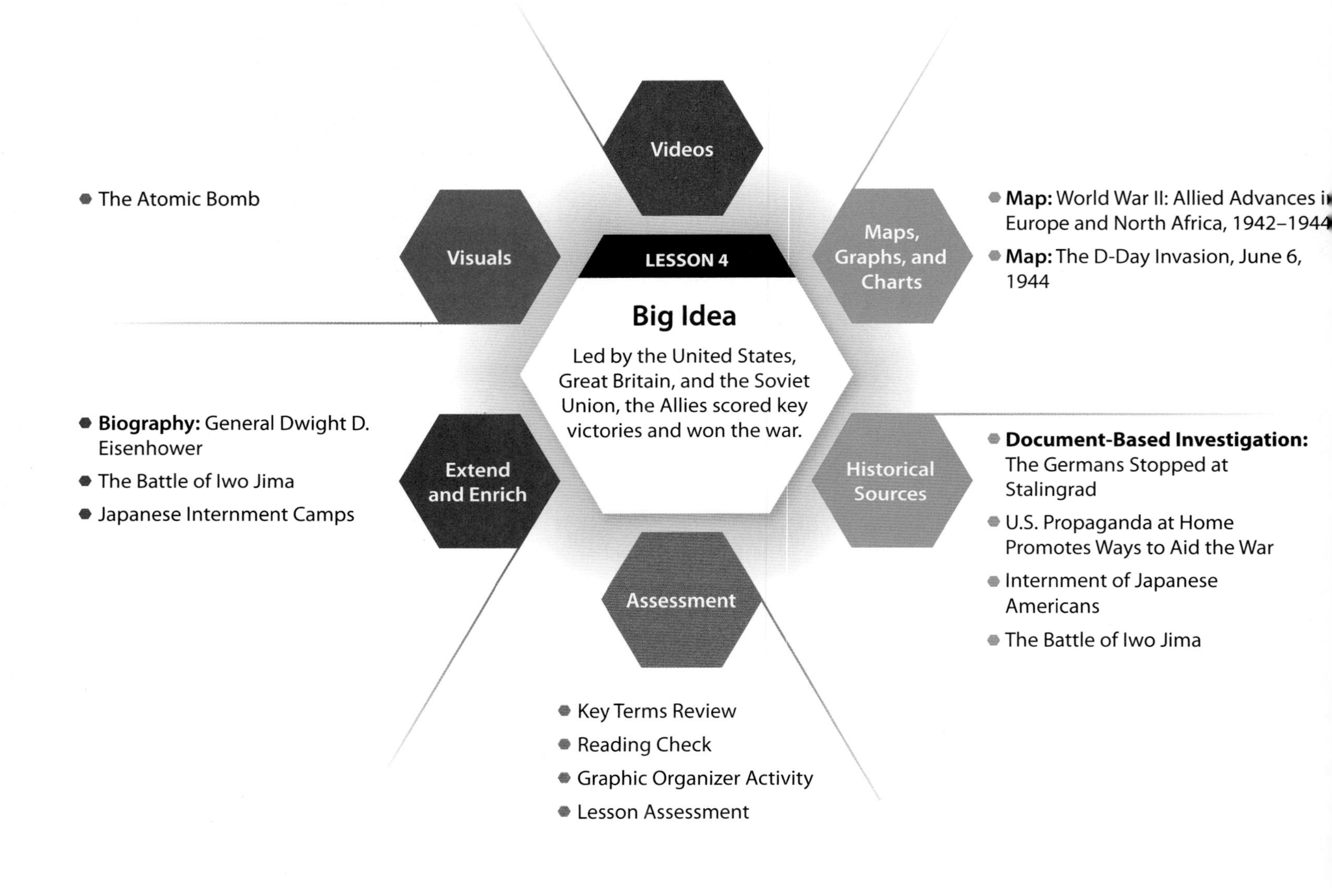

- The Atomic Bomb

- **Map:** World War II: Allied Advances in Europe and North Africa, 1942–1944
- **Map:** The D-Day Invasion, June 6, 1944

- **Biography:** General Dwight D. Eisenhower
- The Battle of Iwo Jima
- Japanese Internment Camps

- **Document-Based Investigation:** The Germans Stopped at Stalingrad
- U.S. Propaganda at Home Promotes Ways to Aid the War
- Internment of Japanese Americans
- The Battle of Iwo Jima

- Key Terms Review
- Reading Check
- Graphic Organizer Activity
- Lesson Assessment

Online Lesson 4 Enrichment Activities

The Battle of Iwo Jima

Eyewitness Account Students read a U.S. Marine correspondent's description of the fighting in the Battle of Iwo Jima near the end of the war, in which Japan lost 21,000 soldiers and the United States 6,800. Then students answer the following questions: What attitude do you think the soldiers on both sides had to adopt to fight in such a bloody conflict as this? How might this type of warfare have influenced the decision ultimately to use atomic weapons to defeat Japan?

Japanese Internment Camps

Article Students read about the treatment of Japanese Americans in the United States following the attack at Pearl Harbor. Then they search the Internet to find photographs taken at Japanese internment camps. Next, they write a paragraph conveying their impression of life in the camps.

Teach the Big Idea

1. **Whole Class Open/Introduction** Discuss what students already know about World War II battles. *Students might be familiar with major battles or war heroes. They might mention films like* Patton *or* Saving Private Ryan *or television series such as* Band of Brothers *and* Flags of Our Fathers.
2. **Direct Teach** Read students the Big Idea: *Led by the United States, Great Britain, and the Soviet Union, the Allies scored key victories and won the war.* Review the following lesson objectives with students to aid in their understanding of the Big Idea.
   - Describe the Allied strategy in Europe.
   - List efforts made on the home fronts.
   - Summarize events that led to the surrender of Germany.
   - Summarize events that led to the surrender of Japan.
3. **Whole Group Close/Reflect** Have students make an illustrated flow chart that shows how the Allies were able to claim victory in Europe and the Pacific.

ONLINE DOCUMENT-BASED INVESTIGATION

World War II

The Germans Stopped at Stalingrad is the fourth of five historical sources that students will analyze in the World War II module. Both distance and a harsh winter challenged the Germans in their quest for control of the city of Stalingrad. Have students explore the image and answer the associated question.

DOCUMENT-BASED INVESTIGATION HISTORICAL SOURCE

The Germans Stopped at Stalingrad

At Stalingrad, the Russians used the city's environment to their advantage, fighting a deadly urban war. Stalingrad's great distance from Germany also aided Russia, making it hard for the Germans to supply and reinforce troops. And the Soviet

ONLINE GRAPHIC ORGANIZER

The Allied Victory

As students read the lesson, have them use the graphic organizer to take notes. Students can review their graphic organizer notes at the end of the lesson to answer the following question:

Analyze Events Why was the D-Day invasion such an important event in the war? *It allowed the Allies to land a huge army and equipment for battle in France and put Germany on the retreat for the first time on the Western front.*

Lesson 4

The Allied Victory

The Big Idea

Led by the United States, Great Britain, and the Soviet Union, the Allies scored key victories and won the war.

Why It Matters Now

The Allies' victory in World War II set up conditions for both the Cold War and today's post-Cold War world.

Key Terms and People

Dwight D. Eisenhower
Battle of Stalingrad
D-Day
Battle of the Bulge
kamikaze

Setting the Stage

On December 22, 1941, just after Pearl Harbor, Winston Churchill and President Roosevelt met at the White House to develop a joint war policy. Stalin had asked his allies to relieve German pressure on his armies in the east. He wanted them to open a second front in the west. This would split the Germans' strength by forcing them to fight major battles in two regions instead of one. Churchill agreed with Stalin's strategy. The Allies would weaken Germany on two fronts before dealing a deathblow. At first, Roosevelt was torn, but ultimately he agreed.

The Tide Turns on Two Fronts

Churchill wanted Britain and the United States to strike first at North Africa and southern Europe. The strategy angered Stalin. He wanted the Allies to open the second front in France. The Soviet Union, therefore, had to hold out on its own against the Germans. All Britain and the United States could offer in the way of help was supplies. Nevertheless, late in 1942, the Allies began to turn the tide of war both in the Mediterranean and on the Eastern Front.

The North African Campaign General Erwin Rommel took the key Libyan port city of Tobruk in June 1942. With Tobruk's fall, London sent General Bernard Montgomery—"Monty" to his troops—to take control of British forces in North Africa. These included British, Indian, and British Commonwealth troops from Canada, Australia, South Africa, and New Zealand. By the time Montgomery arrived, however, the Germans had advanced to an Egyptian village called El Alamein (al•uh•MAYN), west of Alexandria. (See the map World War II: Allied Advances, 1942–1945.) They were dug in so well that British forces could not go around them. The only way to dislodge them, Montgomery decided, was with a massive frontal attack. The Battle of El Alamein began on the night of October 23. The roar of approximately

1100 Module 28

COLLABORATIVE LEARNING

D-Day Presentations

1. Assign groups and inform students that you would like each group to find out more about the D-Day invasion.
2. Explain that their task is create a visual related to the D-Day invasion and use it as they explain the actions that took place during the invasion. The visual may be a model, a mural, an animation, or a diagram.
3. Allow time for student groups to prepare their visuals and construct their explanations. Emphasize that students should apply reasoning and sequence events correctly as they plan their presentations.
4. Ask members of the nonpresenting groups to provide feedback. Presenting students should be able to explain their rationale for the information they included and omitted. They should be encouraged to acknowledge both the strengths and weaknesses of the explanations.

STRUGGLING READERS

Battles in North Africa and the Mediterranean

Materials: outline maps of North Africa and the Mediterranean region

1. Organize students into groups of four and five. Have each group conduct research to follow the progress of the battles in North Africa from 1941 to 1943.

1,000 British guns took the Axis soldiers totally by surprise. They fought back fiercely and held their ground for several days. By November 4, however, Rommel's army had been beaten. He and his forces fell back.

As Rommel retreated west, the Allies launched Operation Torch. On November 8, an Allied force of more than 100,000 troops—mostly Americans— landed in Morocco and Algeria. American general **Dwight D. Eisenhower** led this force. Caught between Montgomery's and Eisenhower's armies, Rommel's Afrika Korps was finally crushed in May 1943.

The Battle for Stalingrad As Rommel suffered defeats in North Africa, German armies also met their match in the Soviet Union. The German advance had stalled at Leningrad and Moscow late in 1941. The bitter winter made the situation worse. When the summer of 1942 arrived, however, Hitler sent his Sixth Army, under the command of General Friedrich Paulus, to seize the oil fields in the Caucasus Mountains. The army was also to capture Stalingrad (now Volgograd), a major industrial center on the Volga River. (See the map World War II: Allied Advances, 1942–1945.)

The **Battle of Stalingrad** began on August 23, 1942. The Luftwaffe went on nightly bombing raids that set much of the city ablaze and reduced the rest to rubble. The situation looked desperate. Nonetheless, Stalin had already told his commanders to defend the city named after him to the death.

By early November 1942, Germans controlled 90 percent of the ruined city. Then another Russian winter set in. On November 19, Soviet troops outside the city launched a counterattack. Closing in around Stalingrad, they trapped the Germans inside and cut off their supplies. General Paulus begged Hitler to order a retreat. But Hitler refused, saying the city was "to be held at all costs."

On February 2, 1943, some 90,000 frostbitten, half-starved German troops surrendered to the Soviets. These pitiful survivors were all that remained of an army of 330,000. Stalingrad's defense had cost the Soviets over one million soldiers. The city was 99 percent destroyed. However, the Germans were now on the defensive, with the Soviets pushing them steadily westward.

Soviet troops launch an attack during the battle for Stalingrad.

Objectives

You may wish to discuss the following questions with students to help them frame the content as they read.

- What did the debate about a second front imply about relationships among the Allies? *Britain and the United States were closer to each other than to the Soviet Union.*
- How did the North African campaign show the value of international cooperation? *British and American forces combined to win.*
- How would you compare Midway and Stalingrad? *Both halted expansion, but Stalingrad was longer, bloodier, and on land.*

More About . . .

The Battle of Stalingrad With most of the city in rubble from bombing and shelling, the Soviets defended Stalingrad street by street and house by house in one of the fiercest of all battles of the war. As German soldiers advanced, the Soviets moved back, setting mines and booby traps everywhere they could. In one instance, a Soviet soldier died beside a German tank upon which he had written a message in his own blood proclaiming that while he will die, his country will ultimately win.

Mussolini and World War II Mussolini and Hitler had pledged to support each other as they waged war. This agreement has become known as the Pact of Steel. Italy's war efforts did not go so well. Italian soldiers suffered defeat after an attempted assault on Greece. In addition, Italian troops supporting German soldiers in the Soviet Union faced many hardships and losses during the harsh Soviet winter. Many Italians gave up on Mussolini after the Allied attack on Sicily, but his agreement with Hitler helped save him. After freeing the Italian leader from captivity, Hitler allowed Mussolini to lead a government in northern Italy, but it was a puppet government, with the Nazis pulling the strings.

Have each group make a chart listing the battles, their locations, the major participants, and their outcomes.

2. Give each group an outline map of North Africa and the Mediterranean. Have each group work together to map the battles in North Africa, labeling them with their names and dates.
3. Conduct a discussion of the war in North Africa. Point out that much of North Africa is desert, and ask students to explain North Africa's strategic importance. *controlled the Suez Canal; provided a launching pad for the invasion of Italy*

ENGLISH LANGUAGE LEARNERS

News Report from Stalingrad

1. Divide students into small groups. Have each group reread the information about the Battle of Stalingrad. Encourage groups to use glossaries or dictionaries to help them understand challenging words.
2. Then have each group write a radio news broadcast from the point of view of an American reporter witnessing the battle. News reports should be from 30 to 90 seconds long and may include notations of sound effects. Reports should explain who is fighting, why the battle is important, and what the outcome of the battle could mean. Encourage students to include facts, details, and quotations from the text and to use vivid, descriptive language.
3. Have each group elect a member to perform the news report for the class.

ONLINE LESSON FLIP CARDS

Review Key Terms and People

Students can use the flip cards in the Lesson Review at any time to review the lesson's key terms and people: *Dwight D. Eisenhower, Battle of Stalingrad, D-Day, Battle of the Bulge,* and *kamikaze.*

ONLINE INTERACTIVE MAPS

World War II: Allied Advances in Europe and North Africa, 1942–1944

Have students explore the map using the interactive features and answer the associated questions.

Movement How did Allied forces reach Italy? *northeast through Sicily*

In print edition, see map titled World War II: Allied Advances, 1942–1945.

1. **Region** Which European countries remained neutral during World War II? *Ireland, Spain, Portugal, Sweden, Switzerland*
2. **Movement** What seems to be the destination for most of the Allied advances that took place in Europe during 1943–1944? *Germany*

ONLINE DOCUMENT-BASED INVESTIGATION

The Germans Stopped at Stalingrad

Both distance and a harsh winter challenged the Germans in their quest for control of Stalingrad. Have students explore the image and answer the associated question.

Analyze Sources In what way was the strategy the same for Hitler and Stalin at Stalingrad? *Much like at Leningrad and Moscow, both planned to win the battle at all costs, regardless of casualties, destruction, or length of time.*

DOCUMENT-BASED INVESTIGATION HISTORICAL SOURCE

The Germans Stopped at Stalingrad

At Stalingrad, the Russians used the city's environment to their advantage, fighting a deadly urban war. Stalingrad's great distance from Germany also aided Russia, making it hard for the Germans to supply and reinforce troops. And the Soviet winter killed many German soldiers and ruined equipment.

READING CHECK

Make Inferences What advantages might a weaker army fighting on its home soil have over a stronger invading army? *The army fighting at home would know the territory better than the invading army, would have the support of the local population, and would have the additional passion that comes with defending one's own home.*

Explore ONLINE!

World War II: Allied Advances, 1942–1945

Interpret Maps

1. **Region** Which European countries remained neutral during World War II?
2. **Movement** What seems to be the destination for most of the Allied advances that took place in Europe during 1943–1944?

The Invasion of Italy As the Battle of Stalingrad raged, Stalin continued to urge the British and Americans to invade France. However, Roosevelt and Churchill decided to attack Italy first. On July 10, 1943, Allied forces landed on Sicily and captured it from Italian and German troops about a month later.

1102 Module 28

SUMMARIZE THE BATTLE OF STALINGRAD

Below Level Have students read "The Battle of Stalingrad" text. Then have them create a numbered list that briefly describes important events in the order they took place.

At Level After students have read "The Battle of Stalingrad" text, ask them to create a multipanel graphic comic strip that summarizes what they have learned.

Above Level Have students find at least three primary sources or quotations related to the Battle of Stalingrad. Students should then analyze each source. Who wrote or spoke each? What was the person's point of view? Did this point of view have an effect on the battle? Is there a relationship between the different primary sources? Next, students should write a summary of the events of the Battle of Stalingrad, incorporating evidence from the various primary sources.

The conquest of Sicily toppled Mussolini from power. On July 25, King Victor Emmanuel III had the dictator arrested. On September 3, Italy surrendered. But the Germans seized control of northern Italy and put Mussolini back in charge. Finally, the Germans retreated northward, and the victorious Allies entered Rome on June 4, 1944. Fighting in Italy, however, continued until Germany fell in May 1945. On April 27, 1945, Italian resistance fighters ambushed some German trucks near the northern Italian city of Milan. Inside one of the trucks, they found Mussolini disguised as a German soldier. They shot him the next day and later hung his body in downtown Milan for all to see.

Reading Check
Make Inferences What advantages might a weaker army fighting on its home soil have over a stronger invading army?

The Allied Home Fronts

Wherever Allied forces fought, people on the home fronts rallied to support them. In war-torn countries like the Soviet Union and Great Britain, civilians endured extreme hardships. Many lost their lives. Except for a few of its territories, such as Hawaii, the United States did not suffer invasion or major bombing. Nonetheless, Americans at home made a crucial contribution to the Allied war effort. Americans produced the weapons and equipment that would help win the war.

Mobilizing for War Defeating the Axis powers required mobilizing for total war. In this feature of warfare in the 20th century, entire national economies were directed toward the war effort. Increased armament production in the United States provided an indispensable boost to the Allied war effort. In 1939, the United States manufactured 3,000 military aircraft. From 1941–1945, the United States produced 300,000 more, as well as 61,000 tanks; 200 submarines; 27 aircraft carriers; and much more military weaponry and materials. Factories converted their peacetime operations to wartime production and made everything from machine guns to boots. Automobile factories produced tanks. A typewriter company made armor-piercing shells. By 1944, between 17 and 18 million U.S. workers had jobs in war industries. Production boomed as citizens—many of them women entering the work force for the first time—flocked to meet the labor demand, working long hours to help win the war.

With factories turning out products for the war, a shortage of consumer goods hit the United States. From meat and sugar to tires and gasoline, from nylon stockings to laundry soap, the American government rationed scarce items. Setting the speed limit at 35 miles per hour also helped to save gasoline and rubber. In European countries directly affected by the war, rationing was even more drastic.

Vocabulary
rationed distributed in limited amounts

To inspire their people to greater efforts, Allied governments conducted highly effective propaganda campaigns, in which citizens were asked to do their part to conserve and contribute resources to the war effort. In the Soviet Union, a Moscow youngster collected enough scrap metal to produce 14,000 artillery shells. A Russian family used its life savings to buy a tank for the Red Army. Other propaganda campaigns used nationalistic sentiment to request money to support the troops fighting for freedom.

STRUGGLING READERS

Create Posters for the Home Front

1. Pair a struggling reader with a more proficient reader, and have the pairs use information from this segment to create a World War II poster. Posters might encourage civilians to work in a factory or buy war bonds.
2. Next, have students use library resources or the Internet to research World War II posters.
3. Display researched posters, and ask students to compare them with the posters students made.

ADVANCED/GIFTED

Make a Presentation on Home Fronts

1. Divide students in to groups, and ask each group to brainstorm topics about the home fronts that they would like to find out more about. Possible topics include attitudes, home gardens, news reports, propaganda, war bonds, movies, and songs.
2. Have each group research three topics.
3. Ask each group to prepare a multimedia presentation that describes and connects the topics.

Objectives

You may wish to discuss the following questions with students to help them frame the content as they read.

- How would you summarize the difference between the home fronts of the United States and its major allies? *Possible answer: Life was harder for Soviet and British civilians than for Americans.*
- Why were so many women needed to work in war industries? *Millions of men were serving as soldiers.*
- How would you contrast the way Japanese Americans were treated with how they acted during World War II? *The government treated them as security risks, but many volunteered for the military.*

More About . . .

Attack on Dresden On February 13, 1945, Allied bombers launched a massive attack on Dresden, a city southeast of Berlin with little military value. The assault created raging firestorms that killed up to 135,000 people, mostly civilians. One author described the city as a "furnace fueled by people." Dresden is now a symbol of "total war."

The Home Front While many people in Britain were collecting pots and pans for scrap metal, in the United States war bond rallies were held across the nation. Movie stars and other celebrities often appeared at these rallies and were very effective in helping raise billions of dollars in bonds sales.

ONLINE HISTORICAL SOURCES

U.S. Propaganda at Home Promotes Ways to Aid the War

Invite students to view the image and answer the associated question.

Analyze Sources In general, what do you think citizens in the United States thought about the propaganda efforts related to rationing, recycling, and buying war bonds? *In general, they were eager to contribute to the war effort because they believed in the cause and felt their sacrifices were little compared to the soldiers fighting.*

ONLINE HISTORICAL SOURCES

Internment of Japanese Americans

Invite students to view the image and answer the associated question.

Analyze Sources Judging from the photograph, what was the government's attitude toward Japanese Americans? *They were potentially dangerous and needed to be segregated and controlled.*

Objectives

You may wish to discuss the following questions with students to help them frame the content as they read.

- Why do you think Hitler ordered the massive counterattack that led to the Battle of the Bulge? *Possible answer: He wanted to make one last-ditch effort to turn back the Allies.*
- What caused Germany to surrender? *Allied and Soviet troops were preparing to take Berlin; Hitler had committed suicide.*

More About . . .

Largest Allied Offensive Operation The largest Allied offensive operation of World War II took place in the Soviet Union, not on the shores of Normandy. In the summer of 1944, a Soviet offensive called Operation Bagration inflicted far more damage to the Germans than the D-Day landings. Stalin's campaign wiped out three Axis armies to support the Allied invasion of France, free Soviet territory from the Germans, and break the German war machine.

D-Day Invasion The D-Day invasion was the largest sea-to-land invasion ever attempted. More than 5,000 ships were needed to bring Allied soldiers and equipment to the beaches. Additional troops parachuted from more than 800 planes. Other planes had already dropped bombs on the area in advance of the landing. The beaches of Normandy were carefully chosen as the landing location. Military leaders had determined that this area would be less closely guarded then coastal areas closer to Britain. The landing took place at Utah, Omaha, Gold, Juno, and Sword Beaches.

Students may wonder how D-Day got its name. Military planners call the day of a future attack a D-day, with the D standing for "designated." The actual date of the attack will be determined later. The D-Day of World War II is one of many D-days that have been planned, but it is the one that is most remembered in U.S. military history.

READING CHECK
Analyze Issues What were some costs and benefits for workers and businesses in converting factories to wartime production? Benefits—Workers had abundant job opportunities; businesses had a high demand for their products. Costs—converting peace-time industries to war production was challenging; maintaining production required long hours and hard work.

American school children helped the war effort by recycling scrap metal and rubber and by buying war bonds.

In the United States, youngsters saved their pennies and bought government war stamps and bonds to help finance the war.

War Limits Civil Rights Government propaganda also had a negative effect. After Pearl Harbor, a wave of prejudice arose in the United States against Japanese Americans. Most lived in Hawaii and on the West Coast. The bombing of Pearl Harbor frightened Americans. This fear, encouraged by government propaganda, was turned against Japanese Americans. They were suddenly seen as "the enemy." On February 19, 1942, President Roosevelt issued an executive order calling for the internment of Japanese Americans because they were considered a threat to the country.

In March, the military began rounding up "aliens" and shipping them to relocation camps. The camps were restricted military areas located far away from the coast. Such locations, it was thought, would prevent these "enemy aliens" from assisting a Japanese invasion. However, two-thirds of those interned were Nisei, native-born American citizens whose parents were Japanese. Many of them volunteered for military service and fought bravely for the United States, even though their families remained in the camps.

Reading Check
Analyze Issues
What were some costs and benefits for workers and businesses in converting factories to wartime production?

Victory in Europe

While the Allies were dealing with issues on the home front, they also were preparing to push toward victory in Europe. In 1943, the Allies began secretly building an invasion force in Great Britain. Their plan was to launch an attack on German-held France across the English Channel.

The D-Day Invasion By May 1944, the invasion force was ready. Thousands of planes, ships, tanks, and landing craft and more than three million troops awaited the order to attack. General Dwight D. Eisenhower, the commander of this enormous force, planned to strike on the coast of Normandy, in northwestern France. The Germans knew that an attack was coming. But they did not know where it would be launched. To keep Hitler guessing, the Allies set up a huge dummy army with its own headquarters and equipment. This make-believe army appeared to be preparing to attack the French seaport of Calais (ka•LAY).

FOLLOW CHRONOLOGICAL ORDER

Put Events in Time Sequence

1. Explain that chronological thinking is an important part of our lives. Putting events in the order they occurred is often a key to understanding relationships between events, particularly between causes and effects and between problems and solutions.
2. Ask students to describe clues in text that help establish chronological order. They may mention dates and words such as *after, next,* and *as.*
3. Have small groups put the events described in the "Victory in Europe" segment in chronological order using a timeline or flow chart.

MAKE INFERENCES

What if D-Day Had Failed

1. Remind students that Allied casualties were high during the D-Day Invasion. Guide a discussion with students about what might have happened if the Allies' D-Day invasion of France had failed. How might it have affected the outcome of the war?
2. Have students write a scenario about what could have happened if the Germans had been expecting the attack and turned back the invasion.
3. Have volunteers read their scenarios to the class.

The D-Day Invasion, June 6, 1944

Explore ONLINE!

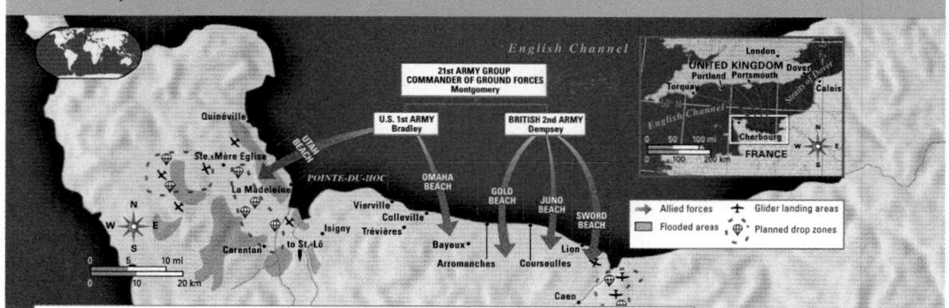

Interpret Maps

1. **Human-Environment Interaction** What environmental problem might have been encountered by 1st Army soldiers landing at Utah Beach?
2. **Movement** Looking at the map, what might have been the Allied strategy behind parachuting troops into France?

Code-named Operation Overlord, the invasion of Normandy was the largest land and sea attack in history. The invasion began on June 6, 1944—known as **D-Day**. At dawn on that day, British, American, French, and Canadian troops fought their way onto a 60-mile stretch of beach in Normandy. (See the map The D-Day Invasion, June 6, 1944.) The Germans had dug in with machine guns, rocket launchers, and cannons. They sheltered behind concrete walls three feet thick. Not surprisingly, the Allies took heavy casualties. Among the American forces alone, more than 2,700 men died on the beaches that day.

BIOGRAPHY

General Dwight D. Eisenhower
(1890–1969)

In his career, U.S. General Dwight Eisenhower had shown an uncommon ability to work with all kinds of people—even competitive Allies. His chief of staff said of Eisenhower, "The sun rises and sets on him for me." He was also wildly popular with the troops, who affectionately called him "Uncle Ike."

So it was not a surprise when, in December 1943, U.S. Army Chief of Staff George Marshall named Eisenhower as supreme commander of the Allied forces in Europe. The new commander's "people skills" enabled him to join American and British forces together to put a permanent end to Nazi aggression.

ONLINE INTERACTIVE MAPS

The D-Day Invasion, June 6, 1944

Have students explore the map and answer the associated questions.

Human-Environment Interaction The army that landed at which beach would have encountered flooding problems? *Utah Beach*

In print edition, see map of same title

1. **Human-Environment Interaction** What environmental problem might have been encountered by 1st Army soldiers landing at Utah Beach? *flooding*
2. **Movement** Looking at the map, what might have been the Allied strategy behind parachuting troops into France? *to move quickly into the interior*

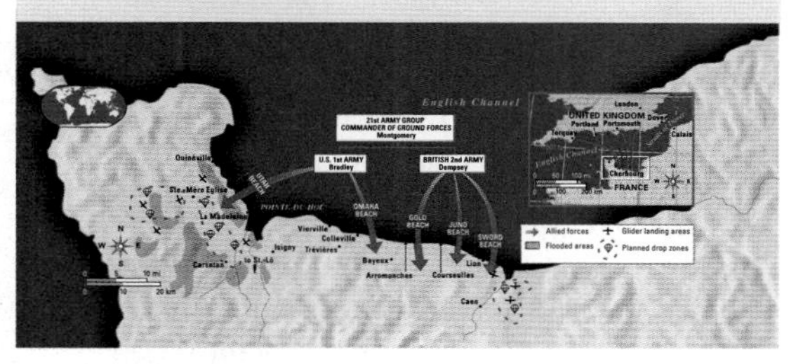

BIOGRAPHY

General Dwight D. Eisenhower

Have students read the biography of the supreme Allied commander in Europe during World War II who led the Allied invasions of North Africa and of France (D-Day) and later became president of the United States.

Objectives

You may wish to discuss the following questions with students to help them frame the content as they read.

- How was the Battle of Leyte Gulf similar to the Battle of the Bulge? *Both were last, desperate efforts that failed.*
- What does the use of kamikazes indicate about the strength of the Japanese navy? *It was so weak they had to hope that suicidal missions would halt the American advance.*
- What alternatives did the United States have to making a full-scale invasion of Japan or to using atomic bombs there? *Possible answer: using conventional weapons, seizing selected targets, blockading Japan, supporting leaders who saw defeat coming, negotiating a treaty*

More About . . .

Kamikaze The word *kamikaze* means "divine wind." It refers to a typhoon that in 1281 saved Japan by destroying the Mongol navy. The Japanese hoped that the kamikaze pilots would be able to save Japan from an Allied invasion.

Iwo Jima The most famous photograph of this period of time shows U.S. servicemen raising the American flag on Iwo Jima after winning one of the bloodiest battles of the war. The tiny island was honeycombed with caves and tunnels, protecting many guns. After attacking the island for more than two months with shells and bombs, some 30,000 U.S. marines stormed ashore in February of 1945. Japanese resistance was so fierce that after three days of combat, the marines had advanced only about 700 yards inland.

The photograph was taken on top of Iwo Jima's Mount Suribachi on February 23, 1945, while the battle was going on. The image was immediately popular in the United States and was used by the U.S. government as part of a campaign to help raise money for the war effort. It later won the Pulitzer Prize for photography.

Vocabulary
beachheads enemy shoreline captured just before invading forces move inland

Despite heavy losses, the Allies held the beachheads. Within a month of D-Day, more than one million additional troops had landed. Then, on July 25, the Allies punched a hole in the German defenses near Saint-Lô (san•LOH), and the United States Third Army, led by General George Patton, broke out. A month later, the Allies marched triumphantly into Paris. By September, they had liberated France, Belgium, and Luxembourg. They then set their sights on Germany.

The Battle of the Bulge As Allied forces moved toward Germany from the west, the Soviet army was advancing toward Germany from the east. Hitler now faced a war on two fronts. In a desperate gamble, he decided to counterattack in the west. Hitler hoped a victory would split American and British forces and break up Allied supply lines. Explaining the reasoning behind his plan, Hitler said, "This battle is to decide whether we shall live or die. . . . All resistance must be broken in a wave of terror."

On December 16, German tanks broke through weak American defenses along a 75-mile front in the Ardennes. The push into Allied lines gave the campaign its name—the **Battle of the Bulge**. Although caught off guard, the Allies eventually pushed the Germans back. The Germans had little choice but to retreat, since there were no reinforcements available.

Germany's Unconditional Surrender After the Battle of the Bulge, the war in Europe rapidly drew to a close. In late March 1945, the Allies rolled across the Rhine River into Germany. By the middle of April, a noose was closing around Berlin. About three million Allied soldiers approached Berlin from the southwest. Another six million Soviet troops approached from the east. By April 25, 1945, the Soviets had surrounded the capital and were pounding the city with artillery fire.

While Soviet shells burst over Berlin, Hitler prepared for his end in an underground headquarters beneath the crumbling city. On April 29, he married his long-time companion, Eva Braun. The next day, Hitler and Eva Braun committed suicide. Their bodies were then carried outside and burned.

On May 7, 1945, General Eisenhower accepted the unconditional surrender of the Third Reich from the German military. President Roosevelt, however, did not live to witness the long-awaited victory. He had died suddenly on April 12, as Allied armies were advancing toward Berlin. Roosevelt's successor, Harry Truman, received the news of the Nazi surrender. On May 9, the surrender was officially signed in Berlin. The United States and other Allied powers celebrated V-E Day—Victory in Europe Day. After nearly six years of fighting, the war in Europe had ended.

Reading Check
Find Main Ideas
How did the Allies try to conceal the true location for the D-Day landings?

Victory in the Pacific

Although the war in Europe was over, the Allies were still fighting the Japanese in the Pacific. With the Allied victory at Guadalcanal, however, the Japanese advances in the Pacific had been stopped. For the rest of the war, the Japanese retreated before the counterattack of the Allied powers.

READING CHECK

Find Main Ideas How did the Allies try to conceal the true location for the D-Day landings? *The Allies prepared a dummy army to attack north of Normandy, at Calais.*

CONNECTIONS ACROSS TIME AND CULTURES

Make Warfare Recommendations

1. Tell students that it is 1945 and they are advisers to President Truman. The Allies have captured Okinawa, and they plan to invade the major islands of Japan.
2. Have each student write a memorandum recommending an action to bring the war to an end. Students should weigh the feasibility of usingtraditional methods, such as strategic air strikes backed up by marines on shore, as opposed to more radical options, such as dropping an atomic bomb. Students should also look at the ethical and long-term consequences of their recommendations.
3. Have students list pros and cons of each in their memorandums and make a final recommendation.Ask for volunteers to read their memorandums to the class. Guide the class in a discussion of students' memorandums.

LINK TO ART

Analyze the Iwo Jima Photograph

1. Project an image of the original Iwo Jima photograph in black and white.
2. Allow students a few minutes to study it as a work of art.
3. Then have them discuss the elements that make it so successful as photographic art. You may want to probe with questions such as:

The Japanese in Retreat By the fall of 1944, the Allies were moving in on Japan. In October, Allied forces landed on the island of Leyte (LAY•tee) in the Philippines. General Douglas MacArthur, who had been ordered to leave the islands before their surrender in May 1942, waded ashore at Leyte with his troops. On reaching the beach, he declared, "People of the Philippines, I have returned."

Actually, the takeover would not be quite that easy. The Japanese had devised a bold plan to halt the Allied advance. They would destroy the American fleet, thus preventing the Allies from resupplying their ground troops. This plan, however, required risking almost the entire Japanese fleet. They took this gamble on October 23, in the Battle of Leyte Gulf. Within four days, the Japanese navy had lost disastrously—eliminating it as a fighting force in the war. Now, only the Japanese army and the feared kamikaze stood between the Allies and Japan. The **kamikazes** were Japanese suicide pilots. They would sink Allied ships by crash-diving their bomb-filled planes into them.

U.S. marines raise the Stars and Stripes after their victory at Iwo Jima.

Vocabulary
kamikaze Japanese word for "divine wind"; the term was originally applied to a storm that saved Japan from a Mongol invasion in 1281

In March 1945, after a month of bitter fighting and heavy losses, American Marines took Iwo Jima (EE•wuh-JEE•muh), an island 760 miles from Tokyo. On April 1, U.S. troops moved onto the island of Okinawa, only about 350 miles from southern Japan. The Japanese put up a desperate fight. Nevertheless, on June 21, one of the bloodiest land battles of the war ended. The Japanese lost over 100,000 troops, and the Americans 12,000.

The Japanese Surrender After Okinawa, the next stop for the Allies had to be Japan. President Truman's advisers had informed him that an invasion of the Japanese homeland might cost the Allies half a million lives. Truman had to make a decision whether to use a powerful new weapon called the atomic bomb, or A-bomb. Most of his advisers felt that using it would bring the war to the quickest possible end. The bomb had been developed by the top-secret Manhattan Project, headed by General Leslie Groves and Jewish scientist J. Robert Oppenheimer. Truman first learned of the new bomb's existence when he became president.

ONLINE HISTORICAL SOURCES

The Battle of Iwo Jima

Invite students to view the image and answer the associated question.

Analyze Sources Why do you think the photograph atop Mount Suribachi was often reprinted by the U.S. government during the war? *It is a powerful image that represents a hard-fought Allied victory, and it could be used to increase morale and promote the war effort.*

HISTORICAL SOURCE

The Battle of Iwo Jima

During the month-long battle for the tiny island of Iwo Jima, nearly 7,000 Americans died. Of the more than 20,000 Japanese defenders of the island, all but a thousand of them fought to the death. This Pulitzer Prize-winning photograph shows U.S. Marines raising the American flag on the top of Mount Suribachi after their victory at Iwo Jima.

What immediately catches your eye? What additional details interest you? How do lines, color, and the position of elements add power to the image? What is the mood presented in the photograph? Was shooting in black and white a good strategy? Why or why not? What do you think the different elements in the photograph symbolize?

ADVANCED/GIFTED

Create an Illustrated Map of Japan's Retreat

1. Have students make an illustrated map showing the Japanese retreat in the Pacific.
2. Guide students to research the battles that resulted in the Japanese retreat. Tell students to take notes on key places, dates, and events.
3. Encourage students to plan and execute their illustrated maps. Encourage creativity and originality.
4. Have students prepare a timeline to accompany the illustrated map and offer descriptions of events featured on the map. Tell students that they should match each event on the timeline to a place on the map.
5. Request that each student prepare a two-minute talk in which he or she presents the final product. Have students take turns showing their work and explaining it.

ONLINE INTERACTIVE VISUALS

Carousel: The Atomic Bomb

Have students navigate through the carousel and note similarities and differences among the images or identify a unifying theme.

In print edition, see History in Depth, titled The Atomic Bomb.

Critical Thinking

1. **Develop Historical Perspective** If you were to design a memorial to the victims of the Hiroshima and Nagasaki bombings, what symbol would you use? Make a sketch of your memorial. *Possible answer: A diagram of an atom splitting would highlight the source of the power. A peace symbol might emphasize the hope that such a terrible weapon would never be used again. A mushroom cloud would focus attention on the explosion. A Japanese flag with an American flag would remind viewers of the nations that participated in the conflict.*

History in Depth

The Atomic Bomb

On the eve of World War II, scientists in Germany succeeded in splitting the nucleus of a uranium atom, releasing a huge amount of energy. Albert Einstein wrote to President Franklin Roosevelt and warned him that Nazi Germany might be working to develop atomic weapons. Roosevelt responded by giving his approval for an American program, later code-named the Manhattan Project, to develop an atomic bomb. In 1942, a Nobel Prize-winning Italian physicist at the University of Chicago, Enrico Fermi, produced the first nuclear chain reaction. In 1945, the Manhattan Project completed its goal of creating the world's first atomic bomb.

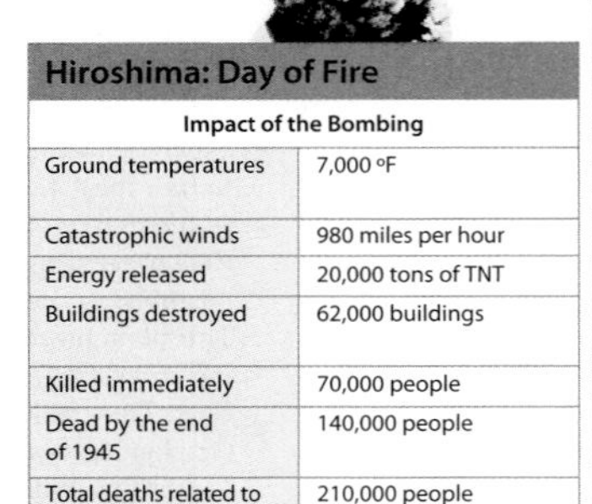

▶ At precisely 8:16 a.m., the atomic bomb exploded above Hiroshima, a city on the Japanese island of Honshu.

▼ On the morning of August 6, 1945, the B-29 bomber *Enola Gay*, flown by Colonel Paul W. Tibbets, Jr., took off from Tinian Island in the Mariana Islands.

Hiroshima: Day of Fire

Impact of the Bombing	
Ground temperatures	7,000 °F
Catastrophic winds	980 miles per hour
Energy released	20,000 tons of TNT
Buildings destroyed	62,000 buildings
Killed immediately	70,000 people
Dead by the end of 1945	140,000 people
Total deaths related to A-bomb	210,000 people

The overwhelming destructive power of the Hiroshima bomb, and of the bomb dropped on Nagasaki three days later, changed the nature of war forever. Nuclear destruction also led to questions about the ethics of scientists and politicians who chose to develop and use the bomb.

Nagasaki citizens trudge through the still smoldering ruins of their city in this photograph by Yosuke Yamahata. ▼

Critical Thinking

1. **Develop Historical Perspective** If you were to design a memorial to the victims of the Hiroshima and Nagasaki bombings, what symbol would you use? Make a sketch of your memorial.

The first atomic bomb was exploded in a desert in New Mexico on July 16, 1945. President Truman then warned the Japanese. He stated that unless they surrendered, they could expect a "rain of ruin from the air." The Japanese did not reply. So, on August 6, 1945, the United States dropped an atomic bomb on Hiroshima, a Japanese city of nearly 350,000 people. Between 70,000 and 80,000 people died in the attack. Three days later, on August 9, a second bomb was dropped on Nagasaki, a city of 270,000. More than 70,000 people were killed immediately. Radiation fallout from the two explosions killed many more.

The Japanese finally surrendered to General Douglas MacArthur on September 2. The ceremony took place aboard the United States battleship *Missouri* in Tokyo Bay. With Japan's surrender, the war had ended. Now, countries faced the task of rebuilding a war-torn world.

Reading Check
Find Main Ideas
What brought about Japan's surrender?

J. Robert Oppenheimer (left) and General Leslie Groves inspect the site of the first atomic bomb test near Alamogordo, New Mexico.

Lesson 4 Assessment

1. Organize Information Which battle do you think was most important in turning the war in favor of the Allies? Why?

Battle	Outcome
Battle of El Alamein	
Battle of Stalingrad	
D-Day Invasion	

2. Key Terms and People For each key term or person in the lesson, write a sentence explaining its significance.
3. Synthesize How do governments gather support for a war effort on the home front?
4. Analyze Issues Should governments have the power to limit the rights of their citizens during wartime? Explain your answer.
5. Form Opinions Did President Truman make the correct decision in using the atomic bomb? What would the consequences have been if he had chosen not to drop the bomb?

READING CHECK
Find Main Ideas What brought about the Japanese surrender? *the use of atomic weapons*

Print Assessment

1. **Organize Information** Which battle do you think was most important in turning the war in favor of the Allies? Why? *El Alamein—Rommel defeated. Stalingrad—Victory on the eastern front. D-Day—The recapture of Western Europe began. Most important—Stalingrad, because it put Hitler on the defensive.*
2. **Key Terms and People** For each key term or person in the lesson, write a sentence explaining its significance. *Explanations of the lesson's key terms can be found on the following pages: Dwight D. Eisenhower, p. 1101; Battle of Stalingrad, p. 1101; D-Day, p. 1105; Battle of the Bulge, p. 1106; kamikaze, p. 1107.*
3. **Synthesize** How do governments gather support for a war effort on the home front? *Possible answer: rationing materials that are essential to the war effort; raising money; using propaganda*
4. **Analyze Issues** Should governments have the power to limit the rights of their citizens during wartime? Explain your answer. *Possible answer: No—Rights must still be protected. Yes—Short-term restrictions may provide long-term protection.*
5. **Form Opinions** Did President Truman make the correct decision in using the atomic bomb? What would the consequences have been if he had chosen not to drop the bomb? *Possible answer: Yes—It ended the war quickly. No—It killed many innocent people. Without the bomb, there would have been many more U.S. casualties.*

Online Assessment

1. What strategy did Stalin want the other Allied forces to follow in Europe in 1943?
   - ● He wanted them to invade France first.
   - ○ He wanted them to send troops to Africa.
   - ○ He wanted them to attack Germany in Berlin.
   - ○ He wanted them to remove Mussolini from power.

   Alternate Question *Select the answer choice from the drop-down list to complete the sentence correctly.*
   Stalin was irritated by the strategy that the other Allied forces were choosing to follow. He wanted them to *invade France* so that the Nazis would be divided on more than one front.

2. During World War II, how did the United States government try to conserve precious resources for the war effort?
   - ○ More airplanes were built than before the war.
   - ○ Children were encouraged to save their pennies.
   - ● The speed limit was lowered to 35 miles per hour.
   - ○ Typewriter companies made armor-piercing shells.

   Alternate Question *Select the answer choice from the drop-down list to complete the sentence correctly.*
   The United States government needed to make sure that the war effort had the supplies it needed for victory. So, because *gasoline and tire rubber* were particularly valuable, the speed limit was lowered to 35 miles per hour.

3. Why was the Battle of the Bulge so important to the Allies in World War II?
   - ○ The Allies were able to reclaim Paris from the Nazis.
   - ○ The Italians were free from having Mussolini as their leader.
   - ○ The Nazis were finally pushed out of the Soviet Union's territory.
   - ● The war in Europe quickly came to an end after the Allies won this battle.

   Alternate Question *Select the answer choice from the drop-down list to complete the sentence correctly.*
   After the Battle of the Bulge, the Allies moved across the Rhine River and then into *Germany*. The war in Europe was winding to a close.

4. What did the battles fought on Okinawa show the Allied forces?
   - ○ The war with Japan would be over quickly.
   - ○ The Japanese were reluctant to use kamikaze pilots.
   - ● The Japanese people would not go down without a fight.
   - ○ The islands of Japan were too isolated to be fought individually.

   Alternate Question *Select the answer choice from the drop-down list to complete the sentence correctly.*
   When the Allies fought Japan on Okinawa, Japan lost 100,000 soldiers and the United States lost 12,000. This showed the Allies that Japan would *put up a desperate fight*.

5. **Sequence** What events led to the Allied victory in North Africa?

   Possible answer: First, General Bernard Montgomery took control over the British forces in North Africa. He decided to lead a massive frontal attack on Rommel's forces in the Battle of El Alamein. This was a significant defeat for Rommel, who was forced back with his troops to the west. As he retreated, Operation Torch was launched. More than 100,000 troops who were mostly American landed in Morocco and Algeria, led by Dwight D. Eisenhower. Rommel found himself caught between these two Allied armies, and his Afrika Korps was crushed by May 1943.

6. **Cause and Effect** What led to the establishment of relocation camps in the United States?

   Possible answer: After Pearl Harbor, many Americans became afraid of Japanese people, fearing that their loyalties would be with Japan instead of the United States. This fear was encouraged by government propaganda. The Japanese were seen as the enemy. Roosevelt issued an executive order in 1942 that required that all Japanese be interned in camps because they were considered a threat to the country. These camps were located far away from the coasts.

7. **Elaborate** What was Operation Overlord, and why was it so important to the Allied cause?

   Possible answer: Operation Overlord was the code name for the Normandy invasion. This invasion was hugely important to the Allied cause. Its success allowed the Allies to gain a foothold in France, which led to the liberation of not only France but also the neighboring countries of Belgium and Luxembourg.

8. **Draw Conclusions** Why did Truman ultimately decide to drop the atomic bombs on Hiroshima and Nagasaki?

   Possible answer: This decision came in response to the predicted loss of life if Allied troops were to invade Japan. Some of Truman's advisers had told Truman that it was predicted that half a million Allied lives would be lost in this invasion. The advisers believed that the atomic bomb would end the war quickly and would save those lives. Based on this analysis, it was deemed better to use the bombs and try to end the war quickly with fewer Allied lives lost.

Lesson 5 Planner

Europe and Japan in Ruins

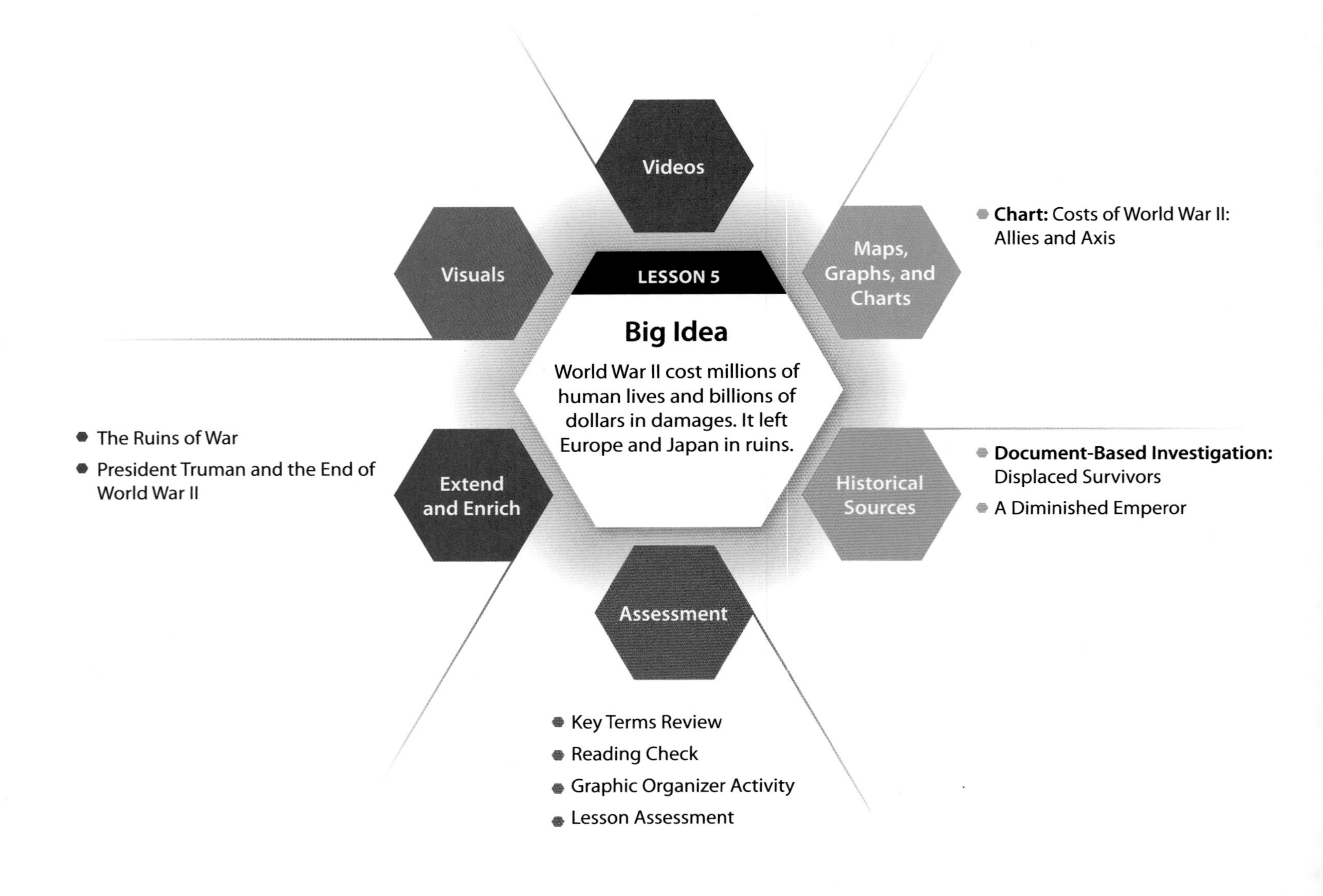

- **Chart:** Costs of World War II: Allies and Axis

- The Ruins of War
- President Truman and the End of World War II

- **Document-Based Investigation:** Displaced Survivors
- A Diminished Emperor

- Key Terms Review
- Reading Check
- Graphic Organizer Activity
- Lesson Assessment

Online Lesson 5 Enrichment Activities

The Ruins of War

Writing Activity Students conduct research to find photographs depicting damage as a result of World War II. Then they create a photo report that describes the war damage evidenced in each selected photograph.

President Truman and the End of World War II

Article Students read how Harry S. Truman led the United States through the final months of World War II following Franklin Roosevelt's death. Then they imagine they are advisers to President Truman and write a memorandum recommending an action to bring the war to an end.

Teach the Big Idea

1. **Whole Class Open/Introduction** Discuss whether military aggression achieves goals. *Possible answer: did not for Germany and Japan in World War II*
2. **Direct Teach** Read students the Big Idea: *World War II cost millions of human lives and billions of dollars in damages. It left Europe and Japan in ruins.* Review the following lesson objectives with students to aid in their understanding of the Big Idea.
   - Describe conditions in Europe in 1945.
   - Identify the political consequences of the Allied victory in postwar Europe.
   - Summarize how defeat and occupation affected political and civic life in Japan.
   - Describe Japan's postwar constitution.
3. **Whole Group Close/Reflect** Have students imagine that they are planning a photo essay for an online magazine. The topic would be "Europe and Japan After World War II." Request that students describe five photographs that they would like to include and tell why it is important for each to be included.

ONLINE DOCUMENT-BASED INVESTIGATION

World War II

Displaced Survivors is the fifth of five historical sources that students will analyze in the World War II module. Simon Wiesenthal vividly described the postwar experience of Holocaust survivors who were among the millions displaced. Students can click on the audio button beneath the historical source to hear the excerpt read aloud.

ONLINE GRAPHIC ORGANIZER

Europe and Japan in Ruins

Compare and contrast the physical destruction in Germany and Japan as a result of the war. *Cities in both countries suffered mass destruction from bombing. While most major cities in Germany were at least partially destroyed by bombing campaigns, damage from the atomic bombs dropped on Japan would have longer-lasting consequences for some survivors.*

ONLINE LESSON FLIP CARDS

Review Key Terms and People

Students can use the flip cards in the Lesson Review at any time to review the lesson's key terms and people: *Nuremberg trials, demilitarization,* and *democratization.*

Lesson 5

Europe and Japan in Ruins

The Big Idea
World War II cost millions of human lives and billions of dollars in damages. It left Europe and Japan in ruins.

Why It Matters Now
The United States survived World War II undamaged, allowing it to become a world leader.

Key Terms and People
Nuremberg Trials
demilitarization
democratization

Setting the Stage

After six long years of war, the Allies finally were victorious. However, their victory had been achieved at a very high price. World War II had caused more death and destruction than any other conflict in history. It left over 60 million dead. About one-third of these deaths occurred in one country, the Soviet Union. Another 50 million people had been uprooted from their homes and wandered the countryside in search of somewhere to live. Property damage ran into billions of U.S. dollars.

Devastation in Europe

By the end of World War II, Europe lay in ruins. Close to 40 million Europeans had died, two-thirds of them civilians. Constant bombing and shelling had reduced hundreds of cities to rubble. The ground war had destroyed much of the countryside. Displaced persons from many nations were left homeless.

A Harvest of Destruction A few of the great cities of Europe—Paris, Rome, and Brussels—remained largely undamaged by war. Many, however, had suffered terrible destruction. The Battle of Britain left huge areas of London little more than blackened ruins. Warsaw, the capital of Poland, was almost completely destroyed. In 1939, Warsaw had a population of nearly 1.3 million. When Soviet soldiers entered the city in January 1945, only 153,000 people remained. Thousands of tons of Allied bombs had demolished 95 percent of the central area of Berlin. One U.S. officer stationed in the German capital reported, "Wherever we looked we saw desolation. It was like a city of the dead." Civilians had died by the millions as a result of military operations, concentration camps, the bombing of towns and cities, and starvation and disease.

Many of the surviving civilians stayed where they were and tried to get on with their lives. Some lived in partially

COLLABORATIVE LEARNING

Economic Profiles of Countries Affected by War

1. Divide the class into groups. Tell the groups to use the Internet to find out more about the aid that the United States granted countries impacted by World War II. Ask each group to select a country to investigate further.
2. Direct students to find out about their country's economy from the end of the war to the present. You might have students focus their inquiry by posing these questions: What was the country's economy like immediately after the war? What steps did the country take to improve its economy? What economic help did it receive? What is its economy like today? What economic help does it currently receive or give?
3. Have groups compile an economic profile for their country based on their research.
4. Initiate a discussion on the role economically independent nations should play in helping developing countries throughout the world.

destroyed homes or apartments. Others huddled in cellars or caves made from rubble. They had no water, no electricity, and very little food. Most no longer had a workplace to provide income or a farm that supplied food.

A large number of people did not stay where they were. Rather, they took to the roads. These displaced persons included the survivors of concentration camps, prisoners of war, and refugees who found themselves in the wrong country when postwar treaties changed national borders. They wandered across Europe, hoping to find their families or to find a safe place to live.

Simon Weisenthal, a prisoner at Auschwitz, described the search made by Holocaust survivors:

> *"Across Europe a wild tide of frantic survivors was flowing. . . . Many of them didn't really know where to go. . . . And yet the survivors continued their pilgrimage of despair. . . . 'Perhaps someone is still alive. . . .' Someone might tell where to find a wife, a mother, children, a brother—or whether they were dead. . . . The desire to find one's people was stronger than hunger, thirst, fatigue."*
>
> —Simon Weisenthal, quoted in *Never to Forget: The Jews of the Holocaust*

Costs of World War II: Allied Powers and Axis Powers

	Direct War Costs	Military Killed/Missing	Civilians Killed
United States	$288.0 billion*	292,131**	—
Great Britain	$117.0 billion	272,311	60,595
France	$111.3 billion	205,707***	173,260†
Soviet Union	$93.0 billion	13,600,000	7,720,000
Germany	$212.3 billion	3,300,000	2,893,000††
Japan	$41.3 billion	1,140,429	953,000
China	unknown	1,310,224†††	unknown

* In 1945 dollars
** An additional 115,187 servicemen died from nonbattle causes.
*** Before surrender to Nazis
† Includes 65,000 murdered Jews
†† Includes about 170,000 murdered Jews and 56,000 foreign civilians in Germany
††† Includes China's war with Japan beginning in 1937

Interpret Charts
1. **Draw Conclusions** Which of the nations listed in the chart suffered the greatest human costs?

Objectives

You may wish to discuss the following questions with students to help them frame the content as they read.

- Compare the devastation in Europe after World War I and World War II. *World War II resulted in far more deaths and dislocated many more people.*
- Why was World War II more destructive than any previous war? *New technologies made destruction more efficient.*

More About . . .

Displaced Persons To help them cross European borders on their way to Palestine, Jews donned uniforms with the insignia CAJR and carried papers stamped with an authentic-looking seal. Few questioned the insignia, which stood for Committee for Assistance to Jewish Refugees.

ONLINE INTERACTIVE CHARTS

Costs of World War II: Allies and Axis

Have students explore the chart and answer the associated questions.

Interpret Charts Which of the nations listed in the chart suffered the greatest human costs? *Soviet Union* and *Germany.*

ONLINE DOCUMENT-BASED INVESTIGATION

Displaced Survivors

The war uprooted millions of people in Europe and Asia, including survivors of Nazi concentration camps and people who had fled the fighting or been forced from their homes. Simon Wiesenthal vividly described the postwar experience of Holocaust survivors. Students can click on the audio button beneath the historical source to hear the excerpt read aloud.

Analyze Sources Why did World War II result in so many displaced people? *Because the Allied and Axis countries devoted so many resources to war, in the aftermath there were unprecedented numbers of affected soldiers and civilians.*

ENGLISH LANGUAGE LEARNERS

Argument for Accepting Displaced Persons

1. Tell small groups that they will create brochures urging Americans to help displaced persons in Europe.
2. Have group members reread the segment, searching for information useful to the brochures such as facts and statistics about the number of refugees, who they are and why they are homeless, what their living conditions are like, and what or whom they are seeking.
3. Direct students to use descriptive, persuasive language as they write their copy for the brochure. Encourage them to add illustrations to add interest.

ANALYZE VISUALS

After the War

1. Have students conduct research to find photographs depicting war damage. If possible, students should find photographs that show the same locations before and after the war.
2. Ask students to research the location of the photo using the following questions as guidelines: How extensive was the damage? What happened to the people who lived there? How long did it take to rebuild?
3. Have students present their photo and describe the war's damage.

Objectives

You may wish to discuss the following questions with students to help them frame the content as they read.

- What evidence indicates that the people of Belgium, Holland, Denmark, and Norway did not blame their leaders for the war's aftermath? *Prewar governments returned to power.*
- Under what conditions should leaders be charged with waging a war of aggression? *Possible answer: when world opinion is strongly united*

More About . . .

Nuremberg Trials Long before World War II ended, the Allied leaders vowed to punish those who were responsible for killing millions of Jews and other innocent civilians. The Nuremberg trials would be the first time nations joined together to prosecute war crimes. The procedures that the international trials would follow were determined in the London Charter of the International Military Tribunal. In all, there were 13 different Nuremberg trials, but the Trial of Major War Criminals is the most famous. Other trials included the Doctors Trial and the Justice Trial.

NOW & THEN

A New War Crimes Tribunal

The former Yugoslavia was a country cobbled together after World War II. It contained many different ethnic groups arbitrarily placed under one government. Yugoslavia included six republics: Croatia, Serbia, Bosnia and Herzegovina, Macedonia, Montenegro, and Slovenia. Different customs, religions, and beliefs caused much friction. In time, the country began to break apart. During the fragmentation, ethnic cleansing in the republics led to relocations, imprisonments, and killings. The International Criminal Tribunal for the former Yugoslavia was created to try cases related to these injustices.

READING CHECK

Analyze Effects What were some immediate after-effects of the war in Europe? *cities of rubble with famine and disease; ruined agriculture in the countryside; displaced people roaming helplessly*

READING CHECK

Identify Problems Why might it have been difficult to find democratic government leaders in post-Nazi Germany? *Since Germany's entire leadership had been Nazi for 12 years, no real democratic leadership had been allowed to develop.*

Misery Continues After the War The misery in Europe continued for years after the war. The fighting had ravaged Europe's countryside, and agriculture had been completely disrupted. Most able-bodied men had served in the military, and the women had worked in war production. Few remained to plant the fields. With the transportation system destroyed, the meager harvests often did not reach the cities. Thousands died as famine and disease spread through the bombed-out cities. The first postwar winter brought more suffering as people went without shoes and coats.

Reading Check **Analyze Effects** What were some immediate after-effects of the war in Europe?

Postwar Governments and Politics

Despairing Europeans often blamed their leaders for the war and its aftermath. Once the Germans had lost, some prewar governments—like those in Belgium, Holland, Denmark, and Norway—returned quickly. In countries like Germany, Italy, and France, however, a return to the old leadership was not desirable. Hitler's Nazi government had brought Germany to ruins. Mussolini had led Italy to defeat. The Vichy government had collaborated with the Nazis. Much of the old leadership was in disgrace. Also, in Italy and France, many resistance fighters were communists.

After the war, the Communist Party promised change, and millions were ready to listen. In both France and Italy, Communist Party membership skyrocketed. The communists made huge gains in the first postwar elections. Anxious to speed up a political takeover, the communists staged a series of violent strikes. Alarmed French and Italians reacted by voting for anticommunist parties. Communist Party membership and influence began to decline. And they declined even more as the economies of France and Italy began to recover.

The Nuremberg Trials While nations were struggling to recover politically and economically, they also tried to deal with the issue of war crimes. During 1945 and 1946, an International Military Tribunal representing 23 nations put Nazi war criminals on trial in Nuremberg, Germany. In the first of these **Nuremberg Trials**, 22 Nazi leaders were charged with waging a war of aggression. They were also accused of committing "crimes against humanity"—the murder of 11 million people.

Adolf Hitler, SS chief Heinrich Himmler, and Minister of Propaganda Joseph Goebbels had committed suicide long before the trials began. However, Hermann Göring, the commander of the Luftwaffe; Rudolf Hess, Hitler's former deputy; and other high-ranking Nazi leaders remained to face the charges.

Hess was found guilty and was sentenced to life in prison. Göring received a death sentence, but cheated the executioner by committing suicide. Ten other Nazi leaders were hanged on October 16, 1946. Hans Frank, the "Slayer of Poles," was the only convicted Nazi to express remorse: "A thousand years will pass," he said, "and still this guilt of Germany will not have been erased." The bodies of those executed were burned at the concentration camp of Dachau (DAHK•ow). They were cremated in the same ovens that had burned so many of their victims.

Reading Check **Identify Problems** Why might it have been difficult to find democratic government leaders in post-Nazi Germany?

ADVANCED/GIFTED

Compare the World Wars

1. Pair students to create and complete a compare-and-contrast poster about the two world wars.
2. Instruct students to review the modules that describe the two world wars.
3. Ask students to come up with their own topics to compare or provide them with questions such as the following to get them started.
   - How did imperialism set the stage for each war?
   - What military alliances pushed European nations into each war?
   - What was Germany's military plan for fighting a two-front war? What was the outcome?
   - In what ways did governments wage total war?
4. Ask students to make a generalization about how the two wars were similar and how they differed. *Possible answer: Similarities—Massive loss of life, new technologies invented, effects lasted for generations. Differences—Conscious attempt after World War II not to plant the seeds of a future war; World War II led to the creation of atomic and nuclear weapons.*

Now and Then

A New War Crimes Tribunal

In 1993, the UN established the International Criminal Tribunal for the former Yugoslavia (ICTY) to prosecute war crimes committed in the Balkan conflicts of the 1990s. This was the first international war crimes court since those held in Nuremberg and Tokyo after World War II.

The ICTY, located in The Hague, Netherlands, issued its first indictment in 1994 and began trial proceedings in 1996. By mid-2007, a total of 161 defendants had been indicted. The most prominent of these, Slobodan Milosevic (shown), the former president of Yugoslavia, was charged with 66 counts of genocide, crimes against humanity, and other war crimes. On March 11, 2006, Milosevic, who had suffered from poor health, was found dead in his cell. Radovan Karadzic and Ratko Mladic, the leaders of the Bosnian Serbs, were arrested in 2008 and 2011, respectively. Both were put on trial in The Hague, charged with multiple war crimes.

Postwar Japan

The defeat suffered by Japan in World War II left the country in ruins. Two million lives had been lost. The country's major cities, including the capital, Tokyo, had been largely destroyed by bombing raids. The atomic bomb had turned Hiroshima and Nagasaki into blackened wastelands. The Allies had stripped Japan of its colonial empire.

Occupied Japan General Douglas MacArthur, who had accepted the Japanese surrender, took charge of the U.S. occupation of Japan. MacArthur was determined to be fair and not to plant the seeds of a future war. Nevertheless, to ensure that peace would prevail, he began a process of **demilitarization**, or disbanding the Japanese armed forces. He achieved this quickly, leaving the Japanese with only a small police force. MacArthur also began bringing Japan's major war criminals to trial. The Tokyo Trials took place from 1946 to 1948, prosecuting the same war crimes as those introduced at Nuremberg. All of the 25 surviving defendants were found guilty. Former Premier Hideki Tojo and six others were condemned to hang. The Nuremberg and Tokyo Trials were the first international criminal tribunals to prosecute high-level political and military leaders for war crimes.

World War II 1113

STRUGGLING READERS

Practice Reading Aloud

1. Have students practice reading this segment aloud.
2. As a prereading activity, write on the board *prevail, demilitarization, prosecuting, Nuremberg, condemned, tribunal, democratization, absentee, subsidies,* and *prosperous.* Pronounce each word, and ask students for possible definitions.
3. Read the first paragraph aloud as students listen. After you have modeled reading a paragraph, review with students tips for reading aloud, such as enunciating words carefully and using expression.
4. Then have a volunteer read the paragraph aloud a second time.
5. Have several students take turns reading aloud the next two paragraphs.

Objectives

You may wish to discuss the following questions with students to help them frame the content as they read.

- Why did General MacArthur and his advisers and not the Japanese people draw up Japan's postwar constitution? *MacArthur was in control of Japan; the Allies wanted to make sure that the new constitution was based on democratic principles.*
- Japan continues to have a small military. How might this help its economy? *A larger military would absorb more money that could be used for other investments.*

More About . . .

Tip for English Language Learners Explain that the prefix *de-*, as in *demilitarization* or *decode*, often means to undo an action.

Demilitarization MacArthur dismissed all Japanese senior military officials actively involved in promoting aggression since 1931. In Japan, just under 0.5 percent of the population were barred from public office. In Germany, 2.5 percent were.

Democratization After World War II, the United States has continued to encourage democratization throughout the world. It believes that more democracies will lead to peace in regions where this type of political system has taken root. It also believes that democratic societies with market economies are the most likely societies to prosper. India and Brazil are examples of relatively new democracies that have become models of economic growth.

Since the end of the cold war, many former Communist nations have become democratic, including Poland, Ukraine, and Bulgaria. Today, the United States encourages democratization through example, financial assistance, and support of human rights worldwide. More than 110 nations can now be categorized as democracies.

NOW & THEN

Demilitarization in Japan

As was the case with Japan, nations may be ordered to demilitarize as part of a peace agreement ending a war. Sometimes, just a part of a country or countries is demilitarized following a war. After the Korean War, a demilitarized zone was established between North Korea and South Korea. Sometimes, a country makes its own decision to demilitarize. For example, it may no longer feel threatened or may not want to devote a large portion of their budget to the military.

Objectives

You may wish to discuss the following questions with students to help them frame the content as they read.

- How did Japan's postwar constitution compare to the U.S. Constitution? *Both had an elected legislature, voting rights for men and women, and a bill of rights. Japan's had a prime minister and lacked power to make war.*
- How did changes in the emperor's postwar role symbolize the changes in Japan? *It marked the end of some of the traditions that had led Japan into war and the beginning of a new and more democratic era.*

More About . . .

Japan's Government Today The two houses that make up the Japanese legislative body known as the Diet are the House of Representatives and the House of Councilors. The House of Representatives has 480 members that are elected to represent the people of various regions of the country. Representatives are elected to four-year terms. The 242 members of the House of Councilors are also elected, but for six-year terms. The two lawmaking bodies have the same basic function for the most part. Japan's executive authority rests with the country's prime minister and its ministers of state, which together make up the Cabinet. The government also has a judiciary body called the Supreme Court. Japan still has an emperor, but this hereditary position is ceremonial.

ONLINE HISTORICAL SOURCES

A Diminished Emperor

Have students explore the image and answer the associated question.

Analyze Sources Why do you think MacArthur and Emperor Hirohito look uncomfortable in this photograph? *They had previously represented enemy nations at war, and MacArthur's power in Japan now usurped the power of the emperor.*

READING CHECK

Make Inferences How would demilitarization and a revived economy help Japan achieve democracy? *The reduced influence of military leaders and increased economic power of the Japanese people resulted in a wider sharing of power in Japan.*

MacArthur then turned his attention to **democratization**, the process of creating a government elected by the people. In February 1946, he and his American political advisers drew up a new constitution. It changed the empire into a constitutional monarchy like that of Great Britain. The Japanese accepted the constitution. It went into effect on May 3, 1947.

MacArthur was not told to revive the Japanese economy. However, he was instructed to broaden land ownership and increase the participation of workers and farmers in the new democracy. To this end, MacArthur put forward a plan that required absentee landlords with huge estates to sell land to the government. The government then sold the land to tenant farmers at reasonable prices. These land reforms, as well as government agricultural subsidies and price supports, quickly led to a prosperous agricultural economy. This, in turn, contributed to Japan's growth as a consumer economy. Other reforms pushed by MacArthur gave workers the right to create independent labor unions.

Reading Check
Make Inferences How would demilitarization and a revived economy help Japan achieve democracy?

Occupation Brings Deep Changes

The new constitution was the most important achievement of the occupation. It brought deep changes to Japanese society. A long Japanese tradition had viewed the emperor as divine. He was also an absolute ruler whose will was law. The emperor now had to declare that he was not divine. That admission was as shocking to the Japanese as defeat. His power was also dramatically reduced. Like the ruler of Great Britain, the emperor became largely a figurehead—a symbol of Japan.

Emperor Hirohito and U.S. General Douglas MacArthur look distant and uncomfortable as they pose here. Although Hirohito's power was greatly reduced after the war, MacArthur felt retaining him as the head of a constitutional monarchy would help the Japanese accept the changes imposed upon them.

ADVANCED/GIFTED

Compare Japan Before, During, and After the War

1. Have students form groups of four to prepare a country brief describing facts about Japan at different times, with each focusing on one time period: World War II years, 1946–1980, 1980–2005, today. Students should find out more about the economy, government, society, and challenges of Japan during their time frame.
2. Ask each group to create an illustrated chart that compares and contrasts Japan at different times.
3. Next, request that group members discuss what they predict the future will hold for Japan. Ask them to support their prediction with evidence.

The new constitution guaranteed that real political power in Japan rested with the people. The people elected a two-house parliament, called the Diet. All citizens over the age of 20, including women, had the right to vote. The government was led by a prime minister chosen by a majority of the Diet. A constitutional bill of rights protected basic freedoms. One more key provision of the constitution—Article 9—stated that the Japanese could no longer make war. They could fight only if attacked.

In September 1951, the United States and 47 other nations signed a formal peace treaty with Japan. The treaty officially ended the war. Some six months later, the U.S. occupation of Japan was over. However, with no armed forces, the Japanese agreed to a continuing U.S. military presence to protect their country. The United States and Japan, once bitter enemies, were now allies.

In the postwar world, enemies not only became allies. Sometimes, allies became enemies. World War II had changed the political landscape of Europe. The Soviet Union and the United States emerged from the war as the world's two major powers. They also ended the war as allies. However, it soon became clear that their postwar goals were very different. This difference stirred up conflicts that would shape the modern world for decades.

Reading Check
Analyze Causes Why did the Americans choose the British system of government for the Japanese, instead of the American system?

Lesson 5 Assessment

1. **Organize Information** How did the aftermath of the war in Europe differ from the aftermath of the war in Japan?

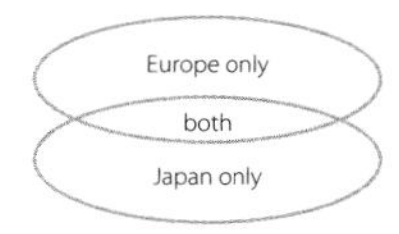

2. **Key Terms and People** For each key term or person in the lesson, write a sentence explaining its significance.
3. **Analyze Causes** Why do you think that many Europeans favored communism after World War II?
4. **Form Opinions** Do you think it was right for the Allies to try only Nazi and Japanese leaders for war crimes? Why or why not?
5. **Make Inferences** How do you think MacArthur's reforms impacted Japan culturally?
6. **Compare and Contrast** Compare and contrast how life in Europe was affected in the immediate aftermath of World War I and World War II.

ENGLISH LANGUAGE LEARNERS

Visualize the Written Word

1. Read aloud the second paragraph of this segment to students, one sentence at a time.
2. Have students read aloud each sentence after you have read it. You may have students read the sentences in unison or select different students to read each sentence. Provide constructive criticism for readers.
3. To see how well they understand what they have read, ask students to draw pictures or diagrams that visually show the structure of the new Japanese government.
4. Have students review each other's illustrations and offer comments to improve them.

READING CHECK

Analyze Causes Why did the Americans choose the British system of government for the Japanese instead of the American system? *The Japanese wanted to keep their emperor—a monarch. The American system had no place for monarchs.*

Print Assessment

1. **Organize Information** How did the aftermath of the war in Europe differ from the aftermath of the war in Japan? *Possible answer: Europe—more displaced persons, famine, communism. Japan—new constitution, radiation from atomic weapons. Both—death and destruction*
2. **Key Terms and People** For each key term or person in the lesson, write a sentence explaining its significance. *Explanations of the lesson's key terms can be found on the following pages: Nuremberg trials, p. 1112; demilitarization, p. 1113; democratization, p. 1114*
3. **Analyze Causes** Why do you think that many Europeans favored communism after World War II? *Possible answer: People lost faith in leaders of the past who had started or conducted the war; communism promised change for people who were suffering.*
4. **Form Opinions** Do you think it was right for the Allies to try only Nazi and Japanese leaders for war crimes? Why or why not? *Possible answer: Yes—The acts were horrendous, and Nazi and Japanese leaders deserved punishment. The Allies were not guilty of war crimes because they were fighting to defend themselves and did not commit horrendous crimes. No—Bloodshed and destruction are always a part of war. Also both sides caused death and destruction.*
5. **Make Inferences** How do you think MacArthur's reforms impacted Japan culturally? *Possible answer: Land and labor reforms and a constitution brought Western ideas to the tradition-based Japanese culture. These changes allowed more participation from the general population in the political and economic life of the country.*
6. **Compare and Contrast** Compare and contrast how life in Europe was affected in the immediate aftermath of World War I and World War II. *Possible answer: In both wars, millions of soldiers and civilians were killed, much of the continent destroyed, and economies devastated. More British and French military were killed in World War I than in World War II, while more Russia/Soviet Union and German soldiers were killed in World War II.*

Online Assessment

1. What was one reason that famine took the lives of thousands in Europe after the war ended?
   - ○ The farmlands had all been destroyed.
   - ● Food could not reach the people in the cities.
   - ○ People spent their money on war bonds instead of food.
   - ○ All of the continent's farmers had died in the concentration camps.

   Alternate Question *Select the answer choice from the drop-down list to complete the sentence correctly.* Many of the *transportation networks* in Europe were destroyed during the war. Because of that, it was difficult to get food to the people who lived in the cities. Famine resulted, killing thousands.

2. Why did the Communist Party briefly become popular in Italy and France at the end of World War II?
   - ● People were looking for a change in government.
   - ○ People were worried that their leaders had fascist inclinations.
   - ○ People were afraid that their old way of life would never resume.
   - ○ People were hoping that their economy would recover without capitalism.

   Alternate Question *Select the answer choice from the drop-down list to complete the sentence correctly.* The Communist Party attracted supporters in *France and Italy* after the war ended until violent labor strikes caused them to vote for anti-Communist parties.

3. What did MacArthur do in Japan to help address the needs of Japan's economy?
   - ● He broadened land ownership.
   - ○ He allowed absentee landlords to buy more land.
   - ○ He limited the participation of farmers in the new government.
   - ○ He set up a program by which the government could give away land to farmers.

   Alternate Question *Select the answer choice from the drop-down list to complete the sentence correctly.* In order to *address the needs of the economy* in Japan, MacArthur instituted land reforms.

4. Why did Japan need to have continued U.S. military presence after the U.S. occupation officially ended?
   - ● Japan had no armed forces.
   - ○ Japan had few natural resources.
   - ○ Japan was a small nation geographically.
   - ○ Japan wanted to become a constitutional monarchy.

   Alternate Question *Select the answer choice from the drop-down list to complete the sentence correctly.*
   Because Japan had no armed forces, it needed continued protection from the *United States*.

5. **Elaborate** What were conditions like in many places in Europe following the war?

   Possible answer: Many places in Europe had been extensively bombed during the war and thereby were destroyed. Homes, buildings, and apartments were leveled. People had to live in partially destroyed homes, in cellars, or in caves that they made out of the rubble. Electricity and water were scarce. Very little food and very little paid work, if any, was available. Much of the transportation system throughout Europe was destroyed. Few people had proper clothing for the winter months. Disease and famine were rampant throughout the continent.

6. **Make Inferences** What happened to some of the Nazi leaders before the war ended, and why did this most likely happen?

   Possible answer: Before the war ended, some of the Nazi leaders committed suicide. Adolf Hitler, SS chief Heinrich Himmler, and Joseph Goebbels were among them. They most likely did this because they didn't want to get captured by the Allies for fear of what their punishment would be for the crimes that they committed.

7. **Draw Conclusions** Why did MacArthur most likely institute demilitarization and democratization in Japan?

   Possible answer: MacArthur wanted to be fair to the Japanese. He also wanted to avoid planting any seeds of a future war. Because of his actions, it can be concluded that he believed that stripping the Japanese of their military and setting up a democracy would allow peace to continue in the region.

8. **Compare and Contrast** Why did the relations between Japan and the United States improve after the war and the relations between the Soviet Union and the United States deteriorate?

   Possible answer: One of the reasons that the relations between Japan and the United States improved is that the United States stepped in and helped rebuild Japan. The United States also set Japan up with a democratic government. Because they now had the same political ideologies, it was easier for the two nations to be friendly with each other. The Soviet Union had very different ideologies from the United Sates. Its goal was to spread communism around the world, which was the polar opposite of democracy. This caused a great amount of tension to exist between the Soviet Union and the United States.

Print Assessment

Key Terms and People

For each term or name below, write a sentence explaining its connection to World War II.

1. blitzkrieg
2. Battle of Britain
3. Atlantic Charter
4. Battle of Midway
5. Douglas MacArthur
6. Holocaust
7. genocide
8. D-Day
9. Battle of the Bulge
10. Nuremberg Trials
11. Demilitarization

Explanations of the significance of the module's key terms and people can be found on the following pages: blitzkrieg, p. 1079; Battle of Britain, p. 1082; Atlantic Charter, p. 1085; Battle of Midway, p. 1090; Douglas MacArthur, p. 1091; Holocaust, p. 1093; genocide, p. 1095; D-Day, p. 1105; Battle of the Bulge, p. 1106; Nuremberg trials, p. 1112; demilitarization, p. 1113

Main Ideas

Use your notes and the information in the module to answer the following questions.

Hitler's Lightning War

1. How was Hitler's pact with Stalin and Germany's invasion of Poland a direct cause of World War II? *The pact and surprise invasion occurred within days and quickly after Britain and France declared war on Germany.*
2. How did German blitzkrieg tactics rely on new military technology? *The Germans used state-of-the-art fighter and bomber planes to conduct air raids and fast tanks and trucks to surprise and overwhelm the Allies.*
3. Why were the early months of World War II referred to as the "phony war"? *Both sides made preparations for war, but very little action took place.*
4. Why was capturing Egypt's Suez Canal so important to the Axis powers? *It was the key for access to the oil fields of Southwest Asia.*
5. What was the Atlantic Charter, and what did it state? *It was a joint declaration by Roosevelt and Churchill stating their objectives for the war: to ensure free trade and democracy, and not to gain territory.*

Japan's Pacific Campaign

6. What was Yamamoto's objective at Pearl Harbor? *to destroy the United States Fleet*
7. How did Japan try to win support from other Asian countries? *by appealing to their hatred for the colonial powers and by pushing the idea of "Asia for the Asiatics"*
8. In what way was the Battle of the Coral Sea a new kind of naval warfare? *Planes from aircraft carriers dominated the fight.*
9. What was General Douglas MacArthur's island-hopping strategy? *seize weakly held islands first*

The Holocaust

10. What was the new racial order proposed by the Nazis? *The Aryans were a "master race," and all other groups were inferior.*

Module 28 Assessment

Key Terms and People

For each term or name below, write a sentence explaining its connection to World War II.

1. blitzkrieg
2. Battle of Britain
3. Atlantic Charter
4. Battle of Midway
5. Douglas MacArthur
6. Holocaust
7. genocide
8. D-Day
9. Battle of the Bulge
10. Nuremberg Trials
11. demilitarization

Main Ideas

Use your notes and the information in the module to answer the following questions.

Hitler's Lightning War

1. How was Hitler's pact with Stalin and Germany's invasion of Poland a direct cause of World War II?
2. How did German blitzkrieg tactics rely on new military technology?
3. Why were the early months of World War II referred to as the "phony war"?
4. Why was capturing Egypt's Suez Canal so important to the Axis powers?
5. What was the Atlantic Charter and what did it state?

Japan's Pacific Campaign

6. What was Yamamoto's objective at Pearl Harbor?
7. How did Japan try to win support from other Asian countries?
8. In what way was the Battle of the Coral Sea a new kind of naval warfare?
9. What was General Douglas MacArthur's island-hopping strategy?

The Holocaust

10. What was the new racial order proposed by the Nazis?
11. Name two tactics that Hitler used to rid Germany of Jews before creating his Final Solution.
12. What Nazi action marked the final stage of the Final Solution?
13. How did some non-Jews oppose Hitler's war on the Jews?

The Allied Victory

14. Why did Stalin want the United States and Britain to launch a second front in the west?
15. Why were consumer goods rationed during the war?
16. What was Operation Overlord?

Europe and Japan in Ruins

17. Why did so many Europeans take to the roads and wander the countryside after the war?
18. How did the governments of non-Axis nations respond to the issue of genocidal war crimes in Europe?
19. What were two of the most important steps that MacArthur took in Japan following the war?

ONLINE DOCUMENT-BASED INVESTIGATION

World War II

Have students complete and review all of the DBI activities in **Part 1.**

Use this Compare-and-Contrast Essay Rubric to score students' work in **Part 2.**

RUBRIC Students' essays should

- identify similarities and differences appropriate to the topic
- attempt comparisons from parallel categories of items
- cite at least three sources of appropriate text evidence from Part 1 in support of their comparisons
- be organized into a distinct introduction, a main body consisting of several paragraphs, and a conclusion that sums up the main points

Write a Compare-and-Contrast Essay Each principal Allied and Axis nation experienced total war in ways that greatly impacted both personnel on the battlefield and their civilian populations. Write an essay in which you compare and contrast the ways that the total war approach defined each Allied and Axis nation during World War II.

Be sure to cite specific evidence from at least three of the sources in your response.

Module 28 Assessment, continued

Critical Thinking

1. Organize Information Copy the chart into your notebook and specify for each listed battle or conflict whether the Axis powers or the Allied powers gained an advantage.

Battle/ Conflict	Allied or Axis Powers?
Battle of Britain	
War in the Balkans	
Pearl Harbor	
Battle of the Coral Sea	
Battle of Midway	

2. Draw Conclusions Consider the personalities, tactics, and policies of Hitler, Rommel, MacArthur, and Churchill. What qualities make a good war leader?
3. Compare And Contrast Compare and contrast Japan's and Germany's goals in World War II. What actions did they take in pursuit of these goals that caused Britain, France, and then the United States to declare war?
4. Evaluate Why do you think the governments of the United States and other countries encouraged people on the home front to organize programs for such activities as scrap collection?

Engage with History

Reread the quotation from Elie Wiesel's *Night* in Lesson 3. Then find other sources of personal reflections on the Holocaust from survivors, as well as from non-Jews living in Germany during World War II. Determine how these writings help contribute to an understanding of the Holocaust. What kind of voice and perspective is apparent? How are events interpreted? Consider how these reflections may help shape your interpretation of the past.

Focus on Writing

Conduct research on the scientific and technological developments used in the Allied war effort. Use your findings to create several **information cards** for a card series titled "Science and Technology During World War II." Organize the information on your cards in the following categories:

- name of invention or development
- country
- year
- use in the war
- use today

Multimedia Activity

During World War II, many consumer-goods manufacturers switched to the production of military goods. Many of these companies still exist. Working with a partner, use the Internet to research one such company. Find out what products the company made before and during the war, and how the company's wartime role affected its reputation.

Present the results of your research in a well-organized paper. Be sure to

- apply a search strategy when using directories and search engines to locate web resources
- judge the usefulness and reliability of each website
- correctly cite your web sources
- edit for organization and correct use of language

Essential Question ESSAY

Why did the Allies win World War II?

RUBRIC Students' essays should

- respond to the Essential Question with a specific position
- illustrate valid reasoning supporting their position
- cite persuasive evidence supporting their position
- identify key people, events, and/or turning points that demonstrate understanding of the module content
- be organized into a distinct introduction, main body, and conclusion

Write an argument answering this question. Your essay should include key people, events, and turning points in World War II. Be sure to cite evidence to support your position and organize your essay into an introduction, body, and conclusion.

Alternative Activity Instead of writing essays, address the Essential Question through activities such as holding debates, creating multimedia presentations, or writing journal entries.

11. Name two tactics that Hitler used to rid Germany of Jews before creating his "Final Solution." *forced emigration, relocation to ghettos, work in concentration camps*
12. What Nazi action marked the final stage of the "Final Solution"? *extermination camps*
13. How did some non-Jews oppose Hitler's war on the Jews? *They hid Jews in their homes or helped them escape Germany.*

The Allied Victory

14. Why did Stalin want the United States and Britain to launch a second front in the west? *to relieve pressure on the Soviets*
15. Why were consumer goods rationed during the war? *Governments needed to supply their armies with materials. Many industries switched to producing war-related goods, causing a shortage of consumer goods.*
16. What was Operation Overlord? *the name used by Allied military leaders for the invasion of Europe in June 1944*

Europe and Japan in Ruins

17. Why did so many Europeans take to the roads and wander the countryside after the war? *Many cities were in ruins, so people went in search of a place to live; prisoners of war and Holocaust survivors looked for their families; postwar treaties forced some people to move.*
18. How did the governments of non-Axis nations respond to the issue of genocidal war crimes in Europe? *established International Military Tribunal to try Nazi leaders*
19. What were two of the most important steps that MacArthur took in Japan following the war? *demilitarization and democratization*

Critical Thinking

1. **Organize Information** Copy the chart into your notebook and specify for each listed battle or conflict whether the Axis powers or the Allied powers gained an advantage.

Battle/Conflict	Allied or Axis Powers?
Battle of Britain	*Allies*
War in the Balkans	*Axis*
Pearl Harbor	*Axis*
Battle of the Coral Sea	*Allies*
Battle of Midway	*Allies*

2. **Draw Conclusions** Consider the personalities, tactics, and policies of Hitler, Rommel, MacArthur, and Churchill. What qualities make a good war leader? *ability to unite people behind a common cause; ability to persuade people that the cause the leader represents is noble; powerful personality*

(continued)

Print Assessment *(continued)*

3. **Compare and Contrast** Compare and contrast Japan's and Germany's goals in World War II. What actions did they take in pursuit of these goals that caused Britain, France, and then the United States to declare war? *Japan wanted European colonial powers and the United States out of Asia. Germany wanted Germans to be ethnically pure and also wanted to make up for losses suffered after World War I. Both wanted to expand their territory, resources, and wealth. German's invasion of Poland led to Britain and France's entry into the war. Japan's attack on Pearl Harbor led directly to a United States declaration of war.*
4. **Evaluate** Why do you think the governments of the United States and other countries encouraged people on the home front to organize programs for such activities as scrap collection? *These programs made a positive contribution to the war effort—providing scrap metal for use in making weapons and ammunition, for example. These programs also got the people on the home front involved and gave them the feeling that they were a part of the war effort.*

Engage with History

Reread the quotation from Elie Wiesel's *Night* in Lesson 3. Then find other sources of personal reflections on the Holocaust from survivors, as well as from non-Jews living in Germany during World War II. Determine how these writings help contribute to an understanding of the Holocaust. What kind of voice and perspective is apparent? How are events interpreted? Consider how these reflections may help shape your interpretation of the past. *Answers will vary, but students should show an understanding of voice and perspective in primary sources and how to use these to interpret events in history.*

Focus on Writing

Conduct research on the scientific and technological developments used in the Allied war effort. Use your findings to create several **information cards** for a card series titled "Science and Technology During World War II." Organize the information on your cards in the following categories:

- name of invention or development
- country
- year
- use in the war
- use today

RUBRIC Information cards should
- record information accurately
- present information clearly and succinctly
- include graphic representations of information where appropriate

Multimedia Activity

During World War II, many consumer-goods manufacturers switched to the production of military goods. Many of these companies still exist. Working with a partner, use the Internet to research one such company. Find out what products the company made before and during the war, and how the company's wartime role affected its reputation.

RUBRIC Present the results of your research in a well-organized paper. Be sure to
- apply a search strategy when using directories and search engines to locate web resources
- judge the usefulness and reliability of each website
- correctly cite your web sources
- edit for organization and correct use of language

Online Assessment

1. *Select the correct button in the table to show whether each statement about the Soviet invasion of Finland is true or false.*

	True	False
Stalin had to accept the Finnish surrender terms.	○	●
The Finns gave up easily when the Soviets invaded.	○	●
The Soviets suffered heavy losses when they invaded Finland.	●	○
Finnish soldiers moved about on skis as they fought the Soviets.	●	○

2. How did the British people respond to the attacks they received by the Nazis?
   - ● They refused to give in.
   - ○ They wanted to negotiate peace.
   - ○ They tried to convince the Soviets to help.
   - ○ They let France set up a puppet government within their borders.
3. *Select the correct button in the table to show whether each statement about Operation Barbarossa is true or false.*

	True	False
Hitler began planning his invasion of the Soviet Union in 1940.	●	○
The Soviet army was much larger and much better trained than the Nazi army.	○	●
Part of Hitler's plan to invade the Soviet Union included building bases in the Balkans.	●	○
After one million people died of starvation, Leningrad finally surrendered to the Nazis.	○	●
The Nazi soldiers were wearing only lightweight summer uniforms during the winter of 1941.	●	○
Hitler did not want to repeat Napoleon's mistakes, so he refused to allow his troops to retreat.	●	○
The Nazi army was depleted by 500,000 by 1943 because of Hitler's attack on the Soviet Union.	●	○

4. Why did the Japanese admiral Isoroku Yamamoto feel it was necessary to attack Pearl Harbor?
   - ● He believed that it posed a danger for the empire of Japan.
   - ○ He hoped Hitler would see Japan as a force to be reckoned with.
   - ○ He wanted to obtain the natural resources of the Hawaiian island chain.
   - ○ He thought his country would gain more respect from other Asian nations.
5. Which locations fell immediately after the attack on Pearl Harbor?
   - ○ the Philippines
   - ○ Burma and India
   - ● Guam and Wake Island
   - ○ Java, Sumatra, and Borneo
6. What were **two** results of Doolittle's raid on Japan in April 1942?
   - ● American morale was significantly raised.
   - ○ The Allied forces lost more battles in the Pacific.
   - ● The Japanese stopped thinking they were invincible.
   - ○ Airplanes were known to be effective battle weapons.
   - ○ The Japanese decided to increase the size of their empire.

7. *Select the correct button in the table to show whether each statement about the initial treatment of the European Jews by the Nazis is true or false.*

	True	False
The Nazis wanted to forbid Jews from immigrating to other countries.	○	●
The Nuremberg Laws of 1935 stripped Jews of their German citizenship.	●	○
Jews and non-Jews were not allowed be married in Germany after 1935.	●	○
Jews were forced to leave their homes and move into crowded Jewish areas of the city.	●	○
Blaming the Jews for a country's misfortunes was a new idea brought about by the Nazis.	○	●
The action of one Jew could cause the entire Jewish population to be punished by the Nazis.	●	○

8. *Select the correct button in the table to show whether each statement about the Holocaust is true or false.*

	True	False
Six million Jews died in the death camps and Nazi massacres.	●	○
Slave labor prisons were the final stage of Hitler's "Final Solution."	○	●
Non-Jews tried to save Jews by using their homes as hiding places.	●	○
Food was so scarce in the camps that some of the Jews ate soup that had fallen into the mud.	●	○

9. *Select the correct button in the table to show whether each statement about Auschwitz is true or false.*

	True	False
It was the largest of all the extermination camps.	●	○
Cyanide gas was used to fuel the ovens in the crematoriums.	○	●
When prisoners arrived, the SS decided who would live or die.	●	○
The elderly and sick were taken immediately to the camp's hospital.	○	●

10. Why were the Nazis ultimately defeated in Stalingrad?

○ The Soviet soldiers had better military training.
○ The Soviet soldiers had better access to armored vehicles.
○ The Nazi soldiers were being led by inexperienced leaders.
● The Nazi soldiers were not prepared for the cold Russian winters.

11. *Select the correct button in the table to show whether each statement about the home front in the United States during World War II is true or false.*

	True	False
The United States only produced 3,000 tanks in 1939.	●	○
From 1941 to 1945, the United States built 300,000 aircraft carriers.	○	●
Nearly all of the nation's economy was directed toward the war effort.	●	○
American consumers had limited goods to choose from, and necessities were rationed.	●	○

12. *Select the correct button in the table to show whether each characteristic is associated with the D-Day invasion or the Battle of the Bulge.*

	D-Day Invasion	Battle of the Bulge
Hitler knew this would determine if the Nazis lived or died.	○	●
The Allied troops had to fight their way onto a 60-mile beach.	●	○
The Nazis pushed into the Allied lines with great force.	○	●
It occurred on the beaches of Normandy, France.	●	○
It opened the way for the Allies to march triumphantly into Paris.	●	○
It occurred in the Ardennes, a region of rough terrain and forests.	○	●
German tanks broke through a 75-mile front.	○	●

13. *Drag the name of each city next to the correct description. Each city will be used only once.*

was called a "city of the dead" by a U.S. officer	●	Berlin
remained largely undamaged after the war	●	Brussels
population declined from 1.3 million in 1939 to 153,000 in 1945	●	Warsaw
was subjected to a prolonged bombing campaign by the Luftwaffe	●	London

14. *Drag the name of each person to the correct description. Each name will be used only once.*

the only convicted Nazi who expressed any remorse	●	Hans Frank
Hitler's former deputy, tried for war crimes at the Nuremberg trials	●	Rudolf Hess
SS chief who committed suicide before the war ended	●	Heinrich Himmler
Minister of Propaganda, committed suicide before the war ended	●	Joseph Goebbels
received a death sentence but committed suicide first	●	Hermann Göring

15. *Drag each characteristic into the correct column in the table to show whether it is associated with the demilitarization or democratization of Japan.*

Demilitarization	Democratization
disbanded the armed forces	created a government elected by the people
only allowed to have a small police force	included a constitution, which was accepted by the people in May 1947
brought war criminals to trial	changed the empire into a constitutional monarchy

Online Multimedia Connections

In this activity, students will learn about several key events in World War II. They will watch and discuss short video clips on American mobilization for the war, the air war over Germany, and D-Day and then read and discuss a soldier's letter home.

HISTORY MULTIMEDIA CONNECTIONS

Memories of WORLD WAR II

A global conflict, World War II shaped the history of both the United States and the world. Americans contributed to the war effort in numerous ways. Many enlisted in the military and served in Africa, Europe, and the Pacific. Others contributed by working in factories to produce the massive amounts of ships, planes, guns, and other supplies necessary to win the war. In the process, these Americans left behind firsthand accounts of their experiences during the war, both at home and abroad. Explore some of the personal stories and recollections of World War II online. You can find a wealth of information, video clips, primary sources, activities, and more through your online textbook.

1117 MC1 MULTIMEDIA CONNECTIONS

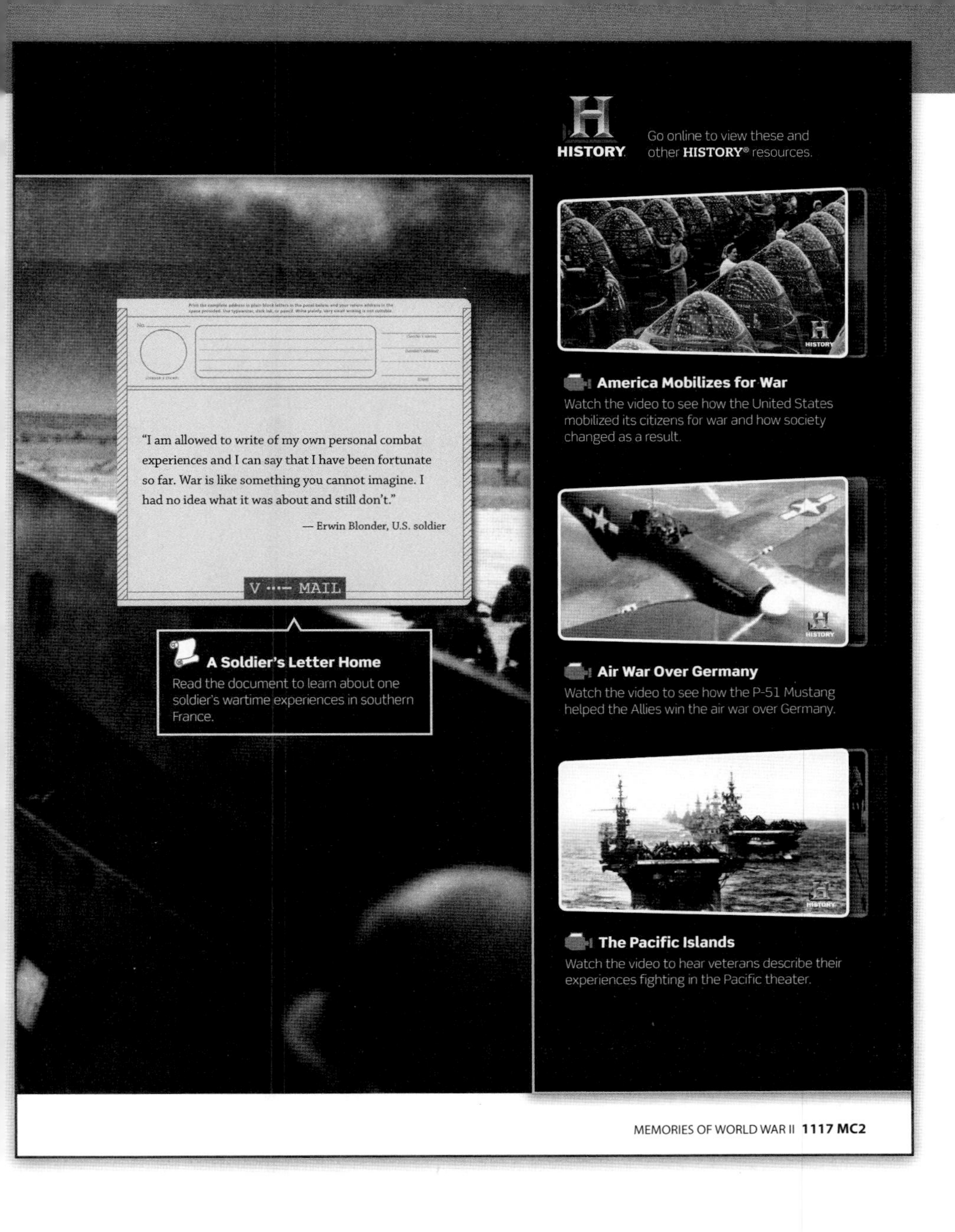

"I am allowed to write of my own personal combat experiences and I can say that I have been fortunate so far. War is like something you cannot imagine. I had no idea what it was about and still don't."

— Erwin Blonder, U.S. soldier

V ··· MAIL

A Soldier's Letter Home

Read the document to learn about one soldier's wartime experiences in southern France.

HISTORY

Go online to view these and other **HISTORY®** resources.

America Mobilizes for War

Watch the video to see how the United States mobilized its citizens for war and how society changed as a result.

Air War Over Germany

Watch the video to see how the P-51 Mustang helped the Allies win the air war over Germany.

The Pacific Islands

Watch the video to hear veterans describe their experiences fighting in the Pacific theater.

Essential Question Preview

Why did the Cold War never develop into a direct military conflict between the United States and the Soviet Union?

Have students consider the Essential Question and capture their initial responses.

Explore the Essential Question

- Tell students that the United States and the Soviet Union battled each other through other countries, using a variety of methods.
- Point out how nations all over the world were pressured and enticed to take sides.

Help students plan inquiries and develop their own supporting questions such as:

What actions did other countries take in response to the Cold War confrontations between the United States and the Soviet Union?

In what ways were nations pressured or enticed by the United States and the Soviet Union to take sides?

You may want to assign students to write a short essay in response to the Essential Question when they complete the module. Encourage students to use their notes and responses to inform their essays.

Explore the Online Video

ANALYZE VIDEOS

Korea: The Forgotten War

Invite students to watch the video to learn how the Soviets gambled that the United States would not defend South Korea.

History Why were the South Koreans unprepared for the invasion from the North? *Many soldiers were also farmers who had been given leave to work in their rice paddies.*

Module 29

Cold War Conflicts

Essential Question

Why did the Cold War never develop into a direct military conflict between the United States and the Soviet Union?

About the Photo: South Korean citizens wave flags to cheer on U.S. First Cavalry Division soldiers on their way to battle Communist troops during the Korean War.

Explore ONLINE!

VIDEOS, including...
- Korea: The Forgotten War
- Arriving in Vietnam
- Ayatollah Khomeini

HISTORY

- Document Based Investigations
- Graphic Organizers
- Interactive Games
- Image Compare: Political Boundaries Before and After World War II
- Carousel: War in Vietnam

In this module you will learn that the United States and the Soviet Union competed for dominance in the post–World War II world, with important consequences for other nations.

What You Will Learn ...

1118 Module 29

Lesson 1 Big Idea

The opposing economic and political philosophies of the United States and the Soviet Union led to global competition.

Why It Matters Now

The conflicts between the United States and the Soviet Union played a major role in reshaping the modern world.

Lesson 2 Big Idea

After World War II, Chinese Communists defeated Nationalist forces and two separate Chinas emerged.

Why It Matters Now

China remains a Communist country and a major power in the world.

Lesson 3 Big Idea

In Asia, the Cold War flared into actual wars supported mainly by the superpowers.

Why It Matters Now

Today, Vietnam is a Communist country, and Korea is split into Communist and non-Communist nations.

Lesson 4 Big Idea

The superpowers supported opposing sides in Latin American and Middle Eastern conflicts.

Why It Matters Now

Many of these areas today are troubled by political, economic, and military conflict and crisis.

Timeline of Events 1945–Present

Explore ONLINE!

World

1945

- 1945 United Nations formed.
- 1947 Independent India partitioned into India and Pakistan.
- 1949 Communists take control of China.
- 1957 Ghana achieves independence from Great Britain.
- 1957 Soviets launch *Sputnik*.
- 1959 Cuba becomes Communist under Fidel Castro.
- 1969 U.S. lands astronauts on the moon.
- 1973 Arab forces attack Israel in Yom Kippur War.
- 1975 Vietnam War ends.
- 1989 Berlin Wall in Germany is knocked down.
- 1990 Communists voted out of power in Nicaragua.
- 1994 First all-race election in South Africa is held. (Nelson Mandela)
- 2000 South Korea and North Korea meet to improve relations.
- 2006 North Korea tests a nuclear weapon.

2010

Cold War Conflicts 1119

Lesson 5 Big Idea

The Cold War began to thaw as the superpowers entered an era of uneasy diplomacy.

Why It Matters Now

The United States and the countries of the former Soviet Union continue to cooperate and maintain a cautious peace.

Explore the Timeline

Interpret Timelines: The Cold War

Have students examine the timeline and then answer the following question.

History How long after the Soviets launched *Sputnik* did it take for U.S. astronauts to land on the moon? *about 12 years*

Interpret Timeline of Events: Timeline of Events 1945–Present

To further explore the timeline, have students discuss the following questions.

1. During what ten-year period did Communism experience the most successes? What were they? *1949–1959; Communists gained control of China and Cuba and launched Sputnik.*
2. After the Berlin Wall was knocked down, what other defeat for the Communists is shown on the timeline? *Communists voted out of power in Nicaragua*

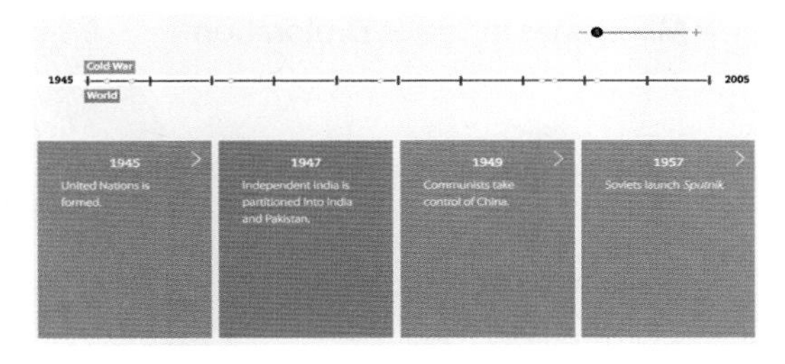

Online Module Flip Cards

Use the flip cards as a whole class activity or in student pairs to preview the module's Key Terms and People. Students can guess the meaning of each word, then review its definition, or do the reverse, using the flip card's toggle button to switch from Term to Definition mode. Students can also use the flip cards at the end of the module as a review tool before taking the Module Assessment.

Online Sequencing Activity

Students can use this sequencing activity to review the chronology of events in the Cold War Conflicts module. To complete, have students drag each event to the correct year on the timeline.

Year	Event
1946	*North Korea attacks South Korea.*
1949	*Communists take control of China.*
1950	*Bay of Pigs invasion*
1957	*Winston Churchill makes his "Iron Curtain" speech.*
1961	*Soviets launch* Sputnik.
1975	*The Vietnam War ends.*

Cold War: Superpowers Face Off

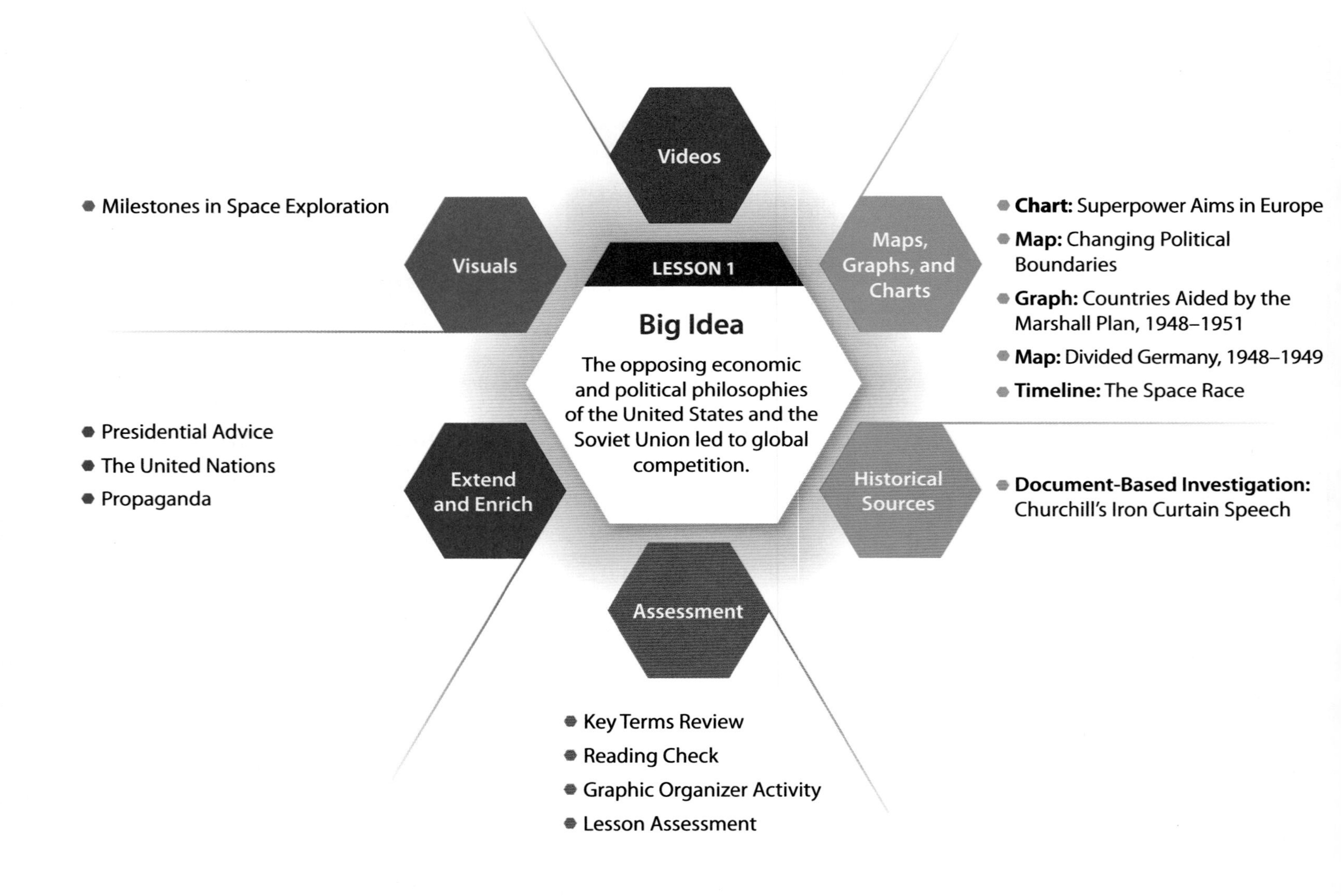

Visuals
- Milestones in Space Exploration

Maps, Graphs, and Charts
- **Chart:** Superpower Aims in Europe
- **Map:** Changing Political Boundaries
- **Graph:** Countries Aided by the Marshall Plan, 1948–1951
- **Map:** Divided Germany, 1948–1949
- **Timeline:** The Space Race

Extend and Enrich
- Presidential Advice
- The United Nations
- Propaganda

Historical Sources
- **Document-Based Investigation:** Churchill's Iron Curtain Speech

Assessment
- Key Terms Review
- Reading Check
- Graphic Organizer Activity
- Lesson Assessment

Online Lesson 1 Enrichment Activities

Presidential Advice

Memo Students imagine they are political advisers and write a memo to the leader of a superpower identifying steps he or she should take to gain allies. Students should include three or four points in their memo, along with their advice and opinions about the best actions to take. The memo should include formal language written in a respectful tone appropriate for a world leader.

The United Nations

Article Students read about the goals and organization of the United Nations. Then they write a position paper stating whether they think Taiwan should be admitted to the UN as a separate nation. They should list reasons both for and against admission.

Propaganda

Article Students read about the purpose and use of propaganda during the Cold War. Then they conduct Internet research to find examples of Cold War propaganda posters. They should study how the posters were used to gain public support for different policies. Students then draw their own Cold War poster that attempts to influence others' beliefs about communism or capitalism.

Teach the Big Idea

1. **Whole Class Open/Introduction** Ask students to name the world's superpowers. Ask if there have been other superpowers in the past. *Possible answer: United States, Soviet Union, United Kingdom*
2. **Direct Teach** Read the Big Idea: *The opposing economic and political philosophies of the United States and the Soviet Union led to global competition.* Review the following lesson objectives with students to aid in their understanding of the Big Idea.
   - Identify consequences of World War II.
   - Analyze the U.S.-Soviet postwar split.
   - Explain how Soviet domination of Eastern Europe developed.
   - Describe U.S. containment of Communist expansion.
   - Define the Cold War.
3. **Whole Group Close/Reflect** Ask students to imagine they are president of the United States after World War II. What policies would they follow to gain allies? Have them discuss the issues and identify ways in which the United States could influence other countries.

ONLINE DOCUMENT-BASED INVESTIGATION

Cold War Conflicts

Churchill's Iron Curtain Speech is the first of five document-based investigations that students will analyze in the Cold War Conflicts module. Winston Churchill delivered this speech in 1946 to urge the United States and Great Britain to stand together against the Soviet Union. Students can click on the audio button beneath the historical source to hear the excerpt read aloud.

DOCUMENT-BASED INVESTIGATION HISTORICAL SOURCE

Churchill's Iron Curtain Speech

Winston Churchill delivered this speech at a college in Missouri in 1946, nine months after he was defeated for reelection as prime minister. He urged the United States and Great Britain to stand together against the Soviet Union, which had been their ally just a year earlier.

ONLINE LESSON FLIP CARDS

Review Key Terms and People

Students can use the flip cards in the Lesson Review at any time to review the lesson's key terms and people: *United Nations, iron curtain, containment, Truman Doctrine, Marshall Plan, Cold War, NATO, Warsaw Pact,* and *brinkmanship.*

Lesson 1

Cold War: Superpowers Face Off

The Big Idea

The opposing economic and political philosophies of the United States and the Soviet Union led to global competition.

Why It Matters Now

The conflicts between the United States and the Soviet Union played a major role in reshaping the modern world.

Key Terms and People

United Nations
iron curtain
containment
Truman Doctrine
Marshall Plan
Cold War
NATO
Warsaw Pact
brinkmanship

Setting the Stage

In late 1943, as World War II raged, leaders of the United States, Britain, and the Soviet Union met together at Tehran, the capital of Iran, to discuss a joint strategy for defeating Germany and to open discussion about how to set national borders after the war. Starting in June 1944, the Soviet army marched west, and the American army, joined by other European allies, marched east. When the two forces met at the Elbe River in Germany on April 25, 1945, they embraced each other warmly because they had defeated the Nazis. Their national leaders, however, regarded each other much more coolly. This animosity caused by competing political philosophies would lead to a nearly half-century of conflict called the Cold War.

Long-term Consequences of World War II

World War II was the most destructive war in history. The death toll of military personnel and civilians in Europe, Africa, and Asia during the conflict may have reached over 60 million. The total represented almost 3 percent of the world's population at the time. Loss of life was only one short-term consequence of the war. Massive land and property destruction, environmental changes, social issues, and problems involving hunger and disease also occurred. These problems would have a long-term impact on the continent.

Demographic and Social Consequences World War II was the first war in which civilian deaths outnumbered military ones. Many civilian deaths occurred in connection with battles, bombings, or enemy occupations. Several ethnic groups, such as Jews and Roma, were singled out for destruction, and their elimination changed the demographic makeup of countries such as Poland, Czechoslovakia, and Hungary. In addition, the fighting and destruction as well as

Objectives

You may wish to discuss the following questions with students to help them frame the content as they read.

- In what ways was World War II the most destructive war in history? *loss of life, property destruction, environmental damage, social issues, hunger, disease*
- What was a long-term consequence of World War II? *forests were depleted; farmland was destroyed*

More About . . .

Global Conflict The repressive governments and conflicts discussed in this lesson were nothing new to the world. What set this period apart was the global scale of the conflict as two superpowers competed for dominance. The competition reached to all parts of the world and repeatedly brought the nations to the brink of nuclear war.

changes in national borders caused millions of civilians to abandon their homes and property and move to new areas. Families were often split up, and many fathers died. Hunger and disease also took their toll on populations in the long term. Medical experts noted increased incidences of diabetes, depression, and heart disease following the war. Many soldiers and civilians also suffered adverse health effects as a result of exposure to chemical, biological, and atomic weapons.

Reading Check
Analyze Effects What demographic changes did Europe undergo as a result of World War II?

Economic and Environmental Consequences Tank battles and bombing raids during the war caused a great deal of destruction both to the infrastructure (buildings, bridges, and roads) of countries and to the physical environment. Forests were depleted, and farmland was destroyed. It would take several years for crop production to reach prewar levels again. Countries began rebuilding soon after the war, and economies improved in most Western European nations. Countries under Soviet control took longer to rebound during the Cold War, as you will read below.

Allies Become Enemies

Even before World War II ended, the U.S. alliance with the Soviet Union had begun to unravel. The United States was upset that Joseph Stalin, the Soviet leader, had signed a nonaggression pact with Germany in 1939. Later, Stalin blamed the Allies for not invading German-occupied Europe earlier than 1944. Driven by these and other disagreements, the two allies began to pursue opposing goals.

Yalta Conference: A Postwar Plan The war was not yet over in February 1945. But the leaders of the United States, Britain, and the Soviet Union met again at the Soviet Black Sea resort of Yalta. There, they agreed to divide Germany into zones of occupation controlled by the Allied military forces. Germany also would have to pay the Soviet Union to compensate for its loss of life and property during the war. Stalin agreed to join the war against Japan once Germany surrendered. He also promised that Eastern Europeans would have free elections. A skeptical Winston Churchill predicted that Stalin would keep his pledge only if the Eastern Europeans followed "a policy friendly to Russia." Events after the war proved Churchill right, as the Soviet Union under Stalin never permitted free elections.

Winston Churchill, Franklin D. Roosevelt, and Joseph Stalin meet at Yalta in 1945.

Objectives

You may wish to discuss the following questions with students to help them frame the content as they read.

- How were the occupation forces for Germany chosen? *nations primarily responsible for defeating Germany occupied the country*
- What made 1945 an especially good time to found the United Nations? *Possible answer: Superpowers were still on good terms. With war fresh on their minds, most people supported the effort to promote peace.*

More About . . .

Connect to Geography Geography played an important role in the development of U.S. and Soviet Cold War strategies. The huge landmass of the Soviet Union and the two oceans that surround the United States were important factors that influenced the countries' policies. For example, the oceans offered the United States natural defense and motivated its leaders to build air and sea power. By contrast, the Soviet Union was vulnerable to land invasion, which led Soviet leaders to build massive armies.

The Security Council Membership in the Security Council currently consists of five permanent member states (China, France, the Russian Federation, the United Kingdom, and the United States) and ten nonpermanent members. Nonpermanent members are elected by the UN General Assembly and serve two years. Members are chosen for regional balance. Five members come from Africa or Asia, one from Eastern Europe, two from Latin America, and two from Western Europe.

ONLINE GRAPHIC ORGANIZER

Cold War: Superpowers Face Off

As students read the lesson, have them use the graphic organizer to take notes. Students can review their graphic organizer notes at the end of the lesson to answer the following question.

Draw Conclusions Which effect of the Cold War was the most significant? Explain. *The Marshall Plan because it rebuilt Europe.*

COLLABORATIVE LEARNING

The Tehran Conference

1. Have students use a map or globe to locate Tehran, Iran, which is mentioned at the beginning of this lesson.
3. Have students work with partners or in small groups to research the Tehran Conference. Students should identify when and where it took place, who was involved, and its purpose.
4. Have students present their findings to the class and then engage in a group discussion about the results of the Tehran Conference. Was it successful? Have students explain their thinking.

ADVANCED/GIFTED

Changing Demographics

1. Have students conduct outside research using both print and Internet sources to learn more about the ethnic groups that were singled out for destruction during World War II.
2. Have students write a summary about the ways in which these groups were singled out, why this occurred, and what happened as a result to both the ethnic groups and the countries in which they lived.
3. Have volunteers present their summaries to the class.

READING CHECK

Recognize Effects What demographic changes did Europe undergo as a result of World War II? *Millions of military personnel and civilians died. The destruction of certain ethnic groups caused a change in population balance in several countries. Many people migrated to new lands because their homes were destroyed or their countries' boundaries changed.*

ONLINE INTERACTIVE CHARTS

Superpower Aims in Europe

Have students explore the chart and answer the associated question.

Interpret Charts Which U.S. and Soviet goals were the same? *Rebuild*

In print edition, see chart of same title.

Contrast Which U.S. and Soviet aims in Europe conflicted? *Encourage democracy (U.S.), keep Germany divided (Soviet)*

READING CHECK

Summarize Why did the United States and the Soviet Union split after the war? *Their philosophies and aims were in conflict: the United States wanted to promote the economic recovery and growth of capitalist countries in Western Europe; the Soviet Union wanted to protect itself and spread communism.*

Creation of the United Nations and Geneva Conventions In June 1945, the United States and the Soviet Union temporarily set aside their differences. They joined 48 other countries in forming the **United Nations** (UN). This international organization was intended to protect the members against aggression. It was to be based in New York.

The new peacekeeping organization included a large General Assembly, in which each UN member nation could vote on a broad range of issues. An 11-member body called the Security Council had the real power to investigate and settle disputes, though. Its five permanent members were Britain, China, France, the United States, and the Soviet Union (now Russia). Each could veto any council action. This provision was intended to prevent any members of the council from voting as a bloc to override the others.

Many nations also joined together after the war in adopting a series of treaties on the treatment of civilians, prisoners of war (POWs), and those injured during wartime. Known as the Geneva Conventions, the treaties were adopted in 1949, added to in later years, and are still in force today.

Differing U.S. and Soviet Philosophy and Goals Despite agreement at Yalta and their presence on the UN Security Council, the United States and the Soviet Union split sharply after the war. The two "superpowers" were leaders both in military strength and in political and economic influence among the world's nations. The United States promoted the capitalist economic philosophy, while the Soviet Union promoted communism.

Reading Check
Summarize Why did the United States and the Soviet Union split after the war?

The war had affected the two superpowers very differently. The United States suffered 400,000 deaths, but its cities remained intact. The Soviet Union had at least 50 times as many fatalities. Also, many Soviet cities were demolished. These contrasting situations, as well as political and economic differences, affected the two countries' postwar goals and decisions.

Superpower Aims in Europe

United States	Soviet Union
Encourage democracy in other countries to help prevent the rise of Communist governments	Encourage communism in other countries as part of a worldwide workers' revolution
Gain access to raw materials and markets to fuel booming industries	Rebuild its war-ravaged economy using Eastern Europe's industrial equipment and raw materials
Rebuild European governments to promote stability and create new markets for U.S. goods	Control Eastern Europe to protect Soviet borders and balance the U.S. influence in Western Europe
Reunite Germany to stabilize it and increase the security of Europe	Keep Germany divided to prevent its waging war again

Analyze Charts
Contrast Which U.S. and Soviet aims in Europe conflicted?

STRUGGLING READERS

Map Analysis

1. Display a world map that shows the United States and the Soviet Union in 1949. Point out the boundaries and scale.
2. Have students brainstorm a list of questions regarding the relationship between the United States and the Soviet Union. For example: *What was the capital of the Soviet Union? How far is it from the U.S. capital? How far apart were the Soviet Union and the United States at their closest point?*
3. Divide the questions among students and have them find the answers using classroom resources. Have students share their answers in class discussion.

COLLABORATIVE LEARNING

Peacekeeping Institutions

1. Display a three-column chart with these headings for the second and third columns: League of Nations, United Nations. Students will use this graphic organizer to compare and contrast the two organizations.
2. Have students copy the chart and then compare the two organizations according to their purpose, when they were established, when they disbanded, their member nations, and their accomplishments. Add these labels to five different rows in the first column of the chart.

Eastern Europe's Iron Curtain

A major goal of the Soviet Union was to shield itself from another invasion from the west. Centuries of history had taught the Soviets to fear invasion. Because it lacked natural western borders, Russia fell victim to each of its neighbors in turn. In the 17th century, the Poles captured the Kremlin. During the next century, the Swedes attacked. Napoleon overran Moscow in 1812. The Germans invaded Russia during World Wars I and II.

Soviets Build a Buffer As World War II drew to a close, the Soviet troops pushed the Nazis back across Eastern Europe. At war's end, these troops occupied a strip of countries along the Soviet Union's own western border. Stalin regarded these countries as a necessary buffer, or wall of protection. He ignored the Yalta agreement and installed or secured Communist governments in Albania, Bulgaria, Hungary, Czechoslovakia, Romania, Poland, and Yugoslavia.

The Soviet leader's American partner at Yalta, Franklin D. Roosevelt, had died on April 12, 1945. To Roosevelt's successor, Harry S. Truman, Stalin's reluctance to allow free elections in Eastern European nations was a clear violation of those countries' rights. Truman, Stalin, and Churchill met at Potsdam, Germany, in July 1945. There, Truman pressed Stalin to permit free elections in Eastern Europe. The Soviet leader refused. In a speech in early 1946, Stalin declared that communism and capitalism could not exist in the same world.

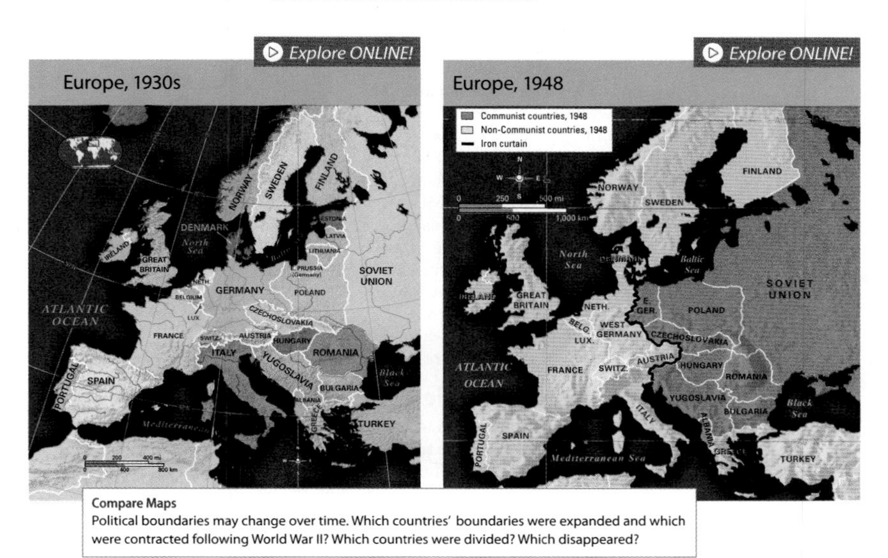

Compare Maps
Political boundaries may change over time. Which countries' boundaries were expanded and which were contracted following World War II? Which countries were divided? Which disappeared?

Objectives

You may wish to discuss the following questions with students to help them frame the content as they read.

- Why did Stalin refuse to allow free elections in Eastern Europe? *He wanted Eastern Europe under Communist control as a buffer against invasion.*
- How is *iron curtain* an apt term for the division between democratic and Communist Europe? *Iron is visually and physically impenetrable and cuts off contact between each side.*

More About . . .

Tip for Struggling Readers Winston Churchill's language may give some students difficulty. Explain that Stettin and Trieste are cities in Europe; the Baltic and Adriatic are seas. The *Soviet sphere* refers to the circle or area of influence. Help students paraphrase the quotation for greater understanding.

Close Read

"Iron Curtain" Speech Have students explore the Close Read feature to aid in comprehension and understanding.

ONLINE INTERACTIVE MAPS

Changing Political Boundaries

Have students explore the map using the interactive features and answer the associated questions.

Interpret Maps Which nation's boundaries expanded after World War II? *Soviet Union*

In print edition, see maps titled Europe, 1930s and Europe, 1948.

Compare Maps Political boundaries may change over time. Which countries' boundaries were expanded and which were contracted following World War II? Which countries were divided? Which disappeared? *Expanded: Soviet Union, Poland, Czechoslovakia; Contracted: Germany, Austria; Divided: Germany; Disappeared: Estonia, Latvia, Lithuania*

3. Then have students consider why the League failed and the UN has endured and been somewhat successful in promoting world peace.

COLLABORATIVE LEARNING

Political Cartoon

1. Call students' attention to the political cartoon in this lesson. Discuss the symbols with students: the iron wall represents the iron curtain; the hammer and sickle represents the Soviet Union or communism; the arm represents the people of Czechoslovakia; the torch represents liberty.
2. Discuss the meaning of the cartoon: The iron curtain has come down on the people of Czechoslovakia, squelching their attempt to achieve liberty. Explain that political cartoons typically use strong symbolism to communicate an opinion about events.
3. Have students work in two groups and assign each of the parts of this segment to a different group. Tell each group to read and discuss their section. Have them evaluate and discuss their ideas and thoughts about the events. Then, have them brainstorm ideas for expressing an opinion in a political cartoon about one or more of the events. Allow them to work individually or as a group to create a cartoon. Have students present and explain their cartoons to the class.

ONLINE DOCUMENT-BASED INVESTIGATION

Churchill's Iron Curtain Speech

Winston Churchill delivered this speech in 1946 to urge the United States and Great Britain to stand together against the Soviet Union. Students can click on the audio button beneath the historical source to hear the excerpt read aloud.

Analyze Sources What do the descriptive details in the first two sentences emphasize? *They emphasize the vast amount of territory that was under Soviet control.*

Objectives

You may wish to discuss the following questions with students to help them frame the content as they read.

- How were the Truman Doctrine and the Marshall Plan alike? *Both provided economic assistance to countries opposed to communism.*
- Why didn't Russia want the occupied zones of Germany to be reunited? *feared Germany would again become a military threat*

More About . . .

The Truman Doctrine When Stalin broke his promise to hold free elections in Europe, Truman saw a repetition of Hitler's broken promises to Britain and France before World War II. He was determined not to mimic the British and French indecision that led to such a disaster in the war. He therefore took a tough line with Stalin. "A totalitarian state is no different whether you call it Nazi, Fascist, Communist, or Franco's Spain," he wrote in a letter to his daughter. "I went to Potsdam [the final wartime conference of the Big Three in 1945] with the kindliest feeling toward Russia—in a year and a half they cured me of it."

The Berlin Airlift The Soviets believed the blockade would force the allies to give up Berlin. In fact, the allies were able to turn the tables on the Soviet Union. First, the airlift operated in two directions, both supplying the Berliners with needed goods and also keeping Berlin's economy alive by allowing industry to continue exporting goods. Second, the allies placed an embargo on exports from the Communist nations, bringing about economic hardships that helped force the Soviet Union to release its grip on Berlin.

An Iron Curtain Divides East and West Europe now lay divided between East and West. Germany had been split into two sections. The Soviets controlled the eastern part, including half of the capital, Berlin. Under a Communist government, East Germany was named the German Democratic Republic. The western zones were occupied by forces and supporting personnel from the United States, Britain, and France. The population in West Germany, devastated by the war, relied on the Allies for goods and services. The Allies soon became concerned about the costs of continuing to support their German sectors and slowly began withdrawing from the country. In 1949, the united West German sectors officially became the Federal Republic of Germany.

Winston Churchill described the division of Europe following the war by referring to Soviet efforts to take control of its neighbors as establishing an "**iron curtain**." Churchill's phrase came to represent Europe's division into mostly democratic Western Europe and Communist Eastern Europe.

> *"From Stettin in the Baltic to Trieste in the Adriatic, an iron curtain has descended across the continent. Behind that line lie all the capitals of the ancient states of Central and Eastern Europe. . . . All these famous cities and the populations around them lie in the Soviet sphere and all are subject in one form or another, not only to Soviet influence but to a very high and increasing measure of control from Moscow."*
>
> —Winston Churchill, "Iron Curtain" speech, March 5, 1946

Nine days after Churchill's speech, Stalin responded angrily in an interview with the Soviet press. He said, "Mr. Churchill now stands as a firebrand of war." The Soviet Union suffered much greater losses than either Great Britain or the United States, Stalin explained. "One can ask, therefore, what can be surprising in the fact that the Soviet Union, in a desire to ensure its security for the future, tries to achieve that these countries should have governments whose relations to the Soviet Union are loyal?"

The Iron Curtain is shown dropping on Czechoslovakia in this 1948 political cartoon.

Reading Check
Draw Conclusions What meanings do Churchill and Stalin hope to convey in using the phrases *iron curtain* and *firebrand of war*? Discuss this question with several classmates before writing your answer.

United States Tries to Contain Soviets

U.S.-Soviet relations continued to worsen in 1946 and 1947. An increasingly worried United States tried to offset the growing Soviet threat to Eastern Europe. President Truman adopted a foreign policy called **containment**. It was a policy directed at blocking Soviet influence and stopping the expansion of communism. Containment policies included forming alliances and helping weak countries resist Soviet advances.

READING CHECK
Draw Conclusions What meanings do Churchill and Stalin hope to convey in using the phrases *iron curtain* and *firebrand of war*? *Churchill wants to show that the Soviet Union is trapping other countries in a stronghold. Stalin wants to suggest that Churchill is trying to provoke another war.*

READING CHECK (Print)
Draw Conclusions What meanings do Churchill and Stalin hope to convey in using the phrases *iron curtain* and *firebrand of war*? Discuss this question with several classmates before writing your answer. *Churchill wants to show that the Soviet Union is trapping other countries in a stronghold. Stalin wants to suggest that Churchill is trying to provoke another war.*

ENGLISH LANGUAGE LEARNERS

Compare and Contrast Maps

1. Display political maps of Europe before and after World War I, after World War II, and as it is today.
2. Have students compare the maps and identify similarities and differences among them (e.g., boundaries, country names).
3. Have students make a list or graphic organizer for the similarities and differences they found.

ADVANCED/GIFTED

The Marshall Plan

1. Have students conduct outside research to learn more about the Marshall Plan, what it entailed, and its consequences in Europe and within the United States.
2. Have students write an economic and political analysis about the ways in which the Marshall Plan helped make the United States a superpower. Students should include charts and graphs with economic data to support the arguments in their analyses.
3. Have volunteers present their papers. Then discuss the importance and effectiveness of the Marshall Plan.

The Truman Doctrine In a speech asking Congress for foreign aid for Turkey and Greece, Truman contrasted democracy with communism:

> *"One way of life is based upon the will of the majority, and is distinguished by free institutions . . . free elections . . . and freedom from political oppression. The second way of life is based upon the will of a minority forcibly imposed upon the majority. It relies upon terror and oppression . . . fixed elections, and the suppression of personal freedoms. I believe it must be the policy of the United States to support free people . . . resisting attempted subjugation [control] by armed minorities or by outside pressures."*
>
> —President Harry S. Truman, speech to Congress, March 12, 1947

Truman's support for countries that rejected communism was called the **Truman Doctrine**. It caused great controversy. Some opponents objected to American interference in other nations' affairs. Others argued that the United States could not afford to carry on a global crusade against communism. Congress, however, immediately authorized more than $400 million in aid to Turkey and Greece. The Truman Doctrine established an ongoing U.S. commitment to offer assistance to protect other democratic countries when it was deemed to be in the best interest of the United States.

The Marshall Plan Much of Western Europe lay in ruins after the war. There was also economic turmoil—a scarcity of jobs and food. In 1947, U.S. Secretary of State George Marshall proposed that the United States give aid to needy European countries. This assistance program, called the **Marshall Plan**, would provide food, machinery, and other materials to rebuild Western Europe. As Congress debated the $12.5 billion program in 1948, the Communists seized power in Czechoslovakia. Congress immediately voted approval. The plan was a spectacular success. Even Communist Yugoslavia received aid after it broke away from Soviet domination.

The Berlin Airlift While Europe began rebuilding, the United States and its allies clashed with the Soviet Union over Germany. The Soviets wanted to keep their former enemy weak and divided. But in 1948, France, Britain, and the United States decided to withdraw their forces from Germany and allow their occupation zones to form one nation. The Soviet Union responded by holding West Berlin hostage.

Although Berlin lay well within the Soviet occupation zone of Germany, it too had been divided into four zones. The Soviet Union cut off highway, water, and rail traffic into Berlin's western zones. The city faced starvation. Stalin gambled that the Allies would surrender West Berlin or give up their idea of reunifying Germany. But American and British officials flew food and supplies into West Berlin for nearly 11 months. In May 1949, the Soviet Union admitted defeat and lifted the blockade.

Reading Check
Make Inferences
What was Truman's major reason for offering aid to other European countries?

ONLINE INTERACTIVE GRAPHS

Countries Aided by the Marshall Plan, 1948–1951

Have students explore the graph and answer the associated question.

Interpret Graphs What is the mean, or average, amount of Marshall Plan aid received by the countries that are identified in the chart (excluding the category "other")? *$713 million*

ONLINE INTERACTIVE MAPS

Divided Germany, 1948–1949

Have students explore the map using the interactive features and answer the associated question.

Interpret Maps Which nation occupied Munich before the formation of West Germany? *The United States*

READING CHECK

Make Inferences What was Truman's major reason for offering aid to other European countries? *to help European countries rebuild and become strong enough to resist Communist expansion*

STRUGGLING READERS

The Berlin Airlift

1. Remind students that allied planes made 278,000 flights over 11 months to keep West Berlin out of the hands of the Soviet Union.
2. Have pairs of students answer the following questions.
   - Why did the Soviet Union set up a blockade around West Berlin? *to force the Allies to either give up their parts of the city or give up the idea of allowing Germany to become one nation*
   - Why did the Allies fly food and supplies into Berlin? *They didn't want to give in to Stalin because they disliked and distrusted him. They were opposed to communism.*

Objectives

You may wish to discuss the following questions with students to help them frame the content as they read.

- How did the arms race help prevent war between the superpowers? *weapons were so devastating neither side was willing to risk war*
- How did a Soviet dominance in space pose a threat to the United States? *Space could be used against the United States for surveillance and military purposes; technology developed for space would give Soviets an advantage in all kinds of military technology.*

More About . . .

U-2 The U-2 was first flown in 1955 and became central to U.S. strategic surveillance during the 1960s. It flew at 494 miles per hour and cruised at about 70,000 feet. In addition to its use over the Soviet Union, it was used to observe the Soviet missile buildup in Cuba in 1962. The U-2 was in service only until the mid-1960s when it was replaced by a new, much faster surveillance plane, the SR-71 Blackbird.

Current Space Exploration The exploration of space goes forward with many projects. First among them is the International Space Station, which is the largest and most sophisticated space craft ever built. It has been continuously occupied since November 2, 2000. The MER mission of the United States landed two robot rovers to explore the surface of Mars in 2004. The Hubble Space Telescope continues to provide scientists with detailed views of deep space that were never possible from Earth. The United States has many other projects underway and planned. Some projects are in cooperation with other nations.

READING CHECK

Summarize What Soviet action led to the Berlin airlift? *the Soviet blockade of West Berlin*

History in Depth

The Berlin Airlift

From June 1948 to May 1949, Allied planes took off and landed every three minutes in West Berlin. On 278,000 flights, pilots brought in 2.3 million tons of food, fuel, medicine, and even Christmas gifts to West Berliners.

Explore ONLINE!

Divided Germany, 1948–1949

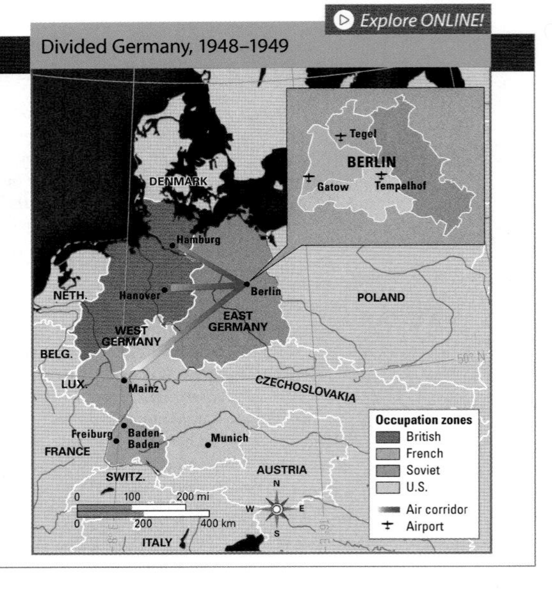

Reading Check
Summarize
What Soviet action led to the Berlin airlift?

Assistance to Asian Nations The Marshall Plan was designed to help European nations recover from the war. President Truman also initiated a similar program to provide technical assistance for non-European nations, such as those in Southeast Asia as well as Pakistan, Israel, and Iran, which had been impacted by the war. The Point Four program provided technical expertise to help build up agriculture, public health, and education within affected countries. It gave rise to other assistance programs administered by an agency of the UN but funded largely by the United States.

The Cold War Divides the World

These conflicts marked the start of the **Cold War** between the United States and the Soviet Union. A cold war is a struggle over political differences carried on by means short of military action or war. Beginning in 1949, the superpowers used spying, propaganda, diplomacy, and secret operations in their dealings with each other. Much of the world allied with one side or the other. In fact, until the Soviet Union finally broke up in 1991, the Cold War not only dictated U.S. and Soviet foreign policy but influenced world alliances as well.

Superpowers Form Rival Alliances The Berlin blockade heightened Western Europe's fears of Soviet aggression. As a result, in 1949, ten western European nations joined with the United States and Canada to form a defensive military alliance. It was called the North Atlantic Treaty

COLLABORATIVE LEARNING

Sputnik Research

1. Provide five or six questions about *Sputnik* and Soviet-American relations that are not covered in the text and a list of websites where the answers can be found. Use questions that encourage students to examine the broad issues while they hone in on the details. Here are some sample questions:
   - What was the reaction of U.S. rocket scientists to news of *Sputnik*'s weight?
   - How did Soviet leaders relate the launching of *Sputnik* to socialism?
   - What role did the launch of *Sputnik* play in the 1959 "kitchen debate" between Vice President Richard M. Nixon and Soviet Premier Nikita S. Khrushchev?
   - How did the United States react to the launch of *Sputnik*?
2. Have students navigate websites to find the answers.

Countries Aided by the Marshall Plan, 1948–1951

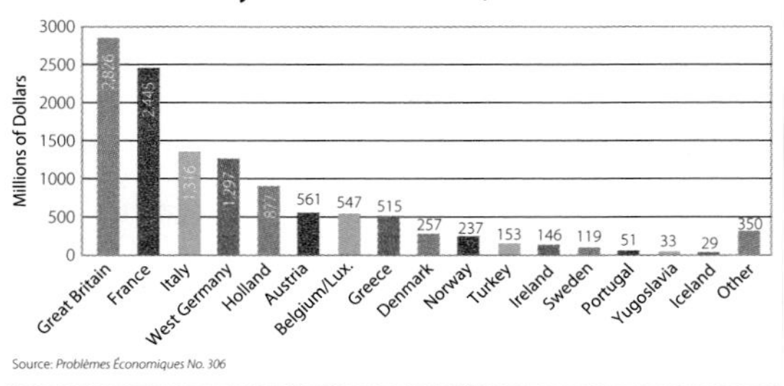

Interpret Charts

1. **Draw Conclusions** Which country received the most aid from the United States?
2. **Make Inferences** Why do you think Great Britain and France received so much aid?

Organization (**NATO**). An attack on any NATO member would be met with armed force by all member nations.

The Soviet Union saw NATO as a threat and formed its own alliance in 1955. It was called the **Warsaw Pact** and included the Soviet Union, East Germany, Czechoslovakia, Poland, Hungary, Romania, Bulgaria, and Albania. In 1961, the East Germans built a wall to separate East and West Berlin. The Berlin Wall symbolized a world divided into rival camps. However, not every country joined the new alliances. Some, like India, chose not to align with either side. And China, the largest Communist country, came to distrust the Soviet Union. It remained nonaligned.

In the Western Hemisphere, the United States pushed for the formation of an organization of countries in North, Central, and South America and the Caribbean. Formed in 1948, the Organization of American States (OAS) hoped to bring peace and security to its member nations and to increase economic and social cooperation.

The Threat of Nuclear War As these alliances were forming, the Cold War threatened to heat up enough to destroy the world. The United States already had atomic bombs, thanks to the work of scientists in America such as Italian-born Enrico Fermi, who directed early experiments in splitting atoms in the early 1940s. Fermi was one of the architects of the nuclear age. In 1949, the Soviet Union exploded its own atomic weapon. President Truman was determined to develop a more deadly weapon before the Soviets did. He authorized work on a thermonuclear weapon in 1950.

The hydrogen or H-bomb would be much more powerful than the A-bomb. Its power came from the fusion, or joining together, of atoms rather than the splitting of atoms, as in the A-bomb. Edward Teller, a Hungarian-born American nuclear physicist, was a leading proponent of the H-bomb and played an important role in its design. The team that

GRAPHS

Countries Aided by the Marshall Plan, 1948–1951

Have students interpret the chart and answer the associated questions.

Draw Conclusions Which country received the most aid from the United States? *Great Britain*

Make Inferences Why do you think Great Britain and France received so much aid? *They were the principal U.S. allies during World War II.*

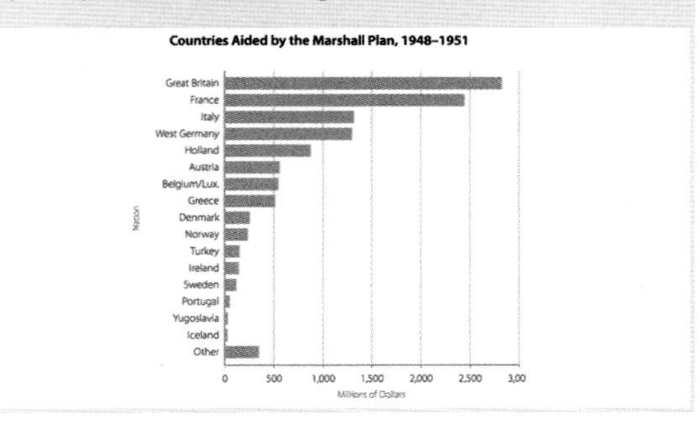

ADVANCED/GIFTED

Literature of the Cold War

1. Explain to students that the Cold War affected not only politics but also literature. Fiction took on new dimensions as writers reflected on the realities of life during the Cold War and the possibilities that the war opened up. Spy novels such as John le Carre's *The Spy Who Came in from the Cold*, for example, include agents with double agendas and sophisticated technology. Science fiction works such as Ray Bradbury's *The Martian Chronicles* and Jack Finney's *The Body Snatchers* explore what the world might be like if Cold War trends in nuclear weapons and pervasive fear continued. Tim O'Brien's *The Nuclear Age* provides a realistic view of what it was like living during the Cold War.
2. Have students read one of these books and write a report that analyzes how realistic it seems in today's world.

ONLINE INTERACTIVE TIMELINES

The Space Race

Have students explore the timeline using the interactive features and answer the associated questions.

Interpret Timelines According to the timeline, which destination did both the United States and the Soviet Union explore? *Mars*

In print edition, see timeline of same title.

Compare Which destinations in space did both the United States and the Soviet Union explore? *Mars*

Make Inferences What role might space continue to play in achieving world peace? *Joint space explorations may build trust and cooperation among participating nations. The sharing of science and technology may prevent one nation from gaining an advantage over other nations that might lead to new weapons used to control others.*

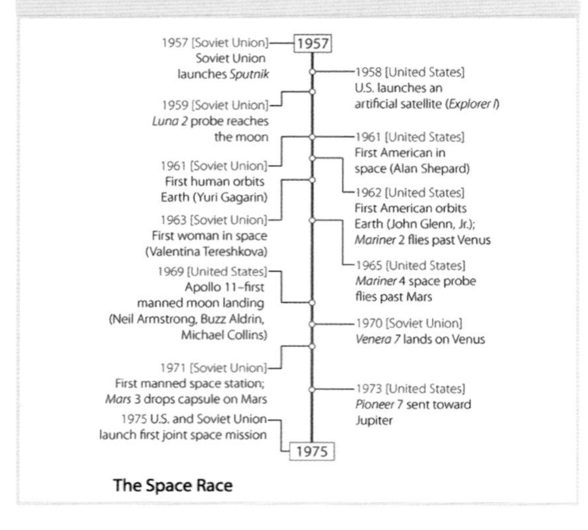

The Space Race

SCIENCE AND TECHNOLOGY

The Space Race

Beginning in the late 1950s, the United States and the Soviet Union competed for influence not only among the nations of the world, but in the skies as well. Once the superpowers had ICBMs (intercontinental ballistic missiles) to deliver nuclear warheads and aircraft for spying missions, they both began to develop technology that could be used to explore—and ultimately control—space. However, after nearly two decades of costly competition, the two superpowers began to cooperate in space exploration.

In a major technological triumph, the United States put human beings on the moon on July 20, 1969. Astronaut Buzz Aldrin is shown on the lunar surface with the lunar lander spacecraft.

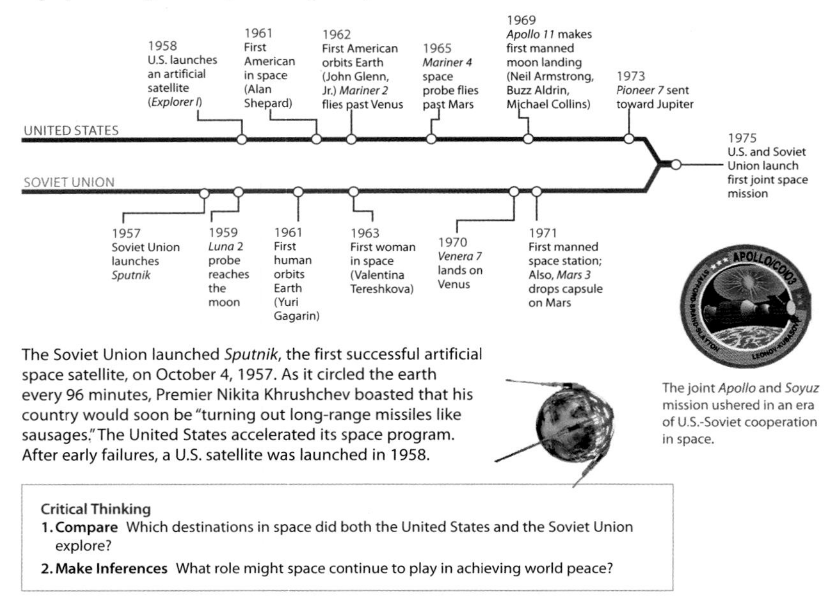

The Soviet Union launched *Sputnik*, the first successful artificial space satellite, on October 4, 1957. As it circled the earth every 96 minutes, Premier Nikita Khrushchev boasted that his country would soon be "turning out long-range missiles like sausages." The United States accelerated its space program. After early failures, a U.S. satellite was launched in 1958.

The joint *Apollo* and *Soyuz* mission ushered in an era of U.S.-Soviet cooperation in space.

Critical Thinking

1. **Compare** Which destinations in space did both the United States and the Soviet Union explore?
2. **Make Inferences** What role might space continue to play in achieving world peace?

developed the new weapon was based in Los Alamos, New Mexico. In 1952, the United States tested the first H-bomb on a group of coral islands in the Pacific. It yielded an explosion equivalent to 10 million tons (10 megatons) of TNT, more than 600 times more powerful than the atomic bomb dropped on Hiroshima, Japan. The Soviets were also hard at work on their own H-bomb and exploded one in 1953.

ONLINE INTERACTIVE VISUALS

Milestones in Space Exploration

Have students navigate through the carousel and note similarities and differences among the images or identify a unifying theme.

Dwight D. Eisenhower became the U.S. president in 1953. He appointed the firmly anti-Communist John Foster Dulles as his secretary of state. If the Soviet Union or its supporters attacked U.S. interests, Dulles threatened, the United States would "retaliate instantly, by means and at places of our own choosing." This willingness to go to the brink, or edge, of war became known as **brinkmanship**. Brinkmanship required a reliable source of nuclear weapons and airplanes to deliver them. So, the United States strengthened its air force and began producing stockpiles of nuclear weapons. The Soviet Union responded with its own military buildup, beginning an arms race that would go on for four decades.

The Cold War in the Skies The Cold War also affected the science and education programs of the two countries. In August 1957, the Soviets announced the development of a rocket that could travel great distances—an intercontinental ballistic missile, or ICBM. On October 4, the Soviets used an ICBM to push *Sputnik*, the first unmanned satellite, above the earth's atmosphere. Americans felt they had fallen behind in science and technology, and the government poured money into science education. In 1958, the United States launched its own satellite. A German-born rocket scientist named Wehrner von Braun was the driving force behind the U.S. ballistic missile program. He would play a major role in the American space program for more than 30 years.

In 1960, the skies again provided the arena for a superpower conflict. Five years earlier, Eisenhower had proposed that the United States and the Soviet Union be able to fly over each other's territory to guard against surprise nuclear attacks. The Soviet Union said no. In response, the U.S. Central Intelligence Agency (CIA) started secret high-altitude spy flights over Soviet territory in planes called U-2s. In May 1960, the Soviets shot down a U-2 plane, and its pilot, Francis Gary Powers, was captured. This U-2 incident heightened Cold War tensions.

While Soviet Communists were squaring off against the United States, Communists in China were fighting a civil war for control of that country.

Reading Check
Analyze Effects How did the U.S. policy of brinkmanship contribute to the arms race?

Lesson 1 Assessment

1. Organize Information Which action or event of the Cold War was the most significant? Explain.

1945 — 1960
Yalta conference — U-2 incident

2. Key Terms and People For each key term or person in the lesson, write a sentence explaining its significance.
3. Analyze Causes How was formation of the United Nations a response to World War II?
4. Evaluate Do you consider the Marshall Plan and Berlin Airlift to have been successful? Explain.
5. Compare and Contrast What factors help to explain why the United States and the Soviet Union became rivals instead of allies?
6. Analyze Motives What were Stalin's objectives in supporting Communist governments in Eastern Europe?
7. Analyze Issues Why might Berlin have been a likely spot for trouble to develop during the Cold War?

READING CHECK

Analyze Effects How did the U.S. policy of brinkmanship contribute to the arms race? *The United States and the Soviet Union began a contest to see who could amass the greater number of nuclear weapons more quickly.*

Print Assessment

1. **Organize Information** Which effect of the Cold War was the most significant? Explain. *Students may say the Marshall Plan was most significant because it rebuilt Europe.*
2. **Key Terms and People** For each key term or person in the lesson, write a sentence explaining its significance. *Explanation of the lesson's key terms can be found on the following pages: United Nations, p. 1122; iron curtain, p. 1124; containment, p. 1124; Truman Doctrine, p. 1125; Marshall Plan, p. 1125; Cold War, p. 1126; NATO, p. 1127; Warsaw Pact, p. 1127; brinkmanship, p. 1129.*
3. **Analyze Causes** How was formation of the United Nations a response to World War II? *The United Nations was formed to protect members against aggression, which was a direct result of World War II.*
4. **Evaluate** Do you consider the Marshall Plan and Berlin Airlift to have been successful? Explain. *Possible answer: Both were successful since the Marshall Plan helped stop the spread of communism and the Berlin Airlift caused the Soviet Union to lift its blockade of Berlin.*
5. **Compare and Contrast** What factors help to explain why the United States and the Soviet Union became rivals instead of allies? *competition for leadership; different goals; conflicting political and economic ideologies*
6. **Analyze Motives** What were Stalin's objectives in supporting Communist governments in Eastern Europe? *to protect borders; to counteract U.S. influence; to have access to raw materials; to keep Germany from rebuilding and threatening the Soviet Union*
7. **Analyze Issues** Why might Berlin have been a likely spot for trouble to develop during the Cold War? *The West wanted to keep Berlin free even though it was inside Communist East Germany.*

Online Assessment

1. How was World War II different from any other war to that point in history?
   - ○ It included tank battles.
   - ● It decimated farmlands.
   - ○ It was the most destructive.
   - ○ It caused hunger and disease.

   Alternate Question *Select the answer choice from the drop-down list to complete the sentence correctly.*
   World War II was different from any other war in history to that point because of the *massive loss of life and destruction of property*.

2. What is one way in which Stalin broke a promise that was made at the Yalta Conference?
   - ○ He wouldn't allow Germany to rebuild its urban areas.
   - ○ He wouldn't allow Germany to be divided into zones of occupation.
   - ● He wouldn't allow Eastern European countries to have free elections.
   - ○ He wouldn't allow Eastern European countries to house Allied forces.

   Alternate Question *Select the answer choice from the drop-down list to complete the sentence correctly.* At the Yalta Conference, Stalin promised to let the *Eastern Europeans have free elections*, but he never fulfilled that promise.

3. What did Churchill's phrase *iron curtain* come to mean?
   - ○ Europe was forever changed by the Nazi regime.
   - ○ Europe would still have Allied and Axis powers after the war.
   - ○ Europe would need a continued military presence for decades.
   - ● Europe was divided between democratic and Communist countries.

   Alternate Question *Select the answer choice from the drop-down list to complete the sentence correctly.* Churchill's phrase *iron curtain* came to represent the division between *democratic and Communist countries*.

4. How were the Marshall Plan and Berlin Airlift similar to each other?
   - ○ They both intended to stop communism.
   - ● They both provided aid to people in need.
   - ○ They both were crucial in ending the Cold War.
   - ○ They both gave inspiration for the Warsaw Pact.

   Alternate Question *Select the answer choice from the drop-down list to complete the sentence correctly.* The *Marshall Plan* and the Berlin Airlift were similar to each other because they both provided aid for people in need.

5. What was the Soviet Union's response to the formation of NATO?
   - ○ It launched *Sputnik*.
   - ○ It engaged in brinkmanship.
   - ● It organized the Warsaw Pact.
   - ○ It developed an intercontinental ballistic missile.

   Alternate Question *Select the answer choice from the drop-down list to complete the sentence correctly.* In 1949, the western European nations and the United States and Canada formed the North Atlantic Treaty Organization (NATO). In response, the Soviet Union *set up the Warsaw Pact*.

6. **Elaborate** What caused World War II to have so many more civilian deaths than military deaths?

   Possible answer: There were many reasons that more civilians than military were killed in World War II. Many civilians died in connection with battles, bombings, and enemy occupations. Yet, the bulk of the civilians died when groups such as Jews and Roma were singled out for destruction. Hunger and disease also took a major toll on populations across the world.

7. **Cause and Effect** What caused the United States and the Soviet Union to have differing postwar goals?

   Possible answer: The United States and the Soviet Union had different postwar goals for various reasons. For one, they operated by different economic philosophies. The United States had a capitalist economy while the Soviet Union had a Communist system. Also, the Soviet Union had suffered tremendous loss in human life and property as a result of the war in comparison with the United States. The United States lost 400,000 soldiers, but its cities and factories remained intact. In contrast, the Soviet Union had 50 times more casualties, and many of its cities and factories were destroyed. Because of these differences, the two countries responded differently after the war.

8. **Elaborate** Why did the Soviet Union feel the need to shield itself from a western invasion, and what did it do to shield itself?

   Possible answer: For centuries, Russia had been invaded by other countries such as Poland in the 17th century, the Swedes in the 18th century, France in the 19th century, and Germany in the 20th century. This was due to the fact that Russia lacked a natural western border—meaning there wasn't any significant geographic barrier that separated Russia from countries in the west. The Soviets felt a need to create a shield for their country because of all of this. The shield they chose was Eastern Europe. If the Eastern European countries all had Communist governments, they would be loyal to the Soviets and wouldn't invade Russia.

9. **Cause and Effect** Why did the Soviets block off access to West Berlin, and what was the result of this action?

   Possible answer: The Soviets wanted to convince the West that Germany couldn't be reunified and to just give up on holding on to West Berlin. The Soviets wanted to control the entire capital city. When the Soviets blocked off access to West Berlin, the West began the Berlin Airlift. This is when the West started sending food and supplies to West Berlin via aircraft. They continued this for 11 months and finally the Soviets had to lift the blockade when they realized their plan wasn't going to work.

10. **Draw Conclusions** What role did brinkmanship play in the Cold War?

    Possible answer: Brinkmanship required a reliable source of nuclear weapons and airplanes to deliver them. This idea caused both the United States and the Soviet Union to increase their military strength. Both built up their air forces and nuclear stockpiles in what would be known as the arms race. The arms race would continue for four decades.

ADDITIONAL LESSON CONTENT

COLLABORATIVE LEARNING

World Conflict Presentation

1. Remind students that World War II was a long, devastating conflict that involved almost every country in the world. Point out that new conflicts over government, land, and control of people continue to emerge between and among countries.
2. Organize students into two or three large groups. Have them imagine they are responsible for security and peace around the world. They should consider the following questions: *How would you reduce the conflict and solve the disputes between nations? What steps would you take to prevent another war?*
3. Have groups work together to discuss the issues and reach a consensus. Then have students from each group present their ideas to the class.

Lesson 2 Planner

Communists Take Power in China

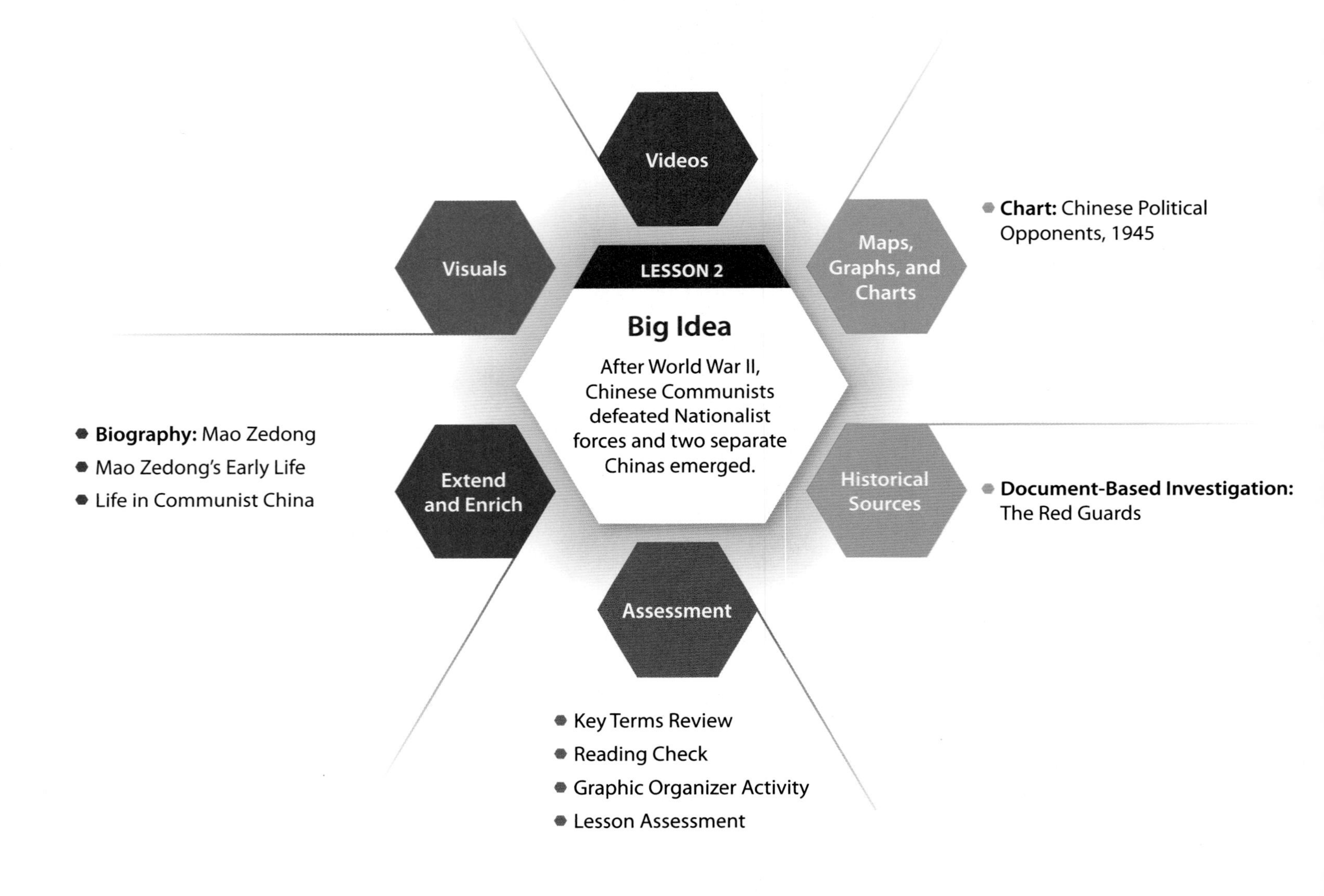

- **Chart:** Chinese Political Opponents, 1945

- **Biography:** Mao Zedong
- Mao Zedong's Early Life
- Life in Communist China

- **Document-Based Investigation:** The Red Guards

- Key Terms Review
- Reading Check
- Graphic Organizer Activity
- Lesson Assessment

Online Lesson 2 Enrichment Activities

Mao Zedong's Early Life

Biography Students read about Mao Zedong's background and early life as a soldier and student. Then they write an opinion paper about whether they think Mao's views would have been different if he grew up in a wealthy family.

Life in Communist China

Journal Entry Students imagine they are teenagers in China during the Cold War. They need to decide whether or not they will join the Red Guards. In a journal entry, they should describe the events happening around them and make a decision about whether they should join the Red Guards. The journal entries should be written in an informal, but passionate, tone.

Teach the Big Idea

1. **Whole Class Open/Introduction** Have students list the qualities that can make someone a great leader. Then explain that when China underwent a civil war, each side was led by a charismatic leader. Tell students to evaluate these leaders as they read and decide which shares more of the qualities they've listed.
2. **Direct Teach Read** Read the Big Idea: *After World War II, Chinese Communists defeated Nationalist forces and two separate Chinas emerged.* Review the following lesson objectives with students to aid in their understanding of the Big Idea.
   - Analyze the civil war between the Nationalists and the Communists.
   - Explain how China split into two nations.
   - Describe how Mao's Marxist regime transformed China.
3. **Whole Group Close/Reflect** Have students write a diary entry of someone their age living during the civil war in China. What would his or her life be like? Invite students to share their work.

ONLINE DOCUMENT-BASED INVESTIGATION

Cold War Conflicts

The Red Guards is the second of five document-based investigations that students will analyze in the Cold War Conflicts module. The Red Guards were students who pledged their devotion to Chairman Mao and the Cultural Revolution. Students can study the image and read the accompanying text.

Lesson 2

Communists Take Power in China

The Big Idea
After World War II, Chinese Communists defeated Nationalist forces, and two separate Chinas emerged.

Why It Matters Now
China remains a Communist country and a major power in the world.

Key Terms and People
Mao Zedong
Jiang Jieshi
commune
Red Guards
Cultural Revolution

Setting the Stage

In World War II, China fought on the side of the victorious Allies. But the victory proved to be a hollow one for China. During the war, Japan's armies had occupied and devastated most of China's cities. China's civilian death toll alone was estimated to be between 10 and 22 million persons. This vast country suffered casualties second only to those of the Soviet Union. However, conflict did not end with the defeat of the Japanese. In 1945, opposing Chinese armies faced one another.

Communists vs. Nationalists

A bitter civil war was raging between the Nationalists and the Communists when the Japanese invaded China in 1937. During World War II, the political opponents temporarily united to fight the Japanese. But they continued to jockey for position within China.

World War II in China Under their leader, **Mao Zedong** (mow-dzuh•dahng), the Communists had a stronghold in northwestern China. From there, they mobilized peasants for guerrilla war against the Japanese in the northeast. Thanks to their efforts to promote literacy and improve food production, the Communists won the peasants' loyalty. By 1945, they controlled much of northern China.

Meanwhile, the Nationalist forces under **Jiang Jieshi** (jee•ahng-jee•shee) dominated southwestern China. Protected from the Japanese by rugged mountain ranges, Jiang gathered an army of 2.5 million men. From 1942 to 1945, the United States sent the Nationalists at least $1.5 billion in aid to fight the Japanese. Instead of benefiting the army, however, these supplies and money often ended up in the hands of a few corrupt officers. Jiang's army actually fought few battles against the Japanese. Instead, the Nationalist army saved its strength for the coming battle against Mao's Red Army. After Japan surrendered, the Nationalists and Communists resumed fighting.

ONLINE GRAPHIC ORGANIZER

Communists Take Power in China

As students read the lesson, have them use the graphic organizer to take notes. Students can review their graphic organizer notes at the end of the lesson to answer the following question.

Draw Conclusions Which effect of the Communist Revolution in China do you think had the most permanent impact? Explain. *the transformation of industry and business, which remade the economy*

Communist Revolution in China		
Causes	→	Effects
Causes	→	Effects
Causes	→	Effects

COLLABORATIVE LEARNING

Main Idea Ladder

1. Organize the class into three groups. Assign each group one of the topics in this lesson: Communists vs. Nationalists, The Two Chinas Affect the Cold War, The Communists Transform China.
2. Draw three ladders for students to see. Label the tops of the ladders with the names of the topics in this lesson. Have students draw a ladder on their own paper and label it with their assigned topic.
3. Group members should work together to fill in the rungs of the ladder with the main ideas of their topic.
4. Have each group present and explain its ladder to the class.

COLLABORATIVE LEARNING

Geography

1. Have students examine a map and contrast the topography, cities, and resources of northern and southern China.
2. Have them decide which area seems to be better developed and more economically important.
3. Ask students to discuss how Mao triumphed over Jiang despite his weaker geographic position.

Civil War Resumes The renewed civil war lasted from 1946 to 1949. At first, the Nationalists had the advantage. Their army outnumbered the Communists' army by as much as three to one. And the United States continued its support by providing nearly $2 billion in military aid. The Nationalist forces, however, did little to win popular support. With China's economy collapsing, thousands of Nationalist soldiers deserted to join the Communists. In spring 1949, China's major cities fell to the well-trained Red forces. Mao's troops were also enthusiastic about his promise to return land to the peasants. The remnants of Jiang's shattered army fled south. In October 1949, Mao Zedong gained control of the country. He proclaimed it the People's Republic of China. Jiang and other Nationalist leaders retreated to the island of Taiwan, which Westerners called Formosa.

Mao Zedong's victory fueled U.S. anti-Communist feelings. Those feelings grew stronger after the Chinese and Soviets signed a treaty of friendship in 1950. Many people in the United States viewed the takeover of China as another step in a Communist campaign to conquer the world.

The Chinese Revolution had several things in common with earlier and later social revolutions. For example, like the French Revolution that began in 1789, the Russian Revolution of 1917, and the Cuban Revolution that began in 1959, a central purpose of the Chinese Revolution was to break down the existing class structure and provide more economic and political opportunity for those other than the ruling class, including land ownership. In all of the revolutions, peasants played a key role.

Reading Check
Recognize Effects
How did the outcome of the Chinese civil war contribute to Cold War tensions?

Chinese Political Opponents, 1945

Nationalists		Communists
Jiang Jieshi	**Leader**	Mao Zedong
Southern China	**Area Ruled**	Northern China
United States	**Foreign Support**	Soviet Union
Defeat of Communists	**Domestic Policy**	National liberation
Weak due to inflation and failing economy	**Public Support**	Strong due to promised land reform for peasants
Ineffective, corrupt leadership and poor morale	**Military Organization**	Experienced, motivated guerrilla army

Interpret Charts
1. **Draw Conclusions** Which party's domestic policy might appeal more to Chinese peasants? Why?
2. **Form and Support Opinions** Which aspect of the Communist approach do you think was most responsible for Mao's victory? Explain.

STRUGGLING READERS

Understanding Charts

1. Explain that charts provide a visual presentation of information that clarifies the relationships among ideas. In a chart, information is grouped into categories.
2. Point out that reading down the columns and across the rows offers a quick summary of a category. It also makes the comparison between entries clear.
3. Display the chart in this segment, and ask students:
   - Based on the chart, which characteristics did the Nationalists and Communists share? *none*
   - Which category indicates that the conflict in China was part of the Cold War? *foreign support*
   - Which category indicates that the Nationalists and the Communists were directly opposed? *domestic policy*

Objectives

You may wish to discuss the following questions with students to help them frame the content as they read.

- How did Mao's use of money compare to Jiang's? *Mao spent money on the peasants; Jiang allowed money to be taken by corrupt officers.*
- What might have been the strongest reason for Jiang's defeat? *Possible answer: He failed to gain popular support.*

More About . . .

Tip for English Language Learners When students examine the chart in this segment, make sure they understand that the middle column identifies the topic of each row. Point out that the last three rows help explain why the Nationalists lost to the Communists.

ONLINE INTERACTIVE CHARTS

Chinese Political Opponents, 1945

Have students explore the chart and answer the associated questions.

Interpret Charts Who supported the Nationalists? *The United States*

In print edition, see chart of same title.

Draw Conclusions Which party's domestic policy might appeal more to Chinese peasants? Why? *Communists; They promised land reform.*

Form and Support Opinions Which aspect of the Communist approach do you think was most responsible for Mao's victory? Explain. *Possible answer: military organization that enabled them to win key battles and appeals to public support that won the peasants over to their side*

ONLINE LESSON FLIP CARDS

Review Key Terms and People

Students can use the flip cards in the Lesson Review at any time to review the lesson's key terms and people: *Mao Zedong, Jiang Jieshi, commune, Red Guards,* and *Cultural Revolution.*

READING CHECK
Recognize Effects How did the outcome of the Chinese civil war contribute to Cold War tensions? *The victory of the Chinese Communists reinforced U.S. belief that the Communist leaders planned to take over the world.*

Objectives

You may wish to discuss the following question with students to help them frame the content as they read.

- How did Chinese promises to the Tibetan people resemble the Soviet Union's promises to the countries of Eastern Europe? *Both promised autonomy but later took control away.*

More About . . .

Mao Zedong In 1972, when President Nixon told Mao Zedong that his teachings had transformed China and affected the whole world, Mao replied, "All I have done is change Beijing and a few of its suburbs." Considering the size of China's population (a quarter of the world's total), however, Mao may have been the most influential leader of the 20th century.

Dalai Lama From his exile in India, the Dalai Lama has been an advocate for nonviolent opposition to China's occupation of Tibet. In 1989, he was awarded the Nobel Peace Prize. The Nobel Committee emphasized that his philosophy of peace was based on a reverence for all living things and that he showed willingness to compromise and seek reconciliation.

BIOGRAPHY

Mao Zedong

Have students read the biography of Mao Zedong, the leader of the Chinese Communists who led a successful revolution and established a Communist government in China in 1949.

READING CHECK

Draw Conclusions How did the Cold War contribute to Jiang's survival? *It ensured aid and protection from the United States, which wanted to maintain some influence in China.*

The Two Chinas Affect the Cold War

China had split into two nations. One was the island of Taiwan, or Nationalist China, with an area of 13,000 square miles. The mainland, or People's Republic of China, had an area of more than 3.5 million square miles. The existence of two Chinas, and the conflicting international loyalties they inspired, intensified the Cold War.

The Superpowers React After Jiang Jieshi fled to Taiwan, the United States helped him set up a Nationalist government on that small island. It was called the Republic of China. The Soviets gave financial, military, and technical aid to Communist China. In addition, the Chinese and the Soviets pledged to come to each other's defense if either was attacked. The United States tried to halt Soviet expansion in Asia. For example, when Soviet forces occupied the northern half of Korea after World War II and set up a Communist government there, the United States supported a separate state in the south.

China Expands Under the Communists In the early years of Mao's reign, Chinese troops expanded into Tibet, India, and southern, or Inner, Mongolia. Northern, or Outer, Mongolia, which bordered the Soviet Union, remained in the Soviet sphere.

In a brutal assault in 1950 and 1951, China took control of Tibet. The Chinese promised autonomy to Tibetans, who followed their religious leader, the Dalai Lama. When China's control over Tibet tightened in the late 1950s, the Dalai Lama fled to India. India welcomed many Tibetan refugees after a failed revolt in Tibet in 1959. As a result, resentment between India and China grew. In 1962, they clashed briefly over the two countries' unclear border. The fighting stopped but resentment continued.

BIOGRAPHY

Mao Zedong
(1893–1976)

Born into a peasant family, Mao embraced Marxist socialism as a young man. Though he began as an urban labor organizer, Mao quickly realized the revolutionary potential of China's peasants. In 1927, Mao predicted:

The force of the peasantry is like that of the raging winds and driving rain. . . . They will bury beneath them all forces of imperialism, militarism, corrupt officialdom, village bosses and evil gentry.

Mao's first attempt to lead the peasants in revolt failed in 1927. But during the Japanese occupation, Mao and his followers won widespread peasant support by reducing rents and promising to redistribute land.

STRUGGLING READERS

Understanding Communist China

1. Tell students to choose a date during the 1930s through 1960s. Then have them imagine that they are living at this time. Remind them that important events were occurring in China throughout this period, including the Chinese civil war between the Communists and the Nationalists, the invasion of Tibet, the establishment of the communes, the Cold War, and the Cultural Revolution.
2. Explain to students that they have a friend who lives in China. Ask them to write a letter to their friend in which they ask questions about life and events in China at that time. They should limit their questions to information that can be found or inferred from details in the text. You may wish to review the format of a friendly letter with students before they begin to write.
3. When students have finished writing, have them exchange letters and write a response. When they've finished these letters, tell them to meet with their partner to review their letters and check the accuracy of their answers.

ADVANCED/GIFTED

Research

1. Have students consider whether Taiwan should be admitted to the United Nations as a separate nation. What are the reasons both for and against admission?

The Communists Transform China

For decades, China had been in turmoil, engaged in civil war or fighting with Japan. So, when the Communists took power, they moved rapidly to strengthen their rule over China's 550 million people. They also aimed to restore China as a powerful nation.

Communists Consolidate Power After taking control of China, the Communists began to tighten their hold. The party's 4.5 million members made up just 1 percent of the population. But they were a disciplined group. Like the Soviets, the Chinese Communists set up two parallel organizations, the Communist Party and the national government. Mao headed both until 1959.

Mao's Brand of Marxist Socialism Mao was determined to reshape China's economy based on Marxist socialism. Eighty percent of the people lived in rural areas, but most owned no land. Instead, 10 percent of the rural population controlled 70 percent of the farmland. Under the Agrarian Reform Law of 1950, Mao seized the holdings of these landlords. His forces killed more than a million landlords who resisted. He then divided the land among the peasants. Later, to further Mao's socialist principles, the government forced peasants to join collective farms. Each of these farms was comprised of 200 to 300 households.

Mao's changes also transformed industry and business. Gradually, private companies were nationalized, or brought under government ownership. In 1953, Mao launched a five-year plan that set high production goals for industry. By 1957, China's output of coal, cement, steel, and electricity had increased dramatically.

"The Great Leap Forward" To expand the success of the first Five-Year Plan, Mao proclaimed the "Great Leap Forward" in early 1958. This plan called for still larger collective farms, or **communes**. By the end of 1958, about 26,000 communes had been created. The average commune sprawled over 15,000 acres and supported more than 25,000 people. In the strictly controlled life of the communes, peasants worked the land together. They ate in communal dining rooms, slept in communal dormitories, and raised children in communal nurseries. And they owned nothing. The peasants had no incentive to work hard when only the state profited from their labor.

The Great Leap Forward was a giant step backward. Poor planning and inefficient "backyard," or home, industries hampered growth. The program was ended in 1961 after crop failures caused a famine that killed about 20 million people.

Soviet Competition and Global Politics China was facing external problems as well as internal ones in the late 1950s. The spirit of cooperation that had bound the Soviet Union and China together began to fade. The two countries clashed several times in territorial disputes along their

Objectives

You may wish to discuss the following questions with students to help them frame the content as they read.

- What was the significance of Mao's role as head of both the Communist party and the national government? *nation was united behind single leader, had clear goals and political philosophy*
- How did nationalizing industry further the Communist goal of social equality? *eliminated private ownership and with it the wealth of some compared to moderate or low income of others*
- Why were intellectuals targeted in the Cultural Revolution? *They were the elite, not consistent with social equality.*

More About . . .

Mandate of Heaven The Mandate of Heaven is an ancient Chinese belief that dates back thousands of years. It states that emperors' right to rule is granted by heaven and is based on their ability to govern well and fairly. They do not need to be of noble birth. The Communists claimed this idea to support their right to rule China.

The Red Guards The Cultural Revolution gave rise to a new class system in China from which the Red Guard arose. At the new bottom was the "Black Five" class. It was made up of people unacceptable to the revolutionaries—landlords, rich peasants, and others labeled "counter-revolutionaries" or "Bad People." The "Red Five" class included the heroes of the revolution—poor peasants, workers, and revolutionary soldiers. Only youth in the Red Five class were allowed to join Mao's Red Guards.

2. Have students explain how reading about the Chinese civil war and the retreat of the Nationalists to Taiwan affects their thoughts on this topic.
3. Encourage students to conduct research online about the relationship between Taiwan and mainland China today. How has the situation changed since the civil war?

ENGLISH LANGUAGE LEARNERS

Break Down Words

1. Encourage students to make a list of unfamiliar words as they read. Whenever possible, point out word parts (roots, affixes) that might help students determine meaning.
2. To demonstrate, point out the words *symbolizes, nationalized,* and *intellectual* in this segment. Write the words on the board. Underline the base word in each (*symbol, nation, intellect*). Challenge students to define these words, using a dictionary if necessary.
3. Then circle the word ending in each and explain how it changes the meaning of the word. Finally, help students name other more familiar words that share either the base word or word ending in common. How are their meanings similar or different?
4. Remind students to try to break down new words in this manner when they read them.

ONLINE DOCUMENT-BASED INVESTIGATION

The Red Guards

The Red Guards were students who pledged their devotion to Chairman Mao and the Cultural Revolution. Have students study the image and answer the associated question.

Analyze Sources How did the dress of the Red Guards help to promote its goals? *Everyone is dressed the same, in simple garb, which shows not only that the Red Guards were unified but also that they were working-class people who didn't wear fancy clothes.*

DOCUMENT-BASED INVESTIGATION HISTORICAL SOURCE

The Red Guards

The Red Guards were students, mainly teenagers. They pledged their devotion to Chairman Mao and the Cultural Revolution. From 1966 to 1968, 20 to 30 million Red Guards roamed China's cities and countryside causing widespread chaos. To smash the old, non-Maoist way of life, they destroyed buildings and beat and even killed Mao's alleged enemies. They lashed out at professors, government officials, factory managers, and even parents.

Eventually, even Mao turned on them. Most were exiled to the countryside. Others were arrested and some executed.

long shared border. They also were involved in political clashes as each sought to be viewed as the leader of a worldwide Communist movement.

Mao's revolution had an impact on global politics from the 1950s through the 1970s. Close to home, the Chinese provided military, advisory, and financial support to Communist leaders in Korea and Vietnam. Farther away, Mao took a particular interest in Communist expansion in Latin American countries such as Cuba, Peru, and Bolivia. Latin American Communist leaders came to China to learn from Mao about political organization and guerilla fighting, which they put into practice during periods of unrest in their own countries during the 1960s and 1970s. African revolutionaries also took lessons from the Chinese Communist leaders and then employed what they learned in their own countries.

The Cultural Revolution After the failure of the Great Leap Forward and the split with the Soviet Union, Mao reduced his role in China's government. Other leaders moved away from Mao's strict socialist ideas. For example, farm families were permitted to live in their own homes and could sell crops they grew on small private plots. Factory workers could compete for wage increases and promotions.

Mao thought China's new economic policies weakened the Communist goal of social equality. He was determined to revive the revolution. In 1966, he urged China's young people to "learn revolution by making revolution." Millions of high school and college students responded. They left their classrooms and formed militia units called **Red Guards**.

The Red Guards led a major uprising known as the **Cultural Revolution**. Its goal was to establish a society of peasants and workers in which all were equal. The new hero was the peasant who worked with his hands.

History in Depth

The Red Guards

The Red Guards were students, mainly teenagers. They pledged their devotion to Chairman Mao and the Cultural Revolution. From 1966 to 1968, 20 to 30 million Red Guards roamed China's cities and countryside, causing widespread chaos. To smash the old, non-Maoist way of life, they destroyed buildings and beat and even killed Mao's alleged enemies. They lashed out at professors, government officials, factory managers, and even parents.

Eventually, even Mao turned on them. Most were exiled to the countryside. Others were arrested and some executed.

The life of the mind—intellectual and artistic activity—was considered useless and dangerous. To stamp out this threat, the Red Guards shut down colleges and schools. They targeted anyone who resisted the regime. Intellectuals had to "purify" themselves by doing hard labor in remote villages. Thousands were executed or imprisoned.

Chaos threatened farm production and closed down factories. Civil war seemed possible. By 1968, even Mao admitted that the Cultural Revolution had to stop. The army was ordered to put down the Red Guards. Zhou Enlai (joh-ehn•leye), Chinese Communist party founder and premier since 1949, began to restore order. While China was struggling to become stable, the Cold War continued to rage. In addition, two full-scale "hot" wars broke out—in Korea and in Vietnam.

Reading Check
Analyze Issues What aspects of Marxist socialism did Mao try to bring to China?

Lesson 2 Assessment

1. **Organize Information** Which effect of the Communist Revolution in China do you think had the most permanent impact? Explain.

Cause	Effect
1.	1.
2.	2.
3.	3.

2. **Key Terms and People** For each key term or person in the lesson, write a sentence explaining its significance.
3. **Analyze Issues** What policies or actions enabled the Communists to defeat the Nationalists in the Chinese civil war?
4. **Make Inferences** Why did the United States support the Nationalists in the civil war in China?
5. **Identify Problems** What circumstances prevented Mao's Great Leap Forward from bringing economic prosperity to China in the late 1950s and early 1960s?
6. **Analyze Effects** Why was the Cultural Revolution led by the Red Guards a failure?

READING CHECK
Draw Conclusions Why did the Cultural Revolution fail? *The social upheaval it caused brought about economic chaos and threatened civil war.*

READING CHECK (Print)
Analyze Issues What aspects of Marxist socialism did Mao try to bring to China? *collective ownership of land, communal living, government control of industry*

Print Assessment

1. **Organize Information** Which effect of the Communist Revolution in China do you think had the most permanent impact? Explain. *Possible answer: land distribution remade the economy; Cultural Revolution caused chaos*
2. **Key Terms and People** For each key term or person in the lesson, write a sentence explaining its significance. *Explanation of the lesson's key terms can be found on the following pages: Mao Zedong, p. 1130; Jiang Jieshi, p. 1130; commune, p. 1133; Red Guards, p. 1134; Cultural Revolution, p. 1134.*
3. **Analyze Issues** What policies or actions enabled the Communists to defeat the Nationalists in the Chinese civil war? *won peasants' loyalty; trained troops in guerilla techniques; promised land reform*
4. **Make Inferences** Why did the United States support the Nationalists in the civil war in China? *The United States did not want Communists to control another country.*
5. **Identify Problems** What circumstances prevented Mao's Great Leap Forward from bringing economic prosperity to China in the late 1950s and early 1960s? *lack of privacy and personal life; lack of incentives for working hard; poor planning; crop failure*
6. **Analyze Effects** Why was the Cultural Revolution led by the Red Guards a failure? *The social upheaval it caused brought about economic chaos and threatened civil war.*

Online Assessment

1. Which of the following is a reason that Communists were able to win the peasants' loyalty in northern China?
   - ● The Communists promoted literacy.
   - ○ The Communists signed up for the Warsaw Pact.
   - ○ The Communists encouraged religious freedoms.
   - ○ The Communists allowed the Nationalists to control the south.

   Alternate Question *Select the answer choice from the drop-down list to complete the sentence correctly.* The Communists gained favor with the *peasants* in northern China due to increased food production and increases in literacy.

2. What caused resentment to increase between China and India?
   - ● China took control over Tibet.
   - ○ China changed the state religion.
   - ○ China offered education for peasants.
   - ○ China forced the Nationalists to Formosa.

   Alternate Question *Select the answer choice from the drop-down list to complete the sentence correctly.* Resentment increased between China and India when China tightened its control over *Tibet* in the late 1950s, forcing refugees from this country to flee to India.

3. What was achieved with the Agrarian Reform Law of 1950?
   - ● The government seized private land.
   - ○ The government educated peasants.
   - ○ The government encouraged home businesses.
   - ○ The government increased natural resource consumption.

   Alternate Question *Select the answer choice from the drop-down list to complete the sentence correctly.* In the Agrarian Reform Law of 1950, Mao seized private land in an effort to *make all things equal*.

4. **Make Inferences** Why did Mao Zedong's victory in China fuel U.S. anti-Communist feelings?

   Possible answer: When Mao Zedong took power in China, many in the United States feared that communism really was spreading around the world. China is a huge nation geographically, and if it fell to communism, what might be next? This fear increased when the Chinese and Soviets signed a treaty of friendship in 1950.

5. **Make Judgments** Why did the existence of two Chinas intensify the Cold War?

   Possible answer: Mainland China was Communist, but the island of Taiwan was not. It was a Nationalist government that was set up by Jiang Jieshi with the help of the United States. The island became known as the Republic of China. The Soviets supported Communist China with financial, military, and technical aid. The two nations (the Soviets and mainland China) also promised to give each other support if either was attacked. This split of democratic support for the Republic of China and Soviet support for mainland China (the People's Republic of China) increased Cold War tensions throughout Asia.

6. **Elaborate** What was the goal of the Cultural Revolution and what role did the Red Guard play in it?

   Possible answer: The Cultural Revolution was an effort to establish a society of peasants and workers in which all were equal. The hero was the peasant; the villain was the intellectual. To achieve this aim, colleges and schools were closed and anyone who resisted was at risk of execution. The Red Guard, militia formed from high school and college students, carried out this uprising.

Lesson 3 Planner

Wars in Korea and Vietnam

Online Lesson 3 Enrichment Activities

Korean War Timeline

Timeline Students create a timeline that identifies key dates and events of the Korean War. They should determine the date range of their timeline, including specific starting and ending dates. Students should consider topics such as North Korea's actions, the Chinese in the Korean peninsula, American activities in Korea, and South Korea's actions.

Vietnam War Movies

Article Students read about how the Vietnam War has been portrayed in U.S. movies. Then, they write an opinion paper about why they think the public's perception of veterans has changed over time. Students should also consider which type of portrayal they think is most accurate.

Teach the Big Idea

1. **Whole Class Open/Introduction** Ask students to recall the problems faced by the divided Germany. Explain that Korea and Vietnam were also divided. What kinds of problems do they think these countries faced? *Possible answer: Cold War pressures from the United States and Soviet Union; internal pressure to reunite the countries*
2. **Direct Teach** Read the Big Idea: *In Asia, the Cold War flared into actual wars supported mainly by the superpowers.* Review the following lesson objectives with students to aid in their understanding of the Big Idea.
   - Trace the course and consequences of the Korean War.
   - Summarize the causes of the Vietnam War and describe its aftermath.
   - Explain why the United States entered the Vietnam War and the results of its involvement.
   - Describe conditions in Cambodia and Vietnam after the Vietnam War.
3. **Whole Group Close/Reflect** Ask students to imagine they are students living in Vietnam during the Vietnam War. Would they agree with the war? Which side would they be on? How would they feel about U.S. involvement? Have them write a letter to Ho Chi Minh or President Johnson, putting their thoughts and opinions into words.

ONLINE DOCUMENT-BASED INVESTIGATION

Cold War Conflicts

The Effects of War is the third of five document-based investigations that students will analyze in the Cold War Conflicts module. Pol Pot's attempts to turn Cambodia into a Communist society resulted in the deaths of 2 million Cambodian citizens. Students can study the image and answer the associated question.

DOCUMENT-BASED INVESTIGATION HISTORICAL SOURCE

The Effects of War

The stakes were high for the various factions that fought during the Cold War. Pol Pot's attempts to turn Cambodia into a Communist society resulted in the deaths of 2 million

ONLINE LESSON FLIP CARDS

Review Key Terms and People

Students can use the flip cards in the Lesson Review at any time to review the lesson's key terms and people: *38th parallel, Douglas MacArthur, Ho Chi Minh, domino theory, Ngo Dinh Diem, Vietcong, Vietnamization,* and *Khmer Rouge.*

Lesson 3

Wars in Korea and Vietnam

The Big Idea

In Asia, the Cold War flared into actual wars supported mainly by the superpowers.

Why It Matters Now

Today, Vietnam is a Communist country, and Korea is split into Communist and non-Communist nations.

Key Terms and People

38th parallel
Douglas MacArthur
Ho Chi Minh
domino theory
Ngo Dinh Diem
Vietcong
Vietnamization
Khmer Rouge

Setting the Stage

When World War II ended, Korea became a divided nation. North of the **38th parallel**, a line that crosses Korea at 38 degrees north latitude, Japanese troops surrendered to Soviet forces. South of this line, the Japanese surrendered to American troops. As in Germany, two nations developed. One was the Communist industrial north, whose government had been set up by the Soviets. The other was the non-Communist rural south, supported by the Western powers.

War in Korea

By 1949, both the United States and the Soviet Union had withdrawn most of their troops from Korea. The Soviets gambled that the United States would not defend South Korea. So they supplied North Korea with tanks, airplanes, and money in an attempt to take over the peninsula.

Standoff at the 38th Parallel On June 25, 1950, North Koreans swept across the 38th parallel in a surprise attack on South Korea. Within days, North Korean troops had penetrated deep into the south. President Truman was convinced that the North Korean aggressors were repeating the types of actions that Hitler, Mussolini, and the Japanese had taken in the 1930s. Truman's policy of containment was being put to the test. And Truman resolved to help South Korea resist communism.

South Korea also asked the United Nations to intervene. When the matter came to a vote in the Security Council, the Soviets were absent. They had refused to take part in the council to protest admission of Nationalist China (Taiwan), rather than Communist China, into the UN. As a result, the Soviet Union could not veto the UN's plan to send an international force to Korea to stop the invasion. A total of 15 nations, including the United States and Britain, participated under the command of General **Douglas MacArthur**.

COLLABORATIVE LEARNING

Pro-and-Con Charts

1. Divide students into small groups. Have groups reread the segments War Breaks Out in Vietnam and The United States Gets Involved.
2. Guide a discussion of why the United States entered the Vietnam War. Point out that many Americans opposed the war, and explain that thousands of people demonstrated against it.
3. Create a pro-and-con chart to summarize the positions. Tell students to consider the arguments and decide whether they are for continuing the war or for pulling out of Vietnam.

Meanwhile, the North Koreans continued to advance. By September 1950, they controlled the entire Korean peninsula except for a tiny area around Pusan in the far southeast. That month, however, MacArthur launched a surprise attack. Troops moving north from Pusan met with forces that had made an amphibious landing at Inchon. Caught in this "pincer action," about half of the North Koreans surrendered. The rest retreated.

The Fighting Continues The UN troops pursued the retreating North Koreans across the 38th parallel into North Korea. They pushed them almost to the Yalu River at the Chinese border. The UN forces were mostly from the United States. The Chinese felt threatened by these troops and by an American fleet off their coast. In October 1950, they sent 300,000 troops into North Korea.

The Chinese greatly outnumbered the UN forces. By January 1951, they had pushed UN and South Korean troops out of North Korea. The Chinese then moved into South Korea and captured the capital, Seoul. "We face an entirely new war," declared MacArthur. He called for a nuclear attack against China. Truman viewed MacArthur's proposals as reckless. "We are trying to prevent a world war, not start one," he said. MacArthur tried to go over the president's head by taking his case to Congress and the press. In response, Truman removed him from his command.

Over the next two years, UN forces fought to drive the Chinese and North Koreans back. By 1952, UN troops had regained control of South Korea. Finally, in July 1953, the UN forces and North Korea signed a cease-fire agreement. The border between the two Koreas was set near the 38th parallel, almost where it had been before the war. In the meantime, 4 million soldiers and civilians had died.

Aftermath of the War After the war, Korea remained divided. A demilitarized zone, which still exists, separated the two countries. In North Korea, the Communist dictator Kim Il Sung established collective farms, developed heavy industry, and built up the military. At Kim's death in

UN forces landing at Inchon in South Korea in 1950

Objectives

You may wish to discuss the following questions with students to help them frame the content as they read.

- Why would the Soviet Union boycott the Security Council, thereby allowing the UN to enter the Korean War? *They didn't think the UN would go to war.*
- How were UN forces able to push back the Chinese, who had many more soldiers? *better equipped*

More About . . .

Connect to Language Arts Point out the word *amphibious*. Tell students that it means that the soldiers invaded Korea from the water and then came ashore. Explain that this word comes from the same base word as *amphibian*, a class of animals that live in the water part of their lives and on land part of their lives. Examples include frogs and salamanders.

ONLINE GRAPHIC ORGANIZER

Wars in Korea and Vietnam

As students read the lesson, have them use the graphic organizer to take notes. Students can review their graphic organizer notes at the end of the lesson to answer the following question.

Compare In what ways were the causes and effects of the wars in Korea and Vietnam similar? *U.S. and Soviet involvement stemmed from Cold War; land was destroyed; millions of people died*

Korean War	Similar	Different	Vietnam War

COLLABORATIVE LEARNING

Korean War Timeline

1. Make sure students understand that the map in this segment traces the course of the Korean War over time. Ask: Which color line marks the extent of the first North Korean surge? *red* From which direction did Chinese troops attack in 1950? *northwest*
2. Have students create a timeline that shows the advances and retreats of troops in the Korean War. Have them use the information on this map to create the framework for their timeline and use print or Internet resources to add more detailed information.
3. Invite volunteers to present their timelines to the whole group.

ONLINE INTERACTIVE MAPS

War in Korea, 1950–1953

Have students explore the map using the interactive features and answer the associated questions.

Interpret Maps What was the northernmost Korean city UN troops had reached by November 1950? *Chosan*

In print edition, see map of same title.

Movement What was the northernmost Korean city UN troops had reached by November 1950? *Chosan*

Changing Boundaries If the war had ended in January 1951, where would the southern border of North Korea have been located? *along the boundary marked by the yellow line on the map*

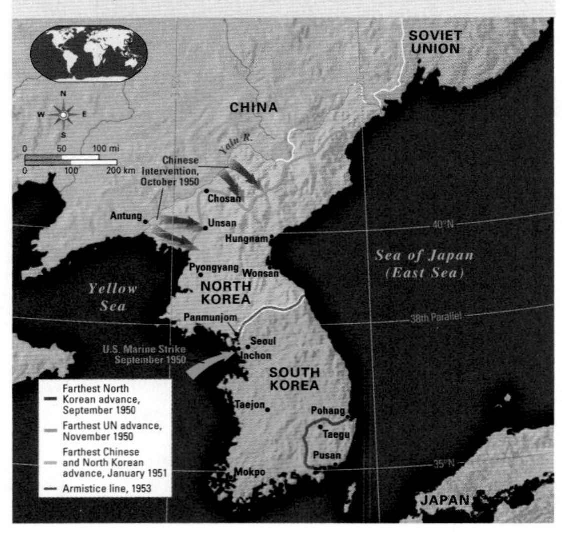

READING CHECK

Recognize Effects What effects did the Korean War have on the Korean people and nation? *About 4 million Koreans and soldiers died and neither North nor South Korea had gained any territory.*

1994, his son Kim Jong Il took power. Under his rule, Communist North Korea developed nuclear weapons but had serious economic problems.

On the other hand, South Korea prospered, thanks partly to massive aid from the United States and other countries. In the 1960s, South Korea concentrated on developing its industry and expanding foreign trade. A succession of dictatorships ruled the rapidly developing country. With the 1987 adoption of a democratic constitution, however, South Korea established free elections. During the 1980s and 1990s, South Korea had one of the highest economic growth rates in the world.

Political differences have kept the two Koreas apart, despite periodic discussions of reuniting the country. North Korea's possession of nuclear weapons is a major obstacle. The United States still keeps troops in South Korea.

Reading Check
Recognize Effects What effects did the Korean War have on the Korean people and nation?

Explore ONLINE!

War in Korea, 1950–1953

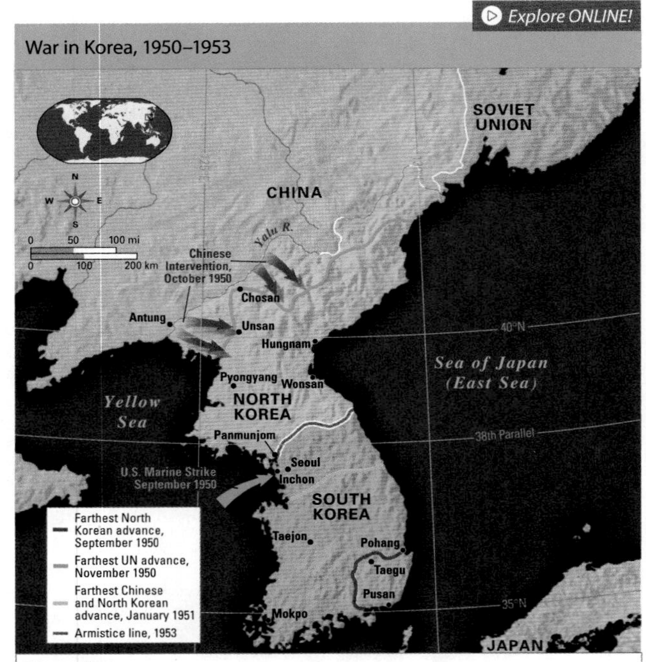

Interpret Maps

1. **Movement** What was the northernmost Korean city UN troops had reached by November 1950?
2. **Changing Boundaries** If the war had ended in January 1951, where would the southern border of North Korea have been located?

War Breaks Out in Vietnam

Much like its involvement in the Korean War, the involvement of the United States in Vietnam stemmed from its Cold War containment policy. After World War II, stopping the spread of communism was the principal goal of U.S. foreign policy.

The Road to War In the early 1900s, France controlled most of resource-rich Southeast Asia. (French Indochina included what are now Vietnam, Laos, and Cambodia.) But nationalist independence movements had begun to develop. A young Vietnamese nationalist, **Ho Chi Minh**, turned to the Communists for help in his struggle. During the 1930s, Ho's Indochinese Communist Party led revolts and strikes against the French.

The French responded by jailing Vietnamese protesters. They also sentenced Ho to death. He fled into exile but returned to Vietnam in 1941, a year after the Japanese seized control of his country during World War II. Ho and other nationalists founded the Vietminh (Independence) League. The Japanese were forced out of Vietnam after their defeat in 1945. Ho Chi Minh believed that independence would follow, but France intended to regain its colony.

The Fighting Begins Vietnamese Nationalists and Communists joined to fight the French armies. The French held most major cities, but the Vietminh had widespread support in the countryside. The Vietminh used hit-and-run tactics to confine the French to the cities. In France the people began to doubt that their colony was worth the lives and money the struggle cost. In 1954, the French suffered a major military defeat at Dien Bien Phu. They surrendered to Ho.

The United States had supported France. With France's defeat, the United States saw a rising threat to the rest of Asia. President Eisenhower described this threat in terms of the **domino theory**. The Southeast Asian nations were like a row of dominos, he said. The fall of one to communism would lead to the fall of its neighbors. This theory became a major justification for U.S. foreign policy during the Cold War era.

Vietnam: A Divided Country After France's defeat, an international peace conference met in Geneva, Switzerland, to discuss the future of Indochina. Based on these talks, Vietnam was divided at 17° north latitude. This is similar to the way Korea was divided at the 38th parallel. North of that line, Ho Chi Minh's Communist forces governed. To the south, the United States and France set up an anti-Communist government under the leadership of **Ngo Dinh Diem** (NOH dihn D'YEM).

Diem ruled the south as a dictator. Opposition to his government grew. Communist guerrillas, called **Vietcong**, began to gain strength in the south. While some of the Vietcong were trained soldiers from North Vietnam, most were South Vietnamese who hated Diem. Gradually, the Vietcong won control of large areas of the countryside. In 1963, a group of South Vietnamese generals had Diem assassinated. But the new leaders were no more popular than Diem had been. It appeared that a takeover by the Communist Vietcong, backed by North Vietnam, was inevitable.

Reading Check
Make Inferences What actions might the United States have justified by the domino theory?

Objectives

You may wish to discuss the following questions with students to help them frame the content as they read.

- How were the Vietnamese Nationalists and Communists different from the Nationalists and Communists in China after World War II? *China—Nationalists and Communists fought each other; Vietnam—they fought together against the French*
- How did the Cold War influence the international peace conference's decision to invade Vietnam? *It responded to the pressures of the Soviet Union and United States.*

More About . . .

Dien Bien Phu The battle of Dien Bien Phu effectively ended the eight-year conflict between Vietnam and France known as the First Indochina War. The battle was waged by Vietminh forces fighting for independence from France. The decisive Vietnamese victory led to French withdrawal from Indochina and independence for Vietnam, Laos, and Cambodia.

READING CHECK
Make Inferences What actions might the United States have justified by the domino theory? *intervention in any situation that might otherwise result in gains of territory or power by the Communists*

COLLABORATIVE LEARNING

Ho Chi Minh

1. In 1945, Ho Chi Minh sent two telegrams to President Truman seeking a seat on a British-American-Russian-Chinese Advisory Commission that would decide the fate of Indochina. Truman ignored him.
2. Have students work together to discuss why they think the United States refused to deal with Ho. Have them consider how events might have been different if Truman responded to Ho and involved him in the process.

STRUGGLING READERS

Vietnamese Geography

1. Have students compare the map of Vietnam in this segment to one that shows the country's terrain and vegetation.
2. Ask students to think about what problems those geographic features might create for armies conducting a ground war. Have students explain in their own words what the problems might be. *Possible answer: Swampy coastal plains and densely jungled mountains would make troop movement difficult.*

ONLINE INTERACTIVE MAPS

War in Vietnam, 1957–1975

Have students explore the map using the interactive features and answer the associated question.

Interpret Maps Through which other countries did North Vietnamese troops move to invade South Vietnam? *Laos and Cambodia*

ONLINE INTERACTIVE VISUALS

Carousel: War in Vietnam

Have students navigate through the carousel and note similarities and differences among the images or identify a unifying theme.

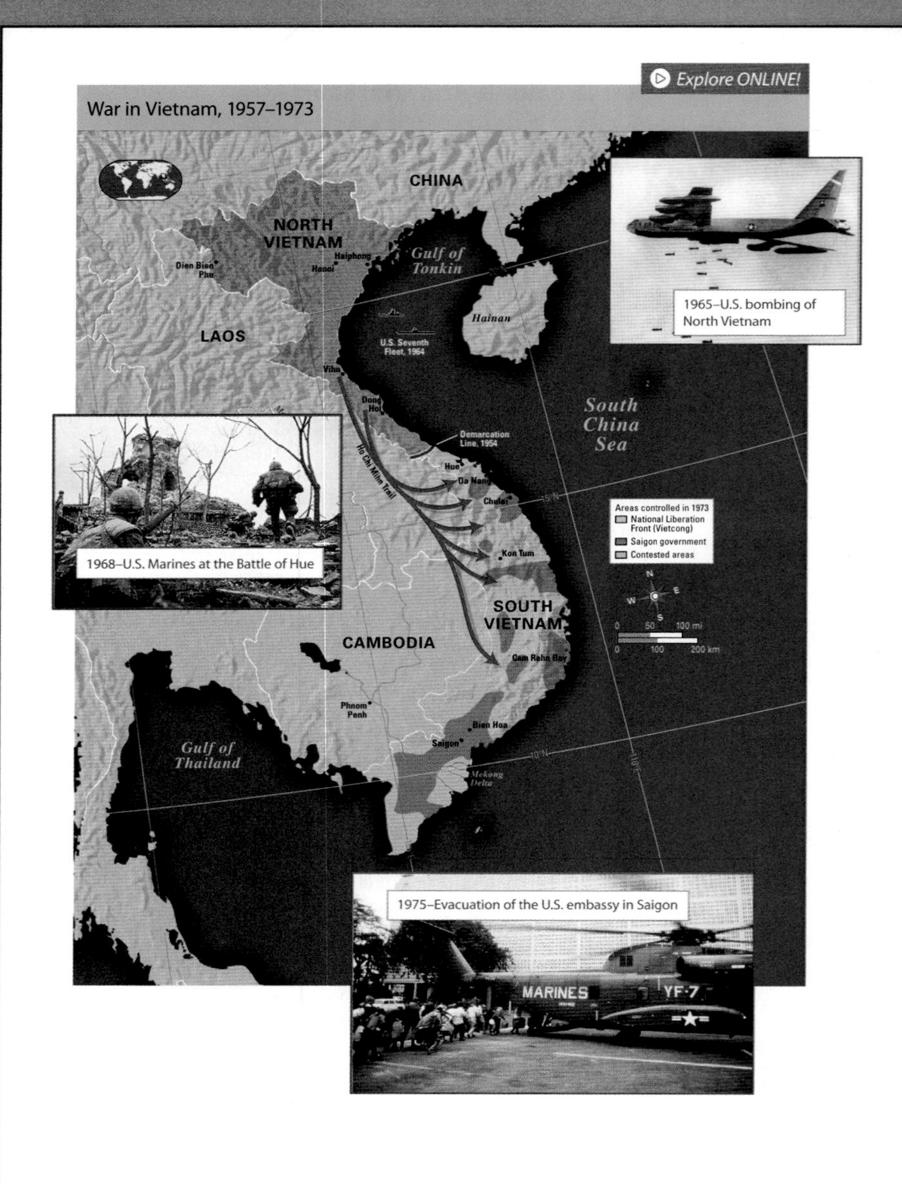

ADVANCED/GIFTED

Art and War

1. Display a work of art that was created by a Vietnamese artist during the time of the Vietnam War. Discuss the imagery and details.
2. Have students do Internet research to learn more about art produced during the war and to view more examples. Have them find one painting or other art object to examine in detail.
3. Ask students to present it to the group. As a group, talk about the dominant themes of Vietnamese war art.

BIOGRAPHY

Ho Chi Minh
(1890–1969)

When he was young, the poor Vietnamese Nguyen Tat Thanh (WEE•un tat thawn) worked as a cook on a French steamship. In visiting U.S. cities where the boat docked, he learned about American culture and ideals. He later took a new name—Ho Chi Minh, meaning "He who enlightens." In proclaiming Vietnam's independence from France in 1945, he declared, "All men are created equal," echoing the words of the American Declaration of Independence.

His people revered him, calling him Uncle Ho. However, Ho Chi Minh did not put his democratic ideals into practice. He ruled North Vietnam by crushing all opposition.

The United States Gets Involved

Faced with the possibility of a Communist victory, the United States decided to escalate, or increase, its involvement. Some U.S. troops had been serving as advisers to the South Vietnamese since the late 1950s. But their numbers steadily grew, as did the numbers of planes and other military equipment sent to South Vietnam.

U.S. Troops Enter the Fight In August 1964, U.S. President Lyndon Johnson told Congress that North Vietnamese patrol boats had attacked two U.S. destroyers in the Gulf of Tonkin. As a result, Congress authorized the president to send U.S. troops to fight in Vietnam. By late 1965, more than 185,000 U.S. soldiers were in combat on Vietnamese soil. U.S. planes had also begun to bomb North Vietnam. By 1968, more than half a million U.S. soldiers were in combat there.

The United States had the best equipped, most advanced army in the world. Yet it faced two major difficulties. First, U.S. soldiers were fighting a guerrilla war in unfamiliar jungle terrain. Second, the South Vietnamese government that they were defending was becoming more unpopular. At the same time, support for the Vietcong grew, with help and supplies from Ho Chi Minh, the Soviet Union, and China. Unable to win a decisive victory on the ground, the United States turned to air power.

The United States began widespread "carpet bombing" of millions of acres of farmland and forests in an attempt to destroy enemy hideouts and deter guerilla attacks. The bombers spread two deadly chemicals, napalm (a jellied oil product) and Agent Orange (a powerful weed killer). Both had terrible side effects. Napalm killed vegetation but also stuck to humans, burning their skin. Agent Orange did clear the jungles but also destroyed cropland and caused sickness in some farm animals. This bombing strengthened peasants' opposition to the South Vietnamese government and to the American forces inside their country.

COLLABORATIVE LEARNING

Vietnam War Movie Scene

1. Have students work in small groups to brainstorm a scene for a movie about the Vietnam War. They may choose any perspective: that of U.S. soldiers, Vietcong, or South Vietnamese civilians, for example.
2. Emphasize that students should focus on a single dramatic situation. Tell them that the setting and plot of their scene should be as realistic as possible. Encourage them to consider the following:
   - Where does the scene take place? What time is it?
   - What is the weather like? What season is it?
   - What events have led up to the scene they are describing?
   - Who are their characters? What do they think of their situation?
3. Have students work together to write the scene. Remind them that their scripts should include stage directions and realistic dialogue.
4. Have students meet with other groups and share their ideas and read their dialogue.

Objectives

You may wish to discuss the following question with students to help them frame the content as they read.

- How were the South Vietnamese and American people alike? Why? *Both opposed the war because of the many casualties.*

More About . . .

The Gulf of Tonkin Incident The Gulf of Tonkin incident took place at night during a storm. The two U.S. destroyers picked up the images of 22 torpedoes on their tracking systems. No one saw the Vietnamese attackers, however, and the next morning Captain Herrick, who commanded the ships, decided his radar might have mistaken "freak weather effects" for an attack. To this day, no one knows whether the attacks used to justify American escalation of the Vietnam War ever really took place.

BIOGRAPHY

Ho Chi Minh

Have students read the biography of Ho Chi Minh, the Vietnamese nationalist and revolutionary leader who was president of the Democratic Republic of Vietnam (North Vietnam) from 1945 to 1969.

ONLINE ANALYZE VIDEOS

Arriving in Vietnam

HISTORY

Have students watch the video individually or as a class. You may wish to use the associated question as a discussion prompt.

Analyze Videos What did soldiers encounter when they first arrived in Vietnam? *white sand beaches; palm trees; hot, humid weather; tanned soldiers in worn uniforms; pale new recruits in new uniforms*

Objectives

You may wish to discuss the following questions with students to help them frame the content as they read.

- How accurately did the domino theory explain events in Southeast Asia? *not very; Cambodia is democratic*
- How has Vietnam changed since the first years after the war? *fewer economic restrictions; strong economy*

More About . . .

Pol Pot Pol Pot was the French-educated leader of the Communist government in Cambodia known as the Khmer Rouge. The Communists captured Phnom Penh, the Cambodian capital, in April of 1975 and reset the calendars to "year zero." In an effort to turn Cambodia into a rural society, everyone living in cities and towns was expelled to work in agricultural communes. The Khmer Rouge also outlawed money, private property, and religion.

READING CHECK
Clarify Why did the attack on U.S. destroyers provide a reason for sending troops into Vietnam? *It was considered a direct attack on the United States.*

READING CHECK (Print)
Analyze Causes What were two reasons U.S. troops had trouble fighting the war on Vietnamese soil? *They were fighting in unfamiliar jungle terrain, and the government they were supporting was unpopular.*

The United States Withdraws During the late 1960s, the war grew increasingly unpopular in the United States. Dissatisfied young people began to protest the tremendous loss of life in a conflict on the other side of the world. Bowing to intense public pressure, President Richard Nixon began withdrawing U.S. troops from Vietnam in 1969.

Nixon had a plan called **Vietnamization**. It allowed for U.S. troops to gradually pull out, while the South Vietnamese increased their combat role. To pursue Vietnamization while preserving the South Vietnamese government, Nixon authorized a massive bombing campaign against North Vietnamese bases and supply routes. He also authorized bombings in neighboring Laos and Cambodia to destroy Vietcong hiding places.

Reading Check
Analyze Causes
What were two reasons U.S. troops had trouble fighting the war on Vietnamese soil?

In response to protests and political pressure at home, Nixon kept withdrawing U.S. troops. The last left in 1973. Two years later, the North Vietnamese overran South Vietnam. The war ended, but more than 1.5 million Vietnamese and 58,000 Americans had lost their lives.

Postwar Southeast Asia

War's end did not bring an immediate halt to bloodshed and chaos in Southeast Asia. Cambodia (also known as Kampuchea) was under siege by Communist rebels. During the war, it had suffered U.S. bombing when it was used as a sanctuary by North Vietnamese and Vietcong troops.

Cambodia in Turmoil In 1975, Communist rebels known as the **Khmer Rouge** set up a brutal Communist government under the leadership of Pol Pot. In a ruthless attempt to transform Cambodia into a Communist society, Pol Pot's followers carried out mass killings of 2 million people. This was almost one quarter of the nation's population. The Vietnamese invaded in 1978. They overthrew the Khmer Rouge and installed a less repressive government. But fighting continued. The Vietnamese withdrew in 1989. In 1993, under the supervision of UN peacekeepers, Cambodia adopted a democratic constitution and held free elections.

Vietnam After the War After 1975, the victorious North Vietnamese imposed tight controls over the South. Officials sent thousands of people to "reeducation camps" for training in Communist thought. They nationalized industries and strictly controlled businesses. They also renamed Saigon, the South's former capital, Ho Chi Minh City. Communist oppression caused 1.5 million people to flee Vietnam. Most escaped in dangerously overcrowded ships. More than 200,000 "boat people" died at sea. The survivors often spent months in refugee

The skulls and bones of Cambodian citizens form a haunting memorial to the brutality of its Communist government in the 1970s.

1142 Module 29

ONLINE DOCUMENT-BASED INVESTIGATION

The Effects of War

Pol Pot's attempts to turn Cambodia into a Communist society resulted in the deaths of 2 million Cambodian citizens. Have students study the image and answer the associated question.

Analyze Sources How does this image help viewers understand the enormity of the slaughter during Pol Pot's regime? *There are skulls and bones lying all over in the image. This leads viewers to understand the enormity of the violence. In addition, since the bones have not been buried, it makes viewers realize that the slaughter may have been so great that no one was left to bury the dead.*

COLLABORATIVE LEARNING

Compare and Contrast

1. Have students compare and contrast two world leaders mentioned in this lesson. Tell them to take notes about their importance and the role each played during the Cold War, Korean War, or Vietnam War.
2. Encourage students to make a Venn diagram to compare and contrast the two individuals they chose.
3. Ask students to write a brief paragraph describing the biggest similarities and differences between these two people.
4. Invite volunteers to read their paragraphs aloud.

Now and Then

Vietnam Today

Vietnam remains a Communist country. But, like China, it has introduced elements of capitalism into its economy. The changes prompted a Western travel magazine in 1997 to claim that Hanoi, the capital of Vietnam, "jumps with vitality, its streets and shops jammed with locals and handfuls of Western tourists and businesspeople." The photo on the right shows two executives touring the city.

Along Hanoi's shaded boulevards, billboards advertise U.S. and Japanese motorcycles, copiers, video recorders, and soft drinks. On the streets, enterprising Vietnamese business people offer more traditional services. These include bicycle repair, a haircut, a shave, or a tasty snack.

Reading Check
Recognize Effects What was one of the effects of Pol Pot's efforts to turn Cambodia into a Communist peasant society?

camps in Southeast Asia. About 70,000 eventually settled in the United States or Canada. Although Communists still govern Vietnam, the country now welcomes foreign investment. The United States normalized relations with Vietnam in 1995.

While the superpowers were struggling for advantage during the Korean and Vietnam wars, they also were seeking influence in other parts of the world.

Lesson 3 Assessment

1. **Organize Information** In what ways were the causes and effects of the wars in Korea and Vietnam similar?

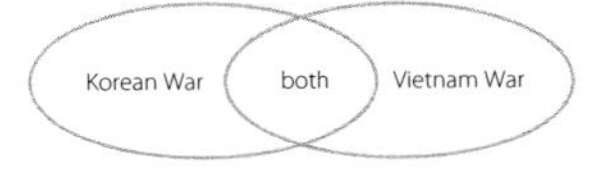

2. **Key Terms and People** For each key term or person in the lesson, write a sentence explaining its significance.
3. **Make Inferences** When President Truman told General MacArthur, "We are trying to prevent a world war, not start one," what did he mean?
4. **Analyze Motives** What role did the policy of containment play in the involvement of the United States in wars in Korea and Vietnam?
5. **Identify Causes** How might imperialism be one of the causes of the Vietnam War?
6. **Form Opinions** Do you think U.S. involvement in Vietnam was justified? Why or why not?
7. **Analyze Motives** Why did the North Vietnamese change the name of Saigon to Ho Chi Minh City?

NOW & THEN

Vietnam Today

In seeking economic growth through foreign investment, Vietnam is following the example of China, South Korea, and other East Asia countries. One victim of this growth has been the environment. The number of elephants in Vietnam, for example, dropped from 2,000 to 150 in 2005.

READING CHECK
Analyze Effects What was one of the effects of Pol Pot's efforts to turn Cambodia into a rural society? *His followers killed nearly 2 million people.*

Print Assessment

1. **Organize Information** In what ways were the causes and effects of the wars in Korea and Vietnam similar? *Possible answer: U.S. and Soviet involvement stemmed from the Cold War; land was destroyed; millions of people died*
2. **Key Terms and People** For each key term or person in the lesson, write a sentence explaining its significance. *Explanation of the lesson's key terms can be found on the following pages: 38th parallel, p. 1136; Douglas MacArthur, p. 1136; Ho Chi Minh, p. 1139; domino theory, p. 1139; Ngo Dinh Diem, p. 1139; Vietcong, p. 1139; Vietnamization, p. 1142; Khmer Rouge, p. 1142.*
3. **Make Inferences** When President Truman told General MacArthur, "We are trying to prevent a world war, not start one," what did he mean? *Truman thought MacArthur's plan to attack China with a nuclear weapon was reckless and would lead to war with China.*
4. **Analyze Motives** What role did the policy of containment play in the involvement of the United States in wars in Korea and Vietnam? *The United States tried to prevent Korea and Vietnam from becoming Communist.*
5. **Identify Causes** How might imperialism be one of the causes of the Vietnam War? *The struggle against French colonialism began the fighting in Vietnam.*
6. **Form Opinions** Do you think U.S. involvement in Vietnam was justified? Why or why not? *Possible answer: Yes—important to stop communism; No—nations should decide for themselves*
7. **Analyze Motives** Why did the North Vietnamese change the name of Saigon to Ho Chi Minh City? *They won the war and changed the name to honor their leader.*

Online Assessment

DIGITAL ASSESSMENT

1. What allowed the UN to intervene when North Korea invaded South Korea?
   - ○ The Chinese had entered the war to support North Korea.
   - ○ The North Koreans had moved all the way to the 38th parallel.
   - ○ The countries had decided to place Douglas MacArthur in charge.
   - ● The Soviet Union was purposely absent when the vote was taken.

   Alternate Question *Select the answer choice from the drop-down list to complete the sentence correctly.*
   The UN was able to intervene in the Korean conflict because the *Soviets* refused to be present when the Security Council voted on the matter.

2. What was the main goal of the Vietnamese nationalists for the country of Vietnam?
   - ○ to disprove the domino theory
   - ○ to establish democratic elections
   - ● to remove the French from power
   - ○ to provide natural resources to the Soviets

   Alternate Question *Select the answer choice from the drop-down list to complete the sentence correctly.*
   Ho Chi Minh's primary goal for Vietnam was to *remove the French from power* in Vietnam. He was willing to align with the Communists to receive the assistance he needed.

3. Which of the following was a characteristic of "carpet bombing"?
   - ● Chemical warfare was used.
   - ○ Beaches and ports were avoided.
   - ○ Guerilla warfare was a key component.
   - ○ Bases and supply routes were off-limits.

   Alternate Question *Select the answer choice from the drop-down list to complete the sentence correctly.*
   "Carpet bombing" was a strategy used by the *United States* in order to destroy enemy hideouts and deter guerilla attacks. Huge areas of forests and farmland were the targets, and the bombs contained deadly chemicals.

4. What strategy did Pol Pot use to take control in Cambodia?
   - ○ He set up free elections.
   - ● He carried out mass killings.
   - ○ He utilized reeducation camps.
   - ○ He worked with international peacekeepers.

   Alternate Question *Select the answer choice from the drop-down list to complete the sentence correctly.*
   In order for Pol Pot and his followers to gain control of the government in Cambodia, they *murdered 2 million people*.

5. **Compare and Contrast** What is the difference between North and South Korea after the Korean War?

   Possible answer: North Korea has a Communist government, collective farms, heavy industry, and a strong military. South Korea has a democratic government, as of 1987, which includes free elections. Prior to that, a succession of dictators ruled South Korea. South Korea has a highly developed industry and expansive foreign trade.

6. **Draw Conclusions** Why did the members of the international peace conference in Geneva most likely feel that dividing Vietnam in half was the best idea for the region, and what was the result of that decision?

   Possible answer: The members of the peace conference most likely felt that by dividing the country into north and south, everyone would be happy and peace would be restored to the region. The north would be given to the Communists and the south would be given to the anti-Communists. The problem was that the government established in the south was led by a dictator. Opposition against his government grew and the Vietcong, or Communist Vietnamese, began increasing in strength and numbers. The Vietcong slowly started taking over large areas of the south.

7. **Analyze Issues** What were the ideas behind Nixon's Vietnamization and what were the outcomes of this plan?

   Possible answer: This plan allowed the U.S. troops to gradually pull out of Vietnam while the South Vietnamese increased their combat role. The goal was for the United States to get out of the conflict while at the same time preserving the South Vietnamese government. Nixon did this by authorizing a massive bombing campaign against the North Vietnamese bases and supply routes and in neighboring Laos and Cambodia so as to destroy Vietcong hiding places. The result of this plan was that the U.S. troops were finally all pulled out of Vietnam—the last ones left in 1973. However, without the U.S. troops' presence in the region, the South Vietnamese government fell to the North Vietnamese two years later.

8. **Make Inferences** Why would the people of South Vietnam have been forced to attend "reeducation camps"?

   Possible answer: The South had different ideas from the North about the types of government and economic systems that they wanted to live under. The North was Communist, and the South was not. So when the North took over, the people in the South would have needed to be indoctrinated into a new way of thinking. They would have needed to be convinced that communism was the only right way to live. They would have needed to be convinced that it was best for the businesses and industries in the country to be controlled by the government instead of by individuals.

Lesson 4 Planner

The Cold War Divides the World

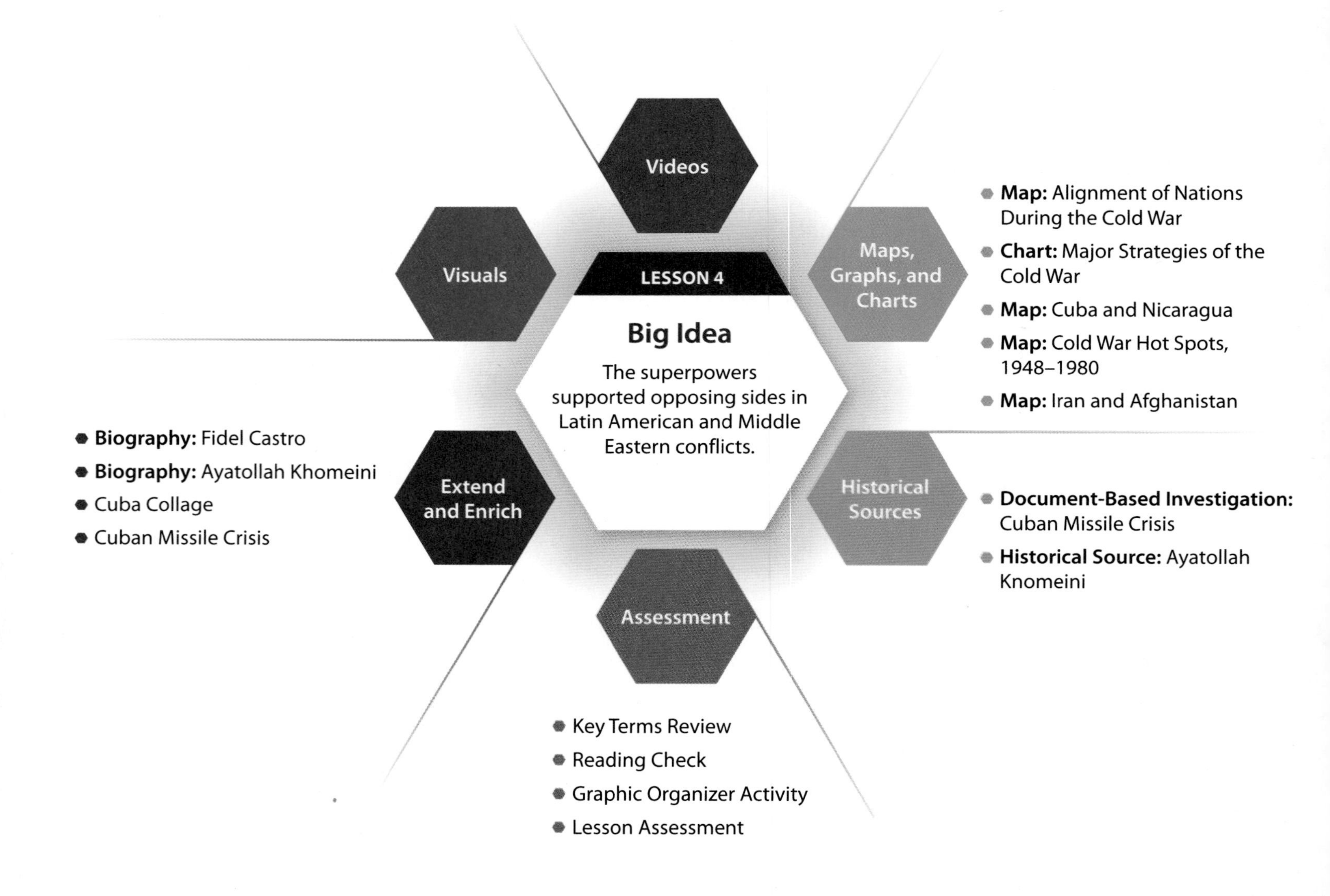

- **Map:** Alignment of Nations During the Cold War
- **Chart:** Major Strategies of the Cold War
- **Map:** Cuba and Nicaragua
- **Map:** Cold War Hot Spots, 1948–1980
- **Map:** Iran and Afghanistan

- **Biography:** Fidel Castro
- **Biography:** Ayatollah Khomeini
- Cuba Collage
- Cuban Missile Crisis

- **Document-Based Investigation:** Cuban Missile Crisis
- **Historical Source:** Ayatollah Knomeini

- Key Terms Review
- Reading Check
- Graphic Organizer Activity
- Lesson Assessment

Online Lesson 4 Enrichment Activities

Cuba Collage

Collage Students conduct research about Cuba to create a collage on the history of the country since 1950. They should identify events they want to use in the collage. For example, they could use key words such as *Fidel Castro, Bay of Pigs invasion, Cuban Missile Crisis,* or *communism in China* as a starting point.

Cuban Missile Crisis

Video Documentary Students write an outline for a video documentary about the Cuban Missile Crisis. They should identify items to include in the outline, such as President Kennedy, Fidel Castro, U.S. and Cuban citizens, and Nikita Khrushchev. Students should conduct research as necessary and include the most important facts in the correct sequence.

Teach the Big Idea

1. **Whole Class Open/Introduction** When businesses compete for customers, they may advertise, give extra service, have sales, and give prizes away. Ask what superpowers might do to win the loyalty of poor nations. *Possible answer: foreign aid, espionage, propaganda*
2. **Direct Teach** Read the Big Idea: *The superpowers supported opposing sides in Latin American and Middle Eastern conflicts.* Review the following lesson objectives with students to aid in their understanding of the Big Idea.
   - Explain how the Cold War affected developing nations.
   - Describe superpower confrontations in Latin America after World War II.
   - Identify Cold War conflicts in the Middle East.
3. **Whole Group Close/Reflect** Have students imagine how the world today would be different if the Cuban Missile Crisis had led to war. What would be different? What would be the same?

ONLINE DOCUMENT-BASED INVESTIGATION

Cold War Conflicts

Cuban Missile Crisis is the fourth of five document-based investigations that students will analyze in the Cold War Conflicts module. President Kennedy gave this televised speech at the height of the crisis. Students can click on the audio button beneath the historical source to hear the excerpt read aloud.

ONLINE GRAPHIC ORGANIZER

The Cold War Divides the World

As students read the lesson, have them use the graphic organizer to take notes. Students can review their graphic organizer notes at the end of the lesson to answer the following question.

Draw Conclusions Which confrontation had the most lasting significance? *Cuba because of its proximity to the United States and the duration.*

ONLINE LESSON FLIP CARDS

Review Key Terms and People

Students can use the flip cards in the Lesson Review at any time to review the lesson's key terms and people: *Third World, nonaligned nations, Fidel Castro, Anastasio Somoza, Daniel Ortega, Ayatollah Ruhollah Khomeini*

Lesson 4

The Cold War Divides the World

The Big Idea

The superpowers supported opposing sides in Latin American and Middle Eastern conflicts.

Why It Matters Now

Many of these areas today are troubled by political, economic, and military conflict and crisis.

Key Terms and People

Third World
nonaligned nations
Fidel Castro
Anastasio Somoza
Daniel Ortega
Ayatollah Ruhollah Khomeini

Setting the Stage

Following World War II, the world's nations were grouped politically into three "worlds." The first was the industrialized capitalist nations, including the United States and its allies. The second was the Communist nations led by the Soviet Union. The **Third World** consisted of developing nations, often newly independent, who were not aligned with either superpower. These nonaligned countries provided yet another arena for competition between the Cold War superpowers.

Fighting for the Third World

The Third World nations were located in Latin America, Asia, and Africa. They were economically poor and politically unstable. This was largely due to a long history of colonialism. They also suffered from ethnic conflicts and lack of technology and education. Each needed a political and economic system around which to build its society. Soviet-style communism and U.S.-style free-market democracy were the main choices.

Cold War Strategies The United States, the Soviet Union, and, in some cases, China, used a variety of techniques to gain influence in the Third World. They backed wars of revolution, liberation, or counterrevolution. The U.S. and Soviet intelligence agencies—the CIA and the KGB—engaged in various covert, or secret, activities, ranging from spying to assassination attempts. The United States also gave military aid, built schools, set up programs to combat poverty, and sent volunteer workers to many developing nations. The Soviets offered military and technical assistance as well as economic aid, mainly to India, Egypt, and newly independent countries in central and west Africa, such as Congo, Angola, and Mozambique.

Association of Nonaligned Nations Other developing nations also needed assistance. They became important

COLLABORATIVE LEARNING

Cold War Thermometer

1. Explain to students that the levels of tension between the United States and Soviet Union varied over time. Some confrontations, such as the Cuban Missile Crisis, raised tensions to especially high levels; it could easily have erupted in war. Other individual events weren't nearly so hot, but during the late 1940s and early 1950s, a lot of events happened during a short period. The frequency of events increased the overall tensions.
2. Have students work in groups and brainstorm ways of tracking the rise and fall of Cold War tensions on a temperature scale. You might suggest, for example, that they consider a scale such as degrees C—degrees of crisis—and assign a number to each confrontation or avoidance of confrontation between the superpowers.
3. Then, have small groups each choose a Cold War incident, write a short description of their incident, and assign it a rating on the crisis scale.
4. Have the groups meet and plot their individual incidents on a crisis temperature chart. As a group, they might assign a higher temperature to a period when events were frequent.

History in Depth

Explore ONLINE!

How the Cold War Was Fought

During the Cold War, the United States and the Soviet Union both believed that they needed to stop the other side from extending its power. What differentiated the Cold War from other 20th-century conflicts was that the two enemies did not engage in a shooting war. Instead, they pursued their rivalry by using the strategies shown below.

Egypt built the Aswan High Dam with Soviet aid.

European Alignments, 1955

NATO, 1955
Warsaw Pact, 1955
Non-aligned, 1955

MAJOR STRATEGIES OF THE COLD WAR

FOREIGN AID
The two superpowers tried to win allies by giving financial aid to other nations. For instance, Egypt took aid from the Soviet Union to build the Aswan High Dam.

ESPIONAGE
Fearing the enemy might be gaining the advantage, each side spied on the other. One famous incident was the Soviet downing of a U.S. U-2 spy plane in 1960.

MULTINATIONAL ALLIANCES
To gain the support of other nations, both the Soviet Union and the United States entered into alliances. Two examples of this were NATO and the Warsaw Pact (shown on map above).

PROPAGANDA
Both superpowers used propaganda to try to win support overseas. For example, Radio Free Europe broadcast radio programs about the rest of the world into Eastern Europe.

BRINKMANSHIP
The policy of brinkmanship meant going to the brink of war to make the other side back down. One example was the Cuban Missile Crisis.

SURROGATE OR PROXY WARS
The word *surrogate* means "substitute" and *proxy* means "representing someone else." Although the United States and the Soviet Union did not fight each other directly, they fought indirectly by backing opposing sides in many smaller conflicts.

Interpret Visuals

1. **Generalize** Judging from the map, how would you describe the effect on Europe of multinational alliances?
2. **Analyze Motives** What motive did the two superpowers have for fighting surrogate or proxy wars?

Cold War Conflicts 1145

ENGLISH LANGUAGE LEARNERS

Make a Collage

1. The text in this segment mentions many different countries with which students may not be familiar: India, Egypt, Congo, Angola, Mozambique, and Indonesia. Each of these countries played a role in the Cold War.
2. Ask partners to choose one of these countries and use the Internet and library resources to find photographs, headlines, quotations, and other artifacts concerning the country during the Cold War.
3. Have students make copies of the images they find or use colored markers to copy quotations and newspaper headlines. Then, have them work together to assemble a collage about their country and the events of the Cold War.
4. Encourage partners to share their finished collages with the entire class.

Objectives

You may wish to discuss the following questions with students to help them frame the content as they read.

- Should the United States sometimes engage in assassination? *Possible answer: Yes—it may save lives by ending despotic governments; No—United States should never condone murder.*
- Why was it hard for countries to remain nonaligned? *Possible answer: superpowers might pressure them, use propaganda, support opposing forces*

More About . . .

The Third World This term for the developing nations of Asia, Africa, and Latin America arose during the Cold War. It originally referred to nonaligned nations. The United States, Western European countries, and some of their allies comprised the First World. The Soviet Union, China, Cuba, and some of their allies represented the Second World. Today, these terms have mostly fallen out of usage.

ONLINE INTERACTIVE MAPS

Alignment of Nations During the Cold War

Have students explore the map using the interactive features and answer the associated questions.

Interpret Maps According to the map, which nation was not aligned with NATO or the Warsaw Pact in 1955? *Yugoslavia*

In print edition, see History in Depth feature.

Generalize Judging from the map, how would you describe the effect on Europe of multinational alliances? *Europe was pretty much split down the middle in its allegiance to the two superpowers.*

Analyze Motives What motive did the two superpowers have for fighting surrogate or proxy wars? *to stop the other superpower from gaining control of the country where the surrogate war was taking place*

ONLINE INTERACTIVE CHARTS

Major Strategies of the Cold War

Have students explore the chart and answer the associated question.

Interpret Charts According to the chart, the Cuban Missile Crisis is an example of which strategy? *Brinkmanship*

Objectives

You may wish to discuss the following questions with students to help them frame the content as they read.

- How did the U.S. policy toward Cuba backfire? *By supporting Batista, and then opposing Castro, the United States drove Cuba into the Soviet sphere.*
- What did the Cuban Missile Crisis reveal about the policy of the United States? *demonstrated United States would stand firm against Communist expansion*

More About . . .

The Sandinistas The Sandinista National Liberation Front was formed in 1961. It drew its support from students, workers, and peasants. The Sandinista government included non-Communists as well as Communists, although during the long civil war, many non-Communists dropped out of the party, allowing it to drift more into the Soviet camp. Even so, the Sandinistas never adopted the Soviet economic plan. Small and medium-sized farms and businesses remained private. Some political opposition was also tolerated, which ultimately allowed Nicaraguans to vote the Sandinistas out of power. They remained in opposition until Daniel Ortega won the presidency in 2006.

Fidel Castro After 1959, when he overthrew the Batista regime, Castro withstood numerous attempts to topple his regime through assassination, invasion, and economic pressure. Castro served as prime minister and president of Cuba from 1959–2008.

Kennedy's Reaction President Kennedy's reaction to the Cuban Missile Crisis was not one of diplomatic negotiation. His plan was to isolate Cuba in order to prevent more military shipments from the Soviet Union. His next move was to address the Soviets in a televised statement on the evening of October 22, 1962. A few days later, the Soviets agreed to remove the missiles.

READING CHECK
Summarize How did the superpowers try to influence Third World nations? *They offered military backing and aid, propaganda, and economic and technical assistance.*

READING CHECK (Print)
Analyze Motives Why did some nations choose to be nonaligned? *They wanted to remain neutral.*

Explore ONLINE!

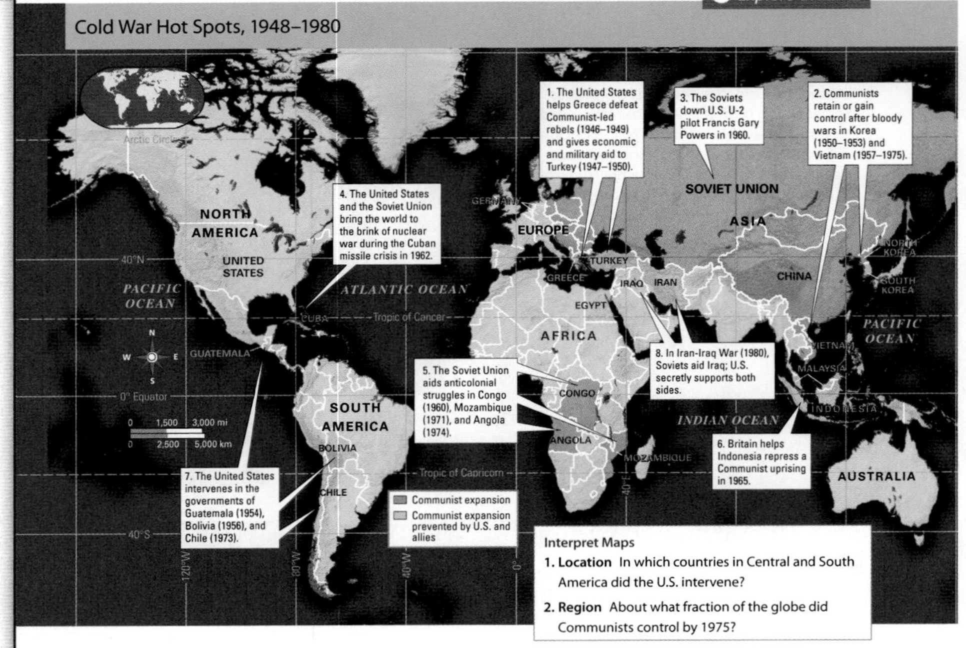

Interpret Maps
1. **Location** In which countries in Central and South America did the U.S. intervene?
2. **Region** About what fraction of the globe did Communists control by 1975?

players in the Cold War competition between the United States, the Soviet Union, and later, China. But not all Third World countries wished to play a role in the Cold War. For example, India vowed to remain neutral. Indonesia, a populous island nation in Southeast Asia, also struggled to stay uninvolved. In 1955, it hosted many leaders from Asia and Africa at the Bandung Conference. They met to form what they called a "third force" of independent countries, or **nonaligned nations**. Some nations, such as India and Indonesia, maintained their neutrality. Others took sides with the superpowers or played competing sides against each other. For example, Egypt first accepted Soviet aid to help build the Aswan High Dam and Soviet weapons for its conflicts with Israel. Later, Egypt switched allegiance to the United States following the 1973 Yom Kippur War.

Reading Check
Analyze Motives
Why did some nations choose to be nonaligned?

Confrontations in Latin America

After World War II, rapid industrialization, population growth, and a lingering gap between the rich and the poor led Latin American nations to seek aid from both superpowers. At the same time, many of these countries alternated between short-lived democracy and harsh military rule. U.S. involvement in Latin America began long before World War II.

ADVANCED/GIFTED

Hot Spot Outcomes

1. Tell students to use the Cold War Hot Spots map in this segment to identify two Cold War hot spots they want to learn more about.
2. Have students conduct research to determine the outcome of interventions by the United States and the Soviets in those two places.
3. Have student compare and contrast the outcomes and then present their findings to the group.

American businesses backed leaders who protected U.S. interests but who also often oppressed their people. After the war, communism and nationalistic feelings inspired revolutionary movements. These found enthusiastic Soviet support. In response, the United States provided military and economic assistance to anti-Communist dictators.

Fidel Castro and the Cuban Revolution In the 1950s, Cuba was ruled by an unpopular dictator, Fulgencio Batista, who had U.S. support. Cuban resentment led to a popular revolution, which overthrew Batista in January 1959. A young lawyer named **Fidel Castro** led that revolution. At first, many people praised Castro for bringing social reforms to Cuba and improving the economy. Yet Castro was a harsh dictator. He suspended elections, jailed or executed his opponents, and tightly controlled the press.

Castro nationalized U.S.-owned sugar mills and refineries. In response, President Eisenhower ordered an embargo on all trade with Cuba. Castro then turned to the Soviets for economic and military aid.

In 1960, the CIA began to train anti-Castro Cuban exiles. In April 1961, they invaded, landing in southwestern Cuba at the Bay of Pigs. However, the United States did not provide the hoped-for air support. Castro's forces easily defeated the invaders, humiliating the United States.

Nuclear Face-off: The Cuban Missile Crisis The failed Bay of Pigs invasion convinced Soviet leader Nikita Khrushchev that the United States would not resist Soviet expansion in Latin America. So, in July 1962, Khrushchev secretly began to build 42 missile sites in Cuba. In October, an American spy plane discovered the sites. President John F. Kennedy declared that missiles so close to the U.S. mainland were a threat. He demanded their removal and also announced a naval blockade of Cuba. Kennedy explained his actions to the American people and the rest of the world in a televised address:

> *"Our policy has been one of patience and restraint, as befits a peaceful and powerful nation which leads a worldwide alliance. We have been determined not to be diverted from our central concerns by mere irritants and fanatics. But now further action is required, and it is under way; and these actions may only be the beginning. We will not prematurely or unnecessarily risk the costs of worldwide nuclear war in which even the fruits of victory would be ashes in our mouth; but neither will we shrink from that risk at any time it must be faced."*
>
> —John F. Kennedy, October 22, 1962

Castro protested that his country was being used as a pawn and that he did not intend for Cuba to get involved in the Cold War. But Castro and Cuba were deeply involved. Kennedy's demand for the removal of Soviet missiles put the United States and the Soviet Union on a collision course. People around the world feared nuclear war. Fortunately, Khrushchev agreed to remove the missiles in return for a U.S. promise not to invade Cuba.

ONLINE DOCUMENT-BASED INVESTIGATION

Cuban Missile Crisis

President Kennedy gave this televised speech at the height of the crisis. Students can click on the audio button beneath the historical source to hear the excerpt read aloud.

Analyze Sources How does Kennedy feel about a nuclear war, even if victorious? *He thinks the costs of war will be too high ("ashes in our mouth"), even if victorious.*

DOCUMENT-BASED INVESTIGATION HISTORICAL SOURCE

Cuban Missile Crisis

Kennedy explained his actions to the American people and the rest of the world in a televised address:

ONLINE INTERACTIVE MAPS

Cold War Hot Spots, 1948–1975

Have students explore the map using the interactive features and answer the associated questions.

Interpret Maps Where is Guatemala in relation to the United States? *south of the United States*

In print edition, see map of same title.

Location In which countries in Central and South America did the U.S. intervene? *Guatemala, Bolivia, and Chile*

Region About what fraction of the globe did Communists control by 1975? *about one-third*

BIOGRAPHY

Fidel Castro

Have students read the biography of Fidel Castro, the Communist political leader of Cuba who helped overthrow the Cuban government in 1959 and seized control of the country, exercising total control of the government and economy.

ONLINE INTERACTIVE MAPS

Cuba and Nicaragua

Have students explore the map and answer the associated question.

Interpret Maps According to the map, where is Nicaragua? *southwest of Cuba.*

BIOGRAPHY

Fidel Castro
(1926–2016)

The son of a wealthy Spanish-Cuban farmer, Fidel Castro became involved in politics at the University of Havana. He first tried to overthrow the Cuban dictator, Batista, in 1953. He was imprisoned but made this vow to continue the struggle for independence:

"Personally, I am not interested in power, nor do I envisage assuming it at any time. All that I will do is to make sure that the sacrifices of so many compatriots should not be in vain."

Despite this declaration, Castro ruled Cuba as a dictator for nearly 50 years. In 2008, his younger brother, Raul Castro, succeeded him as president.

The resolution of the Cuban Missile Crisis left Castro completely dependent on Soviet support. In exchange for this support, Castro backed Communist revolutions in Latin America and Africa. Soviet aid to Cuba, however, ended abruptly with the breakup of the Soviet Union in 1991. This loss dealt a crippling blow to the Cuban economy. Eventually, Castro loosened state control of Cuba's economy and sought better relations with other countries.

Civil War in Nicaragua Just as the United States had supported Batista in Cuba, it had also funded the Nicaraguan dictatorship of **Anastasio Somoza** and his family since 1933. In 1979, Communist Sandinista rebels toppled Somoza's son. Both the United States and the Soviet Union initially gave aid to the Sandinistas and their leader, **Daniel Ortega** (awr•TAY•guh). The Sandinistas, however, gave assistance to other Marxist rebels in nearby El Salvador. To help the El Salvadoran government fight those rebels, the United States supported Nicaraguan anti-Communist forces called the Contras or *contrarevolucionarios*.

The civil war in Nicaragua lasted more than a decade and seriously weakened the country's economy. In 1990, President Ortega agreed to hold free elections, the first in the nation's history. Violeta Chamorro, a reform candidate, defeated him. The Sandinistas also lost elections in 1996 and 2001. However, Ortega won the election once again in 2006 and returned to power.

Reading Check
Analyze Motives
Why did the U.S. switch its support from the Sandinistas to the Contras in Nicaragua?

Coup in Guatemala In 1950, the people of Guatemala elected a new president, Jacobo Arbenz, who promised economic reforms. When Arbenz began a land reform program and nationalized foreign industries in his country, the United States became concerned that his government might turn Communist. President Eisenhower and CIA director Allen Dulles devised a two-part strategy to overthrow Arbenz. First, the CIA began a propaganda campaign that turned the people and the army against their leader. Then, in June 1954, a group of CIA-backed troops led a rebellion and forced Arbenz to flee the country. The U.S.-chosen leader of the military coup, Carlos Castillo Armas, assumed control of the government and promoted American interests in Guatemala.

Confrontations in the Middle East

As the map on page 1146 shows, Cold War confrontations continued to erupt around the globe. The oil-rich Middle East attracted both superpowers.

Religious and Secular Values Clash in Iran Throughout the Middle East, oil industry wealth fueled a growing clash between traditional Islamic values and modern Western materialism. In no country was this cultural conflict more dramatically shown than in Iran (Persia before 1935). After World War II, Iran's leader, Shah Mohammed Reza Pahlavi (PAH•luh•vee), embraced Western governments and wealthy Western oil companies. Iranian nationalists resented these foreign alliances and united under Prime Minister Muhammed Mossadeq (moh•sah•DEHK). They nationalized a British-owned oil company and, in 1953, forced the shah to flee. Fearing Iran might turn to the Soviets for support, the United States helped restore the shah to power.

The United States Supports Secular Rule With U.S. support, the shah westernized his country. By the end of the 1950s, Iran's capital, Tehran, featured gleaming skyscrapers, foreign banks, and modern factories. Millions of Iranians, however, still lived in extreme poverty. The shah tried to weaken the political influence of Iran's conservative Muslim leaders, known as ayatollahs (eye•uh•TOH•luhz), who opposed Western influences. The leader of this religious opposition, **Ayatollah Ruholla Khomeini** (koh•MAY•nee), was living in exile. Spurred by his tape-recorded messages, Iranians rioted in every major city in late 1978. Faced with overwhelming opposition, the shah fled Iran in 1979. A triumphant Khomeini returned to establish an Islamic state and to export Iran's militant form of Islam.

Khomeini's Anti-U.S. Policies Strict adherence to Islam was at the core of Khomeini's domestic policies. But hatred of the United States, because of U.S. support for the shah, was at the heart of his foreign policy. In 1979, with the ayatollah's blessing, young Islamic revolutionaries seized the U.S. embassy in Tehran. They took more than 60 Americans hostage and demanded the United States force the shah to face trial. Most hostages remained prisoners for 444 days before being released in January 1981.

Objectives

You may wish to discuss the following questions with students to help them frame the content as they read.

- Was communism the cause of the ouster of Shah Pahlavi from Iran? *No. Nationalism and protecting traditional Islamic values were.*
- Could the United States have gained Khomeini's support by withdrawing aid to the shah? *No. He opposed the threat of Western influence and values on Islamic values.*

More About . . .

Connect to Geography Use a world map or globe to point out the region known as the Middle East. These countries are roughly located where Africa, Europe, and Asia meet. The name for this region dates back to the early 20th century and was used to distinguish the area from the "Near East" (centered around Turkey) and the "Far East" (centered around China).

ONLINE HISTORICAL SOURCES

Ayatollah Khomeini

Invite students to watch the video and answer the associated question.

Analyze Sources Why was Iran important to American foreign policy? *Losing Iran meant losing oil and influence.*

READING CHECK

Analyze Motives Why did the United States switch its support from the Sandinistas to the Contras in Nicaragua? *The Sandinistas were supporting socialist rebels in El Salvador.*

COLLABORATIVE LEARNING

Cold War Timeline

1. Display a timeline that stretches from 1953 to 1996. Above the timeline, write the heading Latin America. Below the timeline, write the heading Middle East.
2. Have students brainstorm and add three or four events to the timeline for each region.
3. Alternatively, have students work in small groups and use print and Internet resources to complete the timeline as much as they can.

BIOGRAPHY

Ayatollah Khomeini

Have students read the biography of Ayatollah Khomeini, the Iranian political and religious leader who led a revolution to overthrow the shah of Iran's government in 1979 and then ruled the country for the next ten years.

NOW & THEN

The Taliban

The Taliban had little support outside of Afghanistan. Most countries opposed their policy toward women, their severe criminal punishments, and their destruction of non-Islamic art relics. One of the worst crimes against non-Islamic art was the destruction of two giant Buddhas that dated from the fourth and fifth centuries.

ONLINE INTERACTIVE MAPS

Iran and Afghanistan

Have students explore the map and answer the associated question.

Interpret Maps According to the map, where is Afghanistan? *east of Iran*

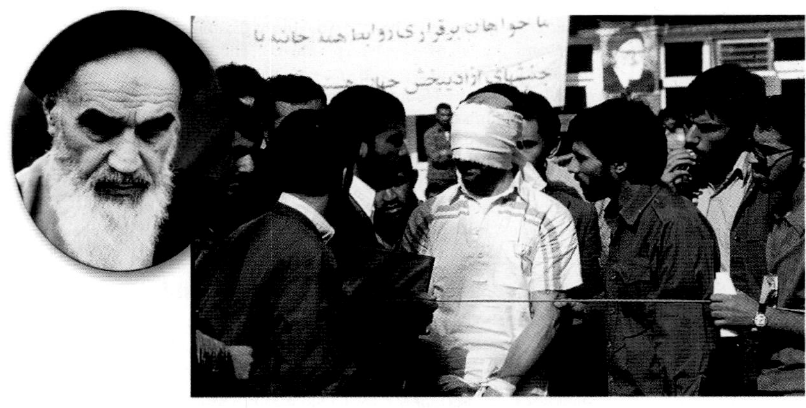

Ayatollah Khomeini (inset) supported the taking of U.S. hostages by Islamic militants in Tehran in 1979.

Khomeini encouraged Muslim radicals elsewhere to overthrow their secular governments. Intended to unify Muslims, this policy heightened tensions between Iran and its neighbor and territorial rival, Iraq. A military leader, Saddam Hussein (hoo•SAYN), governed Iraq as a secular state.

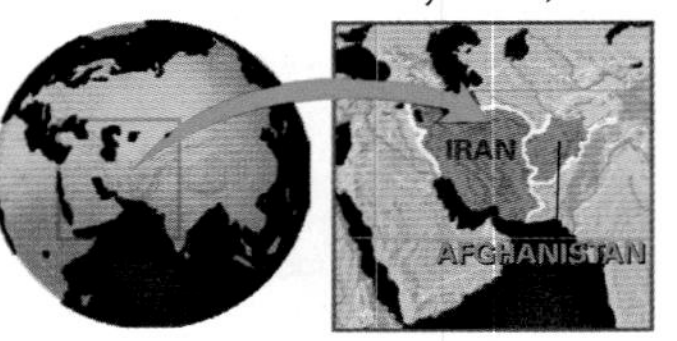

War broke out between Iran and Iraq in 1980. The United States secretly gave aid to both sides because it did not want the balance of power in the region to change. The Soviet Union, on the other hand, had long been a supporter of Iraq. A million Iranians and Iraqis died in the war before the United Nations negotiated a ceasefire in 1988.

The Superpowers Face Off in Afghanistan For several years following World War II, Afghanistan maintained its independence from both the neighboring Soviet Union and from the United States. In the 1950s, however, Soviet influence in the country began to increase. In the late 1970s, a Muslim revolt threatened to topple Afghanistan's Communist regime. This revolt led to a Soviet invasion in 1979.

The Soviets expected to prop up the Afghan Communists and quickly withdraw. Instead, just like the United States in Vietnam, the Soviets found themselves stuck. And like the Vietcong in Vietnam, rebel forces outmaneuvered a military superpower. Supplied with American weapons, the Afghan rebels, called *mujahideen*, or holy warriors, fought on.

Now and Then

The Taliban

Islamic religious students, or taliban, were among the *mujahideen* rebels who fought the Soviet occupation of Afghanistan. Various groups of students loosely organized themselves during a civil war among *mujahideen* factions that followed the Soviet withdrawal in 1989.

In 1996, one of these groups, called the Taliban, seized power and established an Islamic government. They imposed a repressive rule especially harsh on women and failed to improve people's lives. They also gave sanctuary to international Islamic terrorists. In 2001, an antiterrorist coalition led by the United States drove them from power. However, they have regrouped and have been fighting NATO forces in Afghanistan since 2006.

Reading Check
Contrast Which leader in Iran pushed for modernization? Which wanted to establish a more traditional culture? How did this lead to tensions within the country?

The United States had armed the rebels because they considered the Soviet invasion a threat to Middle Eastern oil supplies. President Jimmy Carter warned the Soviets against any attempt to gain control of the Persian Gulf. To protest the invasion, he stopped U.S. grain shipments to the Soviet Union and ordered a U.S. boycott of the 1980 Moscow Olympics. In the 1980s, a new Soviet president, Mikhail Gorbachev, acknowledged the war's devastating costs. He withdrew all Soviet troops by 1989. By then, internal unrest and economic problems were tearing apart the Soviet Union itself.

Lesson 4 Assessment

1. **Organize Information** Which confrontation had the most lasting significance?

Country	Conflict
Cuba	
Nicaragua	
Iran	

2. **Key Terms and People** For each key term or person in the lesson, write a sentence explaining its significance.
3. **Draw Conclusions** What reasons might have prompted Daniel Ortega to permit free elections in Nicaragua in 1990?
4. **Analyze Causes** What differences between the leaders of Iran and Iraq led to war in 1980?
5. **Make Inferences** What advantages and disadvantages might being nonaligned have offered a developing nation during the Cold War?
6. **Compare** What similarities do you see among U.S. actions in Nicaragua, Cuba, and Iran?
7. **Analyze Causes** What were the reasons that Islamic fundamentalists took control of Iran?

READING CHECK

Compare In what ways were U.S. involvement in Vietnam and Soviet involvement in Afghanistan similar? *Both superpowers became mired in long, bloody struggles with guerrilla forces who ultimately defeated them.*

READING CHECK (Print)

Contrast Which leader in Iran pushed for modernization? Which wanted to establish a more traditional culture? How did this lead to tensions within the country? *Shah Reza Pahlavi wanted to modernize and secularize Iran. Ayatollah Khomeini wanted to restore strict religious rule and reduce Western influence in the country. These differences led to coups in 1954 (restoring the shah) and again in 1979 (overthrowing the shah).*

Print Assessment

1. **Organize Information** Which confrontation had the most lasting significance? *Possible answer: Cuba because of its proximity to the United States and the duration.*
2. **Key Terms and People** For each key term or person in the lesson, write a sentence explaining its significance. *Explanation of the lesson's key terms can be found on the following pages: Third World, p. 1144; nonaligned nations, p. 1146; Fidel Castro, p. 1147; Anastasio Somoza, p. 1148; Daniel Ortega, p. 1148; Ayatollah Ruhollah Khomeini, p. 1149.*
3. **Draw Conclusions** What reasons might have prompted Daniel Ortega to permit free elections in Nicaragua in 1990? *Possible answer: country's economy was seriously weakened; Ortega thought he could win*
4. **Analyze Causes** What differences between the leaders of Iran and Iraq led to war in 1980? *Ayatollah Khomeini led Iran with a religious government. Saddam Hussein led Iraq with a secular government.*
5. **Make Inferences** What advantages and disadvantages might being nonaligned have offered a developing nation during the Cold War? *Advantages—control over own politics and economies; ability to accept help from either side; Disadvantages—lack of economic and military support from superpowers*
6. **Compare** What similarities do you see among U.S. actions in Nicaragua, Cuba, and Iran? *United States supported dictators who were overthrown by popular uprisings. It intervened in all three countries to protect its interests—a takeover by Communist Sandinistas in Nicaragua and by Castro in Cuba, and loss of vital oil supplies from Iran.*
7. **Analyze Causes** What were the reasons that Islamic fundamentalists took control of Iran? *wanted to return to traditional values; they were opposed to Western influences*

Online Assessment

1. What did India and Indonesia have in common during the Cold War?
   - They were both nonaligned countries.
   - They both received aid from the Soviet Union.
   - They were both favorable to the United States.
   - They both wanted to host conferences about nuclear weapons.

   Alternate Question *Select the answer choice from the drop-down list to complete the sentence correctly.*
   During the Cold War, some countries joined with the United States and others joined with the Soviet Union. However, some, like *India and Indonesia*, chose to stay neutral and were called the nonaligned countries.

2. What is the primary reason that the United States funded Batista in Cuba and Somoza in Nicaragua?
   - to help the countries stay nonaligned
   - to allow the countries to educate their populations
   - to prevent the countries from becoming Communist
   - to give the countries a chance to build a nuclear arsenal

   Alternate Question *Select the answer choice from the drop-down list to complete the sentence correctly.*
   The United States wanted to prevent its neighbors in the Americas from *becoming Communist*, so the United States provided funding in an effort to keep certain leaders in power.

3. Why did the United States secretly fund both Iraq and Iran during the war between the two countries in 1980?
   - The United States wanted the Cold War to stay out of the region.
   - The United States wanted the two countries to fight the Soviet Union.
   - The United States wanted the two countries to be able to still produce oil.
   - The United States wanted the balance of power in the region to remain the same.

   Alternate Question *Select the answer choice from the drop-down list to complete the sentence correctly.*
   In 1980, the nations of Iran and Iraq went to war with each other. The United States *funded both sides*, in order to maintain the balance of power in the region.

4. **Elaborate** What strategies did both the United States and the Soviet Union use to gain influence among Third World countries?

   Possible answer: Both the United States and the Soviet Union used aid as a way to gain favor in various Third World countries. The United States built schools, gave military aid, set up programs to combat poverty, and sent volunteer workers to help as needed. The Soviet Union offered military support and technical assistance along with economic aid. Both of the countries also employed covert activities and backed wars of revolution, liberation, and counterrevolution.

5. **Draw Conclusions** What was the Cuban Missile Crisis and why was the resolution of the crisis so important for the world?

   Possible answer: In 1962, the Soviet Union's leader Khrushchev secretly began building missile sites in Cuba. When the United States found out about it, it ordered the Soviets to stop. President Kennedy also ordered a naval blockade around Cuba and said it would not be removed until the missile program was halted. This became an extremely tense time between the United States and the Soviet Union, and a nuclear war between the two nations could have easily resulted. Fortunately, the two countries were able to come to an agreement and no missiles were fired.

6. **Compare and Contrast** How was Iran different under the shah's rule versus under Khomeini's rule?

   Possible answer: The shah wanted to westernize Iran. Under his rule, the country prospered. Tehran had gleaming skyscrapers, foreign banks, and modern factories. However, millions of Iranians were still extremely poor. The shah began to be quite unpopular. Under Khomeini's rule, the people had to strictly adhere to Islamic teachings. At the heart of Khomeini's foreign policy was a hatred for the United States, because the United States had supported the shah. Khomeini encouraged radical Muslims around the world to overthrow their secular governments.

Lesson 5 Planner

The Cold War Thaws

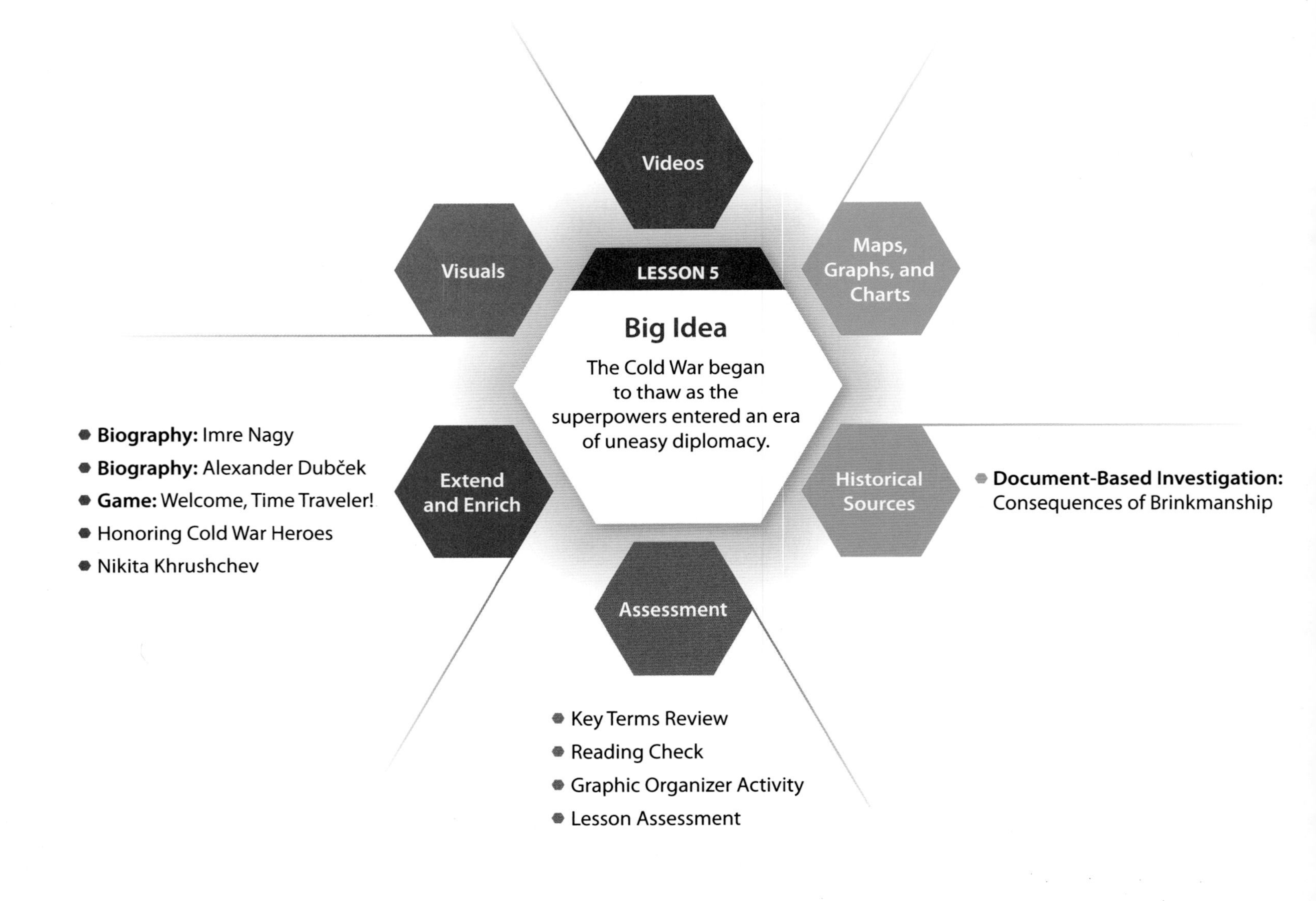

Extend and Enrich:

- **Biography:** Imre Nagy
- **Biography:** Alexander Dubček
- **Game:** Welcome, Time Traveler!
- Honoring Cold War Heroes
- Nikita Khrushchev

Historical Sources:

- **Document-Based Investigation:** Consequences of Brinkmanship

Assessment:

- Key Terms Review
- Reading Check
- Graphic Organizer Activity
- Lesson Assessment

Online Lesson 5 Enrichment Activities

Honoring Cold War Heroes

Testimonial Students write a testimonial honoring a Cold War figure they admire. The testimonial should honor the person's contributions to history and explain why the student admires this person. Students should incorporate visual details if possible and be written in a tone that conveys the personality of the figure.

Nikita Khrushchev

Biography Students read about Nikita Khrushchev and his leadership of the Soviet Union. Then they consider whether they think Khrushchev's brash style helped or hindered him throughout his life and career. Students should explain and justify their ideas.

Teach the Big Idea

1. **Whole Class Open/Introduction** Ask students if Stalin's name belongs on a list of famous bullies. Point out that real-life bullies can be punished, although not always in their lifetime.
2. **Direct Teach** Read the Big Idea: *The Cold War began to thaw as the superpowers entered an era of uneasy diplomacy*. Review the following lesson objectives with students to aid in their understanding of the Big Idea.
   - Analyze Soviet domination of Eastern Europe and the Soviet Union–China split.
   - Trace the origins of détente and its effects on the Cold War.
   - Describe the renewal of Cold War tensions in the 1980s.
3. **Whole Group Close/Reflect** During the Cold War, many events changed the way people looked at the world. Write a brief essay about key events and how they changed common people's lives and ideas.

ONLINE DOCUMENT-BASED INVESTIGATION

Cold War Conflicts

Consequences of Brinkmanship is the fifth of five document-based investigations that students will analyze in the Cold War Conflicts module. President Kennedy's CIA director John McCone predicted the potential for a major war with the Soviet Union. Students can click on the audio button beneath the historical source to hear the excerpt read aloud.

ONLINE GRAPHIC ORGANIZER

The Cold War Thaws

As students read the lesson, have them use the graphic organizer to take notes. Students can review their graphic organizer notes at the end of the lesson to answer the following question.

Draw Conclusions What do you consider the most significant reason for the collapse of détente? *Détente collapsed because of refusal to ratify SALT II, Soviet invasion of Afghanistan, and the SDI.*

ONLINE LESSON FLIP CARDS

Review Key Terms and People

Students can use the flip cards in the Lesson Review at any time to review the lesson's key terms and people: *Nikita Khrushchev, Leonid Brezhnev, John F. Kennedy, Lyndon Johnson, détente, Richard M. Nixon, SALT, Ronald Reagan,* and *Margaret Thatcher.*

Lesson 5

The Cold War Thaws

The Big Idea
The Cold War began to thaw as the superpowers entered an era of uneasy diplomacy.

Why It Matters Now
The United States and the countries of the former Soviet Union continue to cooperate and maintain a cautious peace.

Key Terms and People
Nikita Khrushchev
Leonid Brezhnev
John F. Kennedy
Lyndon Johnson
détente
Richard M. Nixon
SALT
Ronald Reagan
Margaret Thatcher

Setting the Stage

In the postwar years, the Soviet Union kept a firm grip on its satellite countries in Eastern Europe. These countries were Poland, Czechoslovakia, Hungary, Romania, Bulgaria, Albania, and East Germany. (Yugoslavia had broken away from Soviet control in 1948, although it remained Communist.) The Soviet Union did not allow them to direct and develop their own economies. Instead, it insisted that they develop industries to meet Soviet needs. These policies greatly hampered Eastern Europe's economic recovery.

Soviet Policy in Eastern Europe and China

More moderate Soviet leaders came to power after Stalin's death in 1953. They allowed satellite countries somewhat more independence, as long as they remained allied with the Soviet Union. During the 1950s and 1960s, however, growing protest movements in countries such as Poland (in 1952), Hungary (in 1956), and Czechoslovakia (in 1968) threatened the Soviet grip on the region. The Soviets clamped down hard on these protests. In addition, increasing tensions with China also diverted Soviet attention and forces.

Destalinization and Rumblings of Protest After Stalin died, **Nikita Khrushchev** became the dominant Soviet leader. In 1956, the shrewd, tough Khrushchev denounced Stalin for jailing and killing loyal Soviet citizens. His speech signaled the start of a policy called *destalinization*, or purging the country of Stalin's memory. Workers destroyed monuments of the former dictator. Khrushchev called for "peaceful competition" with capitalist states.

But this new Soviet outlook did not change life in the satellite countries. Their resentment at times turned to active protest. In October 1956, for example, the Hungarian army

1152 Module 29

COLLABORATIVE LEARNING

Cold War Debate

1. Divide students into three groups, and assign each group one of the general events mentioned in this lesson: destalinization in Eastern Europe, détente, and the collapse of détente.
2. Explain to students that they will take part in a class debate and argue that their assigned event had the most significant impact on the Cold War.
3. Encourage students to conduct additional online research, if necessary. Students should work together to identify key events, main ideas, and important people. They should also work together to form a persuasive argument for why their event was so influential.
4. Act as moderator for a class debate among all three groups. Ensure the debate remains civil and respectful and that all students who wish to contribute have an opportunity to do so.

joined protesters in an attempt to overthrow Hungary's Soviet-controlled government. Storming through the capital, Budapest, mobs waved Hungarian flags with the Communist hammer-and-sickle emblem cut out. "From the youngest child to the oldest man," one protester declared, "no one wants communism."

A popular and liberal Hungarian Communist leader named Imre Nagy (IHM•ray-nahj) formed a new government. Nagy promised free elections and demanded Soviet troops leave. In response, Soviet tanks and infantry entered Budapest in November. Thousands of Hungarian freedom fighters armed themselves with pistols and bottles but were overwhelmed. A pro-Soviet government was installed, and Nagy was eventually executed.

The Revolt in Czechoslovakia Despite the show of force in Hungary, Khrushchev lost prestige in his country as a result of the Cuban Missile Crisis in 1962. In 1964, party leaders voted to remove him from power. His replacement, **Leonid Brezhnev**, quickly adopted repressive domestic

BIOGRAPHY

Imre Nagy
(1896–1958)

Imre Nagy was born into a peasant family in Hungary. During World War I, he was captured by the Soviets and recruited into their army. He then became a Communist.

Nagy held several posts in his country's Communist government, but his loyalty remained with the peasants. Because of his independent approach, he fell in and out of favor with the Soviet Union. In October 1956, he led an anti-Soviet revolt. After the Soviets forcefully put down the uprising, they tried and executed Nagy.

In 1989, after Communists lost control of Hungary's government, Nagy was reburied with official honors.

Czech demonstrators fight Soviet tanks in 1968.

Alexander Dubček
(1921–1992)

Alexander Dubček was the son of a Czech Communist Party member. He moved rapidly up through its ranks, becoming party leader in 1968.

Responding to the spirit of change in the 1960s, Dubček instituted broad reforms during the so-called Prague Spring of 1968. The Soviet Union reacted by sending tanks into Prague to suppress a feared revolt. The Soviets expelled Dubček from the party. He regained political prominence in 1989, when the Communists agreed to share power in a coalition government. When Czechoslovakia split into two nations in 1992, Dubček became head of the Social Democratic Party in Slovakia.

COLLABORATIVE LEARNING

Satellite Nations

1. Have students identify all of the Soviet satellite nations mentioned in this segment. Encourage students to conduct additional Internet research to identify others.
2. Distribute a blank world map to students and have them identify the satellite nations on the map and then trace the extent of Soviet influence throughout Europe and Asia.
3. Have students present their map to the whole group and use the visual to explain why it was so important for the Soviet Union to maintain control over these satellite nations.

Objectives

You may wish to discuss the following questions with students to help them frame the content as they read.

- Why was the Soviet Union determined to keep Hungary as a satellite? *to keep it as a buffer zone; to prevent other Eastern European nations from rebelling*
- How was "Prague Spring" a good name for Dubček's policies? *Freedom spread, or bloomed, in the spring of 1968, just as flowers bloom in the spring.*

More About . . .

The Brezhnev Doctrine Leonid Brezhnev's claim that the Soviet Union had a right to prevent its satellite countries from rejecting communism came to be known as the Brezhnev Doctrine. This policy was invoked as late as 1979 to justify the Soviet invasion of Afghanistan.

Imre Nagy and Alexander Dubček Imre Nagy and Alexander Dubček were unlikely heroes. Nagy seemed to be more of an idealistic bookworm than a man of action. Nevertheless, he not only agreed to lead the Hungarian uprising but also defended his country's bid for independence with his life. A Hungarian supporter said, "If his life was a question mark, his death was an answer." By contrast, Dubček played by Communist rules and rose steadily through the ranks. He revealed his reformist colors, however, in 1967 when he won the support of political and economic reformers. He granted greater freedom of expression to the press and in 1968 proposed a full-blown reform program designed to democratize the country.

BIOGRAPHY

Imre Nagy

Have students read the biography of Imre Nagy, the Hungarian Communist who led a revolt against the Soviet Union in 1956.

BIOGRAPHY

Alexander Dubček

Have students read the biography of Alexander Dubček, the Communist party leader of Czechoslovakia who instituted broad reforms during the Prague Spring of 1968.

Objectives

You may wish to discuss the following questions with students to help them frame the content as they read.

- Who was the Soviet leader who blinked? What happened to him? *Khrushchev; removed from power*
- How was the SALT I Treaty an example of realpolitik? *practical, flexible solution to arms race*

More About . . .

Tip for English Language Learners Read Secretary Rusk's statement and call attention to the metaphor "eyeball to eyeball . . . just blinked." Tell students that when two people confront each other, it's sometimes said they're standing eyeball to eyeball, or staring at each other. If one blinks, it's because that person has lost courage and given up.

ONLINE DOCUMENT-BASED INVESTIGATION

Consequences of Brinkmanship

President Kennedy's CIA director John McCone predicted the potential for a major war with the Soviet Union. Students can click on the audio button beneath the historical source to hear the excerpt read aloud.

Analyze Sources What consequences does CIA Director McCone see if the United States takes action against the Soviets? *increasing tensions, casualties, retaliation against the United States*

DOCUMENT-BASED INVESTIGATION HISTORICAL SOURCE

Consequences of Brinkmanship

READING CHECK

Analyze Issues Why was Nikita Khrushchev removed from power in 1964? *He lost face during the Cuban Missile Crisis of 1962.*

policies. The party enforced laws to limit such basic human rights as freedom of speech and worship. Government censors controlled what writers could publish. Brezhnev clamped down on those who dared to protest his policies. For example, the secret police arrested many dissidents, including Aleksandr Solzhenitsyn, winner of the 1970 Nobel Prize for literature. They then expelled him from the Soviet Union.

Brezhnev made clear that he would not tolerate dissent in Eastern Europe either. His policy was put to the test in early 1968. At that time, Czech Communist leader Alexander Dubček (DOOB•chehk) loosened controls on censorship to offer his country socialism with "a human face." This period of reform, when Czechoslovakia's capital bloomed with new ideas, became known as Prague Spring. However, it did not survive the summer. On August 20, armed forces from the Warsaw Pact nations invaded Czechoslovakia. Brezhnev justified this invasion by claiming the Soviet Union had the right to prevent its satellites from rejecting communism, a policy known as the Brezhnev Doctrine.

The Soviet-Chinese Split While many satellite countries resisted Communist rule, China was committed to communism. In fact, to cement the ties between Communist powers, Mao and Stalin had signed a 30-year treaty of friendship in 1950. Their spirit of cooperation, however, ran out before the treaty did.

The Soviets assumed the Chinese would follow Soviet leadership in world affairs. As the Chinese grew more confident, however, they resented being in Moscow's shadow. They began to spread their own brand of communism in Africa and other parts of Asia. In 1959, Khrushchev punished the Chinese by refusing to share nuclear secrets. The following year, the Soviets ended technical economic aid. The Soviet-Chinese split grew so wide that fighting broke out along their common border. After repeated incidents, the two neighbors maintained a fragile peace.

Reading Check
Analyze Issues Why was Nikita Khrushchev removed from power in 1964?

From Brinkmanship to Détente

In the 1970s, the United States and the Soviet Union finally backed away from the aggressive policies of brinkmanship that they had followed during the early postwar years. The superpowers slowly moved to lower tensions.

Brinkmanship Breaks Down The brinkmanship policy followed during the presidencies of Eisenhower, Kennedy, and Johnson led to one terrifying crisis after another. Though these crises erupted all over the world, they were united by a common fear. Nuclear war seemed possible. It was never certain, however, whether the possibility of nuclear attack was a real threat or was being used as a means to deter the other side from attacking.

In 1960, the U-2 incident prevented a meeting between the United States and the Soviet Union to discuss the buildup of arms on both sides. Then, during the administration of **John F. Kennedy** in 1962, the Cuban Missile Crisis made the superpowers' use of nuclear weapons a real

COLLABORATIVE LEARNING

Cold War Posters

1. Divide students into six groups. Have each group create a poster about a key Cold War event. Possible events include the following: 1956 Hungarian uprising, Prague Spring, Cuban Missile Crisis, expansion of the war in Vietnam, President Nixon's visit to China, Soviet invasion of Afghanistan, signing of the SALT I Treaty.
2. Have students provide a heading, slogan, or very brief caption for their posters. The posters can be a straightforward representation of the event, or they can present an editorial comment on the events.
3. Have students share responsibilities for presenting their posters to the whole group.

possibility. The crisis ended when Soviet ships turned back to avoid a confrontation at sea. "We're eyeball to eyeball," the relieved U.S. Secretary of State, Dean Rusk, said, "and I think the other fellow just blinked." Luckily, the United States and the world had avoided the potential for a major war that Kennedy's CIA Director John McCone predicted might occur:

> *"Consequences of action by the United States will be the inevitable 'spilling of blood' of Soviet military personnel. This will increase tension everywhere and undoubtedly bring retaliation against U.S. foreign military installations, where substantial U.S. casualties would result. . . ."*
>
> —John McCone, CIA director, in memo to President Kennedy

Tensions remained high. After the assassination of Kennedy in 1963, **Lyndon Johnson** assumed the presidency. Committed to stopping the spread of communism, President Johnson escalated U.S. involvement in the war in Vietnam.

The United States Turns to Détente Widespread popular protests wracked the United States during the Vietnam War. And the turmoil did not end with U.S. withdrawal. As it tried to heal its internal wounds, the United States backed away from its policy of direct confrontation with the Soviet Union. **Détente**, a policy of lessening Cold War tensions, replaced brinkmanship under **Richard M. Nixon**.

Vocabulary
détente a French word meaning "a loosening"

President Nixon's move toward détente grew out of a philosophy known as *realpolitik*. This term comes from the German word meaning "realistic politics." In practice, realpolitik meant dealing with other nations in a practical and flexible manner. While the United States continued to try to contain the spread of communism, the two superpowers agreed to pursue détente and to reduce tensions.

U.S. President Nixon visits China in 1972, accompanied by Chinese premier Zhou Enlai (left).

Nixon and Brezhnev Sign SALT and ABM Treaties Nixon's new policy represented a personal reversal as well as a political shift for the country. His rise in politics in the 1950s was largely due to his strong anti-Communist position. Twenty years later, he became the first U.S. president to visit Communist China. The visit made sense in a world in which three, not just two, superpowers eyed each other suspiciously. "We want the Chinese with us when we sit down and negotiate with the Russians," Nixon explained.

Three months after visiting Beijing in February 1972, Nixon visited the Soviet Union. After a series of meetings called the Strategic Arms Limitation Talks (**SALT**), Nixon and

GAME

Welcome, Time Traveler!

Have students play the game to test their knowledge of Cold War presidents by answering the questions.

Objectives

You may wish to discuss the following questions with students to help them frame the content as they read.

- What would have been two effects of the refusal of Congress to ratify SALT II? *Possible answer: expansion of nuclear arsenals; greater risk of nuclear war*
- How did SDI increase world tensions? *threatened détente and started new arms race*

More About . . .

Margaret Thatcher Margaret Thatcher served as British prime minister from 1979 to 1990. She was the longest-serving British prime minister of the 20th century, and she is the only woman to have held the office. Informally, she was known as the "Iron Lady" for her determination, bold leadership style, and firm grasp on politics. This name was given to her by a Soviet journalist.

READING CHECK

Synthesize Why did the United States adopt a policy of détente? *It was a practical solution, even though many U.S. leaders held anti-Communist positions.*

Brezhnev signed the SALT I Treaty. This five-year agreement limited to 1972 levels the number of intercontinental ballistic missiles (ICBMs) and submarine-launched missiles each country could have. The two sides also negotiated a treaty regulating the number of antiballistic missiles (ABMs) each country could maintain. ABMs could be used to destroy incoming ICBMs. The idea behind the ABM treaty was that with only a limited number of missiles, each country could protect only part of its territory. This would keep both sides fearful of each other and thus serve as a deterrent to nuclear war. In 1975, 33 nations joined the United States and the Soviet Union in signing a commitment to détente and cooperation, the Helsinki Accords.

The Collapse of Détente

Under Presidents Nixon and Gerald Ford, the United States improved relations with China and the Soviet Union. In the late 1970s, however, President Jimmy Carter was concerned over harsh treatment of protesters in the Soviet Union. This threatened to prevent a second round of SALT negotiations. In 1979, Carter and Brezhnev finally signed the SALT II agreement. When the Soviets invaded Afghanistan later that year, however, the U.S. Congress refused to ratify SALT II. Concerns mounted as more nations, including China and India, began building nuclear arsenals.

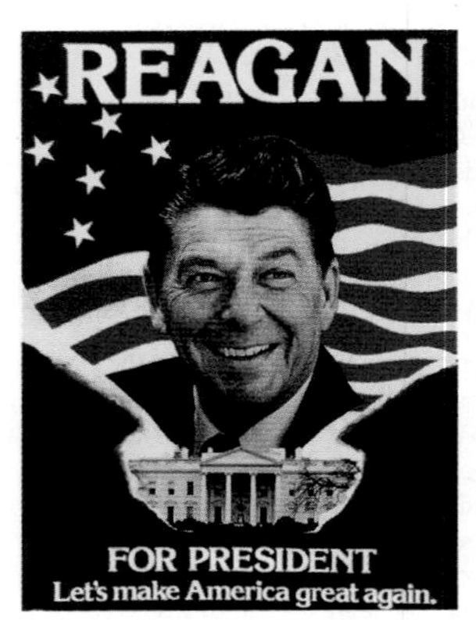

Ronald Reagan's 1980 political button highlights the strong patriotic theme of his campaign.

Reagan Takes an Anti-Communist Stance A fiercely anti-Communist U.S. president, **Ronald Reagan**, took office in 1981. His election was a high point in a new period in American politics known as the New Conservative or New Right era. The New Conservatives were opposed not only to communism but also to a variety of social and economic issues ranging from abortion to affirmative action (special treatment for minority members and women) to any increases in taxes.

Under Reagan, the United States continued to move away from détente. Reagan increased defense spending, putting both economic and military pressure on the Soviets. In 1983, Reagan also announced the Strategic Defense Initiative (SDI), a program to protect against enemy missiles. It was not put into effect but remained a symbol of U.S. anti-Communist sentiment. British prime minister **Margaret Thatcher**, who served as England's leader from 1979 to 1990, supported Reagan's policy. Her anti-Communist stance was so strong that Soviet reporters nicknamed her the "Iron Lady." Soon people in Great Britain also began using the nickname for their strong-willed leader.

Tensions increased as U.S. activities such as arming Nicaragua's Contras pushed the United States and Soviet Union further from détente. However, a change in Soviet leadership in 1985 brought a new policy toward the United States, economic and political changes in the Soviet Union, and

COLLABORATIVE LEARNING

Arms Control Treaties

1. Review with students the information in the text about SALT I and II. Have students work in pairs to write brief summaries of the information in the text about the talks.
2. Guide students in a discussion of the importance, effectiveness, and limitations of treaties that prevent or limit development of weapons and missiles. Have students take notes during the discussion.
3. Have students use the information in their written summaries and class discussion notes to write a paragraph supporting or opposing arms control treaties. Have students work in pairs to review their first-draft paragraphs and incorporate corrections into their final drafts.

the beginnings of a final thaw in the Cold War. This new policy, known as *perestroika* [pehr•ih•STROY•kuh], a Russian word meaning "restructuring," led to a reduction of the power of the Communist Party in the Soviet Union and an expansion of economic opportunities for private businesses there. The country even allowed Soviet republics to establish their own congresses and hold elections with a choice of candidates. Within a few years the Soviet Union would disband, and the Cold War would end. Meanwhile, developing countries in Asia, Africa, and Latin America continued their own struggles for independence.

Reading Check
Contrast In what ways did Nixon's and Reagan's policies toward the Soviet Union differ?

Lesson 5 Assessment

1. Organize Information What do you consider the most significant reason for the collapse of détente?

   I. Soviet Policy in Eastern Europe and China
      A.
      B.
   II. From Brinkmanship to Detente

2. Key Terms and People For each key term or person in the lesson, write a sentence explaining its significance.
3. Draw Conclusions Why did protests of Soviet satellite countries probably begin after Stalin's death and not before?
4. Analyze Motives Why was the policy of brinkmanship replaced?
5. Develop Historical Perspective In view of Soviet policies toward Eastern Europe in the postwar era, what reasons did people in Eastern Europe have for resistance?
6. Evaluate Decisions Do you think it was a wise political move for President Nixon to visit Communist China and the Soviet Union? Why or why not?
7. Recognize Effects What was the result of Reagan's move away from détente?

READING CHECK

Contrast In what ways did Nixon's and Reagan's policies toward the Soviet Union differ? *Nixon pursued a policy of détente, or easing of tensions. Reagan brought tensions to a new height.*

Print Assessment

1. **Organize Information** What do you consider the most significant reason for the collapse of détente? *Possible answer: Détente collapsed because of refusal to ratify SALT II, Soviet invasion of Afghanistan, and SDI.*
2. **Key Terms and People** For each key term or person in the lesson, write a sentence explaining its significance. *Explanation of the lesson's key terms can be found on the following pages: Nikita Khrushchev, p. 1152; Leonid Brezhnev, p. 1153; John F. Kennedy, p. 1154; Lyndon Johnson, p. 1155; détente, p. 1155; Richard M. Nixon, p. 1155; SALT, p. 1155; Ronald Reagan, p. 1156; Margaret Thatcher, p. 1156.*
3. **Draw Conclusions** Why did protests of Soviet satellite countries probably begin after Stalin's death and not before? *Possible answer: Stalin clamped down on protests; Soviet leaders after Stalin were more moderate and allowed satellite countries more independence.*
4. **Analyze Motives** Why was the policy of brinkmanship replaced? *United States decided to reduce tensions*
5. **Develop Historical Perspective** In view of Soviet policies toward Eastern Europe in the postwar era, what reasons did people in Eastern Europe have for resistance? *absence of freedom; subordination to Communist control and Soviet interests*
6. **Evaluate Decisions** Do you think it was a wise political move for Nixon to visit Communist China and the Soviet Union? Why or why not? *Possible answer: Wise—Nuclear war threatened world. China could not be ignored. Unwise—Visit hurt efforts to contain communism*
7. **Recognize Effects** What was the result of Reagan's move away from détente? *Possible answer: Tensions increased between the superpowers. The United States began a weapons buildup.*

COLD WAR PERSONALITIES

Arms Control Treaties

Below Level Review with students the content of this lesson and point out world leaders who had an effect on the Cold War: Nikita Khrushchev, Leonid Brezhnev, John F. Kennedy, Richard Nixon, Ronald Reagan, Mao Zedong, and Margaret Thatcher. Help students name the country each represents, and challenge them to identify each person's views toward communism.

At Level Have students reread this lesson and identify four or five world leaders who had an effect on the Cold War. Ask students to work together and make a chart that shows the rulers, their countries, and their views toward communism. Encourage students to conduct additional research online.

Above Level Have students independently complete the At Level assignment. Then ask students to identify which leader was most committed to ending the Cold War. Could this person have done more than he or she did to end the Cold War? If so, what could he or she have done and how might that have changed history?

Online Assessment

1. What was Khrushchev's main goal when he took power in 1953?
   - to end the Cold War
   - to build missiles in Cuba
   - **to purge the country of Stalin's memory**
   - to allow democracy in satellite countries

   Alternate Question *Select the answer choice from the drop-down list to complete the sentence correctly.*
   When Khrushchev came to power in 1953, he enacted a policy called *destalinization* by which he aimed to purge the country of *Stalin's memory*.

2. What was significant about the Helsinki Accords?
   - The countries that signed it refused to engage in détente.
   - The countries that signed it refused to send satellites into space.
   - **The countries that signed it agreed to cooperate with each other.**
   - The countries that signed it promised to remain neutral in the Cold War.

   Alternate Question *Select the answer choice from the drop-down list to complete the sentence correctly.*
   The Helsinki Accords was a monumental agreement signed by 33 nations who agreed to participate in *détente*.

3. Why was Margaret Thatcher known as the "Iron Lady"?
   - She disagreed with the domino effect.
   - She was an ardent supporter of détente.
   - **She took a hard stance against communism.**
   - She wanted more countries to build nuclear weapons.

   Alternate Question *Select the answer choice from the drop-down list to complete the sentence correctly.*
   Margaret Thatcher, the British prime minister, became known as the "Iron Lady" because she *was strong in her stance against communism*.

4. **Cause and Effect** What were Brezhnev's policies in the 1960s, and what were the results of these policies in the Soviet Union and its satellite countries?

   Possible answer: Brezhnev had very repressive domestic policies. He limited basic human rights such as freedom of speech and freedom of religion. He placed strict control on what writers could publish. He clamped down on anyone who protested his policies. He made it known that he wouldn't tolerate dissent in Eastern Europe. He invaded Czechoslovakia, for example, to squelch a reform movement started by the country's leader Alexander Dubček. Brezhnev justified this invasion by saying that the satellite countries were not allowed to reject communism. This became known as the Brezhnev Doctrine. The results of his policies were that the people of this region lived under very repressive conditions with very few individual liberties.

5. **Make Inferences** What was détente and why did Nixon most likely feel that this was a better policy than brinkmanship for handling the Cold War?

   Possible answer: Détente was a policy of lessening the Cold War tensions. This is in direct contrast to brinkmanship, which was an aggressive Cold War policy that pushed both sides to the edge of war. In brinkmanship, both sides garnered as many nuclear weapons as they could get. In Nixon's détente, the weaponry was purposefully limited on both sides. After decades of trying brinkmanship policies and having them ultimately be unsuccessful at ending the Cold War, Nixon likely felt that an opposite approach would be worth trying.

6. **Compare and Contrast** How were Reagan's policies different from Nixon's policies regarding the Cold War?

   Possible answer: Reagan moved away from détente, which was started by Nixon. Reagan increased defense spending, putting both economic and military pressures on the Soviets. He also started the Strategic Defense Initiative (SDI), which protected the United States from enemy missiles. Nixon wanted to decrease weapons in détente, while Reagan increased them.

Print Assessment

Key Terms and People

For each term or name below, briefly explain its connection to restructuring of the postwar world since 1945.

1. containment
2. Cold War
3. Mao Zedong
4. Cultural Revolution
5. 38th parallel
6. Vietnamization
7. Fidel Castro
8. Nikita Khrushchev
9. détente
10. SALT

Explanations of the significance of the lesson's key terms and people can be found on the following pages: containment, p. 1124; Cold War, p. 1126; Mao Zedong, p. 1130; Cultural Revolution, p. 1134; 38th parallel, p. 1136; Vietnamization, p. 1142; Fidel Castro, p. 1147; Nikita Khrushchev, p. 1152; détente, p. 1155; SALT, p. 1155.

Main Ideas

Use your notes and the information in the module to answer the following questions.

Cold War: Superpowers Face Off

1. What problems did the Americans and British have to overcome to carry out the Berlin Airlift? *They had to fly over Soviet-occupied territory, risk being shot down or crashing, they also had to keep enough supplies moving.*
2. Why did some Americans oppose the Truman Doctrine? *They believed the United States should not interfere with other nations' affairs, that it lacked resources to carry out a worldwide war on communism, and that economic aid might support dictators.*
3. How did the Soviet Union respond to the U.S. policy of brinkmanship? *It proved that it would go to the brink itself by building up a nuclear arsenal and competing aggressively in the arms race.*

Communists Take Power in China

4. Whom did the superpowers support in the Chinese civil war? *The United States supported the Nationalists. The Soviet Union supported the Communists.*
5. What were the results of Mao Zedong's Great Leap Forward and Cultural Revolution? *Both programs failed to create the powerful socialist nation Mao envisioned and actually weakened it.*

Wars in Korea and Vietnam

6. What effects did the Korean War have on Korea's land and its people? *Four million people died, and North and South Korea remained divided at the 38th parallel, as before the war.*
7. What difficulties did the U.S. Army face fighting the war inside Vietnam? *unfamiliar jungle terrain, guerrilla warfare, and lack of popular support for the South Vietnamese government they were bolstering*
8. What happened in Cambodia during and after the Vietnam War? *During the war, Cambodia was under seige by Communist rebels and bombed by the United States. After the war, Khmer Rouge set up a brutal communistic government.*

Module 29 Assessment

Key Terms and People

For each term or name below, briefly explain its connection to the restructuring of the postwar world since 1945.

1. containment
2. Cold War
3. Mao Zedong
4. Cultural Revolution
5. 38th parallel
6. Vietnamization
7. Fidel Castro
8. Nikita Khrushchev
9. détente
10. SALT

Main Ideas

Use your notes and the information in the module to answer the following questions.

Cold War: Superpowers Face Off

1. What problems did the Americans and British have to overcome to carry out the Berlin Airlift?
2. Why did some Americans oppose the Truman Doctrine?
3. How did the Soviet Union respond to the U.S. policy of brinkmanship?

Communists Take Power in China

4. Whom did the superpowers support in the Chinese civil war?
5. What were the results of Mao Zedong's Great Leap Forward and Cultural Revolution?

Wars in Korea and Vietnam

6. What effects did the Korean War have on Korea's land and its people?
7. What difficulties did the U.S. Army face fighting the war inside Vietnam?
8. What happened in Cambodia during and after the Vietnam War?

The Cold War Divides the World

9. Why did developing nations often align themselves with one of the two superpowers?
10. How did the Soviet Union respond to the Bay of Pigs invasion?
11. Why did the Ayatollah Khomeini have strong feelings against the United States government?

The Cold War Thaws

12. In what ways did Soviet actions hamper Eastern Europe's economic recovery after World War II?
13. What policies characterized realpolitik?
14. Which leaders were in office in the U.S. and Great Britain when détente collapsed in the 1980s?

ONLINE DOCUMENT-BASED INVESTIGATION

Cold War Conflicts

Have students complete and review all the DBI activities in **Part 1**.

Use this Analytical Essay Rubric to score students' work in **Part 2**.

RUBRIC Students' essays should

- present an analysis of the topic that is detailed and relevant
- develop the analysis logically, clearly, and accurately
- cite at least three sources of relevant text evidence from Part 1 in support of their analysis
- be organized into a distinct introduction, a main body consisting of several paragraphs, and a conclusion that sums up the main points

Write an Analytical Essay What was at stake for each side in the Cold War? Write an essay explaining the most significant goals and fears that motivated the United States, the Soviet Union, and their allies. Be sure to cite specific evidence from at least three sources in your response.

Module 29 Assessment, continued

Critical Thinking

1. Compare In what ways were the United States and the Soviet Union more similar than different?
2. Hypothesize How might the Cold War have proceeded differently if the United States had been economically and physically damaged in World War II?
3. Draw Conclusions Which two Cold War events do you think had the greatest impact on the U.S. decision to pursue détente?
4. Make Inferences Why do you think the United States and the Soviet Union chose cooperation in space after years of competition?
5. Compare and Interpret Maps Find a map that shows the borders of present-day European countries. Compare the map to the one on page 1123 showing borders of countries following World War II. Which countries' borders have changed significantly? In which regions do countries appear on the present-day map that did not exist in the late 1940s?

Engage with History

On page 1124, you saw a 1948 political cartoon predicting the negative impact of the Iron Curtain on Czechoslovakia. Then, on page 1153, you saw a visual image of Soviet repression of Czech protesters in 1968, 20 years later. Now that you have read the module, consider how people in countries in Europe and the rest of the world were impacted by the spread of communism during the Cold War.

Consider the following questions:

- Which countries were taken over by Communists against their people's wills?
- Which countries turned to Communist leaders to replace dictators or unpopular leaders?
- Which countries were divided as a result of Communist intervention?
- Which countries eventually chose to break from Communist control or influence?

Discuss these questions with a small group.

Focus on Writing

Study the information in the infographic on page 1145 describing how the Cold War was fought. Write a two-page persuasive essay on which strategy was the most successful for the United States and which was the most successful for the Soviet Union. Consider the following:

- who received foreign aid
- whether propaganda was successful
- how strong the military alliances were
- what was gained in surrogate wars

Multimedia Activity

Create an Interactive Timeline

In October 1962, President John F. Kennedy and his advisers had to defuse a potentially devastating nuclear standoff with the Soviet Union. Using books, the Internet, and other resources, create an interactive timeline of the Cuban Missile Crisis. Use graphics software to add maps and photographs. In addition to noting key dates, use the timeline to address some of the following:

- Who were members of Kennedy's inner circle during the crisis?
- What did Kennedy say about the events in his first public address to the nation?
- How did Soviet premier Nikita Khrushchev approach the crisis in Cuba?
- Which details did Americans learn only after the crisis had been resolved?

Essential Question ESSAY

Why did the Cold War never develop into a direct military conflict between the United States and the Soviet Union?

RUBRIC Students' essays should

- respond to the Essential Question with a specific position
- illustrate valid reasoning supporting their position
- cite persuasive evidence supporting their position
- identify key people, events, and/or turning points that demonstrate understanding of the module content
- be organized into a distinct introduction, main body, and conclusion

Write an argument answering this question. Your essay should explore the key people, events, and turning points in the history of the Cold War. Be sure to cite evidence to support your position, and organize your essay into an introduction, body, and conclusion.

Alternative Activity Instead of writing essays, address the Essential Question through activities such as holding debates, creating multimedia presentations, or writing journal entries.

The Cold War Divides the World

9. Why did developing nations often align themselves with one or the other superpower? *They needed financial aid and investment to help them industrialize, as well as a political and economic system on which to model their governments.*
10. How did the Soviet Union respond to the Bay of Pigs? *It secretly built 42 missile sites in Cuba.*
11. Why did the Ayatollah Khomeini have strong feelings against the United States government? *because the United States had supported the shah*

The Cold War Thaws

12. In what ways did Soviet actions hamper Eastern Europe's economic recovery after World War II? *It did not allow the Eastern Europeans to run their own economies or give them enough money to repair war damages. It also promoted industries necessary to the Soviets not to the satellite countries.*
13. What policies characterized realpolitik? *Dealing with nations in a realistic manner, which meant giving up long-held fear and hatred of communism. Pursuit of this policy helped ease Cold War tensions*
14. Which leaders were in office in the U.S. and Britain when détente collapsed in the 1980s? *Ronald Reagan and Margaret Thatcher*

Critical Thinking

1. **Compare** In what ways were the United States and the Soviet Union more similar than different? *Both the United States and Soviet Union wanted to be the dominant world power. Both became involved in conflicts to achieve that end. Both felt their political and economic systems were best.*
2. **Hypothesize** How might the Cold War have proceeded differently if the United States had been economically and physically damaged in World War II? *The Cold War might not have developed, because the Soviet Union might not have felt it necessary to build a wall of satellite nations to protect itself; the United States might not have had the resources to offer aid such as the Marshall Plan or Berlin Airlift.*
3. **Draw Conclusions** Which two Cold War events do you think had the greatest impact on the U.S. decision to pursue détente? *Possible answer: Vietnam War was the most significant event to change U.S. policy because the war failed to stop the spread of communism in Vietnam and it was opposed at home.*
4. **Make Inferences** Why do you think the United States and the Soviet Union chose cooperation in space after years of competition? *The costs of the space race to each country, and the fact that the United States and the Soviet Union wanted to step back from brinkmanship, led to cooperation.*

(continued)

Print Assessment *(continued)*

5. **Compare and Interpret Maps** Find a map that shows the borders of present-day European countries. Compare the map to the one on page 893 showing borders of countries following World War II. Which countries' borders have changed significantly? In which regions do countries appear on the present-day map that did not exist in the late 1940s? *Possible answer: Borders have changed in Germany and Czechoslovakia. New countries have been established within the former Yugoslavia and the former Soviet Union.*

Engage with History

On page 894, you saw a 1948 political cartoon predicting the negative impact of the Iron Curtain on Czechoslovakia. Then, on page 923, you saw a visual image of Soviet repression of Czech protesters in 1968, 20 years later. Now that you have read the module, consider how people in countries in Europe and the rest of the world were impacted by the spread of communism during the Cold War. Consider the following questions:

- Which countries were taken over by Communist regimes against the people's wills?
- Which countries turned to Communist leaders to replace dictators or unpopular leaders?
- Which countries were divided as a result of Communist intervention?
- Which countries eventually chose to break from Communist control or influence?

Discuss these questions with a small group.

Students should consider the consequences of their answers. Effects on the economy, on political support, on the military, and the society should be reviewed.

Focus on Writing

Study the information in the infographic on page 915 describing how the Cold War was fought. Write a two-page persuasive essay on which means was the most successful for the United States and which was most successful for the Soviet Union. Consider the following:

- who received foreign aid
- whether propaganda was successful
- how strong the military alliances were
- what was gained in surrogate wars

RUBRIC The persuasive essay should
- reflect the student's understanding of the basic concepts of the Cold War
- clearly state the selection for the United States and for the Soviet Union
- present supporting reasons for the selections

Multimedia Activity

Create an Interactive Timeline In October 1962, President John F. Kennedy and his advisers had to defuse a potentially devastating nuclear standoff with the Soviet Union. Using books, the Internet, and other resources, create an interactive timeline of the Cuban Missile Crisis. Use graphics software to add maps and photographs. In addition to noting key dates, use the timeline to address some of the following:

- Who were members of Kennedy's inner circle during the crisis?
- What did Kennedy say about the events in his first public address to the nation?
- How did Soviet premier Nikita Khrushchev approach the crisis in Cuba?
- What details did Americans learn only after the crisis had been resolved?

RUBRIC Interactive timelines should
- identify the key players
- explain the events
- give statements by Kennedy and Khrushchev
- discuss the problems faced
- explain the resolution

Online Assessment

1. *Select the button in the table to show whether each statement is true or false about the former Allied leaders after World War II.*

	True	False
Stalin believed that communism and capitalism could coexist with each other.	○	●
Truman didn't think that Stalin needed to allow free elections in Eastern Europe.	○	●
Stalin made certain promises at the Potsdam Conference that he ended up not keeping.	○	●
Churchill believed that the Soviets were trying to set up an "iron curtain" by taking over its neighbors.	●	○

2. What spurred Congress to fund the Marshall Plan?
   - ○ The Soviets started the Point Four program.
   - ● The Soviets seized power in Czechoslovakia.
   - ○ The Soviets divided Germany into four zones.
   - ○ The Soviets blocked Berlin to all ground transportation.

3. *Select the button in the table to show whether each characteristic is associated with* ***Sputnik*** *or Apollo.*

	Sputnik	Apollo
With this program, humans first landed on the moon.	○	●
Wehrner von Braun was influential with this program.	○	●
This was the first unmanned satellite to orbit the Earth.	●	○
This program was designed to explore and control space.	○	●
This was pushed into Earth's atmosphere by an intercontinental ballistic missile.	●	○
As a result of this, the United States poured money into science education.	●	○

4. What played a key role in the French, Russian, Chinese, and Cuban revolutions?
   - ○ the nobility's goals to control all of the land
   - ○ the monarchy's desire to decrease servants' wages
   - ● the peasants' desire to break down class structures
   - ○ the government's desire to guarantee individual liberties

5. *Drag the name of each leader to the description that matches it. Each leader will be used only once.*

religious leader who had to flee to India	●	Dalai Lama
leader who set up a Nationalist government	●	Jiang Jieshi
leader who sought to control all of his neighboring countries	●	Mao Zedong

6. *Drag the characteristic into the correct column to show whether it is associated with the Great Leap Forward or the Cultural Revolution.*

Great Leap Forward	Cultural Revolution
Larger collective farms, called communes, were deemed necessary.	Red Guard high school and college students led the movement.
Peasants worked the land together in communes of 25,000 people.	The goal was to achieve equality among peasants and workers.
Children were raised in communal nurseries.	Intellectual and artistic activities were considered dangerous.
No individual property ownership was allowed.	Thousands of intellectuals were imprisoned or executed.
Incentive to work was nonexistent since the state owned everything.	Colleges and schools were shut down.
	Intellectuals were ordered to purify themselves with hard labor.

7. What caused the Chinese to send 300,000 troops to North Korea?

○ The UN regained control of South Korea.

● The UN troops pushed North Koreans to the Yalu River.

○ The UN voted to support South Korea in the conflict with North Korea.

○ The UN decided to place the troops under the command of Douglas MacArthur.

8. *Drag the events into chronological order from top to bottom.*

○ France controls most of Indochina.

○ Ho Chi Minh joins the Communists and strikes against the French.

○ Protesters are imprisoned.

○ Japanese seize control of Vietnam.

○ French suffers a major defeat at Dien Bien Phu.

○ International peace conference meets in Geneva and divides Vietnam into north and south.

9. *Select the button in the table to show whether each statement about the Vietnam War is true or false.*

	True	False
Fewer than 100,000 U.S. troops served in Vietnam.	○	●
"Carpet bombing" helped garner U.S. support among Vietnamese peasants.	○	●
War protests on the home front eventually encouraged the end of the Vietnam War.	●	○
The United States got involved in Vietnam after two U.S. destroyers were attacked in the Gulf of Tonkin.	●	○

10. Which country did the Soviets provide aid to during the Cold War?

● Angola

○ Britain

○ France

○ Italy

11. Why did Eisenhower order an embargo against Cuba?

○ Castro shut down the Bay of Pigs.

○ Castro set up a naval blockade of Cuba.

○ Castro allowed the Soviets to build missile sites.

● Castro took over all of the U.S.-owned sugar mills.

12. *Select the button in the table to show whether each characteristic is associated with Afghanistan or Iran in the 1980s.*

	Afghanistan	Iran
This country was invaded by the Soviet Union in 1979.	●	○
The country's leader encouraged revolutionaries to take over the U.S. embassy.	○	●
This country received aid from the United States in its fight against the Soviets.	●	○
The invasion of this country led to the U.S. boycott of the 1980 Moscow Olympics.	●	○
Americans were held hostage here for 444 days.	○	●
War broke out between this country and Iraq in 1980.	○	●

13. What actions were evidence that Nikita Khrushchev did not approve of Joseph Stalin?

○ Khrushchev sent tanks into Budapest in November 1956.

○ Khrushchev called for "peaceful competition" with capitalist states.

○ Khrushchev lost power after the Cuban Missile Crisis.

● Khrushchev encouraged the destruction of all statues and monuments.

14. *Select the button in the table to show whether each statement is true or false about Nixon's policies during the Cold War.*

	True	False
Nixon based his ideas for détente on realpolitik.	●	○
Nixon felt that it was important to talk to the Soviet Union and China.	●	○
Nixon convinced the Cubans to back down during the Cuban Missile Crisis.	○	●
Nixon wanted the United States to have fewer missiles than the Soviet Union.	○	●

15. *Drag the characteristic into the correct column in the table to show whether it is associated with the United States, Great Britain, or the Soviet Union during the 1980s.*

United States	Great Britain	Soviet Union
This country elected a leader who was a New Conservative.	This country had a leader who became known as the "Iron Lady."	This country brought about a new policy that helped thaw the Cold War.

Online Multimedia Connections

In this Multimedia Connection, students will describe the sequence of events and understand the tension of the Cuban Missile Crisis. They will explain the significance of the crisis and chart the factors that escalated or diminished the nuclear war threat. Students will also explore firsthand accounts of the Cold War and compare the crisis to the current level of nuclear threat.

HISTORY

MULTIMEDIA CONNECTIONS

OCTOBER FURY: THE CUBAN MISSILE CRISIS

The Cuban missile crisis was perhaps the most dangerous event of the Cold War period. For several days in October 1962, the United States and the Soviet Union stood on the brink of nuclear war. The crisis began when the Soviet Union sent weapons, including nuclear missiles, to Cuba. It deepened when the United States blockaded Cuba to prevent the Soviets from delivering more missiles. With Soviet ships sailing toward the blockade, a confrontation seemed inevitable. However, at the last moment, the Soviet ships turned back and war was averted.

Explore the development and resolution of the Cuban missile crisis online. You can find a wealth of information, video clips, primary sources, activities, and more through your online textbook.

1159 MC1 MULTIMEDIA CONNECTIONS

HISTORY
Go online to view these and other HISTORY® resources.
Prelude to Crisis
Watch the video to learn about the buildup to the Cuban missile crisis.
UNITED KINGDOM
UNITED STATES
Getting Ready for War
Watch the video to see how the missiles in Cuba created tension between the United States and the Soviet Union.
FALLOUT SHELTER IN BASEMENT
Crisis Averted?
Watch the video to see how the Cuban missile crisis brought the United States and the Soviet Union to the brink of nuclear war.
Lessons Learned
Watch the video to learn about the impact of the Cuban missile crisis.
THE CUBAN MISSILE CRISIS 1159 MC2

Essential Question Preview

How can leaders of nations unify diverse populations of people?
Have students consider the Essential Question and capture their initial responses.

Explore the Essential Question

- Describe to students how political, economic, and social factors contributed to movements for independence.
- Explain to students that a leader's strategy or lack of strategy to unify diverse populations directly impacted the success or failure of independent movements.

Help students plan inquiries and develop their own supporting questions, such as:

What were some of the violent outcomes of religious strife in India?

Describe the political upheaval Burma experienced after gaining freedom.

You may want to assign students to write a short essay in response to the Essential Question when they complete the module. Encourage students to use their notes and responses to inform their essays.

Explore the Online Video

ANALYZE VIDEOS

Mahatma Gandhi
Invite students to watch the video to learn how Mahatma Gandhi helped poor Indians with no weapons fight powerful Britain for independence from British rule.

History Why did Gandhi break with Western custom and wear traditional clothing? *to protest the authority of Britain over the Indian people*

Module 30

The Colonies Become New Nations

Essential Question
How can leaders of nations unify diverse populations of people?

About the Photo: Citizens celebrate India's independence from British rule in the streets of Calcutta. After World War II, independence movements swept Africa and Asia. The emergence of new nations from European- and U.S.-ruled colonies brought a change in ownership of vital resources. It also brought new rights and opportunities for the people in these nations.

Explore ONLINE!

VIDEOS, including...
- Mahatma Gandhi: Pilgrim of Peace
- Mahatma Gandhi
- The Power of Tsunamis
- Blood Diamonds: Angola
- Yitzhak Rabin
- Suez Canal

- Document Based Investigations
- Graphic Organizers
- Interactive Games
- Carousel: Changing Times in Southeast Asia
- Carousel: Signs of Hope

In this module, you will learn about how nations and peoples around the world struggled to gain their independence from colonial powers.

What You Will Learn ...

1160 Module 30

Lesson 1 Big Idea

New nations emerged from the British colony of India.

Why It Matters Now
India today is the largest democracy in the world.

Lesson 2 Big Idea

Former colonies in Southeast Asia worked to build new governments and economies.

Why It Matters Now
The power and influence of the Pacific Rim nations are likely to expand during the next century.

Lesson 3 Big Idea

After World War II, African leaders threw off colonial rule and created independent countries.

Why It Matters Now
Today, many of those independent countries are engaged in building political and economic stability.

Lesson 4 Big Idea

Division of the Palestine Mandate after World War II made the Middle East a hotbed of competing nationalist movements.

Why It Matters Now
The Arab-Israeli conflict is one of several conflicts in the region today.

Timeline of Events 1920–2005

Explore ONLINE!

Colonies	World
1920 Gandhi leads Indian campaign of civil disobedience.	
1945 Sukarno proclaims Indonesian independence.	
1947 India gains independence from Britain.	1948 State of Israel is created.
	1948 South Africa establishes apartheid system.
1957 Ghana wins independence. (first prime minister Kwame Nkrumah)	
	1965 Mao Zedong launches Cultural Revolution in China.
	1975 Communist North Vietnam conquers South Vietnam.
	1982 Britain defeats Argentina in war over Falkland Islands.
1986 Election of Corazón Aquino ends Marcos dictatorship in the Philippines.	
	1991 Soviet Union breaks up into 15 republics.
1997 Mobutu dictatorship in Zaire falls.	
	2003 United States drives Saddam Hussein from power in Iraq.
2005 Liberia elects Africa's first female president.	

BLANKE INGANG
EUROPEAN ENTRANCE

Lesson 5 Big Idea

Lands controlled or influenced by the Soviet Union struggle with the challenges of establishing new nations.

Why It Matters Now

The security issues in these nations pose a threat to world peace and security.

Explore the Timeline

Interpret Timelines: The Colonies Become New Nations, 1920–2005

Have students examine the timeline and then answer the following question:

History Which Southeast Asian nation dealt with dictatorship in the years immediately following World War II? *the Philippines*

Interpret Timeline of Events: Timeline of Events, 1920–2005

To further explore the timeline, have students discuss the following questions:

1. What countries in Africa and Asia shown on the timeline fought to become independent nations? In what years? *Indonesia—1945; India—1947; Israel—1948; Ghana—1957*
2. What happened in the Soviet Union in 1991? How does this event reflect the general pattern of the timeline? *Soviet Union broke up, shows general tendency to move away from old governing patterns*

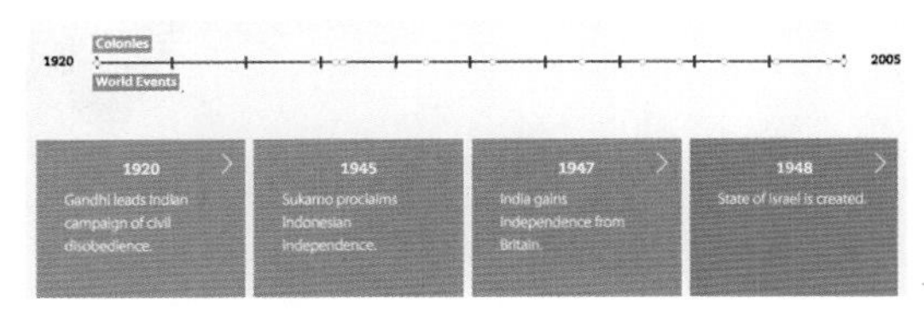

Online Module Flip Cards

Use the flip cards as a whole class activity or in student pairs to preview the module's Key Terms and People. Students can guess the meaning of each word, then review its definition, or do the reverse, using the flip card's toggle button to switch from Term to Definition mode. Students can also use the flip cards at the end of the module as a review tool before taking the Module Assessment.

Online Sequencing Activity

Students can use this sequencing activity to review the chronology of events in The Colonies Become New Nations module. To complete, have students drag each event to the correct year on the timeline.

Year	Event
1947	*India gains independence from Britain.*
1948	*State of Israel created; South Africa establishes apartheid system.*
1957	*Ghana wins independence.*
1965	*Mao Zedong launches Cultural Revolution in China.*
1975	*Communist North Vietnam conquers South Vietnam.*
1991	*Soviet Union breaks up into 15 republics.*

Lesson 1 Planner

The Indian Subcontinent Achieves Freedom

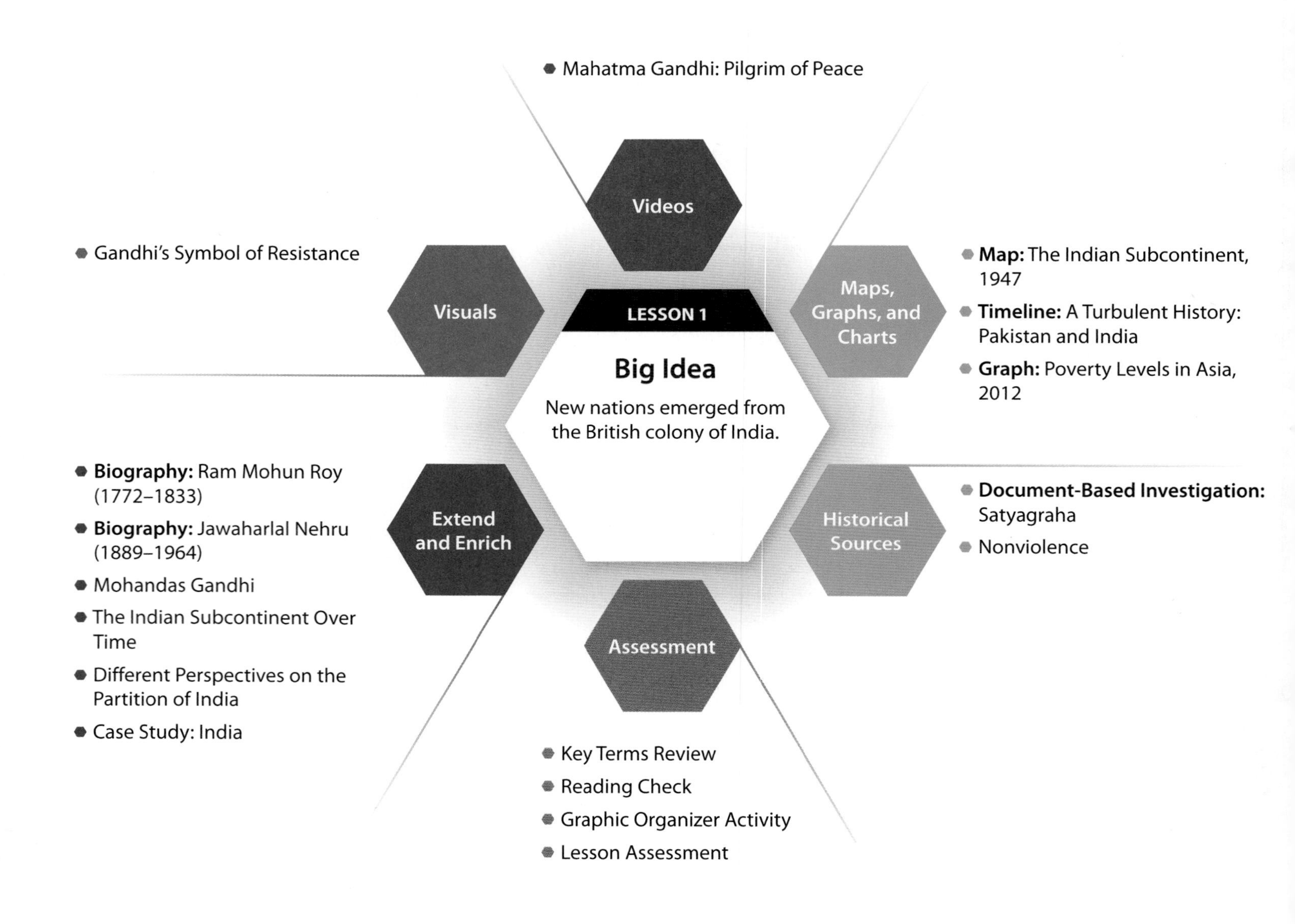

Online Lesson 1 Enrichment Activities

Mohandas Gandhi

Writing Activity Students will read about the Salt March and then create journal entries similar to those that one of Gandhi's followers may have written to chronicle the trip. The activity walks students through prewriting, writing, and reviewing and proofreading their journal entries.

The Indian Subcontinent Over Time

Research Students will conduct research to explore the geographic changes that have occurred in the Indian subcontinent during the time period studied. Then they will draw a series of maps that shows how nations have changed on the Indian subcontinent over time.

Different Perspectives on the Partition of India

Writing Activity Students will read about the partition of India and then write political statements that represent the views of different factions on the partition of India. This activity walks students through prewriting, writing, and reviewing and proofreading their political statements.

Case Study: India

Article Students will read about the contrasts and challenges that exist in India. They will learn about India's population, economy, industry, and culture. Then students will use a Venn diagram to compare urban living in an American city with urban living in an Indian city.

Teach the Big Idea

1. **Whole Class Open/Introduction** Ask students to think of specific times in their own lives when finding a peaceful way to get a need met has been more successful than making demands or beginning a conflict over the matter.
2. **Direct Teach** Read students the Big Idea: *New nations emerged from the British colony of India.* Review the following lesson objectives with students to aid in their understanding of the Big Idea:
   - Trace nationalist activity in India.
   - Summarize Gandhi's nonviolent tactics.
   - Explain how Indian self-rule heightened conflicts between Muslims and Hindus.
   - Describe the rise of independence movements in Southwest Asia.
   - Identify Indian leaders who came into office once India gained its independence.
   - Explain the causes of tension between East and West Pakistan.
   - Summarize the issues facing Sri Lanka and Bangladesh.
3. **Whole Group Close/Reflect** Have students write a one-paragraph summary of the major changes in India during this time.

Lesson 1

The Indian Subcontinent Achieves Freedom

The Big Idea
New nations emerged from the British colony of India.

Why It Matters Now
India today is the largest democracy in the world.

Key Terms and People
Rowlatt Acts
Amritsar Massacre
Mohandas K. Gandhi
civil disobedience
Salt March
Congress Party
Muslim League
Muhammad Ali Jinnah
partition
Jawaharlal Nehru
Indira Gandhi
Benazir Bhutto

Setting the Stage

After World War II, dramatic political changes began to take place across the world. This was especially the case with regard to the policy of colonialism. Countries that held colonies began to question the practice. After the world struggle against dictatorship, many leaders argued that no country should control another nation. Others questioned the high cost and commitment of holding colonies. Meanwhile, the people of colonized regions continued to press even harder for their freedom. All of this led to independence for one of the largest and most populous colonies in the world: British-held India.

Modern-day India is a mix of old and new.

ONLINE DOCUMENT-BASED INVESTIGATION

The Colonies Become New Nations

Satyagraha is the first of five document-based investigations that students will analyze in The Colonies Become New Nations module. The passage explores Gandhi's philosophy of nonviolence, called *satyagraha,* meaning "soul-force" or "truth-force." Students can click on the audio button beneath the historical source to hear the excerpt read aloud

ONLINE GRAPHIC ORGANIZER

The Indian Subcontinent Achieves Freedom

As students read the lesson, have them use the graphic organizer to take notes. Students can review their graphic organizer notes at the end of the lesson to answer the following question:

Compare How were the strategies of these leaders similar and different? *Most leaders wanted peaceful relations with others, but some wanted to achieve peace only through nonviolence while others were willing to fight, or become a separate state.*

COLLABORATIVE LEARNING

Debate the Issues of India

1. Divide the class into groups and assign each group an issue facing India: Pakistani and Indian nuclear arms, overpopulation, terrorism, education, environmental pollution, human trafficking, poverty
2. Ask groups to act as legislators and have them use the Internet library for data to convince the rest of the class, through debate, that their issue is the most important and most deserving of resources and funding.
3. Each group should reference at least four different sources and provide ten facts about their issue to support its importance.
4. Lead the class in a debate, and then ask each student to vote for the issue they feel is most important.
5. Present the results of the vote.

Nationalism Surfaces in India

Growing nationalism led to the founding of two nationalist groups, the primarily Hindu Indian National Congress, or Congress Party, in 1885 and the Muslim League in 1906. At first, such groups concentrated on specific concerns for Indians. By the early 1900s, however, they were calling for self-government. Though deep divisions existed between Hindus and Muslims, they found common ground. They shared the heritage of British rule and an understanding of democratic ideals. These two groups both worked toward the goal of independence from the British.

The nationalists were further inflamed in 1905 by the partition of Bengal. The province was too large for administrative purposes, so the British divided it into a Hindu section and a Muslim section. Keeping the two religious groups apart made it difficult for them to unite in calling for independence. In 1911, the British took back the order and divided the province in a different way.

World War I Increases Nationalist Activity Until World War I, the vast majority of Indians had little interest in nationalism. The situation changed as over a million Indians enlisted in the British army. In return for their service, the British government promised reforms that would eventually lead to self-government.

In 1918, Indian troops returned home from the war. They expected Britain to fulfill its promise. Instead, they were once again treated as second-class citizens. Radical nationalists carried out acts of violence to show their hatred of British rule. To curb dissent, in 1919 the British passed the **Rowlatt Acts**. These laws allowed the government to jail protesters without trial for as long as two years. To Western-educated Indians, denial of a trial by jury violated their individual rights.

BIOGRAPHY

Ram Mohun Roy
(1772–1833)

In the early 1800s, some Indians began demanding more modernization and a greater role in governing themselves. Ram Mohun Roy, a modern-thinking, well-educated Indian, began a campaign to move India away from traditional practices and ideas. Ram Mohun Roy saw arranged child marriages and the rigid caste separation as parts of Indian life that needed to be changed. He believed that if the practices were not changed, India would continue to be controlled by outsiders. Roy's writings inspired other Indian reformers to call for adoption of Western ways. Roy also founded a social reform movement that worked for change in India.

Besides modernization and Westernization, nationalist feelings started to surface in India. Indians hated a system that made them second-class citizens in their own country. They were barred from top posts in the Indian Civil Service. Those who managed to get middle-level jobs were paid less than Europeans. A British engineer on the East India Railway, for example, made nearly 20 times as much money as an Indian engineer.

Objectives

You may wish to discuss the following questions with students to help them frame the content as they read:

- Why were the Rowlatt Acts considered a violation of civil rights? *People were jailed without a trial, which is unjust.*
- The Amritsar Massacre is similar to what event in Russian history that also sparked a revolution? *During Bloody Sunday, peaceful protesters were killed at St. Petersburg.*

More About . . .

Colonialism In the 1930s, an aggressive new colonialism promoted by the Axis Powers (Germany, Italy, Japan) created a new colonial doctrine, the goal of which was to repartition the world's colonial areas. The Axis Powers claimed justification in the name of racial superiority, higher birth rates, and greater productivity.

Nationalism Nationalism is an ideology based on the premise that an individual's loyalty to the nation surpasses any individual or group interests. Nationalists believe that their nation is above all others and that the best interest of the nation takes importance over smaller groups or individuals.

BIOGRAPHY

Ram Mohun Roy

Have students read the biography of Ram Mohun Roy, a modern-thinking, well-educated Indian who began a campaign to move India away from traditional practices and ideas. Roy started a social reform movement for change in India, and his writings inspired reform throughout the country.

COLLABORATIVE LEARNING

Interviews: A Response to the Amritsar Massacre

1. Organize the class into small groups.
2. Ask groups to prepare interview questions directed at activists who want to win independence through non-violence in the wake of the Amritsar Massacre. Invite groups to research the massacre further as needed.
3. Have groups exchange interview questions with other groups, and ask all of them to prepare responses.
4. Ask groups to role-play interviewing one another.

ADVANCED/GIFTED

Evaluate the Rowlatt Act

1. Ask students to research the Rowlatt Act further to discover the details of the legislation, its reception by Indian leaders and the public, events that followed the passing of the Act, and its eventual repeal.
2. Have students prepare a multimedia presentation covering the Act from its inception to its repeal. Encourage students to use images, audio clips, text, timelines, and props.
3. Have students share their presentations and ask them to offer constructive feedback to one another pertaining to organization, content, creativity, and presentation.

ONLINE LESSON FLIP CARDS

Review Key Terms and People

Students can use the flip cards in the Lesson Review at any time to review the lesson's key terms and people: Rowlatt Acts, Amritsar Massacre, Mohandas K. Gandhi, civil disobedience, Salt March, *Congress Party, Muslim League, Muhammad Ali Jinnah, partition, Jawaharlal Nehru, Indira Gandhi, and Benazir Bhutto.*

Objectives

You may wish to discuss the following questions with students to help them frame the content as they read:

- Why was civil disobedience a popular solution for Indians? *They felt helpless to fight the British physically.*
- How did the media influence the Indian independence movement? *Support increased when newspapers worldwide reported the attack on peaceful Salt March protesters.*

More About . . .

Tips for English Learners Remind students that a boycott is a form of peaceful protest in which people decide as a group to refuse to buy certain products or goods in order to show disapproval of those who produce them. Explain that Captain Charles Boycott was isolated and shunned because he attempted to evict protesting tenants in 1880 in Ireland. Using names to create words is one of the ways the English language has developed.

Gandhi's Views Gandhi's emphasis on the traditional values of village life and on handcrafted items made it clear to the majority of Indians that he understood and sympathized with their problems. Gandhi realized that any feeling of Indian nationalism had to begin with the village.

Close Read

Satyagraha Have students explore the Close Read feature to aid in comprehension and understanding.

ONLINE ANALYZE VIDEOS

Mahatma Gandhi: Pilgrim of Peace HISTORY

Have students watch the video individually or as a class. You may wish to use the associated question as a discussion prompt.

Analyze Videos Why did Gandhi connect with people, even in massive crowds? *People, even in crowds, felt as if he was talking to them personally.*

READING CHECK

Analyze Effects What changes resulted from the Amritsar Massacre? *The spirit of nationalism grew more intense; more Indians demanded independence.*

Amritsar Massacre To protest the Rowlatt Acts, around 10,000 Hindus and Muslims flocked to Amritsar, a major city in the Punjab, in the spring of 1919. At a huge festival in an enclosed square, they intended to fast and pray and to listen to political speeches. The demonstration, viewed as a nationalist outburst, alarmed the British. They were especially concerned about the alliance of Hindus and Muslims.

Most people at the gathering were unaware that the British government had banned public meetings. However, the British commander at Amritsar believed they were openly defying the ban. He ordered his troops to fire on the crowd without warning. The shooting in the enclosed courtyard continued for ten minutes. Official reports showed nearly 400 Indians died and about 1,200 were wounded. Others estimate the numbers were higher.

Reading Check
Recognize Effects
What changes resulted from the Amritsar Massacre?

News of the slaughter, called the **Amritsar Massacre**, sparked an explosion of anger across India. Almost overnight, millions of Indians changed from loyal British subjects into nationalists. These Indians demanded independence.

Gandhi's Tactics of Nonviolence

The massacre at Amritsar set the stage for **Mohandas K. Gandhi** (GAHN•dee) to emerge as the leader of the independence movement. Gandhi's strategy for battling injustice evolved from his deeply religious approach to political activity. His teachings blended ideas from all of the major world religions, including Hinduism, Jainism, Buddhism, Islam, and Christianity. Gandhi attracted millions of followers. Soon they began calling him the Mahatma (muh•HAHT•muh), meaning "great soul."

Noncooperation When the British failed to punish the officers responsible for the Amritsar Massacre, Gandhi urged the Indian National Congress to follow a policy of noncooperation with the British government. In 1920, the Congress Party endorsed **civil disobedience**, the deliberate and public

Gandhi adopted the spinning wheel as a symbol of Indian resistance to British rule. The wheel was featured on the Indian National Congress flag, a forerunner of India's national flag.

1164 Module 30

ENGLISH LANGUAGE LEARNERS

Indian Protests and British Responses

1. Review with students the political tension between India and the British government during the independence movement.
2. Draw a two-column chart for students to see. One column should be labeled "Indian Actions" and the other should be labeled "Response."
3. Have students copy the chart and complete it by listing actions Gandhi and his followers took, including specific boycotts, strikes and demonstrations, and highlights of the Salt March. In the second column, ask students to list responses to those actions.
4. Using the information from their lists, students will create a poster that shows Indian protests and British responses. Students can use photographs, drawings, and captions to persuade others to join the independence movement.

refusal to obey an unjust law, and nonviolence as the means to achieve independence. Gandhi then launched his campaign of civil disobedience to weaken the British government's authority and economic power over India.

Boycotts Gandhi called on Indians to refuse to buy British goods, attend government schools, pay British taxes, or vote in elections. Gandhi staged a successful boycott of British cloth, a source of wealth for the British. He urged all Indians to weave their own cloth. Gandhi himself devoted two hours each day to spinning his own yarn on a simple handwheel. He wore only homespun cloth and encouraged Indians to follow his example. As a result of the boycott, the sale of British cloth in India dropped sharply.

DOCUMENT-BASED INVESTIGATION Historical Sources

Satyagraha

A central element of Gandhi's philosophy of nonviolence was called *satyagraha*, often translated as "soul-force" or "truth-force."

"Passive resistance is a method of securing rights by personal suffering; it is the reverse of resistance by arms. When I refuse to do a thing that is repugnant to my conscience, I use soul-force. For instance, the government of the day has passed a law which is applicable to me: I do not like it, if, by using violence, I force the government to repeal the law, I am employing what may be termed body-force. If I do not obey the law and accept the penalty for its breach, I use soul-force. It involves sacrifice of self."

—Gandhi, Chapter XVII, *Hind Swaraj*

Nonviolence

In *Pledge of Resistance in Transvaal Africa*, 1906, Gandhi offered a warning to those who were contemplating joining the struggle for independence.

"[I]t is not at all impossible that we might have to endure every hardship that we can imagine, and wisdom lies in pledging ourselves on the understanding that we shall have to suffer all that and worse. If some one asks me when and how the struggle may end, I may say that if the entire community manfully stands the test, the end will be near. If many of us fall back under storm and stress, the struggle will be prolonged. But I can boldly declare, and with certainty, that so long as there is even a handful of men true to their pledge, there can only be one end to the struggle, and that is victory."

—Gandhi, *Pledge of Resistance in Transvaal Africa*, 1906

Analyze Historical Sources

1. How is soul-force different from body-force?
2. What do Gandhi's writings suggest about his view of suffering? Give examples from each document.

INVESTIGATE CIVIL DISOBEDIENCE

Below Level Have students conduct research and find an organization that is committed to effecting change using nonviolent strategies. Provide them with examples of environmental, animal rights, and political activist movements to help them get started. Have them write a paragraph describing the group's goals and citing specific examples of nonviolent tactics, such as marches, demonstrations, boycotts, and advertising campaigns.

At Level Have students identify two different groups or movements that are dedicated to the principles of nonviolence as a strategy for effecting change. Ask students to evaluate similarities and differences between the two groups and to compare and contrast the two groups in an essay. Student essays should include goals, methods, and specific examples of nonviolent tactics. Students should conclude by offering and supporting an opinion regarding which group's approach and methods are the most effective and why.

Above Level Have students investigate Henry David Thoreau's essay, "Civil Disobedience." Ask students to research the connection between Gandhi and Henry David Thoreau and to draw parallels between "Civil Disobedience" and the writings of Gandhi. Have them analyze the influence of Thoreau on Gandhi and present their findings in an essay.

ONLINE DOCUMENT-BASED INVESTIGATION

Satyagraha

Students will read a passage about Gandhi's philosophy of nonviolence, called *satyagraha*, meaning "soul-force" or "truth-force." Students can click on the audio button beneath the historical source to hear the excerpt read aloud.

Analyze Sources Why did Gandhi believe that suffering oneself, rather than inflicting suffering on others, was the key to victory? *He believed that there could only be one end if everyone stood together against a wrong.*

In print edition, see historical sources titled Satyagraha and Nonviolence.

1. **Compare** How is soul-force different from body-force? *Body-force involves the use of violence but not necessarily the sacrifice of self as soul-force does.*
2. **Make Inferences** What do Gandhi's writings suggest about his view of suffering? Give examples from each document. *Gandhi believes that suffering must take place to achieve the goal. Hind Swaraj states: "Passive resistance is a method of securing rights by personal suffering." The Pledge of Resistance in Transvaal Africa, 1906, states: "[T]here can only be one end to the struggle, and that is victory."*

ONLINE HISTORICAL SOURCES

Nonviolence

Invite students to read or listen to the excerpt and answer the associated question.

Analyze Sources What do Gandhi's writings suggest about his view of suffering? *Gandhi believes that suffering must take place to achieve the goal.*

HISTORICAL SOURCE

Nonviolence

In *Pledge of Resistance in Transvaal Africa*, 1906, Gandhi offered a warning to those who were contemplating joining the struggle for independence.

ONLINE INTERACTIVE VISUALS

Carousel: Gandhi's Symbol of Resistance

Have students navigate through the carousel and identify a common theme.

Objectives

You may wish to discuss the following questions with students to help them frame the content as they read:

- In what ways was civil disobedience a more successful method than violence? *Boycotts and noncooperation took away the British government's economic power and authority.*
- What was the source of tension between Hindus and Muslims in India? *different religious beliefs; Muslims feared the power of the more numerous Hindus.*

More About . . .

Government of India Acts The first several acts passed by the British Parliament to regulate the government of India between 1773 and 1830 were called East India Company Acts. These acts were named so because they were perpetuated to establish a dual system of control by the British government and the East India Company. Acts passed in 1833 through 1935 were titled Government of India Acts.

READING CHECK
Make Inferences How did the Salt March represent Gandhi's methods for change? *The protest against British rule was based on noncooperation and civil disobedience.*

Strikes and Demonstrations Gandhi's weapon of civil disobedience took an economic toll on the British. They struggled to keep trains running, factories operating, and overcrowded jails from bursting. Throughout 1920, the British arrested thousands of Indians who had participated in strikes and demonstrations. But despite Gandhi's pleas for nonviolence, protests often led to riots.

The Salt March In 1930, Gandhi organized a demonstration to defy the hated Salt Acts. According to these British laws, Indians could buy salt from no other source but the government. They also had to pay sales tax on salt. To show their opposition, Gandhi and his followers walked about 240 miles to the seacoast. There they began to make their own salt by collecting seawater and letting it evaporate. This peaceful protest was called the **Salt March**.

Soon afterward, some demonstrators planned a march to a site where the British government processed salt. They intended to shut this salt-works down. Police officers with steel-tipped clubs attacked the demonstrators. An American journalist was an eyewitness to the event. He described the "sickening whacks of clubs on unprotected skulls" and people "writhing in pain with fractured skulls or broken shoulders." Still the people continued to march peacefully, refusing to defend themselves against their attackers. Newspapers across the globe carried the journalist's story, which won worldwide support for Gandhi's independence movement.

Reading Check
Make Inferences How did the Salt March represent Gandhi's methods for change?

More demonstrations against the salt tax took place throughout India. Eventually, about 60,000 people, including Gandhi, were arrested.

Britain Grants Limited Self-Rule

Gandhi and his followers gradually reaped the rewards of their civil disobedience campaigns and gained greater political power for the Indian people. In 1935, the British Parliament passed the Government of India Act. It provided local self-government and limited democratic elections but not total independence.

However, the Government of India Act also fueled mounting tensions between Muslims and Hindus. These two groups had conflicting visions of India's future as an independent nation. Indian Muslims, outnumbered by Hindus, feared that Hindus would control India if it won independence.

A Movement Toward Independence The British had ruled India for almost two centuries. Indian resistance to Britain intensified in 1939, when Britain committed India's armed forces to World War II without first consulting the colony's elected representatives. The move left Indian nationalists stunned and humiliated. Indian leader Mohandas Gandhi launched a nonviolent campaign of noncooperation with the British. Officials imprisoned numerous nationalists for this action. In 1942, the British tried to gain the support of the nationalists by promising governmental changes after the war. But the offer did not include Indian independence.

COLLABORATIVE LEARNING

The Congress Party or the Muslim League?

1. Pair students and ask them to imagine themselves as members of the Congress Party or the Muslim League.
2. Ask students to create a recruitment poster for their group.
3. Request that students include imagery representing the historical roots of the group as well as imagery that would appeal to new members.
4. Ask students to present their posters to the class. Before the presentation, guide the class in guessing the group and the appeal.

ADVANCED/GIFTED

Presentation: How the Muslim League Was Formed

1. Ask students to research factors and events that influenced the formation of the Muslim League and the League's aims and objectives in preparation for creating an expository presentation.
2. Have students create an outline for their presentation, including an introduction, pertinent points, and an obvious conclusion.

As they intensified their struggle against the British, Indians also struggled with each other. The Indian National Congress, or the **Congress Party**, was India's national political party. Most members of the Congress Party were Hindus, but the party at times had many Muslim members.

Muhammad Ali Jinnah

In competition with the Congress Party was the **Muslim League**, an organization founded to protect Muslim interests. Members of the league felt that the mainly Hindu Congress Party looked out primarily for Hindu interests. The leader of the Muslim League, **Muhammad Ali Jinnah** (mu•HAM•ihd-ah•LEE-JIHN•uh), insisted that all Muslims resign from the Congress Party. The Muslim League stated that it would never accept Indian independence if it meant rule by the Hindu-dominated Congress Party. Jinnah stated, "The only thing the Muslim has in common with the Hindu is his slavery to the British."

Reading Check
Summarize What were the two main political parties and two main religions in India during this period?

Freedom Brings Turmoil

When World War II ended, Britain found itself faced with enormous war debts. As a result, British leaders began to rethink the expense of maintaining and governing distant colonies. With India continuing to push for independence, the stage was set for the British to hand over power. However, a key problem emerged: Who should receive the power—Hindus or Muslims?

Partition and Bloodshed Muslims resisted attempts to include them in an Indian government dominated by Hindus. Rioting between the two groups broke out in several Indian cities. In August 1946, four days of clashes in Calcutta left more than 5,000 people dead and more than 15,000 hurt.

British officials soon became convinced that partition, an idea first proposed by India's Muslims, would be the only way to ensure a safe and secure region. **Partition** was the term given to the division of India into separate Hindu and Muslim nations. The northwest and eastern regions of India, where most Muslims lived, would become the new nation of Pakistan. Pakistan comprised two separate states in 1947: West Pakistan and East Pakistan. (See map, The Indian Subcontinent, 1947.)

The British House of Commons passed an act on July 16, 1947, that granted two nations, India and Pakistan, independence in one month's time. In that short period, more than 500 independent native princes had to decide which nation they would join. The administration of the courts, the military, the railways, and the police—the whole of the civil service—had to be divided down to the last paper clip. Most difficult of all, millions of Indian citizens—Hindus, Muslims, and yet another significant religious group, the Sikhs—had to decide where to go.

During the summer of 1947, 10 million people were on the move in the Indian subcontinent. As people scrambled to relocate, violence among the different religious groups erupted. Muslims killed Sikhs who were

Objectives

You may wish to discuss the following questions with students to help them frame the content as they read:

- Why did British officials enforce a partition? *They were convinced that a partition would ensure a safe and secure region.*
- What challenge was created for the people of India and Pakistan when the British House of Commons granted India and Pakistan independence on July 16, 1947? *Millions of Indian citizens (Hindus, Muslims, Sikhs) had to decide where to go. Over 500 independent native princes had to decide which nation they would join. All of civil service had to be divided. A total of 10 million people had to make a decision and move.*

More About . . .

Partition and Bloodshed Leading up to the partition, a widespread series of religious massacres occurred, starting in Calcutta in 1946 where 5,000 people were killed. As violence and unrest escalated, the British began to realize they had lost control and acted quickly to implement the partition and make their exit.

READING CHECK
Summarize What were the two main political parties and two main religions in India during this period? *the Congress Party (mostly Hindu) and the Muslim League (mostly Muslim)*

3. Then ask students to create their presentations, explaining how the Muslim League was formed along with its aims and objectives. Suggest that they use images, timelines, graphs, and text to highlight significant people and events.
4. Allow students time to rehearse their presentations.
5. Have students give their presentations to the class or another World Studies class. Allow time for questions and answers.

ADVANCED/GIFTED

Identify Points of View: the Partition

1. Ask students to imagine themselves as a Hindu or Muslim leader worried about the partition. Have each student write an editorial to support his or her position either for or against the partition.
2. Editorials should include a position statement, present at least two strong reasons to support the position, and provide evidence (such as examples or statistics) to support each reason.
3. Remind students that some of the readers of their editorials will have different points of view on the issue. Students should try to address audience concerns and convince them to change their positions.
4. Ask for volunteers to read their editorials aloud.

ONLINE INTERPRET MAPS

The Indian Subcontinent, 1947

Have students explore the map using the interactive features and answer the associated questions.

Location Which Muslim country, divided into two states, bordered India on the east and the west? *Pakistan*

In print edition, see map of same title.

1. **Location** Which Muslim country, divided into two states, bordered India on the east and the west? *Pakistan*
2. **Location** Which Buddhist countries bordered India to the north and the south? *Bhutan to the north; Ceylon (Sri Lanka) to the south*

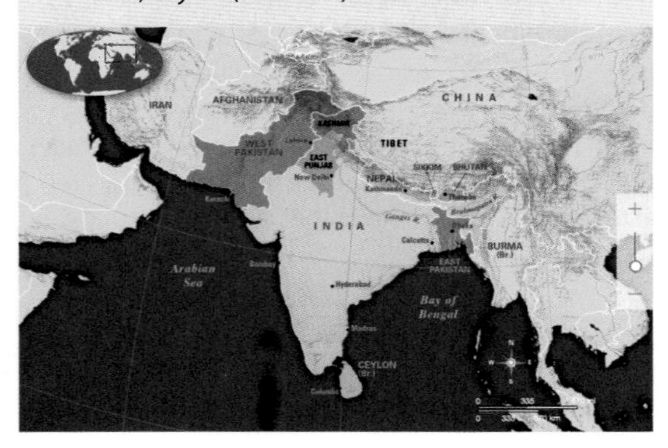

READING CHECK

Analyze Causes What was the cause of the conflict between India and Pakistan over Kashmir? *Kashmir had a large Muslim population but was ruled by a Hindu. Since it bordered both India and Pakistan, both groups staked a claim to it.*

NOW & THEN

The Battle of Kashmir

In 1999, Pakistani troops crossed into an area of Kashmir called Kargil, which brought India and Pakistan alarmingly close to a nuclear exchange. Though the two countries have experienced brief, random gestures toward peace negotiations, they remain in conflict, depleting much-needed resources to invest in defense.

Explore ONLINE!

The Indian Subcontinent, 1947

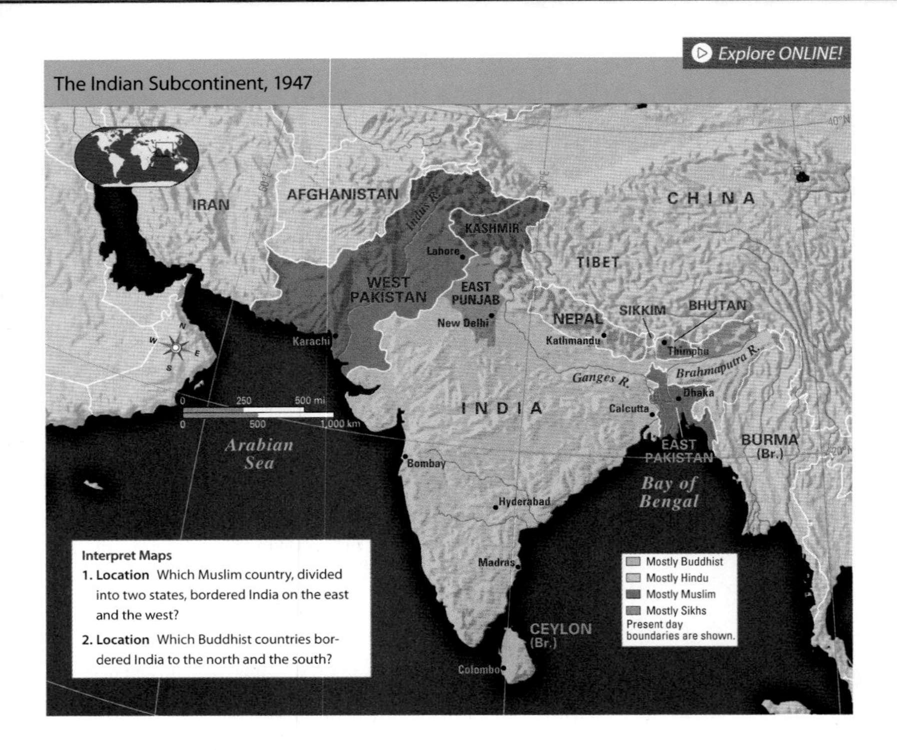

Interpret Maps

1. **Location** Which Muslim country, divided into two states, bordered India on the east and the west?
2. **Location** Which Buddhist countries bordered India to the north and the south?

moving into India. Hindus and Sikhs killed Muslims who were headed into Pakistan. In all, an estimated 1 million died.

"What is there to celebrate?" Gandhi mourned. "I see nothing but rivers of blood." Gandhi personally went to the Indian capital of Delhi to plead for fair treatment of Muslim refugees. While there, he himself became a victim of the nation's violence. A Hindu extremist who thought Gandhi too protective of Muslims shot and killed him on January 30, 1948.

The Battle for Kashmir As if partition itself didn't result in enough bloodshed between India's Muslims and Hindus, the two groups quickly squared off over the small region of Kashmir. Kashmir lay at the northern point of India next to Pakistan. Although its ruler was Hindu, Kashmir had a majority Muslim population. Shortly after independence, India and Pakistan began battling each other for control of the region. The fighting continued until the United Nations arranged a ceasefire in 1949. The ceasefire left a third of Kashmir under Pakistani control and the rest under Indian control. The two countries continue to fight over the region today.

Reading Check
Analyze Causes What was the cause of the conflict between India and Pakistan over Kashmir?

Now and Then

The Coldest War

No part of Kashmir is beyond a fight for India and Pakistan—including the giant Siachen glacier high above the region. The dividing line established by the 1949 cease-fire did not extend to the glacier because officials figured neither side would try to occupy such a barren and frigid strip of land.

They figured wrong. In 1984, both sides sent troops to take the glacier, and they have been dug in ever since. At altitudes nearing 21,000 feet, Indian and Pakistani soldiers shoot at each other from trenches in temperatures that reach 70 degrees below zero. This bitterly cold war was interrupted in 2003 when Pakistan and India declared a cease-fire.

Modern India

With the granting of its independence on August 15, 1947, India became the world's largest democracy. As the long-awaited hour of India's freedom approached, **Jawaharlal Nehru** became the independent nation's first prime minister.

Nehru Leads India Nehru served as India's leader for its first 17 years of independence. He had been one of Gandhi's most devoted followers. Educated in Britain, Nehru won popularity among all groups in India. He emphasized democracy, unity, and economic modernization. Unlike Gandhi, he promoted industrialization as the key to improving India's economy. After independence, he worked to enhance India's heavy manufacturing industries.

Nehru used his leadership to move India forward. He led other newly independent nations of the world in forming an alliance of countries that were neutral in the Cold War conflicts between the United States and the Soviet Union. On the home front, Nehru called for a reorganization of the states by language. He also pushed for industrialization and sponsored social reforms. He tried to elevate the status of the lower castes, or those at the bottom of society, and help women gain the rights promised by the constitution.

Vocabulary
neutralism/nonalignment a policy in which a nation does not side with any major powers

BIOGRAPHY

Jawaharlal Nehru
(1889–1964)

Nehru's father was an influential attorney, and so the first prime minister of India grew up amid great wealth. As a young man, he lived and studied in England. "In my likes and dislikes I was perhaps more an Englishman than an Indian," he once remarked.

Upon returning to India, however, he became moved by the horrible state in which many of his fellow Indians lived. "A new picture of India seemed to rise before me," he recalled, "naked, starving, crushed, and utterly miserable." From then on, he devoted his life to improving conditions in his country.

COLLABORATIVE LEARNING

Introducing India and Pakistan

1. Divide the classroom with one side representing India, the opposite side Pakistan, and the middle representing both countries.
2. Organize students into pairs, and give each pair a piece of paper containing a fact pertaining to India, Pakistan, or both countries.
3. Allow pairs ten minutes to research the fact using classroom materials or the Internet.
4. Pairs place themselves in the room location corresponding to their fact.
5. Each pair shares their fact. The rest of the class or the teacher verifies the accuracy.

Objectives

You may wish to discuss the following questions with students to help them frame the content as they read:

- How did Jawaharlal Nehru use his leadership to move India forward? *Emphasized democracy, unity, and economic globalization; promoted industrialization to improve India's economy; worked to enhance India's manufacturing industries; led other newly independent nations of the world in forming an alliance of countries that were neutral in the Cold War; called for a reorganization of the states by language; sponsored social reforms; tried to help elevate the status of the lower castes; tried to help women gain their constitutional rights*
- Why did Indian army groups overrun the Golden Temple in 1984? *to retaliate against Sikh nationalists*

More About . . .

Indira Gandhi Prime Minister Indira Gandhi proclaimed a state of emergency in India on June 26, 1975. Under the provisions of the Emergency, freedom of the press was halted, and India turned silent for Westerners. Gandhi's opponents were arrested under the Emergency powers, newspapers were closed, and individual freedoms curtailed.

BIOGRAPHY

Jawaharlal Nehru, 1889–1964

Have students read the biography of Jawaharlal Nehru, the first prime minister of an independent India at the end of British colonial rule. Nehru devoted his life to improving living conditions in India.

ONLINE INTERACTIVE TIMELINES

A Turbulent History: Pakistan and India

Have students explore the timeline and answer the associated question.

Analyze Timelines How many politically related deaths are referenced in this timeline? *5*

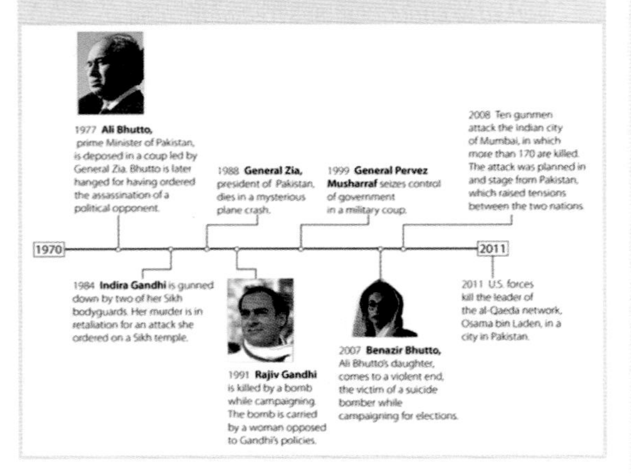

A Turbulent History

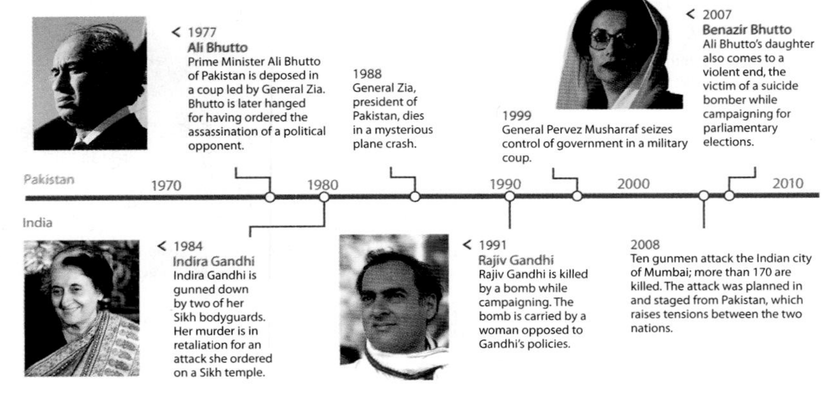

Troubled Times Nehru died in 1964. His death left the Congress Party with no leader strong enough to hold together the many political factions that had emerged with India's independence. Then, in 1966, Nehru's daughter, **Indira Gandhi**, was chosen prime minister. After a short spell out of office, she was reelected in 1980.

Although she ruled capably, Gandhi faced many challenges, including the growing threat from Sikh extremists who themselves wanted an independent state. The Golden Temple at Amritsar stood as the religious center for the Sikhs. From there, Sikh nationalists ventured out to attack symbols of Indian authority. In June 1984, Indian army troops overran the Golden Temple. They killed about 500 Sikhs and destroyed sacred property. In retaliation, Sikh bodyguards assigned to Indira Gandhi gunned her down. This violent act was met by a murderous frenzy that led to the deaths of thousands of Sikhs.

In the wake of the murder of Indira Gandhi, her son, Rajiv (rah•JEEV) Gandhi, took over as prime minister. His party, however, lost its power in 1989 because of accusations of widespread corruption. In 1991, while campaigning again for prime minister near the town of Madras, Rajiv was killed by a bomb. Members of a group opposed to his policies claimed responsibility.

Twenty-first Century Challenges India's prime minister, Manmohan Singh, is a Sikh—the first non-Hindu to hold the job. He and his nation face a number of problems. Simmering religious tensions still occasionally boil over in episodes of violence and reprisal. Also, India's population continues to increase and is expected to surpass that of China by 2035. More acutely, Maoist rebels in the nation's eastern states continue to pose a serious military threat to the government's authority.

Even more troubling are India's tense relations with its neighbor Pakistan and the fact that both have become nuclear powers. In 1974, India exploded a "peaceful" nuclear device. For the next 24 years, the nation quietly worked on building up its nuclear capability. In 1998, Indian officials conducted five underground nuclear tests. Meanwhile, the Pakistanis had been building their own nuclear program. Shortly after India conducted its nuclear tests, Pakistan demonstrated that it too had nuclear weapons. The presence of these weapons in the hands of such bitter enemies and neighbors has become a matter of great international concern, especially in light of their continuing struggle over Kashmir.

Reading Check
Analyze Challenges
What are some of the issues modern-day India must face?

In 2002, the two nations came close to war over Kashmir. However, in 2003 a peace process began to ease tension. From 2004 to 2014, the Congress Party led the nation. The Congress Party focused on jobs and the economy, but still the economy worsened. When this happened, voters deserted the Congress Party. In 2014, two-thirds of the people voted for the Bharatiya Janata Party (BJP) candidate, Narenda Modi. The BJP is a pro-Hindu party.

Pakistan Copes with Freedom

The history of Pakistan since independence has been no less turbulent than that of India. Pakistan actually began as two separate and divided states, East Pakistan and West Pakistan. East Pakistan lay to the east of India, West Pakistan to the northwest. These regions were separated by more than 1,000 miles of Indian territory. In culture, language, history, geography, economics, and ethnic background, the two regions were very different. Only the Islamic religion united them.

Civil War From the beginning, the two regions of Pakistan experienced strained relations. While East Pakistan had the larger population, it was often ignored by West Pakistan, home to the central government. In 1970, a giant cyclone and tidal wave struck East Pakistan and killed an estimated 266,000 residents. While international aid poured into Pakistan, the government in West Pakistan did not quickly transfer that aid to East Pakistan. Demonstrations broke out in East Pakistan, and protesters called for an end to all ties with West Pakistan.

On March 26, 1971, East Pakistan declared itself an independent nation called Bangladesh. A civil war followed between Bangladesh and Pakistan. Eventually, Indian forces stepped in and sided with Bangladesh. Pakistani forces surrendered. More than 1 million people died in the war. Pakistan lost about one-seventh of its area and about one-half of its population to Bangladesh.

Objectives

You may wish to discuss the following questions with students to help them frame the content as they read:

- What were some of the differences between East and West Pakistan? *culture, language, history, geography, economics, ethnic background*
- What factors contributed to the strained relations between East and West Pakistan? *West Pakistan often ignored East Pakistan, and West Pakistan did not quickly offer aid when natural disasters struck East Pakistan.*
- What were some of the repercussions of the 2010 floods in Pakistan? *food and water shortages, disease, looting, transportation and communication problems, shortages of raw materials*

More About . . .

Benazir Bhutto Benazir Bhutto graduated from Oxford, survived five years of imprisonment and house arrest and a succession of political crises and conspiracies. She was 35 when she became the first female prime minister of a Muslim country, and one of the youngest prime ministers in the world.

READING CHECK
Analyze Challenges What are some of the issues modern-day India must face? *religious tensions, a large population, military threats, Pakistan's nuclear arsenal*

COLLABORATIVE LEARNING

Human Placards: A Timeline of Historical Events

1. Pair students and give each pair a historical event pertaining to the history of Pakistan or India.
2. Have pairs research the event using the Internet and library resources.
3. Ask pairs to create a placard containing the event, date, summary, and visual of the event.
4. Request that students work together to create a human timeline, placing themselves in historical order.
5. Going in chronological order, ask each pair to hold up their placard and share their historical event.

Objectives

You may wish to discuss the following questions with students to help them frame the content as they read:

- How did the war with Pakistan affect Bangladesh? *ruined its economy and fractured its communications system*
- What are some of the natural disasters that have struck Bangladesh? *cyclones, tidal waves, storms*
- Why did the Tamils of Sri Lanka form a rebel group? *They wanted to create a separate Tamil nation.*

More About . . .

Sheik Mujibur Rahman Sheik Mujibur Rahman, leader of the Bengalis and popularly known as Mujib, campaigned for autonomy for East Pakistan and gained a clear majority in Pakistan's parliamentary election in December 1970. In March 1971 the Pakistani army, responding to Bengali mass demonstrations, arrested Mujib and took him to West Pakistan. They banned his party and massacred his supporters.

The Tamil Tigers The Liberation Tigers of Tamil Eelam were defeated in May 2009 after 26 years of conflict that divided Sri Lanka. The leader of the Tigers, Velupillai Prabhakaran, was known as one of the most successful guerrilla leaders of modern times. The Sri Lankan Army launched a three-year offensive which proved to be brutally effective in defeating the insurgency of the Tigers. Despite its victory, the Sri Lankan government was criticized for the Army's final offensive by many, including Secretary of State Hillary Clinton, who spoke of the "untold suffering" caused by the Army's efforts to end the war.

READING CHECK

Compare How does the history of Pakistan in 1971 parallel the history of India in 1947? *As India was partitioned into India and Pakistan, Pakistan was divided into Pakistan and Bangladesh.*

A Pattern of Instability Muhammad Ali Jinnah, the first governor-general of Pakistan, died shortly after independence. Beginning in 1958, Pakistan went through a series of military coups. Ali Bhutto took control of the country following the civil war. A military coup in 1977 led by General Zia removed Bhutto, who was later executed for crimes allegedly committed while in office.

After Zia's death, Bhutto's daughter, **Benazir Bhutto**, was twice elected prime minister. However, she was removed from office in 1996. Nawaz Sharif became prime minister after the 1997 elections. In 1999, army leaders led by General Pervez Musharraf ousted Sharif in yet another coup and imposed military rule over Pakistan. By 2007, however, he faced growing political opposition at home. Meanwhile, Benazir Bhutto had returned from exile abroad, only to be assassinated in December 2007. By August 2008, Musharraf had resigned, with Bhutto's widower, Asif Ali Zardari, winning the presidency the following month.

In 2010, Pakistan endured the worst floods in recorded history. The disaster led to food and water shortages, disease, looting, and transportation and communications problems. Pakistan is a nation that relies on agriculture. The floods destroyed farmland and killed farm animals, which led to shortages of food and raw materials.

In 2011, U.S. forces located the leader of the al-Qaeda network, Osama bin Laden, in a city near Islamabad in Pakistan. On May 2, the U.S. military staged an operation in which bin Laden was killed. Before the operation, Pakistani officials had denied that bin Laden was living in Pakistan. The U.S. military action increased distrust between the United States and Pakistan. In 2013, Nawaz Sharif entered his third term as prime minister.

Reading Check
Compare How does the history of Pakistan in 1971 parallel the history of India in 1947?

Bangladesh and Sri Lanka Struggle

Meanwhile, the newly created nations of Bangladesh and Sri Lanka struggled with enormous problems of their own in the decades following independence.

Bangladesh Faces Many Problems The war with Pakistan had ruined the economy of Bangladesh and fractured its communications system. Rebuilding the shattered country seemed like an overwhelming task. Sheik Mujibur Rahman became the nation's first prime minister. He soon took over all authority and declared Bangladesh a one-party state. In August 1975, military leaders assassinated him.

Over the years Bangladesh has attempted with great difficulty to create a more democratic form of government. Charges of election fraud and government corruption are common. In recent years, however, the government has become more stable.

STRUGGLING READERS

Effects of Independence: Bangladesh and Sri Lanka

1. Review with students the positive and negative effects of independence as experienced by Bangladesh and Sri Lanka.
2. Draw a two-column chart for students to see. One column should be labeled "Positive Effects" and the other should be labeled "Negative Effects."
3. Have students copy the chart.
4. Guide students in completing the chart by listing the positive and negative effects these countries faced in the decades following independence.

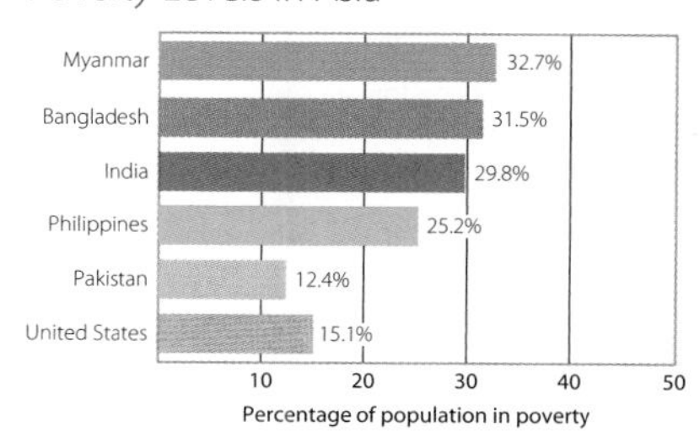

Source: *The World Factbook 2013–14*. Washington, DC: Central Intelligence Agency, 2013.

Overcrowded and poor villages are a common sight throughout Bangladesh.

Bangladesh also has had to cope with crippling natural disasters. Bangladesh is a low-lying nation that is subject to many cyclones and tidal waves. Massive storms regularly flood the land, ruin crops and homes, and take lives. A cyclone in 1991 killed approximately 139,000 people. Such catastrophes, along with a rapidly growing population, have put much stress on the country's economy. Bangladesh is one of the poorest nations in the world. The per capita income there is about $360 per year. About half the workers are employed in agriculture and fishing jobs.

This emblem of the separatist group Liberation Tigers of Tamil Eelam represents the struggle for independence of the Tamils.

Civil Strife Grips Sri Lanka Another newly freed and deeply troubled country on the Indian subcontinent is Sri Lanka, a small, teardrop-shaped island nation just off the southeast coast of India. Formerly known as Ceylon, Sri Lanka gained its independence from Britain in February 1948. Two main ethnic groups dominate the nation. Three-quarters of the population are Sinhalese, who are Buddhists. One-fifth are Tamils, a Hindu people of southern India and northern Sri Lanka.

Sri Lanka's recent history has also been one of turmoil. A militant group of Tamils has long fought an armed struggle for a separate Tamil nation. Since 1981, thousands of lives have been lost. In an effort to end the violence, Rajiv Gandhi and the Sri Lankan president tried to reach an accord in 1987. The agreement called for Indian troops to enter Sri Lanka and help disarm Tamil rebels. This effort was unsuccessful, and Indian troops left in 1990. But in 2009, a government military offensive decisively defeated Tamil separatist forces.

ONLINE INTERACTIVE GRAPHS

Poverty Levels in Asia, 2012

Have students explore the graph and answer the associated question.

Interpret Graphs Which nations had more than 30 percent of the population in poverty? *Bangladesh and Myanmar*

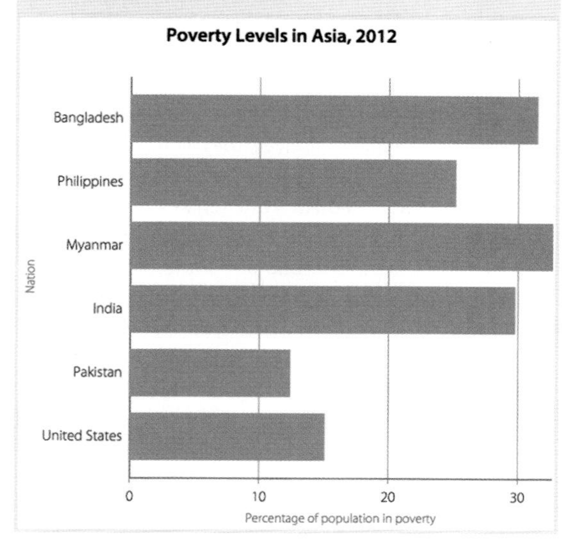

> **READING CHECK**
> **Compare and Contrast** What issues do Bangladesh and Sri Lanka face? *natural disasters, poverty, and civil strife*

Print Assessment

1. **Organize Information** Make a timeline that lists the leaders of India and Pakistan. What tragic connection did many of the leaders share? *Possible answer: Jawaharlal Nehru, Indira Gandhi, Rajiv Gandhi, Atal Bihari Vajpayee; they were killed or faced violence.*
2. **Key Terms and People** For each key term or person in the lesson, write a sentence explaining its significance. *Explanations of the lesson's key terms can be found on the following pages: Rowlatt Acts, p. 1163; Amritsar Massacre, p. 1164; Mohandas K. Gandhi, p. 1164; civil disobedience, p. 1164; Salt March, p. 1166; Congress Party, p. 1167; Muslim League, p. 1167; Muhammad Ali Jinnah, p. 1167; partition, p. 1167; Jawaharlal Nehru, p. 1169; Indira Gandhi, p. 1170; Benazir Bhutto, p. 1172*
3. **Draw Conclusions** Why did British officials partition India into India and Pakistan? *They were burdened with enormous war debt and wanted to reduce the expense of maintaining and governing distant colonies.*
4. **Synthesize** Why might India's political and economic success be so crucial to the future of democracy in Asia? *India is a very populous country and the world's largest democracy. It has great influence in the area.*
5. **Analyze Issues** How did religious and cultural differences create problems for newly emerging nations? *They led to a partition of India, a battle for Kashmir, and civil strife in Sri Lanka.*
6. **Draw Conclusions** What is the main cause today of civil strife in Sri Lanka? *the Tamils' struggle for independence*
7. **Synthesize** How did imperialism contribute to unity and to the growth of nationalism in India? *Hindus and Muslims were united in hating British rule. All Indians resented job discrimination, lower pay, and condescension.*

Sri Lanka began to recover from its long civil war. The economy grew, and at first the government had strong support. The parliament amended Sri Lanka's constitution to give the president greater powers. Over time, however, these greater powers led to human rights abuses against Tamils. In an upset victory in 2015, voters elected a new president.

Reading Check
Compare and Contrast What issues do Bangladesh and Sri Lanka face?

As difficult as postindependence has been for the countries of the Indian subcontinent, other former colonies encountered similar problems. A number of formerly held territories in Southeast Asia faced challenges as they became independent nations.

Lesson 1 Assessment

1. **Organize Information** Make a timeline, similar to the one shown, that lists the leaders of India and Pakistan. What tragic connection did many of the leaders share?

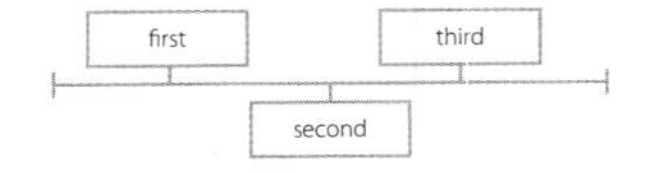

2. **Key Terms and People** For each key term or person in the lesson, write a sentence explaining its significance.
3. **Draw Conclusions** Why did British officials partition India into India and Pakistan?
4. **Synthesize** Why might India's political and economic success be so crucial to the future of democracy in Asia?
5. **Analyze Issues** How did religious and cultural differences create problems for newly emerging nations?
6. **Draw Conclusions** What is the main cause today of civil strife in Sri Lanka?
7. **Synthesize** How did imperialism contribute to unity and to the growth of nationalism in India?

Online Assessment

1. Why did radical nationalists in India gain more support for their cause after World War I?
   - ● The British had broken pre–World War I promises.
   - ○ The nationalists had lost many battles during World War I.
   - ○ The British had set up a new government in India after World War I.
   - ○ The nationalists had refused to send soldiers to fight in World War I.

   Alternate Question *Select the answer choice from the drop-down list to complete the sentence correctly.*
   After World War I, troops of Indian soldiers returned to the war. The *British* didn't keep their promises to allow India to self-govern. Because of this, the radical nationalist movement gained support among the Indian people.

2. What is one reason that a wide variety of people were most likely attracted to the teachings of Mohandas K. Gandhi?
   - ● He blended ideas from major world religions.
   - ○ He believed self-governance in India should come at any cost.
   - ○ He required that people who follow him give up their worldly possessions.
   - ○ He refused to align with the British over matters relating to India's economy.

   Alternate Question *Select the answer choice from the drop-down list to complete the sentence correctly.*
   Mohandas K. Gandhi blended ideas from *all of the major world religions*, which made his teachings attractive to many different kinds of people.

3. Why did Indian resistance to Britain intensify in 1939?
   - ○ Britain insisted upon a one-party political system.
   - ○ Britain promised to give more power to Muslims than to Hindus.
   - ○ Britain granted some self-government to Indians, but not total independence.
   - ● Britain committed India's armed forces to World War II without consulting elected representatives.

   Alternate Question *Select the answer choice from the drop-down list to complete the sentence correctly.*
   In 1939, the Indian people began to resist Britain's rule even more when World War II started and Britain committed India's *armed forces to fight in the war* without first consulting with the colony's elected representatives.

4. What caused the clashes in Calcutta in 1946?
   - ○ British police forced people to vote in elections.
   - ○ British government refused to grant India its independence.
   - ○ Hindus wanted to have their own country with no Muslim leadership.
   - ● Muslims didn't want the Indian government to be dominated by Hindus.

   Alternate Question *Select the answer choice from the drop-down list to complete the sentence correctly.*
   In 1946, the city of Calcutta experienced four days of riots when the *Hindus and Muslims* battled each other due to clashes over leadership in the new government.

5. Why did Rajiv Gandhi's party lose power in 1989?
   - ● He established a one-party system.
   - ○ He discouraged peaceful demonstrations.
   - ○ He was accused of widespread corruption.
   - ○ He had an inability to incorporate economic reforms.

   Alternate Question *Select the answer choice from the drop-down list to complete the sentence correctly.*
   Rajiv Gandhi's party lost power in 1989 because this leader was accused of widespread corruption.

6. What was the one thing that both East Pakistan and West Pakistan had in common with each other?
   - ● They both practiced the Islamic religion.
   - ○ They both had industrialized economies.
   - ○ They both had abundant natural resources.
   - ○ They both were frequently struck by cyclones.

   Alternate Question *Select the answer choice from the drop-down list to complete the sentence correctly.*
   Pakistan was divided into East and West Pakistan. These two areas had many differences and only one thing in common—they both *were predominantly Muslim*.

7. What ruined the economy of Bangladesh and fractured its communication system?
   - ● Bangladesh's war with Pakistan
   - ○ Bangladesh's alliance with India
   - ○ Bangladesh's rapidly growing population
   - ○ Bangladesh's election of Sheik Mujibur Rahman

   Alternate Question *Select the answer choice from the drop-down list to complete the sentence correctly.*
   Because of the war with Pakistan, Bangladesh had to rebuild its *economy* and its communication system.

8. **Elaborate** What was the Amritsar Massacre, and what were the results from this event?

   Possible answer: The Amritsar Massacre occurred in 1919. About 10,000 Hindus and Muslims came to a major city in the Punjab (Amritsar) to protest the Rowlatt Acts. They came to a huge festival in an enclosed square and intended to fast and pray and listen to political speeches. The British didn't think it was going to be a peaceful demonstration but instead viewed it as a nationalist outburst. The British had banned public meetings, which was not to the knowledge of many people who gathered there. The British commander ordered his troops to fire on the crowd without warning. They shot in an enclosed courtyard for 10 minutes, leaving 400 people dead and 1,200 or more people wounded. This massacre sparked an explosion of anger across India. Overnight, millions changed their loyalty from the British side to the nationalist side.

(continued)

Online Assessment *(continued)*

9. **Cause and Effect** What effect did the media have on Gandhi's nationalist movement?

   Possible answer: An American journalist was an eyewitness to the Salt March demonstration and how the British mistreated the demonstrators. He described the "sickening whacks of clubs on unprotected skulls" and people "writhing in pain with fractured skulls or broken shoulders." He observed how the demonstrators were peaceful and the authorities behaved brutally. His story was carried by newspapers across the globe. People were horrified by what they read, which garnered more support for Gandhi's cause.

10. **Make Judgments** Why was the year 1935 a time of both celebration and disappointment in India?

    Possible answer: In this year, the British Parliament passed the Government of India Act. It allowed the Indians to have limited democratic elections and a local self-government. However, it did not give total independence. This was cause to celebrate since it was a move forward in a good direction. However, it was also a time of disappointment since total independence was not granted and that was the ultimate goal of the nationalists.

11. **Make Inferences** What did the British hope to achieve with partition?

    Possible answer: Partition was the term given to the division of India into two countries: India for Hindus and Pakistan for Muslims. These two groups of people were antagonistic toward each other and it didn't seem like either group would be happy to have one or the other ruling over them. Separating them into two nations, each with its own government, seemed like the best compromise to keep the peace.

12. **Elaborate** How did Nehru try to transform India during his time as prime minister?

    Possible answer: He organized the states by language. He also encouraged industrialization, feeling that this was the key to help improve India's economy. After he was elected, he helped India's heavy manufacturing industries. He also sponsored social reforms. He tried to elevate the status of the lower castes, or those at the bottom of society, and helped women gain the rights promised by the constitution.

13. **Draw Conclusions** Why did the incident with Osama bin Laden in 2011 worsen relations between the United States and Pakistan?

    Possible answer: In 2011, the United States was still searching for Osama bin Laden, the leader of the al-Qaeda network. Ever since the terrorist attacks in September 11, 2001, the Pakistani officials had denied that bin Laden was living in Pakistan. The United States found him in a city near Islamabad in Pakistan. The United States military staged an operation in which bin Laden was killed. Pakistan was critical of the United States for the death of bin Laden, and the United States distrusted Pakistan for its denial of bin Laden's presence there.

14. **Elaborate** How did the Sri Lankan president attempt to establish peace in his country in 1987?

    Possible answer: In 1987, the Sri Lankan president signed an accord with the Indian leader Rajiv Gandhi. The agreement called for Indian troops to enter Sri Lanka and help disarm Tamil rebels. These rebels were a militant group that had long fought an armed struggle for a separate Tamil nation. The effort, however, from the accord was fruitless. Indian troops finally left in 1990.

Lesson 2 Planner

Southeast Asian Nations Gain Independence

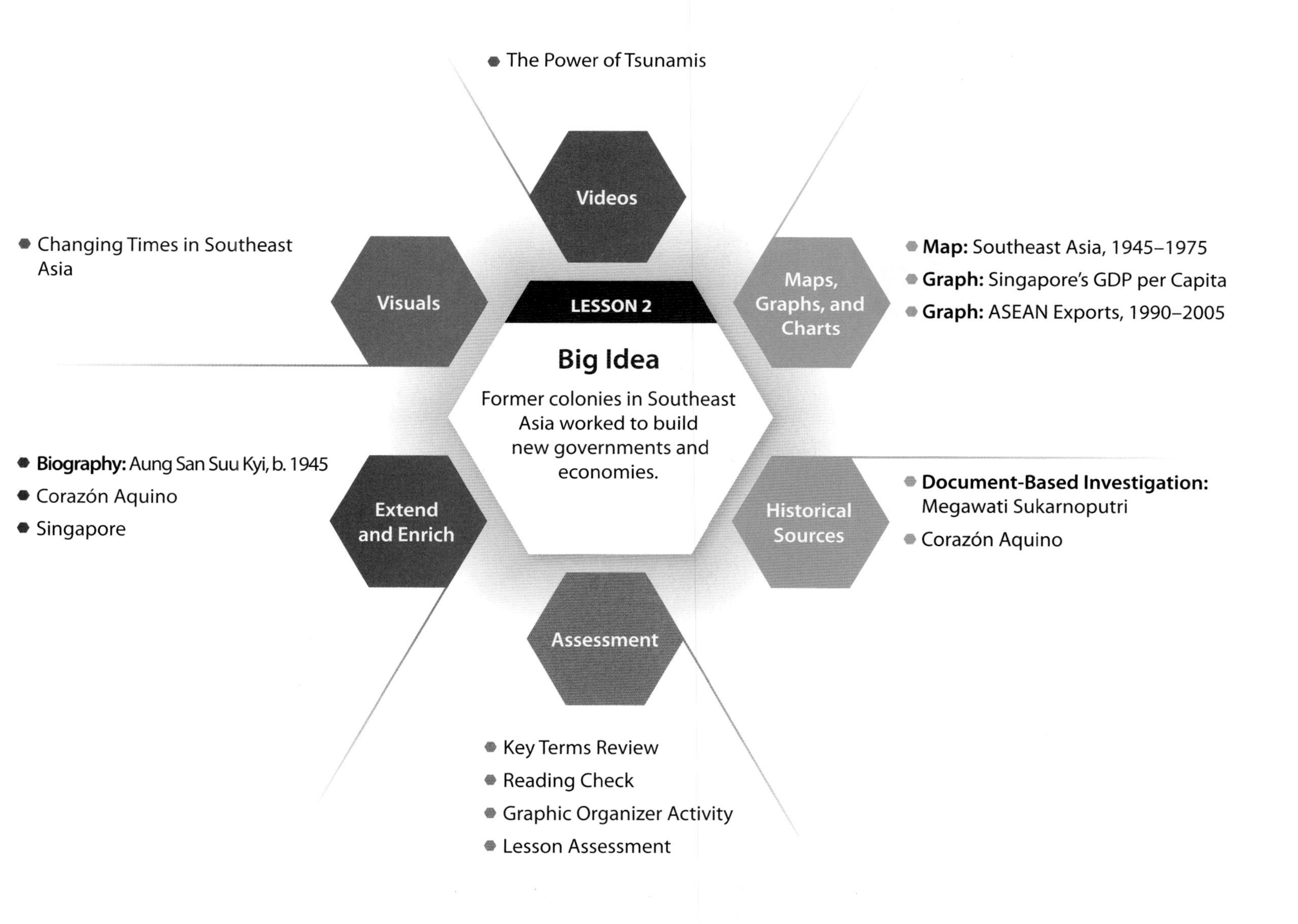

Online Lesson 2 Enrichment Activities

Corazón Aquino

Political Cartoon Students will study the political cartoon about Corazón Aquino's election victory in 1986 and think about what the cartoon shows specific to the task that lay ahead for Aquino after her election. Then students will draw a political cartoon that might have run in a newspaper in the Philippines in the 1900s, either during Marcos' authoritarian regime or after Aquino's election. The cartoon should show how people of the Philippines feel about what is happening in their nation.

Singapore

Article Students will read about modern-day Singapore and then create a brochure promoting it. This activity walks students through prewriting, putting together the brochure, and reviewing and proofreading the final copy.

Lesson 2

Southeast Asian Nations Gain Independence

The Big Idea

Former colonies in Southeast Asia worked to build new governments and economies.

Why It Matters Now

The power and influence of the Pacific Rim nations are likely to expand during the next century.

Key Terms and People

Ferdinand Marcos
Corazón Aquino
Aung San Suu Kyi
Sukarno
Suharto

Setting the Stage

World War II had a significant impact on the colonized groups of Southeast Asia. During the war, the Japanese seized much of Southeast Asia from the European nations that had controlled the region for many years. The Japanese conquest helped the people of Southeast Asia see that the Europeans were far from invincible. When the war ended and the Japanese themselves had been forced out, many Southeast Asians refused to live again under European rule. They called for and won their independence, and a series of new nations emerged.

A floating market in Bangkok, Thailand

The Philippines Achieves Independence

The Philippines became the first of the world's colonies to achieve independence following World War II. The United States granted the Philippines independence in 1946, on the anniversary of its own Declaration of Independence, the Fourth of July.

Teach the Big Idea

1. **Whole Class Open/Introduction** Have students discuss the pros and cons of children or spouses taking over on a leader's death or retirement. *Possible answers: Pros—familiarity, similar goals; Cons—no ability to lead, interested only in power or profit*
2. **Direct Teach** Read students the Big Idea: *Former colonies in Southeast Asia worked to build new governments and economies.* Review the following lesson objectives with students to aid in their understanding of the Big Idea:
   - Summarize the Philippines' independence movement.
   - Identify problems facing Burma, Malaysia, and Singapore.
   - Trace Indonesia's fight for independence.
3. **Whole Group Close/Reflect** Have students write a one-paragraph summary about the Pacific Rim nations that achieved their independence.

ONLINE DOCUMENT-BASED INVESTIGATION

The Colonies Become New Nations

Megawati Sukarnoputri is the second of five document-based investigations that students will analyze in The Colonies Become New Nations module. Students will read a passage by Sukarnoputri hailing the virtues of democracy and urging her fellow Indonesians to do what they could to maintain such a form of government. Students can click on the audio button beneath the historical source to hear the excerpt read aloud.

Objectives

You may wish to discuss the following questions with students to help them frame the content as they read.

- Why was the location of the Philippines a factor in the United States' desire to have a presence there? *It is near the USSR and China.*
- How could constitutional term limits prevent abuse of power such as that of Marcos? *force change in leaders*

More About . . .

Women and the Moro National Liberation Front The Moros established a Women's Committee and provided weapons training for women. Women held roles of critical importance with the Moros. They helped raised awareness of the cause, recruited, made uniforms, collected monetary contributions, and prepared food. Additionally, women aided in communication between Moro members in urban areas and those in rural areas. Women also delivered weapons, information, and supplies.

ONLINE GRAPHIC ORGANIZER

Southeast Asian Nations Gain Independence

As students read the lesson, have them use the graphic organizer to take notes. Students can review their graphic organizer notes at the end of the lesson to answer the following question:

Summarize Which nation faced the greatest challenges? Why? *Indonesia; it had to face many of the problems the other nations faced, as well as natural disasters.*

ONLINE INTERACTIVE MAPS

Southeast Asia, 1945–1975

Have students explore the map using interactive features and answer the associated question.

Location Which former Dutch colony is made up of a series of islands spread out from the Indian Ocean to the Pacific Ocean? *Indonesia*

In print edition, see map of same title.

1. **Location** Which former Dutch colony is made up of a series of islands spread out from the Indian Ocean to the Pacific Ocean? *Indonesia*
2. **Region** From what European country did the most colonies shown gain their independence? *France*

ONLINE LESSON FLIP CARDS

Review Key Terms and People

Students can use the flip cards in the Lesson Review at any time to review the lesson's key terms and people: *Ferdinand Marcos, Corazón Aquino, Aung San Suu Kyi, Sukarno, Sukarno, and Suharto.*

The United States and the Philippines The Filipinos' immediate goals were to rebuild the economy and to restore the capital of Manila. The city had been badly damaged in World War II. The United States had promised the Philippines $620 million in war damages. However, the U.S. government insisted that Filipinos approve the Bell Act in order to get the money. This act would establish free trade between the United States and the Philippines for eight years, to be followed by gradually increasing tariffs. Filipinos were worried that American businesses would exploit the resources and environment of the Philippines. In spite of this concern, Filipinos approved the Bell Act and received their money.

The United States also wanted to maintain its military presence in the Philippines. With the onset of the Cold War, the United States needed to protect its interests in Asia. Both China and the Soviet Union were rivals of the United States at the time. Both were Pacific powers with bases close to allies of the United States and to resources vital to U.S. interests. Therefore, the United States demanded a 99-year lease on its military and naval bases in the Philippines. The bases, Clark Air Force Base and Subic Bay Naval Base near Manila, proved to be critical to the United States later in the staging of the Korean and Vietnam wars.

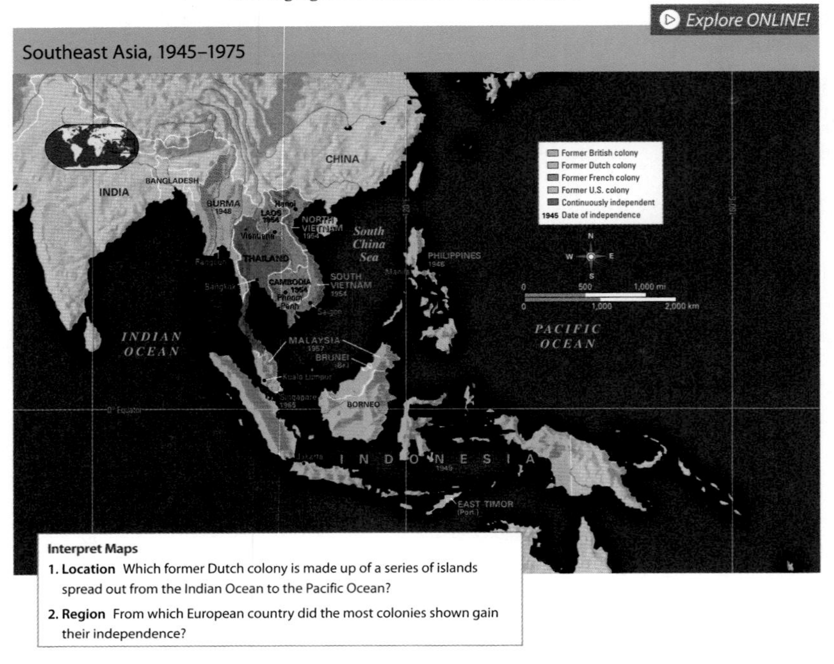

Interpret Maps

1. **Location** Which former Dutch colony is made up of a series of islands spread out from the Indian Ocean to the Pacific Ocean?
2. **Region** From which European country did the most colonies shown gain their independence?

ADVANCED/GIFTED

Write the Story of Aquino's Victory

1. Review the dramatic elements of the 1986 Philippine presidential election: both Marcos and Aquino declared victory; international observers charged Marcos with voting fraud; supporters changed sides; and the public forced Marcos into exile.
2. Ask students to imagine they are foreign correspondents covering the election and have them write a story, or series of stories, for U.S. newspapers.
3. Have students use the Internet to conduct further research, encouraging them to locate 1986 issues of newspapers and magazines.
4. After students complete their stories, have them share the stories in discussion groups.

These military bases also became the single greatest source of conflict between the United States and the Philippines. Many Filipinos regarded the bases as proof of American imperialism. Later agreements shortened the terms of the lease, and the United States gave up both bases in 1992.

After World War II, the Philippine government was still almost completely dependent on the United States economically and politically. The Philippine government looked for ways to lessen this dependency. It welcomed Japanese investments. It also broadened its contacts with Southeast Asian neighbors and with nonaligned nations.

From Marcos to Ramos **Ferdinand Marcos** was elected president of the Philippines in 1965. The country suffered under his rule from 1966 to 1986. Marcos imposed an authoritarian regime and stole millions of dollars from the public treasury. Although the constitution limited Marcos to eight years in office, he got around this restriction by imposing martial law from 1972 to 1981. Two years later, his chief opponent, Benigno Aquino, Jr., was assassinated as he returned from the United States to the Philippines, lured by the promise of coming elections.

In the elections of 1986, Aquino's widow, **Corazón Aquino**, challenged Marcos. Aquino won decisively, but Marcos refused to acknowledge her victory. When he declared himself the official winner, a public outcry resulted. He was forced into exile in Hawaii, where he later died. In 1995, the Philippines succeeded in recovering $475 million Marcos had stolen from his country and deposited in Swiss banks.

During Aquino's presidency, the Philippine government ratified a new constitution. It also negotiated successfully with the United States to end the lease on the U.S. military bases. In 1992, Fidel V. Ramos succeeded Aquino as president. Ramos was restricted by the constitution to a single six-year term. The single-term limit is intended to prevent the abuse of power that occurred during Marcos's 20-year rule.

As she took the oath of office, Aquino promised to usher in a more open and democratic form of government:

Reading Check
Make Inferences
Use context clues to explain the meaning of the word *vigilance* in the quotation by Corazón Aquino.

Historical Source

Excerpt from Corazón Aquino's Inaugural Speech

"I pledge a government dedicated to upholding truth and justice, morality and decency in government, freedom and democracy. I ask our people not to relax, but to maintain more vigilance in this, our moment of triumph. The Motherland can't thank them enough, yet we all realize that more is required of each of us to achieve a truly just society for our people. This is just the beginning."

—Corazón Aquino, *inaugural speech, Feb. 24, 1986*

Analyze Historical Sources
According to Aquino, what is needed to achieve a just society?

ONLINE HISTORICAL SOURCES

Corazón Aquino

Invite students to read the excerpt and answer the associated question.

Analyze Sources Use context clues to explain the meaning and importance of the word *vigilance*. *The word vigilance means not to relax, to remain alert; Aquino knows the Filipinos have waited a long time to gain their freedom, and urges them to protect their new democracy to help it grow stronger.*

In print edition, see historical source, Excerpt from Corazon Aquino's Inaugural Speech.

Analyze Sources According to Aquino, what is needed to achieve a just society? *a government dedicated to upholding truth, justice, morality and decency in government, freedom and democracy*

READING CHECK (DIGITAL)
Make Inferences Why might the United States have been interested in maintaining military bases in the Philippines? *to protect its economic and political interests; the Philippines were located within striking distance of many potential hot spots in the region.*

READING CHECK (Print)
Make Inferences Use context clues to explain the meaning of the word *vigilance* in the quotation by Corazon Aquino. *not to relax, to remain alert*

COLLABORATIVE LEARNING

Create a Visual Biography

1. Organize students into pairs.
2. Allow pairs time to research 15 facts about Ferdinand Marcos, Corazón Aquino, or Aung San Suu Kyi using classroom materials and the Internet.
3. Have pairs create a visual biography of the person they choose using words and symbols. A picture of the person can be drawn, cut out, in the form of a caricature, or any other creative display. Around each picture, students will identify attributes, ideas, or perspectives relating to each historical figure using words, symbols, or imagery.
4. Ask students to display the visual biography on any size paper and include the following: religion, time period, philosophy about leadership, greatest achievement, and how the person influenced history.
5. Request that each pair present and explain their visual biographies.

Objectives

You may wish to discuss the following questions with students to help them frame the content as they read.

- Why might military governments such as Burma's dislike democratic ideals? *Possible answer: Military works by authority rather than by consensus.*
- Why do you think ethnic groups in Malaya resisted British efforts to unite them? How is this similar to uniting people of different religions? *Possible answer: want separate identities; both problems require getting people to tolerate differences*

More About . . .

New Economies Gross domestic product (GDP) is one way that economists measure prosperity in a nation. They measure the dollar value of the goods and services a nation produces. To find the GDP per capita, economists divide the GDP by the number of workers in a nation. In 1965, soon after independence, Singapore had a GDP per capita under $1,000. By 1991, this tiny nation had a GDP per capita of about $13,000. In 2001, the figure was $20,544. The Philippines' GDP per capita was under $1,000 in 1965 and changed very little in the years to 1991. By 2006, that number was $5,100.

World's Tallest Buildings As of 2016, nine out of the ten tallest buildings in the world are located in Asia. The Burj Khalifa skyscraper in Dubai is the tallest building in the world at 2,722 feet. The skyscraper has a total of 57 elevators, 8 escalators, and154 usable floors.

ONLINE INTERACTIVE MAPS

Southeast Asia, 1945–1975

Have students explore the map and answer the associated question.

Location Where is Singapore in relation to Kuala Lumpur? *south*

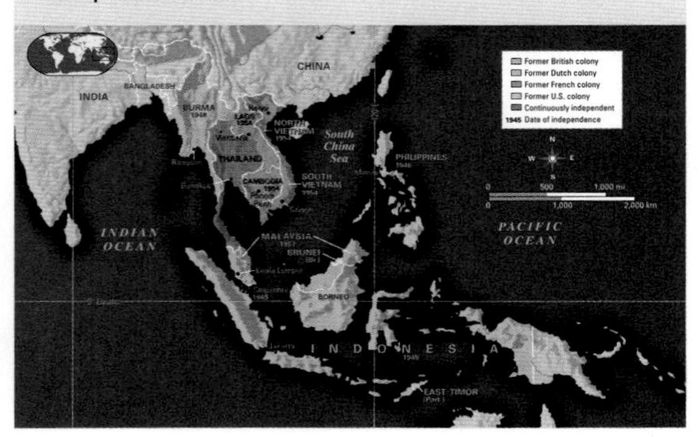

This cartoon is showing the political situation in the Philippines as a mess that Corazón Aquino needed to clean up when she was elected president.

The Government Battles Rebels Since gaining its independence, the Philippines has had to battle its own separatist group. For centuries, the southern part of the country has been a stronghold of Muslims known as the Moros. In the early 1970s, a group of Moros formed the Moro National Liberation Front (MNLF). They began an armed struggle for independence from Philippine rule.

In 1996, the government and rebels agreed to a cease-fire, and the Moros were granted an autonomous region in the southern Philippines. The agreement, however, did not satisfy a splinter group of the MNLF called Abu Sayyaf. These rebels have continued fighting the government, often using terror tactics to try to achieve their goals. In 2000, they kidnapped 21 people including foreign tourists. While the group eventually was freed, subsequent kidnappings and bombings by Abu Sayyaf have killed and injured hundreds of people. President Gloria Macapagal Arroyo launched an all-out military response to this group. The United States provided military assistance to the government's efforts.

Arroyo faced widespread crime, including kidnappings. She was accused of corruption, which led to two attempted coups in 2003 and 2006. After the 2006 coup attempt, Arroyo banned public demonstrations. Many people looked upon this action as evidence of her authoritarian rule.

In 2010, the people elected as president Benigno S. Aquino III, son of Corazón Aquino. He faced many issues, including a powerful typhoon in 2013, which killed thousands of people and left hundreds of thousands homeless.

Reading Check
Make Inferences Why might the United States have been interested in maintaining military bases in the Philippines?

British Colonies Gain Independence

Britain's timetable for granting independence to its Southeast Asian colonies depended on local circumstances. Burma had been pressing for independence from Britain for decades. It became a sovereign republic in 1948. In 1989, Burma was officially named Myanmar (mee•AHN•mahr), its name in the Burmese language.

Burma Experiences Turmoil After gaining freedom, Burma suffered one political upheaval after another. Its people struggled between repressive military governments and prodemocracy forces. Conflict among Communists and ethnic minorities also disrupted the nation. In 1962, General Ne Win set up a military government, with the goal of making Burma a socialist state. Although Ne Win stepped down in 1988, the military continued to rule repressively.

1178 Module 30

READING CHECK

Make Inferences Why might the United States have been interested in maintaining military bases in the Philippines? *to protect its economic and political interests; the Philippines were located within striking distance of many potential hot spots in the region.*

In 1988, **Aung San Suu Kyi** (owng sahn soo chee) returned to Burma after many years abroad. Her father was Aung San, a leader of the Burmese nationalists' army killed years before by political rivals. Aung San Suu Kyi became active in the newly formed National League for Democracy (NLD). For her prodemocracy activities, she was placed under house arrest for six years by the government. In the 1990 election—the country's first multiparty election in 30 years—the National League for Democracy won 80 percent of the seats. The military government refused to recognize the election, and it kept Aung San Suu Kyi under house arrest. She was finally released in 1995, only to be placed under house arrest again in 2000. Freed in 2002, she was detained again in 2003. In June 2007, Aung San Suu Kyi's house arrest was extended.

Vocabulary
house arrest confinement to one's quarters, or house, rather than to prison

In 2010, Burma passed new laws. Among other things, the laws said that people married to foreign nationals could not run for political office. This law disqualified Aung San Suu Kyi, who was married to a British citizen, from running for office. Most international groups, including the United Nations, thought that the 2010 election was not fair. Aung San Suu Kyi was released from house arrest six days after the election.

On February 4, 2011, members of the legislature elected Thein Sein, a former general, president of Myanmar. Thein Sein made many reforms. He removed restrictions on the press and released many political prisoners. He allowed unions to form, and people to demonstrate peacefully. He even relaxed the restrictions on Aung San Suu Kyi.

In December, the NLD became an official party. In 2012, Aung San Suu Kyi ran for office. She and other NLD candidates won 43 of 45 seats. Since the elections, the United States and European Union have lifted restrictions on Myanmar. In addition, Myanmar officials are working to increase investment in the nation and to attract tourists.

BIOGRAPHY

Aung San Suu Kyi
(1945–)

Aung San Suu Kyi won the Nobel Peace Prize in 1991 for her efforts to establish democracy in Myanmar. She could not accept the award in person, however, because she was still under house arrest.

The Nobel Prize committee said that in awarding her the peace prize, it intended the following:

to show its support for the many people throughout the world who are striving to attain democracy, human rights, and ethnic conciliation by peaceful means. Suu Kyi's struggle is one of the most extraordinary examples of civil courage in Asia in recent decades.

BIOGRAPHY

Aung San Suu Kyi

Have students read the biography of Aung San Suu Kyi, who won the Nobel Peace Prize in 1991 for her effort to establish democracy in Myanmar. Aung San became active in the National League for Democracy and subsequently lived under house arrest for six years.

ONLINE INTERACTIVE GRAPHS

Singapore's GDP per Capita

Have students explore the graph and answer the associated question.

Interpret Graphs What was Singapore's GDP per capita in 1965? *$1,000*

STRUGGLING READERS

Analyze Geographic Impact

1. Project a map of Southeast Asia for students, and explain that U.S. business has strong interests in Hong Kong, Singapore, and Indonesia.
2. Ask students to note how close the Philippines is to these areas.
3. Discuss why having military bases in the area would support the strategic and economic interests of the United States.
4. Ask students what international changes might have supported the United States giving up the bases.
5. Give students an outline map of the Pacific region and ask them to circle and name the various countries in the region without the projected map.

Objectives

You may wish to discuss the following questions with students to help them frame the content as they read.

- Why do you think the United States and UN supported Indonesia's independence? *Possible answer: believed Indonesia deserved self-determination*
- What are the possible challenges to uniting Indonesia? *Possible answer: geography, ethnic tensions, language barriers, religious hatreds*

More About . . .

Tips for English Learners Review and explain colloquial language. For example: bloodbath, police state, rules of the game, and main pillars of democracy.

East Timor Before Indonesia took control of East Timor, the island had seen other colonizers. The Portuguese arrived in the early 1500s, followed soon after by the Spanish. Britain also had a short period of control over Timor. However, apart from Japanese occupation during World War II, the Portuguese mostly retained control of East Timor. Indonesian forces then invaded in 1976 and absorbed East Timor as a province. Unlike Indonesia, where religious differences abound, most East Timorese are Christian. East Timor is now Timor-Leste.

READING CHECK
Make Inferences What do the top economies listed by the Geneva World Economic Forum have in common? *They are capitalist economies.*

Malaysia and Singapore During World War II, the Japanese conquered the Malay Peninsula, formerly ruled by the British. The British returned to the peninsula after the Japanese defeat in 1945. They tried, unsuccessfully, to organize the different peoples of Malaya into one state. They also struggled to put down a Communist uprising. Ethnic groups resisted British efforts to unite their colonies on the peninsula and in the northern part of the island of Borneo. Malays were a slight majority on the peninsula, while Chinese were the largest group on the southern tip, the island of Singapore.

In 1957, officials created the Federation of Malaya from Singapore, Malaya, Sarawak, and Sabah. The two regions—on the Malay Peninsula and on northern Borneo—were separated by 400 miles of ocean. In 1965, Singapore separated from the federation and became an independent city-state. The federation, consisting of Malaya, Sarawak, and Sabah, became known as Malaysia. A coalition of many ethnic groups maintained steady economic progress in Malaysia.

Singapore, which has one of the busiest ports in the world, has become an extremely prosperous nation. Lee Kuan Yew ruled Singapore as prime minister from 1959 to 1990. Under his guidance, Singapore emerged as a banking center as well as a center of trade. It had a standard of living far higher than any of its Southeast Asian neighbors. In 2011, the Geneva World Economic Forum listed the world's strongest economies. Singapore's economy ranked third, behind Switzerland and Sweden and ahead of the United States, Germany, and Japan.

Reading Check
Make Inferences What do the top economies listed by the Geneva World Economic Forum have in common?

In addition, efforts are underway in Singapore to make health care, public housing, and education more affordable for all of its people. A national health care plan went into effect at the end of 2015.

Indonesia Gains Independence from the Dutch

Like members of other European nations, the Dutch, who ruled the area of Southeast Asia known as Indonesia, saw their colonial empire crumble with the onset of World War II. The Japanese conquered the region and destroyed the Dutch colonial order. When the war ended and the defeated Japanese were forced to leave, the people of Indonesia moved to establish a free nation.

Sukarno Leads the Independence Movement Leading the effort to establish an independent Indonesia was **Sukarno** (soo•KAHR•noh), known only by his one name. In August 1945, two days after the Japanese surrendered, Sukarno proclaimed Indonesia's independence and named himself president. A guerrilla army backed him. The Dutch, supported initially by Britain and the United States, attempted to regain control of Indonesia. But after losing the support of the United Nations and the United States, the Dutch agreed to grant Indonesia its independence in 1949.

The new Indonesia became the world's fourth most populous nation. It consisted of more than 13,600 islands, with 300 different ethnic groups, 250 languages, and most of the world's major religions. It contained the world's largest Islamic population. Sukarno, who took the official title of "life-time president," attempted to guide this diverse nation in a parliamentary democracy.

Instability and Turmoil Sukarno's efforts to build a stable democratic nation were unsuccessful. He was not able to manage Indonesia's economy, and the country slid downhill rapidly. Foreign banks refused to lend money to Indonesia, and inflation occasionally soared as high as 1,000 percent. In 1965, a group of junior army officers attempted a coup. A general named **Suharto** (suh•HAHR•toh) put down the rebellion. He then seized power for himself and began a bloodbath in which 500,000 to 1 million Indonesians were killed.

Vocabulary
coup the sudden overthrow of a government by a small group of people

Suharto, officially named president in 1967, turned Indonesia into a police state and imposed frequent periods of martial law. Outside observers heavily criticized him for his annexation of nearby East Timor in 1976 and for human rights violations there. Suharto's government also showed little tolerance for religious freedoms.

Bribery and corruption became commonplace. The economy improved under Suharto for a while, but from 1997 through 1998 the nation suffered one of the worst financial crises in its history. Growing unrest over both government repression and a crippling economic crisis prompted Suharto to step down in 1998. While turmoil continued to grip the country, it moved slowly toward democracy. The daughter of Sukarno, Megawati Sukarnoputri, was elected to the presidency in 2001.

Upon taking office, the new president hailed the virtues of democracy:

DOCUMENT-BASED INVESTIGATION Historical Source

Excerpt from Megawati Sukarnoputri's Inaugural Speech

"Democracy requires sincerity and respect for the rules of the game. Beginning my duty, I urge all groups to sincerely and openly accept the outcome of the democratic process . . . . In my opinion, respect for the people's voice, sincerity in accepting it, and respect for the rules of game are the main pillars of democracy which we will further develop. I urge all Indonesians to look forward to the future and unite to improve the life and our dignity as a nation."

—Megawati Sukarnoputri, July 23, 2001

Analyze Historical Sources
According to Sukarnoputri, what are the cornerstones of democracy?

ONLINE DOCUMENT-BASED INVESTIGATION

Megawati Sukarnoputri

Students will read a passage by Sukarnoputri hailing the virtues of democracy and urging her fellow Indonesians to do what they could to maintain such a form of government. Students can click on the audio button beneath the historical source to hear the excerpt read aloud.

Analyze Sources Do you think Gandhi would agree with Sukarnoputri's desire for "respect for the rules of the game"? *He would agree if a situation were just, but if it was not just, he would disagree.*

In print edition, see historical source, Excerpt from Megawati Sukarnoputri's Inaugural Speech.

Analyze Sources According to Sukarnoputri, what are the cornerstones of democracy? *respect for the people's voice and respect for the rule of the law*

DOCUMENT-BASED INVESTIGATION HISTORICAL SOURCE

Megawati Sukarnoputri

Upon taking office, the new president hailed the virtues of democracy and urged her fellow Indonesians to do what they could to maintain such a form of government:

"Democracy requires sincerity and respect for the rules of the game. Beginning my duty, I urge all groups to sincerely and openly accept the outcome of the democratic process . . . . In my opinion, respect for the people's voice, sincerity in accepting it, and respect for the rules of game are the main pillars of democracy which we will

ENGLISH LANGUAGE LEARNERS

Clarify Sequence: The Independence of Southeast Asia

1. Review the section material with students using the Spanish edition of the GRW and then organize them into groups of six.
2. Ask each group to list the nations discussed in this lesson. *Philippines, Malaysia, East Timor, Singapore, Burma/Myanmar, Indonesia*
3. Assign each group member a different nation, and then ask each group to arrange themselves in the order in which these six nations achieved independence.
4. Ask each student to make a statement telling when, how, and from whom his or her country achieved independence.

Social History

Changing Times in Southeast Asia

Ask students which of the photographs on these pages show Southeast Asia the way they envision it. Which photographs are the most surprising? Why? *Answers will vary.*

What characteristics of Indonesian housing indicate a gap between rich and poor? *Possible answer: high-rise, modern tower next to decrepit shacks*

Draw Conclusions Why might some countries in Southeast Asia have more successful economies than others? *Possible answer: The countries of the Association of Southeast Asian Nations (ASEAN) might be more prosperous because they are part of a trading alliance.*

Forming and Supporting Opinions Are the issues facing Southeast Asians discussed here also a concern for Americans? Why or why not? *Bridging the gap between rich and poor is a problem facing Americans, though perhaps less dramatically. U.S. transportation systems are fairly modern throughout the nation, but modern markets are displacing farmers' markets and family-owned stores in some places. In other places, farmers' markets have made a comeback as Americans seek fresh or organic produce.*

ONLINE INTERACTIVE VISUALS

Carousel: Changing Times in Southeast Asia

Have students navigate through the carousel and note similarities and differences among the images or identify a unifying theme. You may wish to use the associated question as a discussion prompt.

Analyze Visuals Why might some countries in Southeast Asia have more successful economies than others? *Some nations, like Singapore, have ports that improve trade.*

SOCIAL HISTORY

Changing Times in Southeast Asia

As you have read, many countries in Southeast Asia have undergone revolutionary changes in their political and social organization. The region continues to struggle with its past and to face new challenges, but democratic reforms are becoming more common.

The past and present exist side by side throughout much of Southeast Asia. For an increasing number of Southeast Asians, housing, transportation, even purchasing food are a mixture of old and new. These images explore the differences between traditional and modern, rich and poor, past and present.

TRANSPORTATION
The water buffalo-drawn cart (above) is a common sight in rural Thailand. It is a mode of transport that reaches deep into the past.

In Bangkok, Thailand (right)—with its cars, motorcycles, and public buses—transportation is very different. These distinctly past and present modes of transportation symbolize the changes many Southeast Asian countries are facing.

▲ HOUSING
The luxury apartment building (background) in Jakarta, Indonesia, towers over the shabby and polluted slum of Muarabaru (foreground). Indonesia declared its independence in 1945 but was not recognized by the United Nations until 1950. Since independence, Indonesians have enjoyed relative economic prosperity, but bridging the gap between rich and poor is an issue that faces Indonesia and much of Southeast Asia.

1182 Module 30

MARKETS
As the postcolonial economies of Southeast Asia grow, traditional markets, like the floating market in Thailand (above), give way to the modern convenience of stores with prepackaged foods, like this street-side store (below) in Vietnam.

SOUTHEAST ASIA

GEOGRAPHY

- Eleven countries are generally referred to as Southeast Asia: Brunei, Cambodia, East Timor, Indonesia, Laos, Malaysia, Myanmar, the Philippines, Singapore, Thailand, and Vietnam.

POPULATION

- About 9 percent of the world's population lives in Southeast Asia.
- Indonesia is the world's fourth most populous country, behind China, India, and the United States.

ECONOMICS

- Ten Southeast Asian nations— Indonesia, Malaysia, the Philippines, Singapore, Brunei, Cambodia, Laos, Vietnam, Myanmar, and Thailand—make up a trading alliance known as the Association of South-East Asian Nations (ASEAN).

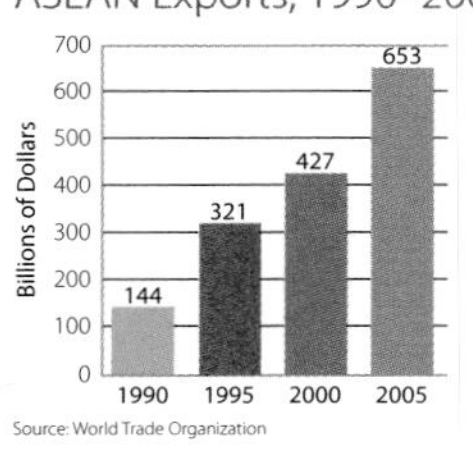

Critical Thinking

1. **Draw Conclusions** Why might some countries in Southeast Asia have more successful economies than others?
2. **Form and Support Opinions** Are the issues facing Southeast Asians discussed here also a concern for Americans? Why or why not?

ONLINE INTERACTIVE GRAPHS

ASEAN Exports, 1990–2005

Have students explore the graph and answer the associated question.

Interpret Graphs By how much did the value of exports change from 1990 to 1995? *The value more than doubled.*

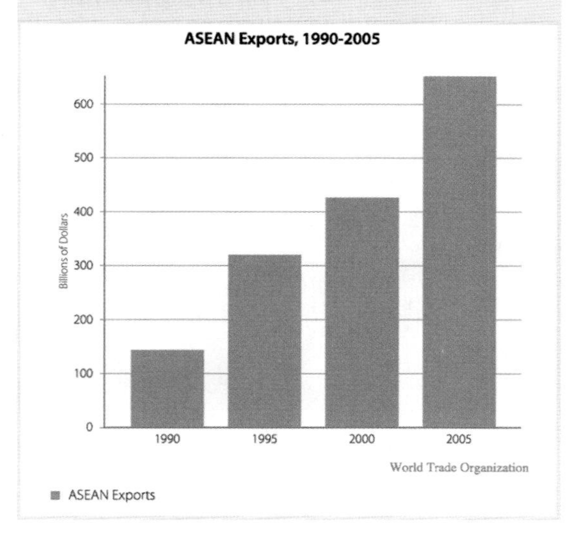

ONLINE ANALYZE VIDEOS

The Power of Tsunamis

Have the students watch the video individually or as a class. You may wish to use the associated question as a discussion prompt.

Analyze Videos According to the video, if the Indonesian tsunami had hit New York's Manhattan Island, how deeply would it have been buried in water? *The water would have been five miles deep in Manhattan.*

An earthquake off the coast of Indonesia on December 26, 2004, triggered a devastating tsunami. The tidal waves and floods killed more than 150,000 people.

Indonesia's next president, Susilo Bambang Yudhoyono, faced enormous challenges, including ethnic strife and government corruption. In 2004, an earthquake caused a large tsunami that flooded Indonesia's western coast. The tsunami caused many deaths and great damage. In spite of this disaster, Yudhoyono improved the nation's economy. In 2009, he was elected to a second term.

Soon after the election, however, Yudhoyono faced more natural disasters. These natural disasters included a major earthquake, tsunamis, and a volcanic eruption. Despite this, Yudhoyono led Indonesia to continued prosperity and peace. Economic growth slowed in 2013, however, and inflation rose. In 2014, Joko Widodo became Indonesia's new president.

East Timor Wins Independence As Indonesia worked to overcome its numerous obstacles, it lost control of East Timor. Indonesian forces had ruled the land with brutal force since Suharto had seized it in the 1970s. The East Timorese, however, never stopped pushing to regain their freedom. Jose Ramos-Horta, an East Timorese independence campaigner, won the 1996 Nobel Peace Prize (along with East Timor's Roman Catholic bishop) for his efforts to gain independence for the region without

COLLABORATIVE LEARNING

Create a Biography

1. Refer students to the biography of Aung San Suu Kyi as a model for creating a biography.
2. Have students conduct independent research using the Internet to create their own biographies for either Sukarno or Suharto. Biographies should include years lived, interesting facts about the person, and a question at the end pertaining to the person.
3. Collect the biographies and redistribute them. Each student should have a biography written by another student.
4. Ask students to read the biographies and answer the questions.
5. Have students share their questions and answers.

violence. In a United Nations-sponsored referendum held in August 1999, the East Timorese voted for independence. The election angered pro-Indonesian forces. They ignored the referendum results and went on a bloody rampage. They killed hundreds and forced thousands into refugee camps in West Timor, which is a part of Indonesia. UN intervention forces eventually brought peace to the area. In 2002, East Timor celebrated independence. In May 2007, Jose Ramos-Horta won the presidency, but in 2008, he was injured in an assassination attempt. Ramos-Horta recovered, but he lost his second bid for president. Ramos-Horta appointed Xanana Gusmão to be prime minister.

During Gusmão's first term, the economy grew. But many people still lived in poverty. The government did little to improve their condition. In February 2015, Gusmão stepped down as prime minister. He was succeeded by Rui Maria de Araújo.

Reading Check
Summarize
How did East Timor achieve independence?

As on the Indian subcontinent, violence and struggle were part of the transition in Southeast Asia from colonies to free nations. The same would be true in Africa, where numerous former colonies shed European rule and created independent countries in the wake of World War II.

Lesson 2 Assessment

1. **Organize Information** Use a table to show challenges nations faced following independence. Which nation faced the greatest challenges? Why?

Nation	Challenges Following Independence
The Philippines	
Burma	
Indonesia	

2. **Key Terms and People** For each key term or person in the lesson, write a sentence explaining its significance.
3. **Draw Conclusions** Why did the retention of U.S. military bases in the Philippines so anger Filipinos?
4. **Synthesize** What was the outcome of the 1990 Myanmar election? How did the government respond?
5. **Clarify** How did World War II play a role in the eventual decolonization of Southeast Asia?
6. **Make Inferences** Why do you think that the United States demanded a 99-year lease on military and naval bases in the Philippines?
7. **Compare and Contrast** What was similar and different about the elections that brought defeat to the ruling governments in the Philippines and in Burma?

READING CHECK (DIGITAL)
Summarize What are the cornerstones of democracy, according to Sukarnoputri? *respect for the people's voice and respect for the rule of law*

READING CHECK (Print)
Summarize How did East Timor achieve independence? *They kept fighting for their freedom; the efforts of Jose Ramos-Horta; the UN intervened*

Print Assessment

1. **Organize Information** Use a table to show challenges nations faced following independence. Which nation faced the greatest challenges? Why? *Possible answers: Philippines—election corruption, power abuse, rebel groups; Burma—repressive military; Malaysia—ethnic differences, Communist uprising; Indonesia—many islands, ethnic groups, languages, religions; East Timor—conflict over independence. Possible answer: Indonesia, due to size and diversity*
2. **Key Terms and People** For each key term or person in the lesson, write a sentence explaining its significance. *Explanations of the lesson's key terms can be found on the following pages: Ferdinand Marcos, p. 1177; Corazón Aquino, p. 1177; Aung San Suu Kyi, p. 1179; Sukarno, p. 1180; Suharto, p. 1181*
3. **Draw Conclusions** Why did the retention of U.S. military bases in the Philippines so anger Filipinos? *many saw bases as imperialistic*
4. **Synthesize** What was the outcome of the 1990 Myanmar election? How did the government respond? *National League for Democracy gained majority, but military refused to honor results and arrested NLD leader*
5. **Clarify** How did World War II play a role in the eventual decolonization of Southeast Asia? *Japanese occupied area and ejected previous colonial powers.*
6. **Make Inferences** Why do you think that the United States demanded a 99-year lease on military and naval bases in the Philippines? *to protect U.S. economic and political interests; to remind surrounding nations of U.S. military force*
7. **Compare and Contrast** What was similar and different about the elections that brought defeat to the ruling governments in the Philippines and in Burma? *Both governments ignored results; Philippine government finally stepped down; Myanmar retained power.*

Online Assessment

1. What is one reason that the United States wanted to maintain its military presence in the Philippines after World War II?
   - ○ to relocate its home fleet
   - ○ to retrieve prisoners of war
   - ● to protect its interests in Asia
   - ○ to increase its trading network

   Alternate Question *Select the answer choice from the drop-down list to complete the sentence correctly.*
   After World War II, the United States wanted to keep its military presence in *the Philippines* so that it could protect its interests in Asia.

2. What is one reason that Singapore has developed as a center of trade?
   - ○ It has an economy based on industrial factories.
   - ● Its location allows it to be one of the busiest ports.
   - ○ It is the only way to get to China from the United States.
   - ○ Its landscape is rich in natural resources such as coal and petroleum.

   Alternate Question *Select the answer choice from the drop-down list to complete the sentence correctly.*
   Singapore has one of the busiest ports in the world because of its accessible location. It is now a center of trade in Asia.

3. Why did the Dutch grant Indonesia its independence?
   - ○ The Dutch lost some of their land during World War II.
   - ○ The Dutch wanted to set up colonies in other parts of the world.
   - ● The Dutch lost the support of the United States and the United Nations.
   - ○ The Dutch suffered major economic losses putting down uprisings in Indonesia.

   Alternate Question *Select the answer choice from the drop-down list to complete the sentence correctly.*
   Once the United Nations and the United States stopped supporting the Dutch in *Indonesia*, the Dutch finally agreed to grant the island nation its independence.

4. **Evaluate** What was the purpose of the Bell Act, and why did the Filipinos oppose it?

   Possible answer: The Bell Act would establish free trade between the United States and the Philippines for eight years after it was signed, and then it would be followed by gradually increasing tariffs. The U.S. government insisted that the Filipinos sign this if they wanted to get the $620 million in war damages from the United States that the United States offered. The Filipinos were worried that American businesses would exploit the resources and environment of the Philippines.

5. **Elaborate** What did the British try to do in Malaya after World War II?

   Possible answer: After the war, the British tried to organize the different people of Malaya into one state. However, the British were unsuccessful in this attempt. The British also struggled to put down a Communist uprising.

6. **Cause and Effect** What was Suharto's leadership of Indonesia like and what prompted Suharto to step down from the presidency in 1998?

   Possible answer: Suharto immediately turned Indonesia into a police state when he was elected in 1967. He frequently imposed martial law. He annexed nearby Timor in 1976 and was criticized by the outside world for his human rights violations in that area. His government showed little tolerance for religious freedom. Bribery and corruption were commonplace. The economy did improve for a short time, but then the country suffered an enormous financial crisis in 1998. It was this economic crisis and the government repression that caused Suharto to step down that same year.

Lesson 3 Planner

New Nations in Africa

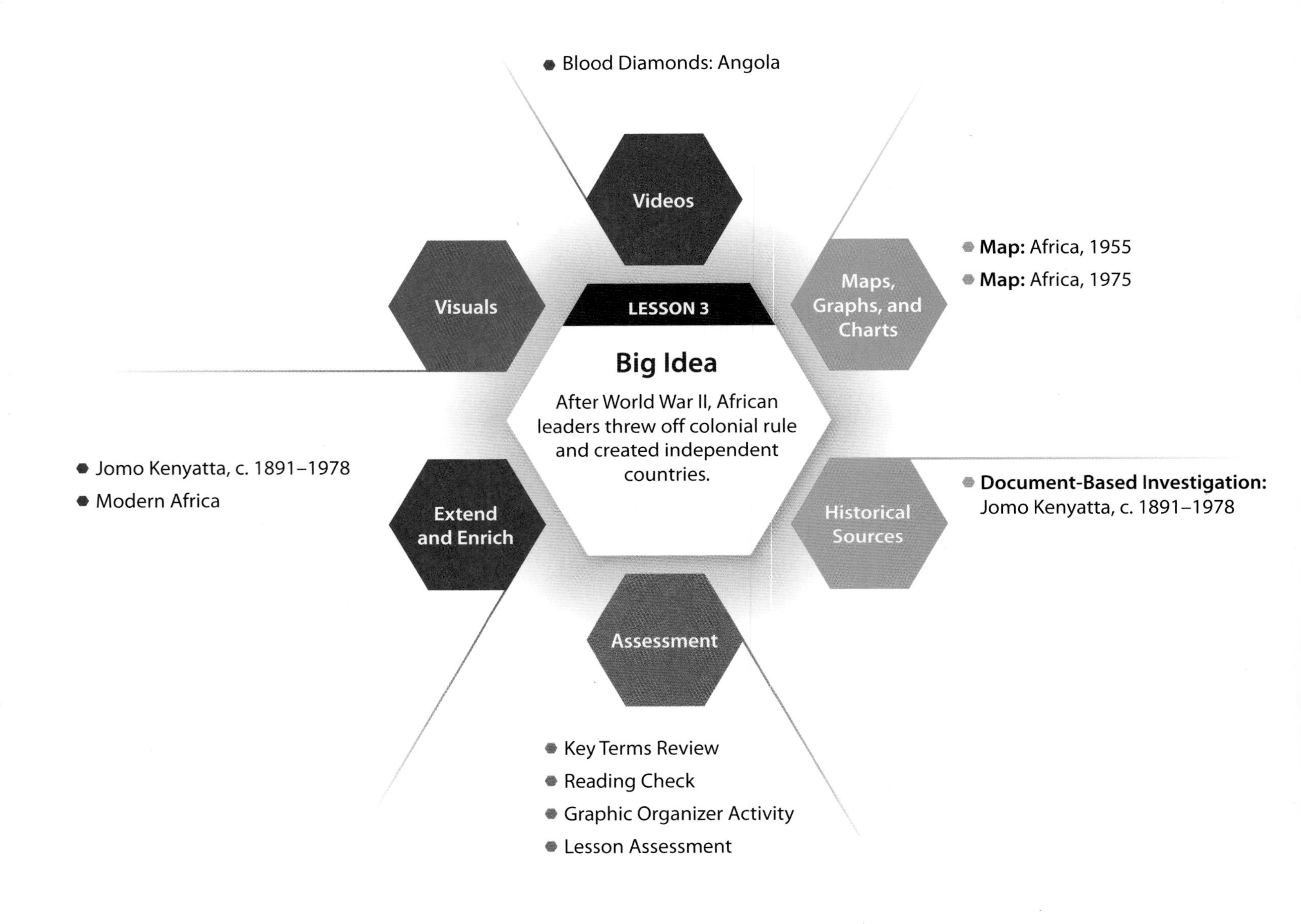

Online Lesson 3 Enrichment Activities

Jomo Kenyatta, c. 1891–1978

Article Students will read about the life of Jomo Kenyatta and his start as a political activist. Then they will answer a question about the lasting effects of Kenyatta's work to help Kenya achieve independence.

Modern Africa

Article Students will read about the formation of the African Union (AU). Then students will draw a map of Africa today that outlines and names the nations in the AU and includes the names of the leaders of these nations.

Teach the Big Idea

1. **Whole Class Open/Introduction** Tell students that many newly independent African nations struggled under rulers who would not share power. How does the U.S. government create shared power? *Possible answer: Constitution mandates three branches and shared power with states.*
2. **Direct Teach** Read students the Big Idea: *After World War II, African leaders threw off colonial rule and created independent countries.*

   Review the following lesson objectives with students to aid in their understanding of the Big Idea:

   - Identify factors affecting the success of African independence efforts.
   - Profile the tactics that Nkrumah used to liberate the Gold Coast from the British.
   - Describe the independence movements of Ghana and Kenya.
   - Explain civil wars and independence struggles in Congo and Angola.
3. **Whole Group Close/Reflect** Have each student write a newspaper article about the main topics in this section.

ONLINE DOCUMENT-BASED INVESTIGATION

The Colonies Become New Nations

The featured selection by Jomo Kenyatta is the third of five document-based investigations that students will analyze in The Colonies Become New Nations module. Jomo Kenyatta's words express his view of independence as the only option for Africa. Students can use the interactivity of the feature to learn more about this man who was willing to spend years in jail for his belief in freedom.

ONLINE GRAPHIC ORGANIZER

New Nations in Africa

As students read the lesson, have them use the graphic organizer to take notes. Students can review their graphic organizer notes at the end of the lesson to answer the following question:

Draw Conclusions What item in your notes had the biggest impact on a nation and why? *Jomo Kenyatta's leadership in Kenya—without his efforts Kenya may have struggled longer to gain freedom; civil war in Angola—it lasted for two decades, and land mines made it difficult to return after the war ended.*

Lesson 3

New Nations in Africa

The Big Idea
After World War II, African leaders threw off colonial rule and created independent countries.

Why It Matters Now
Today, many of those independent countries are engaged in building political and economic stability.

Key Terms and People
Negritude movement
Kwame Nkrumah
Jomo Kenyatta
Ahmed Ben Bella
Mobutu Sese Seko

Setting the Stage

Throughout the first half of the 20th century, Africa resembled little more than a European outpost. As you recall, the nations of Europe had marched in during the late 1800s and colonized much of the continent. Like the diverse groups living in Asia, however, the many different peoples of Africa were unwilling to return to colonial domination after World War II. And so, in the decades following the great global conflict, they too won their independence from foreign rule and went to work building new nations.

Achieving Independence

The African push for independence actually began in the decades before World War II. French-speaking Africans and West Indians began to express their growing sense of black consciousness and pride in traditional Africa. They formed the **Negritude movement**, a movement to celebrate African culture, heritage, and values.

When World War II erupted, African soldiers fought alongside Europeans to "defend freedom." This experience made them unwilling to accept colonial domination when they returned home. The war had changed the thinking of Europeans too. Many began to question the cost, as well as the morality, of maintaining colonies abroad. These and other factors helped African colonies gain their freedom throughout the 1950s and 1960s.

Objectives

You may wish to discuss the following questions with students to help them frame the content as they read.

- How would indirect rule better prepare a nation for independence? *Possible answer: more practice with governing*
- What were the main differences between direct and indirect rule? *Indirect rule: local officials governed, colonists enjoyed limited self-governance and an easier transition to independence. Direct rule: foreigners governed at all levels and no self-rule existed, independence was difficult*

More About . . .

Negritude French-speaking black writers and intellectuals led the Negritude movement. The term "Negritude" comes from Aimé Césaire, and in his words it means "the simple recognition of the fact that one is black, the acceptance of this fact, and of our destiny as blacks, and of our history and culture."

Algeria Algeria was part of France from 1830 until it gained independence in 1962. France sometimes recruited Algerian men and women against their will to fight in France's wars. During World War I, some 173,000 Algerian troops fought for France, and 23,000 died. The Algerian struggle for independence that began in 1954 was filled with conflict.

The ways in which African nations achieved independence, however, differed across the continent. European nations employed two basic styles of government in colonial Africa—direct and indirect. Under indirect rule, local officials did much of the governing and colonists enjoyed limited self-rule. As a result, these colonies generally experienced an easier transition to independence. For colonies under direct rule, in which foreigners governed at all levels and no self-rule existed, independence came with more difficulty. Some colonies even had to fight wars of liberation, as European settlers refused to surrender power to African nationalist groups.

No matter how they gained their freedom, however, most new African nations found the road to a strong and stable nation to be difficult. They had to deal with everything from creating a new government to establishing a postcolonial economy. Many new countries were also plagued by great ethnic strife. In colonizing Africa, the Europeans had created artificial borders that had little to do with the areas where ethnic groups actually lived. While national borders separated people with similar cultures, they also enclosed traditional enemies who began fighting each other soon after the Europeans left. For many African nations, all of this led to instability, violence, and an overall struggle to deal with their newly gained independence.

Reading Check
Recognize Effects How were the struggles of newly independent nations in Africa and Southeast Asia similar?

Ghana Leads the Way

The British colony of the Gold Coast became the first African colony south of the Sahara to achieve independence. Following World War II, the British in the Gold Coast began making preparations. For example, they allowed more Africans to be nominated to the Legislative Council. However, the Africans wanted full freedom. The leader of their largely nonviolent movement was **Kwame Nkrumah** (KWAH•mee-uhn•KROO•muh). Starting in 1947, he worked to liberate the Gold Coast from the British. Nkrumah organized strikes and boycotts and was often imprisoned by the British government. Ultimately, his efforts were successful.

On receiving its independence in 1957, the Gold Coast took the name Ghana. This name honored a famous West African kingdom of the past. Nkrumah became Ghana's first prime minister and later its president-for-life. Nkrumah pushed through new roads, new schools, and expanded health facilities. These costly projects soon crippled the country. His programs for industrialization, health and welfare, and expanded educational facilities showed good intentions. However, the expense of the programs undermined the economy and strengthened his opposition.

In addition, Nkrumah was often criticized for spending too much time on Pan-African efforts and neglecting economic problems in his own country. He dreamed of a "United States of Africa." In 1966, while Nkrumah was in China, the army and police in Ghana seized power. Since then, the country has shifted back and forth between civilian and military rule and has struggled for economic stability. In 2000, Ghana held its first open elections.

Vocabulary
Pan-African refers to a vision of strengthening all of Africa, not just a single country

Objectives

You may wish to discuss the following questions with students to help them frame the content as they read.

- What might be the advantages to having a president for life? *Possible answer: able to follow through on agenda or major changes*
- What might be the advantages of a United States of Africa? *Possible answer: global bargaining power in economic and political matters*

More About . . .

Kwame Nkrumah Kwame Nkrumah was baptized a Roman Catholic and after graduating from college in 1930, began a career of teaching in Roman Catholic schools and seminaries. Because of a keen interest in politics, Nkrumah came to the United States in 1935 to pursue political studies. He became immersed in political work and was imprisoned several times early in his political endeavors for advocating self-government.

Ghana As the first black African country to achieve independence from colonial rule, Ghana remains one of the leading countries of Africa. In 2015, it was Africa's second-biggest gold producer and second-largest cocoa producer. Though small in area and population, the country boasts coastal and forest zone environments that are rich in varied animal life. Mammal inhabitants include wild hogs, leopards, lions, hyenas, and all types of monkeys. The rivers and lagoons hold crocodiles, manatees, and hippopotamuses. Among the snakes are pythons, cobras, adders, and green mambas.

READING CHECK

Analyze Effects How were the struggles of newly independent nations in Africa and Southeast Asia similar? *Both began after World War II, and both had ethnic divisions.*

COLLABORATIVE LEARNING

Creating Art: The Harlem Renaissance

1. Explain to students that the Harlem Renaissance inspired Negritude, and introduce students to the art of Harlem Renaissance painters.
2. Ask groups to use the Internet to research the work of Jacob Lawrence, Aaron Douglas, and Romare Bearden.
3. Have groups choose one artist and create a collage or work of art that mimics the style of their chosen artist.
4. Ask groups to present and explain their works of art, with a brief commentary on the artist's style and subject matter.

ADVANCED/GIFTED

Journal Responses to Poems of the Negritude Movement

1. Ask students to use the Internet to find and read one poem by Léopold Senghor, Aimé Césaire, or Léon Damas.
2. Have students write a journal response to the poem that includes the poem's theme and its purpose.
3. Have students do a read aloud of the poems they chose and share their responses.

ONLINE LESSON FLIP CARDS

Review Key Terms and People

Students can use the flip cards in the Lesson Review at any time to review the lesson's key terms and people: *Negritude movement, Kwame Nkrumah, Jomo Kenyatta, Ahmed Ben Bella,* and *Mobutu Sese Seko.*

Objectives

You may wish to discuss the following questions with students to help them frame the content as they read.

- Why were the British willing to let Ghana go, but not Kenya? *British colonists living there opposed it.*
- How might unemployment in Algeria have led to the rise of Islamic fundamentalism? *Possible answer: It may have offered answers or solutions to their dissatisfaction.*

More About . . .

Mau Mau The Mau Mau (the origin of the name is uncertain) militant African nationalist movement began in the 1950s with the Kikuyu people of Kenya. This movement pushed for violent resistance to British rule in Kenya and was banned by British authorities in 1950. Mau Mau terrorists were linked with a campaign of sabotage and assassination and in 1952, the British government of Kenya began four years of military operations against the Mau Mau. By the end of 1956, more than 11,000 rebels had been killed and more than 20,000 imprisoned.

ONLINE DOCUMENT-BASED INVESTIGATION

Jomo Kenyatta, c. 1891–1978

Jomo Kenyatta's words express his view of independence as the only option for Africa. Students can use the interactivity of the feature to learn more about this man who was willing to spend years in jail for his belief in freedom.

Analyze Sources Why did Kenyatta think self-rule was important in Africa? *Without self-rule, Africans were not free to govern their own nations and participate in their own government.*

DOCUMENT-BASED INVESTIGATION HISTORICAL SOURCE

Jomo Kenyatta (c. 1891–1978)

A man willing to spend years in jail for his beliefs, Kenyatta viewed independence as the only option for Africans.

On the official day that freedom finally came to Kenya, December 12, 1963, Kenyatta recalls watching with overwhelming delight as the British flag came down and the new flag of Kenya rose up. He called it "the greatest day in Kenya's history and the happiest day in my life."

READING CHECK

Analyze Causes How did Nkrumah's policies undermine Ghana's economy? *The expenses of his projects—new roads, schools, hospitals—were more than the nation could afford.*

In 2001, the people elected a new president: Agyekum Kufuor. This transition was the first peaceful transfer of power between elected governments since 1957. In 2004, the people reelected Kufuor.

In Ghana's 2008 presidential elections, the people elected John Evans Atta Mills, and there was again a peaceful transfer of power. In 2012, Mills died. He was succeeded by his vice president, John Dramani Mahama. In the next election, Mahama ran against seven other candidates and narrowly won reelection.

Reading Check
Analyze Causes
How did Nkrumah's policies undermine Ghana's economy?

Fighting for Freedom

In contrast to Ghana, nations such as Kenya and Algeria had to take up arms against their European rulers to win their freedom.

Kenya Claims Independence The British ruled Kenya, and many British settlers resisted Kenyan independence—especially those who had taken over prize farmland in the northern highlands of the country. They were forced to accept African self-government as a result of two developments. One was the strong leadership of Kenyan nationalist **Jomo Kenyatta**. The second was the rise of a group known as the Mau Mau (MOW mow). This was a secret society made up mostly of native Kenyan farmers forced out of the highlands by the British.

Using guerrilla war tactics, the Mau Mau sought to push the white farmers into leaving the highlands. Kenyatta claimed to have no connection to the Mau Mau. However, he refused to condemn the organization. As a result, the British imprisoned him for nearly a decade. By the time the British granted Kenya independence in 1963, more than 10,000 Africans and 100 settlers had been killed.

BIOGRAPHY

Jomo Kenyatta
(1891–1978)

A man willing to spend years in jail for his beliefs, Kenyatta viewed independence as the only option for Africans.

The African can only advance to a "higher level" if he is free to express himself, to organize economically, politically and socially, and to take part in the government of his own country.

On the official day that freedom came to Kenya, December 12, 1963, Kenyatta recalls watching with delight as the British flag came down and the new flag of Kenya rose up. He called it "the greatest day in Kenya's history and the happiest day in my life."

COLLABORATIVE LEARNING

Interview Jomo Kenyatta

1. Organize students into pairs.
2. Request that students work in pairs to create mock interviews with Jomo Kenyatta.
3. First have the pairs use the Internet or library to research Jomo Kenyatta's life and political accomplishments.
4. Then have them plan and perform an interview in which one person plays a journalist and the other person plays Jomo Kenyatta.

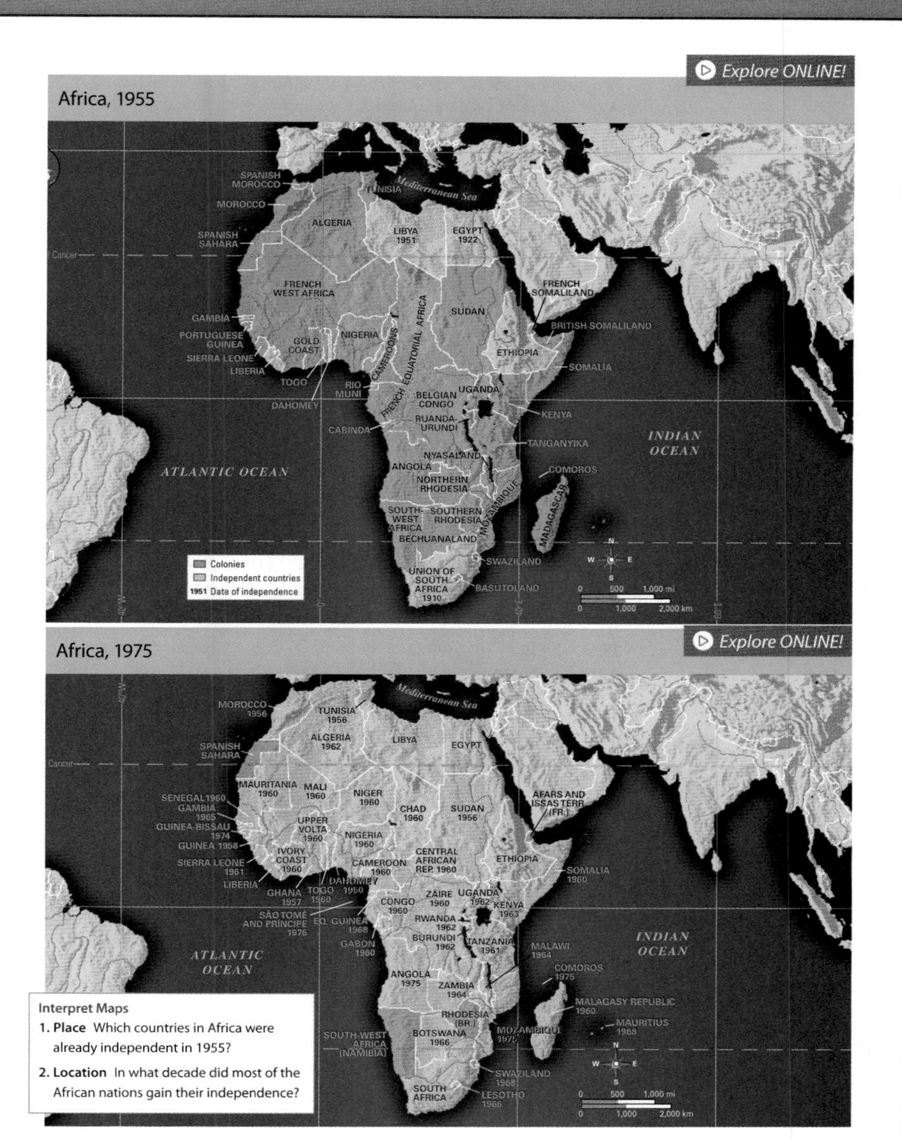

ONLINE INTERPRET MAPS

Africa, 1955

Have students explore the map using the interactive features and answer the associated questions.

Location Which country in Africa was NOT independent in 1955? *Algeria*

In print edition, see map of same title.

1. **Place** Which countries in Africa were already independent in 1955? *Libya, Egypt, Ethiopia, South Africa, Liberia*
2. **Location** In what decade did most African nations gain their independence? *1960s*

ONLINE INTERPRET MAPS

Africa, 1975

Have students explore the map using the interactive features and answer the associated questions.

Location In what decade did most African nations gain their independence? *1960s*

In print edition, see map of same title.

1. **Place** Which countries in Africa were already independent in 1955? *Libya, Egypt, Ethiopia, South Africa, Liberia*
2. **Location** In what decade did most African nations gain their independence? *1960s*

COLLABORATIVE LEARNING

Analyze Historical Decisions

1. Organize students into pairs.
2. Ask students to review this section, "Ghana Leads the Way."
3. Give students the following questions, and ask them to work together to develop responses: For what sorts of programs in Ghana was Nkrumah criticized? What were other criticisms of Nkrumah? What are alternative ways Nkrumah might have handled the economy?
4. Ask each pair to share one question, their response, and their opinion of Nkrumah's leadership.

READING CHECK

Contrast How did the granting of independence to the British colonies of Ghana and Kenya differ? *The British granted Ghana its independence peacefully, while British settlers in Kenya fought to remain in control.*

Kenyatta became president of the new nation. He worked to unite the country's many cultures and language groups. Kenyatta died in 1978. His successor, Daniel arap Moi, had a more difficult time running the nation. Some people disagreed with his one-party rule and accused his government of corruption. Ethnic conflicts killed hundreds and left thousands homeless. Moi stepped down in 2002. A new party gained power through free elections.

A record high number of voters turned out for the 2007 presidential elections. It was one of the closest elections in Kenya's history. Disputes over the close results led to violence. More than 1,000 people were killed and more than 600,000 injured in the violence that followed the election.

In August 2010, Kenyan voters adopted a new constitution. This constitution gave more control to local governments and limited the president's power.

Although many people feared the worst, the presidential election of 2013 was mostly peaceful. The people elected Uhuru Kenyatta, Jomo Kenyetta's son, with 50.07 percent of the vote.

In 2011, Kenyan troops joined a fight against an Islamic militant group, al-Shabaab, in Somalia. In retaliation, the group began to attack Kenya. One attack occurred in 2013, when al-Shabaab gunmen attacked a shopping mall in Nairobi. At least 65 people were killed. In late 2014, al-Shabaab killed dozens of non-Muslims in northern Kenya. On April 2, 2015, al-Shabaab attacked a Kenyan university, killing more than 140 people.

Algeria Struggles with Independence France's principal overseas colony, Algeria, had a population of 1 million French colonists and 9 million Arabs and Berber Muslims. After World War II, the French colonists refused to share political power with the native Algerians. In 1954, the Algerian National Liberation Front, or FLN, announced its intention to fight for independence. The French sent about half a million troops into Algeria to fight the FLN. Both sides committed atrocities. The FLN prevailed, and Algeria gained its independence in July 1962.

The leader of the FLN, **Ahmed Ben Bella**, became first president of the newly independent Algeria. He attempted to make Algeria a socialist state but was overthrown in 1965 by his army commander. From 1965 until 1988, Algerians tried unsuccessfully to modernize and industrialize the nation. Unemployment and dissatisfaction with the government contributed to the rise of religious fundamentalists who wanted to make Algeria an Islamic state. The chief Islamic party, the Islamic Salvation Front (FIS), won local and parliamentary elections in 1990 and 1991. However, the ruling government and army refused to accept the election results. As a result, a civil war broke out between Islamic militants and the government. The war continues, on and off, to this day.

Reading Check
Contrast How did the granting of independence to the British colonies of Ghana and Kenya differ?

COLLABORATIVE LEARNING

Write and Present: A Speech on Independence

1. Have students work in pairs and use the Internet to research an independence movement in one of the countries studied in this module.
2. Ask students to imagine they have been tasked with writing a speech for a leader of the movement.
3. Request that students write and present a speech for followers that includes these topics: current government, conditions inspiring the movement, goals of the movements, segments of the population supporting the movement, and the current status of the movement.
4. Have pairs exchange speeches and ask for volunteers to read speeches aloud.

Civil War in Congo and Angola

Civil war also plagued the new nations of Congo and Angola. Congo's problems lay in its corrupt dictatorship and hostile ethnic groups. Meanwhile, Angola's difficulties stemmed from intense political differences.

Freedom and Turmoil for Congo Of all the European possessions in Africa, one of the most exploited was the Belgian Congo. Belgium had ruthlessly plundered the colony's rich resources of rubber and copper. In addition, Belgian officials ruled with a harsh hand and provided the population with no social services. They also had made no attempt to prepare the people for independence. Not surprisingly, Belgium's granting of independence in 1960 to the Congo (known as Zaire from 1971 to 1997) resulted in upheaval.

In 1960, **Patrice Lumumba** became the Congo's first prime minister. He worked for a united Congo because he didn't want to divide the nation along ethnic or regional lines. Like many other African leaders, he supported Pan-Africanism, neutralism, and an end to colonial territories. Soon after he came to power, however, he was murdered. People throughout Africa mourned his death.

Mobuto Sese Seko

After years of civil war, an army officer, Colonel Joseph Mobutu, later known as **Mobutu Sese Seko** (moh•BOO•too-SAY•say-SAY•koh), seized power in 1965. For 32 years, Mobutu ruled the country that he renamed Zaire. He maintained control though a combination of force, one-party rule, and gifts to supporters. Mobutu successfully withstood several armed rebellions. He was finally overthrown in 1997 by rebel leader Laurent Kabila after months of civil war. Shortly thereafter, the country was renamed the Democratic Republic of the Congo.

On becoming president, Kabila promised a transition to democracy and free elections by April 1999. Such elections never came. By 2000 the nation endured another round of civil war, as three separate rebel groups sought to overthrow Kabila's autocratic rule. In January 2001, a bodyguard assassinated Kabila.

His son, Joseph Kabila, took power and began a quest for peace. In 2002, the government signed peace deals with rebel groups and neighboring countries. In 2006, Kabila was elected president under a new constitution. In 2008, the government and more than 20 rebel groups signed a peace agreement. They wanted to end the fighting in the eastern part of the nation. Later in the year, however, rebels attacked. The truce broke down. Tens of thousands of people were displaced.

Objectives

You may wish to discuss the following questions with students to help them frame the content as they read.

- How was Kabila's rule similar to that of other leaders in newly independent nations? *Possible answer: He promised democracy but seized autocratic rule once in power.*
- How did interference by outside forces affect the war in Angola? *Possible answer: Aid from outside forces kept the war going and reduced the chance of a peaceful end to the war.*

More About . . .

Mobutu Sese Seko In 1997 Mobutu Sese Seko, Zaire's longtime dictator and the last of the Cold War rulers, died from cancer at age 66 while he was in exile in Morocco. His ideology, known as Mobutuism, sought to benefit his own rule by reawakening pride in Africans for their unique cultural values. His political career was marked by violence, cunning, and his use of state funds to buy off enemies.

ONLINE ANALYZE VIDEOS

Blood Diamonds: Angola

Have students watch the video individually or as a class. You may wish to use the associated question as a discussion prompt.

Analyze Videos How did the two sides in Angola's civil war finance their operations? *They both used Angola's natural resources. The MPLA used oil; UNITA took over the diamond mines.*

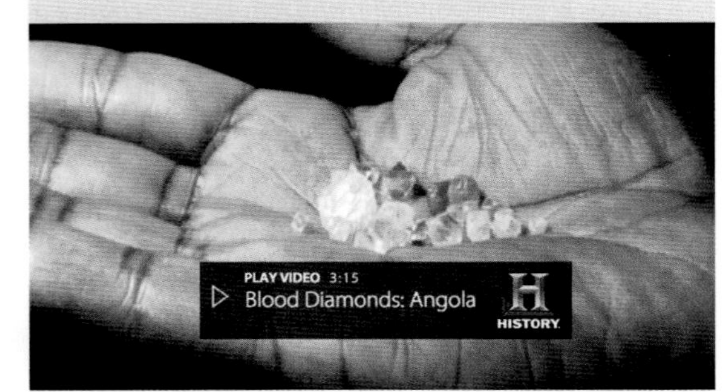

Eleven candidates ran for election in 2011. Kabila, with 49 percent of the vote, was declared the winner. Former prime minister Etienne Tshisekedi, with 32 percent of the vote, was second. The Supreme Court later confirmed the results, but Tshisekedi's party rejected the results. Tshisekedi declared himself the nation's rightful president. Kabila's party, however, had won more than half of the seats in the National Assembly.

War Tears at Angola To the southwest of Congo lies Angola, a country that not only had to fight to gain its freedom but to hold itself together after independence. The Portuguese had long ruled Angola and had no desire to stop. When an independence movement broke out in the colony, Portugal sent in 50,000 troops. The cost of the conflict amounted to almost half of Portugal's national budget. The heavy cost of fighting, as well as growing opposition at home to the war, prompted the Portuguese to withdraw from Angola in 1975.

Almost immediately, the Communist-leaning MPLA (Popular Movement for the Liberation of Angola) declared itself the new nation's rightful government. This led to a prolonged civil war, as various rebel groups fought the government and each other for power. Each group received help from outside sources. The MPLA was assisted by some 50,000 Cuban troops and by the Soviet Union. The major opposition to the MPLA was UNITA (National Union for the Total Independence of Angola),

History in Depth

Genocide in East Africa

In East Africa, both Rwanda and Darfur, a region in Sudan, have suffered from campaigns of genocide.

In the spring of 1994, the Rwandan president, a Hutu, died in a suspicious plane crash. In the months that followed, Hutus slaughtered about 1 million Tutsis before Tutsi rebels put an end to the killings. The United Nations set up a tribunal to punish those responsible for the worst acts of genocide.

In 2004, Sudanese government forces and progovernment militias began killing villagers in Darfur as part of a campaign against rebel forces. In 2007, President Bush announced fresh sanctions against Sudan.

In 2009 an International Criminal Court (ICC) issued an arrest warrant for president Omar al-Bashir, president of Sudan. The ICC accused Bashir of genocide, war crimes, and crimes against humanity. The Sudan government said that Bashir was innocent.

In spite of the presence of United Nations troops, terror in Darfur continues. In 2014, the UN stated that more than 3,000 villages in Darfur had been burned down. It said also that there was widespread violence against the people there.

STRUGGLING READERS

Explore Leadership Styles

1. Use the Guided Reading worksheet and Guided Reading Workbook for Section 3 to review the section material with students.
2. Assign groups of students the roles of various leaders they have read about in this section: Kwame Nkrumah, Jomo Kenyatta, Mobutu Sese Seko, Ahmed Ben Bella.
3. Within their groups, have students discuss their leader's methods of ruling the country. Then have them discuss the success or failure of the leader's style of governing.
4. Ask each group to give a brief report describing the leadership style and its success or failure.

to which South Africa and the United States lent support. For decades, the two sides agreed to and then abandoned various cease-fire agreements. In 2002, the warring sides agreed to a peace accord, and the 27-year-long civil war ended.

The Angolan government had to rebuild the country, which had been destroyed by warfare. Epidemics and cholera outbreaks occurred because of poor sanitation. The civil war left more than 4 million people homeless. Hundreds of thousands of refugees outside the nation wanted to return home.

Thousands of land mines buried across the country limited farmers' ability to farm again. The Angolan government had to work with separatist groups, who demanded independence. When the government and the main separatist group reached an agreement in 2006, Angolans hoped that peace had finally come to their nation.

In 2008, Angola held elections. The MPLA won about four-fifths of the vote. A new constitution let the president be elected by the party with the most votes. The MPLA party selected José dos Santos to be president. In the 2012 elections, the MPLA easily won a majority, and dos Santos became president again.

Reading Check
Recognize Effects
Why was the Congo vulnerable to turmoil after independence?

As the colonies of Africa worked to become stable nations, the new nation of Israel was emerging in the Middle East. However, its growth upset many in the surrounding Arab world and would prompt one of the longest-running conflicts in modern history.

Lesson 3 Assessment

1. Organize Information Use a two-column table to list important items in the history of African nations. Which item had the greatest impact on its country? Why?

Ghana	
Kenya	
Zaire	
Algeria	
Angola	

2. Key Terms and People For each key term or person in the lesson, write a sentence explaining its significance.
3. Draw Conclusions Who were the Mau Mau of Kenya? What was their goal?
4. Synthesize What ignited the genocide in Rwanda, and how was the issue resolved by the United Nations?
5. Draw Conclusions How did the way in which European colonialists carved up Africa in the 1800s lead to civil strife in many new African nations?
6. Analyze Motives What prompted Portugal to grant Angola its freedom? Why do you think the United States and the Soviet Union participated in Angola's civil war?
7. Analyze Issues Why do you think revolution swept so many African nations following their independence from European rule?

READING CHECK

Analyze Effects Why was the Congo vulnerable to turmoil after independence? *The Belgians left it with a ruined economy and no social services, and provided no preparation for independence.*

Print Assessment

1. **Organize Information** Use a two-column table to list important items in the history of African nations. Which item had the greatest impact on its country? Why? *Possible answers: Ghana—Nkrumah damaged economy through costly projects; Kenya—Kenyatta fought against British; Zaire—Mobutu overthrown; Algeria—French colonists fought independence; long civil war; Angola—Portuguese fought to keep country but gave up; long civil war.*
2. **Key Terms and People** For each key term or person in the lesson, write a sentence explaining its significance. *Explanations of the lesson's key terms can be found on the following pages: Negritude movement, p. 1186; Kwame Nkrumah, p. 1187; Jomo Kenyatta, p. 1188; Ahmed Ben Bella, p. 1190; Mobutu Sese Seko, p. 1191*
3. **Draw Conclusions** Who were the Mau Mau of Kenya? What was their goal? *resistance group of Kenyan farmers; force British farmers from the land*
4. **Synthesize** What ignited the genocide in Rwanda, and how was the issue resolved by the United Nations? *The Rwandan genocide started when Rwanda's president died in a plane crash. It was finally resolved when the UN punished those responsible for the worst acts of the genocide.*
5. **Draw Conclusions** How did the way in which European colonialists carved up Africa in the 1800s lead to civil strife in many new African nations? *Possible answer: Europeans created artificial borders, dividing ethnic groups and enclosing those at odds. Groups fought after Europeans left.*
6. **Analyze Motives** What prompted Portugal to grant Angola its freedom? Why do you think the United States and the Soviet Union participated in Angola's civil war? *high cost of fighting for control, opposition at home to colonialism; Soviets wanted to support Communist government; United States wanted to stop it.*
7. **Analyze Issues** Why do you think revolution swept so many African nations following their independence from European rule? *desire for freedom had been building; colonial departure left instability*

Online Assessment

1. Why were Africans unwilling to accept colonial domination after World War II?
   - ○ Africans had set up their own independent governments during the war.
   - ○ Europeans had diminished the size of European militaries during the war.
   - ● Africans had served as soldiers alongside Europeans to defend freedom during the war.
   - ○ Europeans had used up all of the natural resources in their own countries during the war.

   Alternate Question *Select the answer choice from the drop-down list to complete the sentence correctly.*
   During World War II, Africans served as soldiers alongside Europeans. Because of that, Africans were unwilling to accept *colonial domination* after the war.

2. How were Nkrumah and Gandhi similar to each other?
   - ● They both encouraged strikes and boycotts.
   - ○ They both used violence to refuse imprisonment.
   - ○ They both wanted self-governance at any cost.
   - ○ They both included religious teachings in their speeches.

   Alternate Question *Select the answer choice from the drop-down list to complete the sentence correctly.*
   Nkrumah and Gandhi were similar to each other because they both encouraged their followers to *use nonviolent demonstrations*.

3. Which of the following is a development that forced British settlers in Africa to accept African self-government?
   - ○ the seizing of prize farmland
   - ○ the promise of free elections
   - ○ the acceptance of Islamic law
   - ● the rise of the Mau Mau group

   Alternate Question *Select the answer choice from the drop-down list to complete the sentence correctly.*
   The *British settlers* who lived in Kenya finally accepted African self-government because of the strong leadership of Jomo Kenyatta and the rise of the Mau Mau group.

4. What was the main reason that the Portuguese finally withdrew from Angola?
   - ○ The Angolans joined with the government of the Congo.
   - ○ The Angolans offered to pay the Portuguese a monthly tribute.
   - ● The Portuguese found it too expensive to fight off the revolutionaries.
   - ○ The Portuguese had already taken all of the natural resources they wanted.

   Alternate Question *Select the answer choice from the drop-down list to complete the sentence correctly.*
   The *Portuguese* finally withdrew from Angola when they realized that it was too expensive for them to keep fighting the revolutionary forces.

5. **Compare and Contrast** What are things that the African nations had in common after they gained their freedom?

   Possible answer: They all had to figure out how to create a new government. They also had to determine what kind of postcolonial economy they wanted to have. They were all plagued by great ethnic strife. When the Europeans had colonized Africa, they created artificial borders that separated people with similar cultures and enclosed traditional enemies in the same country. So, when the Europeans left, fighting broke out between these factious groups.

6. **Elaborate** How did Nkrumah try to turn Ghana into the "United States of Africa" and what were the results of these actions?

   Possible answer: Nkrumah wanted new roads and new schools to be built in Ghana. He also wanted to expand health facilities. These were all good intentions, but they undermined the economy. He seemed to be more concerned about Pan-African efforts than on focusing on the problems within the country. While he was in China in 1966, the army and police seized power in Ghana.

7. **Draw Conclusions** Why were the population sizes of the French, Arabs, and Berbers in Algeria most likely included in the text?

   Possible answer: The purpose of including population numbers might have been to point out the disparity that although only about 1 million French but 9 million Arabs and Berbers lived in Algeria, it was the French who ruled. After World War II, the French refused to share political power with the native peoples.

8. **Elaborate** Which characteristics describe the way Belgium ruled the Belgian Congo?

   Possible answer: The Belgians ruled very harshly. They provided the local population with no social services. They also exploited the country, taking most of the natural resources (rubber and copper). They made no attempt to help prepare the people for independence. When the Belgians granted the people in the Congo independence, the people did not know how to govern themselves.

Lesson 4 Planner

Conflicts in the Middle East

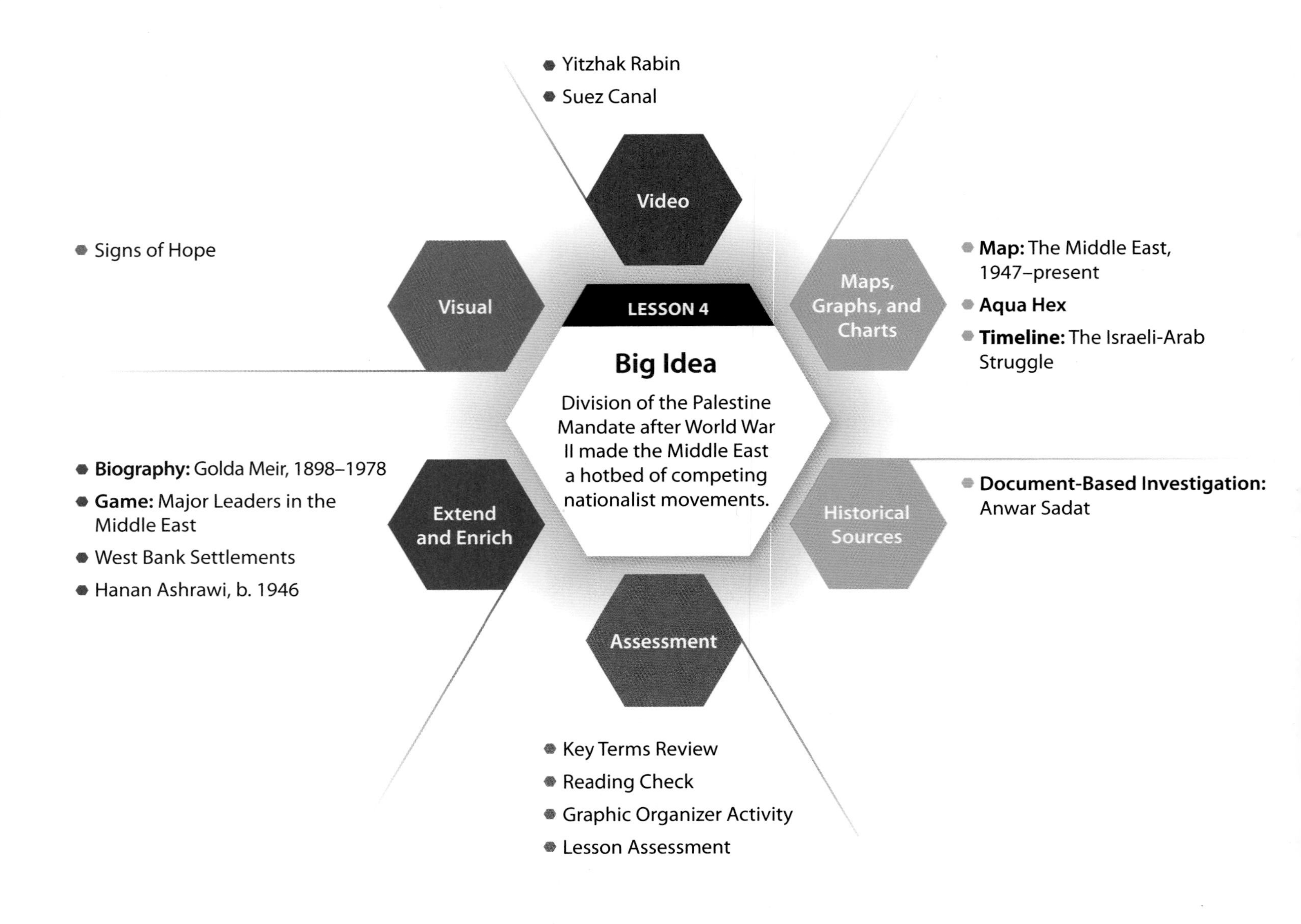

Online Lesson 4 Enrichment Activities

West Bank Settlements

Writing Activity Students will write an unbiased essay that explores all sides of the issue of West Bank Settlements. The activity walks students through prewriting, writing their essays, and reviewing and proofreading.

Hanan Ashrawi (b. 1946)

Article Students will read about the contributions of Hanan Ashrawi to the Middle East peace process. Then they will answer questions about Ashrawi's role and his skills as a commentator on the Palestinian side of Middle Eastern politics.

Teach the Big Idea

1. **Whole Class Open/Introduction** Explain that, in response to terrorism, Israelis live daily with heightened security measures. What security measures do students face in their schools or communities? *Possible answers: metal detectors in schools or airports, police presence*
2. **Direct Teach** Read students the Big Idea: *Division of the Palestine Mandate after World War II made the Middle East a hotbed of competing nationalist movements.* Review the following lesson objectives with students to aid in their understanding of the Big Idea:
   - Describe the formation of Israel.
   - Trace the conflicts between Israel and Arab states.
   - Describe the Palestinian struggle against Israel.
   - Explain Arab-Israeli peace efforts.
3. **Whole Group Close/Reflect** Have students select one conflict in the Middle East and write a short summary describing it and the outcome.

ONLINE DOCUMENT-BASED INVESTIGATION

The Colonies Become New Nations

The selection from Anwar Sadat's speech is the fourth of five document-based investigations that students will analyze in The Colonies Become New Nations module. Students will read a speech by Anwar Sadat, which he gave in a dramatic gesture before the Israeli parliament, inviting his enemies to join him in a quest for peace. Students can click on the audio button beneath the historical source to hear the excerpt read aloud.

ONLINE GRAPHIC ORGANIZER

Conflicts in the Middle East

As students read the lesson, have them use the graphic organizer to take notes. Students can review their graphic organizer notes at the end of the lesson to answer the following question:

Draw Conclusions Which military or political event in the Middle East between Israel and its existing Arab neighbors was most important? Why? *Six-Day War. It is the war in which Israel seized much of the now-disputed land.*

Lesson 4

Conflicts in the Middle East

The Big Idea

Division of the Palestine Mandate after World War II made the Middle East a hotbed of competing nationalist movements.

Why It Matters Now

The Arab-Israeli conflict is one of several conflicts in the region today.

Key Terms and People

Anwar Sadat
Golda Meir
PLO
Yasir Arafat
Menachem Begin
Camp David Accords
intifada
Oslo Peace Accords
Yitzhak Rabin

Setting the Stage

In the years following World War II, the Jewish people won their own state. The gaining of their ancient homeland along the eastern coast of the Mediterranean Sea, however, came at a heavy price. A Jewish state was unwelcome in this mostly Arab region, where Arab nationalism, or Pan-Arabism, was a common sentiment. The resulting Arab hostility led to a series of wars. Perhaps no Arab people, however, have been more opposed to a Jewish state than the Palestinian Arabs who claim that the entire Jewish land belongs to them.

Israel Becomes a State

The former Palestine Mandate now consists of Israel, the West Bank, and the Gaza Strip. To Jews, their claim to the land dates back 3,000 years, when Jewish kings ruled the region from Jerusalem. To Palestinian Arabs, the land has belonged to them since their conquest of the area in the 7th century.

After being forced out of Jerusalem during the second century AD, many Jews were dispersed throughout the world. Those who remained in the newly named Roman province of Palestinia were unable to establish their own state. The global dispersal of the Jews, which had begun many centuries before, is known as the Diaspora. During the late 19th and early 20th centuries, a Jewish nationalist movement began supporting the return of Jews to the region. Known as Zionists, they planned to reestablish the Jewish national homeland. At this time, the region known as Palestine was still part of the Ottoman Empire, ruled by Islamic Turks. After the Ottomans' defeat in World War I, the League of Nations gave Britain a mandate to oversee Palestine until it was ready for independence.

Vocabulary
Pan-Arabism refers to the idea of cultural and political unity among Arab nations

1194 Module 30

Objectives

You may wish to discuss the following questions with students to help them frame the content as they read.

- How could the claims to land in British Palestine be true for both Jews and Palestinian Arabs? *Both groups claimed lands based on previous residence.*
- Why was the United Nations given the task of dividing the former Palestine Mandate? *The League of Nations established the mandates and Britain turned responsibility over to the new world body, the UN.*

More About . . .

Ottoman Empire The Ottoman Empire was created by Turkish tribes in Anatolia and grew to be one of the world's most powerful states during the 15th and 16th centuries. Spanning more than 600 years, the Ottoman period ended in 1922 when it was replaced by the Turkish Republic and other successor states in the Middle East and southeastern Europe. The term "Ottoman" comes from Osman I, the nomadic Turkmen chief who founded the dynasty and empire about 1300.

Both Jews and Arabs had moved to the area in large numbers, and the Jews were pressing for their own nation in the territory. The Arabs living in the region strongly opposed such a move. In a 1917 letter to Zionist leaders, British Foreign Secretary Sir Arthur Balfour promoted the idea of creating a Jewish homeland in Palestine while protecting the "rights of existing non-Jewish communities." The British also promised the Arabs a state and gave part of the Palestine Mandate—Transjordan—to Abdullah for a kingdom in 1921.

At the end of World War II, the United Nations took action. In 1947, the UN General Assembly voted to partition the Palestine Mandate into an Arab state and a Jewish state. Jerusalem was to be an international city owned by neither side. The terms of the partition gave Jews and Arabs land according to their population centers. In the wake of the war and the Holocaust, the United States and many European nations felt great sympathy for the Jews.

All of the Islamic countries voted against partition, and the Palestinian Arabs rejected it outright. They argued that the UN did not have the right to partition a territory without considering the wishes of the majority of its people. Finally, the date was set for the formation of Israel, May 14, 1948. On that date, David Ben-Gurion, long-time leader of the Jews residing in Palestine, announced the creation of an independent Israel.

Reading Check
Summarize What recommendations did the UN make for the Palestine Mandate?

Israel and Arab States in Conflict

The new nation of Israel got a hostile greeting from its neighbors. The day after it proclaimed itself a state, six Islamic states—Egypt, Iraq, Jordan, Lebanon, Saudi Arabia, and Syria—invaded Israel. The first of many Arab-Israeli wars, this one ended within months in a victory for Israel. Full-scale war broke out again in 1956, 1967, and 1973. Arab governments forced out 700,000 Jews living in Arab lands. Most moved to Israel.

The state that the UN had set aside for Arabs never came into being because the Arabs rejected it. Israel gained part of the land in the 1948–1949 fighting. Meanwhile, Egypt took control of the Gaza Strip, and Jordan annexed the West Bank of the Jordan River and the Old City of Jerusalem. (See map, The Middle East, 1947–present.) While the fighting raged, at least 600,000 Arab Palestinians fled, migrating from the areas under Israeli control. They settled in refugee camps in the areas designated for the Arab state and in neighboring Arab countries.

Objectives

You may wish to discuss the following questions with students to help them frame the content as they read.

- What prevented the establishment of the Arab state in 1948? *Possible answer: Palestinian Arabs rejected the partition plan.*
- How did Israel triumph so quickly in the Six-Day War? *Possible answer: by moving preemptively; by being highly motivated and better equipped*

More About . . .

Six-Day War The Six-Day War, also called the June War or Third Arab-Israeli War, resulted in a decisive victory for Israel. The UN called for a ceasefire on June 7 that Israel and Jordan immediately accepted. Egypt accepted the next day, but Syria continued firing on villages in northern Israel. After Israel launched an assault on Golan Heights and captured it from Syria, the Syrians finally accepted the ceasefire on June 10, 1967.

Palestine Liberation Organization (PLO) The PLO sought to centralize the leadership of various Palestinian groups that previously operated as clandestine resistance movements. It came into prominence after the Six-Day War. The PLO engaged in a protracted guerrilla war against Israel during the 1960s, '70s, and '80s before entering into peace negotiations with that country in the 1990s.

READING CHECK
Summarize What recommendations did the UN make for the Palestine Mandate? *The UN recommended the partition of the Palestine Mandate into an Arab state and a Jewish state, with Jerusalem as an international city.*

ADVANCED/GIFTED

Explore the Balfour Declaration

1. Have students research the Balfour Declaration using the Internet.
2. Then ask students if they think that Jews and non-Jews living in Palestine might have understood the Balfour Declaration differently. Use these questions to guide the discussion: How might Muslims, Jews, and Christians already living there have understood the document? Why would some non-Jews and the British government be sympathetic to Zionist goals?
3. Prompt students to consider historical connections and religious reasons.

ONLINE LESSON FLIP CARDS

Review Key Terms and People

Students can use the flip cards in the Lesson Review at any time to review the lesson's key terms and people: *Anwar Sadat, Golda Meir, PLO, Yasir Arafat, Camp David Accords, intifada, Oslo Peace Accords, Menachem Begin,* and *Yitzhak Rabin.*

ONLINE INTERPRET MAPS

The Middle East, 1947–present

Have students explore the map and answer the associated question.

Location What is the southernmost point in Israel, and what is its strategic value? *Eilat. It gives Israel access to the Red Sea.*

In print edition, see map of the same title.

1. **Location** What is the southernmost point in Israel, and what is its strategic value? *Eilat. It gives Israel access, by way of the Gulf of Aqaba, to the Red Sea.*
2. **Region** What country lies due north of Israel? east? northeast? *Lebanon; Jordan; Syria*

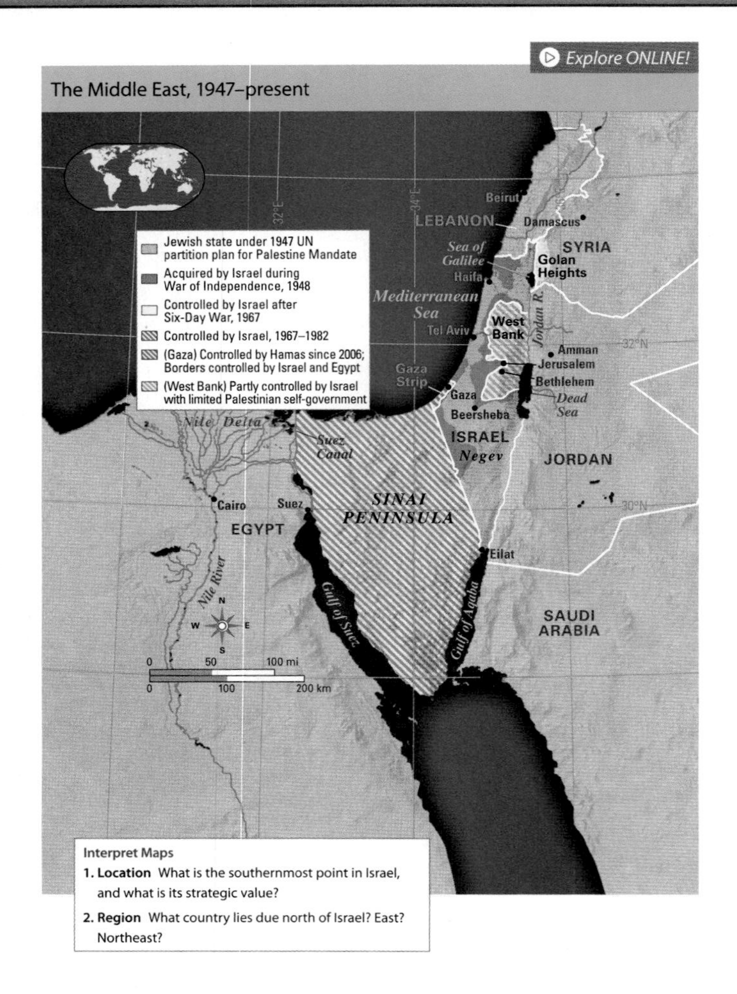

Interpret Maps
1. **Location** What is the southernmost point in Israel, and what is its strategic value?
2. **Region** What country lies due north of Israel? East? Northeast?

COLLABORATIVE LEARNING

Create Maps: Israel and Its Neighbors

1. Organize students into small groups and give them white paper and markers or colored pencils.
2. Ask students to use the maps in this section and the Internet to create a map of Israel and neighboring countries.
3. Have students add capitals, major cities, and physical features.
4. Ask students to trace the events in this section about Arab-Israel conflicts on their maps, showing land lost and gained, areas of dispute, and where wars took place.
5. When students have finished, guide them in a discussion of the role of geography in Middle East conflicts, and remind them of the size of the region.

The 1956 Suez Crisis The second Arab-Israeli war followed in 1956. That year, Egypt seized control of the Suez Canal, which ran along Egypt's eastern border between the Gulf of Suez and the Mediterranean Sea. Egyptian president Gamal Abdel Nasser blockaded Israeli shipping and took the canal, which was controlled by British interests. The military action was prompted in large part by Nasser's anger over the loss of U.S. and British financial support for the building of Egypt's Aswan Dam.

Outraged, the British made an agreement with France and Israel to retake the canal. With air support provided by their European allies, the Israelis marched on the Suez Canal and quickly defeated the Egyptians. However, pressure from the world community, including the United States and the Soviet Union, forced Israel and the Europeans to withdraw from Egypt. This left Egypt in charge of the canal and thus ended the Suez Crisis.

Arab-Israeli Wars Continue Tensions between Israel and the Arab states began to build again in the years following the resolution of the Suez Crisis. By early 1967, Nasser and his Arab allies, equipped with Soviet tanks and aircraft, felt ready to confront Israel. "We are eager for battle in order to force the enemy to awake from his dreams," Nasser announced, "and meet Arab reality face to face." He moved to close off the Gulf of Aqaba, Israel's outlet to the Red Sea.

Arab armies massed on Israel's borders. The Israelis struck airfields in Egypt, Iraq, Jordan, and Syria. Safe from air attack, Israeli ground forces struck like lightning on three fronts. Israel defeated the Arab states in what became known as the Six-Day War, because it was over in six days. Israel lost 800 troops in the fighting, while Arab losses exceeded 15,000.

Anwar Sadat

As a consequence of the Six-Day War, Israel gained control of the old city of Jerusalem, the Sinai Peninsula, the Golan Heights, and the West Bank. Israelis saw these new holdings as a key buffer zone against further Arab attacks and expected to exchange the land for peace agreements. Arabs who lived in Jerusalem were given the choice of Israeli or Jordanian citizenship. Most chose the latter. People who lived in the other areas came under Israel's control pending a peace treaty.

A fourth Arab-Israeli conflict erupted in October 1973. Nasser's successor, Egyptian president **Anwar Sadat** (AHN•wahr-suh•DAT), planned a joint Arab attack on the date of Yom Kippur, the holiest of Jewish holidays. This time the Israelis were caught by surprise. Arab forces inflicted heavy casualties and recaptured some of the territory lost in 1967. The Israelis, under their prime minister, **Golda Meir** (MY•uhr), launched a counter attack and regained most of the lost territory. Both sides agreed to a truce after several weeks of fighting, and the Yom Kippur war came to an end.

ONLINE ANALYZE VIDEOS

Suez Canal

Have students watch the video individually or together. You may use the question as a discussion prompt.

Analyze Videos What is the importance of the Suez Canal? *It gives ships access to the Mediterranean Sea from the Gulf of Suez.*

COLLABORATIVE LEARNING

Investigating Camp David

1. Organize students into pairs.
2. Tell students that two U.S. presidents have invited Arab and Jewish leaders to Camp David to work out a path to peace. In 1978, President Carter invited Anwar Sadat of Egypt and Menachem Begin of Israel to a meeting that resulted in the Camp David Accords. In 2000, President Clinton invited Ehud Barak of Israel and Yasir Arafat of the Palestinian Authority to Camp David. That meeting ended in failure to reach a compromise.
3. Request that student pairs research one of the meetings at Camp David. Ask them to describe the major participants in terms of their personalities and personal histories, identify the major issues under negotiation, and describe the outcome of the meeting.
4. Have students gather evidence from multiple sources and ask them to include sound reasoning, examples and details, and to organize their presentations sequentially.
5. After students have completed their research, have them share their findings with the class.

Objectives

You may wish to discuss the following questions with students to help them frame the content as they read.

- Why do you think Sadat's peace initiative enraged Arabs? *Possible answer: It offered to recognize Israel.*
- How are Yitzhak Rabin and Anwar Sadat similar? *Possible answer: Both were courageous leaders who were killed for their willingness to compromise in the interest of peace.*

More About . . .

Lebanon's Civil War Conflicts between Lebanese Christians and Muslims supported by the PLO erupted into a civil war in 1975. In 1982, Israel invaded southern Lebanon in an effort to drive out PLO troops and leaders. By 1985, Israel had withdrawn its troops except for a security zone at the Lebanese-Israeli border.

Oslo Peace Agreement The achievements of PLO chairman Yasir Arafat, Israeli prime minister Yitzhak Rabin, and Israeli foreign minister Shimon Peres were recognized in 1994 when the Nobel Peace Prize was awarded jointly to the three of them. Have students compare the Camp David Accords with the Oslo Peace Agreement.

BIOGRAPHY

Golda Meir, 1898–1978

Have students read the biography of Golda Meir, who served as ambassador to the Soviet Union, minister of labor, and foreign minister before becoming prime minister. She was the prime minister of Israel during the Yom Kippur War and sought assistance from the United States.

READING CHECK

Analyze Effects What were some of the effects of the Arab-Israeli conflicts? *Some territory changed hands; hostilities continued; instability threatened the region.*

BIOGRAPHY

Golda Meir (1898–1978)

Meir was born in Kiev, Russia, but grew up in the American heartland. Although a skilled carpenter, Meir's father could not find enough work in Kiev. So he sold his tools and other belongings and moved his family to Milwaukee, Wisconsin. Meir would spend more than a decade in the United States before moving to the Palestine Mandate.

The future Israeli prime minister exhibited strong leadership qualities early on. When she learned that many of her fellow fourth-grade classmates could not afford textbooks, she created the American Young Sisters Society, an organization that succeeded in raising the necessary funds.

The Palestine Liberation Organization As Israel fought for its existence, the Palestinians struggled for recognition. While the United Nations had granted both Jews and Arabs their own states, the Arabs rejected their state and the Arab countries launched a war to destroy Israel. The Arabs refused to negotiate peace with Israel.

In 1964, Palestinian officials formed the Palestine Liberation Organization (**PLO**) to push for the formation of an Arab Palestinian state that would include all of Israel. Originally, the PLO was an umbrella organization made up of different groups—laborers, teachers, lawyers, and guerrilla fighters. Soon, guerrilla groups came to dominate the organization and insisted that the only way to achieve their goal was through armed struggle. In 1969 **Yasir Arafat** (YAH•sur-AR•uh•FAT) became chairman of the PLO. Throughout the 1960s and 1970s the group carried out numerous terrorist attacks against Israel. Some of Israel's Arab neighbors supported the PLO's goals by allowing PLO guerrillas to operate from their lands.

Reading Check
Recognize Effects What were some of the effects of the Arab-Israeli conflicts?

Efforts at Peace

In November 1977, just four years after the Yom Kippur war, Anwar Sadat stunned the world by extending a hand to Israel. No Arab country up to this point had recognized Israel's right to exist. In a dramatic gesture, Sadat went before the Knesset, the Israeli parliament, and invited his one-time enemies to join him in a quest for peace.

Sadat emphasized that in exchange for peace Israel would have to recognize the rights of Palestinians. Furthermore, it would have to withdraw from territory captured in 1967 from Egypt, Jordan, and Syria.

DOCUMENT-BASED INVESTIGATION Historical Source

Excerpt from Sadat's Knesset Speech

"Today, through my visit to you, I ask you why don't we stretch our hands with faith and sincerity and so that together we might . . . remove all suspicion of fear, betrayal, and bad intention? Why don't we stand together with the courage of men and the boldness of heroes who dedicate themselves to a sublime [supreme] aim? Why don't we stand together with the same courage and daring to erect a huge edifice [building] of peace? An edifice that . . . serves as a beacon for generations to come with the human message for construction, development, and the dignity of man."

—Anwar Sadat, Knesset speech, November 20, 1977

Analyze Historical Sources
What conditions for peace did Sadat request?

U.S. President Jimmy Carter recognized that Sadat had created a historic opportunity for peace. In 1978, Carter invited Sadat and Israeli prime minister **Menachem Begin** (mehn•AHK•hehm-BAY•gihn) to Camp David, the presidential retreat in rural Maryland. Isolated from the press and from domestic political pressures, Sadat and Begin worked to reach an agreement. After 13 days of negotiations, Carter triumphantly announced that Egypt recognized Israel as a legitimate state. In exchange, Israel agreed to return the Sinai Peninsula to Egypt. Signed in 1978, the **Camp David Accords** ended 30 years of hostilities between Egypt and Israel and became the first signed agreement between Israel and an Arab country.

President Sadat (left), President Carter, and Prime Minister Begin celebrate the signing of the Camp David Accords.

ONLINE DOCUMENT-BASED INVESTIGATION

Anwar Sadat

Students will read a speech by Anwar Sadat, which he gave in a dramatic gesture before the Israeli parliament, inviting his enemies to join him in a quest for peace. Students can click on the audio button beneath the historical source to hear the excerpt read aloud.

Analyze Sources How is Sadat's message similar to the messages from Gandhi, Kenyatta, and Sukarnoputri? *He, like the others, wanted to work together for peace.*

In print edition, see historical source, Excerpt from Sadat's Knesset Speech.

Analyze Sources What conditions for peace did Sadat request? *Israel would have to recognize the rights of Palestinians, and it would have to withdraw from territory captured in 1967 from Egypt, Jordan, and Syria.*

DOCUMENT-BASED INVESTIGATION HISTORICAL SOURCE

Anwar Sadat

In a dramatic gesture, Sadat went before the Knesset, the Israeli parliament, and invited his one-time enemies to join him in a quest for peace.

"Today, through my visit to you, I ask you why don't we stretch our hands with faith and sincerity and so that together we might . . . remove all suspicion of fear, betrayal, and bad intention? Why don't we stand together with the courage of men and the boldness of heroes who dedicate themselves to a sublime [supreme] aim? Why

ONLINE INTERACTIVE TIMELINES

The Israeli-Arab Struggle

Have students explore the timeline and answer the associated question.

Analyze Timelines How did the event of 1947 lead to conflict? *The partitioning in 1947 led to conflict between different factions in the Middle East.*

The Israeli-Arab Struggle

The Israeli-Arab Struggle

While world leaders praised Sadat, his peace initiative enraged many Arab countries. In 1981, a group of Muslim extremists assassinated him. However, Egypt's next leader, Hosni Mubarak (HAHS•nee-moo•BAHR•uhk), worked to maintain peace with Israel.

Israeli-Palestinian Tensions Increase One Arab group that continued to clash with the Israelis were the Palestinians, a large number of whom lived in the West Bank and Gaza Strip—lands controlled by Israel. During the 1970s and 1980s, the military wing of the PLO conducted a campaign against Israel. Israel responded forcefully, bombing suspected rebel bases in Palestinian towns. In 1982, the Israeli army invaded Lebanon in an attempt to destroy strongholds in Palestinian villages. The Israelis became involved in Lebanon's civil war and were forced to withdraw.

In 1987, Palestinians began to express their frustrations in a widespread **intifada**, or "uprising." The intifada took the form of boycotts, demonstrations, violent attacks on Israelis, rock throwing, shootings, and use of explosives. The intifada continued into the 1990s, with little progress made toward a solution. However, the intifada affected world opinion, which, in turn, put pressure on Israel and the Palestinians to negotiate. Finally, in October 1991, Israeli and Palestinian delegates met for a series of peace talks.

The Oslo Peace Accords Negotiations between the two sides made little progress, as the status of the Palestinian

Yitzhak Rabin, Bill Clinton, and Yasir Arafat at the Oslo Peace Accords.

ENGLISH LANGUAGE LEARNERS

Organize Events Chronologically

1. Review the section material with students taking turns reading aloud.
2. Whenever a reader encounters a date, ask students what occurred on that date, and have students write down the date and the event.
3. Lists should include the following: birth of new state of Israel, Six-Day War, Suez Crisis, PLO formed, Sadat assassinated, first intifada, Rabin assassinated, second intifada, Yom Kippur war, Jordan-Israel peace treaty, Sadat offers peace, and the Camp David Accords.
4. Have students compare their lists with the timeline in this section and correct any errors. Have them create a class timeline.

History in Depth

Signs of Hope

Amid the cycle of violence and disagreement in the Middle East, there are small but inspiring efforts to bring together Israelis and Palestinians. One is Seeds of Peace, a summer camp that hosts teenagers from opposing sides of world conflicts in the hopes of creating lasting friendships. Another is the West-Eastern Divan, an orchestra made up of Jewish and Arab musicians—the creation of famous Jewish conductor Daniel Barenboim and prominent Palestinian writer Edward Said.

▾ Palestinian and Israeli campers bond at Seeds of Peace, located in Maine.

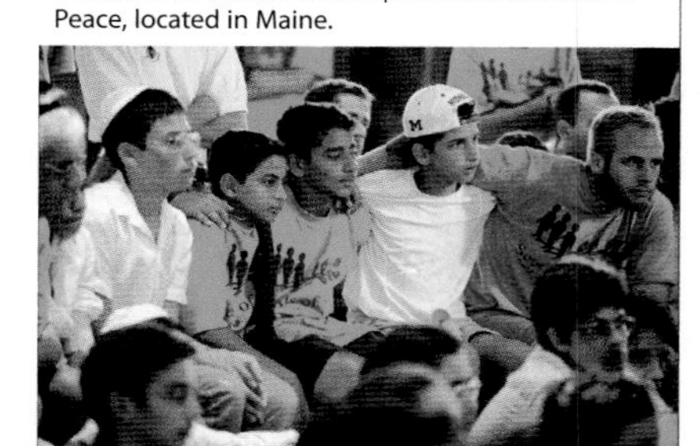

Edward Said and Daniel Barenboim (left) talk about their orchestra (right).

territories proved to be a bitterly divisive issue. In 1993, secret talks in Oslo, Norway, produced a surprise agreement: the **Oslo Peace Accords**. Israel agreed to grant the Palestinians self-rule in the Gaza Strip and the West Bank, beginning with Jericho. The Palestinians agreed to end violence and recognize Israel. Prime Minister **Yitzhak Rabin** (YIHTS•hahk-rah•BEEN) and Arafat signed the agreement in 1993. In 1994, Jordan and Israel signed a peace treaty.

ONLINE ANALYZE VIDEOS

Yitzhak Rabin

Have students watch the video individually or together. You may use the question as a discussion prompt.

Analyze Videos What event did Rabin consider to be the end of his childhood? *the death of his mother, Rosa Cohen Rabin*

GAME

Who Am I? Major Leaders in the Middle East

Have students play the game to test their knowledge of major leaders in the Middle East by selecting the correct person based on the actions and events provided.

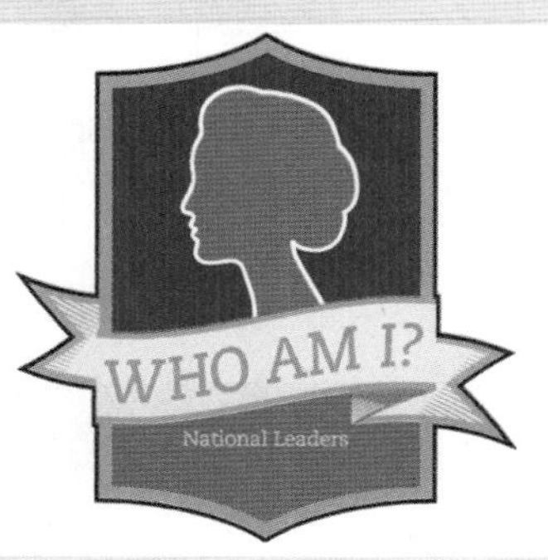

Objectives

You may wish to discuss the following questions with students to help them frame the content as they read.

- Why do you think Sharon's visit to the Temple Mount angered Palestinians given that the Temple Mount is sacred to both Jews and Muslims? *Possible answer: Palestinians objected to his visiting a Muslim holy site. The Temple Mount is a Jewish holy site.*
- What do you think are the main obstacles to peace between Israel and the Arab states? How has each side caused problems? *Possible answers: mistrust, extremists on both sides, with continued aggression and violence*

More About . . .

Mahmoud Abbas Abbas and Yasir Arafat worked together after co-founding the organization Fatah, which is part of the PLO. Abbas was born in 1935 in British Mandate Palestine, in an area now part of Israel. Known also as Abu Mazen, Abbas is highly educated and brought that education to bear as a fundraiser and then negotiator. Many credit him with the main ideas of the Oslo Accords. In September of 2003, Abbas resigned as prime minister after the peace plan known as "the road map" came apart and violence escalated once again. After the death of Arafat in 2004, Abbas was elected as the new Palestinian president.

READING CHECK

Clarify What was the significance of the Camp David Accords? *It was the first signed agreement between Israel and an Arab country.*

ONLINE INTERACTIVE VISUALS

Carousel: Signs of Hope

Have students navigate through the carousel and note similarities and differences among the images or identify a unifying theme.

Reading Check
Clarify What was the significance of the Camp David Accords?

Continuing Palestinian terrorist attacks against Israelis and the assassination of Rabin in 1995 by a right-wing Jewish extremist demonstrated the difficulty of making the agreement work. Rabin was succeeded as prime minister by Benjamin Netanyahu (neh•tan•YAH•hoo), who had opposed the Oslo Accords. Still, Netanyahu made efforts to keep to the agreement. In January 1997, Netanyahu met with Arafat to work out plans for a partial Israeli withdrawal from the West Bank.

Peace Slips Away

In 1999, the slow and difficult peace negotiations between Israel and the Palestinians seemed to get a boost. Ehud Barak won election as Israeli prime minister. Many observers viewed him as a much stronger supporter of the peace plan than Netanyahu had been. The world community, led by the United States, was determined to take advantage of such a development.

In July of 2000, U.S. President Bill Clinton hosted a 15-day summit meeting at Camp David between Ehud Barak and Yasir Arafat. Arafat rejected American and Israeli proposals and offered no alternatives, so the peace process once again stalled. Just two months later, Israeli political leader Ariel Sharon visited Jerusalem's Temple Mount, a site holy to both Jews and Muslims. The next day, the Voice of Palestine, the Palestinian Authority's official radio station, called upon Palestinians to protest the visit. Riots broke out in Jerusalem and the West Bank, and a second intifada, sometimes called the Al-Aqsa intifada, was launched.

The Conflict Intensifies The second intifada began much like the first with demonstrations, attacks on Israeli soldiers, and rock throwing. Palestinian groups also used suicide bombers as a weapon against Israelis. Their attacks on Jewish settlements and on civilian locations throughout Israel significantly raised the level of bloodshed. As the second intifada continued through 2007, thousands of Israelis and Palestinians had died in the conflict.

In response to the uprising, Israeli forces moved into Palestinian refugee camps and clamped down on terrorists. Troops destroyed buildings in which they suspected extremists were hiding and bulldozed entire areas of Palestinian towns and camps. The Israeli army bombed Arafat's headquarters, trapping him inside his compound for many days.

Arab-Israeli relations did not improve with Israel's next prime minister, Ariel Sharon. Sharon, a former military leader, refused to negotiate with the Palestinians until attacks on Israelis stopped. Eventually, under intense pressure from the world community, Arafat agreed to take a less prominent role in peace talks.

In early 2003, the Palestinian Authority appointed its first-ever prime minister, PLO official Mahmoud Abbas. Shortly afterward, U.S. President George W. Bush brought together Sharon and Abbas to begin working on a new peace plan known as the "road map." But violence increased again in 2003, and talks stalled.

Shifting Power and Alliances In the summer of 2005, Israel unilaterally evacuated all its settlers and military from the Gaza Strip. Then in 2006, Hamas, a militant terrorist group intent on replacing Israel with an Islamic state, won majority control in Palestinian Authority elections.

Israel refused to recognize the new Hamas government. However, in August 2007, Israeli Prime Minister Ehud Olmert began talks with Palestinian leader Mahmoud Abbas. In 2010, Olmert was replaced as prime minister by Benjamin Netanyahu and, after three weeks, the talks broke down when Israel refused to stop building Jewish housing in the West Bank.

In 2012, Abbas asked the UN General Assembly to recognize Palestinian statehood. He requested that the UN upgrade the status of Palestine to "nonmember observer state." This status, which is less than full UN membership, allowed Palestinians to become members of international groups, such as the International Criminal Court. The resolution passed.

In 2014, Netanyahu's governing coalition collapsed and early elections were held. However, Netanyahu's Likud party (a nationalist party that is against a Palestinian state) won more seats than any other party and Netanyahu remained as prime minister.

Reading Check
Evaluate What do you think it will take to achieve peace between Palestinians and Israelis?

Lesson 4 Assessment

1. Organize Information Make notes about the major events of the Arab-Israeli conflict. What is the significance of the 1967 war to Jews and Palestinians?

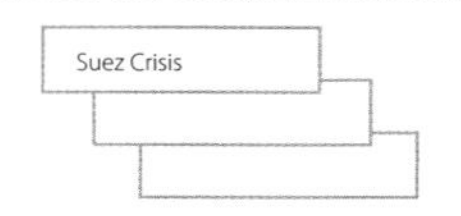

2. Key Terms and People For each key term or person in the lesson, write a sentence explaining its significance.
3. Analyze Issues What historic claim do both Palestinians and Jews make to the same land?
4. Summarize What land did Israel gain from the wars against its Arab neighbors?
5. Synthesize What were the terms of the Oslo Accords?
6. Compare How was the creation of Israel similar to the establishment of an independent India?
7. Draw Conclusions Why do you think all of the Israeli-Palestinian accords ultimately have failed? Some have said that this conflict represents the struggle of right against right. Explain why you agree or disagree.

STRUGGLING READERS

Determine Main Ideas

1. Have pairs of students use the Guided Reading Workbook and the module to review section material.
2. Start by turning heads and subheads into questions.
3. After the questions have been written, request that the pairs trade questions with another pair and write out answers for each question.
4. The pair writing the questions should check the answers for accuracy.

READING CHECK

Evaluate What do you think it will take to achieve peace between Palestinians and Israelis? *strong world leaders who are willing to compromise*

Print Assessment

1. **Organize Information** Make notes about the major events of the Arab-Israeli conflict. What is the significance of the 1967 war to Jews and Palestinians? *Suez Crisis; Six-Day War; Yom Kippur war; PLO formed; Camp David Accords; Sadat killed; first intifada; Oslo Peace Accords; Rabin killed; second intifada. Possible answer: To Jews, the unification of Jerusalem and access to their holiest site, the Western Wall. To Palestinians, Israeli control of the West Bank and Gaza.*
2. **Key Terms and People** For each key term or person in the lesson, write a sentence explaining its significance. *Explanations of the lesson's key terms can be found on the following pages: Anwar Sadat, p. 1197; Golda Meir, p. 1197; PLO, p. 1198; Yasir Arafat, p. 1198; Menachem Begin, p. 1199; Camp David Accords, p. 1199; intifada, p. 1200; Oslo Peace Accords, p. 1201; Yitzhak Rabin, p. 1201*
3. **Analyze Issues** What historic claim do both Palestinians and Jews make to this land? *Jews—ancient kingdom in the area; continuous Jewish presence since then; Palestinians—claim the land since Arab invasion in the 7th century.*
4. **Summarize** What land did Israel gain from the wars against its Arab neighbors? *Israel took the old city of Jerusalem, West Bank, Gaza, Golan Heights, and Sinai Peninsula in 1967.*
5. **Synthesize** What were the terms of the Oslo Accords? *Palestinian self-rule in West Bank and Gaza, Palestinian renunciation of terrorism, Palestinian recognition of Israel's right to exist*
6. **Compare** How was the creation of Israel similar to the establishment of an independent India? *both involved partitioning a region*
7. **Draw Conclusions** Why do you think all the Israeli-Palestinian accords ultimately have failed? Some have said that this conflict represents the struggle of right against right. Explain why you agree or disagree. *Possible answers: most Israelis willing to compromise for peace; many Palestinians reject Israel's right to exist. Both sides have legitimate claims to the land and have reasonable arguments to make.*

Online Assessment

1. What was one of the terms for the partition of the Palestinian Mandate?
   - ● Jerusalem would be an international city.
   - ○ United Nations officials would set up the government.
   - ○ Jews would be allowed to live in any region of Palestine.
   - ○ Arabs could travel from one region to another without harassment.

   Alternate Question *Select the answer choice from the drop-down list to complete the sentence correctly.*
   When members of the United Nations General Assembly voted to partition the Palestinian Mandate, they agreed that they would make *an Arab state* and a Jewish state. The land would be divided up according to population centers, and Jerusalem would be an international city that was not controlled by either side.

2. What was a consequence of the Six-Day War?
   - ○ Arabs attained their own state.
   - ● Israel gained control of Jerusalem.
   - ○ Egypt retained control of the Suez Canal.
   - ○ Jordanians were allowed to flee Israeli-held territory.

   Alternate Question *Select the answer choice from the drop-down list to complete the sentence correctly.*
   As a result of the Six-Day War, the state of Israel was able to gain control of *Jerusalem* among other areas, which seemed to buffer against Arab attacks.

3. Which group was involved in the intifadas of the 1980s and 1990s?
   - ○ Israelis
   - ○ Egyptians
   - ○ Lebanese
   - ● Palestinians

   Alternate Question *Select the answer choice from the drop-down list to complete the sentence correctly.*
   In the *1980s and 1990s*, the Palestinians expressed their frustrations in the form of intifadas, or uprisings. These took the form of boycotts, demonstrations, violent attacks on Israelis, rock throwing, shooting, and the use of explosives.

4. How did Israel respond to the second intifada?
   - ○ It selected a new Palestinian prime minister.
   - ○ It allowed Arafat to form his own government.
   - ○ It refused to meet with U.S. President George W. Bush.
   - ● It clamped down on terrorists in Palestinian refugee camps.

   Alternate Question *Select the answer choice from the drop-down list to complete the sentence correctly.*
   When terrorists began attacking Israelis in the second intifada, the Israelis fought back by moving into *Palestinian refugee camps* and routing out the terrorists there.

5. **Draw Conclusions** Why did the Islamic countries and Palestinian Arabs reject the formation of Israel?

   Possible answer: They felt that the United Nations should have considered the wishes of the people who lived in the area. The majority of the people in the area were not in favor of having a country established for the Jewish people.

6. **Make Inferences** Why would the state of Israel have been opposed to the formation of the Palestinian Liberation Organization (PLO) in 1964?

   Possible answer: The PLO had one main goal—the formation of an Arab Palestinian state that would include all of the land presently held by Israel. Obviously, this would have been opposed by Israel because it would mean that country's demise. The PLO also believed that the only way to achieve its goal was through armed struggle. The PLO carried out terrorist attacks on Israel throughout the 1960s and 1970s. These activities affected Israelis' safety, security, and their lives.

7. **Elaborate** What was the Camp David Accords agreement and what significance did it have on the Middle East?

   Possible answer: The Camp David Accords was an agreement between Egypt and Israel. It was orchestrated by President Jimmy Carter, who invited the leaders of those nations to Camp David so they could come to some agreements for peace. In these accords, Egypt recognized the existence of Israel as a legitimate state. Israel agreed to return the Sinai Peninsula to Egypt. This agreement was the first signed agreement between Israel and an Arab nation. It also ended 30 years of hostilities between these two nations.

8. **Draw Conclusions** Why would Israel have refused to recognize the new Hamas government that won control of the Palestinian Authority elections in 2006?

   Possible answer: The Hamas government's intent was to replace Israel with an Islamic state. Because Israel obviously would not have been in favor of that, it would not have been willing to recognize the legitimacy of this new governing power.

Lesson 5 Planner

Central Asia Struggles

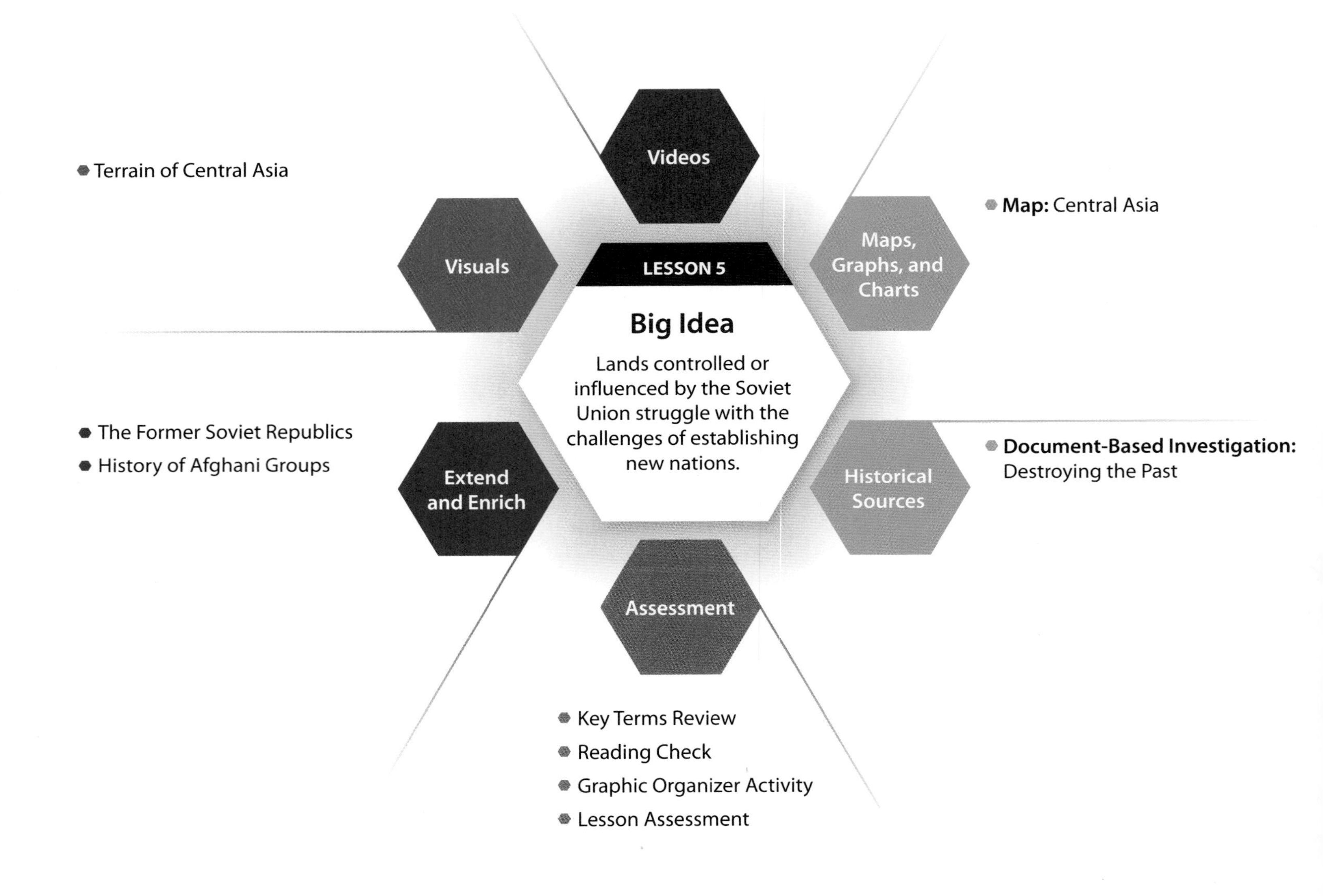

- Terrain of Central Asia

- **Map:** Central Asia

- The Former Soviet Republics
- History of Afghani Groups

- **Document-Based Investigation:** Destroying the Past

- Key Terms Review
- Reading Check
- Graphic Organizer Activity
- Lesson Assessment

Online Lesson 5 Enrichment Activities

The Former Soviet Republics

Table Students will create a table to show more about each of the fifteen former Soviet republics. This activity walks students through outlining the table, conducting additional research, and completing the table. Students will conclude by summarizing their findings beneath the table.

History of Afghani Groups

Writing Activity Students will conduct research about the history of one of an Afghani group: the mujahideen or the Taliban. They will use their research to write a paper that includes the purpose of the group, the group's actions, international reactions to the group, and the future of the group. This activity walks students through planning, creating their historical outlines, writing, reviewing and proofreading.

Teach the Big Idea

1. **Whole Class Open/Introduction** Ask students what challenges a nation faces after becoming independent. *Keeping the economy going, protecting its citizens, solving issues of education and social concern.*
2. **Direct Teach** Read students the Big Idea: *Lands controlled or influenced by the Soviet Union struggle with the challenges of establishing new nations.* Review the following lesson objectives with students to aid in their understanding of the Big Idea.
   - Identify challenges facing the nations of the former Soviet Union.
   - Describe Afghanistan's struggle for independence and possible role in global terrorism.
3. **Whole Group Close/Reflect** Have students write a one-paragraph summary describing the ethnic and religious strife in Central Asia during Soviet rule.

ONLINE DOCUMENT-BASED INVESTIGATION

The Colonies Become New Nations

Destroying the Past is the last of five document-based investigations that students will analyze in The Colonies Become New Nations. Students will read a passage which describes the impact of Taliban policies on Afghanistan's most prized artifacts. Students can use the interactivity of the feature to learn about why the Taliban chose to exercise their power in this way.

ONLINE GRAPHIC ORGANIZER

Central Asia Struggles

As students read the lesson, have them use the graphic organizer to take notes. Students can review their graphic organizer notes at the end of the lesson to answer the following question:

Synthesize Which challenges for the Central Asian nations are most difficult to overcome? *Religious disagreements; terrorism; poverty*

ONLINE FLIP CARDS

Review Key Terms and People

Students can use the flip cards in the Lesson Review at any time to review the lesson's key terms and people: *Transcaucasian Republics, Central Asian Republics, mujahideen,* and *Taliban.*

Lesson 5

Central Asia Struggles

The Big Idea
Lands controlled or influenced by the Soviet Union struggled with the challenges of establishing new nations.

Why It Matters Now
The security issues in these nations pose a threat to world peace and security.

Key Terms and People
Transcaucasian Republics
Central Asian Republics
mujahideen
Taliban

Setting the Stage

For thousands of years, the different peoples of Central Asia suffered invasions and domination by powerful groups such as the Mongols, Byzantines, Ottomans, and finally the Communist rulers of the Soviet Union. While such occupation brought many changes to this region, its various ethnic groups worked to keep alive much of their culture. They also longed to create nations of their own, a dream they realized in the early 1990s with the collapse of the Soviet Union. In the decade since then, however, these groups have come to know the challenges of building strong and stable independent nations.

Freedom Brings New Challenges

In 1991, the Soviet Union collapsed, and the republics that it had conquered emerged as 15 independent nations. Among them were those that had made up the Soviet empire's southern borders. Geographers often group these new nations into two geographic areas.

Armenia, Azerbaijan, and Georgia make up the **Transcaucasian Republics**. These three nations lie in the Caucasus Mountains between the Black and Caspian seas. East of the Caspian Sea and extending to the Tian Shan and Pamir mountains lie the five nations known as the **Central Asian Republics**. They are Uzbekistan, Turkmenistan, Tajikistan, Kazakhstan, and Kyrgyzstan.

COLLABORATIVE LEARNING

Debate: The Taliban and US Troops After 9/11

1. Provide students with a brief summary of the 9/11 attacks in 2001 and how US troops defeated the Taliban and largely drove them from Afghanistan.
2. Organize students into groups of three or four. Ask them to prepare for a debate, arguing against or in support of President Obama's decision to send more US troops to Afghanistan the summer after 9/11.
3. Explain that students will need to use the Internet to research both sides of the debate. They will find out which side they will argue immediately before the debate starts.
4. Arguments must include significant evidence from multiple sources.
5. Assign "for" or "against" to groups and begin the debate.
6. Ask the class to vote on the winner of the debate, and have groups critique one another on the use of evidence, reasoning, and supporting details.

Economic Struggles Since gaining independence, these nations have struggled economically and are today some of the poorest countries in the world. Much of the problem stems from their heavy reliance on the Soviet Union for economic help. As a result, they have had a difficult time standing on their own. Economic practices during the Soviet era have created additional problems. The Soviets, for example, converted much of the available farmland in the Central Asian Republics to grow "white gold"—cotton. Dependence on a single crop has hurt the development of a balanced economy in these nations.

Azerbaijan, which is located among the oil fields of the Caspian Sea, has the best chance to build a solid economy based on the income from oil and oil products. Meanwhile, Kazakhstan and Turkmenistan are working hard to tap their large reserves of oil and natural gas.

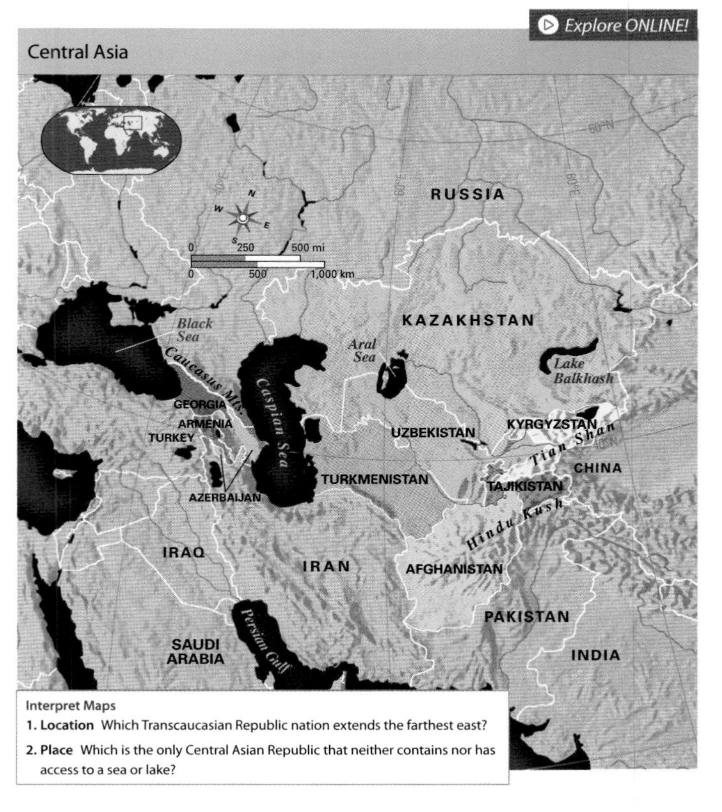

Interpret Maps
1. **Location** Which Transcaucasian Republic nation extends the farthest east?
2. **Place** Which is the only Central Asian Republic that neither contains nor has access to a sea or lake?

Objectives

You may wish to discuss the following questions with students to help them frame the content as they read.

- What problems could result from a dependence on a single crop? *Possible Answer: Crop failures or disease could wipe out the economy.*
- How is the problem of ethnic hostility in the former Soviet republics similar to that of post-colonial Africa? *Possible Answer: Outside authority kept control of ethnic hostility; without that control, hostilities flared.*

More About . . .

Azerbaijan Azerbaijan occupies an area fringing the southern flanks of the Caucasus Mountains. Russia lies to the north, the Caspian Sea to the east, Iran to the south, and Armenia to the west. Azerbaijan is characterized by a wide variety of landscapes, which include lowlands as well as peaks higher than 14,000 feet. With deep gorges of mountain streams that cut the land into beautiful spurs and ridges, Azerbaijan holds regions of incredible natural beauty but is also dangerous due to a high degree of seismic activity.

Uzbekistan Uzbekistan lies between two major rivers, the Syr Darya on the northeast and the Amu Arya on the southwest. These rivers only partly form the boundaries of Uzbekistan as it is also bordered by five other nations. Almost four-fifths of Uzbekistan territory, the sundried western area, appears as wasteland. The Turan Plain in the northwest rises 200 to 300 feet above sea level and then merges on the south with the Kyzylkum Desert. Farther west, it becomes the Ustyurt Plateau, a region of low ridges, salt marshes, sinkholes, and caverns.

STRUGGLING READERS

Pronouncing Soviet Republic Names

1. Highlight the names of the 15 former Soviet republics.
2. Ask volunteers to attempt pronunciation.
3. Then demonstrate correct pronunciation yourself, using this list:
   - Armenia: ahr•MEE•nee•uh
   - Azerbaijan: AZ•uhr•by•JAHN
   - Georgia: JAWR•juh
   - Uzbekistan: uz•BEHK•ih•STAN
   - Turkmenistan: TURK•mehn•ih•STAN
   - Tajikistan: tah•JIHK•ih•STAN
   - Kazakhstan: KAH•zahk•STAHN
   - Kyrgyzstan: KEER•gee•STAHN
4. Work with students to create a two-column chart with headings "Proper Noun" and "Proper Adjective."
5. Clarify how to turn each proper noun type into a proper adjective in order to describe a person from that nation.

ONLINE INTERPRET MAPS

Central Asia

Have students explore the map using interactive features and answer the associated question.

Place Which Central Asian Republic does not have access to a sea or lake? *Tajikistan*

In print edition, see map of same title.

1. **Location** Which Transcaucasian Republic nation extends the farthest east? *Kazakhstan*
2. **Place** Which is the only Central Asian Republic that neither contains nor has access to a sea or lake? *Tajikistan*

Objectives

You may wish to discuss the following questions with students to help them frame the content as they read.

- Why might access to the Indian Ocean be important to Russia? *Possible Answer: eased trade from that part of a vast nation*
- Why might people accept a lack of freedom, such as the Taliban created? *Possible Answer: They may think the order and security that such an authority creates is worth the loss of freedom.*

More About . . .

Hamid Karzai Hamid Karzai was selected to rule the country by the Loya Jerga, a traditional assembly of tribal representatives. Mr. Karzai comes from a prominent family whose members have been leaders in Afghanistan for centuries. His father, a parliamentary deputy, was assassinated in 1999, probably by the Taliban.

READING CHECK

Clarify Why was there little ethnic or religious strife in Central Asia during Soviet rule? *The Soviets kept a lid on all such hostilities through repressive rule.*

Ethnic and Religious Strife Fighting among various ethnic and religious groups has created another obstacle to stability for many of the newly independent countries of Central Asia. The region is home to a number of different peoples, including some with long histories of hostility toward each other. With their iron-fisted rule, the Soviets kept a lid on these hostilities and largely prevented any serious ethnic clashes. After the breakup of the Soviet Union, however, long-simmering ethnic rivalries erupted into fighting. Some even became small regional wars.

Such was the case in Azerbaijan. Within this mostly Muslim country lies Nagorno-Karabakh, a small region of mainly Armenian Christians. In the wake of the Soviet Union's collapse, the people of this area declared their independence. Azerbaijan had no intention of letting go of this land, and fighting quickly broke out. Neighboring Armenia rushed to aid the Armenian people in the district. The war raged from 1991 through 1994, when the two sides agreed to a cease-fire. As of 2007, the status of Nagorno-Karabakh remained unresolved.

Reading Check
Clarify Why was there little ethnic or religious strife in Central Asia during Soviet rule?

Afghanistan and the World

Just to the south of the Central Asian Republics lies one of the region's more prominent nations. Afghanistan is a small nation with both mountainous and desert terrain. It is one of the least-developed countries in the world, as most of its inhabitants are farmers or herders. And yet, over the past several decades, this mostly Muslim nation has grabbed the world's attention with two high-profile wars—one against the Soviet Union and the other against the United States.

Struggle for Freedom Afghanistan has endured a long history of struggle. During the 1800s, both Russia and Britain competed for control of its land. Russia wanted access to the Indian Ocean through Afghanistan, while Britain wanted control of the land in order to protect the northern borders of its Indian Empire. Britain fought three separate wars with the Afghanis before eventually leaving in 1919.

That year, Afghanistan declared itself an independent nation and established a monarchy. The government implemented various reforms and tried to modernize the country. In 1964, the country devised a constitution that sought to establish a more democratic style of government. However, officials could not agree on a reform program and most people showed little interest in the effort to transform the government. As a result, a democratic system failed to develop.

Pushing Back the Soviets Nonetheless, Afghanistan had grown stable enough to establish good relations with many Western European nations and to hold its own on the world stage. When the Cold War conflict between the United States and Soviet Union broke out, Afghanistan chose to remain neutral. However, over the years, it received aid from both of the opposing superpowers.

ENGLISH LANGUAGE LEARNERS

Define Difficult Language

1. Clarify that the colloquial language in the text has a meaning different from its literal dictionary definition, and that context is a useful clue to meaning.
2. Have students find the language listed below and take turns reading the appropriate sentence aloud. Discuss what students think each phrase means.
   - hold its own on the world stage
   - banded together
   - troops rolled in
   - guerrilla tactics
   - superpowers
   - lopsided affair
   - war-torn
   - took up arms
   - had all the makings
3. Then have students create a list in which they define the language in their own words.
4. For help, have students use the Guided Reading Workbook in Spanish for this section.

Situated so close to the Soviet Union, however, Afghanistan could not hold out against the force of communism forever. In 1973, military leaders overthrew the government. Five years later, in 1978, a rival group with strong ties to the Soviet Union seized control of the country. Much of the population opposed the group and its strong association with communism. Many Afghanis felt that Communist policies conflicted with the teachings of Islam.

The opposition forces banded together to form a group known as the **mujahideen** (moo•JAH•heh•DEEN), or holy warriors. These rebels took up arms and fought fiercely against the Soviet-supported government. The rebellion soon prompted the Soviet Union to step in. In 1979 and 1980, Soviet troops rolled into Afghanistan to conquer the country and add it to their Communist empire.

With the Soviets' superior military force and advanced weaponry, the war had all the makings of a quick and lopsided affair. But the Afghan rebels used the land and guerrilla tactics to their advantage. In addition, the United States provided financial and military assistance. After nearly 10 years of bloody and fruitless fighting, the Soviet Union withdrew its troops. The Afghanis had taken on the world's Communist superpower and won.

Rise and Fall of the Taliban With the Soviets gone, various Afghan rebel groups began battling each other for control of the country. A conservative Islamic group known as the **Taliban** emerged as the victor. By 1998, it controlled 90 percent of the country. Another rebel group, the Northern Alliance, held the northwest corner of the country. Observers initially viewed the Taliban as a positive force, as it brought order to the war-torn nation, rooted out corruption, and promoted the growth of business.

History in Depth

Destroying the Past

Among the Taliban's extreme policies that stemmed from their interpretation of Islam, one in particular shocked and angered historians around the world. In the years after gaining power, Taliban leaders destroyed some of Afghanistan's most prized artifacts—two centuries-old Buddhas carved out of cliffs in the Bamiyan Valley.

The Taliban deemed the giant statues offensive to Islam. Ignoring pleas from scholars and museums, they demolished the ancient figures with dynamite and bombs. One of the two statues was thought to have dated back to the third century AD.

ONLINE DOCUMENT-BASED INVESTIGATION

Destroying the Past

Students will read a passage which describes the impact of Taliban policies on Afghanistan's most prized artifacts. Students can use the interactivity of the feature to learn about why the Taliban chose to exercise their power in this way.

Analyze Sources Based on your interpretation of the image, how large were the giant statues? Why would a group go to such lengths to destroy the statues? *The Buddhas seem to be 40 to 60 feet tall. A group might destroy something like this if they believe it will hurt their cause or conflict with their beliefs.*

DOCUMENT-BASED INVESTIGATION HISTORICAL SOURCE

Destroying the Past

Among the Taliban's extreme policies that stemmed from their interpretation of Islam, one in particular shocked and angered historians around the world. In the years after gaining power, Taliban leaders destroyed some of Afghanistan's most prized artifacts—two centuries-old Buddhas carved out of cliffs.

The Taliban deemed the giant statues offensive to Islam. Ignoring pleas from scholars and museums, they demolished the ancient figures with dynamite and bombs. One of the two statues was thought to have dated back to the third century AD.

ONLINE INTERACTIVE VISUALS

Image Slider: Terrain of Central Asia

Have students explore the image by revealing additional information using the interactive slider.

The terrain of Central Asia varies widely, from mountains to plains.

However, the group followed an extreme interpretation of Islamic law and applied it to nearly every aspect of Afghan society. Taliban leaders restricted women's lives by forbidding them to go to school or hold jobs. They banned everything from television and movies to modern music. Punishment for violating the rules included severe beatings, amputation, and even execution.

Even more troubling to the world community was the Taliban's role in the growing problem of world terrorism. Western leaders accused the Taliban of allowing terrorist groups to train in Afghanistan. The Taliban also provided refuge for terrorist leaders, including Osama bin Laden, whose al-Qaeda organization is thought to be responsible for numerous attacks on the West—including the attacks on the World Trade Center in New York and the Pentagon in Washington, D.C., on September 11, 2001.

In the wake of the September 11 attacks, the U.S. government demanded that the Taliban turn over bin Laden. After its leaders refused, the United States took military action. In October 2001, U.S. forces began bombing Taliban air defense, airfields, and command centers, as well as al-Qaeda training camps. On the ground, the United States provided assistance to anti-Taliban forces, such as the Northern Alliance. By December, the United States had driven the Taliban from power.

Challenges Ahead While the Taliban regrouped in remote parts of Afghanistan and Pakistan, Afghan officials selected a new government under the leadership of Hamid Karzai. Later, in 2004, he was elected president for a five-year term. His government faced the task of rebuilding a country that had endured more than two decades of warfare. However, in 2006, the Taliban appeared resurgent, and NATO troops took

In the Afghanistan elections, the ballot included photographs of the candidates and symbols for each party.

over military operations in the South. Heavy fighting continued. In 2008, civilian casualties reached the highest levels since the war began.

On August 20, 2009, Afghanistan held a presidential election. Karzai won, and later that year he was inaugurated as president for a second term.

By 2012, NATO forces in Afghanistan had reached nearly 150,000. President Barack Obama sent U.S. troops, too. This increase in troops had mixed results. Although NATO troops removed the Taliban from some areas, Taliban fighters attacked military and civilian targets in other areas.

NATO withdrew all troops by 2014. Then Afghanistan held a presidential election. Under Afghanistan's constitution, Karzai could not run again. Two leading candidates, Abdullah Abdullah and Ashraf Ghani, emerged. Because of voter fraud, both candidates declared victory.

On September 21, 2014, Ghani and Abdullah worked out a compromise. Ghani would become president. But Abdullah (or someone from his party) would become chief executive officer, which was a newly created role.

The challenge before Afghanistan is neither unique nor new. Over the past 60 years, countries around the world have attempted to shed their old and often repressive forms of rule and implement a more democratic style of government.

Reading Check
Draw Conclusions
Why do you think the Soviets finally decided to leave Afghanistan?

Lesson 5 Assessment

1. Organize Information Make a list like the one shown. Which challenge for the Central Asian nations is most difficult to overcome?

Freedom Brings New Challenges
A.
B.
Afghanistan and the World
A.
B.

2. Key Terms and People For each key term or person in the lesson, write a sentence explaining its significance.
3. Summarize What countries make up the Central Asian Republics?
4. Draw Conclusions Why did Afghanis oppose the idea of Communist rule? Why might Afghanis have been willing to accept Taliban rule by 1998?
5. Analyze Causes Why did the United States take military action against the Taliban?
6. Make Inferences Some historians call the Soviet-Afghan war the Soviet Union's "Vietnam." What do they mean by this reference? Do you agree with it?
7. Identify Problems Why did the new nations of Central Asia experience such economic difficulties?

READING CHECK

Draw Conclusions Why do you think the Soviets finally decided to leave Afghanistan? *They no longer had the will or desire to continue fighting against the Afghanis and their guerrilla tactics*

Print Assessment

1. **Organize Information** Make a list of challenges for the Central Asian nations. Which challenge is most difficult to overcome? *Possible Answer: I. A. economic struggles, B. ethnic/religious strife. II. A. fight for independence, B. Taliban brings Islamic fundamentalism. C. support for terrorism. Possible Answer: ethnic diversity and tension*
2. **Key Terms and People** For each key term or person in the lesson, write a sentence explaining its significance. *Explanations of the lesson's key terms can be found on the following pages: Transcaucasian Republics, p. 1204; Central Asian Republics, p. 1204; mujahideen, p. 1207; Taliban, p. 1207*
3. **Summarize** What countries make up the Transcaucasian Republics? the Central Asian Republics? *Transcaucasian—Armenia, Azerbaijan, Georgia; Central Asia—Uzbekistan, Turkmenistan, Tajikistan, Kazakhstan, Kyrgyzstan*
4. **Draw Conclusions** Why did Afghanis oppose the notion of Communist rule? Why might Afghanis have been willing to accept Taliban rule by 1998? *felt communism conflicted with Islam; Afghanis might be worn out from war and chaos enough to choose order and security offered by the Taliban.*
5. **Analyze Causes** Why did the United States take military action against the Taliban? *The Taliban refused to hand over bin Laden.*
6. **Make Inferences** Some historians call the Soviet-Afghan war the Soviet Union's "Vietnam." What do they mean by this reference? Do you agree with it? *Possible Answer: Both were long drawn-out wars, in which a strong nation failed to defeat a seemingly weaker enemy. Most will agree, as U.S. also retreated without victory.*
7. **Identify Problems** Why did the new nations of Central Asia experience such economic difficulties? *Possible Answer: too much dependence on single crop, economic development unnecessary under Soviets*

Online Assessment

1. What has caused economic hardship for the Central Asian republics since they gained independence from the Soviet Union?
   - huge national debt
   - lack of a national currency
   - depletion of natural resources
   - dependence on single-crop agriculture

   Alternate Question *Select the answer choice from the drop-down list to complete the sentence correctly.*
   When the Soviet Union controlled the Central Asian Republics, the Soviets mainly grew *cotton*. The dependency on a single-crop agriculture has hurt the region economically.

2. What was significant about the war between the Soviet Union and Afghanistan?
   - Afghanistan won.
   - The Soviets used nuclear bombs.
   - Afghanistan used superior weaponry.
   - The Soviets utilized their knowledge of the terrain.

   Alternate Question *Select the answer choice from the drop-down list to complete the sentence correctly.*
   Afghanistan is a small country and the fact that it took on the world's *Communist superpower* and won was very impressive.

3. **Elaborate** Why were there conflicts in central Asia after the collapse of the Soviet Union?

   Possible answer: The region is home to many different ethnic and religious groups. Many of these groups have long histories of hostilities toward each other. The Soviets ruled the area with an iron fist, keeping the people's conflicts subdued. However, when the Soviets were no longer around, these peoples didn't have anything forcing them to get along. So, they began to fight with each other. Some of this fighting even became small regional wars.

4. **Make Judgments** How did people initially view the Taliban and how did that view change over time?

   Possible answer: At first the Taliban was seen as a positive force. It brought order to the war-torn nation and rooted out corruption. It also promoted the growth of local businesses. However, it was the group's extreme interpretation of Islamic law that led to a changed view of the group. The Taliban restricted women's lives by forbidding them to go to school or hold jobs. It banned everything from television and movies to modern music. Punishment for violating the rules included severe beatings, amputation, and even execution. The Taliban also allowed terrorist groups to train in its country's borders. It provided a refuge for terrorists who were being sought by other countries.

Print Assessment

Key Terms and People

For each term or name below, briefly explain its connection to colonial independence or other international developments after World War II.

1. partition *p. 1167*
2. Jawaharlal Nehru *p. 1169*
3. Indira Gandhi *p. 1170*
4. Corazón Aquino *p. 1177*
5. Jomo Kenyatta *p.1188*
6. Anwar Sadat *p.1197*
7. PLO *p. 1198*
8. Mujahideen *p. 1207*

Main Ideas

The Indian Subcontinent Achieves Freedom

1. What two nations emerged from the British colony of India in 1947? *India and Pakistan*
2. How did Jawaharlal Nehru spur India's economic growth after India became an independent nation? *He promoted industrialization and modernization.*
3. In what way did Pakistan undergo a partition? *Pakistan was divided into two regions: East Pakistan and West Pakistan.*
4. Briefly explain the reason for the civil disorder in Sri Lanka. *Some Tamils, a Hindu people, want to establish a separate nation. The Buddhist majority opposes this.*

Southeast Asian Nations Gain Independence

5. What were some concerns the Filipinos had regarding the Bell Act? *United States got free trading rights; Filipinos feared exploitation of natural resources and environment.*
6. Who is Sukarno and what did he accomplish in Indonesia? *leader of the Indonesian independence movement; nation's first president*

New Nations in Africa

7. Why were Kwame Nkrumah's politics criticized? *for spending too much money on programs nation couldn't afford; too much time on Pan-African affairs*
8. Why did Zaire face such difficulty upon gaining independence? *unprepared for governing freely*
9. What sparked the present-day civil struggle in Algeria? *Religious fundamentalists tried to make Algeria an Islamic state, and the ruling government and army refused to accept the election results.*

Conflicts in the Middle East

10. What was the Suez Crisis? *Egypt seized canal in 1956; Israelis, with British/French air support invaded to recapture, withdrew under world pressure*
11. What were the Camp David Accords? *Israeli-Egyptian agreement: Egypt would recognize Israel as a nation and Israel would return the Sinai Peninsula.*

Central Asia Struggles

12. Which nations comprise the Transcaucasian Republics? *Armenia, Azerbaijan, Georgia*
13. What was the Taliban? *group that controlled Afghanistan in mid-1990s, imposed strict Islamic laws on nation and its people*

Module 30 Assessment

Key Terms and People

For each term or name below, briefly explain its connection to colonial independence or other international developments after World War II.

1. partition
2. Jawaharlal Nehru
3. Indira Gandhi
4. Corazón Aquino
5. Jomo Kenyatta
6. Anwar Sadat
7. PLO
8. mujahideen

Main Ideas

The Indian Subcontinent Achieves Freedom

1. What two nations emerged from the British colony of India in 1947?
2. How did Jawaharlal Nehru spur India's economic growth after India became an independent nation?
3. In what way did Pakistan undergo a partition?
4. Briefly explain the reason for the civil disorder in Sri Lanka.

Southeast Asian Nations Gain Independence

5. What were some concerns the Filipinos had regarding the Bell Act?
6. Who is Sukarno, and what did he accomplish in Indonesia?

New Nations in Africa

7. Why were Kwame Nkrumah's politics criticized?
8. Why did Zaire face such difficulty upon gaining independence?
9. What sparked the present-day civil struggle in Algeria?

Conflicts in the Middle East

10. What was the Suez Crisis?
11. What were the Camp David Accords?

Central Asia Struggles

12. Which nations comprise the Transcaucasian Republics?
13. What was the Taliban?

1210 Module 30

ONLINE DOCUMENT-BASED INVESTIGATION

The Colonies Become New Nations

Have students complete and review all the DBI activities in **Part 1**.

Use this Analytical Essay Rubric to score students' work in **Part 2**.

RUBRIC Students' essays should

- present an analysis of the topic that is detailed and relevant
- develop the analysis logically, clearly, and accurately
- cite at least three sources of relevant text evidence from Part 1 in support of their analysis
- be organized into a distinct introduction, a main body consisting of several paragraphs, and a conclusion that sums up the main points

Write an Analytical Essay Write an analytical essay that examines how leaders are remembered in history based on the types of actions they promote and enact. Be sure to cite specific evidence from each of the three sources in your response.

Module 30 Assessment, continued

Critical Thinking

1. Use a web diagram to show some of the challenges that newly independent nations have faced.

2. **Support Opinions** Do you think there should be a limit to the methods revolutionaries use? Explain your opinion.
3. **Analyze Issues** Why have so many of the new nations that emerged over the past half-century struggled economically?
4. **Draw Conclusions** In your view, was religion a unifying or destructive force as colonies around the world became new nations?
Support your answer with specific examples from the text.
5. **Contrast** Describe the nature of totalitarianism and the police state that existed in Russia, and how it differed from some authoritarian governments you learned about in this lesson.
6. **Compare** Compare the rise of nationalism in Turkey, India, and China.
7. **Analyze** Compare and contrast the methods used by African and Asian nations to achieve independence.
8. **Infer** Use a globe to make a chart that shows the distance from Moscow and Washington, D.C., to Afghanistan, Ghana, the Philippines, and India. What do these distances tell you about the influences of the United States and the Soviet Union on these new nations?
9. With a partner, take turns reading, listening to, summarizing, and discussing the quotation by Anwar Sadat in lesson 4.

Analyze Historical Accuracy

Examine websites, documentaries, movies, newspaper articles, and biographies about one of the leaders in these lessons. Based on what you know, critique the historical accuracy of at least two sources. What specifically can you find that is biased or inaccurate? What is most fair and impartial?

Interact with History

Now that you have read about the efforts by so many former colonies to forge new countries, identify the main factors that determine whether a new nation struggles or thrives. Be sure to cite specific examples from the text.

Focus on Writing

Select one of the leaders discussed in this module. Review the decisions the leader made while in power. Write an evaluation of the leader's decisions and his or her impact on the country. Consider the following:

- the leader's views on government and democracy
- the leader's handling of the economy
- the leader's accomplishments and failures

Multimedia Activity

Creating a Database

Use the Internet, library resources, and other reference materials to create a database showing the economic growth of any four countries discussed in this module. Create one table for each country, with column headings for each measure of economic growth you choose to record and row headings for each 10-year period. Then insert the most current data you can find. Consider the following questions to get started.

- Which statistics will be most useful in making comparisons between nations?
- Which nations have capitalist economies? What other types of economies did you discover?
- Which nations have "one-crop" economies?

Essential Question ESSAY

How can leaders of nations unify diverse populations of people?

RUBRIC Students' essays should

- respond to the Essential Question with a specific position
- illustrate valid reasoning supporting their position
- cite persuasive evidence supporting their position
- identify key people, events, and/or turning points that demonstrate understanding of the module content
- be organized into a distinct introduction, main body, and conclusion

Write an argument answering this question. Your essay should include key people, events, and turning points in the history of Africa and Asia independence movements. Be sure to cite evidence to support your position, and organize your essay into an introduction, body, and conclusion.

Alternative Activity Instead of writing essays, address the Essential Question through activities such as holding debates, creating multimedia presentations, or writing journal entries.

Critical Thinking

1. Use a web diagram to show some of the challenges that newly independent nations have faced. *Possible answers: constant threat of revolution, former colonizers' continued meddling, developing a viable economy and government, civil war, random boundaries*
2. **Support Opinions** Do you think there should be a limit to the methods revolutionaries use? Explain your opinion. *Possible answers: Yes—The ends do not justify the means; No—Sometimes all possible force is necessary.*
3. **Analyze Issues** Why have so many of the new nations that emerged over the past half-century struggled economically? *Possible answer: many were dependent on former colonizer; war and corruption after independence also hurt economies*
4. **Draw Conclusions** In your view, was religion a unifying or destructive force as colonies around the world became new nations? Support your answer with specific examples from the text. *Possible answer: It has mostly been destructive. Hindu and Muslim tension led to death of nearly 1 million Indians and a partitioned nation. Religious differences have led to violence and instability in Sri Lanka, the Middle East, and Africa.*
5. **Contrast** Describe the nature of totalitarianism and the police state that existed in Russia, and how it differed from some authoritarian governments you learned about in this lesson. *Possible answer: Totalitarian governments have absolute and centralized control over every aspect of life. Authoritarian governments are not as strict.*
6. **Compare** Compare the rise of nationalism in Turkey, India, and China. *Possible answer: In Turkey, Mustafa Kemal led nationalists in fighting back the Greeks and their British backers. The nationalists overthrew the last Ottoman sultan. Then church and state were separated, a new legal system established, women granted rights, and the nation industrialized. India's nationalists pressed for independence, and the land was divided among two different religious factions. In China, people overthrew the emperor of the Qing dynasty, but disagreements among factions eventually led to communist control of the government.*
7. **Analyze** Compare and contrast the methods used by African and Asian nations to achieve independence. *Possible answer: Some Asian nations were given independence after World War II because the nation that ruled them could no longer afford the cost. Some African nations already had limited self-rule, so independence came more easily. Other African nations, however, had to fight for independence from European settlers who refused to surrender power.*
8. **Infer** Use a globe to make a chart that shows the distance from Moscow and Washington, D.C., to Afghanistan, Ghana, the Philippines, and India. What do these distances tell you about the influences of the United States and the Soviet Union on these new nations? *Possible answer: Powerful nearby nations often assert a greater influence than nations that are farther away.*

(continued)

Print Assessment *(continued)*

9. With a partner, take turns reading, listening to, summarizing, and discussing the quotation by Anwar Sadat in Lesson 4.

Analyze Historical Accuracy

Examine websites, documentaries, movies, newspaper articles, and biographies about one of the leaders in these lessons. Based on what you know, critique the historical accuracy of at least two sources. What specifically can you find that is biased or inaccurate? What is most fair and impartial?

Interact with History

Now that you have read about the efforts by so many former colonies to forge new countries, identify the main factors that determine whether a new nation struggles or thrives. Be sure to cite specific examples from the text.

Focus on Writing

Select one of the leaders discussed in this chapter. Review the decisions the leader made while in power. Write an evaluation of the leader's decisions and his or her impact on the country. Consider the following:

- the leader's views on government and democracy
- the leader's handling of the economy
- the leader's accomplishments and failures

Multimedia Activity

Creating a Database

Use the Internet, library, and other reference materials to create a database showing the economic growth of any four countries discussed in this chapter. Create one table for each country, with column headings for each measure of economic growth you chose to record and row headings for each 10-year period. Then insert the most current data you can find. Consider the following questions to get started:

- What statistics will be most useful in making comparisons between nations?
- Which nations have capitalist economies? What other types of economies did you discover?
- Which nations have "one-crop" economies?

RUBRIC Databases should

- convey information clearly
- provide a full and comprehensive economic picture of each nation
- identify the sources of information used in the database

Online Assessment

1. *Select the button in the table to show whether each characteristic is true or false about partition.*

	True	False
Gandhi lived many years after partition was complete.	○	●
Pakistan and India decided to share the lands of Kashmir during partition.	○	●
Partition was intended to keep peace between Hindus and Muslims in India.	●	○
Millions of people were killed as they tried to migrate to either Pakistan or India.	●	○

2. What caused people in East Pakistan to want to break ties with West Pakistan in 1970?

○ West Pakistan gave part of its land to India near Kashmir.
○ West Pakistan refused to allow Hindus to practice their religion.
● West Pakistan did not fairly distribute foreign aid to East Pakistan.
○ West Pakistan made an agreement with the Soviet Union during the Cold War.

3. *Select the button in the table to show whether each characteristic is true or false about Bangladesh.*

	True	False
Bangladesh is a mountainous country.	○	●
Massive storms regularly flood Bangladesh.	●	○
Bangladesh is one of the poorest countries on Earth.	●	○
More than half of the people in Bangladesh work in manufacturing.	○	●

4. *Select the button in the table to show whether each characteristic is about Corazón Aquino or Ferdinand Marcos.*

	Corazón Aquino	Ferdinand Marcos
The Philippines ratified a new constitution under this person's leadership.	●	○
The Philippines elected this person president in 1965.	○	●
This president imposed an authoritarian regime and martial law.	○	●
This person won as president, and the previous president refused to acknowledge the victory.	●	○
The Philippines negotiated successfully with the United States to end the lease on the U.S. military bases under this person's leadership.	●	○
This president stole millions of dollars from the public treasury.	○	●

5. *Select the button in the table to show whether each characteristic is true or false about Aung San Suu Kyi.*

	True	False
She was placed under house arrest six days after the 2010 election.	○	●
She was placed under house arrest by the military government in Myanmar.	●	○
She refused to leave the country until a civilian government was restored in Myanmar.	●	○
She was married to a British citizen, which disqualified her from running for political office.	●	○

6. Why did Indonesia slide downhill during Sukarno's leadership?
   - ● He was not able to manage Indonesia's economy.
   - ○ He allowed citizens to protest in peaceful demonstrations.
   - ○ He set up a police state to force people to work in the fields.
   - ○ He confiscated all of the private land and turned it over to the state.

7. *Drag the description to one of the two types of governments that were found in colonial Africa.*

Direct form of government	●	Foreigners governed at all levels and no self-rule existed.
Indirect form of government	●	Local officials did much of the governing and colonists enjoyed limited self-rule.

8. *Select the button in the table to show whether each characteristic describes Kenya or Algeria.*

	Kenya	Algeria
It was ruled by the British prior to receiving its independence.	●	○
It had a population of 1 million French colonists and 9 million Arabs or Berbers.	○	●
The Mau Mau was a secret society made up of native farmers.	●	○
A record high number of voters turned out for the 2007 presidential elections.	●	○
Ahmed Ben Bella became the first president of the newly independent country.	○	●
Civil war between Islamic militants and the government broke out in 1991.	○	●

9. *Drag the characteristic into the correct column in the table to show whether it is associated with the Congo or Angola.*

Congo	Angola
Rich resources of rubber and copper were pilfered by the Belgians.	Thousands of land mines buried across the country limited farmers' ability to farm again after the war.
Patrice Lumumba became the first prime minister.	Portugal sent 50,000 troops to squelch an independence movement.
Leaders promised a transition to democracy and free elections by 1999.	Elections were held in 2008 and the MPLA won four-fifths of the vote.

10. What was the Diaspora?
    - ● the dispersal of the Jews around the globe
    - ○ the partition of Palestine after World War II
    - ○ the defeat of the Ottomans during World War I
    - ○ the return of the Jews to their national homeland

11. *Drag the name of each leader to the description that matches it. Each leader will be used only once.*

Gamal-Abdel Nasser	●	blockaded Israeli shipping and took the Suez Canal
Anwar Sadat	●	planned a surprise attack and recaptured territory lost in 1967
Golda Meir	●	launched a counterattack and regained most of the territory lost during the Yom Kippur war

12. Why did Benjamin Netanyahu most likely oppose the Oslo Peace Accords with the Palestinians?
    - ○ Other Arab nations refused to abide by the treaty.
    - ○ West Bank residents did not want to have self-government.
    - ○ Israel was required to stop building an army to defend itself.
    - ● Terrorist attacks against Israel continued after the agreement was signed.

13. What economic advantage does Azerbaijan have over its other central Asian neighbors?
    - ● The country has large oil reserves.
    - ○ The country is based on a capitalistic system.
    - ○ The country has a young population of workers.
    - ○ The country still has an alliance with the Soviet Union.

14. *Select the button in the table to show whether each characteristic is true or false about Afghanistan.*

	True	False
Afghanistan tried to establish a democratic government in 1964.	●	○
Afghanistan decided to support the Soviets during the Cold War.	○	●
Afghanistan harbored Osama bin Laden after the September 11 attacks.	●	○
Afghanistan received financial and military assistance from Great Britain.	○	●

15. *Drag the characteristic into the correct column in the table to show whether it is associated with the mujahideen or the Taliban.*

Mujahideen	Taliban
known as the holy warriors	conservative Islamic group
took up arms against the Soviet-supported government	became leaders of Afghanistan after the Soviets left
used land and guerilla warfare against Soviet troops	restricted the lives of women
	provided refuge for terrorist leaders

Essential Question Preview

Have the attempts at democracy in China and nations in Latin America, Africa, and the former Soviet bloc been worthwhile?

Have students consider the Essential Question and capture their initial responses.

Explore the Essential Question

- Discuss with students why democracy might be a goal that many nations attempt to achieve.
- Remind students that the collapse of the Soviet Union led many nations to attempt to establish democratic governments.

Help students plan inquiries and develop their own supporting questions such as:

How did China and nations in Latin America, Africa, and the former Soviet bloc struggle for democracy?

What were the major causes and effects of the struggles for democracy in China and nations in Latin America, Africa, and the former Soviet bloc?

You may want to assign students to write a short essay in response to the Essential Question when they complete the module. Encourage students to use their notes and responses to inform their essays.

Explore the Online Video

ANALYZE VIDEOS

Josip Broz Tito: The Rebel Communist

Invite students to watch the video to learn about the impact of Josip Broz Tito's rule in Yugoslavia.

History What did Josip Tito's death tell about his legacy? Possible answer: He was mourned greatly, and people openly feared whether Yugoslavia would descend into violence once he died; their fears came true.

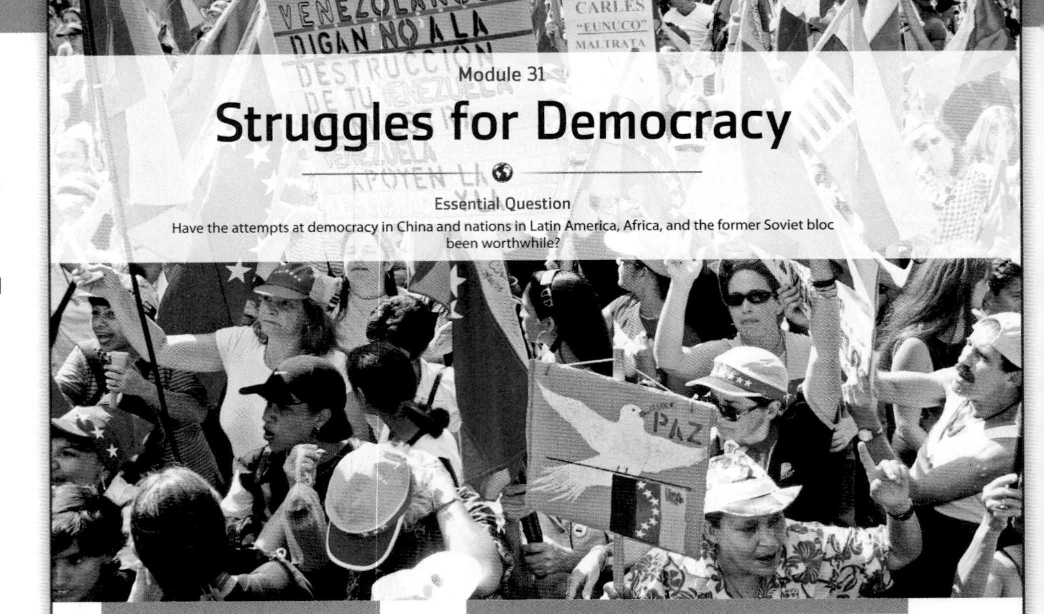

About the Photo: Protesters march in Caracas, Venezuela, in favor of democracy.

In this module, you will learn about the struggles for change in Latin America, Africa, the former Soviet bloc, and China.

Explore ONLINE!

VIDEOS, including...
- Josip Broz Tito: The Rebel Communist
- Eva Perón
- 100 Years of Terror
- The Fall of the Soviet Union
- The Fall of the Berlin Wall
- Tiananmen Square

- Document Based Investigations
- Graphic Organizers
- Interactive Games
- Image Compare: South Africa's Flags
- Carousel: Fall of the Berlin Wall

What You Will Learn ...

Lesson 1 Big Idea

In Latin America, economic problems and authoritarian rule delayed democracy.

Why It Matters Now

By the mid-1990s, almost all Latin American nations had democratic governments.

Lesson 2 Big Idea

As the recent histories of Nigeria and South Africa show, ethnic and racial conflicts can hinder democracy.

Why It Matters Now

In 1996, as Nigeria struggled with democracy, South Africa adopted a bill of rights that promotes racial equality.

Lesson 3 Big Idea

Democratic reforms brought important changes to the Soviet Union.

Why It Matters Now

Russia continues to struggle to establish democracy.

Lesson 4 Big Idea

Changes in the Soviet Union led to changes throughout Central and Eastern Europe.

Why It Matters Now

Many Eastern European nations that overthrew communist governments are still struggling with reform.

Timeline of Events 1945–Present

Explore ONLINE!

United States		World
	1948	
1948 Harry Truman wins second term as president.		1948 South Africa imposes apartheid policy of racial discrimination.
		1959 Fidel Castro seizes power in Cuba.
		1967 Nigerian civil war begins.
1969 Neil Armstrong walks on the moon in first lunar landing.		
		1978 Deng Xiaoping begins economic reforms in China.
1980 Ronald Reagan is elected president.		
1988 George H. W. Bush is elected president.		
		1989 Berlin Wall comes down.
1992 Bill Clinton is elected president.		
		1994 South Africa holds its first multiracial election.
2000 George W. Bush is elected president.		
2008 Barack Obama is elected president.		2008 Kosovo declares independence from Serbia.
		2012 Vladimir Putin begins third term as president.
	Present	

Struggles for Democracy 1213

Lesson 5 Big Idea

In response to contact with the West, China's government has experimented with capitalism but has rejected calls for democracy.

Why It Matters Now

After the 1997 death of Chinese leader Deng Xiaoping, President Jiang Zemin seemed to be continuing Deng's policies.

Explore the Timeline

Interpret Timelines: Struggles for Democracy, 1945–Present

Have students examine the timeline and then answer the following question:

History How many years after apartheid was instituted in South Africa did the nation hold its first multiracial election? *46 years*

Interpret Timeline of Events: Timeline of Events 1945–Present

To further explore the timeline, have students discuss the following questions:

1. Why is 1959 a significant year in the history of Cuba? *That is the year in which Fidel Castro seized power.*
2. During the 1960s, what conflict was the United States involved in? *the war in Vietnam*

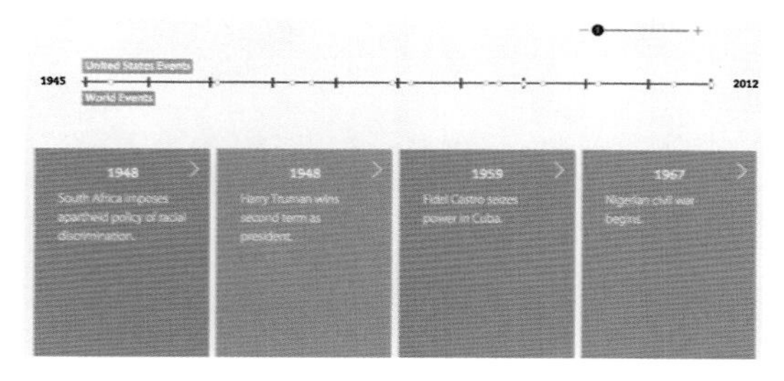

Online Module Flip Cards

Use the flip cards as a whole class activity or in student pairs to preview the module's Key Terms and People. Students can guess the meaning of each word, then review its definition, or do the reverse, using the flip card's toggle button to switch from Term to Definition mode. Students can also use the flip cards at the end of the module as a review tool before taking the Module Assessment.

Online Sequencing Activity

Students can use this sequencing activity to review the chronology of events in the Struggles for Democracy module. To complete, have students drag each event to the correct year on the timeline.

Year	Event
1948	*South Africa imposes apartheid policy of racial discrimination.*
1959	*Fidel Castro seizes power in Cuba.*
1967	*Nigerian civil war begins.*
1978	*Deng Xiaoping begins economic reforms in China.*
1989	*Berlin Wall comes down.*
1994	*South Africa holds its first multiracial election.*

Lesson 1 Planner

Democracy

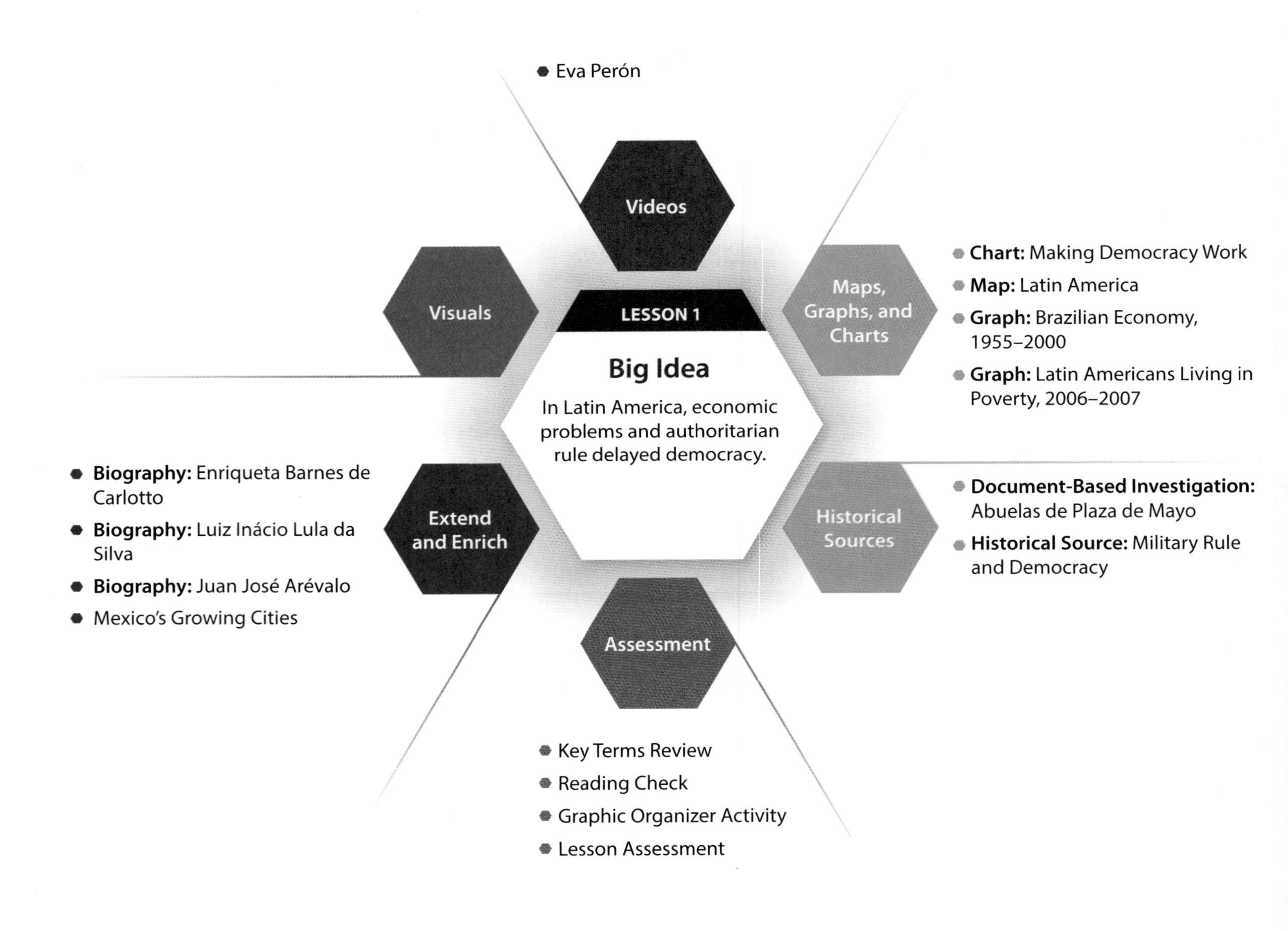

Online Lesson 1 Enrichment Activities

Enriqueta Barnes de Carlotto (1930–)

Biography Students read about the courage Enriqueta has shown in her search for the missing children of Argentina. Then they imagine that the Grandmothers of the Plaza de Mayo has found a missing relative of theirs after many years. Using information from the biography, students write a letter to Enriqueta Barnes de Carlotto thanking her for the group's efforts on behalf of disappeared children.

Luiz Inácio Lula da Silva (1945–)

Biography Students read about Luiz Inácio Lula da Silva, a popular labor leader and former president of Brazil. Then, using information from the biography, they write a speech that Lula da Silva might have given during the 2002 election campaign. Students then rehearse it and deliver it to the class.

Juan José Arévalo (1904–1990)

Biography Students read the biography about Juan José Arévalo, who became president of Guatemala after 14 years of military rule. Then students imagine that they are at a campaign event for Guatemalan presidential candidate Juan José Arévalo. Using information from the biography, students create a sign or banner that tells about one or more of the reforms that Arévalo supports.

Mexico's Growing Cities

Research Activity Students conduct research about the effects of urbanization in Mexico. Then they create a chart showing how industrialization and urbanization have changed Mexico's social institutions.

Teach the Big Idea

1. **Whole Class Open/Introduction** In what ways is U.S. democracy a "work in progress"? *concerns over civil liberties, the influence of lobbyists, campaign funding, and affirmative action*
2. **Direct Teach** Read students the Big Idea: *In Latin America, economic problems and authoritarian rule delayed democracy.* Review the following lesson objectives with students to aid in their understanding of the Big Idea.
   - Identify key features of democracy.
   - Describe Brazil's steps toward democracy.
   - Understand the causes and effects of the Pinochet regime in Chile.
   - Explain attempts to build democracy in Mexico.
   - Describe key events in postwar Argentina.
   - Understand the effects of military rule on Guatemala's struggles for democracy.
3. **Whole Group Close/Reflect** Have students write a letter to the editor of a Latin American newspaper explaining why economic reforms will help pave the way to democratic reform, peace, and stability in Latin America.

ONLINE DOCUMENT-BASED INVESTIGATION

Struggles for Democracy

Abuelas de Plaza de Mayo is the first of five document-based investigations that students will analyze in the Struggles for Democracy module. Groups of Argentine women banded together to protest the government-sponsored torture and murder of thousands of political dissidents. Students can click on three hotspots to learn more about the photograph and its historical context.

ONLINE GRAPHIC ORGANIZER

Democracy

As students read the lesson, have them use the graphic organizer to take notes. Students can review their graphic organizer notes at the end of the lesson to answer the following question:

Critical Thinking Which country has made the most progress? *Mexico has made the most progress because its democracy has not been interrupted by dictatorships, so it has a more stable base.*

Lesson 1

Case Study

Latin American Democracies

Democracy

The Big Idea

In Latin America, economic problems and authoritarian rule delayed democracy.

Why It Matters Now

By the mid-1990s, almost all Latin American nations had democratic governments.

Key Terms and People

Brasília
land reform
standard of living
recession
PRI

Setting the Stage

By definition, democracy—or liberal democracy as it is sometimes called—is government by the people. Direct democracy, in which all citizens meet to pass laws, is not practical for nations. Therefore, democratic nations developed indirect democracies, or republics, in which citizens elect representatives to make laws for them. For example, the United States is a republic. But democracy is more than a form of government. It is also a way of life and an ideal goal. A democratic way of life includes practices such as free and open elections.

Democracy As a Goal

The chart "Making Democracy Work" lists four practices in a democracy, together with conditions that help these democratic practices succeed. Many nations follow these practices to a large degree. However, establishing democracy is a process that takes years.

Even in the United States, the establishment of democracy has taken time. Although the principle of equality is part of the Constitution, many Americans have struggled for equal rights. To cite one example, women did not receive the right to vote until 1920. Democracy is always a "work in progress."

Other political ideologies have existed in the United States as well. Though socialism and communism never became strong political forces in the United States, both have maintained a presence here. The movements have remained a much stronger presence in other parts of the world, including Europe, Asia, and Africa.

Democratic institutions may not ensure stable, civilian government if other conditions are not present. The participation of a nation's citizens in government is essential to democracy. Education and literacy—the ability to read and write—give citizens the tools they need to make political decisions. Also, a stable economy with a strong middle class

1214 Module 31

COLLABORATIVE LEARNING

Return of Democracy

1. Organize students into small groups.
2. Have each group write and rehearse a skit that describes how citizens of a Latin American country of their choice feel about their country becoming democratic. As an alternative, students might wish to create a formal ceremony announcing sweeping democratic reforms to the public.
3. Have students present their skits to the class.

ENGLISH-LANGUAGE LEARNERS

Obstacles to Democracy

1. Divide students into small groups.
2. Tell students to read "Democracy as a Goal."
3. Ask them to redraw the "Making Democracy Work" chart. Have groups replace the second column heading with "Conditions That Stop Those Practices" and rewrite the entries to reflect the new heading.
4. Point out that simply changing words to their opposite will not always result in a logical entry.

Examples from row two follow.

and opportunities for advancement help democracy. It does so by giving citizens a stake in the future of their nation.

Other conditions advance democracy. First, a firm belief in the rights of the individual promotes the fair and equal treatment of citizens. Second, rule by law helps prevent leaders from abusing power without fear of punishment. Third, a sense of national identity helps encourage citizens to work together for the good of the nation. In contrast, a citizen of an authoritarian system receives few or no rights while their rulers demand loyalty and service to the government.

The struggle to establish democracy and to build stable economies continued into the twenty-first century as many nations abandoned authoritarian rule for democratic institutions. As the cold war has faded, nations have worked to establish a New World Order, in which countries work together to promote peace rather than conflict. The Organization of American States (OAS) is one such way the countries of the Americas work together to promote democracy and defend human rights. A United Nations study released in July 2002 warned that the spread of democracy around the world could be derailed if free elections in poor countries are not followed by economic growth. The United Nations Development Program's annual report warned particularly about Latin America.

Reading Check
Make Inferences Why would democracy suffer if citizens didn't participate?

Making Democracy Work

Common	Conditions That Foster Those Practices
Free elections	Having more than one political party Universal suffrage—all adult citizens can vote
Citizen participation	High levels of education and literacy Economic security Freedoms of speech, press, and assembly
Majority rule, minority rights	All citizens equal before the law Shared national identity Protection of such individual rights as freedom of religion Representatives elected by citizens to carry out their will
Constitutional government	Clear body of traditions and laws on which government is based Widespread education about how government works National acceptance of majority decisions Shared belief that no one is above the law

Interpret Charts
How might economic security foster citizen participation?

Objectives

You may wish to discuss the following questions with students to help them frame the content as they read.

- Can one nation force another to become a democracy? *No—Democratization is an organic process. Yes—With enough financial and human resources, it would be possible.*
- Does a nation's wealthiest citizens have more at stake in their nation's future than the poor? *Yes—They have more possessions and freedoms to lose. No—Everyone in a nation has the same stake in the future.*

More About . . .

Rule of Law Rule of law is the idea that nations should be governed by laws, not by the arbitrary decisions of individuals. In a nation governed by rule of law, all people are subject to the laws, including government authorities and lawmakers themselves. According to the World Justice Project, the law must also be "clear, publicized, stable, and fair" and must protect basic human rights.

ONLINE INTERACTIVE CHARTS

Making Democracy Work

Have students explore the chart and answer the associated question.

Interpret Charts Which condition best helps foster the democratic practice of free elections? *universal suffrage*

In print edition, see chart of same title.

Interpret Charts How might economic security foster citizen participation? *It might make citizens feel that they have something worth protecting, and this feeling might lead them to vote.*

READING CHECK

Make Inferences Why would democracy suffer if citizens didn't participate? *If a low percentage of the citizens voted, then a minority would end up making decisions, which contradicts majority rule.*

ONLINE LESSON FLIP CARDS

Review Key Terms and People

Students can use the flip cards in the Lesson Review at any time to review the lesson's key terms and people: *Brasília, land reform, standard of living, recession,* and *PRI.*

Citizen participation

- *Few people can read or go to school.*
- *People don't know if they will have money in the future.*
- *People are not allowed to say what they think to others, in newspapers or magazines, on television or radio, or in public places.*

COLLABORATIVE LEARNING

Human Rights

1. Divide students into small groups.
2. Have each group make a list of all the material things people need in order to survive. Then have students make a list of basic rights and freedoms that people need in order to live in a just and fair society.
3. Have groups share their ideas with the whole class and create a class list for all to see. You may wish to add several amendments from the Bill of Rights to the class list if students do not include them.
4. Ask students to name common traits of dictatorships, such as lack of security, little freedom, poor economy, and poor standard of living.
5. Guide students in a discussion of conditions in countries run by dictators. Why do people in these countries often lack material necessities and basic human rights?

Objectives

You may wish to discuss the following questions with students to help them frame the content as they read.

- What are the potential benefits and drawbacks of the foreign investment encouraged by Kubitschek and his successors? *Benefit—It would allow Brazil to pursue projects it could not finance itself. Drawback—Brazil might have to surrender some control over its domestic affairs to foreign investors.*
- What factors would you consider before introducing land reform? *Possible answers: fairness, how to persuade landowners, how to ensure cooperation of the military and police*
- Why is it significant that Cardoso, a promoter of free markets, was trained as a Marxist scholar? *Marxists see markets as a way for capitalists to take advantage of their wealth.*

More About . . .

Latin American Languages In 1989, several prominent publications attributed this remark to Vice President Dan Quayle: "I was recently on a tour of Latin America, and the only regret I have was that I didn't study Latin harder in school so I could converse with those people." The quotation turned out to be a fabrication, but many people believed it because of the vice president's reputation as a poor public speaker. Of course, the people of Latin America do not speak Latin but rather languages derived from Latin—Romance languages such as Spanish, Portuguese, and French.

Case Study > Brazil

Dictators and Democracy

Many Latin American nations won their independence from Spain and Portugal in the early 1800s. However, three centuries of colonial rule left many problems. These included powerful militaries, economies that were too dependent on a single crop, and large gaps between rich and poor. These patterns persisted in the modern era. Citizens of many Latin American countries worked to gain more rights. Women, indigenous people, and other groups fought for both civil rights—the rights of citizens to political and social freedoms, and for human rights—the basic rights belonging to every person.

After gaining independence from Portugal in 1822, Brazil became a monarchy. This lasted until 1889, when Brazilians established a republican government, which a wealthy elite controlled. Then, in the 1930s, Getulio Vargas became dictator. Vargas suppressed political opposition. At the same time, however, he promoted economic growth and helped turn Brazil into a modern industrial nation.

Kubitschek's Ambitious Program After Vargas, three popularly elected presidents tried to steer Brazil toward democracy. Juscelino Kubitschek (zhoo•suh•LEE•nuh-KOO•bih•chehk), who governed from 1956 to 1961, continued to develop Brazil's economy. Kubitschek encouraged foreign investment to help pay for development projects. He built a new capital city, **Brasília** (bruh•ZIHL•yuh), in the country's interior. Kubitschek's dream proved expensive. The nation's foreign debt soared and inflation shot up.

Kubitschek's successors proposed reforms to ease economic and social problems. Conservatives resisted this strongly. They especially opposed the plan for **land reform**—breaking up large estates and distributing that land to peasants. In 1964, with the blessing of wealthy Brazilians, the army seized power in a military coup.

Military Dictators For two decades military dictators ruled Brazil. Emphasizing economic growth, the generals fostered foreign investment. They began huge development projects in the Amazon jungle. The economy boomed.

The boom had a downside, though. The government froze wages and cut back on social programs. This caused a decline in the **standard of living**, or level of material comfort, which is judged by the amount of goods people have. When Brazilians protested, the government imposed censorship. It also jailed, tortured, and sometimes killed government critics. Nevertheless, opposition to military rule continued to grow.

The Road to Democracy By the early 1980s, a **recession**, or slowdown in the economy, gripped Brazil. At that point, the generals decided to open up the political system. They allowed direct elections of local, state, and national officials.

1216 Module 31

COLLABORATIVE LEARNING

Design an Interactive Map of Latin America

1. Divide the class into heterogeneous groups.
2. Explain to students that they are going to create a design for an interactive map based on the "Latin America, 2003" map. Have them use the textbook to find information about some of the countries on the map.
3. After students have compiled their data, have them create a design that describes how their maps will look and how users will interact with the map. Encourage students to be creative with their designs. Students might want to tailor the visual aspects of their maps to the types of information they have chosen. For example, if they feature economic information, they could incorporate clickable icons shaped like coins. Also, to access the data they have collected, students could have users click on a country's name, answer a multiple-choice question from a pull-down menu, or drag items from a data list to the country with which the data corresponds.

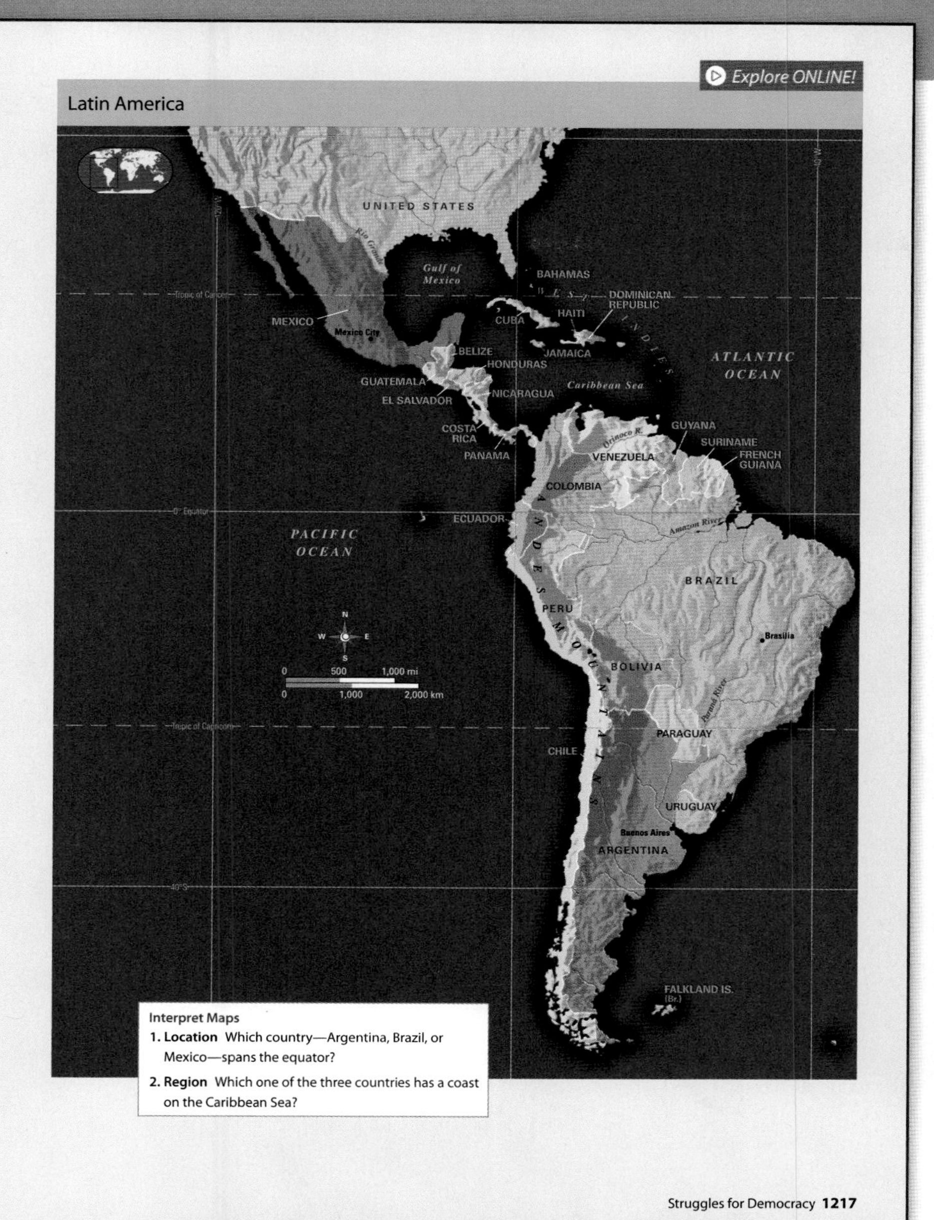

Interpret Maps

1. **Location** Which country—Argentina, Brazil, or Mexico—spans the equator?
2. **Region** Which one of the three countries has a coast on the Caribbean Sea?

MAPS

Latin America

Have students explore the map and answer the associated questions.

Location Which country—Argentina, Brazil, or Mexico—spans the equator? *Brazil*

Region Which one of the three countries has a coast on the Caribbean Sea? *Mexico*

ONLINE INTERACTIVE GRAPHS

Brazilian Economy, 1955–2000

Have students explore the graphs and answer the associated question.

Interpret Graphs By how much did Brazil's foreign debt increase from 1955 to 2000? *about $230 billion*

In the print edition, see graphs of the same title.

Interpret Graphs Of the years shown on the line graph, which was the worst year for inflation? *1990*

READING CHECK

Analyze Motives Why might the wealthy have preferred military rule to land reform? *They feared that land reform would take away their property and believed the army would protect their property rights.*

In 1985, a new civilian president, José Sarney (zhoh•ZAY-SAHR•nay), took office. Sarney inherited a country in crisis because of foreign debt and inflation. He proved unable to solve the country's problems and lost support. The next elected president fared even worse. He resigned because of corruption charges.

In 1994 and again in 1998, Brazilians elected Fernando Henrique Cardoso, who achieved some success in tackling the nation's economic and political problems. Although trained as a Marxist scholar, Cardoso became a strong advocate of free markets. One of his main concerns was the widening income gap in Brazil. He embarked on a program to promote economic reform.

The 2002 Presidential Election In the presidential election of October 2002, Cardoso's handpicked successor to lead his centrist coalition was José Serra. Serra faced two candidates who proposed a sharp break with Cardoso's pro-business policies. These candidates included Luiz Inácio Lula da Silva, a candidate of the leftist Workers Party.

An economic crisis hit many countries in South America, including Brazil, in 2002. Because of stalled economic growth, rising unemployment, and poverty, there was a backlash against free-market economic policies. This made the election of 2002 a close contest. Da Silva, the leftist candidate, won the hotly disputed election, defeating the ruling party candidate, Serra. The election was part of the trend toward socialist governments in Latin America. By 2005, approximately three out of four Latin Americans were living under leftist administrations. This marked a change from the previous era when leaders ruled governments supported by the United States, a country seeking to end the spread of communism.

Da Silva, who was reelected in 2006, proved a more moderate president than his supporters and opponents had expected. In 2010, Dilma Rousseff became the first woman president elected in Brazil. She has faced many challenges, including natural disasters and political scandals. Demonstrators at widespread protests have called for her impeachment. Despite these challenges, Brazil continues on the path of democracy.

Reading Check
Analyze Motives
Why might the wealthy have preferred military rule to land reform?

Brazilian Economy, 1955–2000

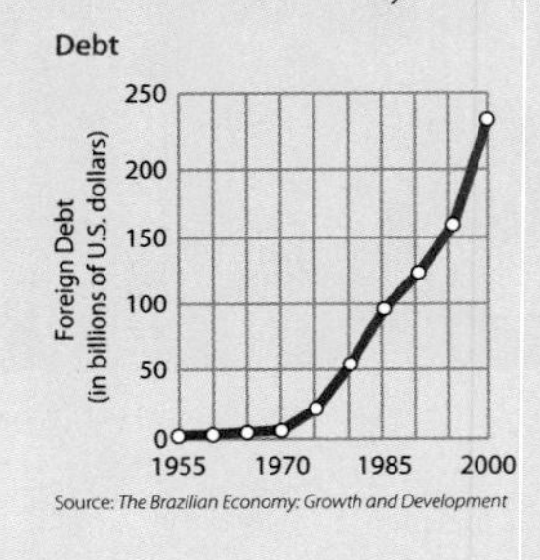

Source: *The Brazilian Economy: Growth and Development*

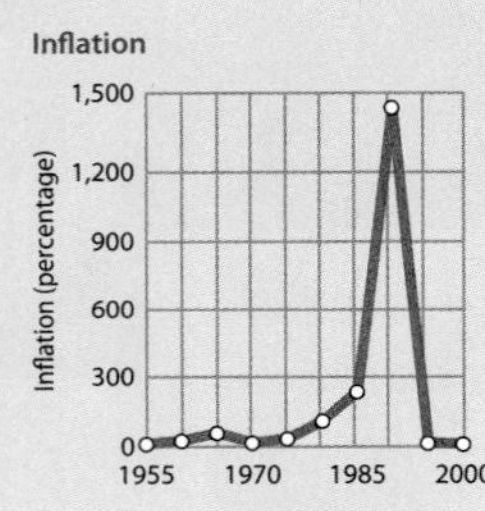

Interpret Graphs
Of the years shown on the line graph, which was the worst year for inflation?

State-Sponsored Terror

In 1970, Chileans elected the leftist Salvador Allende as president. Allende spent huge amounts of money in efforts to improve the lives of the working class and stimulate the economy. The government broke up large estates and distributed the land to peasants. It also nationalized foreign-owned companies. For a time, Allende's measures were successful and widely popular.

Allende's Fall Allende soon ran into trouble. Industrial and farm production fell, prices rose, and food shortages spread. In addition, Allende's Communist policies alienated business owners and worried the U.S. government, which feared that Allende had developed close ties with the Soviet Union. The U.S. Central Intelligence Agency (CIA) began providing secret funding and military training to opposition groups in Chile in hopes of triggering an anti-Allende revolt. As the economy failed, more and more people turned against Allende. On September 11, 1973, the military rebelled. Allende and more than 3,000 others died in the bloodshed.

The Pinochet Regime Several weeks before the coup, Allende had appointed a new commander in chief of the army, Augusto Pinochet (peen•oh•SHAY). General Pinochet was closely involved in the rebellion. He took command of the new military regime and became president in 1974.

Pinochet moved quickly to destroy the opposition. He disbanded congress, suspended the constitution, and banned opposition parties. He also censored the media. His plan to cement his control of the Chilean government can best be described as politically motivated mass murder. Within three years, an estimated 130,000 people were arrested for opposing the government. Thousands of people disappeared, were tortured, killed, or fled into exile.

Despite the political crackdown, Chile's economy experienced rapid growth. Pinochet's government privatized state-owned businesses, slashed government budgets, cut tariffs, and eased government regulations. Exports grew and the economy took off. The cost of living, however, exploded and the gap between rich and poor got wider and wider. Even with a 30 percent unemployment rate, Chile became the fastest-growing economy in Latin America.

Government Reform Under international pressure, Augusto Pinochet agreed to mild reforms in 1980. That year, he allowed for a new constitution. Under the agreement, Pinochet would remain president until 1989 and receive immunity for any crimes he may have committed. However, courts in Europe and Chile continued to seek justice for victims of the Pinochet regime. Pinochet was eventually charged with kidnapping and murder, but the court was not able to convict him before his death in 2006. Today, Chile's government is once again a democracy.

Reading Check
Find Main Ideas State the main idea of the section "The Pinochet Regime." Then cite at least two details that support the main idea.

Objectives

You may wish to discuss the following questions with students to help them frame the content as they read.

- What was life like in Chile during Pinochet's dictatorship? *civil rights restricted, no free speech, no opposition tolerated*
- Were General Pinochet and his army justified in rebelling against Allende? Why or why not? *Possible answers: No, Allende did a lot to improve the lives of his people. Yes, Allende's policies led to an economic downturn.*

More About . . .

Special Movement Chile Because of the political instability and frequent violations of human rights in their own country, many Chileans emigrated in the months following September 11, 1973. Canada, in particular, took in more than 7,000 Chilean refugees in an operation known as "Special Movement Chile." There are now more than 38,000 Chilean Canadians.

READING CHECK

Find Main Ideas What is the main idea of the section "The Pinochet Regime"? Cite at least two details that support the main idea. *Main idea: General Pinochet's rule was marked by extreme changes, mass murder, and an improved economy. Supporting details: Pinochet disbanded congress and suspended the constitution. Chile became the fastest-growing economy in Latin America.*

STRUGGLING READERS

Art as Protest

1. Provide students with construction paper, art supplies, and photographs of *arpilleras* (a type of Latin American tapestry).
2. Tell students that *arpilleras* are tapestries created to show daily life, and that they were first used as a form of protest in Chile.
3. Have students make their own *arpillera* depicting the daily life of a person living in Chile during the military dictatorship.
4. Have students share their work in small groups or with the entire class.

ADVANCED/GIFTED

Political Cartoon

1. Have students review the information about the military coup in Chile, focusing on the effects of the revolt.
2. Have students use the information to create a political cartoon showing the problems in Chile that resulted from the anti-Allende revolt and Pinochet's subsequent regime. Students should create a cartoon and an appropriate caption.
3. Have students share their cartoons in small groups and then post the cartoons for all to see.

Objectives

You may wish to discuss the following questions with students to help them frame the content as they read.

- What benefits and drawbacks might Cárdenas have considered before nationalizing Mexico's oil industry? *Benefit—More revenue for Mexican government. Drawback—Animosity and potential military action of foreign powers divested of property.*
- Why would President Fox concern himself with the legal status of Mexican immigrants in the United States? *The money that immigrants send to their families may contribute to the economic well-being of Mexico.*

More About . . .

Presidential Election 2006 Democracy is still a challenge for Mexico. In July 2006, Mexico held its presidential election. It first seemed that Manuel Lopez Obrador, the favorite of the poor, won. After further calculations and recounts, the PAN candidate, Felipe Calderon, was declared winner by about ½ percent, about 240,000 votes. Controversy erupted over the voting and the accuracy of the counting of ballots. Supporters of Obrador participated in many protests demanding a recount of the votes.

One-Party Rule

Unlike Brazil, Mexico enjoyed relative political stability for most of the 20th century. Following the Mexican Revolution, the government passed the Constitution of 1917. The new constitution outlined a democracy and promised reforms.

Beginnings of One-Party Domination From 1920 to 1934, Mexico elected several generals as president. However, these men did not rule as military dictators. They did create a ruling party—the National Revolutionary Party, which dominated Mexico under various names for the rest of the 20th century. From 1934 to 1940, President Lázaro Cárdenas (KAHR•day•nahs) tried to improve life for peasants and workers. He carried out land reform and promoted labor rights. He nationalized the Mexican oil industry, kicking out foreign oil companies and creating a state-run oil industry. After Cárdenas, however, a series of more conservative presidents turned away from reform.

The Party Becomes the PRI In 1946, the main political party changed its name to the Institutional Revolutionary Party, or **PRI**. In the half-century that followed, the PRI became the main force for political stability in Mexico. Although stable, the government was an imperfect democracy. The PRI controlled the congress and won every presidential election. The government allowed opposition parties to compete, but fraud and corruption tainted the elections.

Even as the Mexican economy rapidly developed, Mexico continued to suffer severe economic problems. Lacking land and jobs, millions of Mexicans struggled for survival. In addition, a huge foreign debt forced the government to spend money on interest payments. In the late 1960s, students and workers began calling for economic and political change. On October 2, 1968, protesters gathered at the site of an ancient Aztec market in Mexico City. Soldiers hidden in the ruins opened fire on the protesters. The massacre claimed several hundred lives.

People also called for change in the United States as the civil rights movement there grew in strength. Between 1942 and 1964, more than four million Mexicans moved to the United States as part of the bracero program. Braceros worked as farm laborers in California and other states. Migrant workers often faced very poor working conditions and received little pay. Labor leaders such as Cesar Chavez worked to improve the rights of these workers.

Chavez effected change by organizing boycotts and encouraging migrant farmers to form labor unions. As the movement grew, Chavez's opponents tried to stop it. When a large grape grower named Schenley sprayed its vineyard workers with pesticides, Chavez and the National Farm Workers Association fought back harder. They organized a massive march that resulted in Schenley agreeing to a bargain with the union.

ADVANCED/GIFTED

Writing About Episodes in Mexico's History

1. After they have finished reading, tell students to use facts and details from the text to write a magazine article about an event described in the passage—for example, nationalization of the Mexican oil industry or the massacre at the Aztec ruins. Tell them to pick an event and to choose a magazine for which they wish to write.
2. Before they begin their essay, students should identify the magazine's readership. Are readers younger or older, more or less educated, progressive or conservative, wealthy or less well off? Tell students to keep this audience in mind as they write their articles.
3. After they have completed their articles, have students add a paragraph at the head of their article that describes the readership. At the end of the article, ask them to write a paragraph that describes how their essay was tailored or not tailored to this readership. (Students might opt to challenge the magazine's readers—at least to an extent allowed by the magazine's editors.)

Historical Source

Military Rule and Democracy

Throughout the 20th century, many Latin American countries were ruled by military dictators or political bosses. Most typically, the dictator's support came from the wealthy and the military. But sometimes the dictator's support came from the people.

"My goodness, if I'd known how badly you wanted democracy I'd have given it to you ages ago."

Analyze Historical Sources
Do dictators typically take into account the opinions of the people they rule? What does this cartoon suggest about the dictator's attitude toward the opinion of the people he rules?

Another critical episode occurred during the early 1980s. By that time, huge new oil and natural gas reserves had been discovered in Mexico. The economy had become dependent on oil and gas exports. In 1981, world oil prices fell, cutting Mexico's oil and gas revenues in half. Mexico went into an economic decline.

Economic and Political Crises The 1980s and 1990s saw Mexico facing various crises. In 1988, opposition parties challenged the PRI in national elections. The PRI candidate, Carlos Salinas, won the presidency. Even so, opposition parties won seats in the congress and began to force a gradual opening of the political system.

Latin Americans Living in Poverty, 2006–2007

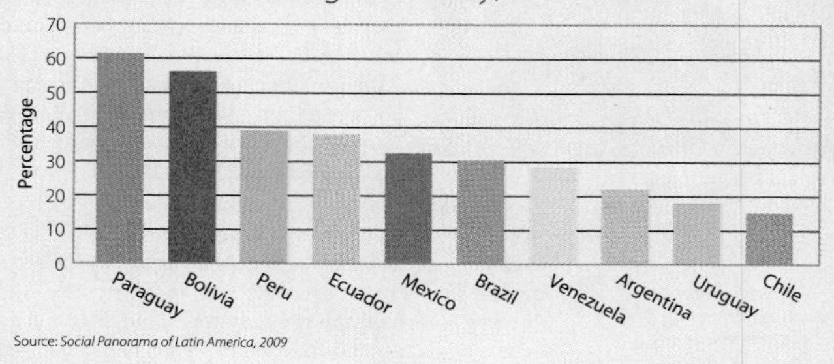

Source: *Social Panorama of Latin America, 2009*

Interpret Graphs
In which three countries of Latin America is the percentage of people living in poverty the lowest? In which three countries is the poverty rate the highest?

HISTORICAL SOURCES

Military Rule and Democracy

Invite students to study the political cartoon and answer the associated question.

Analyze Sources Do dictators typically take into account the opinions of the people they rule? What does this cartoon suggest about the dictator's attitude toward the opinion of the people he rules? *Dictators typically do not concern themselves with the opinions of their subjects. This cartoon suggests that he is ruled by the wishes of the people, which is one source of the cartoon's humor.*

HISTORICAL SOURCE

Military Rule and Democracy

Throughout the 20th century, many Latin American countries were ruled by military dictators or political bosses. Most typically, the dictator's support came from the wealthy and the military. But sometimes the dictator's support came from the people.

GRAPHS

Latin Americans Living in Poverty, 2006–2007

Have students explore the graph and answer the associated question.

Interpret Graphs In which three countries of Latin America is the percentage of people living in poverty the lowest? In which three countries is the poverty rate highest? *Lowest—Argentina, Uruguay, Chile; Highest—Paraguay, Bolivia, Peru*

READING CHECK
Analyze Effects Why does over-reliance on one product weaken an economy? *If prices for that product drop, the economy is severely damaged.*

During his presidency, Salinas signed NAFTA, the North American Free Trade Agreement. NAFTA removed trade barriers between Mexico, the United States, and Canada. In early 1994, peasant rebels in the southern Mexican state of Chiapas (chee•AH•pahs) staged a major uprising. Shortly afterward, a gunman assassinated Luis Donaldo Colosio, the PRI presidential candidate for the upcoming election.

The PRI Loses Control After these events, Mexicans grew increasingly concerned about the prospects for democratic stability. Nevertheless, the elections of 1994 went ahead. The new PRI candidate, Ernesto Zedillo (zuh•DEE•yoh), won. Opposition parties continued to challenge the PRI.

In 1997, two opposition parties each won a large number of congressional seats, denying the PRI control of congress. Then, in 2000, Mexican voters ended 71 years of PRI rule by electing center-right candidate Vicente Fox as president.

Former President Vicente Fox of Mexico

New Policies and Programs Fox's agenda was very ambitious. He advocated reforming the police, rooting out political corruption, ending the rebellion in Chiapas, and opening up Mexico's economy to free-market forces.

Fox also argued that the United States should legalize the status of millions of illegal Mexican immigrant workers. Fox hoped that a negotiated agreement between the United States and Mexico would provide amnesty for these undocumented Mexican workers in the United States. After Felipe Calderon, a conservative, was elected president in 2006, he continued many of Fox's policies. However, tensions between the governments grew over Washington's plan to build a fence along the two countries' border.

The United States' presence has also been felt in Mexico as part of the nation's War on Drugs. Violence connected to the drug trade increased dramatically during Calderon's presidency. Calderon's administration decided to expand the use of military force against drug traffickers. Since 2006, Calderon has sent thousands of troops to the U.S.-Mexico border to fight against drug cartels. Washington continues to support these efforts by supplying military equipment and training to Mexican soldiers.

The War on Drugs has weighed heavily on the nation's economy. Mexico's economy also struggled after the H1N1 flu pandemic hit the nation in 2009. Citizens elected Enrique Peña Nieto in 2012, marking a return to PRI rule. Nieto has worked to improve the economy by increasing foreign investment in the nation's oil industry, but he has met resistance from congress. His administration has had success in implementing political and electoral reforms, however.

Reading Check
Analyze Effects Why does over-reliance on one product weaken an economy?

Case Study > Argentina

Political and Economic Disorder

Mexico and Brazil were not the only Latin American countries where democracy had made progress. By the late 1990s, most of Latin America was under democratic rule.

Perón Rules Argentina
Argentina had struggled to establish democracy. It was a major exporter of grain and beef. It was also an industrial nation with a large working class. In 1946, Argentine workers supported an army officer, Juan Perón, who won the presidency and then established a dictatorship.

Perón did not rule alone. He received critical support from his wife, Eva—known as Evita to the millions of Argentines who idolized her. Together, the Peróns created a welfare state. The state offered social programs with broad popular appeal but limited freedoms. After Eva's death in 1952, Perón's popularity declined and his enemies—the military and the Catholic Church—moved against him. In 1955, the military ousted Perón and drove him into exile.

Eva Perón

Vocabulary
welfare state a government that tries to provide for all its citizens' needs—including health, education, and employment

Repression in Argentina For many years, the military essentially controlled Argentine politics. Perón returned to power once more, in 1973, but ruled for only a year before dying in office. By the mid-1970s, Argentina was in chaos.

In 1976, the generals seized power again. They established a brutal dictatorship and hunted down political opponents. For several years, torture and murder were everyday events. By the early 1980s, several thousand Argentines had simply disappeared, kidnapped by their own government.

Objectives

You may wish to discuss the following questions with students to help them frame the content as they read.

- How might the Catholic Church have become an enemy of President Juan Perón? *Perón may have initiated policies that offended Church officials or harmed Church interests.*
- Why might the Argentine military have attacked the Falkland Islands? *They may have believed that the United Kingdom would be unwilling to defend such a distant and relatively insignificant territory. Undertaking such a campaign may have been perceived as a way to unite Argentines behind their military rulers.*

More About . . .

Eva Perón British composer Andrew Lloyd Webber and lyricist Tim Rice based their hit Broadway musical *Evita* (1978) on the life of Eva Perón. In 1996, the musical was made into a movie starring Madonna and Antonio Banderas.

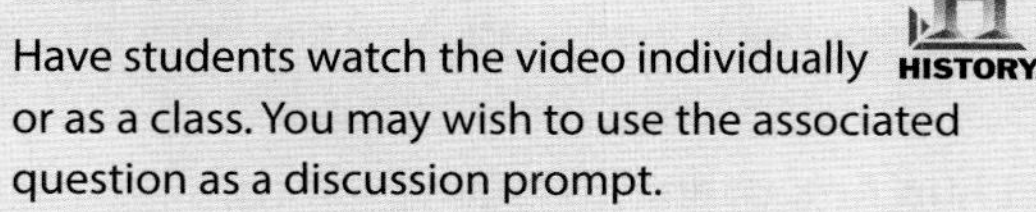

Eva Perón

HISTORY

Have students watch the video individually or as a class. You may wish to use the associated question as a discussion prompt.

Analyze Videos What career did Eva Perón pursue before meeting her future husband? *a movie actress*

STRUGGLING READERS

Child Missing

1. Review the information in the text under "Repression in Argentina."
2. Have students create a "Child Missing" poster for a young Argentine man or woman who became a victim of Argentina's brutal dictatorship.

 ONLINE DOCUMENT-BASED INVESTIGATION

Abuelas de Plaza de Mayo

Groups of Argentine women banded together to protest the government-sponsored torture and murder of thousands of political dissidents. Students can click on three hotspots to learn more about the photograph and its historical context.

Analyze Sources What kind of impact do you think this photograph has on the viewer? Why? *It might make people better empathize with the Argentines who lost people close to them than just reading text.*

DOCUMENT-BASED INVESTIGATION HISTORICAL SOURCE

Abuelas de Plaza de Mayo

From 1976 to 1983, the military government of Argentina tortured and killed thousands of political dissidents and sometimes stole their children. In response, groups of Argentine women banded together to protest these injustices and to demand to know the fate of their relatives. In this photo from a protest in 1979, the banner translates as "Disappeared Children." Abuelas de Plaza de Mayo means "Grandmothers of the Plaza de Mayo."

ONLINE INTERACTIVE GRAPHS

Latin Americans Living in Poverty, 2006–2007

Have students explore the graph and answer the associated question.

Interpret Graphs In which three countries of Latin America is the percentage of people living in poverty the lowest? *Argentina, Uruguay, Chile*

READING CHECK

Analyze Causes What finally caused military rule to end in Argentina? *The military government lost a humiliating war and had to turn the government over to civilians.*

Argentinian women protesting the disappearance of children they believe were taken by the government.

Some groups worked to address these human rights violations. The Mothers of the Plaza de Mayo, an association of Argentine women whose children and grandchildren had disappeared or been killed, were one such group. For nearly 30 years, they held weekly vigils in a park near the presidential palace to call attention to the missing.

Democracy and the Economy In 1982, the military government went to war with Britain over the nearby Falkland Islands and suffered a defeat. Disgraced, the generals agreed to step down. In 1983, Argentines elected Raúl Alfonsín (ahl•fohn•SEEN) president in the country's first free election in 37 years.

During the 1980s, Alfonsín worked to rebuild democracy and the economy. Carlos Menem gained the presidency in 1989 and continued the process. He attempted to stabilize the currency and privatize industry. By the late 1990s, however, economic problems intensified as the country lived beyond its means.

A Growing Crisis In December 2001, the International Monetary Fund (IMF) refused to provide financial aid to Argentina. Then President Fernando de la Rua resigned in the face of protests over the economy. He was succeeded by Eduardo Duhalde, who tried to deal with the economic and social crisis. In 2002, Argentina had an unemployment rate of about 24 percent. The country defaulted on $132 billion in debt, the largest debt default in history, and devalued its currency. In 2003, under then President Nestor Kirchner, the nation renegotiated its debt with the IMF. In 2006, Argentina successfully repaid its debt. Despite high inflation rates, Argentina's economy continued to strengthen throughout the early twenty-first century under the leadership of the nation's first female president, Cristina Fernández de Kirchner.

Reading Check **Analyze Causes** What finally caused military rule to end in Argentina?

Chaos in Central America

Guatemala gained independence from Spain in 1821 and Mexico in 1823. Beginning in 1838, Rafael Carrera ruled Guatemala under a nationalistic policy, giving power to the Church and to aristocracy. He maintained control until his death in 1865. For many decades afterward, different presidents worked to improve infrastructure, increase Guatemalan exports, and better the country's health and education systems. At the same time, however, leaders ruled ineffectively and committed human rights violations. The struggle for economic autonomy and social justice would continue into the 20th century.

Rise of Military Dictatorships As in Argentina, the military controlled Guatemalan politics for many years. In 1931, General Jorge Ubico rose to power via a military coup. He was the fourth military dictator to rule in Guatemala. During his reign, the United Fruit Company, a U.S.-owned company, became the most important business in the country. In 1944, a military group that supported change took control of government. Under this group, political parties were formed and presidential elections were held. Leaders reformed many parts of the country, including giving laborers better benefits. But leaders in other countries worried about the spread of communism in Guatemala. Similar to the situation in Chile, U.S. President Dwight D. Eisenhower directed the CIA to supply weapons and funding to forces fighting against the Guatemalan president.

Civil War Begins A military coup overthrew the democratically elected Guatemalan president in 1954. Its leader, Colonel Carlos Castillo Armas, became the new president. Armas took away many of the reforms that previous leaders had put in place. He removed voting rights for illiterate citizens, took land away from peasants, and imprisoned thousands of Guatemalans labeled as Communists. Thus began the nation's long and torturous civil war. For three decades, right-wing government military forces fiercely battled against leftist groups, including many Mayan revolutionaries who fought for economic and social justice.

Violence and Terror Grows During this period, the government supported armies that caused terrible violence throughout Guatemala. Many people were tortured, murdered, or disappeared. There were few bright spots during this time. In 1966, citizens elected a civilian president. However, his promises for economic reforms and social justice were largely unmet. Violence and social unrest only intensified. Between 1970 and 1983, more than 50,000 Guatemalans were killed and many more fled to other countries.

United States Influence In 1977, U.S. President Jimmy Carter ended military aid to Guatemala. However, six years later President Ronald Reagan overturned Carter's arms embargo, despite continuing massacres.

CURRENT EVENTS IN GUATEMALA

Below Level Have students review the information about conditions in Guatemala today. Then have them find an article about Guatemala in magazines, newspapers, or from reliable online sources. Have students answer the following questions about their articles on a separate sheet of paper: Who was involved? What happened? Where did it happen? When did it happen? Why is it important?

At Level Have students review the information about conditions in Guatemala today. Then have them conduct further research on current conditions and events in Guatemala using reliable print or online sources. Have students create a timeline of recent events in Guatemala and write a one-page summary of their research findings.

Above Level Have students review the information about conditions in Guatemala today. Then have them conduct further research on current conditions and events in Guatemala using reliable print or online sources. Have students write a two-page essay explaining how the Guatemalan Civil War has impacted current conditions in Guatemala.

Objectives

You may wish to discuss the following questions with students to help them frame the content as they read.

- Why might the United States have chosen to get involved in Guatemalan politics in the 1950s? *A United States–owned company, the United Fruit Company, was the most important business in Guatemala. The United States was concerned about the spread of communism in Guatemala, possibly exacerbated by the fact that it had an economic stake in the country.*
- How did the United States influence the Civil War in Guatemala? *It supplied weapons and funding to the Guatemalan military. Finally, in the 1990s, it threatened to impose economic sanctions against Guatemala.*

More About . . .

The Maya The Maya civilization is probably the best known classic civilization of Mesoamerica. From its origins around 2600 BC to its rise to prominence around 250, the Maya occupied lands including what is now Guatemala and parts of Mexico, Honduras, El Salvador, and Belize. Today, people of Maya descent comprise around 40 percent of the population of Guatemala. Maya people were the primary victims of Guatemala's civil war. In attempts to escape the violence, between 500,000 and 1.5 million Maya fled to other parts of the country and the world.

ONLINE HISTORICAL SOURCES

Military Rule and Democracy

Invite students to study the political cartoon and answer the associated question.

Analyze Sources Do dictators typically take into account the opinions of the people they rule? What is the dictator in this cartoon's attitude toward the opinion of the people he rules? *Dictators typically do not concern themselves with the opinions of their subjects. This cartoon suggests that he is ruled by the wishes of the people, which is one source of the cartoon's humor.*

HISTORICAL SOURCE

Military Rule and Democracy

Throughout the 20th century, many Latin American countries were ruled by military dictators or political bosses. Most typically, the dictator's support came from the wealthy and the military. But sometimes the dictator's support came from the people.

READING CHECK

Analyze Causes What led to the breakout of the civil war in Guatemala? *President Armas took away land and rights from many groups and imprisoned civilians.*

Print Assessment

1. **Organize Information** Which country do you think has made the most progress? Explain. *Possible answer: Mexico has made the most progress because its democracy has not been interrupted by dictatorships, so it has a more stable base.*
2. **Key Terms and People** For each key term or person in the lesson, write a sentence explaining its significance. *Explanations of the lesson's key terms can be found on the following pages: Brasília, p. 1216; land reform, p. 1216; standard of living, p. 1216; recession, p. 1216; PRI, p. 1220*
3. **Analyze Effects** What effect did the Falklands war have on the military government in Argentina? *It led to the end of military rule.*
4. **Compare and Contrast** Compare and contrast the rise of military dictatorships in Brazil, Guatemala, and Argentina. *In all three countries, the military overthrew civilian governments but was eventually forced to yield power and allow free elections. However, only in Guatemala did the rise of military dictatorships lead to a civil war.*
5. **Synthesize** What have been some of the obstacles to democracy in Latin America? *Possible answers: powerful militaries, weak rule of law*
6. **Develop Historical Perspective** What are some of the attributes of democracy? *free elections, citizen participation*

The civil war death toll continued to rise throughout the 1980s. In 1993, the United States and European nations threatened to impose economic sanctions after Guatemalan president Jorge Serrano disbanded congress. As a result, business owners, who worried about the economic repercussions, helped force Serrano out of power.

In 1994, peace talks finally began between the Guatemalan government and guerilla insurgents. Two years later, the civil war ended. A United Nations report issued in 1999 found that the Guatemalan military committed a large majority of the human rights crimes that occurred during the civil war. More than 80 percent of the victims were Mayans. Unfortunately, very little progress has been made in bringing human rights violators during the war to justice. Guatemala remains a country plagued by drugs, inequality, and high rates of crime. More than half of its residents live in poverty.

Reading Check **Analyze Causes** What led to the breakout of the civil war in Guatemala?

Indigenous groups suffered human rights violations during Guatemala's decades-long civil war.

Lesson 1 Assessment

1. **Organize Information** Which country do you think has made the most progress? Explain.

Nation	Steps toward democracy
Brazil	
Mexico	
Argentina	

2. **Key Terms and People** For each key term or person in the lesson, write a sentence explaining its significance.
3. **Analyze Effects** What effect did the Falklands War have on the military government in Argentina?
4. **Compare and Contrast** Compare and contrast the rise of military dictatorships in Brazil, Guatemala, and Argentina.
5. **Synthesize** What have been some of the obstacles to democracy in Latin America?
6. **Develop Historical Perspective** What are some of the attributes of democracy?

Online Assessment

1. What happens in poor countries if economic growth does not follow free elections?
   - Communist governments become less attractive.
   - Fewer people want to be part of the middle class.
   - Democratic governments have a hard time succeeding.
   - Migration to urban areas from rural areas is reversed.

   Alternate Question *Select the answer choice from the drop-down list to complete the sentence correctly.* If free elections are not followed by *economic growth*, poor countries often have little incentive to continue with democratic forms of government.

2. What did the generals who ruled Brazil from the 1960s to the 1980s accomplish during their time in power?
   - They reversed the country's recession.
   - They dramatically increased Brazil's national debt.
   - They raised the standard of living for all Brazilians.
   - They began huge development projects in the Amazon jungle.

   Alternate Question *Select the answer choice from the drop-down list to complete the sentence correctly.* The economy boomed during the 1960s to 1980s when the *generals* were in power in Brazil. They fostered foreign investments. They also began huge development projects in the Amazon jungle.

3. How did Augusto Pinochet come to power in Chile?
   - He took command after the president died.
   - He disbanded congress and named himself the king.
   - He won the presidency in the country's first fair election.
   - He inherited the throne when his family member abdicated.

   Alternate Question *Select the answer choice from the drop-down list to complete the sentence correctly.* Allende was assassinated in 1973, and so his commander in chief of the army, General Augusto Pinochet, took command of *Chile*. He became president in 1974.

4. What types of reforms did President Lázaro Cárdenas institute in Mexico during his time in power?
   - He promoted labor rights.
   - He created a two-party political system.
   - He encouraged private ownership in the oil industry.
   - He invited foreign companies to start businesses in the country.

   Alternate Question *Select the answer choice from the drop-down list to complete the sentence correctly.* During his time in power in Mexico, *Lázaro Cárdenas* promoted labor rights. He also carried out land reform and nationalized the oil industry.

5. What type of government did Juan Perón establish in Argentina between 1946 and 1955?
   - communist
   - democratic
   - dictatorship
   - fascist

   Alternate Question *Select the answer choice from the drop-down list to complete the sentence correctly.* Juan Perón took power in *Argentina* in 1946. He established a dictatorship along with the support of his wife, Eva. They provided social programs that had limited freedoms.

6. How were Argentina and Guatemala similar to each other after they achieved independence?
   - They both had politics that were controlled by the military.
   - They both had leaders that strongly opposed communism.
   - They both were investigated by the U.S. Central Intelligence Agency.
   - They both defaulted on their loans to the International Money Fund.

   Alternate Question *Select the answer choice from the drop-down list to complete the sentence correctly.* Argentina and Guatemala were similar to each other because they both had *military-controlled politics* for many years.

7. **Elaborate** What are three conditions that advance democracy?

   Possible answer: The first condition that advances democracy is the firm belief that the rights of the individual promote the fair and equal treatment of citizens. The second condition is that the rule of law helps prevent leaders from abusing powers without fear of punishment. Third, a sense of national identity helps encourage citizens to work together for the good of the nation.

8. **Elaborate** What happened in Brazil under Kubitschek's leadership, and what did his successors do to remediate those issues?

   Possible answer: Kubitschek wanted to develop Brazil's economy. He built a new capital city (Brasilia), which proved to be extremely expensive. It caused the nation's foreign debt to soar and inflation to rise drastically. Kubitschek's successors proposed reforms; some were popular and some were not. The land reforms idea, which called for distributing large estates to peasants, was definitely not popular among the people who owned those estates.

9. **Make Inferences** Why did the United States feel it needed to provide funding to opposition groups in Chile when Allende was in power?

   Possible answer: Allende was engaging in communistic activities. He seized land from the owners of large estates and redistributed it to peasants. He also took over foreign-owned companies and nationalized them, or gave them to the Chilean government. The United States was worried that Allende would turn Chile entirely into a communist state. The United States was also concerned about Allende's close ties to the Soviet Union, so the United States gave money to groups that were trying to take over power from Allende.

10. **Elaborate** What was significant about the election of Vicente Fox, and what was the agenda for his presidency?

    Possible answer: His election was remarkable because it was the first time in 71 years that the country was not ruled by the Institutional Revolutionary Party, or PRI. His agenda included major reforms. He reformed the police. He rooted out political corruption. He ended the rebellion in Chiapas, and he opened up Mexico's economy to free-market forces. He also argued that the United States should legalize the status of millions of illegal Mexican immigrant workers.

(continued)

Online Assessment *(continued)*

11. **Sequence** What happened with Argentina's economy during the first decade of the 21st century?

Possible answer: In 2001, the International Monetary Fund (IMF) refused to provide financial aid to Argentina. This caused protests in the country that led to the resignation of the president. In 2002, the unemployment rate was 24 percent. The country had defaulted on $132 billion in debt. This was the largest debt default in history and caused a devaluation of the nation's currency. A new president in 2003 negotiated the debt with the IMF. In 2006, Argentina repaid its debt. The economy continued to strengthen under the leadership of the nation's first elected female president.

12. **Make Inferences** How did the United States' actions toward Guatemala under the Eisenhower administration end up having different results than what was expected?

Possible answer: The United States was worried that the Guatemalan president was promoting communism. So, under the Eisenhower administration, the United States supplied weapons and money to the forces that were fighting against the president. This backfired because when the president was ousted from office, another president was put in his place who was much worse than the previous president. He removed voting rights for illiterate citizens, took away land from peasants, and imprisoned thousands of Guatemalans. This was all done out of fear of communism, too, but the infringement on human rights was an unintended result when the United States funded this revolutionary group.

Lesson 2 Planner

The Challenge of Democracy in Africa

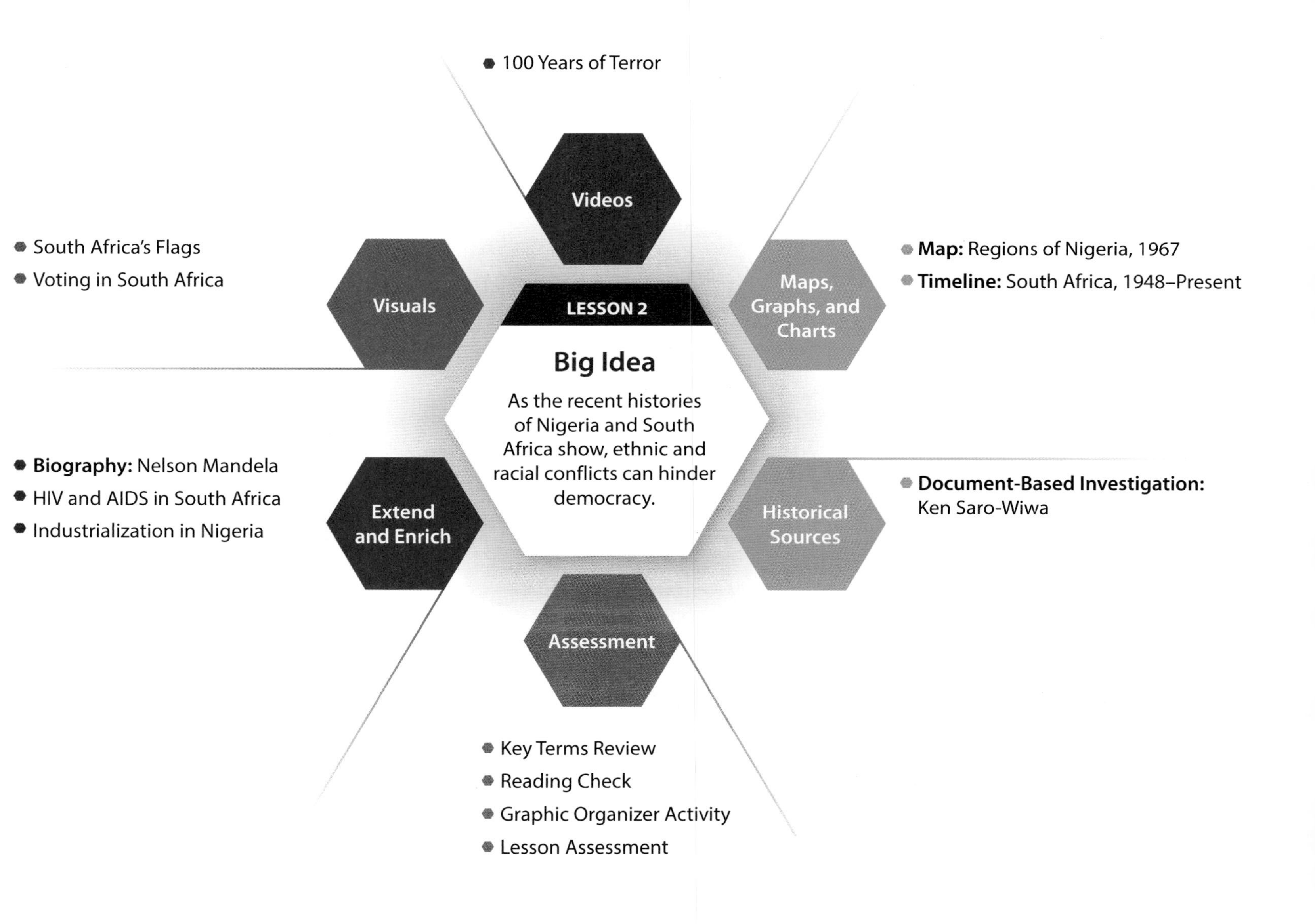

Online Lesson 2 Enrichment Activities

Nelson Mandela

Biography Students read about Nelson Mandela's perseverance in opposing apartheid. Then students imagine that they are Nelson Mandela in the years 1962–1990. Using information from the biography, students write one page of the story of Mandela's life.

HIV and AIDS in South Africa

Report Students research HIV and AIDS in South Africa and then create a report based on their research.

Industrialization in Nigeria

Research Report Students write a report about the impacts of industrialization and urbanization in Nigeria.

Lesson 2

The Challenge of Democracy in Africa

The Big Idea
The ethnic and racial conflicts in Nigeria and South Africa hindered democracy.

Why It Matters Now
In 1996, as Nigeria struggled with democracy, South Africa adopted a bill of rights that promotes racial equality.

Key Terms and People
federal system
martial law
dissident
apartheid
Nelson Mandela

Setting the Stage

Beginning in the late 1950s, dozens of European colonies in Africa gained their independence and became nations. As in Latin America, the establishment of democracy in Africa proved difficult. In many cases, the newly independent nations faced a host of problems that slowed their progress toward democracy. The main reason for Africa's difficulties was the negative impact of colonial rule. European powers had done little to prepare their African colonies for independence.

Colonial Rule Limits Democracy

The lingering effects of colonialism undermined efforts to build stable, democratic economies and states. This can be seen throughout Africa.

European Policies Cause Problems When the Europeans established colonial boundaries, they ignored existing ethnic or cultural divisions. New borders divided peoples of the same background or threw different—often rival—groups together. Because of this, a sense of national identity was difficult to develop. After independence, the old colonial boundaries became the borders of the newly independent states. As a result, ethnic and cultural conflicts remained.

Other problems had an economic basis. European powers had viewed colonies as sources of wealth for the home country. The colonial powers encouraged the export of one or two cash crops, such as coffee or rubber, rather than the production of a range of products to serve local needs. Europeans developed plantations and mines but few factories. Manufactured goods were imported from European countries. These policies left new African nations with unbalanced economies and a small middle class. Such economic problems lessened their chances to create democratic stability.

Teach the Big Idea

1. **Whole Class Open/Introduction** Ask students when legal segregation ended in the United States. *Some students will cite the passage of the 1964 Civil Rights Act.*
2. **Direct Teach** Read students the Big Idea: *As the recent histories of Nigeria and South Africa show, ethnic and racial conflicts can hinder democracy.* Review the following lesson objectives with students to aid in their understanding of the Big Idea.
   - Explain Africa's legacy of colonialism.
   - Describe Nigeria's civil war.
   - Describe Nigeria's nation-building efforts and events in Nigeria since 1970.
   - Trace the history of white rule in South Africa.
   - Examine South Africa's transition to democracy.
3. **Whole Group Close/Reflect** Have students make generalizations to answer this question: Why did African countries turn to dictatorships and one-party governments instead of pursuing democracy and free elections?

ONLINE DOCUMENT-BASED INVESTIGATION

Struggles for Democracy

Ken Saro-Wiwa is the second of five document-based investigations that students will analyze in the Struggles for Democracy module. Ken Saro-Wiwa was a Nigerian writer, political activist, and member of the Ogoni people. Have students read the historical source and answer the associated questions.

ONLINE GRAPHIC ORGANIZER

The Challenge of Democracy in Africa

As students read the lesson, have them use the graphic organizer to take notes. Students can review their graphic organizer notes at the end of the lesson to answer the following question:

Critical Thinking Which country is more democratic, Nigeria or South Africa? *South Africa's institutions make it more democratic.*

ONLINE LESSON FLIP CARDS

Review Key Terms and People

Students can use the flip cards in the Lesson Review at any time to review the lesson's key terms and people: *federal system, martial law, dissident, apartheid,* and *Nelson Mandela.*

Objectives

You may wish to discuss the following questions with students to help them frame the content as they read.

- Do you think colonial powers deliberately ignored ethnic and cultural divisions when they established boundaries? *Possible answers: No—Competition with rival powers determined such decisions. Yes—Such divisions made colonies easier to manage.*
- Why didn't colonial powers encourage the production of a range of products? *They were primarily interested in economic gain; they wanted raw materials so they could manufacture products themselves.*

More About . . .

Sub-Saharan Africa While conditions vary from country to country, poverty and lack of education are widespread in sub-Saharan Africa. About 947 million people live in 49 countries, and 28 of the world's least developed countries are in Africa. The countries' gross national incomes range from \$250 per person in Malawi to over \$14,000 in the Seychelles. In 2012, the number of sub-Saharan Africans living in poverty was about 389 million—almost half of the population.

Connect to Geography: Africa Show students a large map of Africa to make sure they have an overall understanding of the geography of the areas they will be studying in this lesson. Ask students to locate South Africa and Nigeria.

Objectives

You may wish to discuss the following questions with students to help them frame the content as they read.

- Why might ethnic identity in Nigeria be more important than national identity? *The nation's borders are based on artificial colonial borders.*
- Based on the events in Biafra, how significant was Igbo representation in the federal government? *It was probably weak. If the Igbo had been well-represented at the federal level, they might have sought a political resolution to their dispute with the Yoruba.*

More About . . .

Connect to Literature: Biafra Students who are interested in learning more about the war with Biafra might be interested in reading *Half of a Yellow Sun* by Chimamanda Ngozi Adichie, a harrowing historical novel that tells the story of two Igbo sisters' experiences of the war.

ONLINE ANALYZE VIDEOS

100 Years of Terror

HISTORY

Have students watch the video individually or as a class. You may wish to use the associated question as a discussion prompt.

Analyze Videos What caused the Mau Mau movement to grow? *people's anger against colonial repression and limits on freedoms*

READING CHECK

Identify Problems Why did the newly independent African nations have unbalanced economies? *European powers encouraged producing one or two cash crops and did not build factories.*

European rule also disrupted African family and community life. In some cases, colonial powers moved Africans far from their families and villages to work in mines or on plantations. In addition, most newly independent nations still lacked a skilled, literate work force that could take on the task of building a new nation.

Reading Check
Identify Problems Why did the newly independent African nations have unbalanced economies?

Short-Lived Democracies When Britain and France gave up their colonies, they left fragile democratic governments in place. Soon problems threatened those governments. Rival ethnic groups often fought for power. Strong militaries became tools for ambitious leaders. In many cases, a military dictatorship replaced democracy.

Civil War in Nigeria

Nigeria, a former British colony, won its independence peacefully in 1960. Nigeria is Africa's most populous country and one of its richest. However, the country was ethnically divided. This soon created problems that led to war.

A Land of Many Peoples Three major ethnic groups live within Nigeria's borders. In the north are the Hausa-Fulani, who are mostly Muslim. In the south are the Yoruba and the Igbo (also called Ibo), who are mostly Christians, Muslims, or animists, who believe that spirits are present in animals, plants, and natural objects. The Yoruba, a farming people with a tradition of kings, live to the west. The Igbo, a farming people who have a democratic tradition, live to the east.

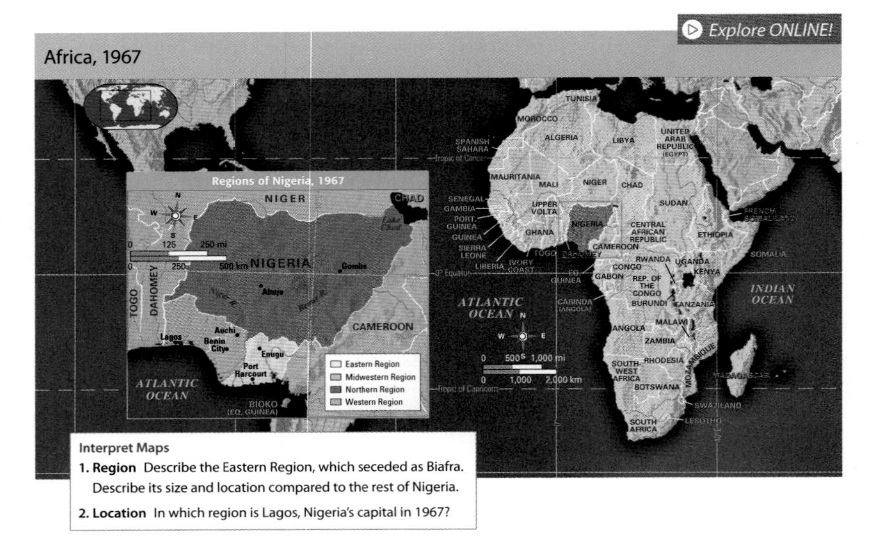

Interpret Maps
1. **Region** Describe the Eastern Region, which seceded as Biafra. Describe its size and location compared to the rest of Nigeria.
2. **Location** In which region is Lagos, Nigeria's capital in 1967?

1228 Module 31

COLLABORATIVE LEARNING

Independence in Africa

1. Organize students into small groups, and have each group list three or four African countries that students want to learn more about.
2. Have each group vote to select one country. Create a class list of each group's country. Try to avoid duplication of countries on the list. Some groups may have to vote again to choose another country.
3. Have groups conduct outside research about their chosen country. Research should focus on current events, problems, challenges, advantages, and resources the country possesses. Remind students to use reliable sources.
4. Have groups prepare multimedia presentations for the class about their chosen countries. Reports should include maps, charts, and graphs as a means of telling the country's story.

After independence, Nigeria adopted a **federal system**. In a federal system, power is shared between state governments and a central authority. The Nigerians set up three states, one for each region and ethnic group, with a political party in each.

War with Biafra Although one group dominated each state, the states also had ethnic minorities. In the Western Region, non-Yoruba minorities began to resent Yoruba control. In 1963, they tried to break away and form their own region. This led to fighting. In January 1966, a group of army officers, most of them Igbo, seized power in the capital city of Lagos. These officers abolished the regional governments and declared **martial law**, or temporary military rule.

The Hausa-Fulani, who did not trust the Igbo, launched an attack from the north. They persecuted and killed many Igbo. The survivors fled east. In 1967, the Eastern Region seceded from Nigeria, declaring itself the new nation of Biafra (bee•AF•ruh).

Reading Check
Analyze Effects
What was the effect of the war on the Igbo?

The Nigerian government then went to war to reunite the country. The Igbo were badly outnumbered and outgunned. In 1970, Biafra surrendered. Nigeria was reunited, but perhaps more than a million Igbo died, most from starvation.

Nigeria's Nation-Building

After the war, Nigerians returned to the process of nation-building. "When the war ended," noted one officer, "it was like a referee blowing a whistle in a football game. People just put down their guns and went back to the business of living." The Nigerian government did not punish the Igbo. It used federal money to rebuild the Igbo region.

Federal Government Restored The military governed Nigeria for most of the 1970s. During this time, Nigerian leaders tried to create a more stable federal system, with a strong central government and a number of regional units. The government also tried to build a more modern economy based on oil income.

In 1979, the military handed power back to civilian rulers. Nigerians were cheered by the return to democracy. Some people, however, remained concerned about ethnic divisions in the nation. Nigerian democracy was short lived. In 1983, the military overthrew the civilian government, charging it with corruption. A new military regime, dominated by the Hausa-Fulani, took charge.

A Return to Civilian Rule In the years that followed, the military governed Nigeria, while promising to bring back civilian rule. The army held elections in 1993, which resulted in the victory of popular leader Moshood Abiola. However, officers declared the results invalid, and a dictator, General Sani Abacha, took control.

General Abacha banned political activity and jailed **dissidents**, or government opponents. Upon Abacha's death in 1998, General Abdulsalami Abubakar seized power and promised to end military rule. He kept his

Objectives

You may wish to discuss the following questions with students to help them frame the content as they read.

- Why do you think the Nigerian government paid to rebuild the rebellious Igbo region? *wanted to reunite the country rather than punish rebellion*
- Is canceling debts incurred by nations such as Nigeria a good idea? *Good—It allows governments to devote more resources to public health and education. Bad—It hurts lenders and sends the message to borrowers that there are no repercussions for financial mismanagement.*

More About . . .

Boko Haram Boko Haram is an Islamic extremist group based in northeastern Nigeria. In 2015, the group declared allegiance to ISIL (Islamic State of Iraq and the Levant). The group is responsible for killing 20,000 and displacing 2.3 million people from their homes. Students, in particular, have been targeted. Boko Haram made international news in 2014 when they kidnapped 276 schoolgirls. The name *Boko Haram* translates to "Western education is forbidden."

ONLINE INTERACTIVE MAPS

Regions of Nigeria, 1967

Have students explore the map using the interactive features and answer the associated question.

In which region is Lagos, Nigeria's capital in 1967? *Western Region*

In the print edition, see the map of the same title.

Describe the Eastern Region, which seceded as Biafra. Describe its size and location compared to the rest of Nigeria. *Biafra is in the southeastern part of Nigeria and is small, though comparable in size to the Western Region.*

In which region is Lagos, Nigeria's capital in 1967? *Lagos is located in the Western Region of Nigeria.*

READING CHECK

Analyze Effects What was the effect of the war on the Igbo? *They were forced to rejoin Nigeria; a million people died.*

COLLABORATIVE LEARNING

Ethnic Groups in Nigeria

1. Divide students into small groups.
2. Ask each group to create a table with three columns, labeled *Ethnic Group, Location,* and *Culture.*
3. Then have students review "Civil War in Nigeria."
4. Ask them to fill in their tables with information about the different ethnic groups in Nigeria as they review the passage.
5. Discuss what conflicts are likely to occur between such groups. *Possible answer: differences over religion and preferred type of government*

ONLINE DOCUMENT-BASED INVESTIGATION

Ken Saro-Wiwa

Ken Saro-Wiwa was a Nigerian writer, political activist, and member of the Ogoni people. Have students read the historical source and answer the associated questions.

Analyze Sources What seems to be Saro-Wiwa's attitude toward his persecutors? *He seems contemptuous of their power; though they have the power to execute him, they are fools.*

In the print edition, see historical source of the same title.

Analyze Sources What do Saro-Wiwa's imprisonment and execution suggest about the government of General Sani Abacha? *government was ruthless and murderous*

Analyze Sources What seems to be Saro-Wiwa's attitude toward his persecutors? *He seems contemptuous of their power; though they have the power to execute him, they are fools.*

READING CHECK

Contrast How did the leadership of General Abacha and General Abubakar differ? *Abacha was a military dictator who banned political activity and jailed dissidents. Abubakar ended military rule, which led to Nigeria's first elected civilian president.*

word. In 1999, Nigerians elected their first civilian president, Olusegun Obasanjo, in nearly 20 years. In 2003, Obasanjo was reelected.

Civilian Presidents Obasanjo was an ethnic Yoruba from southwest Nigeria. As a critic of Nigerian military regimes, he had spent three years in jail (1995–1998) under Sani Abacha. As a former general, Obasanjo had the support of the military.

Obasanjo worked for a strong, unified Nigeria. He made some progress in his battle against corruption. He also attempted to draw the attention of the world to the need for debt relief for Nigeria. Obasanjo saw debt relief as essential to the relief of hunger and the future of democracy in Africa.

The controversial 2007 elections brought President Umaru Yar'Adua to power. Like his mentor Mr. Obasanjo, President Yar'Adua faced a variety of problems. These included war, violence, corruption, poverty, pollution, and hunger. In addition, militant groups threatened Nigeria's oil exports

DOCUMENT-BASED INVESTIGATION Historical Source

Ken Saro-Wiwa

Ken Saro-Wiwa was a Nigerian writer, political activist, and member of the Ogoni people. The Ogoni live in a poor part of the country that has large oil reserves. Mr. Saro-Wiwa denounced the Nigerian oil industry's pollution of his people's land and intimidation of those who spoke out.

In 1994, Saro-Wiwa and eight fellow Ogoni activists were arrested on murder charges. Despite nearly unanimous international agreement that the charges were unsupported, they were convicted and sentenced to death. Shortly before he was hung in November 1995, Saro-Wiwa smuggled several manuscripts out of prison.

"Injustice stalks the land like a tiger on the prowl. To be at the mercy of buffoons [fools] is the ultimate insult. To find the instruments of state power reducing you to dust is the injury. . . . It is also very important that we have chosen the path of non-violent struggle. Our opponents are given to violence and we cannot meet them on their turf, even if we wanted to. Non-violent struggle offers weak people the strength which they otherwise would not have. The spirit becomes important, and no gun can silence that. I am aware, though, that non-violent struggle occasions more death than armed struggle. And that remains a cause for worry at all times. Whether the Ogoni people will be able to withstand the rigors of the struggle is yet to be seen. Again, their ability to do so will point the way of peaceful struggle to other peoples on the African continent. It is therefore not to be underrated."

—Ken Saro-Wiwa, quoted in *A Month and a Day: A Detention Diary*

Analyze Historical Sources

1. What do Saro-Wiwa's imprisonment and execution suggest about the government of General Sani Abacha?
2. What seems to be Saro-Wiwa's attitude toward his persecutors?

ADVANCED/GIFTED

Politics and Oil News Report

- After students have read "Civil War in Nigeria" and "Nigeria's Nation-Building," have them use the Internet or the library to search for information about Nigeria's oil industry.
- Tell students to focus on the oil industry's impact on Nigeria's economy and politics.
- After they have finished their research, ask students to use their findings to create and deliver a brief news report. Tell students they will be reporting for a major news network and that their story will target viewers who know little or nothing about Nigeria. Explain that because they are reporting for a major network, they will be expected to be objective.
- After they complete the project, have students discuss how they made their reports objective and what they might have added if they had been allowed to express a subjective point of view.

Reading Check
Contrast How did the leadership of General Abacha and General Abubakar differ?

and economic growth. Yar'Adua also faced health problems through much of his presidency. After his death in 2010, his vice president, Goodluck Jonathan was sworn in as president. One of the most serious problems facing Jonathan has been Boko Haram, the Islamic militant group that has killed and kidnapped thousands in Nigeria.

South Africa Under Apartheid

In South Africa, racial conflict was the result of colonial rule. From its beginnings under Dutch and British control, South Africa was racially divided. A small white minority ruled a large black majority. In 1910, South Africa gained self-rule as a dominion of the British Empire. In 1931, it became an independent member of the British Commonwealth. Although South Africa had a constitutional government, the constitution gave whites power and denied the black majority its rights.

Apartheid Segregates Society In 1948, the National Party came to power in South Africa. This party promoted Afrikaner, or Dutch South African, nationalism. It also instituted a policy of **apartheid**, complete separation of the races. The minority government banned social contacts between whites and blacks. It established segregated schools, hospitals, and neighborhoods.

In 1959, the minority government set up reserves, called homelands, for the country's major black groups. Blacks were forbidden to live in white areas unless they worked as servants or laborers for whites. The homelands policy was totally unbalanced. Although blacks made up about 75 percent of the population, the government set aside only 13 percent of the land for them. Whites kept the best land.

Blacks Protest The blacks of South Africa resisted the controls imposed by the white minority. In 1912, they formed the African National Congress (ANC) to fight for their rights. The ANC organized strikes and boycotts to protest racist policies. The government banned the ANC and imprisoned many of its members. One was ANC leader **Nelson Mandela** (man•DEHL•uh).

The troubles continued. In 1976, riots over school policies broke out in the black township of Soweto, leaving about 600 students dead. In 1977, police beat popular protest leader Stephen Biko to death while he was in custody. As protests mounted, the government declared a nationwide state of emergency in 1986.

Reading Check
Make Inferences How did the policy of apartheid strengthen whites' hold on power?

Struggle for Democracy

By the late 1980s, South Africa was under great pressure to change. For years, a black South African bishop, Desmond Tutu, had led an economic campaign against apartheid. He asked foreign nations not to do business with South Africa. In response, many nations imposed trade restrictions. They also isolated South Africa in other ways, for example, by banning South Africa from the Olympic Games. (In 1984, Tutu won the Nobel Peace Prize for his nonviolent methods.)

Objectives

You may wish to discuss the following questions with students to help them frame the content as they read.

- Why didn't South Africa's black majority use its greater numbers to overpower the white minority? *Whites had greater military strength. Poverty may have made it difficult to organize resistance.*
- Ask students if the United States had anything comparable to South Africa's "homelands." *Some students might argue that reservations for Native Americans are similar. Others may note that discriminatory policies, such as "redlining"—refusing to offer home mortgages or home insurance to certain areas because of the race or income of the residents—contributed to the formation of ghettos.*

More About . . .

Commonwealth of Nations As the former colonies of the British Empire gained independence, they decided to join Britain in a free, voluntary association called the British Commonwealth. The members have no legal or formal obligation to one another but rather are held together by shared traditions and institutions, as well as by economic self-interest. Today, there are more than 50 members in the Commonwealth. (In 1946, the word *British* was dropped from the organization's title.)

READING CHECK
Make Inferences How did the policy of apartheid strengthen whites' hold on power? *It kept the races separate; forced blacks to use segregated, inferior facilities; and gave whites the best land.*

Objectives

You may wish to discuss the following questions with students to help them frame the content as they read.

- Do you think economic sanctions can help eliminate racism? *No—Sanctions do not change the way people think. Yes—Sanctions gradually contribute to a shift in people's beliefs.*
- Why would the *New York Times* assert that Mbeki's views on AIDS might undermine "all his good work"? *They believed that Mbeki's statements called into question his suitability for public office.*

More About . . .

Thabo Mbeki Former South African president Thabo Mbeki's controversial statements have not been restricted to AIDS. About the 2003 war in Iraq, Mbeki remarked, "The prospect facing the people of Iraq should serve as sufficient warning that in [the] future we too might have others descend on us, guns in hand to force-feed us [with their democracy]." Mbeki insisted that democracy had to be homegrown and practiced within a country's social context, not imported.

ONLINE INTERACTIVE VISUALS

Compare: South Africa's Flags

Have students explore and compare the images using the interactive slider. You may wish to use the associated question as a discussion prompt.

Contrast How did the South African flag change between 1927 and 1994? *The present-day flag no longer has the smaller flags representing other countries.*

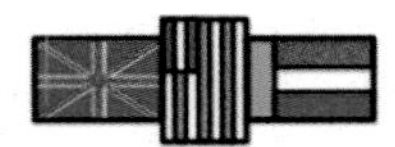

ONLINE INTERACTIVE VISUALS

Carousel: Voting in South Africa

Have students navigate through the carousel and note similarities and differences among the images or identify a unifying theme.

The First Steps In 1989, white South Africans elected a new president, F. W. de Klerk. His goal was to transform South Africa and end its isolation. In February 1990, he legalized the ANC and also released Nelson Mandela from prison.

A young South African poll worker helps an elderly man to vote in the first election open to citizens of all races.

These dramatic actions marked the beginning of a new era in South Africa. Over the next 18 months, the South African parliament repealed apartheid laws that had segregated public facilities and restricted land ownership by blacks. World leaders welcomed these changes and began to ease restrictions on South Africa.

Although some legal barriers had fallen, others would remain until a new constitution was in place. First, the country needed to form a multiracial government. After lengthy negotiations, President de Klerk agreed to hold South Africa's first universal elections, in which people of all races could vote, in April 1994.

Majority Rule Among the candidates for president were F. W. de Klerk and Nelson Mandela. During the campaign, the Inkatha Freedom Party—a rival party to the ANC—threatened to disrupt the process. Nevertheless, the vote went smoothly. South Africans of all races peacefully waited at the polls in long lines. To no one's surprise, the ANC won 63 percent of the vote. They won 252 of 400 seats in the National Assembly (the larger of the two houses in Parliament). Mandela was elected president. Mandela stepped down in 1999, but the nation's democratic government continued.

STRUGGLING READERS

South African Leaders Venn Diagram

1. Ask students to draw a Venn diagram in their notebooks.
2. Then ask them to read the biographies of Nelson Mandela and F. W. de Klerk and fill in the diagram.An example follows. Nelson Mandela: born in 1918; black; inspired by elders' stories of forever freedoms; top official of ANC; joined violent struggle against apartheid; imprisoned 27 years. F. W. de Klerk: born in 1936; white Afrikaner; served in Parliament; backed apartheid but open to reform; liberal religious background. Both: trained as lawyers; presidents of South Africa; sought to bring democracy to South Africa; won Nobel Peace Prize.

BIOGRAPHY

Nelson Mandela
(1918–2013)

Nelson Mandela has said that he first grew interested in politics when he heard elders in his village describe how freely his people lived before whites came. Inspired to help his people regain that freedom, Mandela trained as a lawyer and became a top official in the ANC. Convinced that apartheid would never end peacefully, he joined the armed struggle against white rule. For this, he was imprisoned for 27 years.

After his presidential victory, Mandela continued to work to heal his country.

F. W. de Klerk
(1936–)

Like Mandela, Frederik W. de Klerk also trained as a lawyer. Born to an Afrikaner family with close links to the National Party, de Klerk was elected to Parliament in 1972.

A firm party loyalist, de Klerk backed apartheid but was also open to reform. Friends say that his flexibility on racial issues stemmed from his relatively liberal religious background.

In 1993, de Klerk and Mandela were jointly awarded the Nobel Peace Prize for their efforts to bring democracy to South Africa.

A New Constitution In 1996, after much debate, South African lawmakers passed a new, more democratic constitution. It guaranteed equal rights for all citizens. The constitution included a bill of rights modeled on the United States Bill of Rights. The political and social changes that South Africa had achieved gave other peoples around the world great hope for the future of democracy.

This was South Africa's flag from 1927 to 1994.

South Africa adopted this flag in 1994.

South Africa Today In 1999, ANC official Thabo Mbeki won the election as president in a peaceful transition of power. As Mbeki assumed office, he faced a number of serious challenges. These included high crime rates—South Africa's rape and murder rates were among the highest in the world. Unemployment stood at about 40 percent among South Africa's blacks, and about 60 percent lived below the poverty level. In addition, an economic downturn discouraged foreign investment.

Mbeki promoted a free-market economic policy to repair South Africa's infrastructure and to encourage foreign investors. Investing in the education and training of a nation's workforce can lead to economic growth. In 2002, South Africa was engaged in negotiations to establish free-trade agreements with a number of countries around the world, including those of the European Union as well as Japan, Canada, and the United States. This was an attempt at opening the South African economy to foreign competition and investment, and promoting growth and employment. Investing in the education and training of South Africans led to economic growth as well.

BIOGRAPHY

Nelson Mandela

Have students read the biography of Nelson Mandela, the anti-apartheid revolutionary who served as South Africa's president from 1994 to 1999.

BIOGRAPHY

F. W. de Klerk

Have students read the biography of F. W. de Klerk, the president of South Africa from 1989 to 1994.

ONLINE INTERACTIVE TIMELINES

South Africa, 1948–Present

Have students interpret the timeline and answer the associated question.

Interpret Timelines How many years did Nelson Mandela spend in jail? *28 years*

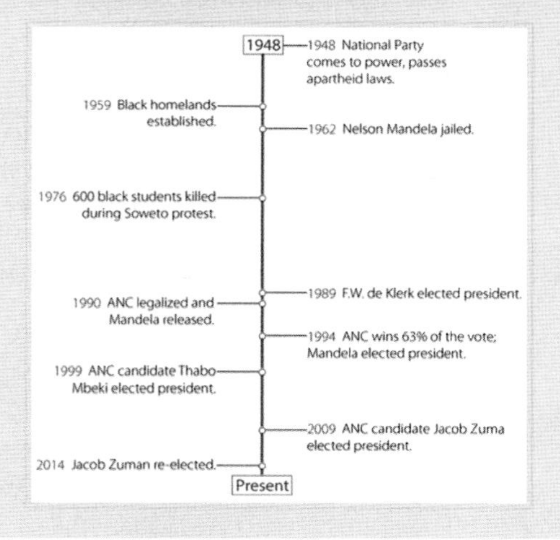

READING CHECK
Analyze Effects How did Desmond Tutu help force South Africa to end apartheid? *He convinced the world to put economic pressure on South Africa.*

Print Assessment

1. **Organize Information** Which country is more democratic? Explain. *Nigeria—Civil war when Biafra seceded; South Africa—Passage of apartheid; Both—Former British colonies. South Africa's institutions make it more democratic.*
2. **Key Terms and People** For each key term or person in the lesson, write a sentence explaining its significance. *Explanations of the lesson's key terms and people can be found on the following pages: federal system, p. 1229; martial law, p. 1229; dissident, p. 1229; apartheid, p. 1231; Nelson Mandela, p. 1231*
3. **Analyze Effects** What effect did old colonial boundaries have on newly independent African states? *dividing people of similar backgrounds or throwing rival groups together*
4. **Identify Problems** What do you think is the main problem that Nigeria must overcome before it can establish a democratic government? *Possible answer: Leaders must end corruption and see that Nigeria's people benefit from its resource wealth.*
5. **Analyze Issues** What are some of the important issues facing South Africa today? *high crime rates, unemployment, economic downturn, AIDS epidemic*
6. **Summarize** What were the main negative effects of the economic policies of European colonizers? *border issues; economic dependence on one or two products*

Timeline: South Africa, 1948–2014

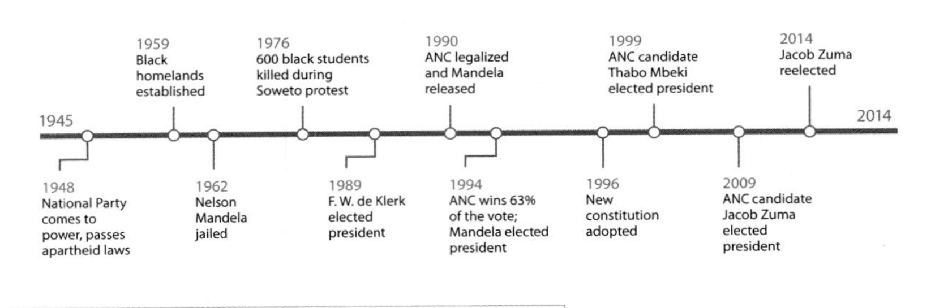

Interpret Timelines
How many years did Nelson Mandela spend in jail?

One of the biggest problems facing South Africa was the AIDS epidemic. Some estimates concluded that 6 million South Africans were likely to die of AIDS by 2010. The economic impact has been widespread as well. The nation's labor supply has been diminished due to the AIDS pandemic. Lower productivity has led to a decline in exports. Mbeki disputed that AIDS was caused by HIV (human immunodeficiency virus). His opinion put South Africa at odds with the scientific consensus throughout the world. However, in 2009, South African president Jacob Zuma broadened the country's AIDS policy. As of 2015, the nation was investing more than one billion dollars each year to run its HIV and AIDS treatment program—the largest program in the world.

Reading Check
Analyze Effects
How did Desmond Tutu help force South Africa to end apartheid?

Lesson 2 Assessment

1. Organize Information Which country is more democratic? Explain.

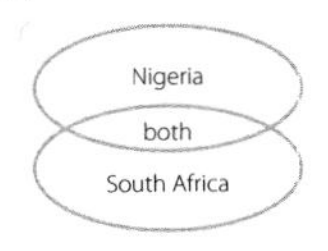

2. Key Terms and People For each key term or person in the lesson, write a sentence explaining its significance.
3. Analyze Effects What effect did old colonial boundaries have on newly independent African states?
4. Identify Problems What do you think is the main problem that Nigeria must overcome before it can establish a truly democratic government?
5. Analyze Issues What are some of the important issues facing South Africa today?
6. Summarize What were the main negative effects of the economic policies of European colonizers?

1234 Module 31

Online Assessment

1. In former European colonies, what would have helped new democratic governments to succeed?
   - ○ strong military leaders
   - ○ one-cash crop economies
   - ● a literate and skilled population
   - ○ more plantations and mines and fewer factories

   Alternate Question *Select the answer choice from the drop-down list to complete the sentence correctly.*
   One of the problems that former European colonies experienced when they tried to become democracies was that they had illiterate populations that lacked the skills necessary to be a productive workforce. Because of this, they were unable to properly govern themselves, and so *strong military leaders* were able to take over the government.

2. Why did the federal system in Nigeria lead to conflicts?
   - ○ There was no national military.
   - ○ There was no way to determine if laws were fair.
   - ○ There were restrictions on travel within the country.
   - ● There were ethnic minorities that were unrepresented in each state.

   Alternate Question *Select the answer choice from the drop-down list to complete the sentence correctly.*
   Even though Nigeria set up a federal government with separate states, many *ethnic minorities* felt unrepresented, and this resulted in serious conflicts.

3. What significant event happened in 1999 in Nigeria that hadn't happened for nearly 20 years?
   - ○ Military rulers were arrested.
   - ○ Warfare ceased in the country.
   - ○ Dissidents were let out of prison.
   - ● An elected civilian president took office.

   Alternate Question *Select the answer choice from the drop-down list to complete the sentence correctly.*
   When Olusegun Obasanjo was elected in 1999, it had been nearly 20 years since a civilian leader served as *president* of Nigeria.

4. Why was the homelands policy of distribution of South African land unbalanced?
   - ○ Whites had to live in the big cities and not on farmland.
   - ○ Blacks were required to show citizenship before they could own land.
   - ○ Whites were not allowed to purchase land unless they hired black servants.
   - ● Blacks made up most of the population but received only a small percentage of the land.

   Alternate Question *Select the answer choice from the drop-down list to complete the sentence correctly.*
   South Africa's homeland policy required that blacks and whites live separately from each other. In this policy, blacks were allowed to live on only about 13 percent of the land even though they made up about *75 percent* of the population.

5. What is one way that F. W. de Klerk transformed South Africa during his presidency?
   - ○ He set up more apartheid laws.
   - ○ He placed Nelson Mandela in prison.
   - ● He legalized the African National Congress.
   - ○ He restricted land ownership to only whites.

   Alternate Question *Select the answer choice from the drop-down list to complete the sentence correctly.*
   During F. W. de Klerk's administration, he was able to transform South Africa into a country with new ideals. One of his first steps in doing so was to *give legal status to the African National Congress* and release Nelson Mandela from prison.

6. **Make Judgments** How were the economies set up by European colonial rule in Africa detrimental to the native peoples?

   Possible answer: The European powers had viewed the colonies only as a source of income for them. They set up one or two cash crops in the colonies rather than developing economies that were diverse and capable of sustaining a population. Europeans set up huge plantations and mines, but they built very few factories. The people were not able to make their own goods, which left them totally dependent upon other nations for those things. Because of these practices, the African colonies had unbalanced economies and a small middle class. This left them less of a chance to be able to establish successful democracies later on.

7. **Cause and Effect** What were the causes and effects of the new nation of Biafra?

   Possible answer: The new nation was formed in 1967 because ethnic minorities in the region no longer wanted to be under the rule of the ethnic majority and wanted to have their own nation. However, the Nigerian government did not want the country to be split apart, so they went to war with Biafra to reunite the country. The country of Biafra finally surrendered in 1970 after more than a million people had died. Nigeria was reunited.

8. **Elaborate** What goals did the Nigerian leaders try to achieve during the 1970s?

   Possible answer: They tried to create a more stable federal government that had a strong central government and a number of regional units. They also wanted to build a more modern economy that was based on oil income. These leaders were military leaders. They wanted to help the country return to democratic rule. They returned the leadership back to civilian rulers in 1979.

(continued)

Online Assessment *(continued)*

9. **Cause and Effect** What were the causes and effects of the African National Congress's activities in South Africa?

   Possible answer: The African National Congress fought for the rights of black people. They were led to this fight based on the unfair treatment of blacks because of the apartheid policies. They organized strikes and boycotts to protest racial policies. The result of these actions was that many of the members and leaders, including Nelson Mandela, were imprisoned by the government. People were also killed in the protests. A national state of emergency was declared in 1986.

10. **Elaborate** What were the key elements of Mbeki's economic policy in South Africa?

   Possible answer: Mbeki promoted a free-market economic policy. He wanted to repair South Africa's infrastructure. He wanted to encourage foreign trade and investors. He also felt it necessary to invest in education and training of the nation's workforce. He knew this would lead the country to grow economically. He wanted to establish free-trade agreements with other nations including the European Union, Japan, Canada, and the United States.

ADDITIONAL LESSON CONTENT

COLLABORATIVE LEARNING

Apartheid Letter to the Editor

1. Review with students the information in the text about apartheid, the Soweto Uprising, and the imprisonment of Nelson Mandela.
2. Have students work in mixed-ability pairs to create a graphic organizer that summarizes the information.
3. Guide students in a discussion of the anti-apartheid movement and have students take notes during the class discussion. Focus students' attention on the embargoes and divestments in businesses that occurred.
4. Have students use their notes and graphic organizers to write a letter to the editor of a South African newspaper encouraging an end to apartheid. Have students review their drafts in mixed-ability pairs, correct their work, and turn in the final letter.

ENGLISH LANGUAGE LEARNERS

Create a South Africa Glossary

1. Have students read "South Africa Under Apartheid."
2. Then have them use the text and a dictionary to create a glossary of challenging words in the passage. Tell students that words should be in alphabetical order and that students should note the number of the paragraph in which the word appears. A sample glossary follows.
   - **African National *Congress*** *organization that wanted to end apartheid (4)*
   - **Afrikaner** *a Dutch South African (2)*
   - **apartheid** *complete separation of races (2)*
   - **homelands** *poor-quality land set aside for South Africa's major black groups (3)*
   - **Nelson Mandela** *African National Congress leader (4)*
   - **Stephen Biko** *popular protest leader killed by police (5)*

Lesson 3 Planner

The Collapse of the Soviet Union

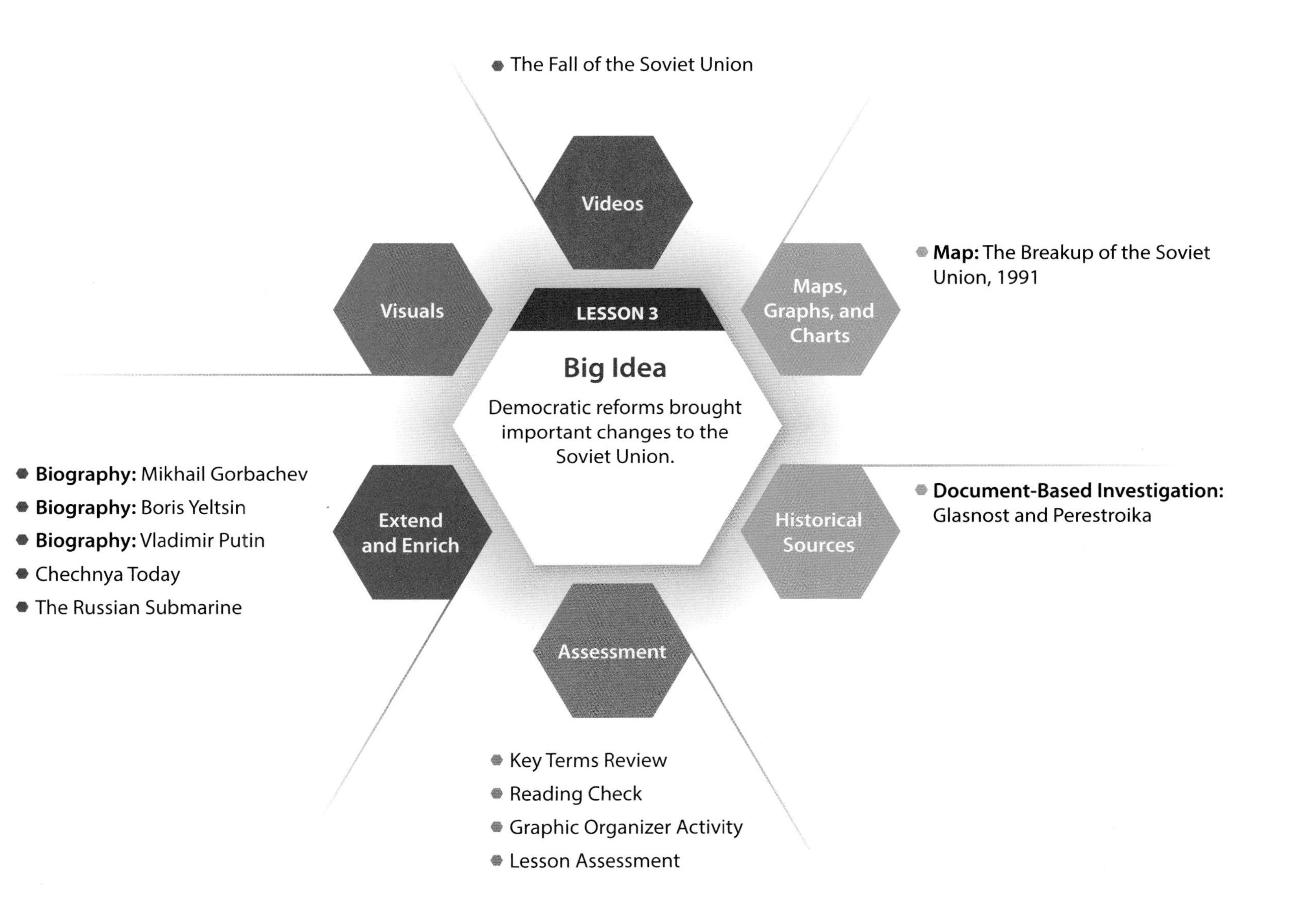

Online Lesson 3 Enrichment Activities

Chechnya Today

Multimedia Poster Students conduct research to learn about the situation in Chechnya today. Then they create a multimedia poster with the results of their findings.

The Russian Submarine

Video Students view a video to discover the significance of the Russian Navy's submarine *Kursk* and its tragic demise. Then they create a diagram of the Russian submarine. Students then write a paragraph explaining the submarine's importance in Russia's political history.

Lesson 3

The Collapse of the Soviet Union

The Big Idea

Democratic reforms brought important changes to the Soviet Union.

Why It Matters Now

Russia continues to struggle to establish democracy.

Key Terms and People

Politburo
Mikhail Gorbachev
glasnost
perestroika
Boris Yeltsin
CIS
"shock therapy"

Setting the Stage

After World War II, the Soviet Union and the United States engaged in a cold war. Each tried to increase its worldwide influence. The Soviet Union extended its power over much of Eastern Europe. By the 1960s, it appeared that communism was permanently established in the region. During the 1960s and 1970s, the Soviet Union's Communist leadership kept tight control over the Soviet people. But big changes, including democratic reforms, were on the horizon.

Gorbachev Moves Toward Democracy

Soviet premier Leonid Brezhnev and the **Politburo**—the ruling committee of the Communist Party—crushed all political disagreement. Censors decided what writers could publish. The Communist Party also restricted freedom of speech and worship. After Brezhnev's death in 1982, the aging leadership of the Soviet Union tried to hold on to power. However, each of Brezhnev's two successors died after only about a year in office. Who would succeed them?

A Younger Leader To answer that question, the Politburo debated between two men. One was **Mikhail Gorbachev** (mih•KYL-GAWR•buh•chawf). Gorbachev's supporters praised his youth, energy, and political skills. With their backing, Gorbachev became the party's new general secretary. In choosing him, Politburo members did not realize they were unleashing another Russian Revolution.

The Soviet people welcomed Gorbachev's election. At 54, he was the youngest Soviet leader since Stalin. Gorbachev was only a child during Stalin's ruthless purge of independent-minded party members. Unlike other Soviet leaders, Gorbachev decided to pursue new ideas.

Teach the Big Idea

1. **Whole Class Open/Introduction** Ask students to describe what happens when a government collapses. *Possible answers: confusion, violence, economic disruption*
2. **Direct Teach** Read students the Big Idea: *Democratic reforms brought important changes to the Soviet Union.* Review the following lesson objectives with students to aid in their understanding of the Big Idea.
   - Discuss Mikhail Gorbachev and his policy of glasnost.
   - Explain Gorbachev's reforms to the economy and political system.
   - Identify events leading to the breakup of the Soviet Union.
   - Describe Russia under Boris Yeltsin.
   - Describe Russia under Vladimir Putin.
3. **Whole Group Close/Reflect** Have students create a presidential campaign advertisement for Gorbachev, Yeltsin, or Putin.

ONLINE DOCUMENT-BASED INVESTIGATION

Struggles for Democracy

Glasnost and Perestroika is the third of five document-based investigations that students will analyze in the Struggles for Democracy module. Mikhail Gorbachev's policies of glasnost and perestroika shook up the traditional way of doing things in the Soviet economy and in the society at large. Have students study the historical source and answer the associated question.

Objectives

You may wish to discuss the following questions with students to help them frame the content as they read.

- Why might youth alone have made Mikhail Gorbachev more willing to pursue new ideas? *Communist ideology seemed less sacred to Gorbachev than it did to previous generations.*
- Why did it take so long for Soviet leaders to reform their system? *They were blinded by political ideology; they were interested in their own power and wealth, not the state's.*

More About . . .

Mikhail Gorbachev Mikhail Gorbachev was the leader of the Soviet Union from 1985 to 1991. The son of Russian peasants, he joined the Soviet Communist Party in the 1950s and rose steadily through the party's ranks. As Soviet leader, Gorbachev's primary goal was to rebuild the nation's stagnant economy. He called for major reforms of the Soviet economic and political system. Under his leadership, the Soviet Union began to end its domination of Eastern Europe. Gorbachev also worked to build better relations with the United States and the West and is credited with helping bring an end to the Cold War. For his efforts to improve international relations, Gorbachev received the Nobel Peace Prize in 1990.

ONLINE GRAPHIC ORGANIZER

The Collapse of the Soviet Union

As students read the lesson, have them use the graphic organizer to take notes. Students can review their graphic organizer notes at the end of the lesson to answer the following question:

Critical Thinking What were the major issues faced by Russia after the breakup of the Soviet Union? *ailing economy; war in Chechnya; increase in social problems such as domestic violence*

ONLINE LESSON FLIP CARDS

Review Key Terms and People

Students can use the flip cards in the Lesson Review at any time to review the lesson's key terms and people: *Politburo, Mikhail Gorbachev, glasnost, perestroika, Boris Yeltsin, CIS,* and *"shock therapy."*

Objectives

You may wish to discuss the following questions with students to help them frame the content as they read.

- Why might Gorbachev have chosen to allow private businesses only on a small scale? *He believed that broader reforms would have harmed the interests of powerful people to whom he was politically vulnerable.*
- Why might people have voted for powerful party bosses rather than for candidates who advocated change? *They may not have dared to risk the anger of the powerful bosses.*

More About . . .

Reagan's "Evil Empire" Speech U.S. President Ronald Reagan favored taking an aggressive stance against the Soviet Union. In his famous March 8, 1983, speech, Reagan declared: "I urge you to beware the temptation of pride—the temptation of blithely declaring yourselves above it all and label both sides equally at fault, to ignore the facts of history and the aggressive impulses of an evil empire, to simply call the arms race a giant misunderstanding and thereby remove yourself from the struggle between right and wrong and good and evil." Five years later—after Gorbachev's reforms—Reagan was asked if he still thought the Soviet Union was an evil empire. He responded that he no longer did, that he used the term in a "different era."

ONLINE HISTORICAL SOURCES

Glasnost

Mikhail Gorbachev's policies of glasnost and perestroika shook up the traditional way of doing things in the Soviet economy and in the society at large. Have students study the historical source and answer the associated questions.

1. One arrow points down the road toward stagnation. Where is the other arrow, pointing in the opposite direction, likely to lead? *away from stagnation to a dynamic new society and economy*
2. Why might the Soviet Union look different to the figure in the cartoon? *Possible answer: because Gorbachev's policies were so different*

READING CHECK

Draw Conclusions What effect would glasnost likely have on the public's opinion of Gorbachev? *Glasnost probably improved the public's opinion of Gorbachev because the majority of people would enjoy the increased rights brought about by glasnost.*

DOCUMENT-BASED INVESTIGATION Historical Source

Glasnost

Mikhail Gorbachev's policies of glasnost and perestroika shook up the traditional way of doing things in the Soviet economy and in the society at large.

Analyze Historical Sources
1. One arrow points down the road toward stagnation. Where is the other arrow, pointing in the opposite direction, likely to lead?
2. Why might the Soviet Union look different to the figure in the cartoon?

Glasnost Promotes Openness Past Soviet leaders had created a totalitarian state. It rewarded silence and discouraged individuals from acting on their own. As a result, Soviet society rarely changed, and the Soviet economy stagnated. Gorbachev realized that economic and social reforms could not occur without a free flow of ideas and information. In 1985, he announced a policy known as **glasnost** (GLAHS•nuhst), or openness.

Glasnost brought remarkable changes. The government allowed churches to open. It released dissidents from prison and allowed the publication of books by previously banned authors. Reporters investigated problems and criticized officials. These changes helped to improve human rights for the Soviet people by giving them more freedom to do and say what they wanted.

Reading Check
Draw Conclusions What effect would glasnost likely have on the public's opinion of Gorbachev?

Reforming the Economy and Politics

The new openness allowed Soviet citizens to complain about economic problems. Consumers protested that they had to stand in lines to buy food and other basics.

Economic Restructuring Gorbachev blamed these problems on the Soviet Union's inefficient system of central planning. Under central planning, party officials told farm and factory managers how much to produce. They also told them what wages to pay and what prices to charge. Because individuals could not increase their pay by producing more, they had little motive to improve efficiency.

In 1985, Gorbachev introduced the idea of **perestroika** (pehr•ih•STROY•kuh), or economic restructuring. In 1986, he made changes to revive the Soviet economy. Local managers gained greater authority over their farms and factories, and people were allowed to open small private businesses. Gorbachev's goal was not to throw out communism, but to make the economic system more efficient and productive.

STRUGGLING READERS

Paraphrase a Passage

Tell students to pick two paragraphs from "Gorbachev Moves Toward Democracy" and paraphrase them. Make the activity more enjoyable for students by encouraging them to use informal language. Sample paragraph:

Glasnost, which means "openness," brought many positive changes to the Soviet Union. Churches reopened. The censorship of books ended. Government officials could now be criticized and investigated. The Soviet people had more freedom and human rights as a result of glasnost.

Democratization Opens the Political System Gorbachev knew that for the economy to improve, the Communist Party would have to loosen its grip on Soviet society. In 1987, he unveiled a third new policy called democratization which was a gradual opening of the political system.

The plan called for the election of a new legislative body. In the past, voters had merely approved candidates who were handpicked by the Communist Party. Now, voters could choose from a list of candidates for each office. The election produced many surprises. In several places, voters chose lesser-known candidates and reformers over powerful party bosses.

Foreign Policy Soviet foreign policy also changed, in part due to President Ronald Reagan's strong anti-Soviet views. Reagan famously called the Soviet Union "an evil empire" during a speech in 1983. To compete militarily with the Soviet Union, Reagan had begun the most expensive military buildup in peacetime history, costing more than $2 trillion. Under pressure from U.S. military spending, Gorbachev realized that the Soviet economy could not afford the costly arms race. Arms control became one of Gorbachev's top priorities. In December 1987, he and Reagan signed the Intermediate-Range Nuclear Forces (INF) Treaty. This treaty banned nuclear missiles with ranges of 300 to 3,400 miles.

Reading Check
Make Inferences Why would it be inefficient for the central government to decide what should be produced all over the country?

The Soviet Union Faces Turmoil

Gorbachev's new thinking led him to support movements for change in both the economic and political systems within the Soviet Union. Powerful forces for democracy were building in the country, and Gorbachev decided not to oppose reform. Glasnost, perestroika, and democratization were all means to reform the system. However, the move to reform the Soviet Union ultimately led to its breakup.

Various nationalities in the Soviet Union began to call for their freedom. More than 100 ethnic groups lived in the Soviet Union. Russians were the largest, most powerful group. However, non-Russians formed a majority in the 14 Soviet republics other than Russia.

Ethnic tensions brewed beneath the surface of Soviet society. As reforms loosened central controls, unrest spread across the country. Nationalist groups in Georgia, Ukraine, and Moldavia (now Moldova) demanded self-rule. The Muslim peoples of Soviet Central Asia called for religious freedom.

Lithuania Defies Gorbachev The first challenge came from the Baltic nations of Lithuania, Estonia, and Latvia. These republics had been independent states between the two world wars until the Soviets annexed them in 1940. Fifty years later, in March 1990, Lithuania declared its independence. To try to force it back into the Soviet Union, Gorbachev ordered an economic blockade of the republic.

Although Gorbachev was reluctant to use stronger measures, he feared that Lithuania's example might encourage other republics to secede. In January 1991, Soviet troops attacked unarmed civilians in Lithuania's capital. The army killed 14 and wounded hundreds.

Objectives

You may wish to discuss the following questions with students to help them frame the content as they read.

- Based on Gorbachev's use of force in Lithuania in 1991, what were his views on the future of the Soviet Union at that time? *He probably had faith in the survival of the Union; otherwise he would not have ordered the attack on unarmed civilians.*
- Why might Soviet military leaders have ignored orders to attack the parliament? *They probably believed that the military would fare better under reformers.*
- Why might the August coup have accelerated the breakup of the Soviet Union? *The central authority was too weak to prevent secessions.*

More About . . .

The August Coup The coup attempt hurt Gorbachev politically by making it appear that he lacked control. Yeltsin, on the other hand, emerged as a triumphant figure. To many Soviets, Gorbachev seemed to represent the past, and Yeltsin symbolized the future.

Word Origins The U.S. state of Georgia is named for England's King George II. The name for the Republic of Georgia is said to derive from *gurj*—a Persian name for the region's inhabitants.

ONLINE DOCUMENT-BASED INVESTIGATION

Glasnost and Perestroika

Mikhail Gorbachev's policies of glasnost and perestroika shook up the traditional way of doing things in the Soviet economy and in the society at large. Have students study the historical source and answer the associated question.

Analyze Sources Why might the Soviet Union look different to the figure in the cartoon? *because Gorbachev's policies were so different*

DOCUMENT-BASED INVESTIGATION HISTORICAL SOURCE

Glasnost and *Perestroika*

Mikhail Gorbachev's policies of *glasnost* and *perestroika* shook up the traditional way of doing things in the Soviet economy and in the society at large.

ENGLISH LANGUAGE LEARNERS

Chart Gorbachev's Reforms

Have students read "Reforming the Economy and Politics" and create a three-column list for details about glasnost, perestroika, and democratization. Details may include the following: Glasnost: "openness," churches opened, political prisoners released. Perestroika: "economic restructuring," managers of farms and factories could make more decisions on their own. Democratization: gradual opening of the political system, election of a new group of lawmakers, Communist Party no longer chose all candidates.

READING CHECK
Make Inferences Why would it be inefficient for the central government to decide what should be produced all over the country? *because the central government would not understand local conditions, needs, or problems*

BIOGRAPHY

Mikhail Gorbachev

Have students read the biography of Mikhail Gorbachev, the Soviet leader whose attempts to reform the Soviet Union ultimately led to its breakup.

BIOGRAPHY

Boris Yeltsin

Have students read the biography of Boris Yeltsin, the first president of post-Soviet Russia, serving from 1991 to 1999.

BIOGRAPHY

Mikhail Gorbachev
(1931–)

Mikhail Gorbachev's background shaped the role he would play in history. Both of his grandfathers were arrested during Stalin's purges. Both were eventually freed. However, Gorbachev never forgot his grandfathers' stories.

After working on a state farm, Gorbachev studied law in Moscow and joined the Communist Party. As an official in a farming region, Gorbachev learned much about the Soviet system and its problems.

He advanced quickly in the party. When he became general secretary in 1985, he was the youngest Politburo member and a man who wanted to bring change. He succeeded. Although he pursued reform to save the Soviet Union, ultimately he triggered its breakup.

Boris Yeltsin
(1931–2007)

Boris Yeltsin was raised in poverty. For ten years, his family lived in a single room.

As a youth, Yeltsin earned good grades but behaved badly. Mikhail Gorbachev named him party boss and mayor of Moscow in 1985. Yeltsin's outspokenness got him into trouble. At one meeting, he launched into a bitter speech criticizing conservatives for working against perestroika. Gorbachev fired him for the sake of party unity.

Yeltsin made a dramatic comeback and won a seat in parliament in 1989. Parliament elected him president of Russia in 1990, and voters reelected him in 1991. Due at least in part to his failing health (heart problems), Yeltsin resigned in 1999.

Yeltsin Denounces Gorbachev The assault in Lithuania and the lack of economic progress damaged Gorbachev's popularity. People looked for leadership to **Boris Yeltsin**. He was a member of parliament and former mayor of Moscow. Yeltsin criticized the crackdown in Lithuania and the slow pace of reforms. In June 1991, voters chose Yeltsin to become the Russian Federation's first directly elected president.

In spite of their rivalry, Yeltsin and Gorbachev faced a common enemy in the old guard of Communist officials. Hardliners—conservatives who opposed reform—were furious that Gorbachev had given up the Soviet Union's role as the dominant force in Eastern Europe. They also feared losing their power and privileges. These officials vowed to overthrow Gorbachev and undo his reforms.

The August Coup On August 18, 1991, the hardliners detained Gorbachev at his vacation home on the Black Sea. They demanded his resignation as Soviet president. Early the next day, hundreds of tanks and armored vehicles rolled into Moscow. However, the Soviet people had lost their fear of the party. They were willing to defend their freedoms. Protesters gathered at the Russian parliament building, where Yeltsin had his office.

Around midday, Yeltsin emerged and climbed atop one of the tanks. As his supporters cheered, he declared, "We proclaim all decisions and decrees of this committee to be illegal. . . . We appeal to the citizens of Russia to . . . demand a return of the country to normal constitutional developments."

1238 Module 31

COLLABORATIVE LEARNING

Create a Travel Guide

1. Divide students into pairs and tell them that they will be assembling a travel guide booklet for Lithuania.
2. Explain that they are to use the library or the Internet to gather information.
3. Tell each group that they will need to allocate responsibility for each section of their booklet before they begin their research. Each booklet should include a short historical essay; details about geography and climate; concise outlines of Lithuania's government, economy, and people; and brief descriptions of its languages and religions.
4. Students can also choose to include additional information, such as the current average cost of airfare; an outline of the country's arts; maps and other visuals; and details about Lithuania's currency, major newspapers and magazines, places to stay and eat, and the best spots to shop or be entertained.
5. Encourage students to think carefully about how to order their information and to be creative in designing their guides.

On August 20, the hardliners ordered troops to attack the parliament building, but they refused. Their refusal turned the tide. On August 21, the military withdrew its forces from Moscow. That night, Gorbachev returned to Moscow.

End of the Soviet Union The coup attempt sparked anger against the Communist Party. Gorbachev resigned as general secretary of the party. The Soviet parliament voted to stop all party activities. Having first seized power in 1917 in a coup that succeeded, the Communist Party now collapsed because of a coup that failed.

The coup also played a decisive role in accelerating the breakup of the Soviet Union. Estonia and Latvia quickly declared their independence. Other republics soon followed. Although Gorbachev pleaded for unity, no one was listening. By early December, all 15 republics had declared independence.

Yeltsin met with the leaders of other republics to chart a new course. They agreed to form the Commonwealth of Independent States, or **CIS**, a loose federation of former Soviet territories. Only the Baltic republics (also called states) and Georgia declined to join. The formation of the CIS meant the death of the Soviet Union. It also signaled the end of the Cold War. On Christmas Day 1991, Gorbachev announced his resignation as president of the Soviet Union, a country that ceased to exist. Fifteen new countries, including Ukraine, Kazakhstan, and the Baltic States, formed in its place.

Reading Check
Analyze Motives Why do you think the Soviet troops refused the order to attack the parliament building?

Explore ONLINE!

The Breakup of the Soviet Union, 1991

Interpret Maps
1. **Place** What are the 15 republics of the former Soviet Union?
2. **Region** Which republic received the largest percentage of the former Soviet Union's territory?

ONLINE ANALYZE VIDEOS

The Fall of the Soviet Union

Have students watch the video individually or as a class. You may wish to use the associated question as a discussion prompt.

Analyze Videos What is one event mentioned in the video that led to the Soviet Union's collapse? *After World War II, Eastern Europe was divided in ways that went against what people in the region wanted.*

ONLINE INTERACTIVE MAPS

The Breakup of the Soviet Union, 1991

Have students explore the map and answer the associated questions.

Region Which republic received the largest percentage of the former Soviet Union's territory? *Russia*

In the print edition, see the map of the same title.

Place What are the 15 republics of the former Soviet Union? *Russia, Kazakhstan, Ukraine, Turkmenistan, Uzbekistan, Belarus, Kyrgyzstan, Tajikistan, Azerbaijan, Georgia, Lithuania, Latvia, Estonia, Moldova, Armenia*

Region Which republic received the largest percentage of the former Soviet Union's territory? *Russia*

READING CHECK
Analyze Motives Why do you think the Soviet troops refused the order to attack the parliament building? *They were inspired by Yeltsin's courage, they were sick of communist rule, or they were unwilling to gun down civilians.*

Objectives

You may wish to discuss the following questions with students to help them frame the content as they read.

- What consequences might result from 800 percent inflation? *development of a black market; widespread poverty; increase in crime*
- How might Yeltsin's response to Chechnya's declaration of independence parallel Gorbachev's reaction to Lithuania's? *Yeltsin may have felt that using force in Chechnya would discourage other regions of the Russian Republic from seceding.*

More About . . .

Boris Yeltsin's Retirement Yeltsin announced his retirement on New Year's Eve of 2000. During his speech to the Russian people, he expressed remorse for the hardship his policies had caused, saying, "I want to ask you for forgiveness, because many of our hopes have not come true, because what we thought would be easy turned out to be painfully difficult. I ask [you] to forgive me for not fulfilling some hopes of those people who believed that we would be able to jump from the gray, stagnating, totalitarian past into a bright, rich, and civilized future in one go. I myself believed in this. But it could not be done in one fell swoop. In some respects I was too naive. Some of the problems were too complex."

A Russian soldier throws away a spent shell case near the Chechnyan capital of Grozny.

Russia Under Boris Yeltsin

As president of the large Russian Federation, Boris Yeltsin was now the most powerful figure in the CIS. He would face many problems, including an ailing economy, tough political opposition, and an unpopular war.

Vocabulary
subsidies government funds given in support of industries

Yeltsin Faces Problems One of Yeltsin's goals was to reform the Russian economy. He adopted a bold plan known as **"shock therapy,"** an abrupt shift to free-market economics. Yeltsin lowered trade barriers, removed price controls, and ended subsidies to state-owned industries.

Initially, the plan produced more shock than therapy. Prices soared; from 1992 to 1994, the inflation rate averaged 800 percent. Many factories dependent on government money had to cut production or shut down entirely. This forced thousands of people out of work. By 1993 most Russians were suffering economic hardship.

Economic problems fueled a political crisis. In October 1993, legislators opposed to Yeltsin's policies shut themselves inside the parliament building. Yeltsin ordered troops to bombard the building, forcing hundreds of rebel legislators to surrender. Many were killed. Opponents accused Yeltsin of acting like a dictator.

ADVANCED/GIFTED

Create a Biography of Boris Yeltsin

1. Tell students that they will write a biography about Boris Yeltsin for young readers.
2. Explain that readers will be about ten years old, so the books need to be written at a level that such an audience can understand.
3. Before students begin their research, ask them to create a preliminary design for their books.
4. Have them decide on a number of chapters or sections. These might include chapters about Yeltsin's childhood and education, his work experience and involvement with the Communist Party, his family life, his presidency, and his retirement.
5. Suggest to students that they include a glossary at the end of their books so that readers can look up difficult terms, such as *Communist Party.*
6. Ask students to think hard about how to enliven the text for young readers. Encourage them to think of ways to connect the information to readers' lives and to incorporate lots of interesting pictures and other visuals—maps and illustrated timelines, for example.

Impact on the World The breakup of the Soviet Union created challenges in many parts of the world. Tensions between Russia and the United States grew as Yeltsin and other Russian leaders worried about U.S. dominance. Leaders in Moscow strengthened relations with China and India in an attempt to challenge the United States. Hostility grew further as the two nations disagreed over issues in Iraq.

Dozens of countries had chosen to stay nonaligned, or neutral, during the Cold War. These nations were also impacted by the collapse of the Soviet Union. Some feared the nonaligned countries that had banded together during the Cold War had lost their purpose to protect nations of the developing world. Internal conflicts among the many diverse members of the movement also presented problems.

Chechnya Rebels Yeltsin's troubles included war in Chechnya (CHEHCH•nee•uh), a largely Muslim area in southwestern Russia. In 1991, Chechnya declared its independence, but Yeltsin denied the region's right to secede. In 1994, he ordered 40,000 Russian troops into the breakaway republic. Russian forces reduced the capital city of Grozny (GROHZ•nee) to rubble. News of the death and destruction sparked anger throughout Russia.

With an election coming, Yeltsin sought to end the war. In August 1996, the two sides signed a ceasefire. That year, Yeltsin won reelection. War soon broke out again between Russia and Chechnya, however. In 1999, as the fighting raged, Yeltsin resigned and named Vladimir Putin as acting president.

Reading Check
Compare Compare Yeltsin's action here to his actions during the August Coup. Which were more supportive of democracy?

Russia Under Vladimir Putin

Putin forcefully dealt with the rebellion in Chechnya—a popular move that helped him win the presidential election in 2000. Nonetheless, violence in the region continues.

BIOGRAPHY

Vladimir Putin (1952–)

Vladimir Putin worked for 15 years as an intelligence officer in the KGB (Committee for State Security). Six of those years were spent in East Germany. In 1990, at the age of 38, he retired from the KGB with the rank of lieutenant colonel.

In 1996, he moved to Moscow where he joined the presidential staff. Eventually, Boris Yeltsin appointed Putin prime minister. When Yeltsin resigned at the end of 1999, he appointed Putin acting president. In 2000 and 2004, Putin won election as president. In 2008, he took the post of prime minister. He returned to the office of president for a third term in 2012.

Objectives

You may wish to discuss the following questions with students to help them frame the content as they read.

- How might Russians have felt about Yeltsin appointing Putin instead of calling an early election? *Some may have seen the move as a setback for democratic reform. Others may have seen the appointment as a wise move that would help maintain stability.*
- Ask students what they think will happen to the Russian Republic if the current economic trend continues. *regional secession movements, a military coup*

Connect to Literature: Chechnya Students who are interested in the war in Chechnya may be interested in reading *A Constellation of Vital Phenomena* by Anthony Marra, a novel about an eight-year-old Chechen girl whose father is abducted by Russian soldiers.

READING CHECK

Compare How does Yeltsin's action here compare to his actions during the August Coup? Which were more supportive of democracy? *He was more supportive of democracy during the August coup, because he defied a military takeover. Here he used the military to stay in power.*

BIOGRAPHY

Vladimir Putin

Have students read the biography of Vladimir Putin, who served as the president of Russia from 2000 to 2008 and was reelected in 2012.

ADVANCED/GIFTED

Recognize Bias in Primary Sources

1. Have students select one country from the former Soviet Union that they wish to know more about.
2. Encourage students to use reliable print or Internet sources to find information about a recent event in their chosen country.
3. Have students find at least three newspaper, magazine, or Internet features on their chosen recent event.
4. Ask students to read the articles carefully and write a summary of each.
5. At the end of each summary, have students write a few sentences describing the bias in each article that they found and the reasons why they believe that the authors may have taken the position they did.

READING CHECK
Make Inferences Why do you think some critics have wondered whether Russian democracy will survive? *because there have been so many issues on the road to Russian democracy*

Print Assessment

1. **Organize Information** In what year did the Soviet Union break apart? *1991*
2. **Key Terms and People** For each key term or person in the lesson, write a sentence explaining its significance. *Explanations of the lesson's key terms can be found on the following pages:* Politburo, p. 1235; Mikhail Gorbachev, p. 1235; glasnost, p. 1236; perestroika, p. 1236; Boris Yeltsin, p. 1238; CIS, p. 1239; "shock therapy", p. 1240
3. **Evaluate** Describe the weaknesses of the Soviet command economy. *Consumers had to stand in long lines to buy food and other basics; workers had little motive to improve efficiency; people could not open businesses.*
4. **Synthesize** How did Gorbachev's reforms help to move the Soviet Union toward democracy? *by initiating glasnost and perestroika, which promoted civic and economic liberalization*
5. **Evaluate** What were some of the consequences of the breakup of the Soviet Union? *some republics prospered, others failed, bloody fighting in Chechnya, ethnic conflicts, market reforms created businesses*
6. **Compare** In what ways were the policies of Gorbachev, Yeltsin, and Putin similar? *All supported glasnost and perestroika; all favored economic reform; all favored greater democratization.*

Putin Struggles with Chechnya Putin's war in Chechnya helped draw terrorism into the Russian capital itself. In October 2002, Chechens seized a theater in Moscow, and more than 150 people died in the rescue attempt by Russian forces.

As the war in Chechnya dragged on, Russian popular support faded, and Putin moved to suppress his critics. The 2005 Chechen elections helped restore order, and as of 2010, under current Russian president, Dmitry Medvedev, the rebels had been largely quieted. But rebellion still simmers.

Economic, Political, and Social Problems Since the collapse of the Soviet Union, Russia has seen growth in homelessness, domestic violence, and unemployment, and a decrease in life expectancy. Concerns over Russia's nuclear weapons have grown. Experts worry that security at nuclear storage sites in Russia is lacking. In addition, several former Soviet republics have stockpiles of nuclear weapons that some worry could get in the hands of rogue states and terrorist organizations.

Observers have wondered whether Russian democracy could survive. Putin's presidency has not settled the question. Russia has been moving toward greater participation in world trade by modernizing banking, insurance, and tax codes. Putin also worked to improve the economy by increasing exports in oil and natural gas. At the same time, attacks on democratic institutions such as a free press have not built the world's confidence.

Reading Check
Make Inferences Why do you think some critics have wondered whether Russian democracy will survive?

The histories of Russia and its European neighbors have always been intertwined. Unrest in the Soviet Union had an enormous impact on Central and Eastern Europe as well.

Lesson 3 Assessment

1. **Organize Information** Add major events from the lesson to a timeline like the one shown here.

   1985 — 2002

2. **Key Terms and People** For each key term or person in the lesson, write a sentence explaining its significance.
3. **Evaluate** Describe the weaknesses of the Soviet command economy.
4. **Synthesize** How did Gorbachev's reforms help to move the Soviet Union toward democracy?
5. **Evaluate** What were some of the consequences of the breakup of the Soviet Union?
6. **Compare** In what ways were the policies of Gorbachev, Yeltsin, and Putin similar?

Online Assessment

1. What key principle inspired the policy of glasnost?
   - Religious institutions have no place in civilized society.
   - Human rights are more important than the rights of the state.
   - Books of questionable nature should be banned from publication.
   - ● Economic and social reforms are not possible without a free flow of ideas.

   Alternate Question *Select the answer choice from the drop-down list to complete the sentence correctly.* Glasnost was inspired by the idea that an economy and society could not improve if people were forbidden from freely expressing their ideas. This policy of openness was put into place by *Gorbachev* in the Soviet Union in 1985.

2. How did the voting process change under Gorbachev's leadership?
   - People could vote regardless of if they were a landowner in the Soviet Union.
   - People could vote only for party bosses and not for lesser-known candidates.
   - People could vote in their own hometowns instead of having to travel to big cities.
   - ● People could vote directly for the leader instead of just approving already-selected candidates.

   Alternate Question *Select the answer choice from the drop-down list to complete the sentence correctly.* Under Gorbachev's leadership, the voting process in the Soviet Union changed. People could now *choose from a list of candidates* instead of just agreeing to the people who had already been selected for the office.

3. What did the formation of the Commonwealth of Independent States signify?
   - ● the end of the Soviet Union
   - the beginning of the Cold War
   - the end of peace in Eastern Europe
   - the beginning of conflict in the Middle East

   Alternate Question *Select the answer choice from the drop-down list to complete the sentence correctly.* When *Yeltsin* and leaders of Eastern Europe met together in December 1991, they agreed to form a loose federation of states called the Commonwealth of Independent States. This union showed that the end of the Soviet Union was official.

4. What was the "shock therapy" instituted during Boris Yeltsin's presidency?
   - a form of punishment for dissidents
   - a way to encourage neutrality in politics
   - an alliance with other communist nations
   - ● an abrupt shift to free-market economics

   Alternate Question *Select the answer choice from the drop-down list to complete the sentence correctly.* Boris Yeltsin did not want to wait around for the Russian economy to eventually improve. He wanted to force the changes to occur immediately. His plan of *shock therapy* was an abrupt shift to free-market economics. He lowered trade barriers, removed price controls, and ended subsidies to state-owned industries.

5. What evidence would a proponent of communism use to support the economic system of communism in Russia over a free-market system?
   - ● There is more homelessness in Russia after the Soviet Union's collapse than there was before.
   - There are more private industries in Russia after the Soviet Union's collapse than there were before.
   - There is an increase in life expectancy in Russia after the Soviet Union's collapse than there was before.
   - There are fewer incidents of domestic violence in Russia after the Soviet Union's collapse than there were before.

   Alternate Question *Select the answer choice from the drop-down list to complete the sentence correctly.*
   Homelessness is on the rise in Russia and so is domestic violence and unemployment. People in Russia are also expected to live shorter lives now than they did during *the Soviet Union era*.

6. **Cause and Effect** What were the effects of glasnost on the Soviet Union?

   Possible answer: Glasnost brought about extraordinary changes in the Soviet Union. Churches were allowed to be opened once again. People imprisoned as dissidents were released. Books that had previously been banned could now be published and read. Reporters were free to do their job uncensored—they investigated problems and were allowed to openly criticize officials. Human rights were improved drastically as people were allowed to say and do what they wanted.

7. **Draw Conclusions** Why was central planning to blame for the Soviet Union's economic problems, and what was Gorbachev's alternative to this system?

   Possible answer: Central planning required that all of the decisions for the economy happen at the central government level. The party officials told farm and factory managers how much to produce and what to produce. They also told them what wages to pay and what prices to charge. Because individuals could not increase their pay by producing more, they had very little incentive to work harder. This economic structure is very ineffective because it should be the people involved in the actual transaction, and not a bureaucrat, making these decisions. Gorbachev's alternative was the idea of perestroika. This was an economic restructuring that allowed local managers to have greater authority over their farms and factories, and people were allowed to open their own small private businesses. Gorbachev didn't want to throw out communism completely; he just wanted to make the Soviet Union's economic system more efficient.

8. **Draw Conclusions** Why did Gorbachev feel he needed to stop Lithuania from leaving the Soviet Union?

   Possible answer: Lithuania was the first of the Soviet republics to declare its independence. Gorbachev wanted to force it back into the Soviet Union by ordering an economic blockade. Gorbachev feared that Lithuania's actions might encourage other states to also want independence. This would be disastrous to the Soviet Union as a country since other members of the union would want to follow in their footsteps. Something needed to be done to show all of the countries that this type of behavior would not be tolerated.

(continued)

Online Assessment *(continued)*

9. **Draw Conclusions** Why did people say Boris Yeltsin was behaving like a dictator?

   Possible answer: In October 1993, the economy was suffering because of Yeltsin's "shock therapy" policies. Legislators who were opposed to Yeltsin's policies shut themselves up inside the parliament building and refused to leave. Yeltsin ordered troops to bombard the building. Hundreds of legislators were forced to surrender, and many were killed. This action caused Yeltsin's opponents to label him as a dictator.

10. **Elaborate** Why are there concerns regarding the former Soviet Union's stockpile of nuclear weapons?

    Possible answer: There are some serious questions on the security of the weapons at storage facilities in both Russia and in the former Soviet republics. If these weapons were to get into the wrong hands, it could have disastrous effects on the world as a whole. If the wrong groups of people had possession of these weapons, they could use them to threaten warfare or to engage in warfare with other countries of the world.

ADDITIONAL LESSON CONTENT

COLLABORATIVE LEARNING

Breakup of Soviet Union Multimedia Presentation

1. Organize students into small groups.
2. Assign each group a country that emerged after the fall of the Soviet Union.
3. Have groups research their country, focusing on how it gained independence, conflicts that may have developed, and the current status of the country.
4. Have each group create a multimedia presentation and present a culmination of its research to the class.

Lesson 4 Planner

Changes in Central and Eastern Europe

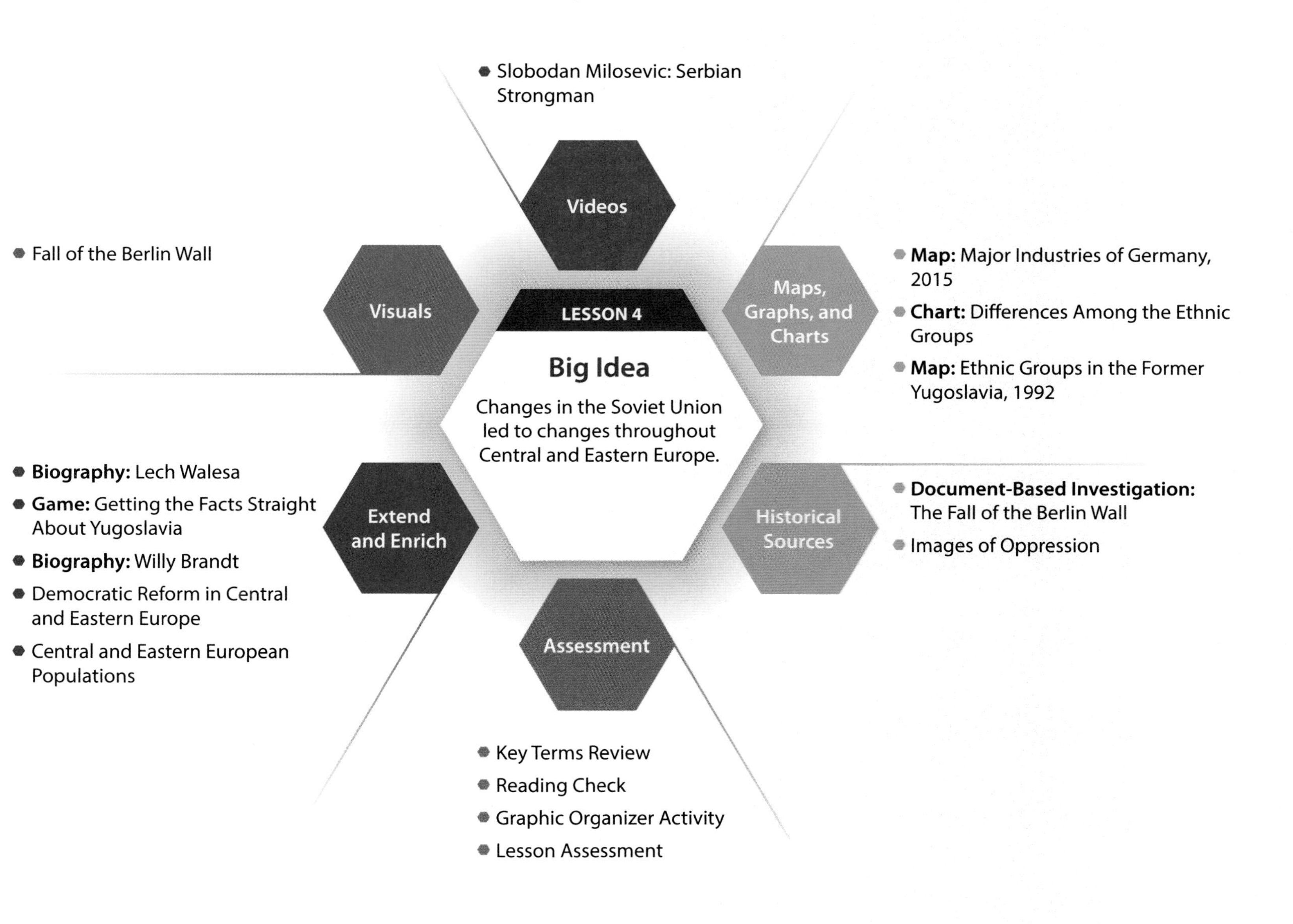

Online Lesson 4 Enrichment Activities

Willy Brandt

Biography Students read a biography about how Willy Brandt served the country of Germany after World War II. Then they imagine that they are going to interview Willy Brandt about his political career. With a partner, students use information from the biography to draft a list of questions and responses for the interview. Then they take parts and perform the interview for the rest of the class.

Democratic Reform in Central and Eastern Europe

Diagram Students create a cause-and-effect diagram about the spread of democratic reform in Central and Eastern Europe.

Central and Eastern European Populations

Graph Students conduct research to find out about the size of the population in different Central and Eastern European countries. Then they create a population circle chart to show the comparative sizes of the countries.

Lesson 4

Changes in Central and Eastern Europe

The Big Idea

Changes in the Soviet Union led to changes throughout Central and Eastern Europe.

Why It Matters Now

Many Eastern European nations that overthrew Communist governments are still struggling with reform.

Key Terms and People

Solidarity
Lech Walesa
reunification
ethnic cleansing

Setting the Stage

The Soviet reforms of the late 1980s brought high hopes to the people of Central and Eastern Europe. For the first time in decades, they were free to make choices about the economic and political systems governing their lives. However, they discovered that increased freedom sometimes challenges the social order. Mikhail Gorbachev's new thinking in the Soviet Union led him to urge Central and Eastern European leaders to open up their economic and political systems.

Poland and Hungary Reform

The aging Communist rulers of Europe resisted reform. However, powerful forces for democracy were building in their countries. In the past, the threat of Soviet intervention had kept such forces in check. Now, Gorbachev was saying that the Soviet Union would not oppose reform.

Poland and Hungary were among the first countries in Eastern Europe to embrace the spirit of change. In 1980, Polish workers at the Gdansk shipyard went on strike, demanding government recognition of their union, **Solidarity**. When millions of Poles supported the action, the government gave in to the union's demands. Union leader **Lech Walesa** (lehk-vah•WEHN•sah) became a national hero.

Solidarity Defeats Communists The next year, however, the Polish government banned Solidarity again and declared martial law. The Communist Party discovered that military rule could not revive Poland's failing economy. In the 1980s, industrial production declined, while foreign debt rose to more than $40 billion.

Public discontent deepened as the economic crisis worsened. In August 1988, defiant workers walked off their jobs. They demanded raises and the legalization of Solidarity. The military leader, General Jaruzelski (yar•uh•ZEHL•skee), agreed to hold talks with Solidarity leaders. In April 1989,

Objectives

You may wish to discuss the following questions with students to help them frame the content as they read.

- What does the early success of Solidarity suggest about Poland's Communist Party? *It was not as ruthless as other communist states in crushing opposition.*
- Why might Hungary's Communist Party have voted itself out of existence? *Communism had a bad reputation, so party members may have wished to regroup under a different name.*

More About . . .

Hungary's 2012 Constitution Hungary's new constitution has received heavy international criticism, including from the United States, other European nations, and Amnesty International. According to the Venice Commission, the changes "threaten democracy and the rule of law." The controversial changes include limits on the role of Hungary's Constitutional Court, limits on political advertising, and giving preference to "traditional" family relationships.

Teach the Big Idea

1. **Whole Class Open/Introduction** Ask students how living in a communist country might change their lives. *Possible answers: limits on speech and worship, fewer consumer goods available*
2. **Direct Teach** Read students the Big Idea: *Changes in the Soviet Union led to changes throughout Central and Eastern Europe.* Review the following lesson objectives with students to aid in their understanding of the Big Idea.
   - Explain reforms in Poland and Hungary.
   - Summarize changes in Germany.
   - Describe the spread of democracy in Czechoslovakia
   - Explain the democratic revolution in Romania.
   - Explain the conflict in the former Yugoslavia.
3. **Whole Group Close/Reflect** Have students create a before-and-after poster showing how society in Eastern Europe changed during the postwar era.

ONLINE DOCUMENT-BASED INVESTIGATION

Struggles for Democracy

The Fall of the Berlin Wall is the fourth of five document-based investigations that students will analyze in Struggles for Democracy. This video discusses the brutal life and catastrophic death of the Berlin Wall, the central symbol of the longest war of the 20th century. Have students watch the video and answer the associated question.

ONLINE GRAPHIC ORGANIZER

Changes in Central and Eastern Europe

As students read the lesson, have them use the graphic organizer to take notes. Students can review their graphic organizer notes at the end of the lesson to answer the following question:

Critical Thinking Which nation seems to have had the most positive changes? Explain. *Slovakia, because it had one of the best economic growth rates in the area*

ONLINE LESSON FLIP CARDS

Review Key Terms and People

Students can use the flip cards in the Lesson Review at any time to review the lesson's key terms and people: *Solidarity, Lech Walesa, reunification,* and *ethnic cleansing.*

BIOGRAPHY

Lech Walesa

Have students read the biography of Lech Walesa, the trade-union activist who later became the president of Poland and a winner of the Nobel Peace Prize.

NOW & THEN

The main goal of NATO is to protect the freedom and security of member nations through political and military means. Every day, civilian and military experts convene at the NATO headquarters in Brussels, Belgium, to share information and ideas to help make decisions on various security issues.

READING CHECK

Analyze Causes How did Solidarity affect Communist rule in Poland? *It undermined communist rule.*

Jaruzelski legalized Solidarity and agreed to hold Poland's first free election since the Communists took power.

In elections during 1989 and 1990, Polish voters voted against Communists and overwhelmingly chose Solidarity candidates. They elected Lech Walesa president.

Poland Votes Out Walesa After becoming president in 1990, Lech Walesa tried to revive Poland's bankrupt economy. Like Boris Yeltsin, he adopted a strategy of shock therapy to move Poland toward a free-market economy. As in Russia, inflation and unemployment shot up. By the mid-1990s, the economy was improving.

Nevertheless, many Poles remained unhappy with the pace of economic progress. In the elections of 1995, they turned Walesa out of office in favor of a former Communist, Aleksander Kwasniewski (kfahs•N'YEHF•skee).

Poland Under Kwasniewski President Kwasniewski led Poland in its drive to become part of a broader European community. In 1999, Poland became a full member of NATO. As a NATO member, Poland provided strong support in the war against terrorism after the attack on the World Trade Center in New York on September 11, 2001.

In 2005, Lech Kaczynski of the conservative Law and Justice party won the presidency. The following year Kaczynski's twin brother Jaroslaw became prime minister. The Kaczynskis fought Poland's pervasive corruption, opposed rapid reforms of the free market, and supported the American-led campaign in Iraq. After Lech Kaczynski was killed in a plane crash in 2010, Bronislaw Komorowski of the Civic Platform party was elected president. Political scandals lowered support of Komorowski's party, however, and Polish citizens elected Andrzej Duda to replace him in 2015.

Hungarian Communists Disband Inspired by the changes in Poland, Hungarian leaders launched a sweeping reform program. To stimulate economic growth, reformers encouraged private enterprise and allowed a small stock market to operate. A new constitution permitted a multiparty system with free elections.

Vocabulary
deposed removed from power

The pace of change grew faster when radical reformers took over a Communist Party congress in October 1989. The radicals deposed the party's leaders and then dissolved the party itself. Here was another first: a European Communist Party had voted itself out of existence. A year later, in national elections, the nation's voters put a non-Communist government in power.

In 1994, a socialist party—largely made up of former Communists—won a majority of seats in Hungary's parliament. The socialist party and a democratic party formed a coalition, or alliance, to rule.

In parliamentary elections in 1998, a liberal party won the most seats in the National Assembly. In 1999, Hungary joined the North Atlantic Treaty Organization as a full member. In the year 2001, there was a general economic downturn in Hungary. This was due to weak exports, a

ENGLISH LANGUAGE LEARNERS

Write Mini-Biographies

1. Ask students to read "Poland and Hungary Reform," listing the people mentioned in the text as they read.
2. Then have students take notes about each individual named in the text.

Sample:
Mikhail Gorbachev *Soviet reformer who encouraged Central and Eastern Europe to change economic and political systems*
Lech Walesa *A leader of Poland's Solidarity union who became president of Poland in 1990*
General Jaruzelski *Poland's military leader who agreed to hold free elections*
Boris Yeltsin *Russian president who introduced economic "shock therapy"*
Aleksander Kwasniewski *Former communist who became president of Poland in 1995*

Reading Check
Analyze Causes
How did Solidarity affect Communist rule in Poland?

decline in foreign investment, excessive spending on state pensions, and increased minimum wages. Economic crises continued through the early part of the twenty-first century, leading to broad legislative actions by the Fidesz administration. In 2012, Hungary adopted a new constitution that emphasized conservative, Christian morals. Many in Hungary protested this constitution, and foreign criticism rose as well.

Germany Reunifies

While Poland and Hungary were moving toward reform, East Germany's 77-year-old party boss, Erich Honecker, dismissed reforms as unnecessary. Then, in 1989, Hungary allowed vacationing East German tourists to cross the border into Austria. From there they could travel to West Germany. Thousands of East Germans took this new escape route to the west.

Fall of the Berlin Wall In response, the East German government closed its borders entirely. By October 1989, huge demonstrations had broken out in cities across East Germany. The protesters demanded the right to travel freely, and later added the demand for free elections. Honecker lost his authority with the party and resigned on October 18.

In June 1987, President Reagan had stood before the Berlin Wall and demanded, "Mr. Gorbachev, tear down this wall!" Two years later, the wall was indeed about to come down. The new East German leader, Egon Krenz, boldly gambled that he could restore stability by allowing people to leave East Germany. On November 9, 1989, he opened the Berlin Wall. The long-divided city of Berlin erupted in joyous celebration. Krenz's dramatic gamble to save communism did not work. By the end of 1989, the East German Communist Party had ceased to exist.

The fall of the Berlin Wall, November 10, 1989

Objectives

You may wish to discuss the following questions with students to help them frame the content as they read.

- Why did Hungary and Austria allow East Germans to cross their borders? *to pressure East German leaders into initiating reforms*
- How might West Germans' views about reunification have changed over time? *At first, they were overjoyed to be reunited. Later, they worried about economic sacrifices.*

More About . . .

Germany's Challenges After communism fell, refugees flooded into Germany from the poorer countries of Eastern Europe. This angered many Germans, who accused foreigners of stealing jobs by working for cheap wages. Thousands of angry young people joined neo-Nazi groups, which began to carry out violent actions against foreigners. In May 1993, five Turkish immigrants died when their house was set on fire. Attacks such as this revived the ugly memories of Nazi violence in the 1930s. By the 1990s, however, Germany had deep democratic roots, and millions of Germans spoke out against racism and anti-foreign violence.

ONLINE INTERACTIVE VISUALS

Carousel: Fall of the Berlin Wall

Have students navigate through the carousel and note similarities and differences among the images or identify a unifying theme. You may wish to use the associated question as a discussion prompt.

Analyze Visuals What was the reaction of citizens in Germany after the fall of the Berlin Wall? *People celebrated and used tools to break down the wall themselves.*

COLLABORATIVE LEARNING

Create a Timeline

1. Divide students into mixed-ability pairs.
2. Have students read "Poland and Hungary Reform" and make a timeline of the events in either Poland or Hungary.
3. Review student timelines as a class, and create class timelines of Poland and Hungary for all to see. Have students correct their work as needed as you fill in the class timeline.
4. Have students identify the events on the class timeline they believe had the biggest impact on democracy in Poland or Hungary.

ONLINE DOCUMENT-BASED INVESTIGATION

The Fall of the Berlin Wall

This video discusses the brutal life and catastrophic death of the Berlin Wall, the central symbol of the longest war of the 20th century. Have students watch the video and answer the associated question.

Analyze Sources Describe one event that led to the fall of the Berlin Wall. *In 1989, the Central Communist Committee made the decision to lift travel restrictions so that people would stop fleeing East Germany.*

ONLINE INTERACTIVE MAPS

Major Industries of Germany, 2015

Have students explore the map using the interactive features and answer the associated questions.

Location Which major industry is found in the city of Leipzig? *Energy & Environment*

In the print edition, see the map titled "Major Industries of Germany."

Location What is the relative location of business centers? Give possible reasons. *They are near borders and ports, which makes international trade easier.*

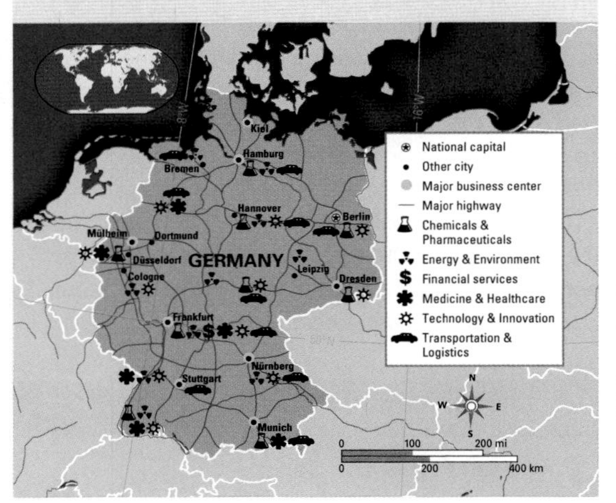

Reunification With the fall of communism in East Germany, many Germans began to speak of **reunification**—the merging of the two Germanys. However, the movement for reunification worried many people who feared a united Germany.

The West German chancellor, Helmut Kohl, assured world leaders that Germans had learned from the past. They were now committed to democracy and human rights. Kohl's assurances helped persuade other European nations to accept German reunification. Germany was officially reunited on October 3, 1990.

Germany's Challenges The newly united Germany faced serious problems. More than 40 years of Communist rule had left eastern Germany in ruins. Its railroads, highways, and telephone system had not been modernized since World War II. East German industries produced goods that could not compete in the global market.

Rebuilding eastern Germany's bankrupt economy was going to be a difficult, costly process. To pay these costs, Kohl raised taxes. As taxpayers tightened their belts, workers in eastern Germany faced a second problem—unemployment. Inefficient factories closed, depriving millions of workers of their jobs.

Explore ONLINE!

Major Industries of Germany

Interpret Maps

1. **Location** What is the relative location of business centers? Give possible reasons.

1246 Module 31

ADVANCED/GIFTED

Fall of the Berlin Wall News Report

1. After students have read "Germany Reunifies," have them use reliable print or Internet sources to conduct further research into the fall of the Berlin Wall.
2. After they have finished their research, ask students to use their findings to create and deliver a brief news report about the fall of the Berlin Wall.
3. Tell students they will be reporting for a major international news network, and their viewers may not know very much about the situation in Berlin.
4. Remind students to be objective in their news reports. After students have completed the project, have them discuss how they made their reports objective.

Reading Check
Synthesize Why would Europeans fear the reunification of Germany?

Economic Challenges In 1998, voters turned Kohl out of office and elected a new chancellor, Gerhard Schroeder, of the Socialist Democratic Party (SDP). Schroeder started out as a market reformer, but slow economic growth made the task of reform difficult. Although Germany had the world's third largest economy, it had sunk to fifth by 2005. Germany's unemployment rate was among the highest in Europe, and rising inflation was a problem. However, in 2006, a year after Angela Merkel of the Christian Democratic Union (CDU) was elected chancellor, unemployment fell below 4 million, and Germany's budget deficit was kept to within EU limits. In 2013, Merkel became only the third chancellor in Germany since World War II to win three elections, and her international popularity remained high.

Reunification has also forced Germany—as Central Europe's largest country—to rethink its role in international affairs.

Democracy Spreads in Czechoslovakia

Changes in East Germany affected other European countries, including Czechoslovakia and Romania.

Czechoslovakia Reforms While huge crowds were demanding democracy in East Germany, neighboring Czechoslovakia remained quiet. A conservative government led by Milos Jakes resisted all change. In 1989, the police arrested several dissidents. Among those was the Czech playwright Václav Havel (VAH•tslahv-HAH•vehl), a popular critic of the government.

On October 28, 1989, about 10,000 people gathered in Wenceslas Square in the center of Prague. They demanded democracy and freedom. Hundreds were arrested. Three weeks later, about 25,000 students inspired by the fall of the Berlin Wall gathered in Prague to demand reform. Following orders from the government, the police brutally attacked the demonstrators and injured hundreds.

The government crackdown angered the Czech people. Huge crowds gathered in Wenceslas Square. They demanded an end to Communist rule. On November 25, about 500,000 protesters crowded into downtown Prague. Within hours, Milos Jakes and his entire Politburo resigned. One month later, a new parliament elected Václav Havel president of Czechoslovakia.

Czechoslovakia Breaks Up In Czechoslovakia, reformers also launched an economic program based on "shock therapy." The program caused a sharp rise in unemployment. It especially hurt Slovakia, the republic occupying the eastern third of Czechoslovakia.

Unable to agree on economic policy, the country's two parts—Slovakia and the Czech Republic—drifted apart. In spite of President Václav Havel's pleas for unity, a movement to split the nation gained support among the people. Havel resigned because of this. Czechoslovakia split into two countries on January 1, 1993.

Objectives

You may wish to discuss the following questions with students to help them frame the content as they read.

- Why is the fall of communism in Czechoslovakia sometimes called the "Velvet Revolution"? *It happened relatively smoothly.*
- What, in addition to economic differences, may have led to the division of Czechoslovakia? *ethnic differences*

More About . . .

The European Union The European Union consists of 28 members and half a billion people, and its accomplishments are notable. For example, there have been no wars between member countries in the past 60 years. In order for a country to join the European Union it must apply and meet certain criteria. Countries must have a stable democratic government with a competitive market economy.

READING CHECK

Synthesize Why would Europeans fear the reunification of Germany? *A reunified Germany would be larger and stronger than the two separate Germanys—and could once again be a military threat as Nazi Germany had been.*

COLLABORATIVE LEARNING

Debate the Merits of Economic "Shock Therapy"

1. Divide students into small groups.
2. Remind students that they learned in Lesson 3 that Boris Yeltsin's plan of economic shock therapy initially produced more shock than therapy.
3. Have groups review Lessons 3 and 4 so that they are able to describe the following in their own words:
   - what economic shock therapy is
   - which governments have tried it
   - what the results have been
4. Have half the groups gather information that shows positive results of this type of economic change. The other groups should look for negative results.
5. As a class, discuss whether the positive results of economic shock therapy are worth the disruption it causes.

Objectives

You may wish to discuss the following questions with students to help them frame the content as they read.

- How could Ceausescu have been shocked by the sudden collapse of his power? *He may have mistaken fear of his power for loyalty.*
- What factors might predispose some postcommunist states to corruption? *antiquated infrastructures; greater distance from democratic countries*

More About . . .

The Romanian Language Isolation of Romanian from other Romance tongues and close contact with Slavic languages and Hungarian caused Romanian phonology and grammar to develop differently.

READING CHECK

Analyze Causes What was the main cause of the breakup of Czechoslovakia? *Disagreements over economic policy caused Czechoslovakia's breakup.*

Havel was elected president of the Czech Republic. He won reelection in 1998. Then, in 2003, Havel stepped down as president, in part because of ill health. The Czech parliament chose Václav Klaus, a right-wing economist and former prime minister, to succeed him. The economy of the Czech Republic has steadily improved in the face of some serious problems, aided by its becoming a full member of the European Union (EU) in 2004. In 2012, the Czech government passed a constitutional amendment to allow direct presidential elections. The following year Milos Zeman was elected in the first presidential election in the country.

Slovakia, too, proceeded on a reformist, pro-Western path. It experienced one of the highest economic growth rates in the region in 2002. In 2004, it elected Ivan Gasparovic president and joined both NATO and the EU. Andrej Kiska, an entrepreneur, became president in 2014.

Reading Check
Analyze Causes What was the main cause of the breakup of Czechoslovakia?

Overthrow in Romania

By late 1989, only Romania seemed unmoved by the calls for reform. Romania's ruthless Communist dictator Nicolae Ceausescu (chow•SHES•koo) maintained a firm grip on power. His secret police enforced his orders brutally. Nevertheless, Romanians were aware of the reforms in other countries. They began a protest movement of their own.

A Popular Uprising In December, Ceausescu ordered the army to fire on demonstrators in the city of Timisoara (tee•mee•SHWAH•rah). The army killed and wounded hundreds of people. The massacre in Timisoara ignited a popular uprising against Ceausescu. Within days, the army joined the people. Shocked by the collapse of his power, Ceausescu and his wife attempted to flee. They were captured, however, and then tried and executed on Christmas Day, 1989. Elections have been held regularly since then. In 2014, Klaus Iohannis was elected president.

SOCIAL HISTORY

The Romanian Language

The Romanians are the only people in Eastern Europe whose ancestry and language go back to the ancient Romans. Romanian is the only Eastern European language that developed from Latin. For this reason, Romanian is very different from the other languages spoken in the region.

Today's Romanians are descended from the Dacians (the original people in the region), the Romans, and tribes that arrived later, such as the Goths, Huns, and Slavs.

Romanian remains the official language today. Minority groups within Romania (such as Hungarians, Germans, Gypsies, Jews, Turks, and Ukrainians) sometimes speak their own ethnic languages among themselves. Nonetheless, almost all the people speak Romanian as well.

ADVANCED/GIFTED

NATO and the European Union

1. Have students choose either the European Union or NATO to learn more about.
2. Ask students to use reliable print or Internet sources to research their chosen organization, including how it functions and what problems it has encountered. In their research, students should investigate how the organization came into being, what its functions are, and how successful it has been in meeting its goals. Students should support their findings with appropriate analytical data.
3. Have students prepare multimedia presentations of their research findings and present them to the class.

COLLABORATIVE LEARNING

Newspaper Article

1. Divide students into mixed-ability pairs.
2. Tell students that they will work with their partner to write a newspaper article about the uprising in Romania. Students should include firsthand observations of the uprising from people who were there (although these observations will be fictional, they must be based in fact).
3. Articles should also include relevant historical background, a photograph, and a map showing where the uprising took place.
4. Invite students to share their newspaper articles with the rest of the class.

A view of downtown Sarajevo through a bullet-shattered window

The Romanian Economy Throughout the 1990s, Romania struggled with corruption and crime as it tried to salvage its economy. In 2001, overall production was still only 75 percent of what it had been in 1989, the year of Ceausescu's overthrow. In the first years of the twenty-first century, two-thirds of the economy was still state owned.

However, the government made economic reforms to introduce elements of capitalism. The government also began to reduce the layers of bureaucracy in order to encourage foreign investors. In 2007, Romania joined the European Union as the Romanian government began to move away from a state controlled economy. Much of Iohannis's campaign focused on ending corruption and raising living standards for Romanians. The nation is the second poorest in the European Union.

Reading Check
Contrast Contrast the democratic revolutions in Czechoslovakia and Romania.

The Breakup of Yugoslavia

Ethnic conflict plagued Yugoslavia. This country, formed after World War I, had eight major ethnic groups—Serbs, Croats, Bosniaks, Slovenes, Macedonians, Albanians, Hungarians, and Montenegrins. Ethnic and religious differences dating back centuries caused many people to develop prejudiced views of other groups, based on long-held stereotypes. After World War II, Yugoslavia became a federation of six republics. Each republic had a mixed population.

A Bloody Breakup Josip Tito, who led Yugoslavia from 1945 to 1980, held the country together. After Tito's death, ethnic resentments boiled over. Serbian leader Slobodan Milosevic (mee•LOH•sheh•vihch) asserted leadership over Yugoslavia. Many Serbs opposed Milosevic and his policies and fled the country.

Struggles for Democracy **1249**

Objectives

You may wish to discuss the following questions with students to help them frame the content as they read.

- Why might it have been easier for Slovenia and Croatia to win independence than Bosnia and Herzegovina? *stronger militarily; ethnically more homogeneous*
- Why might Muslims make up a large percentage of Bosnia and Herzegovina's and Kosovo's populations? *These regions were once part of the Muslim Ottoman Empire.*
- Why was Milosevic extradited instead of being tried in Serbia? *Many Serbians continued to support him.*

More About . . .

Ethnic Differences Most Serbs are Orthodox Christians, unlike Croats, who are primarily Roman Catholic, and Bosniaks, who follow Islam. In the past, Croats and Muslim Turks have dominated Serbs. Muslim Turks ruled Serbia for 400 years. During World War II, Croats joined forces with the Nazis in persecuting Serbs.

Serbo-Croatian Vocabulary and pronunciation differences exist among the Croatian, Bosnian, and Serbian dialects, but these differences are no real obstacle to verbal communication. However, the differences are significant in writing. The Croats and Bosnians use the Roman, or Latin, alphabet. The Serbs and Montenegrins use the Cyrillic alphabet.

Tip for English Language Learners Explain to students that a *broker* is somebody who acts as an intermediary, or go-between. A broker negotiates agreements between different people or groups.

STRUGGLING READERS

Venn Diagram

1. Ask students to draw a Venn diagram with the labels *Czechoslovakia, Both,* and *Romania*.
2. Have students review "Democracy Spreads in Czechoslovakia" and "Overthrow in Romania" and take notes in their Venn diagram, comparing and contrasting the two democratic revolutions.

READING CHECK

Contrast Contrast the democratic revolutions in Czechoslovakia and Romania. *Czechoslovakia struggled with internal divisions over economic policy, which resulted in it being divided into two independent countries. Romania, on the other hand, remained united. In Romania, the army joined forces with the people, and they executed the old communist leader.*

ONLINE INTERACTIVE CHARTS

Differences Among the Ethnic Groups

Have students explore the chart and answer the associated question.

Interpret Charts Which groups are mostly Roman Catholic? *Croats and Slovenes*

In the print edition, see History in Depth: Ethnic Groups in the Former Yugoslavia.

Interpret Visuals Use the chart to find out information about the various groups that lived in Bosnia and Herzegovina (as shown on the map). What were some of the differences among those groups? *There were three major religions practiced there (Catholicism, Orthodox Christianity, and Islam); three different dialects were spoken.*

Group	Language (Slavic unless noted)	Religion
Albanians	Albanian (not Slavic)	mostly Muslim
Croats	dialect of Serbo-Croatian*	mostly Roman Catholic
Hungarians	Magyar (not Slavic)	many types of Christians
Macedonians	Macedonian	mostly Eastern Orthodox
Montenegrins	dialect of Serbo-Croatian*	mostly Eastern Orthodox
Muslims	dialect of Serbo-Croatian*	Muslim (converted under Ottoman rule)
Serbs	dialect of Serbo-Croatian*	mostly Eastern Orthodox
Slovenes	Slovenian	mostly Roman Catholic

ONLINE ANALYZE VIDEOS

Slobodan Milosevic: Serbian Strongman

Have students watch the video individually or as a class and answer the associated question.

Analyze Videos What are Milosevic's main character traits? *ambitious, stubborn, selfish*

Two republics, Slovenia and Croatia, declared independence. In June 1991, the Serbian-led Yugoslav army invaded both republics. After months of bloody fighting, both republics freed themselves from Serbian rule. Early in 1992, Bosnia-Herzegovina joined Slovenia and Croatia in declaring independence. (In April, Serbia and Montenegro formed a new Yugoslavia.) Bosnia's population included Bosniaks (44 percent), Serbs (31 percent), and Croats (17 percent). While Bosniaks and Croats backed independence, Bosnian Serbs strongly opposed it. Supported by the country of Serbia, the Bosnian Serbs launched a war in March 1992.

During the war, Serbian military forces used violence and forced emigration against Bosniaks living in Serb-held lands. Called **ethnic cleansing**, this policy was intended to rid Bosnia of its Bosniak population. The international response focused on providing humanitarian aid to those affected by the war. Critics argue that many nations, including the United States and those in the European Union, could have done more to end the human rights abuses taking place in Bosnia. By 1995, the Serbian military controlled 70 percent of Bosnia. In December of that year, leaders of the three factions involved in the war signed a UN- and U.S.-brokered peace treaty. In September 1996, Bosnians elected a three-person presidency, one leader from each ethnic group. By 2001, Bosnia and Herzegovina began to stand on its own without as much need for supervision by the international community.

Rebellion in Kosovo The Balkan region descended into violence and bloodshed again in 1998, this time in Kosovo, a province in southern Serbia made up almost entirely of ethnic Albanians. As an independence movement in Kosovo grew increasingly violent, Serbian military forces invaded the province. In response to growing reports of atrocities—and the failure of diplomacy to bring peace—NATO began a bombing campaign against Yugoslavia in the spring of 1999. After enduring more than two months of sustained bombing, Yugoslav leaders finally withdrew their troops from Kosovo. In 2007, talks continued over the status of Kosovo.

The Region Faces Its Problems In the early years of the twenty-first century, there were conflicting signs in Yugoslavia. Slobodan Milosevic was extradited to stand trial for war crimes but died in 2006, while his trial was continuing. A large portion of the country's foreign debt was erased. Despite an independence movement in Kosovo, parliamentary elections under UN supervision took place in November 2001 without violence.

ADVANCED/GIFTED

International Criminal Tribunal for the Former Yugoslavia

1. Ask students to use the library or the Internet to learn about the work of the International Criminal Tribunal for the Former Yugoslavia (ICTFY).
2. Explain that the ICTFY was established by a May 1993 UN Security Council resolution for the prosecution of war crimes committed in the former Yugoslavia.
3. Tell students that they will be using their research to prepare an oral report summarizing the work of the tribunal, which they will deliver to the class.
4. Encourage students to include information about the location and structure of the tribunal; important indictments, trials, and appeals (such as the trial of former Yugoslav president Slobodan Milosevic); and efforts to arrest top fugitives, such as Radovan Karadzic and Ratko Mladic.

History in Depth

Ethnic Groups in the Former Yugoslavia

Many ethnic and religious groups lived within Yugoslavia, which was a federation of six republics. The map shows how the ethnic groups were distributed. Some of those groups held ancient grudges against one another. The chart summarizes some of the cultural differences among the groups.

Explore ONLINE!

Ethnic Groups in the Former Yugoslavia, 1992

Differences Among the Ethnic Groups

Group	Language (slavic unless noted)	Religion
Albanians	Albanian (not Slavic)	mostly Bosniak
Croats	dialect of Serbo-Croatian*	mostly Roman Catholic
Hungarians	Magyar (not Slavic)	many types of Christians
Macedonians	Macedonian	mostly Eastern Orthodox
Montenegrins	dialect of Serbo-Croatian*	mostly Eastern Orthodox
Bosniak	dialect of Serbo-Croatian*	Muslim (converted under Ottoman rule)
Serbs	dialect of Serbo-Croatian*	mostly Eastern Orthodox
Slovenes	Slovenian	mostly Roman Catholic

Interpret Visuals
Use the chart to find out information about the various groups that lived in Bosnia and Herzegovina (as shown on the map). What were some of the differences among those groups?

*Since Yugoslavia broke apart, many residents of the former republics have started to refer to their dialects as separate languages: Croatian for Croats, Bosnian for Bosniaks, Serbian for Serbs and Montenegrins.

ONLINE INTERACTIVE MAPS

Ethnic Groups in the Former Yugoslavia, 1992

Have students explore the map using the interactive features and answer the associated question.

Place Kosovo was a province within Serbia. What group was in the majority there? *Albanian*

ONLINE HISTORICAL SOURCE

Images of Oppression

Invite students to view the images and answer the associated question.

Analyze Sources How might these photographs have an impact on human behavior? *Both photographs evoke a strong emotional message about the reality of war that might make viewers want to help.*

HISTORICAL SOURCE

Images of Oppression

As these photographs demonstrate, photojournalists and others have captured many of the democratic struggles that have occurred in the last few decades. In some cases, news photographs have helped protesters or oppressed people gain the support of the world.

GAME

Getting the Facts Straight About Yugoslavia

Have students play the game to test their knowledge of facts about Yugoslavia.

READING CHECK

Identify Problems Why did Bosnia's mixed population cause a problem after Bosnia declared independence? *Bosnia's Serbs did not want to lose their ties to Serbia, while Croats and Muslims did.*

Print Assessment

1. **Organize Information** Which nation seems to have done best since the breakup? Explain. *Yugoslavia—ethnic tensions, loss of Tito's authority, Serbian aggression; Czechoslovakia—economic problems. Best—Slovakia had one of the best economic growth rates in the area.*
2. **Key Terms and People** For each key term or person in the lesson, write a sentence explaining its significance. *Explanations of the lesson's key terms can be found on the following pages:* Solidarity, *p. 1243; Lech Walesa, p. 1243; reunification, p. 1246; ethnic cleansing, p. 1250*
3. **Evaluate** What effect did reunification have on Germany's international role? *It made Germany the largest country in Central Europe, and with that came new international responsibilities.*
4. **Analyze Causes** Why did ethnic tension become such a severe problem in the Soviet Union and Yugoslavia? *In the past, communist leaders had suppressed nationalism. With the spread of democratic reforms, many ethnic groups demanded self-rule.*
5. **Draw Conclusions** What are some of the problems faced in Central and Eastern Europe in the twenty-first century? *ethnic conflict, economic slowdown, and the need for political reform*
6. **Analyze Effects** What effect did economic reform have on Slovakia? *Economic reform caused a sharp rise in unemployment in Slovakia, which undermined Czechoslovakian unity.*

In Montenegro (which together with Serbia made up Yugoslavia), an independence referendum in May 2006 revealed that most voters wanted to separate from Serbia. As the Montenegrins declared independence in 2006, Serbia accepted the new situation peacefully. In 2007, Serbia held a parliamentary election in which the ultra-nationalist Radical Party made some gains, but it could not win enough seats to form a new government.

The nations of Central and Eastern Europe made many gains in the early years of the twenty-first century. Even so, they continued to face serious obstacles to democracy. Resolving ethnic conflicts remained crucial, as did economic progress. If the nations of Central and Eastern Europe and the former Soviet Union can improve their standard of living, democracy may have a better chance to grow.

Reading Check
Identify Problems Why did Bosnia's mixed population cause a problem after Bosnia declared independence?

Lesson 4 Assessment

1. **Organize Information** Which nation seems to have done best since the breakup? Explain.

Former nations	Reasons for breakup
Yugoslavia	
Czechoslovakia	

2. **Key Terms and People** For each key term or person in the lesson, write a sentence explaining its significance.
3. **Evaluate** What effect did reunification have on Germany's international role?
4. **Analyze Causes** Why did ethnic tension become such a severe problem in the Soviet Union and Yugoslavia?
5. **Draw Conclusions** What are some of the problems faced in Central and Eastern Europe in the twenty-first century?
6. **Analyze Effects** What effect did economic reform have on Slovakia?

Online Assessment

1. Why has the new constitution adopted in Hungary in 2012 received criticism?
   - ○ It allows for a one-party system.
   - ○ It does not defend basic human rights.
   - ○ It promotes communism over capitalism.
   - ● It emphasizes conservative Christian morals.

   Alternate Question *Select the answer choice from the drop-down list to complete the sentence correctly.*
   A new constitution adopted in *Hungary* in 2012 has received criticism by opponents because it stresses conservative Christian morals.

2. How did Hungary aid East Germans in their escape to West Germany?
   - ○ Hungary allowed them to obtain Hungarian passports.
   - ● Hungary allowed them to cross the border into Austria.
   - ○ Hungary allowed them to work in its factories to get money.
   - ○ Hungary allowed them to send messages to their families in the West.

   Alternate Question *Select the answer choice from the drop-down list to complete the sentence correctly.*
   In 1989, Hungary started allowing East Germans to cross over the border into *Austria* so they could escape into the West.

3. Why did Czechoslovakia decide to split into two nations in 1993?
   - ○ The two parts of the country could not agree on a state religion.
   - ● The two parts of the country could not agree on an economic policy.
   - ○ The two parts of the country wanted different types of governments.
   - ○ The two parts of the country wanted different types of education systems.

   Alternate Question *Select the answer choice from the drop-down list to complete the sentence correctly.*
   Czechoslovakia split into two nations in *1993* primarily because Slovakia and the Czech Republic could not agree on an economic policy that would be beneficial to both of them.

4. What was different about Romania's uprising against its communist government compared with the other Eastern European countries?
   - ○ The economy thrived as soon as communism fell.
   - ○ The leader was able to escape to Russia with his family.
   - ● The army joined the people and fought against the government.
   - ○ The country released all of its state-owned businesses immediately.

   Alternate Question *Select the answer choice from the drop-down list to complete the sentence correctly.*
   When the Romanians rebelled against their communist government in December 1989, the *military* eventually joined the people and fought against the government.

5. Why did Slobodan Milosevic not have to pay for his war crimes?
   - ● He died before his trial was complete.
   - ○ He blamed his activities on his superiors.
   - ○ He escaped to Russia and was never captured.
   - ○ He found people who would give false testimonies.

   Alternate Question *Select the answer choice from the drop-down list to complete the sentence correctly.*
   Slobodan Milosevic was extradited to stand trial for his war crimes. However, he *died* in 2006 before his trial was complete.

6. **Elaborate** What pathway did Hungary take to stimulate economic growth?

   Possible answer: Hungary encouraged private enterprises. It allowed a small stock market to operate. Its constitution allowed for a multiparty system with free elections. In October 1989, Hungary voted out the communist government, which further allowed it to grow the economy.

7. **Cause and Effect** What caused Egon Krenz to open up the Berlin Wall on November 9, 1989?

   Possible answer: The East Germans had been demanding the right to travel freely and to have free elections. This caused problems in the country and finally led to the resignation of East German president Erich Honecker. The new leader, Egon Krenz, came up with the brilliant idea that he could restore stability in the country if he allowed people to travel freely and leave East Germany. He opened the Berlin Wall. This action didn't save communism as Krenz had hoped but rather took it down, just like the wall was literally taken down.

8. **Make Inferences** What did the events of November 25, 1989, show about the Czech people? Use details from the text to support your answer.

   Possible answer: The events of that day showed that the Czech people had great courage and that they were willing to risk everything for freedom. About a week prior, a group of about 25,000 people had gathered for a demonstration to demand reform. The police brutally attacked the protesters, injuring hundreds. For the demonstration on November 25, some 500,000 people gathered at the same square because of their anger over what had happened at the previous demonstration. They knew that the police could have come back out again and attacked the crowds, and yet 20 times as many people were clearly willing to come out and risk such an attack.

9. **Make Inferences** What are some possible reasons that Romania still remains one of the poorest nations in the European Union?

   Possible answer: In the first years of the 21st century, two-thirds of Romania's economy was still state owned. There was a great deal of corruption in the government that could have contributed to the economic conditions of the country, especially because so much of the industry was state controlled. All of these factors have combined to lead to the fact that Romania has struggled to compete with its fully capitalistic neighbors in Europe.

10. **Compare and Contrast** How was the experience of Montenegro in obtaining its independence different from the experiences of its neighbors in the former Yugoslavia?

    Possible answer: Montenegro was allowed to leave peacefully. Serbia accepted the new situation without any retribution. The same was not true for all of the other nations that were once part of Yugoslavia. When they tried to leave, Slovenia, Croatia, and Bosnia-Herzegovina were each met with a bloody and violent war.

ADDITIONAL LESSON CONTENT

COLLABORATIVE LEARNING

The European Union Map

1. Split the class into small groups.
2. Give each group an unlabeled outline map of Europe.
3. Have students use reliable print or online sources to find out which countries in Europe belong to the European Union and which do not.
4. Ask students to fill in the unlabeled map to create their own map of the European Union. Encourage students to use different colors to differentiate between those countries that belong to the European Union and those that do not. Remind students to create a legend.
5. Guide students in a discussion of the goals of the European Union and how effective it has been in achieving those goals and in unifying Europe.

Lesson 5 Planner

China: Reform and Reaction

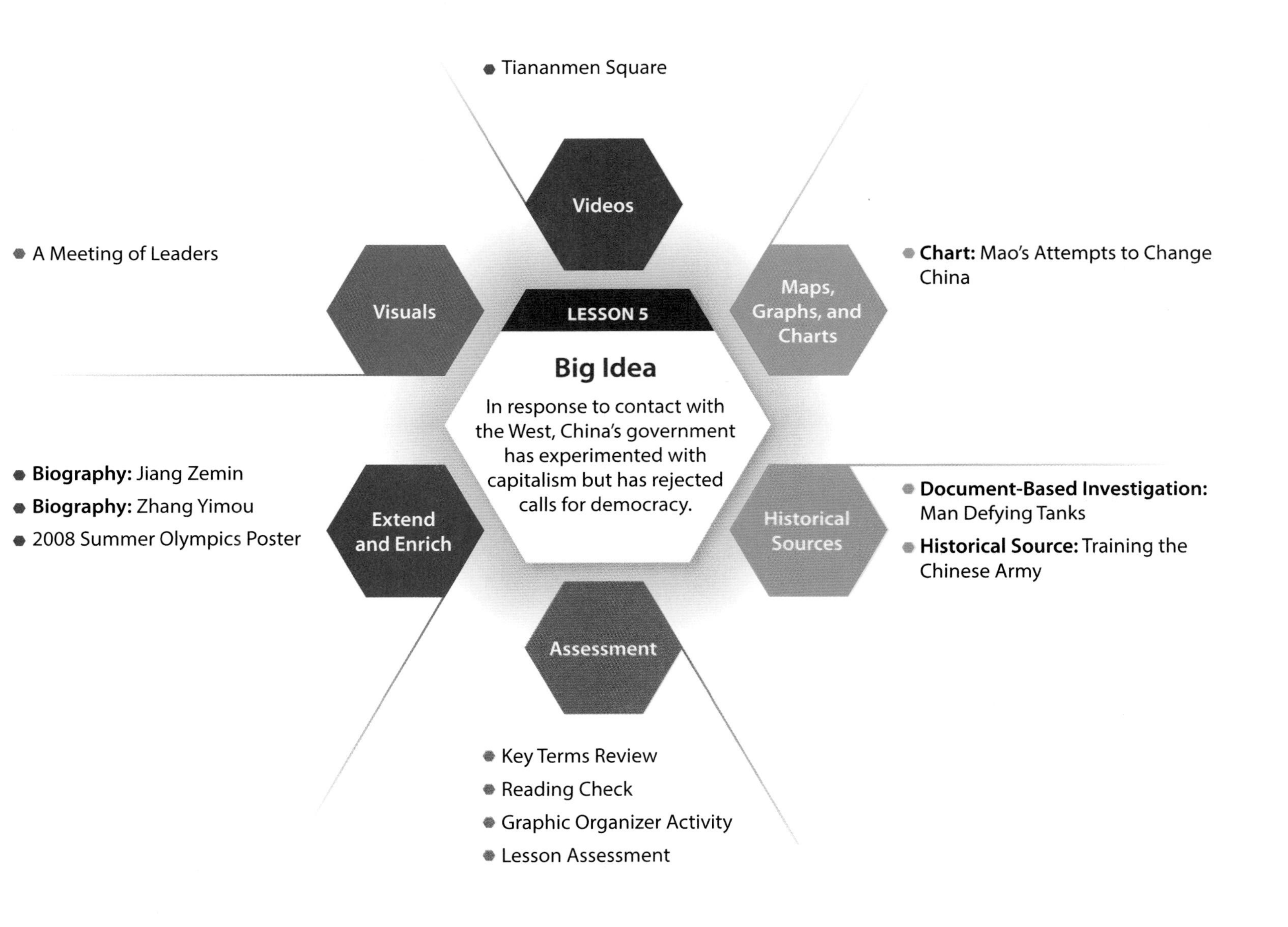

Online Lesson 5 Enrichment Activities

Zhang Yimou

Biography Students read a biography about Zhang Yimou, an Academy Award–nominated film director. Then they write a short story in which the hero finds out that the heart is more important than the sword.

2008 Summer Olympics Poster

Poster Students create a poster about the 2008 Summer Olympics in Beijing.

Lesson 5

China: Reform and Reaction

The Big Idea

In response to contact with the West, China's government has experimented with capitalism but has rejected calls for democracy.

Why It Matters Now

After the 1997 death of Chinese leader Deng Xiaoping, President Jiang Zemin seemed to be continuing Deng's policies.

Key Terms and People

Zhou Enlai
Deng Xiaoping
Four Modernizations
Tiananmen Square
Hong Kong

Setting the Stage

The trend toward democracy around the world also affected China to a limited degree. A political reform movement arose in the late 1980s. It built on economic reforms begun earlier in the decade. However, although the leadership of the Communist Party in China generally supported economic reform, it opposed political reform. China's Communist government clamped down on the political reformers. At the same time, it maintained a firm grip on power in the country.

The Legacy of Mao

After the Communists came to power in China in 1949, Mao Zedong set out to transform China. Mao believed that peasant equality, revolutionary spirit, and hard work were all that was needed to improve the Chinese economy.

However, lack of modern technology damaged Chinese efforts to increase agricultural and industrial output. In addition, Mao's policies stifled economic growth. He eliminated incentives for higher production. He tried to replace

Mao's Attempts to Change China

Mao's Programs	Program Results
First Five-Year Plan 1953–1957	Industry grew 15 percent a year. Agricultural output grew very slowly.
Great Leap Forward 1958–1961	China suffered economic disaster—industrial declines and food shortages. Mao lost influence.
Cultural Revolution 1966–1976	Mao regained influence by backing radicals. Purges and conflicts among leaders created economic, social, and political chaos.

Interpret Charts
Which of Mao's programs do you think had the greatest impact on China?

Teach the Big Idea

1. **Whole Class Open/Introduction** In this section, students will read about the Tiananmen Square massacre. Ask students if they can think of a similar crackdown in U.S. history. (Some students might mention the Boston Massacre.)
2. **Direct Teach** Read students the Big Idea: *In response to contact with the West, China's government has experimented with capitalism but has rejected calls for democracy.* Review the following lesson objectives with students to aid in their understanding of the Big Idea.
   - Summarize Mao Zedong's rule.
   - Explain changes under Deng Xiaoping.
   - Describe China's democracy movement.
   - Describe current conditions and recent events in China.
   - Discuss the relationship between economic and political change in China.
3. **Whole Group Close/Reflect** Have each student write a paragraph about China from 1934 to the present.

Objectives

You may wish to discuss the following questions with students to help them frame the content as they read.

- Do you think Chinese peasants favored a communist takeover of China? *Yes—Communism promised equality. No—Mao's policies were unfavorable to family life and made work less rewarding.*
- What might Mao have hoped to achieve by replacing family life with communes? *focus people on the good of the state rather than families or individuals*

More About . . .

Tip for Advanced/Gifted Students Students may be mystified about what exactly defines communism. Explain that their confusion is warranted. In fact, not long before his death in 1883, Karl Marx, author of *The Communist Manifesto,* remarked to his son-in-law, "One thing I am certain of; that is that I myself am not a Marxist."

ONLINE DOCUMENT-BASED INVESTIGATION

Struggles for Democracy

Man Defying Tanks is the fifth of five document-based investigations that students will analyze in the Struggles for Democracy module. This photograph shows a single Chinese man blocking tanks on their way to crush prodemocracy protests in Tiananmen Square in June 1989. Have students look at the photograph and answer the associated question.

DOCUMENT-BASED INVESTIGATION HISTORICAL SOURCE

Man Defying Tanks

A single Chinese man blocked tanks on their way to crush prodemocracy protests in Tiananmen Square in June 1989. No

ONLINE GRAPHIC ORGANIZER

China: Reform and Reaction

As students read the lesson, have them use the graphic organizer to take notes. Students can review their graphic organizer notes at the end of the lesson to answer the following question:

Critical Thinking Other than the demonstration in Tiananmen Square, which of these events was most important? Explain. *Deng's Four Modernizations was most important because it introduced Western ideas into China.*

Objectives

You may wish to discuss the following questions with students to help them frame the content as they read.

- Why might Zhou have chosen to invite a U.S. table tennis team to China? *It was a politically neutral way to open relations with the West.*
- Ask students if Deng's Four Modernizations are consistent with communism. *No—Motivation by profit and private enterprise are practices that communism was supposed to eliminate.*

More About . . .

Deng Xiaoping Deng Xiaoping embraced economic pragmatism—he was interested in results, not communist theory. He summed up his views by saying, "It doesn't matter whether a cat is black or white, so long as it catches mice." A key figure in world history, Deng is remembered for opening up China's economy while maintaining strict communist rule.

ONLINE INTERACTIVE CHARTS

Mao's Attempts to Change China

Have students explore the chart and answer the associated question.

Interpret Charts Which of Mao's programs had the most positive effect on the Chinese economy? *First Five-Year Plan*

In the print edition, see the chart of the same title.

Interpret Charts Which of Mao's programs do you think had the greatest impact on China? *Possible answer: First Five-Year Plan*

READING CHECK

Analyze Effects What was the ultimate result of Mao's radical communist policies? *The destructiveness of the Cultural Revolution turned many Chinese people away from radical communism.*

ONLINE LESSON FLIP CARDS

Review Key Terms and People

Students can use the flip cards in the Lesson Review at any time to review the lesson's key terms and people: *Zhou Enlai, Deng Xiaoping, Four Modernizations, Tiananmen Square,* and *Hong Kong.*

Zhou Enlai, a translator, Mao Zedong, President Nixon, and Henry Kissinger meet in Beijing in 1972.

family life with life in the communes. These policies took away the peasants' motive to work for the good of themselves and their families.

Facing economic disaster, some Chinese Communists talked of modernizing the economy. Accusing them of "taking the capitalist road," Mao began the Cultural Revolution in 1966 to cleanse China of antirevolutionary influences.

Instead of saving radical communism, however, the Cultural Revolution turned many people against it. In the early 1970s, China entered another moderate period under **Zhou Enlai** (joh-ehn•ly). Zhou had been premier since 1949. During the Cultural Revolution, he had tried to restrain the radicals.

Reading Check
Analyze Effects
What was the ultimate result of Mao's radical Communist policies?

China and the West

Throughout the Cultural Revolution, China played almost no role in world affairs. In the early 1960s, China had split with the Soviet Union over the leadership of world communism. In addition, China displayed hostility toward the United States because of U.S. support for the government on Taiwan.

China Opened Its Doors China's isolation worried Zhou. He began to send out signals that he was willing to form ties to the West. In 1971, Zhou startled the world by inviting an American table-tennis team to tour China. It was the first visit by an American group to China since 1949.

The visit began a new era in Chinese-American relations. In 1971, the United States reversed its policy and endorsed UN membership for the People's Republic of China. The next year, President Nixon made a state visit to China. He met with Mao and Zhou. The three leaders agreed to begin cultural exchanges and a limited amount of trade. In 1979, the United States and China established diplomatic relations.

Economic Reform Both Mao and Zhou died in 1976. Soon, moderates took control of the Communist Party. They jailed several of the radicals who had led the Cultural Revolution. By 1980, **Deng Xiaoping** (duhng-show•pihng) had emerged as the most powerful leader in China. He was the last of the "old revolutionaries" who had ruled China since 1949.

1254 Module 31

ENGLISH LANGUAGE LEARNERS

Write a Glossary

1. Ask students to read "The Legacy of Mao," and list any unfamiliar names or terms as they read.
2. Then have students either use a dictionary or clues from the text to write a sentence defining and explaining the importance of each person or term.

Sample:

Cultural Revolution *a revolution started by Mao in 1966 to cleanse China of antirevolutionary influences*
commune *a group of unrelated people who live together and share all their possessions and responsibilities*
Mao Zedong *communist leader of China whose policies stifled economic growth and political reform*
Zhou Enlai *leader of China in the 1970s; tried to restrain radicals*

Although a lifelong Communist, Deng boldly supported moderate economic policies. Unlike Mao, he was willing to use capitalist ideas to help China's economy. He embraced a set of goals known as the **Four Modernizations**. These called for progress in agriculture, industry, defense, and science and technology. Deng launched an ambitious program of economic reforms.

First, Deng eliminated Mao's communes and leased the land to individual farmers. The farmers paid rent by delivering a fixed quota of food to the government. They could then grow crops and sell them for a profit. Under this system, food production increased by 50 percent in the years 1978 to 1984.

Deng extended his program to industry. The government permitted private businesses to operate. It gave the managers of state-owned industries more freedom to set production goals. Deng also welcomed foreign technology and investment.

Reading Check
Synthesize What were some of Deng Xiaoping's economic reforms?

Deng's economic policies produced striking changes in Chinese life. As incomes increased, people began to buy appliances and televisions. Chinese youths now wore stylish clothes and listened to Western music. Gleaming hotels filled with foreign tourists symbolized China's new policy of openness.

Massacre in Tiananmen Square

Deng's economic reforms produced a number of unexpected problems. As living standards improved, the gap between the rich and poor widened. Increasingly, the public believed that party officials profited from their positions.

Furthermore, the new policies admitted not only Western investments and tourists but also Western political ideas. Increasing numbers of Chinese students studied abroad and learned about the West. In Deng's view, the benefits of opening the economy exceeded the risks. Nevertheless, as Chinese students learned more about democracy, they began to question China's lack of political freedom.

Students Demand Democracy In 1989, students sparked a popular uprising that stunned China's leaders. Beginning in April of that year, more than 100,000 students occupied **Tiananmen** (tyahn•ahn•mehn) **Square**, a huge public space in the heart of Beijing. The students mounted a protest for democracy.

The student protest won widespread popular support. When thousands of students began a hunger strike to highlight their cause, people poured into Tiananmen Square to support them. Many students called for Deng Xiaoping to resign.

Deng Orders a Crackdown Instead of considering political reform, Deng declared martial law. He ordered about 100,000 troops to surround Beijing. Although many students left the square after martial law was declared, about 5,000 chose to remain and continue their protest.

Objectives

You may wish to discuss the following questions with students to help them frame the content as they read.

- Why might Deng have been successful in crushing dissent when so many Eastern European leaders had failed? *He controlled the media. He had made efforts to reform Chinese communism.*
- Why are students so often involved in protest movements? *youthful idealism; they have the time to protest*

More About . . .

Goddess of Democracy The Goddess of Democracy was a 33-foot-tall statue created by students for the Tiananmen Square protests of 1989. It was made in only four days out of foam and papier-mâché. Many people have noted the statue's resemblance to the Statue of Liberty. However, the students specifically decided not to model it after the Statue of Liberty because they were concerned it would seem too "pro-American." The statue was destroyed by soldiers during the massacre. However, the memory of the statue lives on as an icon of liberty, free speech, and democracy. Several replicas of the statue have been created in cities around the world, including Hong Kong, San Francisco, and Vancouver.

READING CHECK

Synthesize What were some of Deng Xiaoping's economic reforms? *limited sales for profit; privatization of some businesses*

STRUGGLING READERS

Causes and Effects of Chinese Reforms

1. After students have read "China and the West," have them create a simple cause-and-effect chart about Deng Xiaoping's Four Modernizations.
2. Point out that an effect (such as incomes increasing) can in turn become a cause for another effect.

ONLINE DOCUMENT-BASED INVESTIGATION

Man Defying Tanks

This photograph shows a single Chinese man blocking tanks on their way to crush prodemocracy protests in Tiananmen Square in June 1989. Have students look at the photograph and answer the associated question.

Analyze Sources Why do you think this protester stood in front of the tanks? *Possible answer: He might have thought that even though he is one person that he could send a message to the Chinese government.*

ONLINE INTERACTIVE VISUALS

Image with Hotspots: A Meeting of Leaders

Have students explore the image using the interactive hotspots.

Objectives

You may wish to discuss the following questions with students to help them frame the content as they read.

- Why might U.S. leaders pressure China to improve its human rights record? *concern about the way the Chinese government treats its citizens; human rights record might interfere with the economic relationship between the United States and China*
- Why might China have promised to respect Hong Kong's economic system and political liberties for 50 years? *It saw Hong Kong as a potential revenue stream. China wanted neither to disturb the economic system nor to cause the emigration of the people who managed and sustained it.*

More About . . .

Jiang Zemin In an October 1995 speech at the UN, Jiang Zemin asserted that "certain big powers, often under the cover of 'freedom,' 'democracy,' and 'human rights,' set out to encroach upon the sovereignty of other countries." Ask students why Jiang Zemin might have been chosen to succeed Deng Xiaoping as president. *Communist Party officials may have seen his administrative competence and industrial background as useful skills in a time of economic transition.*

ONLINE ANALYZE VIDEOS

Tiananmen Square

HISTORY

Have students watch the video individually or as a class. You may wish to use the associated question as a discussion prompt.

Analyze Videos Why did the death of Hu Yaobang spark the Tiananmen Square protests? *Young people felt they needed to commemorate Yaobang, who was a revolutionary leader, and that it was a chance to bring their cause for democratic reforms to a greater audience.*

READING CHECK

Analyze Causes How did economic reform introduce new political ideas to China? *Possible answer: Western businesses and tourists brought Western ideas into the country, and students went to school overseas for economic reasons but learned about democracy.*

Historical Source

Training the Chinese Army

After the massacre in Tiananmen Square, Xiao Ye (a former Chinese soldier living in the United States) explained how Chinese soldiers are trained to obey orders without complaint.

"We usually developed bleeding blisters on our feet after a few days of . . . hiking. Our feet were a mass of soggy peeling flesh and blood, and the pain was almost unbearable. . . . We considered the physical challenge a means of tempering [hardening] ourselves for the sake of the Party. . . . No one wanted to look bad. . . ."

"And during the days in Tiananmen, once again the soldiers did not complain. They obediently drove forward, aimed, and opened fire on command. In light of their training, how could it have been otherwise?"

—Xiao Ye, "Tiananmen Square: A Soldier's Story"

Analyze Historical Sources

1. For whom did the soldiers seem to believe they were making their physical sacrifices?
2. What attitude toward obeying orders did their training seem to encourage in the soldiers?

The students revived their spirits by defiantly erecting a 33-foot statue that they named the "Goddess of Democracy."

On June 4, 1989, the standoff came to an end. Thousands of heavily armed soldiers stormed Tiananmen Square. Tanks smashed through barricades and crushed the Goddess of Democracy. Soldiers sprayed gunfire into crowds of frightened students. They also attacked protesters elsewhere in Beijing. The assault killed hundreds and wounded thousands.

The attack on Tiananmen Square marked the beginning of a massive government campaign to stamp out protest. Police arrested thousands of people. The state used the media to announce that reports of a massacre were untrue. Officials claimed that a small group of criminals had plotted against the government. Television news, however, had already broadcast the truth to the world.

Reading Check **Analyze Causes** How did economic reform introduce new political ideas to China?

China Enters the New Millennium

The brutal repression of the prodemocracy movement left Deng firmly in control of China. During the final years of his life, Deng continued his program of economic reforms.

Although Deng moved out of the limelight in 1995, he remained China's leader. In February 1997, after a long illness, Deng died. Communist Party General Secretary Jiang Zemin (jee•ahng-zeh•meen) assumed the presidency.

COLLABORATIVE LEARNING

Analyze Primary and Secondary Sources

1. Explain that primary sources provide firsthand evidence of historical events. They can include manuscripts, photographs, maps, artifacts, audio and video recordings, oral histories, postcards, and posters. Secondary sources are materials, such as textbooks, that synthesize and interpret primary materials.
2. Have students read "Massacre in Tiananmen Square" and the Historical Sources feature in this section.
3. Lead a class discussion that focuses on how reading the primary source—the excerpt from Xiao Ye's "Tiananmen Square: A Soldier's Story"—changes, or does not change, the impression of the massacre that they received from the secondary source.

China Under Jiang Many questions arose after Deng's death. What kind of leader would Jiang be? Would he be able to hold on to power and ensure political stability? A highly intelligent and educated man, Jiang had served as mayor of Shanghai. He was considered skilled, flexible, and practical. However, he had no military experience. Therefore, Jiang had few allies among the generals. He also faced challenges from rivals, including hard-line officials who favored a shift away from Deng's economic policies.

Other questions following Deng's death had to do with China's poor human rights record, its occupation of Tibet, and relations with the United States. During the 1990s, the United States pressured China to release political prisoners and ensure basic rights for political opponents. China remained hostile to such pressure. Its government continued to repress the prodemocracy movement. Nevertheless, the desire for freedom still ran through Chinese society. If China remained economically open but politically closed, tensions seemed bound to surface.

In late 1997, Jiang paid a state visit to the United States. During his visit, U.S. protesters demanded more democracy in China. Jiang admitted that China had made some mistakes but refused to promise that China's policies would change.

President Jiang Zemin and Premier Zhu Rongji announced their retirement in late 2002. Jiang's successor was Hu Jintao. However, Jiang was expected to wield influence over his successor behind the scenes. Hu became president of the country and general secretary of the Communist Party. Jiang remained political leader of the military. Both supported China's move to a market economy.

BIOGRAPHY

Jiang Zemin
(1926–)

Jiang Zemin was trained as an engineer. After working as an engineer, heading several technological institutes, and serving as minister of the electronics industry, he moved up in politics.

In 1982, he joined the Central Committee of the Communist Party in China. He became mayor of Shanghai in 1985, in which post he proved to be an effective administrator. In 1989, he became general secretary of the Chinese Communist Party. This promotion was largely due to his support for the government's putdown of the prodemocracy demonstrations in that year. In 1993, he became president. In 2003, he stepped down and was replaced by Hu Jintao; however, Jiang retained power behind the scenes.

BIOGRAPHY

Jiang Zemin

Have students read the biography of Jiang Zemin, the president of China from 1993 to 2003.

ONLINE HISTORICAL SOURCES

Training the Chinese Army

Invite students to read the excerpt and answer the associated question.

Analyze Sources For whom did the soldiers seem to believe they were making their physical sacrifices? *the Communist Party*

In the print edition, see the source of the same title.

1. For whom did the soldiers seem to believe they were making their physical sacrifices? *the Communist Party*
2. What attitude toward obeying orders did their training seem to encourage in the soldiers? *to follow orders blindly*

HISTORICAL SOURCE

Training the Chinese Army

After the massacre in Tiananmen Square, Xiao Ye (a former Chinese soldier living in the United States) explained how Chinese soldiers are trained to obey orders without complaint.

ADVANCED/GIFTED

Writing a Poem About Human Rights

1. Tell students to read "China Enters the New Millennium" and "China Beyond 2000."
2. Ask them to pay close attention to the passages that address human rights issues and to think carefully about the statement that "Supporters of [the normalization of trade with China] argue that the best way to prompt political change in China is through greater engagement rather than isolation."
3. Tell students to use these passages as a springboard for creating a poem about human rights issues in today's global society.
4. Encourage volunteers to read their poems in front of the class.

Objectives

You may wish to discuss the following questions with students to help them frame the content as they read.

- What might have happened if China's leaders had adopted a "shock therapy" economic policy? *It might have caused economic upheaval and widespread popular discontent, perhaps even leading to overthrow of the regime.*
- Do you think the best way to prompt political change in China is through greater engagement, not isolation? *Possible answers: Yes—The United States is unlikely to change the human rights situation in China through a boycott. China would simply seek economic and political relationships with other nations. No—Abuse of human rights should not be tolerated.*

More About . . .

China's Economy The Index of Economic Freedom provides annual metrics on economic freedom in 186 countries around the world. This index defines economic freedom as "the fundamental right of every human to control his or her own labor and property." In the 2015 Index of Economic Freedom, China ranked as the 139th freest country in the world and as the 30th out of 42 countries in Asia. According to the index, economic freedom in China has improved only slightly over the past five years. In 2015, China had a gross domestic product (GDP) of $9,844 per capita and a 4.6% unemployment rate.

READING CHECK

Summarize What challenges did Jiang Zemin face when he became president? *ensuring political stability, challenges from rivals who wanted to shift away from Deng's economic reforms, pressure from the United States to improve human rights*

Transfer of Hong Kong Another major issue for China was the status of **Hong Kong**. Hong Kong was a thriving business center and British colony on the southeastern coast of China. On July 1, 1997, Great Britain handed Hong Kong over to China, ending 155 years of colonial rule. As part of the transfer, China promised to respect Hong Kong's economic system and political liberties for 50 years.

Many of Hong Kong's citizens worried about Chinese rule and feared the loss of their freedoms. Others, however, saw the transfer as a way to reconnect with their Chinese heritage. In the first four or five years after the transfer, the control of mainland China over Hong Kong tightened.

Reading Check
Summarize What challenges did Jiang Zemin face when he became president?

China Beyond 2000

The case of China demonstrates that the creation of democracy can be a slow, fitful, and incomplete process. Liberal reforms in one area, such as the economy, may not lead immediately to political reforms.

People celebrate in Tiananmen Square after Beijing won the bid for the 2008 Olympic Games.

Economics and Politics In China, there has been a dramatic reduction in poverty. Some experts argue that China managed to reform its economy and reduce poverty because it adopted a gradual approach to selling off state industries and privatizing the economy rather than a more abrupt approach. China's strategy has paid off; by 2007, the country had the world's fourth largest economy, after the United States, Japan, and Germany. Cheap consumer goods from China are filling shops and department stores worldwide.

But China's economic strength has come with a cost. The wealth gap between urban and rural areas has widened, with inequality leading to social unrest. In addition, rapid industrialization has caused pollution and severe environmental problems.

COLLABORATIVE LEARNING

Research Trade Between U.S. and China

1. Organize students into small groups. Tell students that the U.S. Census Bureau keeps extensive records about trade.
2. Have each group conduct online research about trade between China and the United States. Ask them to find out the total value of trade between the two countries and the specific products that are frequently traded between the countries. Remind students to record information for imports as well as exports.
3. Next, have groups discuss their data, whether or not it is complete, what precisely it represents, and what they can conclude from it. Have each group record its conclusions.
4. Allow class time for groups to share their discoveries with the class.

As countries are increasingly linked through technology and trade, they will have more opportunity to influence each other politically. When the U.S. Congress voted to normalize trade with China, supporters of such a move argued that the best way to prompt political change in China is through greater engagement rather than isolation. Another sign of China's increasing engagement with the world was its successful hosting of the 2008 Summer Olympics in Beijing. Two years later China hosted the Expo 2010, a world exposition in Shanghai that was one of the largest world fairs ever hosted.

In recent years, China's economy has begun to slow. Decreased global demand has caused traditional sources of growth in China, such as investment and manufacturing, to decline. A new five-year plan introduced in 2015 has promised to better balance the economy by focusing on the service and technology industries. The plan also officially ends the controversial one-child policy in China to help increase the future labor supply.

Reading Check
Make Inferences Why has technology led to an increase in political influence among China and other countries?

Lesson 5 Assessment

1. **Organize Information** Other than the demonstration in Tiananmen Square, which events in the lesson were most important? Explain.

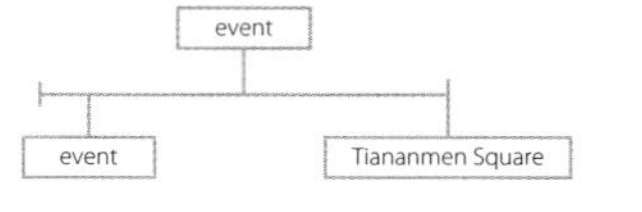

2. **Key Terms and People** For each key term or person in the lesson, write a sentence explaining its significance.
3. **Analyze Effects** What effect did Mao's policies have on economic growth?
4. **Form Opinions** How would you describe China's record on human rights?
5. **Predict** Judging from what you have read about the Chinese government, do you think Hong Kong will keep its freedoms under Chinese rule? Explain.
6. **Summarize** What were some of the events that followed the demonstration in Tiananmen Square?
7. **Compare and Contrast** Has there been greater progress in political or economic reform in China?

READING CHECK
Make Inferences Why has technology led to an increase in political influence among China and other countries? *Technology allows for easier engagement and connection among countries all over the world.*

Print Assessment

1. **Organize Information** Other than the demonstration in Tiananmen Square, which of these events was most important? Explain. *1971—Zhou opens China to West; 1980s—Four Modernizations (most important because changed economy)*
2. **Key Terms and People** For each key term or person in the lesson, write a sentence explaining its significance. *Explanations of the lesson's key terms can be found on the following pages:* Zhou Enlai, *p. 1254; Deng Xiaoping, p. 1254; Four Modernizations, p. 1255; Tiananmen Square, p. 1255; Hong Kong, p. 1258*
3. **Analyze Effects** What effect did Mao's policies have on economic growth? *They undermined economic growth.*
4. **Form Opinions** How would you describe China's record on human rights? *relatively poor*
5. **Predict** Judging from what you have read about the Chinese government, do you think Hong Kong will keep its freedoms under Chinese rule? Explain. *Possible answer: It is difficult to predict, but so far Hong Kong has been given some freedom.*
6. **Summarize** What were some of the events that followed the demonstration in Tiananmen Square? *Chinese government massacred protesters and repressed the prodemocracy movement.*
7. **Compare and Contrast** Has there been greater progress in political or economic reform in China? *economic reform*

History Through Art

Photojournalism

Make a list on the board of the most powerful photojournalistic images students have seen in the last 12 months. Then have students vote for the most powerful image of those listed. Students should explain which elements of the image make it the most powerful.

Critical Thinking

1. **Form Opinions** Choose one of the photographs, and evaluate its impact on human behavior. *Some students may choose the photo of the grandmothers of the Plaza de Mayo because it effectively shows the anger and outrage of the women.*
2. **Evaluate** Use the Internet to find a news photograph that you think effectively shows a recent historic event. Bring a copy of the photograph to class, and explain orally or in writing what it conveys about the event. Be sure to carefully evaluate the website you choose for accuracy. *Students should choose news photos of significant historic events, such as recent terrorist attacks or wars. Their explanation should describe what aspect of the historic event the photograph conveys.*

HISTORY THROUGH ART

Photojournalism

From the earliest days of photography, media such as magazines and newspapers have used photographs to convey the news. Today, websites are a common source of news journalism. Photojournalists must respond quickly to recognize a history-making moment and to record that moment before it passes. As these photographs demonstrate, photojournalists have captured many of the democratic struggles that have occurred in the last few decades. In some cases, news photographs have helped protesters or oppressed people gain the support of the world.

FLIGHT FROM SREBRENICA ▸
During the conflicts in Bosnia and Herzegovina, the United Nations declared the city of Srebrenica a safe area. Even so, the Bosnian Serb army invaded in July 1995 and expelled more than 20,000 Muslims—nearly all of them women, children, or elderly people. In addition, the soldiers held more than 7,000 men and boys prisoner and over a five-day period massacred them.

▴ MAN DEFYING TANKS
A single Chinese man blocked tanks on their way to crush prodemocracy protests in Tiananmen Square in June 1989. No one knows for sure what happened to the man afterward—or even who he was. Even so, this image has become one of the enduring photographs of the 20th century; it has come to stand for one man's courage in defying tyranny.

▲ ABUELAS DE PLAZA DE MAYO
From 1976 to 1983, the military government of Argentina tortured and killed thousands of political dissidents and sometimes stole their children. In this demonstration in December 1979, the *Abuelas de Plaza de Mayo* (Grandmothers of the Plaza de Mayo) demanded to know the fate of their relatives. The banner they carried reads "Disappeared Children."

▲ FALL OF THE WALL
When the East German government opened the Berlin Wall in November 1989, a huge celebration broke out. Some people began to use pickaxes to demolish the wall entirely. Others danced on top of the wall.

▲ VOTING LINE
When South Africa held its first all-race election in April 1994, people were so eager to vote that they stood in lines that sometimes stretched nearly a kilometer (0.62 mile).

Critical Thinking
1. **Form Opinions** Choose one of the photographs, and evaluate its impact on human behavior.
2. **Evaluate** Use the Internet to find a news photograph that you think effectively shows a recent historic event. Bring a copy of the photograph to class, and explain orally or in writing what it conveys about the event. Be sure to carefully evaluate the website you choose for accuracy.

Struggles for Democracy 1261

Online Assessment

1. Based on Mao's policies, what did he believe about communal living for peasants?
   - ● It was superior to family life.
   - ○ It was a way to avoid democracy.
   - ○ It was a way to keep people illiterate.
   - ○ It was more important than modern technology.

   Alternate Question *Select the answer choice from the drop-down list to complete the sentence correctly.*
   Mao replaced *family* life with life in communes. This policy backfired because it gave people less motivation to work hard for the betterment of themselves and their families, thereby lowering rather than raising productivity.

2. How was Deng different from Mao in his approach to improving China's economy?
   - ● He was willing to use capitalistic ideas.
   - ○ He was a proponent of the Cultural Revolution.
   - ○ He was in favor of large agricultural communes.
   - ○ He was interested in cutting off foreign trade with the West.

   Alternate Question *Select the answer choice from the drop-down list to complete the sentence correctly.*
   Deng was different than Mao in his approach to improving China's economy because he was willing to embrace capitalistic ideas. He promoted a set of goals, known as the Four Modernizations, that called for progress in *agriculture*, industry, defense, and science and technology.

3. Where did the students involved in the Tiananmen Square protests get the idea to protest for democracy?
   - ● They had been influenced by Western culture.
   - ○ They had studied the principles taught by Mao Zedong.
   - ○ They had read books written during the Cultural Revolution.
   - ○ They had researched the ideas of ancient Greece on the Internet.

   Alternate Question *Select the answer choice from the drop-down list to complete the sentence correctly.*
   One of the results of *Deng's economic reforms* is that the Chinese people became exposed to Western ideas, and that exposure became one of the leading factors that caused the students to protest for democracy in Tiananmen Square.

4. Which country controlled Hong Kong before it was turned over to China in 1997?
   - ○ France
   - ● Great Britain
   - ○ Japan
   - ○ United States

   Alternate Question *Select the answer choice from the drop-down list to complete the sentence correctly.*
   Prior to being turned over to China in 1997, the city of Hong Kong had been controlled by the *British* for 155 years.

5. What is one reason that China has ended its one-child policy?
   - ● It needs future workers.
   - ○ It has been criticized for human rights violations.
   - ○ It wants to one day have the largest population in the world.
   - ○ It hopes to have more supporters of the communist economic system.

   Alternate Question *Select the answer choice from the drop-down list to complete the sentence correctly.*
   China decided to end its *free-enterprise system* in 2015 in part because it needs to make sure it has a large enough workforce for the future.

6. **Cause and Effect** What caused Mao's economic policies to fail?

   Possible answer: Mao thought that peasant equality, revolutionary spirit, and hard work were all that was needed to improve the Chinese economy. But more than that was needed. The country lacked modern technology, and that affected the peasantry's ability to increase agricultural output. Mao also eliminated incentives for higher production, and he replaced family life with communal life. These policies took away the peasants' motivation to work for the good of themselves and their families.

7. **Draw Conclusions** What did Deng understand about human nature? Use examples from the text to support your answer.

   Possible answer: Deng understood that people need incentives to work hard. If you do not have any incentives to work hard for yourself or your family, you won't. Deng showed that he understood this principle when he privatized agriculture. He leased land to individual farmers and told them that while they had to produce a certain amount for the government, anything produced beyond that amount could be sold by the farmers for their own profit. Food production increased by 50 percent between 1978 and 1984 because of this system. People had the incentive to work hard because they would then personally gain by doing so.

8. **Elaborate** What did Deng do instead of considering political reform when protesters gathered at Tiananmen Square?

   Possible answer: He declared martial law. He ordered about 100,000 troops to descend on the area and surround Beijing. He then ordered the military to drive the tanks into the square and spray gunfire into the crowds of protesters. Hundreds were killed and thousands were wounded in the massacre.

9. **Elaborate** What were some of Jiang Zemin's positive and negative qualities as a political leader in China?

   Possible answer: Jiang was highly intelligent and well educated. He had political experience, having served as mayor of Shanghai. He was skilled, flexible, and practical. But he had no military experience, and he had few allies among the country's generals.

10. **Cause and Effect** What is an effect of China's rapid industrialization?

    Possible answer: Because China has industrialized so quickly, it has not made the necessary efforts to protect the country from pollution. This has caused serious environmental problems in the country.

ADDITIONAL LESSON CONTENT

COLLABORATIVE LEARNING

Mao's Little Red Book

1. Tell students that many Chinese citizens had a copy of *Quotations from Chairman Mao* during his rule. The "Little Red Book" was a guide to life as a loyal Communist.
2. Organize students into small groups. Distribute copies of several quotations from Mao's Little Red Book to each group. Ask groups to discuss their assigned quotations, marking wording that reflects any sort of bias. Have students record the observations expressed by group members about each quotation.
3. Have groups share their results with the class.
4. As homework, have students write a paragraph summarizing Mao Zedong's ideas.

Print Assessment

Key Terms and People

For each term or name below, write a sentence explaining its connection to the democratic movements that took place from 1945 to the present.

1. PRI
2. apartheid
3. Nelson Mandela
4. Mikhail Gorbachev
5. glasnost
6. Lech Walesa
7. Deng Xiaoping
8. Tiananmen Square

Explanations of the lesson's key terms can be found on the following pages: PRI, p. 1220; apartheid, p. 1231; Nelson Mandela, p. 1231; Mikhail Gorbachev, p. 1235; glasnost, p. 1236; Lech Walesa, p. 1243; Deng Xiaoping, p. 1254; Tiananmen Square, p. 1255.

Main Ideas

Use your notes and the information in the module to answer the following questions.

Democracy

1. What are four common democratic practices? *free elections, citizen participation, majority rule, constitutional government*
2. What group held up democratic progress in both Brazil and Argentina until the 1980s? *the military*

The Challenge of Democracy in Africa

3. What brought about the civil war in Nigeria? *Ethnic conflict between the Igbo on one side and the Hausa-Fulani and Yoruba on the other led the Igbo region to secede. The government went to war to reunify the country.*
4. What were three significant steps toward democracy taken by South Africa in the 1990s? *legalization of the ANC, holding of all-race (universal) elections, writing of a new constitution and bill of rights*

The Collapse of the Soviet Union

5. What were the main reforms promoted by Soviet leader Mikhail Gorbachev? *glasnost, perestroika, democratization*
6. What was the August Coup, and how did it end? *an attempt in 1991 by hardline communists to force Gorbachev to resign and to undo his reforms; failed because the people would not go along with it*

Changes in Central and Eastern Europe

7. Which nations overthrew communist governments in 1989? *Poland, Hungary, East Germany, Czechoslovakia, and Romania*
8. What led to the breakup of Yugoslavia? *The loss of Tito's leadership allowed ethnic conflicts to rise to the surface; when Serbia tried to dominate the other republics, several of them declared independence.*

Module 31 Assessment

Key Terms and People

For each term or name below, write a sentence explaining its connection to the democratic movements that took place from 1945 to the present.

1. PRI
2. apartheid
3. Nelson Mandela
4. Mikhail Gorbachev
5. glasnost
6. Lech Walesa
7. Deng Xiaoping
8. Tiananmen Square

Main Ideas

Use your notes and the information in the module to answer the following questions.

Democracy

1. What are four common democratic practices?
2. What group held up democratic progress in both Brazil and Argentina until the 1980s?

The Challenge of Democracy in Africa

3. What brought about the civil war in Nigeria?
4. What were three significant steps toward democracy taken by South Africa in the 1990s?

The Collapse of the Soviet Union

5. What were the main reforms promoted by Soviet leader Mikhail Gorbachev?
6. What was the August Coup, and how did it end?

Changes in Central and Eastern Europe

7. Which nations overthrew Communist governments in 1989?
8. What led to the breakup of Yugoslavia?

China: Reform and Reaction

9. What changes took place in China during the 1970s?
10. How did the Chinese government react to demands for democratic reform?

1262 Module 31

ONLINE DOCUMENT-BASED INVESTIGATION

Struggles for Democracy

Have students complete and review all the DBI activities in **Part 1**.

Use this Informative/Explanatory Essay Rubric to score students' work in **Part 2**.

RUBRIC Students' essays should

- focus on the topic and support it with explanations and facts
- present information logically, clearly, and accurately
- cite at least three sources of relevant, informative text evidence from Part 1 in support of their topic
- be organized into a distinct introduction, a main body consisting of several paragraphs, and a conclusion that sums up the main points

Write an Explanatory Essay The struggle for democracy has spawned human rights movements in many countries as people demand more rights and freedoms. What reasons did people have for taking part in protests in China, Latin America, Africa, and the former Soviet Union? What kinds of changes did these movements create? Write an essay in which you explain the causes and effects of the human rights movements you have learned about. Be sure to cite specific evidence from at least three sources in your response.

Module 31 Assessment, continued

Critical Thinking

1. **Evaluate** List several leaders who helped their nations make democratic progress. For each, cite one positive action.
2. **Analyze Issues** What are some examples from this chapter in which the negative impact of one culture on another blocked democratic progress?
3. **Synthesize** Consider what conditions helped democratic movements succeed and what conditions caused difficulties for them. What do you think were their hardest challenges?
4. **Draw Conclusions** How does a nation's economy affect its democratic progress?
5. **Summarize** It has been said that Gorbachev's reforms led to another Russian Revolution. In your opinion, what did this revolution overthrow? Support your opinion in a two-paragraph essay.
6. **Compare** Choose a revolutionary or independence movement you have read about in this module. Compare and contrast the movement with a revolutionary or independence movement from a previous era. What were people trying to achieve in each movement? Were they successful?

Engage with History

A government official has asked you to evaluate the following three systems: free market capitalism, communism, and socialism. Go through the module and gather information to create a chart comparing the three systems. Then, compile a report to recommend which system you think is the most successful. Consider the following issues:

- unemployment
- inflation
- political effects
- social upheaval

Focus on Writing

Working in small teams, write biographies of South African leaders who were instrumental in the revolutionary overturn of apartheid. Use at least one existing biography and one newspaper article in your research. Include a brief critique of each source's accuracy before writing your own biography.

Multimedia Activity

With two other classmates, plan a two-week virtual field trip to explore the sights in China, including the Forbidden City and the sites of the 2008 Summer Olympics. After selecting and researching the sites you'd like to visit, use maps to determine your itinerary. Consider visiting the following places and enjoying these excursions:

- sites of the 2008 Summer Olympic Games
- sites around Beijing
- Great Wall
- a cruise along the Chang Jiang or Huang He Rivers
- Three Gorges Dam
- Shanghai

For each place or excursion, give one reason why it is an important destination on a field trip to China. Include pictures and sound in your presentation.

Essential Question ESSAY

Have the attempts at democracy in China and nations in Latin America, Africa, and the former Soviet bloc been worthwhile?

RUBRIC Students' essays should

- respond to the Essential Question with a specific position
- illustrate valid reasoning supporting their position
- cite persuasive evidence supporting their position
- identify key people, events, and/or turning points that demonstrate understanding of the module content
- be organized into a distinct introduction, main body, and conclusion

Write an argument answering this question. Your essay should include key people, events, and progress made in the democratization of the countries you studied. Be sure to cite evidence to support your position, and organize your essay into an introduction, body, and conclusion.

Alternative Activity Instead of writing essays, address the Essential Question through activities such as holding debates, creating multimedia presentations, or writing journal entries.

China: Reform and Reaction

9. What changes took place in China during the 1970s? *Zhou Enlai made overtures to the United States, and Deng Xiaoping initiated economic reforms.*
10. How did the Chinese government react to demands for democratic reform? *It massacred demonstrators in Tiananmen Square, publicly lied about what had happened, and continued to repress the prodemocracy movement.*

Critical Thinking

1. **Evaluate** List several leaders who helped their nations make democratic progress. For each, cite one positive action. *Raúl Alfonsín—reformed democracy and economy; Nelson Mandela—protested apartheid and called for economic reform and reconciliation; Mikhail Gorbachev—initiated reforms*
2. **Analyze Issues** What are some examples from this chapter in which the negative impact of one culture on another blocked democratic progress? *The legacy of colonialism hindered democratic progress in Africa; ethnic clashes in Eastern Europe led to civil war.*
3. **Synthesize** Consider what conditions helped democratic movements succeed and what conditions caused difficulties for them. What do you think were their hardest challenges? *Advantages—increasing literacy rates and quality of life, worldwide media; Difficulties—colonial legacy, ethnic and racial conflicts, oppressive governments, centrally controlled economies; Most challenging—ethnic and racial conflicts*
4. **Draw Conclusions** How does a nation's economy affect its democratic progress? *A floundering economy can make political reform difficult. Likewise, political chaos can make it difficult to achieve economic reform.*
5. **Summarize** It has been said that Gorbachev's reforms led to another Russian Revolution. In your opinion, what did this revolution overthrow? Support your opinion in a two-paragraph essay.
   RUBRIC Essays should mention
   - the breakup of the Soviet Union
   - that authoritarian rule was replaced by more democratic practices
   - that conservative communists lost power
6. **Compare** Choose a revolutionary or independence movement you have read about in this module. Compare and contrast the movement with a revolutionary or independence movement from a previous era. What were people trying to achieve in each movement? Were they successful? *Possible answer: American Civil War and Nigerian Civil War. In both wars, one region of the country tried to break away and form an independent nation. Neither was successful. Differences: very different reasons for secession; the U.S. South was not as badly devastated as Biafra.*

(continued)

Print Assessment *(continued)*

Engage with History

A government official has asked you to evaluate the following three systems: free market capitalism, communism, and socialism. Go through the module and gather information to create a chart comparing the three systems. Then compile a report to recommend which system you think is the most successful. Consider the following issues:

- unemployment
- inflation
- political effects
- social upheaval

RUBRIC Reports should mention
- the impact of the profit motive on the economy
- the importance of foreign investment
- the relationship among economics, politics, and human rights

Focus on Writing

Working in small teams, write biographies of South African leaders who were instrumental in the revolutionary overturn of apartheid. Use at least one existing biography and one newspaper article in your research. Include a brief critique of each source's accuracy before writing your own biography.

RUBRIC Biographies should
- describe important events in a person's life
- explain how the person helped overturn apartheid

Multimedia Activity

With two other classmates, plan a two-week virtual field trip to explore the sights in China, including the Forbidden City and the sites of the 2008 Summer Olympics. After selecting and researching the sites you'd like to visit, use maps to determine your itinerary. Consider visiting the following places and enjoying these excursions:

- sites of the 2008 Summer Olympic Games
- sites around Beijing
- Great Wall
- a cruise along the Chang Jiang or Huang He rivers
- Three Gorges Dam
- Shanghai

For each place or excursion, give one reason why it is an important destination on a field trip to China. Include pictures and sound in your presentation.

RUBRIC Virtual field trips should
- list a number of interesting sites to visit
- provide informative details about each site
- give persuasive reasons for visiting each destination
- include relevant pictures and sound

Online Assessment

1. *Select the correct button in the table to show whether each statement is true or false about General Augusto Pinochet and his rule of Chile.*

	True	False
He wrote a new constitution.	○	●
He encouraged freedom of the press.	○	●
He eliminated the country's legislature.	●	○
He turned the country into a one-party state.	●	○

2. Why did the generals step down from power in Argentina in 1982?
   - ○ They were sent into exile with Juan Perón.
   - ○ They allowed foreign countries to own state lands.
   - ● They were disgraced after losing in the Falkland Islands war.
   - ○ They could not secure funding from the International Monetary Fund.

3. *Select the correct button in the table to show whether each statement is true or false about Guatemala.*

	True	False
All of Guatemala's residents live in poverty.	○	●
President Jimmy Carter ended U.S. aid to Guatemala in 1977.	●	○
The death toll in Guatemala's civil war continued to rise in the 1980s.	●	○
Great progress has been made to bring human rights violators to justice in Guatemala.	○	●

4. *Drag each statement into the correct column in the table to show whether it is associated with Olusegun Obasanjo, Umaru Yar'Adua, or both.*

Olusegun Obasanjo	Umaru Yar'Adua	Both
He tried to draw global attention to Nigeria's need for debt relief.	He was mentored by the previous leader.	He faced problems with war, violence, corruption, poverty, pollution, and hunger.
He was the first civilian president in 20 years.	He suffered from health problems and died while in office.	

5. *Select the correct button in the table to show whether each statement is true or false about apartheid.*

	True	False
This policy resulted in the formation of the American National Congress.	●	○
This policy required that blacks live on homelands, or reserves.	●	○
This policy desegregated schools, hospitals, and neighborhoods.	○	●
This policy was enacted by the minority and imposed on the majority.	●	○

6. *Drag the name of the individual into the box next to the correct description of his contribution to South Africa.*

African National Congress leader who was the first president elected in a universal election	●	Nelson Mandela
South African bishop who led an economic campaign against apartheid	●	Desmond Tutu
President of South Africa who agreed to hold South Africa's first universal elections	●	F. W. de Klerk
South African president who promoted a free-market economic policy	●	Thabo Mbeki

7. *Select the correct button in the table to show whether each statement about Gorbachev is true or false.*

	True	False
Gorbachev was considered youthful when he became the Soviet leader.	●	○
Gorbachev ruled very differently than any of the Soviet leaders before him.	●	○
Gorbachev saw that a lack of ideas in society created a country that was stagnated.	●	○
Gorbachev was chosen directly by the people as the Communist Party's general secretary.	○	●

8. What action by Ronald Reagan caused Mikhail Gorbachev to seek an arms control agreement between the two nations?
   - ○ Reagan expressed strong anti-Soviet views.
   - ○ Reagan called the Soviet Union an "evil empire."
   - ○ Reagan signed the Intermediate-Range Nuclear Forces (INF) Treaty.
   - ● Reagan began the most expensive military buildup in U.S. peacetime history.

9. *Select the correct button in the table to show whether each statement is true or false about Russia after the collapse of the Soviet Union.*

	True	False
Russia has since had at least two presidents.	●	○
Russia's political system was united in purpose.	○	●
Russia strengthened its ties with China and India.	●	○
Russia easily transformed into a free-market economy.	○	●

10. *Drag each statement into the correct column in the table to show whether it is associated with Poland, Hungary, or both.*

Poland	Hungary	Both
Workers at a shipyard in this country went on strike to demand that the Soviet Union recognize their labor union.	In 1994, the Socialist Party and the Free Democrats in this country formed a ruling coalition.	In 1999, this country became a member of NATO.
This country was supportive of the United States after the September 11, 2001, terrorist attack.	This country adopted a constitution that many critics have characterized as reflecting conservative Christian values.	

11. *Select the correct button in the table to show whether each statement is true or false about Germany after the fall of the Berlin Wall.*

	True	False
East Germany was still in ruins from World War II.	●	○
Foreign nations were at first leery of a reunified Germany.	●	○
Many factories in West Germany closed due to inefficiency.	○	●
Taxes were raised throughout Germany to pay for the rebuilding of East Germany.	●	○

12. *Select the correct button in the table to show whether each statement is true or false.*

	True	False
Serbian military forces in Bosnia engaged in ethnic cleansing.	●	○
Slovenia and Croatia each won their independence by means of war.	●	○
Many Serbs opposed Slobodan Milosevic and his policies.	●	○
Bosnia's Muslims and Croats were opposed to independence.	○	●

13. What event started a new era for Chinese–American relations?
   - ○ Mao made a visit to the United States.
   - ○ Deng decided to embrace the Four Modernizations.
   - ● Zhou invited an American table-tennis team to tour China.
   - ○ Deng eliminated Mao's communes and leased land to individual farmers.

14. *Select the correct button in the table to show whether each statement is true or false about the Tiananmen Square protests in 1989.*

	True	False
Protesters wanted Deng Xiaoping to resign.	●	○
The troops built a statue called the "Goddess of Liberty."	○	●
Students stole tanks and crashed them into the military.	○	●
Deng declared martial law and sent troops into Tiananmen Square.	●	○
Students began occupying the square in April to demand democracy.	●	○

15. What did protesters in the United States demand when Jiang Zemin visited in 1997?
   - ● more democracy for China
   - ○ higher wages for Chinese workers
   - ○ fewer restrictions on Chinese exports
   - ○ better policies for immigrants from China

Essential Question Preview

Do the benefits of globalization outweigh the problems it causes?
Have students consider the Essential Question and capture their initial responses.

Explore the Essential Question

- Tell students that advances in communication technologies have made the world seem much smaller in the last 30 years.
- Discuss with students what could be some of the downsides of a smaller, more interdependent world.

Help students plan inquiries and develop their own supporting questions, such as

How have advances in science and technology made the world more globally interdependent and affected people's lives?

How has increased globalization affected security and the environment?

You may want to assign students to write a short essay in response to the Essential Question when they complete the module. Encourage students to use their notes and responses to inform their essays.

Explore the Video

ANALYZE VIDEOS

Renewable Energy
Invite students to watch the video to learn about the world's need for new energy sources and alternatives to fossil fuels.

Analyze Videos What factors make working with the marine environment challenging? *Corrosion, the constant movement of the ocean causes infrastructure to bang around, and the high cost to repair parts in the ocean*

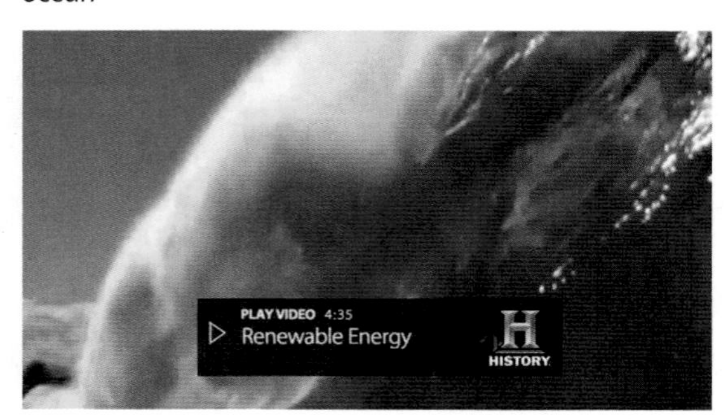

Module 32

Global Interdependence

Essential Question
Do the benefits of globalization outweigh the problems it causes?

About the Photo: This photo taken from the Old City in Shanghai features one of the tallest buildings in the world (Shanghai Tower) and reflects the changes seen in China as the world grew increasingly interconnected.

Explore ONLINE!

VIDEOS, including...
- A World Without Oil
- Battle for Baghdad
- History of Terrorism
- 100 Years of Terror
- A World Without Water

- Document Based Investigations
- Graphic Organizers
- Interactive Games
- Image Compare: Evolution of Computers
- Carousel: The Reality of War: Ethnic and Religious Conflicts

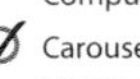

In this module, you will learn how technology, economics, and diplomacy have helped make the world a more interconnected place.

What You Will Learn ...

1264 Module 32

Lesson 1 Big Idea

Advances in technology after World War II led to increased global interaction and improved quality of life.

Why It Matters Now

Advances in science and technology affect the lives of people around the world.

Lesson 2 Big Idea

The economies of the world's nations are so tightly linked that the actions of one nation affect others.

Why It Matters Now

Every individual is affected by the global economy and the environment.

Lesson 3 Big Idea

Since 1945, nations have used collective security efforts to solve problems.

Why It Matters Now

Personal security of the people of the world is tied to security within and between nations.

Lesson 4 Big Idea

Terrorism threatens the safety of people all over the world.

Why It Matters Now

People and nations must work together against the dangers posed by terrorism.

Timeline of Events 1960–2015

Explore ONLINE!

World

1960

< 1968 Many nations sign the Nuclear Non-Proliferation Treaty.

1972 Terrorists carry out attack at the Summer Olympic games in Munich. >

1975 Helsinki Accords support human rights.

1981 U.S. carries out first space shuttle flight. >

1983 French research scientists isolate the AIDS virus.

1986 Accident takes place at Soviet nuclear power plant in Chernobyl.

1995 World Trade Organization is set up.

2001 UN issues the Declaration of Commitment on HIV/AIDS. Terrorists launch attacks in New York and Washington, D.C.

< 2003 Human Genome Project is completed.

2007 NASA space shuttle makes 23rd mission to International Space Station.

2010 British Petroleum drilling rig explodes in the Gulf of Mexico.

2011 Syrian civil war begins.

2013 Malaria epidemic kills 584,000 people in Sub-Saharan Africa.

2014 An outbreak of Ebola virus, the largest in history, begins to spread through western Africa. >

2015 The number of Syrian refugees surges to about 9 million since February 2011.

2015

Lesson 5 Big Idea

Technology, population growth, and industrialization have created environmental challenges that affect the entire world.

Why It Matters Now

Failure to solve environmental problems will threaten the health of the planet.

Lesson 6 Big Idea

Technology has increased contact among the world's people, changing their cultures.

Why It Matters Now

Globalization of culture has changed the ways people live, their perceptions, and their interactions.

Explore the Timeline

Interpret Timelines: A Connected World

Have students examine the timeline and then answer the following question:

Analyze Timelines Identify two events that show how technology contributed to building a globally interconnected world. *creation of the International Space Station, completion of the Human Genome Project*

Interpret Timeline of Events : A Connected World

To further explore the timeline, have students discuss the following questions:

1. Ask students to name an event that marks a major step toward a global economy. *Possible answer: 1995—World Trade Organization is set up.*
2. Ask students to identify an event that had a negative impact on the environment. *1986—accident at Soviet nuclear power plant in Chernobyl*

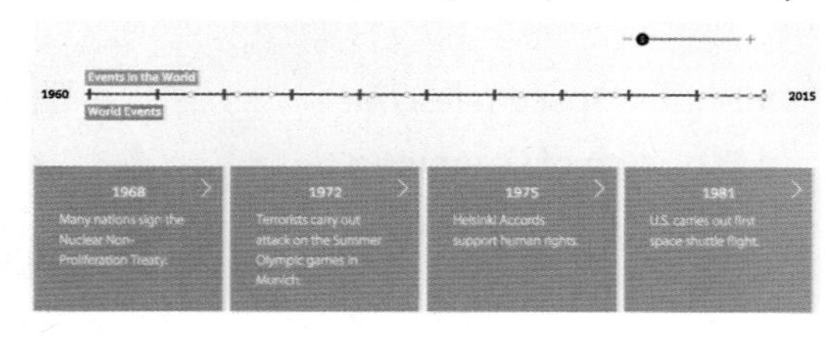

Online Module Flip Cards

Use the flip cards as a whole class activity or in student pairs to preview the module's key terms and people. Students can guess the meaning of each word and then review its definition, or do the reverse, using the flip card's toggle button to switch from Term to Definition mode. Students can also use the flip cards at the end of the module as a review tool before taking the Module Assessment.

Online Sequencing Activity

Students can use this sequencing activity to review the chronology of events in the Global Interdependence module. To complete, have students drag each event to the correct year on the timeline.

Year	Event
1968	*Many nations sign the Nuclear Non-Proliferation Treaty.*
1972	*U.S. and Soviet Union agree to joint space venture. Terrorists carry out attack on the Summer Olympic games in Munich.*
1983	*French research scientists isolate the AIDS virus.*
1995	*World Trade Organization is set up.*
2014	*An outbreak of Ebola virus, the largest in history, begins to spread through western Africa.*
2015	*The number of Syrian refugees surges to about 9 million since 2011 when its civil war began.*

Lesson 1 Planner

Science and Technology Transform Life

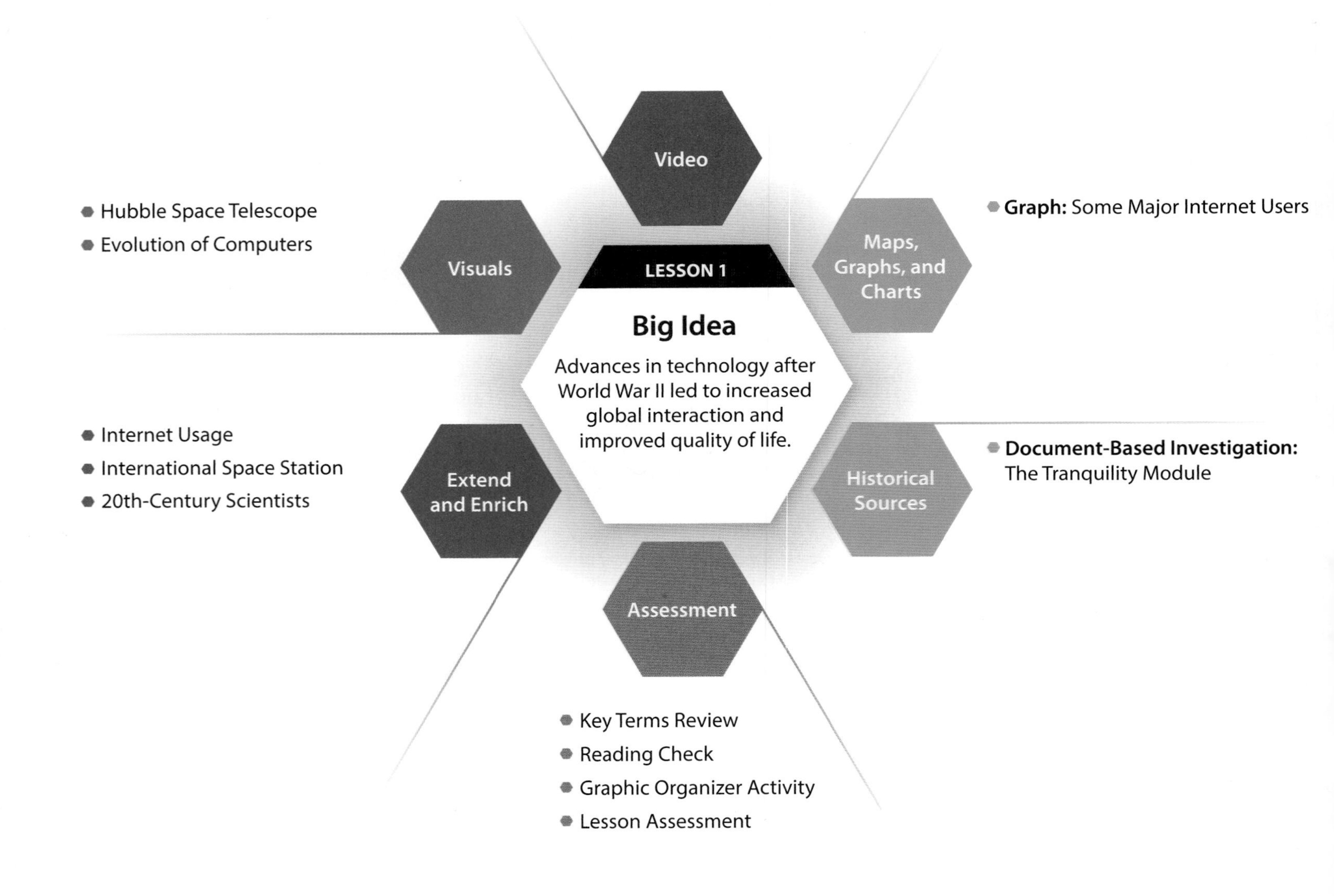

Visuals:
- Hubble Space Telescope
- Evolution of Computers

Maps, Graphs, and Charts:
- **Graph:** Some Major Internet Users

Extend and Enrich:
- Internet Usage
- International Space Station
- 20th-Century Scientists

Historical Sources:
- **Document-Based Investigation:** The Tranquility Module

Assessment:
- Key Terms Review
- Reading Check
- Graphic Organizer Activity
- Lesson Assessment

Online Lesson 1 Enrichment Activities

Internet Usage

Graph Students create a graph showing the most common Internet activities. First, students choose a specific population and activity type to research. Then they create the graph, including a brief written summary that draws a conclusion from the data.

International Space Station

Infographic Students create an infographic about the International Space Station. They research questions about the ISS that interest them and use a digital tool to create the final product.

20th-Century Scientists

Presentation Students create a presentation about the 20th-century scientists Jonas Salk, James Watson, and Francis Crick. In their presentation, students introduce the contributions of each scientist, describe the effects of their discoveries on the world's population, and explain how scientists today continue to build on their discoveries.

Teach the Big Idea

1. **Whole Class Open/Introduction** Discuss ways in which students communicate that have been made possible by advances in technology. *Possible answers: texting, instant messaging, apps, e-mail, cell phones*
2. **Direct Teach** Read students the Big Idea: *Advances in technology after World War II led to increased global interaction and improved quality of life.* Review the following lesson objectives with students to aid in their understanding of the Big Idea.
   - Trace the exploration of outer space.
   - Identify effects of expanding global communications.
   - Evaluate effects of advances in health care, medicine, and agriculture.
3. **Whole Group Close/Reflect** Have students select the scientific or technological breakthrough discussed in the lesson that they feel is the most significant. Then tell them to write a paragraph explaining their choice, using examples of how that breakthrough has affected their own lives.

ONLINE DOCUMENT-BASED INVESTIGATION

Global Interdependence

The Tranquility Module is the first of six document-based investigations that students will analyze in the Global Interdependence module. After the crew of the space shuttle *Endeavour* delivered Tranquility to the space station in 2010, President Obama spoke with the crew. Invite students to read the excerpt and answer the associated question.

ONLINE GRAPHIC ORGANIZER

Science and Technology Transform Life

As students read the lesson, have them use the graphic organizer to take notes. Students can review their graphic organizer notes at the end of the lesson to answer the following question:

Form Opinions Which scientific or technological development had the most impact on the lives of people? *The advances in the green revolution reduced hunger around the world and helped people live longer, healthier lives.*

Lesson 1

Science and Technology Transform Life

The Big Idea

Advances in technology after World War II led to increased global interaction and improved quality of life.

Why It Matters Now

Advances in science and technology affect the lives of people around the world.

Key Terms and People

International Space Station
Internet
genetic engineering
cloning
green revolution

Setting the Stage

Beginning in the late 1950s, the United States and the Soviet Union competed in the exploration of space. The Soviets launched Earth's first artificial satellite and put the first human in orbit around the planet. By the late 1960s, however, the United States had surpassed the Soviets. U.S. astronauts landed on the moon in 1969. The heavy emphasis on science and technology that the space race required led to the development of products that changed life for people across the globe.

Exploring the Solar System and Beyond

In its early years, competition between the United States and the Soviet Union in the space race was intense. Eventually, however, space exploration became one of the world's first and most successful arenas for cooperation between U.S. and Soviet scientists.

This grand design spiral galaxy can be found about twelve million light-years away in the Ursa Major constellation.

Cooperation in Space In 1972, years before the end of the Cold War, the U.S. and Soviet space programs began work on a cooperative project—the docking of U.S. and Soviet spacecraft in orbit. This goal was achieved on July 17, 1975, when spacecraft from the two countries docked some 140 miles above Earth. Television viewers across the globe watched as the hatch between the space vehicles opened and crews from the rival countries greeted each other.

This first cooperative venture in space between the United States and the Soviet Union was an isolated event. People from different countries, however, continued to work together to explore space. The Soviets were the first to send an international crew into space. The crew of *Soyuz 28*, which orbited Earth in 1978, included a Czech cosmonaut. Since the mid-1980s, crews on U.S. space missions have included astronauts from Saudi Arabia, France, Germany, Canada, Italy, Japan, Israel, and Mexico.

COLLABORATIVE LEARNING

Debate the Pros and Cons of Technology

1. Divide the class into groups of four. Have each group choose one of the following statements:
   - New technologies lead to new problems.
   - Someday computers will control humans.
   - New methods of identification will lead to a "police state" where the government monitors everything and everyone.
   - Internet-based communities are not as worthwhile as more traditional communities.
   - People who oppose technology are just afraid of what they don't yet understand.
   - Technology and mass media have led to a new and better global culture.
   - Technology and traditional ways of life can coexist peacefully.
2. Two members of each group should work together to develop arguments in favor of the statement. The other two members should develop arguments against it. Arguments should be based on the text and on students' knowledge or research.
3. When groups have finished, have them debate their question. Poll the class about which side was more effective, and which specific arguments or debate techniques made the difference.

The **International Space Station** (ISS) project came together in 1993 when the United States and Russia agreed to merge their individual space station programs. The European Space Agency (ESA) and Japan also became part of the effort. Beginning in 1998, U.S. shuttles and Russian spacecraft transported sections of the ISS to be assembled in space. In 2011, the ISS was completed, covering an area larger than a six-bedroom home and four times larger than *Mir*, the Russian Space Station. It weighs almost one million pounds. Ongoing experiments aboard the ISS helped lead to advances in medicine and technology and have allowed scientists to study the long-term effects of weightlessness on the human body.

Space Exploration The U.S. space shuttle program began in 1981 with the launch of *Columbia*. Over the next 30 years, space shuttles hosted great numbers of scientific experiments in orbit around Earth and deployed satellites from their enormous cargo bays. The space shuttle program ended on July 21, 2011, when the shuttle *Atlantis* landed at the Kennedy Space Center in Florida.

In 1990, the United States' National Aeronautics and Space Administration (NASA) and the ESA developed and launched the Hubble Space Telescope. More than 20 years later, this orbiting telescope continues

DOCUMENT-BASED INVESTIGATION Historical Source

The Tranquility Module

In February, 2010, the crew of the space shuttle *Endeavor* delivered Tranquility, one of the last pieces of the space station. To mark the occasion, President Obama hosted a video conference with the crew of the shuttle and of the ISS.

> THE PRESIDENT: "*. . .The amazing work that's being done on the International Space Station not only by our American astronauts but also our colleagues from Japan and Russia is just a testimony to the human ingenuity; a testimony to extraordinary skill and courage . . . ; and is also a testimony to why continued space exploration is so important. . . . I wanted you guys to maybe let us know what this new Tranquility Module will help you accomplish. . . .*
> COMMANDER WILLIAMS: *. . . The Tranquility Module . . . is going to serve as a gym, as a hygiene area, as a place a crew can maintain themselves for a long duration. And a long duration living and working in space is what the Space Station is all about—to do the research and the science necessary to take us beyond Earth orbit. That was the ultimate purpose of the Space Station, and the arrival of this module will enable us to do that.*"
>
> —from Remarks by the President in Conversation with the ISS Crew and the Space Shuttle *Endeavor* Crew, February 10, 2010

Analyze Historical Sources
What common goals are the Americans and their Japanese and Russian colleagues working toward on the ISS?

STRUGGLING READERS

Dramatize Space Travel

1. Divide the class into five groups. Each will research space exploration during a particular period: 1950–1967, 1968–1978, 1979–1989, 1990–2000, and 2001–present. Mix students of varying reading abilities in each group.
2. Have students use library and Internet resources to gather firsthand and eyewitness reports of space travel events such as the first walk on the moon in 1969 and the explosion of the space shuttle *Challenger* in 1986.
3. After each group collects two or three accounts, have the groups meet as a class. Select one account from each group and decide in which order to present the accounts.
4. Then ask each group to prepare its own skit or dramatic reading and present it to the class.

Objectives

You may wish to discuss the following questions with students to help them frame the content as they read.

- Why did the crash of the shuttle *Columbia* adversely affect the International Space Station? *Possible answer: Safety questions put the shuttle program on hold; the shuttle transports people and supplies to the ISS.*
- Why are unmanned space probes used for certain kinds of space exploration? *Possible answer: Risks and length of journeys rule out astronauts.*

More About . . .

Moon Colonies The prospect of humans living in colonies on the moon in the not-too-distant future is not so far-fetched in some scientists' minds. Darby Dyer, an astronomer at the Solar System Exploration Research Virtual Institute at Mount Holyoke College, hopes humans will set up a permanent station on the moon in her lifetime. She is studying one of the biggest obstacles to settling on the moon: how to get water. Some possibilities for getting water include extracting it from minerals or obtaining it from comets that crashed on the moon, trapping ice.

ONLINE DOCUMENT-BASED INVESTIGATION

The Tranquility Module

In February 2010, the crew of the space shuttle *Endeavour* delivered Tranquility, one of the last pieces of the space station. To mark the occasion, President Obama hosted a video conference with the crew of the shuttle and of the ISS. Invite students to read the excerpt and answer the associated question.

Analyze Sources What common goals are the Americans and their Japanese and Russian colleagues working toward on the ISS? *They are doing research to learn how humans can eventually travel or live beyond Earth's orbit.*

ONLINE INTERACTIVE VISUALS

Carousel: Hubble Space Telescope

Have students navigate through the carousel and note similarities and differences among the images or identify a unifying theme.

ONLINE LESSON FLIP CHARTS

Review Key Terms and People

Students can use the flip cards in the Lesson Review at any time to review the lesson's key terms and people: *International Space Station, Internet, genetic engineering, cloning,* and *green revolution.*

Objectives

You may wish to discuss the following questions with students to help them frame the content as they read.

- Why does the phrase *global village* describe the results of satellite communication? *Possible answer: Events all over the world can be experienced with the same immediacy of events in one's neighborhood.*
- What power have individuals gained from the miniaturization of computers? *Possible answer: Knowledge once available only to computer experts is available to ordinary people.*

More About . . .

Computer Chips Silicon is used in the making of computer chips because it can be made to conduct electricity at room temperature. The chips that tell computers and other electronic devices what to do are microprocessors. They were first used in desktop calculators in 1971.

Tip for English Language Learners Explain that the word *telecommute* contains the prefix *tele-*, which means "distance" or "far off." Ask students to name other words with this prefix. *Possible answers: telephone, television, telescope.*

READING CHECK

Analyze Motives Why might rival nations cooperate in space activities but not on Earth? *The great expense can be shared. Scientists, not politicians, plan the activities.*

ONLINE INTERACTIVE VISUALS

Carousel: Evolution of Computers

Have students navigate through the carousel and note similarities and differences among the images or identify a unifying theme. You may wish to use the associated question as a discussion prompt.

Analyze Visuals How have computers improved over the years? *They have become smaller and unlike the first computer, they are multipurpose.*

This view of the ISS was taken from the space shuttle *Endeavor*.

to record and send back images of objects many millions of light-years from Earth.

Other NASA programs focus on neighbors in Earth's solar system. In 2004, NASA successfully landed two robotic rovers on Mars. Their mission was to study the planet for signs of water or life (now or in the past). Both rovers, *Spirit* and *Opportunity*, found evidence of water in Mars's past. *Spirit* stopped operating in 2010, while *Opportunity* continues to explore Mars, taking panoramic images. In September 2015, NASA announced that a satellite orbiting Mars found evidence that liquid water exists on Mars under certain conditions. In July 2015, NASA made history when *New Horizons*, a U.S. space probe, flew by Pluto and one of its moons. This was the first time that a space probe had flown by Pluto.

Reading Check **Analyze Motives** Why might rival nations cooperate in space activities but not on Earth?

Expanding Global Communications

Since the 1960s, artificial satellites launched into orbit around Earth have aided worldwide communications. With satellite communication, the world has been transformed into a global village. Today, political and cultural events occurring in one part of the world often are witnessed live by people thousands of miles away. This linking of the globe through worldwide communications is made possible by the miniaturization of the computer.

Smaller, More Powerful Computers In the 1940s, when computers first came into use, they took up a huge room. In the years since then, however, the circuitry that runs the computer has become smaller and more powerful. By the late 1950s, the much smaller transistor had replaced the bulky vacuum tubes used earlier. Today, tiny silicon chips, also called microchips, can contain a billion or more transistors, and that number doubles about every two years.

Tablet computer users have books, newspapers, music, games, and movies at their fingertips.

In light of these developments, industries began to use computers and silicon chips to run assembly lines. Today a variety of consumer products such as microwave ovens, keyboard instruments, smartphones, household thermostats, and cars use computers and chips. Computers have become essential in many industries, and millions of people around the globe have computers in their homes.

Communications Networks Starting in the 1990s, businesses and individuals began using a worldwide network of linked computers known as the **Internet**. The Internet is a voluntary network that began in the late 1960s as a method of linking scientists so they could exchange information about research. Through wired or wireless links, business

STRUGGLING READERS

Summarize the Effects of New Technologies

1. Have pairs of students review the technologies discussed in the text, helping each other with difficult words and concepts.
2. When students have finished, draw the outlines of a concept web on the board.
3. As a class, complete the web so that it summarizes the information in the text as well as students' additional ideas. Explain that a concept web can be a useful way to take notes. *Possible concept web: Central bubble: Computers changed the world. Secondary bubbles: Business > rockets, airplanes, cars, banks; Communication > smartphones, social media, internet*

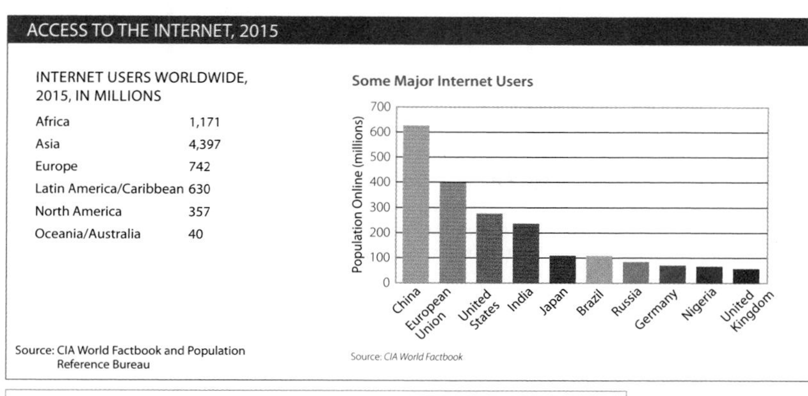

ACCESS TO THE INTERNET, 2015

INTERNET USERS WORLDWIDE, 2015, IN MILLIONS

Africa	1,171
Asia	4,397
Europe	742
Latin America/Caribbean	630
North America	357
Oceania/Australia	40

Source: CIA World Factbook and Population Reference Bureau

Interpret Visuals

1. **Compare** In which world region do most Internet users live?
2. **Draw Conclusions** How would you describe most of the nations with large percentages of their populations online?

and personal computers can connect to these computer networks. These networks allow users to communicate with people across the nation and around the world. The rapid exchange of information over these networks has become so integral to economic activity that this period of human history has come to be known as the Information Age. Between 2000 and the end of 2015, the number of worldwide Internet users soared from 394 million to more than 3 billion.

Conducting business on the Internet has become a way of life, and the Internet has increased personal and business electronic communications to create a global culture. Because it transmits information electronically to remote locations, the Internet paved the way for home offices and telecommuting—working at home using a computer connected to a business network. Once again, as it has many times in the past, technology has changed how and where people work.

It has also changed how people live, affecting not only traditional cultures but also people's values. The ability for one culture to connect electronically with another culture enables cultures to influence one another more easily and rapidly than ever before. This influence can be positive or negative depending on how different cultural values and traditions are perceived and adopted among cultures.

The Internet has also changed social interactions. Social networks allow users to connect with people with similar interests or backgrounds regardless of geographic locations. Social networking services allow people to communicate their ideas, pictures, posts, events, and interests with others in their network.

Reading Check
Summarize What types of technology have recently changed the workplace?

ONLINE INTERACTIVE GRAPHS

Some Major Internet Users

Have students explore the graph and answer the associated questions.

Interpret Which of the following countries has the most Internet users? *Australia*

In print edition, see graph titled Access to the Internet, 2015.

Compare In which world region do most Internet users live? *Asia and the Pacific*

Draw Conclusions How would you describe most of the nations with large percentages of their populations online? *developed nations*

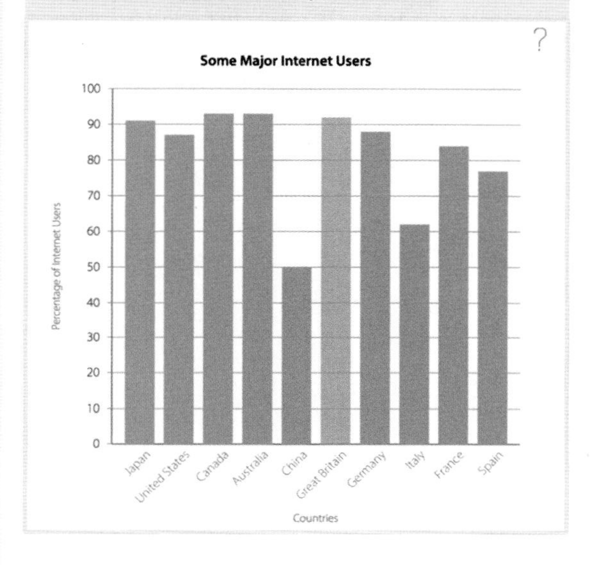

READING CHECK

Summarize What types of technology have recently changed the workplace? *computers, fax machines, Internet*

Global Interdependence 1269

Objectives

You may wish to discuss the following questions with students to help them frame the content as they read.

- How do new medical imaging techniques relate to the need for surgery? *Possible answer: Doctors are able to see inside the body without having to do as much exploratory surgery.*
- In what way was the green revolution not green? *Possible answer: Pesticides and fertilizers are not generally environmentally friendly.*

More About . . .

Green Revolution and the World The green revolution set out to eliminate hunger and famine by developing heartier or more productive varieties of crops. By the 1990s, 75 percent of Asian rice fields were planted with new varieties of rice, and almost 50 percent of the wheat in Africa also consisted of new varieties.

Transforming Human Life

Advances with computers and communications networks have transformed not only the ways people work but also standards of living. Technological progress in the sciences, medicine, and agriculture has improved the quality of the lives of millions of people, whether making life easier, healthier, or more accessible.

Health and Medicine Before World War II, surgeons seldom performed operations on sensitive areas such as the eye or the brain. However, in the 1960s and 1970s, new technologies, such as more powerful microscopes, the laser, and ultrasound, were developed. Many of these technologies advanced surgical techniques to save lives and improve quality of life for those who suffer from chronic disease.

Advances in medical imaging also helped to improve health care. Using data provided by CAT scans and MRI techniques, doctors can build three-dimensional images of different organs or regions of the body. Doctors use these images to diagnose injuries, detect tumors, or collect other medical information. Advanced imaging with MRIs has helped detect neurological injuries and aided neurological studies.

Mapping the human genome

In the 1980s, genetics, the study of heredity through research on genes, became a fast-growing field of science. Found in the cells of all organisms, genes are hereditary units that cause specific traits, such as eye color, in every living organism. Technology allowed scientists to isolate and examine individual genes that are responsible for different traits. Through **genetic engineering**, scientists were able to modify the traits of an organism by changing its genes.

Another aspect of genetic engineering is **cloning**. This is the creation of identical copies of DNA, the chemical chains of genes that determine heredity. Cloning allows scientists to reproduce both plants and animals that are identical to existing plants and animals. The application of genetics has led to many breakthroughs, especially in agriculture.

The Green Revolution In the 1960s, agricultural scientists around the world started a campaign known as the **green revolution**. It was an attempt to increase food production worldwide. Scientists promoted the use of irrigation, fertilizers, pesticides, and high-yield, disease-resistant strains of a variety of crops. The green revolution helped avert famine, which can be caused by natural disasters, armed conflicts, and overused soil, and increased crop yields in many parts of the world.

However, the green revolution had its negative side. Fertilizers and pesticides often contain dangerous chemicals that may cause cancer and pollute the environment. Also, the cost of the chemicals and the equipment to harvest more crops was far too expensive for an average peasant farmer. Consequently, owners of small farms received little benefit from the advances in agriculture. In some cases, farmers were forced off the land by larger agricultural businesses.

ADVANCED/GIFTED

Prepare a News Report

1. Encourage interested students to do additional research on the Internet or in scientific or medical journals concerning advances in modern medicine. Some possible topics to research include
   - imaging techniques such as MRIs and CAT scans
   - surgical methods such as the use of lasers
   - gene therapy
   - organ transplantation
   - the ongoing search for plants with naturally occurring medicinal properties
2. Suggest that students prepare their information in the form of a television or radio news special that they can share with the class. News specials should include a description of a particular medical advance, examples of practical applications, and a conclusion about the significance of the advance.

SOCIAL HISTORY

Molecular Medicine

In 2003, scientists employed on the Human Genome Project completed work on a map of the thousands of genes contained in human DNA—human genetic material. The information provided by this map has helped in the development of a new field of medicine. Called molecular medicine, it focuses on how genetic diseases develop and progress.

Researchers in molecular medicine are working to identify the genes that cause various diseases. This will help scientists detect diseases in early stages of development and find new ways to treat the diseases. Another area of interest to researchers is gene therapy. This involves using genes to treat disease either by replacing a patient's mutated genes with healthy ones, deactivating a mutated gene, or adding a gene that can fight disease. The ultimate aim of workers in this field is to create customizable drugs based on a person's genetic makeup.

Advances in genetics research seem to be helping to fulfill some of the goals of the green revolution. In this new "gene revolution," resistance to pests is bred into plant strains, reducing the need for pesticides. Plants being bred to tolerate poor soil conditions also reduce the need for fertilizers. The gene revolution involves some risks, including the accidental creation of disease-causing organisms. However, the revolution holds great promise for increasing food production in a world with an expanding population.

Science and technology have changed the lives of millions of people. What people produce and even their jobs have changed. These changes have altered the economies of nations. Not only have nations become linked through communications networks but they are also linked in a global economic network, as you will see in lesson 2.

Reading Check
Analyze Effects
What are some of the positive and negative effects of genetic engineering?

Lesson 1 Assessment

1. **Organize Information** List the effects of changes in communications, health and medicine, and agriculture on the chart. Explain which of the three developments you think has had the greatest global effect.

Developments	Effects
Communications	
Health and Medicine	
Agriculture	

2. **Key Terms and People** For each key term or person in the lesson, write a sentence explaining its significance.
3. **Make Inferences** Why do you think that space exploration became an area of cooperation between the Soviet Union and the United States?
4. **Predict** How do you think the Internet will affect the world of work in the future? Create a graph that shows your prediction.
5. **Form Opinions** How do you think scientific and technological advances have changed the quality of life?

STRUGGLING READERS

Make Persuasive Ads

1. Have students review the information about the green revolution and genetically engineered organisms. Discuss the advantages of and concerns about genetic engineering, and have students take notes during the discussion.
2. Have students create a print advertisement to promote or discredit genetically engineered crops. Ads should carry a distinct message, a slogan, and a brief argument or comment supporting the position stated in the ad.
3. Have students present their advertisements to the class.

Print Assessment

Review Ideas, Terms, and People

1. **Organize Information** List the effects of changes in communications, health and medicine, and agriculture on the chart. Explain which of the three developments you think has had the greatest global effect. *Possible answer: Communications—Worldwide television, home offices and telecommuting; Health and Medicine—Improved diagnoses and surgery, genetic engineering; Agriculture—Increased crop yields, decreased use of pesticides. Greatest global effect—Agriculture, because food production affects everyone.*
2. **Key Terms and People** For each key term or person in the lesson, write a sentence explaining its significance. *Explanations of the lesson's key terms can be found on the following pages: International Space Station, p. 1267; Internet, p. 1268; genetic engineering, cloning, green revolution, p. 1270.*
3. **Make Inferences** Why do you think that space exploration became an area of cooperation between the Soviet Union and the United States? *Possible answer: Both nations saw the advantages of sharing costs and information, pooling resources, and increasing goodwill.*
4. **Predict** How do you think the Internet will affect the world of work in the future? Create a graph that shows your prediction. *Possible answer: More telecommuting will decrease office size and reduce the need for business travel.*
5. **Form Opinions** How do you think scientific and technological advances have changed the quality of life? *Possible answer: People now have access to a lot of information and newer tools that can help and improve their quality of life. Scientific and technological advances also help people with physical or mental challenges.*

READING CHECK

Analyze Effects What are some of the positive and negative effects of genetic engineering? *Positive—more food available, reduced need for fertilizer; negative—potential for accidental creation of disease-causing organisms*

Online **Assessment**

1. Which statement accurately describes American and Russian cooperation on space exploration?
   - ◉ The two countries combined their space station programs.
   - ○ The two countries agreed to jointly develop the space shuttle program.
   - ○ The two countries agreed to financially support their efforts to explore Mars.
   - ○ The two countries shared technology in developing better rockets during the Cold War.

   Alternate Question *Drag the answer choice into the box to complete the sentence correctly.* In the 1990s, the United States, Japan, and the European Space Agency joined Russia in developing the International Space Station to replace Russia's *Mir* space station.

2. Which of the following gives an example of an effect of placing communications satellites in Earth's orbit?
   - ○ It has reduced our dependence on fossil fuels.
   - ○ It has allowed people to travel overseas more quickly.
   - ◉ It has allowed people to view live events on other continents.
   - ○ It has decreased the number of armed conflicts around the world.

   Alternate Question *Drag the answer choice into the box to complete the sentence correctly.* The invention of the microchip allowed more *transistors* to be placed in computing devices, greatly increasing their speed and decreasing their size.

3. How has the use of lasers improved medicine?
   - ○ They have allowed doctors to better diagnose cancer.
   - ○ They have allowed doctors to treat contagious diseases.
   - ◉ They have allowed surgeons to perform sensitive brain surgeries.
   - ○ They have allowed radiologists to better diagnose athletic injuries.

   Alternate Question *Drag the answer choice into the box to complete the sentence correctly.* The invention of new imaging techniques, such as *computerized tomography scans*, has allowed doctors to get a better understanding of the size and density of tumors.

4. **Analyze Information** How has the development of the International Space Station increased our knowledge of living in space?

   Possible answer: The International Space Station (ISS) was created, in part, to conduct scientific experiments in space. By placing people on the ISS for long periods of time, we can understand how weightlessness affects the human body. Since we will have to spend long periods of times in zero gravity if we expect to send manned expeditions to explore our solar system and beyond, this information is vital to understanding how to achieve these goals. Experiments on the ISS have increased our scientific knowledge of living in space and have led to technical and medical advances.

5. **Draw Conclusions** How has the creation of the Internet affected people's lives?

   Possible answer: The Internet began as a project to link scientists' computers to better communicate research findings. In the 1990s, individuals, businesses, universities, governments, and so on began linking their computers together. The Internet has allowed people to exchange information more readily and communicate with each other electronically. It has changed how people conduct business and has made it possible to work from remote locations.

6. **Make Judgments** How has the green revolution negatively impacted agriculture?

   Possible answer: The green revolution has greatly increased the ability to feed millions of people by eliminating pests, creating plants that can better adapt to adverse climate conditions, and improving irrigation. However, by creating pesticides and fertilizers to increase crop yields, farmers have often poisoned the environment and the animals that live in it. Genetic engineering of plants has allowed plants to deal with pests and the unpredictable climate better but has had unseen consequences, such as the creation of disease-causing organisms. In addition, industrial agriculture's use of these new technologies has made it difficult for small-plot farmers to compete economically with larger companies.

Lesson 2 Planner

Global Economic Development

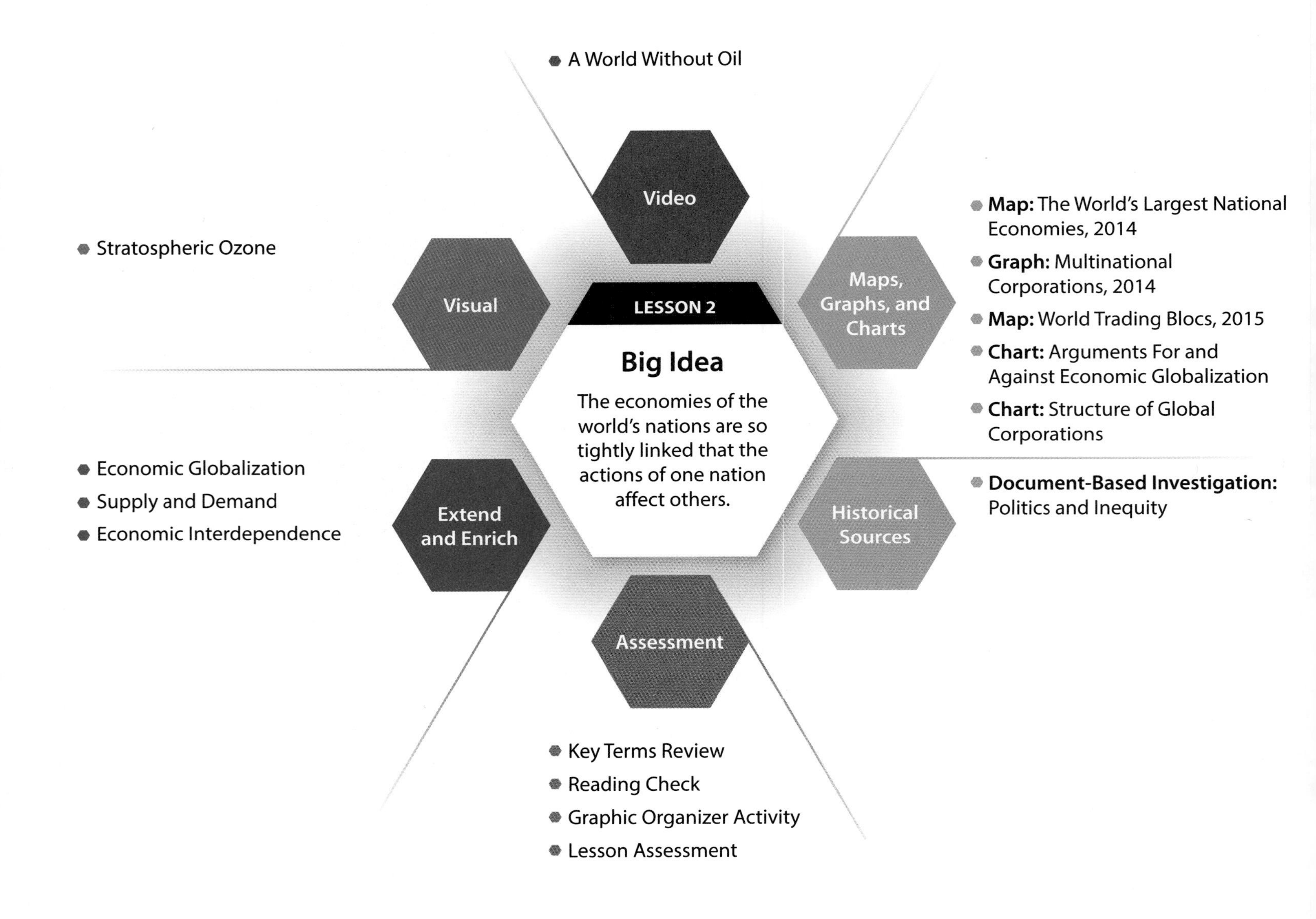

Online Lesson 2 Enrichment Activities

Economic Globalization

Article Students read about the efforts of American businesses to remain competitive in the global economy. Then they consider the different perspectives people have about American companies' decisions to move operations to developing countries and create a political cartoon that might have run in a newspaper in the 1990s.

Supply and Demand

Multimedia Presentation Students create a multimedia presentation explaining the United States economic system with a focus on supply and demand.

Economic Interdependence

Poster Students research multinational companies and choose a consumer product from one of these companies. Then students create a poster or infographic tracing the manufacture of this product. They include a summary paragraph explaining how trade and specialization contribute to economic interdependence.

Teach the Big Idea

1. **Whole Class Open/Introduction** Ask students to name items they or their families have recently bought that were made in another country. *Possible answers: clothing, shoes, consumer electronics, cars*
2. **Direct Teach** Read students the Big Idea: *The economies of the world's nations are so tightly linked that the actions of one nation affect others.* Review the following lesson objectives with students to aid in their understanding of the Big Idea.
   - Discuss the effects of technology on the world economy.
   - Define the global economy.
   - Describe the environmental impact of global development.
3. **Whole Group Close/Reflect** Have students write a memo from the CEO of an American company to his or her employees explaining why the company either will or will not expand its production overseas.

ONLINE DOCUMENT-BASED INVESTIGATION

Global Interdependence

Politics and Inequity is the second of six document-based investigations that students will analyze in the Global Interdependence module. Former Philippine president Gloria Macapagal Arroyo discusses the importance of a political system that does not promote inequity. Invite students to read the excerpt and answer the associated question.

ONLINE GRAPHIC ORGANIZER

Global Economic Development

As students read the lesson, have them use the graphic organizer to take notes. Students can review their graphic organizer notes at the end of the lesson to answer the following question:

Summarize What are the advantages and disadvantages of having a global economy? *advantages—produce where it's most efficient to do so, open markets, spread of technology; disadvantages—economic problems spread quickly, pollution, communication and management challenges in multicultural situations*

Lesson 2

Global Economic Development

The Big Idea

The economies of the world's nations have been so tightly linked that the actions of one nation have affected others.

Why It Matters Now

Every individual is affected by the global economy and the environment.

Key Terms and People

developed nation
emerging nation
gross domestic product
global economy
globalization
free trade
ozone layer
sustainable development

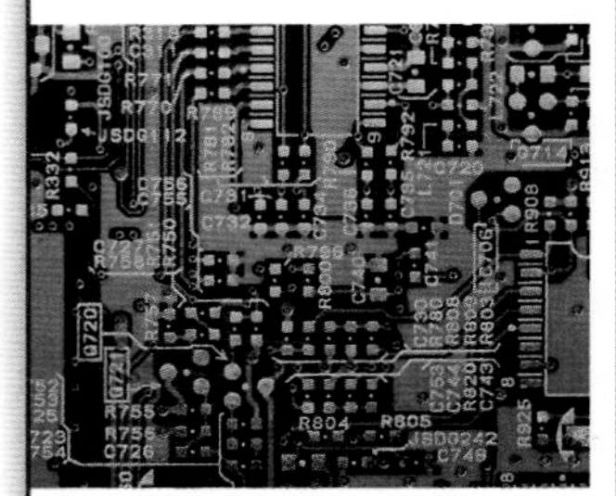

An integrated circuit such as this one was first developed in the 1950s. It was smaller than other circuits and easier to manufacture.

Setting the Stage

At the end of World War II, much of Europe and Asia lay in ruins, with many of the major cities leveled by bombing. The devastation of the war was immense. However, with aid from the United States, the economies of Western European nations and Japan began expanding rapidly within a decade. Their growth continued, long after the United States ceased supplying aid. Advances in science and technology contributed significantly to this ongoing economic growth.

Economic Opportunities and Challenges

In both Asia and the Western world, an explosion in scientific knowledge prompted great progress that led to new industries. Technological advances in plastics, robotics, and computer science changed industrial and business processes, lowered costs, improved quality, and led to large productivity gains. For example, robotic arms on automobile assembly lines made possible the fast and safe manufacture of high-quality cars, and the Internet enabled companies to reach new markets around the world. But these developments did not eliminate economic challenges. Nations routinely monitor their economies and take action to promote growth and reduce risks.

Information Industries Change Economies Technological advances in manufacturing have reduced the need for factory workers, but in other areas of the economy new demands are emerging. Computerization and communications advances changed the processing of information. By the 1980s, people could transmit information quickly and cheaply. Information industries such as financial services, insurance, market research, and communications services boomed. Those industries depended on "knowledge workers," or people whose jobs focus on working with information.

COLLABORATIVE LEARNING

Outsourcing Debate

1. Review the information in the lesson about multinational corporations.
2. Then organize the students into two groups. Have one group represent members of a multinational corporation that believes that outsourcing, or selecting less expensive labor or goods from a foreign source, has a positive worldwide effect; have the other group represent those who oppose outsourcing to foreign countries.
3. Have students use reliable Internet or current print sources to acquire information about both sides of this issue.
4. Have each group prepare its arguments and then debate the effects and consequences of outsourcing. Have all students take notes during the debate.
5. Have students use the information from their notes to write a letter to the editor stating and supporting their own position on this topic.

Nigeria, an emerging nation, produces about 2.2 million barrels of crude oil each day. Its annual petroleum exports are worth about $77 billion.

The Effects of New Economies In the post-World War II era, the expansion of the world's economies led to an increase in the production of goods and services so that many nations benefited. The economic base of some nations shifted. Manufacturing jobs began to move out of **developed nations**, those nations with the industrialization, transportation, and business facilities for advanced production of manufactured goods, into **emerging nations**, those nations in the process of becoming industrialized. Overall there are far more emerging countries in the world than developed countries.

Emerging nations became prime locations for new manufacturing operations. Some economists believe these areas were chosen because they had many eager workers whose skills fit manufacturing-type jobs. Also, these workers would work for less money than those in developed nations. On the other hand, information industries that require better-educated workers who demand higher wages multiplied in the economies of developed nations. Thus the changes brought by technology changed the workplace, resources, and labor of both developed and emerging nations.

Wealth and Inequality Nations measure the strength and stability of their economies in many ways. **Gross domestic product (GDP)** is one key indicator of a country's economic health. GDP is a measure of the total market value of all goods and services produced by a country in a given period of time. Many factors affect GDP, including natural resources, governmental institutions, market structures, technological capabilities, and labor skills. Ongoing changes to these factors may impact the economy in multiple ways.

Developed countries have the highest GDPs. They include the world's wealthiest and most powerful nations and are found mostly in Europe, North America, and parts of Asia. People in developed countries generally have access to good health care, education, and technology. Their standard of living is high compared to that of

Objectives

You may wish to discuss the following questions with students to help them frame the content as they read.

- How has the new economy affected the lives of factory workers in the United States? *Jobs have decreased because of technology and movement of manufacturing to emerging nations.*
- In general, how do education levels in developed countries compare to those in developing countries? *People in developed countries tend to have higher levels of education.*

More About . . .

Multinational Corporations U.S. multinational corporations, also known as multinational enterprises or MNEs, have a total value in the trillions of dollars. These enterprises employ tens of millions of workers, accounting for a large fraction of U.S. private industry employment. Because these corporations carry such weight in the global economy, some policymakers have pushed the World Trade Organization (WTO) to increase regulation of them.

ONLINE LESSON FLIP CARDS

Review Key Terms and People

Students can use the flip cards in the Lesson Review at any time to review the lesson's key terms and people: *developed nation, emerging nation, gross domestic product, global economy, globalization, free trade, ozone layer,* and *sustainable development.*

STRUGGLING READERS

Create Outlines

1. Have students create an outline of the lesson using the heads as main points. Have students identify at least two main ideas under each subheading.
2. Review student outlines as a class. Have students identify the points in their outlines that they feel are most important or most interesting, and have them explain their reasoning to the class.
3. Guide students in a discussion about the ways their lives are affected by international trade and governments' economic policies.

ONLINE INTERACTIVE GRAPHS

The World's Largest National Economies, 2014

Have students explore the graph and answer the associated question.

Interpret Graphs What is the estimated GDP for the world's three largest national economies? *about 53 trillion*

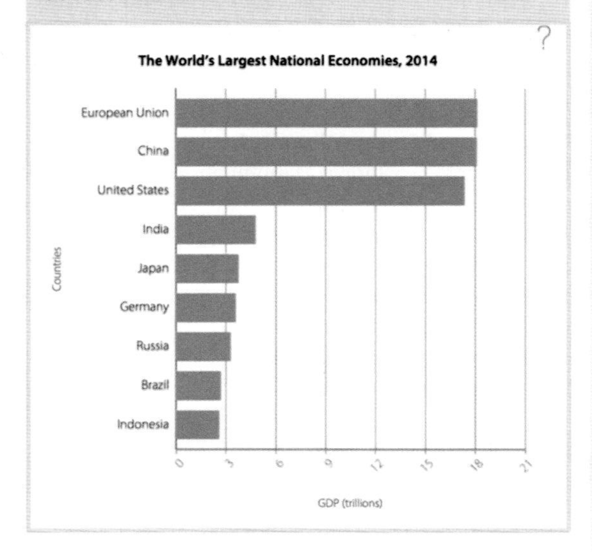

developing countries. The world's poorest countries, those with the lowest GDP, are sometimes called the least developed countries. Most of these countries are located in Africa and southern Asia. They suffer from high levels of poverty, a lack of political and social stability, and often, ongoing war or other conflicts. These challenges make it difficult for the least developed countries to compete in a global economy.

Even within the developed economies, however, there are inequities in the distribution of wealth and income that result in different economic outcomes for individuals, ranging from poverty to extreme wealth. These imbalances present very real challenges and suffering to the people at the lower end of the economic scale. Governments, charitable organizations, and sometimes even businesses design and implement programs to address the suffering that results from poverty. Governments use redistributive measures (such as taxing those with higher incomes and distributing the funds to those with lower incomes) and social programs (such as subsidized health care and housing). An example of how business and charitable organizations work together to address poverty in the United States and in many other countries are the food banks that collect and redistribute excess food to those in need.

Economic Stability The most common factors that contribute to the successful development of an economy are strong legal and judicial institutions, free markets, and economic freedom. Less developed countries tend to have weak political institutions and low rates of participation in the economy, as well as markets that offer fewer products. Countries with a high concentration of governmental control—North Korea, Venezuela, and Cuba, for example—exhibit some of the worst economic outcomes and the greatest political and economic inequality. A lack of educational opportunity and poor-quality infrastructure (roads, bridges, sanitation systems, and so forth) can also contribute to poor economic results.

Most developing countries aim to create stable political, economic, and social conditions for their people. Factors such as affordable health care, educational opportunity, and low levels of crime contribute to social stability, or the well-being of a country's population. Countries that enjoy social stability tend to attract increased investment, leading to the expansion of their economies. A stable society can also promote political order and democratic governance. Political stability and the rule of law, which protects private property, contracts, and other legal agreements, can further foster the growth of the economy. A strong economy leads to the creation of wealth, more jobs, and expanding consumer markets. In the United States and many other nations, economic strength helps enlarge the middle class, which forms the backbone of a stable society. However, in many developing nations in Latin America, Africa, and southern Asia, instability is common. In such situations, investors are unwilling to make the investments that would lead to a stronger economy.

DOCUMENT-BASED INVESTIGATION Historical Source

Politics and Inequity

Former Philippine president Gloria Macapagal Arroyo discusses the importance of the rule of law in government:

"Politics and political power as traditionally practiced and used in the Philippines are among the roots of the social and economic inequities that characterize our national problems. Thus, to achieve true reforms, we need to outgrow our traditional brand of politics based on patronage and personality. Traditional politics is the politics of the status quo. It is a structural part of our problem. We need to promote a new politics of true party programs and platforms, of an institutional process of dialogue with our citizenry. This new politics is the politics of genuine reform. It is a structural part of the solution."

—Gloria Macapagal Arroyo
Inauguration Speech, 2001

Analyze Historical Sources
According to Arroyo, how does traditional politics promote poverty? What do you think she means by "patronage"?

Managing Economies Monetary authorities control the money supply in a country. Monetary policy can include taking short-term actions, such as raising or lowering interest rates, to try to ensure an adequate money supply and to sustain and expand a country's economy. Monetary policy also manages or limits the effects of recessions and inflation.

Many developing countries struggle with poor monetary policies. In some of these countries, the central bank places the government's financial interests above the health of the country's economy. This can result in a weak financial system and an unstable money supply.

Governments can regulate the economy toward different goals, whether to maintain a competitive environment for businesses, increase consumer spending, or to spur economic growth. Governments can use price ceilings (upper limits) and floors (lower limits) on goods and services. Such regulations mean that businesses can only charge prices for a good or service within these limits.

Price ceilings and floors are generally understood to create negative distortions in the economy, resulting in surpluses or shortages of the price-controlled commodity. For example, when the U.S. government tried to control the maximum price of gasoline, shortages appeared, resulting in long lines at gas stations. A minimum wage is an example of a price floor. The government sets a minimum price for labor, and businesses must pay this minimum to workers even if it is higher than what the business can afford to pay. In this situation, some businesses may downsize, or reduce their number of employees, in order to pay the higher wage. Thus, a surplus of labor would enter the economy and could cause unemployment to rise. However, those who support a minimum wage argue that paying workers a higher wage causes those earners to spend more as consumers, which can spur economic growth.

Reading Check
Find Main Ideas
What are some ways that emerging nations can improve their economies?

ONLINE DOCUMENT-BASED INVESTIGATION

Politics and Inequity

Former Philippine president Gloria Macapagal Arroyo discusses the importance of a political system that does not promote inequity. Invite students to read the excerpt and answer the associated question.

Analyze Sources According to Arroyo, how does traditional politics promote poverty? What do you think she means by *patronage*? *Traditional politics have been based on patronage and personality. Patronage refers to the power to appoint people to government jobs.*

DOCUMENT-BASED INVESTIGATION HISTORICAL SOURCE

Politics and Inequity

Former Philippine president Gloria Macapagal Arroyo discusses the importance of a political system that promotes equity.

READING CHECK (DIGITAL)

Find Main Ideas What are some ways that technology can affect economic development? *It changes the job market by creating manufacturing jobs in developing or emerging nations, which changes the job market in developed countries to knowledge-based jobs.*

READING CHECK (PRINT)

Find Main Ideas What are some ways that emerging nations can improve their economies? *They can focus on creating strong legal and judicial institutions and promoting social stability.*

Objectives

You may wish to discuss the following questions with students to help them frame the content as they read.

- Why is improved technology important to multinational corporations? *Possible answer: Some technologies allow use of fewer or less-educated workers.*
- Why might developed countries benefit most from globalization? *Possible answer: higher-paying jobs available; less manufacturing-related pollution*

More About . . .

NAFTA The economic assumptions that led to the creation of NAFTA are the same as those that led to the formation of the European Union: that lowering or eliminating tariffs and other trade barriers should significantly increase regional trade and economic growth. Some U.S. and Canadian citizens opposed NAFTA, fearing that their countries would lose jobs to Mexico, where wages tend to be lower.

The World Trade Organization The Internet and use of email had a major role in the organization of large-scale protests in 1999 against the World Trade Organization (WTO) at its conference in Seattle, Washington. More than 50,000 people voiced their concerns about the impact of globalization and multinational corporations on the environment and labor markets. Critics of the organization come from both developed and developing countries.

Economic Globalization

Economies in different parts of the world have been linked for centuries through trade and through national policies, such as colonialism. However, a true global economy did not begin to take shape until well into the second half of the 1800s. The **global economy** includes all the economic interactions—among people, businesses, and governments—that cross international borders. In recent decades, several factors hastened the process of **globalization**. Huge cargo ships could inexpensively carry enormous supplies of fuels and other goods from one part of the world to another. Technology such as the telephone and computer linkages made global financial transactions quick and easy. In addition, multinational corporations developed around the world.

In order to foster global monetary cooperation, the International Monetary Fund (IMF) was created to facilitate international trade, promote employment and sustainable economic growth, and reduce poverty around the world. The IMF pursues its goals by monitoring financial and economic policy in member countries; providing technical assistance and training, especially for countries with lower and middle income; and providing loans with the expectation that the country receiving the money will put into action IMF policies to improve its economy for sustainable growth.

Multinational Corporations Companies that operate in a number of countries are called multinational or transnational corporations. U.S. companies such as Exxon Mobil and Ford, European companies such as BP and Royal Dutch/Shell, and Japanese companies such as Toyota and Mitsui are all multinational giants.

All of these companies have established manufacturing plants, offices, or stores in many countries. For their manufacturing plants, they select spots where the raw materials or labor are cheapest. This enables them to produce components of their products on different continents. They ship the various components to another

Multinational Corporations, 2014

Based on a comparison of revenues with GDP, some of the top multinationals have economies bigger than those of several countries.

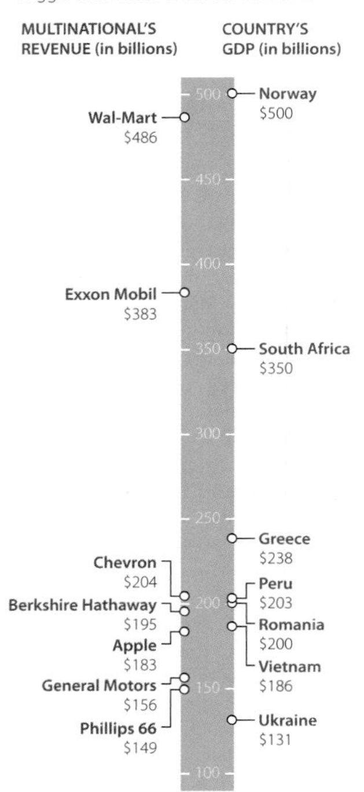

Sources: *Fortune Magazine* and *CIA World Factbook*

Interpret Graphs
1. **Compare** Which has the larger economy, Vietnam or General Motors?
2. **Compare** Which countries have an economy greater than the annual revenue of Chevron but smaller than that of Wal-Mart?

ADVANCED/GIFTED

Analyze Motives of Multinational Corporations

1. Explain that people and governments make decisions and take actions based on many factors, which may be complex and confusing even to the people involved. Among these factors are the motives, or reasons, for why people act as they do. Examining the needs, emotions, prior experiences, and goals of a person or government can help historians understand the motives that lie behind historical decisions.
2. Ask students to examine the text and the graph titled "Multinational Corporations, 2014" and think about the reasons multinational corporations are established. Have them consider these questions:
   - What needs or goals might motivate corporations? *Possible answers: profit, longevity, desire to be successful*
   - What do corporations gain from operating worldwide? *Possible answers: more flexibility, greater profits*
   - What do consumers gain from buying products made by multinational corporations? *Possible answer: lower prices*

location to be assembled. This level of economic integration is beneficial because it allows such companies to view the whole world as the market for their goods. Goods or services are distributed throughout the world as if there were no national boundaries.

Multinational corporations create jobs when they open new locations in host countries. They may increase profits and productivity (the rate of output per unit of input). They often bring technology to an area, which helps to improve production and the area's economy in general. At the same time, multinational corporations face challenges such as management across multiple countries where processes and standards differ. Critics accuse multinational corporations of widening the gap between developed and emerging countries and contributing to economic exploitation, human rights abuses, and the loss of traditional industries in emerging countries.

Expanding Free Trade Opening up the world's markets to trade is a key aspect of globalization. In fact, a major goal of globalization is **free trade**, or the elimination of trade barriers, such as tariffs, among nations. As early as 1947, nations began discussing ways to open trade. The result of these discussions was the General Agreement on Tariffs and Trade (GATT). Over the years, meetings among the nations that signed the GATT have brought about a general lowering of protective tariffs and considerable expansion of free trade. Since 1995, the World Trade Organization (WTO) has overseen the GATT to ensure that trade among nations flows smoothly and freely.

Vocabulary
tariff a tax on goods imported from another country

Global flows, which include the movement of goods, services, finances, and people, have driven global economic growth. They play an important role in creating new international economic relations. In 2014, the value of all exports and imports made up about half of global GDP, and some experts expect this value to increase. Several factors cause global flows growth, including rising prosperity, emerging world markets, regional trade blocs, and the increased use of the Internet.

Regional Trade Blocs A European organization set up in 1951 promoted tariff-free trade among member countries. This experiment in economic cooperation was so successful that six years later, a new organization, the European Economic Community (EEC), was formed. Over time, most of the other Western European countries joined the organization, which has been known as the European Union (EU) since 1992. By 2015, twenty-eight European nations were EU members, and many had adopted the common European currency—the euro (symbol: €). The EU is an economic and political union and is now the largest trading bloc in the world. It acts as a single economic unit but also advocates a united foreign and security policy and works to promote peace and equality.

The success of the EU inspired countries in other regions to make trade agreements with each other. The North American Free Trade Agreement (NAFTA), put into effect in 1994, called for the gradual elimination of tariffs and trade restrictions among Canada, the United States, and Mexico. All three countries received a small positive economic benefit as seen in each country's GDP. Organizations in Asia, Africa, Latin America, and the

ONLINE INTERACTIVE GRAPHS

Multinational Corporations, 2014

Have students explore the graph and answer the associated questions.

Interpret Graphs Which has the larger economy, Vietnam or General Motors? *Vietnam*

In print edition, see graph of the same title.

Compare Which has the larger economy, Vietnam or General Motors? *Vietnam*

Compare Which countries have an economy greater than the annual revenue of Chevron but smaller than that of Wal-Mart? *Greece and South Africa*

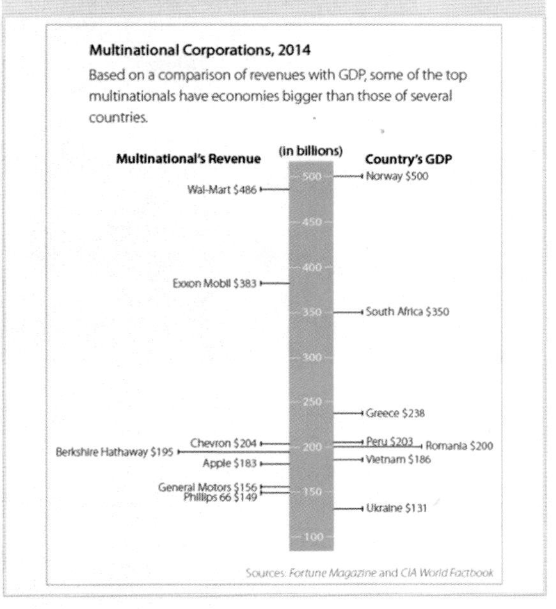

Sources: *Fortune Magazine* and *CIA World Factbook*

ONLINE INTERACTIVE MAPS

World Trading Blocs, 2015

Have students explore the map and answer the associated questions.

Interpret Maps Which OPEC country is located outside of Southwest Asia? *Venezuela*

In print edition, see map of the same title.

Location Which countries in OPEC are located outside of Southwest Asia? *Venezuela, Nigeria, Algeria, Libya, Indonesia, Angola, Ecuador*

Location To which world trade organization does the United States belong? *G8*

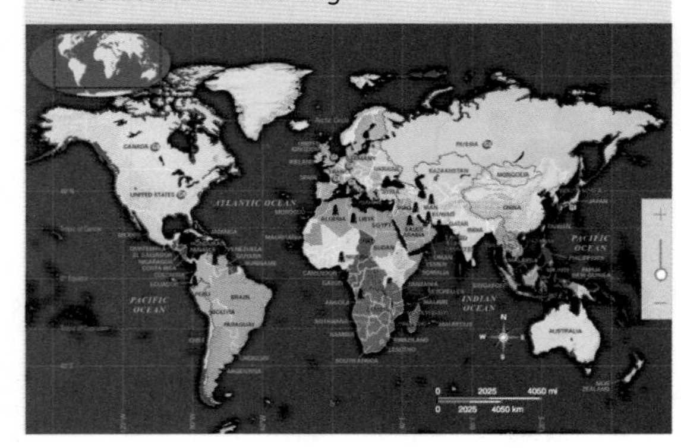

Explore ONLINE!

World Trading Blocs, 2015

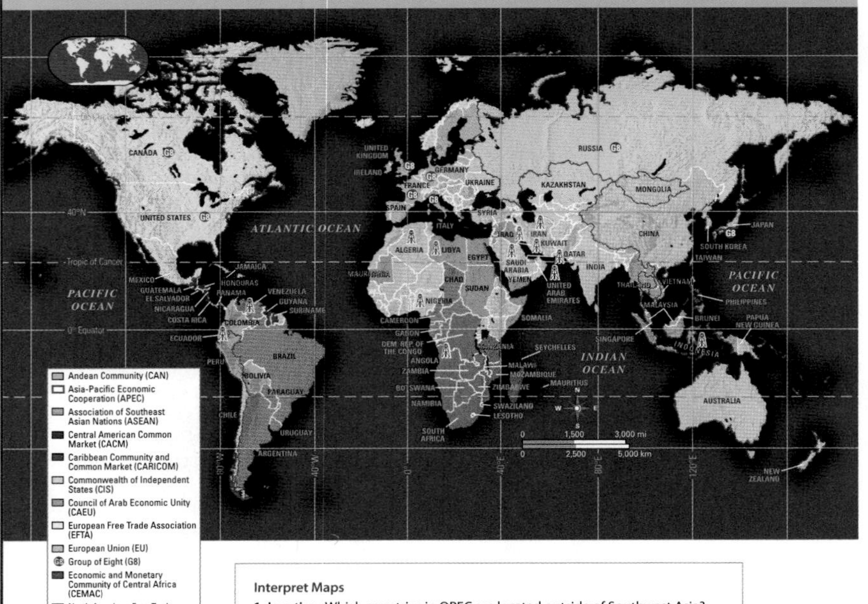

Interpret Maps

1. **Location** Which countries in OPEC are located outside of Southwest Asia?
2. **Location** To which world trade organization does the United States belong?

South Pacific have also created regional trade policies. In 2013, the United States began negotiating a free trade agreement, called the Transatlantic Trade and Investment Partnership (T-TIP), with the EU.

These trade agreements, along with other global economic trends, have made nations economically interdependent, or mutually dependent. Nations depend on other nations for the goods and services that scarcity prevents them from being able to produce themselves. Nations produce those goods or services for which they have a comparative advantage, or an ability to produce at a relatively low cost. They are then able to sell their product or service to other nations that cannot produce it efficiently, at the same time acquiring items they are unable to produce. For example, a nation with extensive forests but no iron ore may harvest timber to export but need to import steel from nations who have the iron ore needed to create it.

Vocabulary
scarcity in economics, having unlimited wants and resources too limited to meet all of the wants

History in Depth

Asia in the G20

The Group of Twenty, known as the G20, is an international group that was founded in 1999 with the goal of promoting discussion of policy affecting the global economy. It forms strategic communications between political leaders and central bank governors. The G20 is comprised of 19 countries, many of which are Asian—China, Japan, India, Indonesia, and the Republic of Korea—and the European Union.

The Asian economies of China, India, Vietnam, and Indonesia have been emerging from the mid- to late 20th and early 21st centuries. The G20 issued a working paper in 2011 predicting that large Asian economies, such as those of China and India, would play a more prominent role in the global economy over time. The G20 works to promote sustainable, balanced growth within an Asian intraregional trade market while also encouraging domestic demand.

A Global Economic Crisis Beginning in 2007, after a long period of relative worldwide prosperity, several factors combined to cause an economic downturn, which later became known as the "Great Recession." Housing prices in the United States and in parts of Europe had increased dramatically over a short time, driven up by lax lending policies that offered mortgage loans to almost anyone and monetary policies that supported the growth of the money supply. The financial industry found it could bundle groups of these mortgages into an investment vehicle called a mortgage-backed security (MBS), which it sold to investors despite hidden risks. When housing prices in the United States and parts of Europe began to plummet, banks and financial institutions across the globe were not prepared to deal with the loss of value in their portfolios of mortgages and mortgage-backed securities. As these entities began to fail, governments around the world stepped in to attempt to stabilize the situation. Meanwhile, unemployment rates skyrocketed.

When economic crises occur, governments enact programs in the hopes of improving economic outcomes. These programs are often based on competing models of how the economy works and what governments can do to address the issues. When the financial crisis hit the U.S. economy in 2007, a Keynesian program of fiscal stimulus was enacted. It consisted of a combination of new government spending (road construction, extended unemployment benefits) and tax cuts (tax rebates). The bulk of the stimulus was implemented in 2008 and 2009. As the economic crisis continued, the U.S. government tried a different approach. It allowed the tax cuts to expire, reduced government spending, and attempted to restrain growth of the federal deficit. Whether despite or in response to these competing programs, the U.S. economy stabilized in the second half of 2009 and began to slowly grow out of the recession, with unemployment declining beginning in 2010.

Vocabulary
Keynesian relating to the theories of economist John Maynard Keynes, who advocated use of government deficit spending to stimulate commerce and decrease unemployment

By 2010, the world economy had stabilized, but it remained weak, as seen especially in the economies of Greece, Spain, Portugal, Italy, and Ireland. In May 2010, the IMF, the European Commission, and the

NOW & THEN

Asia in the G20

The members of the Group of Twenty are Argentina, Australia, Brazil, Canada, China, France, Germany, India, Indonesia, Italy, Japan, Mexico, Russia, Saudi Arabia, South Africa, South Korea, Turkey, United Kingdom, United States, and the European Union. Other participants include the International Monetary Fund and the World Bank.

In print edition, see History in Depth.

ADVANCED/GIFTED

Evaluate NAFTA

1. Explain that NAFTA has been controversial since its enactment in 1994. Proponents touted its advantages for the region and for the U.S. economy. Critics warned of dire consequences in the areas of balance of trade, labor, and the environment.
2. Ask students to research what current thoughts are about the success or failure of the agreement. After preliminary research on the Internet or in newspapers or magazines, have each student choose a particular aspect to follow up in depth.
3. Possible topics to research include
   - how the balance of trade has changed in the region
   - how NAFTA has affected the labor market
   - what impact NAFTA has had on the environment
   - who the key proponents and opponents are
   - how current reality compares to predictions

Make sure students also check the background of their sources. When students have completed their research, have them present a panel discussion to the class.

ONLINE INTERACTIVE CHARTS

Arguments For and Against Economic Globalization

Have students explore the table and answer the associated questions.

Interpret Charts Which of the following statements does NOT support economic globalization? *benefits those who already have money*

In print edition, see Analyze Key Concepts: Globalization.

Make Inferences How do developed countries influence culture around the world? *Wealthy, developed countries that are able to play a larger role in the global economy are more likely to spread their culture around the world.*

Predict How will increased globalization impact the 21st century? *There will be a growing number of countries involved in the WTO, IMF, and World Bank and the lack of limitations on the power of multinational corporations. They might clash with growing grassroots movements dedicated to encouraging the strengthening of local cultures and economies.*

ONLINE INTERACTIVE CHARTS

Structure of Global Corporations

Have students explore the table and answer the associated question.

Interpret Charts Which of the following countries is NOT a manufacturing and production center? *Australia*

NOW & THEN

International Regulation

While the International Monetary Fund and the World Bank may seem similar, there are pronounced differences between the two institutions. The IMF seeks to promote currency exchange stability among all of its member countries. It provides credit for countries that experience short-term financial difficulties, with the goal of avoiding the economic disruption that might otherwise ensue. The World Bank, on the other hand, is focused on improving the economic situation of the poorest countries. It provides loans and financial assistance for long-term development projects within these countries.

ANALYZE KEY CONCEPTS

Globalization

Globalization can be described in broad terms as a process that makes something worldwide in its reach or operation. Currently, globalization is most often used in reference to the spread and diffusion of economic or cultural influences. The graphics below focus on economic globalization. The first shows a global corporation. The second lists some arguments for and against economic globalization.

Global Corporation

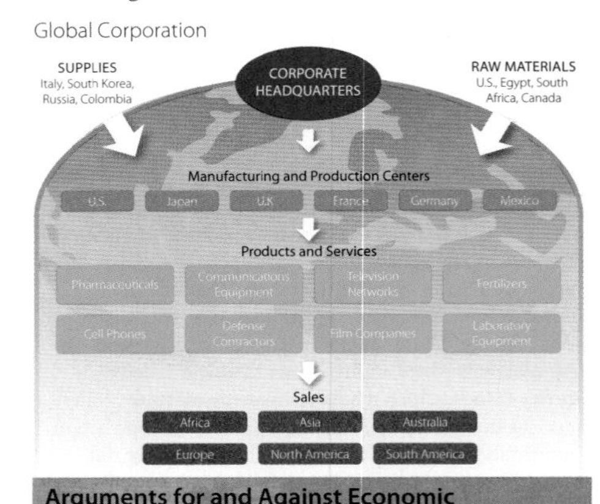

Arguments for and Against Economic Globalization

For	Against
promotes peace through trade	creates conflict because of an inherently unfair system
raises the standard of living around the world	benefits developed nations disproportionately
creates jobs in emerging countries	takes jobs from high-paid laborers in developed countries
promotes investment in less developed countries	benefits those who already have money
creates a sense of world community	erodes local cultures

INTERNATIONAL REGULATION

Many countries have joined international organizations to help regulate and stimulate the global economy. Such groups face the same criticisms against globalization in general.

WORLD TRADE ORGANIZATION (WTO)

- Stated goal: "Help trade flow smoothly, freely, fairly, and predictably"
- About 160 member nations; around 25 nations negotiating for admission
- WTO members account for about 95 percent of world trade.

INTERNATIONAL MONETARY FUND (IMF)

- Stated goal: "Promote international monetary cooperation; to foster economic growth and high levels of employment; and to provide temporary financial assistance to countries"
- 188 member countries
- In September 2015, IMF total resources were $334 billion.

THE WORLD BANK GROUP

- Stated goal: "A world free of poverty"
- 5 organizations
- In 2015, this group provided $42.5 billion to emerging countries.

Critical Thinking

1. **Make Inferences** How do developed countries influence culture around the world?
2. **Predict** How will increased globalization impact the 21st century?

Reading Check
Analyze Causes
What elements helped to accelerate the process of globalization?

European Central Bank provided a loan of 110 billion euro to help finance Greece's debt. This was followed a year later with an additional loan of 130 billion euro and the restructuring of private bank debt. The World Bank also provided financial support and partnered with the IMF and EU on assistance programs.

Impact of Global Development

The development of the global economy has had a notable impact on the use of energy and other resources. Worldwide demand for resources has led to both political and environmental problems.

Political Impacts Manufacturing requires the processing of raw materials. Trade requires the transport of finished goods. These activities, essential for development, require the use of much energy. For the past 50 years, one of the main sources of energy used by developed and emerging nations has been oil. For nations with little of this resource available in their own land, disruption of the distribution of oil causes economic and political problems.

On the other hand, nations possessing oil reserves have the power to affect economic and political situations in countries all over the world. For example, in the 1970s the Arab members of the Organization of Petroleum Exporting Countries (OPEC) declared an oil embargo—a restriction of trade. This contributed to a significant economic decline in many developed nations during that decade. The OPEC crisis also caused a shift in international relations and changes in foreign policies. For example, as a result of the embargo, many developed countries changed their policies toward the Arab-Israeli conflict.

In 1990, Iraq invaded Kuwait and seized the Kuwaiti oil fields. Fears began to mount that Iraq would also invade Saudi Arabia, another major source of oil. This would have destabilized Saudi Arabia and put most of

During the 1991 Persian Gulf War, the Iraqis set hundreds of Kuwaiti oil wells ablaze. Smoke from these fires clouded the skies more than 250 miles away.

READING CHECK

Analyze Causes What elements helped to accelerate the process of globalization? *Better communication and transportation systems and the development of multinational companies*

Objectives

You may wish to discuss the following questions with students to help them frame the content as they read.

- What was the impact of the 1991 Persian Gulf War on the environment? *Possible answer: Burning oil fields polluted the atmosphere.*
- How does United States' dependence on foreign oil make its economy vulnerable? *Possible answer: Without oil from foreign sources, U.S. offices, factories, and transportation systems could not operate. The price of foreign oil affects the price of other goods in the U.S.*

More About . . .

The 1991 Persian Gulf War Interdependence among nations has led to war at times. Southwest Asia has the world's largest known oil reserves. When Iraq threatened to cut off supplies of oil from the region, a coalition of nations worked together to stop that threat. The Persian Gulf War resulted in great environmental damage. Iraq dumped more than 465 million gallons of oil.

Globalization Developing countries have increased their trade overall. Some developing countries have benefited more than others. For example, countries in Asia are profiting, while African nations struggle. Successfully increasing trade and raising the standard of living in developing countries means that the need for international aid is decreasing.

ANALYZE VIDEOS

A World Without Oil

HISTORY

Have students watch the video individually or as a class. You may wish to use the associated question as a discussion prompt.

Analyze Videos What would happen if the world's oil supply suddenly dried up? *Our way of life would drastically change. We would not be able to drive or heat our homes until we found an alternate energy source. We would have to find local sources of food because we could not ship food from place to place. We would have to find new resources to create everyday products, as oil is used to produce many products, from cars to lotions.*

ONLINE INTERACTIVE VISUALS

Carousel: Stratospheric Ozone

Have students navigate through the carousel and note similarities and differences among the images or identify a unifying theme. You may wish to use the associated question as a discussion prompt.

Analyze Visuals Explain how the ozone layer has changed from 1979 to 2015. *The ozone layer is thinning, so there are larger areas with less ozone.*

the world's petroleum supplies under Iraqi control. Economic sanctions imposed by the UN failed to persuade Iraq to withdraw from Kuwait. Then, in early 1991, a coalition of some 39 nations declared war on Iraq. After several weeks of fighting, the Iraqis left Kuwait and accepted a cease-fire. This Persian Gulf War showed the extent to which the economies of nations are globally linked.

Environmental Impacts Economic development has had a major impact on the environment. The burning of coal and oil as an energy source releases carbon dioxide and other gases into the atmosphere, causing health-damaging pollution and acid rain. The buildup of carbon dioxide in the atmosphere also contributes to global warming.

The release of chemicals called chlorofluorocarbons (CFCs), used in refrigerators, air conditioners, and manufacturing processes, has destroyed the ozone layer in Earth's upper atmosphere. The **ozone layer** is our main protection against the sun's damaging ultraviolet rays. With the increase in ultraviolet radiation reaching Earth's surface, the incidence of skin cancer continues to rise in many parts of the world. Increased ultraviolet radiation also may result in damage to populations of plants and plankton at the bases of the food chains, which sustain all life on Earth.

Ozone Levels

A large area of the ozone layer has become much thinner in recent years.

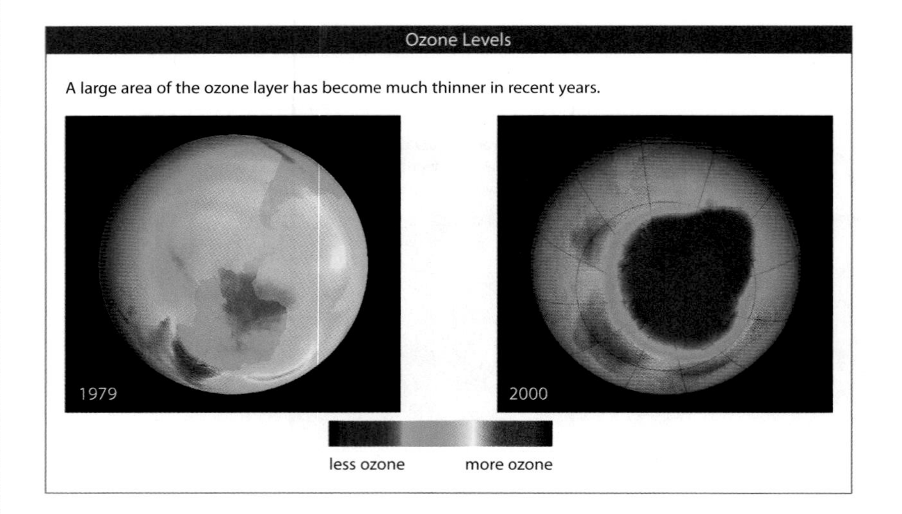

STRUGGLING READERS

Evaluate the Effects of Oil

1. Ask students to reread the text in this section, looking for references to oil and petroleum.
2. As a class, create a concept web that shows the effects oil has on the economy and the environment. *Possible concept web: Center bubble: Oil affects the economy and the environment. Secondary bubbles: source of energy; not all countries have oil; OPEC restricted oil supply in 1970s; Persian Gulf War; causes pollution; may affect global warming*

Economic development has also led to problems with the land. Large-scale soil erosion is a worldwide problem due to damaging farming techniques. The habitat destruction that comes from land development has also led to shrinking numbers of wildlife around the world. At present, the extinction rate of plants and animals is about a thousand times greater than it would naturally be, and it appears to be increasing. This high extinction rate means that certain species can no longer serve as an economic resource. The resulting loss of wildlife could endanger complex and life-sustaining processes that keep Earth in balance.

Sustainable Development Working together, economists and scientists are looking for ways to reduce the negative effect that development has on the environment. Their goal is to manage development so that growth can occur without destroying air, water, and land resources. The concept is sometimes called "green growth." Many people feel that the negative impact of economic growth on the environment will not be completely removed.

Reading Check
Analyze Issues
Explain the influence and importance of the petroleum industry in world politics and in the global economy.

But "green growth," also known as **sustainable development**, is possible. This involves creating economic growth while preserving the environment. Making such plans and putting them into practice have proved to be difficult. Because the economies of nations are tied to their political institutions, such development plans will depend on the efforts of nations in both economic and political areas.

Lesson 2 Assessment

1. **Organize Information** Create a web to list the forces that shape the global economy. Explain which of these forces has had the greatest impact on the development of a global economy.

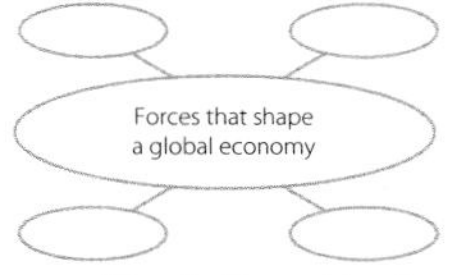

2. **Key Terms and People** For each key term or person in the lesson, write a sentence explaining its significance.
3. **Analyze Effects** In what ways has technology changed the workplace of people across the world?
4. **Draw Conclusions** Describe the impact of the European Union on member nations and non-member nations.
5. **Form Opinions** Do you think that sustainable development is possible? Why or why not?
6. **Form Opinions** Do you think that the euro has provided economic unity and stability among EU members? Use reasoning and evidence in your response.
7. **Evaluate** Do you agree with the actions taken by the IMF and the World Bank during the world economic crisis in 2007? Explain your response.

READING CHECK
Analyze Issues Explain the influence and importance of the petroleum industry in world politics and in the global economy. *Most economies depend on oil, so those who provide oil gain a lot of wealth and power. For example, after OPEC's oil embargo in the 1970s and the shortage it caused, some nations changed their political policies toward the Arab-Israeli conflict because the Arab nations in OPEC were concerned about that conflict.*

Print Assessment

Review Ideas, Terms, and People

1. **Organize Information** Create a web to list the forces that shape the global economy. Explain which of these forces has had the greatest impact on the development of a global economy. *Possible answer: advances in communication and transportation, development of multinational corporations, expanded free trade, regional trade agreements; greatest impact— free trade, because it has removed many economic barriers*
2. **Key Terms and People** For each key term or person in the lesson, write a sentence explaining its significance. *Explanations of the lesson's key terms can be found on the following pages: developed nation, emerging nation, gross domestic product, p. 1273; global economy, globalization, p. 1276; free trade, p. 1277; ozone layer, p. 1282; sustainable development, p. 1283.*
3. **Analyze Effects** In what ways has technology changed the workplace of people across the world? *Possible answer: Developed nations—more people work in information industries, some people telecommute; Emerging nations—More people work in manufacturing.*
4. **Draw Conclusions** Describe the impact of the European Union on member nations and nonmember nations. *Member nations will have an easier time trading and establishing trade laws through the organization; nonmember nations are still developing and will be struggling economically as they do not benefit from the trade agreements.*
5. **Form Opinions** Do you think that sustainable development is possible? Why or why not? *Possible answers: Yes—Industrial practices can be adjusted to limit adverse impact on environment. No—The negative impact of economic growth can never be completely removed.*

(continued)

Print Assessment *(continued)*

6. **Form Opinions** Do you think the euro has provided economic unity and stability among EU members? Use reasoning and evidence in your response. *Possible answers: Yes, I think that having a common currency among EU member nations has made their economies stronger. People and businesses no longer have to exchange currency and be concerned with exchange rates. They can use the euro anywhere in the EU, which promotes the buying and selling of goods and services.*
7. **Evaluate** Do you agree with the actions taken by the IMF and the World Bank during the world economic crisis in 2007? Explain your response. *Yes, I think that the IMF and World Bank had no other choice than to provide funding to countries in need as national debts rose. If they had not, economies like those in Europe may have collapsed, which would have impacted global markets even more so*

▷.Online Assessment

1. How has technology affected many manufacturing companies in the latter half of the 20th century?
   - ○ Technology has increased the need for factory workers.
   - ● Manufacturing jobs have moved out of developed nations.
   - ○ Technology has completely eliminated serious accidents in factories.
   - ○ Manufacturers have increased wages by moving to emerging nations.

   Alternate Question *Drag the answer choice into the box to complete the sentence correctly.*
   Information industries, such as communication services, pay a higher wage than manufacturing industries because their workers tend to be *more educated* than factory workers.

2. Which of the following is an example of economic globalization?
   - ○ governments eliminating intercontinental barriers to trade
   - ○ companies establishing businesses within their own country
   - ● cargo ships carrying large shipments from one continent to another
   - ○ people using computers to purchase items from their local clothing store

   Alternate Question *Drag the answer choice into the box to complete the sentence correctly.* *Multinational corporations* establish manufacturing plants in many nations and employ people of many nationalities.

3. Since the end of World War II, how have industrialized nations been affected by the dependence of their economies on oil?
   - ○ Industrialized nations have started to rely solely on solar energy for electricity production.
   - ○ Industrialized nations have occupied Middle Eastern countries to ensure the continued production of oil.
   - ○ Industrialized nations have entered into military pacts with oil-producing nations in order to provide security in the Middle East.
   - ● Industrialized nations have supported the foreign policies of oil-producing nations in order to ensure the continued supply of crude oil.

   Alternate Question *Select the answer choice from the drop-down list to complete the sentence correctly.*
   The 1990 invasion of *Kuwait* by Iraq was opposed militarily by a coalition of 39 nations that were concerned that Iraq would threaten the region's oil production.

4. **Apply Concepts** How is a country's gross domestic product (GDP) often an indicator of the quality of life of its citizens?

   Possible answer: A country's GDP often indicates whether it is industrially developed or whether it is an emerging country. An industrially developed country with a high GDP generally has good health care and educational systems, and it relies on technology for manufacturing and communication. A country that is fully industrialized is best able to compete with other industrialized countries on a global scale and provide good jobs for its workers. An emerging country with a low GDP generally has not developed a good infrastructure, and the standard of living for the majority of its citizens is low. Emerging countries are often involved in armed conflicts that pose constant dangers to their citizens.

5. **Evaluate** Why do some people criticize multinational corporations?

   Possible answer: Multinational corporations are criticized for widening the economic gap between developed and emerging nations. Multinational corporations establish manufacturing plants in emerging countries because they can take advantage of workers who are willing to work for low wages. Government officials in those countries then complain that the corporations exploit emerging countries economically by keeping wages low and creating unfair competition with traditional industries in those countries.

6. **Cause and Effect** How has the burning of fossil fuels affected the environment?

   Possible answer: The burning of coal and oil since the beginning of the Industrial Revolution has had a profound effect on the earth's environment. The burning of fossil fuels produces pollution and emits carbon dioxide, and it has been blamed for rising global temperatures. The accumulation of pollution in the air, water, and soil poisons animals and has caused health problems in humans. Harmful gases can cause acid rain, which can kill forests and destroy their ecosystems.

Lesson 3 Planner

Global Security Issues

Online Lesson 3 Enrichment Activities

Human Rights

Primary Source Students read an excerpt from *The Universal Declaration of Human Rights* to learn more about the human rights standards set by the United Nations for all nations. They write a paragraph assessing the progress of human rights around the world since the 1948 UN Declaration of Human Rights. Then they identify two countries in which residents do not have these rights and create a chart describing the conditions that exist in these countries that may contribute to human rights violations.

Refugees

Timeline Activity Students create a timeline showing large movements of refugees from 1980 to the present day. They add illustrations or brief descriptions to some or all of the events and write a brief introduction that summarizes the contents of the timeline.

Human Rights Movements

Writing Activity Students write an explanatory essay describing the results of human rights movements and equal rights movements around the world.

UNMIBH: United Nations Mission in Bosnia and Herzegovina

Writing Activity Students write an analysis of the role the United Nations played during the fighting in Bosnia and Herzegovina in the early 1990s.

Teach the Big Idea

1. **Whole Class Open/Introduction** Ask students what kind of world events might threaten their personal security. *Possible answers: violence, including terrorism or war; ethnic, religious, or gender prejudice; infectious disease*
2. **Direct Teach** Read students the Big Idea: *Since 1945, nations have used collective security efforts to solve problems.* Review the following lesson objectives with students to aid in their understanding of the Big Idea.
   - Identify ways that nations deal with issues of war and peace.
   - Give examples of human rights issues.
   - Describe some major world health issues.
   - Explain the increase in migration and discuss its worldwide effects.
3. **Whole Group Close/Reflect** Have students select one of the global challenges discussed in the section and write a proposal containing workable solutions to their chosen problem.

ONLINE DOCUMENT-BASED INVESTIGATION

Global Interdependence

The Universal Declaration of Human Rights is the third of six document-based investigations that students will analyze in the Global Interdependence module. The Universal Declaration of Human Rights contains 30 articles that explain the political, economic, and cultural rights of all people. Invite students to read the excerpt and answer the associated question.

ONLINE GRAPHIC ORGANIZER

Global Security Issues

As students read the lesson, have them use the graphic organizer to take notes. Students can review their graphic organizer notes at the end of the lesson to answer the following question:

Summarize What are some of the collective measures taken by the world's nations to increase global security? *Formation of the UN has helped reduce threats of conflict and promote peace. Nations form arms-control agreements to reduce numbers of weapons of mass destruction, which reduces the threat of mass murder.*

Lesson 3

Global Security Issues

The Big Idea

Since 1945, nations have used collective security efforts to solve problems.

Why It Matters Now

Personal security of the people of the world is tied to security within and between nations.

Key Terms and People

supranational union
refugee
proliferation
Universal Declaration of Human Rights
nonbinding agreement
political dissent
gender inequality
AIDS
refugees

Setting the Stage

World War II was one of history's most devastating conflicts. More than 55 million people died as a result of bombings, the Holocaust, combat, starvation, and disease. Near the end of the war, one of humankind's most destructive weapons, the atomic bomb, killed more than 100,000 people in Hiroshima and Nagasaki in a matter of minutes. Perhaps because of these horrors, world leaders look for ways to make the earth a safer, more secure place to live.

Issues of War and Peace

In the years after World War II, the Cold War created new divisions and tensions among the world's nations. This uneasy situation potentially threatened the economic, environmental, and personal security of people across the world. So, nations began to work together to pursue collective security.

Nations Unite and Take Action Many nations consider that having a strong military is important to their security. After World War II, nations banded together to create military alliances. They formed the North Atlantic Treaty Organization (NATO), the Southeast Asia Treaty Organization (SEATO), the Warsaw Pact, and others. The member nations of each of these alliances generally pledged military aid for their common defense.

In addition to military alliances to increase their security, some world leaders also took steps to reduce the threat of war and promote political and economic unity through the creation of **supranational unions**. *Supranational* refers to something extending beyond national boundaries. One such supranational union was the European Economic Community (EEC), created in 1957 to unify its member states' economies. In 1993 the EEC became part of the European Union, which carried on the EEC's mission and pursued additional goals related to justice, foreign policy,

COLLABORATIVE LEARNING

Challenge Posters

1. Organize students into mixed-ability pairs. Ask students what they think is the biggest challenge facing societies today.
2. Have each pair decide on a challenge and write it on a sheet of paper. (Students may choose a challenge discussed in this lesson, or another challenge, such as an aging population.)
3. Have pairs create a poster to build awareness of the challenge.
4. Display student posters for the class to see.
5. Guide students in a discussion of the challenges they illustrated. Why do they feel it is the most significant challenge? What are the possible consequences of either addressing the challenge successfully or leaving it unaddressed?

and security. Other unions, such as the African Union (AU), pursue similar goals for their member nations. The United Nations (UN) also works in a variety of ways toward increasing collective global security. The Organization of Ibero-American States (OEI) works to advance science, culture, and education in its member countries.

Peacekeeping Activities One of the major aims of the UN is to promote world peace. The UN provides a public forum, private meeting places, and skilled mediators to help nations try to resolve conflicts at any stage of their development. At the invitation of the warring parties, the UN also provides peacekeeping forces. These forces are made up of soldiers from different nations. They work to carry out peace agreements, monitor cease-fires, or end fighting to allow peace negotiations to go forward. They also help to move **refugees**, deliver supplies, and operate hospitals. A refugee is a person who leaves his or her country to find safety in another country.

As of October 2015, the UN had more than 100,000 soldiers, military observers, and police in 16 peacekeeping operations around the world. Some forces, such as those in India, Pakistan, and Cyprus, have been in place for decades.

Weapons of Mass Destruction Nations not only have worked to prevent and contain conflicts, but they also have forged treaties to limit the manufacturing, testing, and trade of weapons. The weapons of most concern are those that cause mass destruction. These include nuclear, chemical, and biological weapons that can kill thousands, even millions of people.

In 1968, many nations signed a Nuclear Non-Proliferation Treaty to help prevent the **proliferation**, or spread, of nuclear weapons to other nations. In the 1970s, the United States and the Soviet Union signed the Strategic Arms Limitation Treaties. In the 1980s, both countries talked about deactivating some of their nuclear weapons. Many nations also signed treaties promising not to produce biological or chemical weapons. Still, at least nine countries are known to possess nuclear weapons, while others are believed to be trying to develop them.

One difficulty in controlling nuclear weapons is that nuclear technology can be used for legitimate purposes, such as generating energy. Many countries and international organizations try to ensure that nuclear technology is used safely. For example, the International Atomic Energy Agency (IAEA) routinely monitors countries suspected of developing nuclear weapons. In addition, countries may sanction other nations they consider to be nuclear threats.

Vocabulary
sanction to impose an economic or political penalty on another country in order to force a change in that country's policy

War in Iraq Other nations, however, have tried to develop weapons of mass destruction (WMD). Iraq, for example, used chemical weapons in conflicts during the 1980s. Many people suspected that the Iraqi leader, Saddam Hussein, had plans to develop biological and nuclear weapons too. As part of the cease-fire arrangements in the Persian Gulf War, Iraq agreed to destroy its weapons of mass destruction. UN inspectors were sent to monitor this disarmament process. However, in 1998, the Iraqis ordered the inspectors to leave.

Objectives

You may wish to discuss the following questions with students to help them frame the content as they read.

- Why might UN peacekeepers be more effective than one nation's forces? *Possible answer: UN forces are from different countries, so they are less likely to take sides.*
- How does weapons limitation promote global security? *by limiting the scope of conflict*

More About . . .

Nuclear Weapons The United States, Russia, United Kingdom, France, China, North Korea, Pakistan, India, and Israel have nuclear weapons. Some countries of the former Soviet Union may also have the ability to produce nuclear weapons.

Running for Freedom During his final year of high school in the central African nation of Burundi, champion runner Gilbert Tuhabonye dreamed of attending college in the United States. Instead, an outbreak of ethnic violence nearly killed him. Tuhabonye is a Tutsi, one of the two main ethnic groups in Burundi. The other group is the Hutu. In October 1993, a mob of Hutus attacked Tuhabonye's village and forced the Tutsis into the school building, which they set on fire. For hours, Tuhabonye lay trapped in the flames, protected only by the bodies of his dead classmates.

Finally, he gathered the strength to break free. With his back on fire, he broke through a window and escaped into the nearby woods. His legs were so badly burned that they barely functioned, but he refused to give up. Tuhabonye made his way to a hospital for treatment, where he had to learn again how to walk and, eventually, to run.

Less than three years after Tuhabonye nearly died, he was a member of Burundi's Olympic team. Soon after, he enrolled in college in the United States—where he was given a running scholarship. Today, Gilbert Tuhabonye lives in the United States, where he trains runners and tells his story of how running helped him survive.

ADVANCED/GIFTED

Understand Ethnic Conflicts

1. Ask students use the Internet, books, newspapers, or magazines to research an example of ethnic conflict. Encourage them to find examples of conflicts in different countries in order to present a variety of experiences.
2. Have students learn how the ethnic conflict affects families, particularly the lives of children and teenagers. Ask them to find personal stories whenever possible. A pair of students might work together to learn about two sides of a conflict—for example, to contrast the experiences of Israeli and Palestinian children. Stories might involve young people as victims, combatants, or peacemakers.
3. Have students prepare short documentaries to share the stories with the class.
4. Use the documentaries as the basis for a class discussion. Ask the class to notice similarities and differences among the experiences of people in different conflicts.

ONLINE LESSON FLIP CARDS

Review Key Terms and People

Students can use the flip cards in the Lesson Review at any time to review the lesson's key terms and people: *supranational union, refugee, proliferation, Universal Declaration of Human Rights, nonbinding agreement, political dissent, gender inequality,* and *AIDS*.

ONLINE ANALYZE VIDEOS

Battle for Baghdad

Have students watch the video individually or as a class. You may wish to use the associated question as a discussion prompt.

Analyze Videos What difficulties did U.S. forces face when entering Baghdad? *The soldiers had to cross collapsed bridges and enter Baghdad under constant fire.*

ONLINE INTERACTIVE VISUALS

Carousel: The Reality of War: Ethnic and Religious Conflicts

Have students navigate through the carousel and note similarities and differences among the images or identify a unifying theme. You may wish to use the associated question as a discussion prompt.

Analyze Visuals Explain a common thread between the conflicts in Rwanda, South Sudan, and the Iran-Iraq war. *The lives of the civilians were disrupted or changed forever either through displacement, relocation, or injury.*

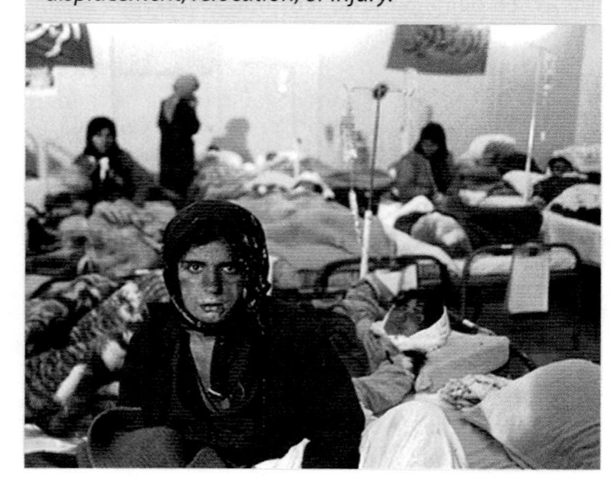

In central Baghdad, a U.S. Marine watches as a statue of Saddam Hussein is pulled down.

In 2002, analysts once again suspected that Hussein might be developing WMD. UN weapons inspectors returned, but Hussein seemed reluctant to cooperate. U.S. President George W. Bush argued that Hussein might be close to building powerful weapons to use against the United States or its allies. In March 2003, Bush ordered American troops to invade Iraq. Troops from Great Britain and other countries supported the attack. After four weeks of fighting, Hussein's government fell.

However, violence in Iraq continued. Factions of Iraqis battled one another for power in the new government. Iraqis angered by the presence of foreign troops in their country fought American soldiers. By the end of 2011, untold thousands of Iraqis and more than 4,486 Americans had been killed. No WMD were ever found.

Chaos in Somalia From 1969 to 1991, a dictator named Mohamed Siad Barre ruled Somalia. Barre banned political parties and arrested or executed political rivals. In 1973, he signed a treaty with the Soviet Union and then enacted Soviet-style economic reforms. The state took control of banks and many businesses. Barre also increased the size of Somalia's military. Beginning in the late 1970s, various clans challenged Barre's rule. In 1991, Barre fled when clan-based militias defeated his military. Those militias then began to fight each other. They killed thousands of civilians in their attempt to gain control of the country. Fighting and mass killings continued for years.

Between 1991 and 2004, there were multiple attempts to negotiate a government. In 2004, the Transitional Federal Government (TFG) was created. Around that time, Somali Islamist groups, including the Islamic Courts Union (ICU) and other affiliated militias, emerged. Concerned

STRUGGLING READERS

Write a Petition

1. Have students review the information in the lesson about the conflicts in Rwanda and the Darfur region of Sudan. Have students locate these two countries on a world map.
2. Then guide students in a discussion of the destruction caused by these two conflicts to the population and to each country.
3. Have students select one of the two conflicts and write a petition to the United Nations, dated during the midst of the conflict, asking for immediate international assistance to help enforce peace within the selected country. Students should discuss the number of people being killed, the reason for the internal conflict, and why immediate assistance is needed.

about terrorist activity in Somalia, the United States began helping the TFG. In 2006, U.S.-backed Ethiopian troops invaded Somalia to support the TFG against the Islamist militias. In 2009, Ethiopian troops withdrew from Somalia. As a result, the TFG lost territory and agreed to a power-sharing deal with Islamist splinter groups. One such group, al Shabaab, separated from the ICU and rejected the peace deal. It continues to operate as a militant group that commits acts of terrorism. Somalia's government is still transitional.

Vocabulary
transitional government a temporary government that prepares the way for elections to establish a permanent government

Ethnic and Religious Conflicts Violence caused by ethnic and religious hatred is a threat to people in many parts of the world. Some conflicts among people of different ethnic or religious groups have roots centuries old. Such conflicts include those between Protestants and Catholics in Ireland, between Palestinians and Israelis in the Middle East, and among Serbs, Bosnians, and Croats in southeastern Europe.

These conflicts have led to terrible violence. The Kurds of southwest Asia have also been the victims of such violence. For decades, Kurds have wanted their own country. But their traditional lands cross the borders of three countries—Turkey, Iran, and Iraq. In the past, the Turks responded to Kurdish nationalism by forbidding Kurds to speak their native language. The Iranians also persecuted the Kurds, attacking them over religious issues. In the late 1980s, the Iraqis dropped poison gas on the Kurds, killing 5,000. Several international organizations, including the UN, worked to end the human rights abuses inflicted upon the Kurds.

South Sudanese refugees

In Rwanda, people of the Hutu ethnic group massacred nearly 1 million people of the Tutsi group. They also killed thousands of Hutus who opposed the killings. Another 2 million Tutsi and Hutu refugees fled to neighboring countries, where food shortages and disease killed thousands more, despite international humanitarian aid. As part of a peacekeeping mission, French and UN troops worked to maintain a ceasefire in Rwanda until a new government could establish order and end the violence. In 1998, some of the people involved in the conflict were tried by the International Criminal Tribunal for Rwanda (ICTR). They were charged with genocide, crimes against humanity, and war crimes. Many were convicted and sentenced to life in prison or executed for their crimes.

A similar situation occurred in the 2000s in the Darfur region of Sudan. There, Arab militias supported by the government attacked African villagers and looted and destroyed their homes. The African Union sent a peacekeeping force to Sudan to try to end the killings, but the violence continued. By 2006, some 400,000 people had been killed in Darfur, and more than 2 million others had fled to refugee camps. In 2011, the southern region of Sudan became a separate state, South Sudan. Unfortunately, a civil war erupted in South Sudan in 2013, and thousands died before a tentative peace agreement was reached in August 2015. Ethnic and religious violence continues in Sudan and South Sudan today.

Reading Check
Analyze Motives Why did nations join supranational organizations in the decades after World War II?

READING CHECK
Analyze Motives Why did nations join supranational organizations in the decades after World War II? *For security, to create and maintain peace, to promote growth, and to pursue common political goals.*

Global Interdependence 1287

Objectives

You may wish to discuss the following questions with students to help them frame the content as they read.

- Why does publicizing human rights violations lead to reform? *Possible answers: The force of public opinion can make governments change. The worst violations often occur in secret.*
- Why is political dissent important in ending human rights abuses? *Possible answer: People must be free to criticize the government in order to gain support for change.*

More About . . .

Aung San Suu Kyi An activist for democracy in her native Myanmar (Burma), Aung San Suu Kyi has long been an opponent of her country's harsh military government. In 1990 her political party won a large majority of the seats in Myanmar's parliament, but the military rulers refused to give up power. Instead, they placed Aung San and other democratic leaders under house arrest. Despite her imprisonment, she continued to fight for democratic reform and free elections in Myanmar. For her nonviolent struggle for democracy, Aung San was awarded the Nobel Peace Prize in 1991. In 2010, she was released from house arrest. In 2012, she won a seat in Parliament.

ONLINE DOCUMENT-BASED INVESTIGATION

The Universal Declaration of Human Rights

The Universal Declaration of Human Rights contains 30 articles that explain the political, economic, and cultural rights of all people. Invite students to read the excerpt and answer the associated question.

Analyze Sources How are some of the words and ideas expressed in the Universal Declaration of Human Rights similar to other historical declarations? *Similar wording and ideas are expressed in the U.S. Declaration of Independence and the French Declaration of the Rights of Man and of the Citizen. The Declaration of Independence claims that all men are equal and have the right to life, liberty, and the pursuit of happiness. The French declaration states that all men are born free and have the right to liberty, property, and security, among other rights.*

DOCUMENT-BASED INVESTIGATION Historical Source

Universal Declaration of Human Rights

The Universal Declaration of Human Rights contains thirty articles that explain the political, economic, and cultural rights of all people.

> "**Article 1**: *All human beings are born free and equal in dignity and rights. They are endowed with reason and conscience and should act towards one another in a spirit of brotherhood.*
> **Article 2**: *Everyone is entitled to all the rights and freedoms set forth in this Declaration, without distinction of any kind, such as race, colour, sex, language, religion, political or other opinion, national or social origin, property, birth or other status. Furthermore, no distinction shall be made on the basis of the political, jurisdictional or international status of the country or territory to which a person belongs, whether it be independent, trust, non-self-governing or under any other limitation of sovereignty.*
> **Article 3**: *Everyone has the right to life, liberty and security of person.*
> **Article 4**: *No one shall be held in slavery or servitude; slavery and the slave trade shall be prohibited in all their forms.*
> **Article 5**: *No one shall be subjected to torture or to cruel, inhuman or degrading treatment or punishment. . . ."*
>
> —quoted from *The Universal Declaration of Human Rights*

Analyze Historical Sources
How are some of the words and ideas expressed in the Universal Declaration of Human Rights similar to other historical declarations?

Human Rights Issues

In 1948, the UN issued the **Universal Declaration of Human Rights**, which set human rights standards for all nations. The declaration listed specific rights, such as the right to liberty and the right to work, that all human beings should have. Later, in the Helsinki Accords of 1975, the UN addressed the issues of freedom of movement and freedom to publish and exchange information.

Both the declaration and the accords are **nonbinding agreements**. A nonbinding agreement means that a nation does not suffer a penalty if it does not meet the terms of the declaration. However, the sentiments in these documents inspired many people around the world. They made a commitment to ensuring that basic human rights are respected. The UN and other private international agencies, such as Amnesty International, identify and publicize human rights violations. They also encourage people to work toward a world in which liberty and justice are guaranteed for all.

Some of the greatest human rights successes have come in the area of political rights and freedoms. In Europe, most countries that were once

COLLABORATIVE LEARNING

Research Nongovernmental Organizations

1. Have groups of students conduct outside research to find an NGO that interests them.
2. Then have each group find the goals of the organization, where it is based, how many people are involved in the group, where it operates, its annual budget, funding sources, and other pertinent information.
3. Have groups compile their research into a multimedia or video presentation and present their finished work to the class.

History in Depth

Human Rights Movements

Human rights movements resisting colonialism, imperialism, slavery, racism, apartheid, patriarchy, and other abuses have reshaped political, social, and economic life around the world. A human rights movement is a social movement that responds to human rights issues. Many national and international government organizations and NGOs have been dedicated to such movements, and the most successful campaigns usually involve a number of organizations working together for a common goal.

Recognizing this, the National Economic and Social Rights Initiative (NESRI) decided to work with many community organizations across the United States. Founded in 2004, NESRI organizes and supports initiatives to integrate social and economic rights into American laws and political culture. Economic and social rights include access to safe work with fair wages; affordable, quality health care; education; nutritious food; and safe, affordable housing.

Analyze Issues
Which human rights does NESRI promote in the United States?

part of the Soviet bloc have opened up their political systems to allow for democratic elections and the free expression of ideas. There have been similar successes in South Africa, where the apartheid system of racial separation came to an end in the early 1990s. Free elections held in South Africa in 1994 finally brought a multiracial government to power.

Vocabulary
nongovernmental organization
a nonprofit group set up by private citizens, businesses, or groups

Combatting Human Rights Abuses Many multinational organizations combat human rights abuses. Non-governmental organizations (NGOs) like Amnesty International and Human Rights Watch research and publicize abuses and campaign to end them. Human Rights Watch's annual world reports detail human rights issues and policy developments around the globe, and the organization works with governments and institutions to promote human rights in more than 90 countries and territories. These and other NGOs have played key roles in the fights against slavery, violence against women, and apartheid. Other groups such as the International Red Cross and Red Crescent are charitable NGOs that offer free assistance to people in times of crisis.

Intergovernmental organizations also play a role. The International Criminal Court (ICC), housed in the Netherlands, prosecutes individuals for genocide, crimes against humanity, and war crimes. By 2015, the ICC had investigated nine situations, including the human rights violations in Darfur.

Continuing Rights Violations Despite the best efforts of various human rights organizations, protecting human rights remains an uphill battle. Serious violations of fundamental rights continue to occur around the world.

HISTORY IN DEPTH

Human Rights Movements

NGOs can take many forms. These include foundations, volunteer organizations, and local, regional, national, and international organizations. Their contributions are wide-ranging and include health aid, disaster recovery assistance, advocacy, supporting entrepreneurs, expanding credit, and helping people confront abuse.

Analyze Issues Which human rights does NESRI promote in the United States? *Possible answer: economic and social rights, such as the rights to work and have health care, education, food, and housing.*

BIOGRAPHY

Mother Teresa

Have students read the biography of Mother Teresa, who devoted her life to helping India's poor and received the Nobel Peace Prize in 1979.

BIOGRAPHY

Mother Teresa (1910–1997)

Mother Teresa was one of the great champions of human rights for all people. Born Agnes Gonxha Bojaxhiu in what today is Macedonia, Mother Teresa joined a convent in Ireland at the age of 18. A short time later, she headed to India to teach at a girls' school. Over time, she noticed many sick and homeless people in the streets. She soon vowed to devote her life to helping India's poor.

In 1948, she established the Order of the Missionaries of Charity in Calcutta, which committed itself to serving the sick, needy, and unfortunate. In recognition of her commitment to the downtrodden, Mother Teresa received the Nobel Peace Prize in 1979.

One type of violation occurs when governments try to stamp out **political dissent**, or the difference of opinion over political issues. In many countries around the world, from Cuba to Iran to Myanmar, individuals and groups have been persecuted for holding political views that differ from those of the people in power. In some countries, like Sudan, ethnic or racial hatreds lead to human rights abuses.

Women's Status Improves In the past, when women in Western nations entered the workforce, they often faced discrimination in employment and salary. In non-Western countries, many women not only faced discrimination in jobs, they were denied access to education. In regions torn by war or ethnic conflict, women have often been victims of violence and abuse. As women suffered, so have their family members, especially children.

In the 1970s, a heightened awareness of human rights encouraged women in many countries to work to improve their lives. They pushed for new laws and government policies that gave them greater equality. In 1975, the UN held the first of several international conferences on women's status in the world. The UN also sponsored a movement toward gender equality, and most countries signed the Convention on the Elimination of All Forms of Discrimination Against Women (1979). In Southeast Asia, all but a few nations, such as Vietnam and Laos, have ratified the treaty. The fourth conference was held in Beijing, China, in 1995. It addressed such issues as preventing violence against women and empowering women to take leadership roles in politics and in business.

Explore ONLINE!

World AIDS Situation, 2014

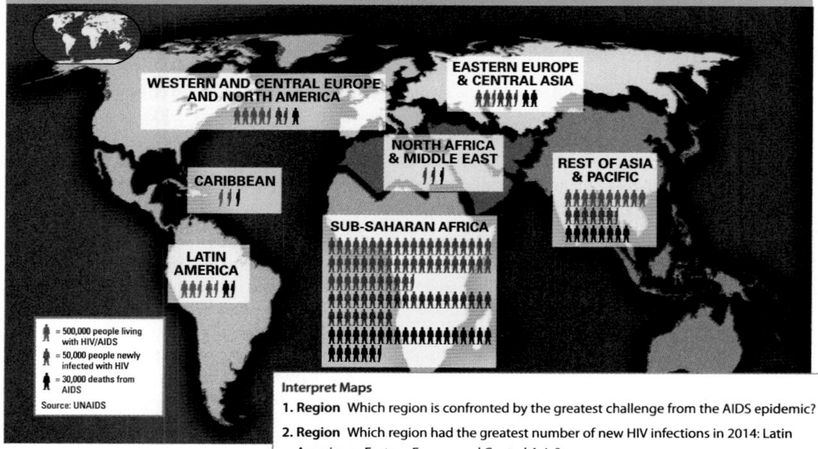

Interpret Maps

1. **Region** Which region is confronted by the greatest challenge from the AIDS epidemic?
2. **Region** Which region had the greatest number of new HIV infections in 2014: Latin America or Eastern Europe and Central Asia?

Reading Check
Analyze Issues
What responsibilities do nations have for protecting human rights in other countries?

In its report *Progress of the World's Women 2015–2016,* the UN found that women had made notable gains in many parts of the world, especially in the areas of education and work. Even so, the report concluded that **gender inequality**—the difference between men and women in terms of wealth and status—still very much exists. It cites discrimination in health care, political representation, employment, and education as reasons for the continued imbalance between men and women.

Health Issues

In recent decades, the enjoyment of a decent standard of health has become recognized as a basic human right. However, for much of the world, poor health is the norm. World health faced a major threat in 2003, with the outbreak of severe acute respiratory syndrome (SARS). This pneumonia-like disease emerged in China and spread worldwide. Afraid of infection, many people canceled travel to Asia. The resulting loss of business hurt Asian economies.

The AIDS Epidemic One of the greatest global health issues is a disease known as **AIDS**, or acquired immune deficiency syndrome. It attacks the immune system, leaving sufferers open to deadly infections. The disease was first detected in the early 1980s. Since that time, AIDS has become a global pandemic: it has claimed the lives of nearly 39 million people worldwide. By the end of 2014, there were almost 37 million people across the world living with HIV (the virus that causes AIDS) or AIDS. And in 2014, two million people were newly infected with HIV.

Vocabulary
pandemic an infectious disease that spreads through a human population in a widespread geographic area

Objectives

You may wish to discuss the following questions with students to help them frame the content as they read.

- What do SARS and AIDS have in common? *Both are infectious diseases.*
- Why is AIDS particularly a problem in poorer countries? *Possible answer: lower standard of living and poorer health-care facilities there*

More About . . .

Tip for Struggling Readers Sub-Saharan Africa refers to the part of the continent that is below, or south of, the Sahara Desert.

Dr. Nafis Sadik Dr. Nafis Sadik studied medicine in Pakistan and the United States. She began her career practicing obstetrics and gynecology in rural Pakistan. In 1970, she was named director-general of Pakistan's Central Family Planning Council, but she left a year later to join the United Nations Population Fund. By 1987, she had become that agency's executive director. She retired in December 2000 but remained active, serving as special adviser to the secretary-general, who in June 2002 appointed Sadik as special envoy for HIV/AIDS in Asia.

READING CHECK

Analyze Issues What responsibilities do nations have for protecting human rights in other countries? *Nations should do all they can to end human rights violations wherever they take place.*

ENGLISH LANGUAGE LEARNERS

Understand Medical Vocabulary

1. Explain that a good strategy to use while reading complicated text is to break down long phrases into parts.
2. Have students analyze the meaning of *severe acute respiratory syndrome* (SARS) and *acquired immune deficiency syndrome* (AIDS). Point out that the first letter of each word is used to create the acronym that is a shorthand word for the disease.
3. Students should create a two-column chart. Have students define the words, using dictionaries as needed.
4. Ask students to notice what word both diseases have in common *(syndrome)*. Ask them to identify the key word or words in each name that describes how and where the disease affects the body. *(SARS—respiratory; AIDS—immune deficiency)*

ONLINE INTERACTIVE MAPS

World AIDS Situation, 2014

Have students explore the map and answer the associated questions.

Interpret Maps Which region below had the greatest number of new HIV infections in 2014? *Eastern Europe and Central Asia*

In print edition, see map of the same title.

Region Which region is confronted by the greatest challenge from the AIDS epidemic? *Sub-Saharan Africa*

Region Which region had the greatest number of new HIV infections in 2014: Latin America or Eastern Europe and Central Asia? *Eastern Europe and Central Asia*

READING CHECK

Synthesize Why are health issues considered a threat to global security? *As a result of globalization, diseases and other health issues can more easily travel from country to country, and epidemics can destabilize societies.*

While AIDS is a worldwide problem, sub-Saharan Africa has suffered most from the epidemic. About 70 percent of all persons infected with HIV live in this region. And in 2014, more than 1.1 million Africans died of AIDS. Many of the people dying are young adults—the age when people are at their most productive economically. AIDS, therefore, is reducing the number of people available as workers, managers, and entrepreneurs.

Since the '90s the world has made some progress in slowing the spread of AIDS. In response to the devastating impact of the disease, the UN issued the Declaration of Commitment on HIV/AIDS in 2001. This document set targets for halting the spread of AIDS and provided guidelines on how countries could pool their efforts.

Other Health Issues Other diseases also threaten world health. For example, in 2015, there were about 214 million malaria cases and an estimated 438,000 malaria deaths. The UN and other global organizations are working to reduce outbreaks of the disease worldwide. As a result, there has been an increase in resources available for prevention and treatment. Cases of tuberculosis are increasing in some regions, and the ability of medical professionals to cure this disease and others caused by bacteria is in jeopardy, as some antibiotics have lost their effectiveness against drug-resistant bacteria.

Reading Check
Synthesize Why are health issues considered a threat to global security?

SOCIAL HISTORY

Syrian Civil War

In 2011, Syrian prodemocracy protesters demanded the resignation of President Bashar al-Assad. In response, the government used military force to end the protests and silence opposition. Violence soon escalated, and a civil war broke out as rebel groups formed to fight against government forces for control of cities and towns. After years of fighting, the conflict has grown into a struggle between the Sunni Muslim majority and the president's Shia Muslim sect. The growth of insurgent groups, such as the Islamic State of Iraq and the Levant (ISIL), have furthered the conflict.

This Syrian refugee family left their home in November 2015 and fled to Turkey along with many other refugee families. The refugee families live in tents, storehouses and rental properties in many different countries as they try to find safety.

As a result of the civil war, more than 220,000 Syrians have lost their lives and more than 11 million have been forced to leave their homes. According to human rights organizations, at least 7 million Syrians have been displaced within Syria, and more than 4 million have fled as refugees to neighboring countries, mostly Turkey, Lebanon, Jordan, and Iraq.

Two Afghan girls quietly wait for food at a refugee camp on the Afghanistan-Iran border.

Population Movement

The global movement of people has increased dramatically in recent years. This migration has taken place for both negative and positive reasons.

Push-Pull Factors People often move because they feel pushed out of their homelands. Lack of food due to drought, natural disasters, and political oppression are examples of push factors of migration. At the end of 2014, the number of **refugees** stood at 19.5 million. Millions more were displaced within their home countries.

Not only negative events push people to migrate. Most people have strong connections to their home countries and do not leave unless strong positive attractions pull them away. They hope for a better life for themselves and for their children, and thus migrate to developed nations. For example, hundreds of thousands of people migrate from Africa to Europe and from Latin America to the United States every year. Many of these people eventually become citizens. Others do not, perhaps because they entered the country illegally. Although their rights are limited, even non-citizens have responsibilities in civic participation, such as paying taxes.

Effects of Migration Everyone has the right to leave his or her country. However, the country to which a migrant wants to move may not accept that person. The receiving country might have one policy about accepting refugees from political situations, and another about migrants coming for economic reasons. Because of the huge volume of people migrating from war-torn, famine-stricken, and politically unstable regions, millions

Objectives

You may wish to discuss the following questions with students to help them frame the content as they read.

- Why do refugees have a more difficult time than other immigrants? *Possible answer: often forced to flee without having any place to go*
- How does a country's labor market affect its attitude toward immigrants? *Possible answer: If unemployment is high, a country may not want immigrants who will compete with citizens for jobs.*

More About . . .

Khaled Hosseini Khaled Hosseini is a physician who was born in Afghanistan. His family moved to the United States in 1980 where he received his bachelor's degree in biology and then his medical degree. The novel *The Kite Runner* was his first attempt at writing a novel, and the work was met with critical success. The novel tells the story of an Afghan whose family immigrates to the United States when the Taliban comes to power, and it recounts life for those who were left to deal with the changes in the country.

ENGLISH LANGUAGE LEARNERS

Commemorate a Natural Disaster

1. Review with students some of the natural disasters that have occurred in the 21st century. Students might mention Hurricane Katrina, tsunamis, tornadoes, or earthquakes. Make a class list for all to see. Then review the ways in which the national and international community responded to each disaster on the list.
2. Have students write a song or poem commemorating one of the events on the class list. Student work should be sensitive to the loss of life, property, and way of life that occurs during a major natural disaster.

COLLABORATIVE LEARNING

Discuss Social Challenges

1. Organize students into groups of four. Assign one of the four topics in the lesson: War and Peace, Human Rights, Health, and Population Movement, to each student in a group.
2. Have students write a summary of their topic and read it to the rest of the group. Have students ask and answer questions about the summaries.
3. Guide students in a discussion of the importance of human rights, and develop a class list of the rights students believe to be most important.

READING CHECK

Analyze Causes What push and pull factors cause people to migrate? *push: natural disasters, political problems, lack of food; pull: hope for a better life*

of people have no place to go. Crowded into refugee camps, often under squalid conditions, these migrants face a very uncertain future.

Those accepted into new countries face many challenges and opportunities. In their adopted countries, they often have more services and opportunities available to them, such as health care, education, and jobs. However, it may be difficult to obtain those services due to language barriers, cost, or lack of knowledge about how to access services. If immigrants don't speak the adopted country's language or if job training obtained in their home country isn't considered valid in the receiving country, they may struggle to find work. Once they do, however, they can sometimes reduce the economic struggles of family and friends still in their home country by sending money to them. At the same time, immigrants bring their home cultures to their adopted countries, helping to create a rich, diverse blended culture.

Immigrants often help offset labor shortages in a variety of industries. Nevertheless, some citizens in receiving countries believe that immigrants take more than they give, a belief that can lead to policies intended to reduce immigration. For example, in Canada, where about 250,000 immigrants arrive each year, government policies enacted in 2015 made it more difficult to obtain Canadian citizenship. Some believe this change is a reaction to recent economic difficulties and job scarcity, because in the past Canada has served as a model for immigration.

Reading Check
Analyze Causes
What push and pull factors cause people to migrate?

Lesson 3 Assessment

1. Use a table to note the methods of global security and examples of each method. Explain which methods have resulted in the greatest contribution to global security.

Method	Examples
Form military alliances	NATO, SEATO, Warsaw Pact

2. **Key Terms and People** For each key term or person in the lesson, write a sentence explaining its significance.
3. **Make Inferences** Why might nations want to retain or develop an arsenal of nuclear, biological, and chemical weapons?
4. **Analyze Effects** How have conflict and cooperation among groups impacted the control of limited resources in the world?
5. **Evaluate** What strategies have been used to resolve conflicts in society and government? Do you think they have been effective?
6. **Identify Problems** How are ethnic and religious conflicts related to problems of global security?
7. **Recognize Effects** How can individuals affect social conditions around the world? Consider the example of Mother Teresa when writing your answer.

Print Assessment

Review Ideas, Terms, and People

1. Use a table to note the methods of global security and examples of each method. Explain which methods have resulted in the greatest contribution to global security. *Possible answer: Formation of the UN—reduced threat of conflict, promoted peace; Arms-control agreements—reduced number of weapons of mass destruction. Most important—arms control, because it lessens the threat of mass destruction*
2. **Key Terms and People** For each key term or person in the lesson, write a sentence explaining its significance. *Explanations of the lesson's key terms can be found on the following pages: supranational union, p. 1284; refugee, proliferation, p. 1285; Universal Declaration of Human Rights, nonbinding agreement, p. 1288; political dissent, p. 1290; gender inequality, AIDS, p. 1291.*
3. **Make Inferences** Why might nations want to retain or develop an arsenal of nuclear, biological, and chemical weapons? *as a deterrent*
4. **Analyze Effects** How have conflict and cooperation among groups impacted the control of limited resources in the world? *Possible answer: Countries and groups that control oil supplies have control over the nations that need the oil, and as a result this control can lead to conflicts such as war. An example of such a conflict was the Persian Gulf War.*
5. **Evaluate** What strategies have been used to resolve conflicts in society and government? Do you think they have been effective? *Possible answer: The UN sets up committees and issues declarations; NGOs and government organizations implement different plans and strategies to help people like refugees. Yes, I think they have been somewhat effective but stricter strategies may be needed because many conflicts such as the one in Darfur (Sudan) continue around the world.*
6. **Identify Problems** How are ethnic and religious conflicts related to problems of global security? *Possible answer: Some ethnic and religious conflicts have lasted for centuries and have led to much violence and persecution of other groups. The conflicts have spread and have led to human rights issues.*
7. **Recognize Effects** How can individuals affect social conditions around the world? Consider the example of Mother Teresa when writing your answer. *Possible answer: Mother Teresa committed herself to serving the sick, needy, and unfortunate, which helped many people around the world.*

Online Assessment

1. Why did many European nations join NATO and the Warsaw Pact?
   - ● They believed that military coalitions could best protect their security.
   - ○ They believed that by eliminating trade barriers their economies would prosper.
   - ○ They needed international organizations to help rebuild their economies after World War II.
   - ○ They needed international organizations to oversee the settlement of refugees after World War II.

   Alternate Question *Select the answer choice from the drop-down list to complete the sentence correctly.* In 1957, (the) *EEC* was formed to promote trade between member nations, binding their economies together in an attempt to avoid future conflicts over resources.

2. Which statement accurately describes the Universal Declaration of Human Rights?
   - ● The United Nations document promotes the right to liberty and the right to work.
   - ○ Governments must sign the document in order to become a United Nations member.
   - ○ The document promotes the freedom to publish information and the freedom of movement.
   - ○ Governments are bound to respect the ideals in the document by threat of economic sanctions.

   Alternate Question *Drag the answer choice into the box to complete the sentence correctly.* Organizations such as (the) *Amnesty International* investigate human rights violations and publish their findings in an effort to pressure governments to cease such activities.

3. Which statement accurately describes the state of the world's health?
   - ○ Doctors have been unable to slow the spread of AIDS.
   - ● Contagious diseases, like SARS, still threaten large populations.
   - ○ Doctors have been able to eliminate tuberculosis with antibiotics.
   - ○ Diseases carried by insects, like malaria, have been eliminated with pesticides.

   Alternate Question *Select the answer choice from the drop-down list to complete the sentence correctly.* Continents that have poor health care systems, like *Africa*, have suffered the most from the spread of AIDS.

4. Why did Syrians rebel against President Bashar al-Assad's rule in 2011?
   - ○ They demanded that the government expel ISIL.
   - ○ They wanted an end to religious warfare in the Middle East.
   - ● Their political protests were met with government oppression.
   - ○ Their government refused to allow immigration to neighboring countries.

   Alternate Question *Select the answer choice from the drop-down list to complete the sentence correctly.* The Syrian civil war escalated into a conflict between al-Assad's *Shia* supporters and the Sunni majority population of the country.

5. **Evaluate** How does the International Atomic Energy Agency (IAEA) promote peace throughout the world?

   Possible answer: The IAEA is an organization that monitors the use of nuclear technology throughout the world. Nuclear energy can be used to create electricity and develop a nation's economy. However, a nation could create nuclear bombs as well. The IAEA is called in to determine whether a nation's nuclear program is peaceful or not. If a country is suspected of building nuclear bombs, the international community may choose to impose economic sanctions on that nation in an effort to influence it to cease the construction of a nuclear bomb.

6. **Evaluate** How effective have reformers been in eliminating gender inequality since the 1979 Convention on the Elimination of All Forms of Discrimination Against Women?

   Possible answer: Judging by the 2016 United Nations report, Progress of the World's Women, 2015–2016, women have made significant advancements in education and employment. However, there are fewer wealthy women in the world than men and their wages are often not equal to men. The authors of the report found that women lack sufficient leadership positions in politics, education, and business. As well, the report concluded that women lack adequate access to good health care.

7. **Make Inferences** How can contagious diseases, like SARS, cause global economic problems?

   Possible answer: With the advent of world travel using passenger airplanes and the globalization of the world's economies, contagious diseases can easily spread from one continent to another. The outbreak of SARS in 2003 is a good example of how quickly a disease can spread from one region to another. Many businesspeople and travelers canceled trips to Asia because they feared contracting the highly contagious disease. These canceled trips and the fear of traveling throughout Asia caused a disruption in business.

8. **Elaborate** What difficulties do immigrants face when moving to other countries?

   Possible answer: Immigrants move to other countries because they are forced out of their country by war, oppression, or famine, or they are encouraged to leave to seek a better life for themselves and their families. Migrants face numerous challenges, such as language barriers, social acceptance, and religious discrimination. In the case of refugees, there is the psychological issue of leaving one's country against their will and the mental scars left from the violence of war.

Lesson 4 Planner

Terrorism

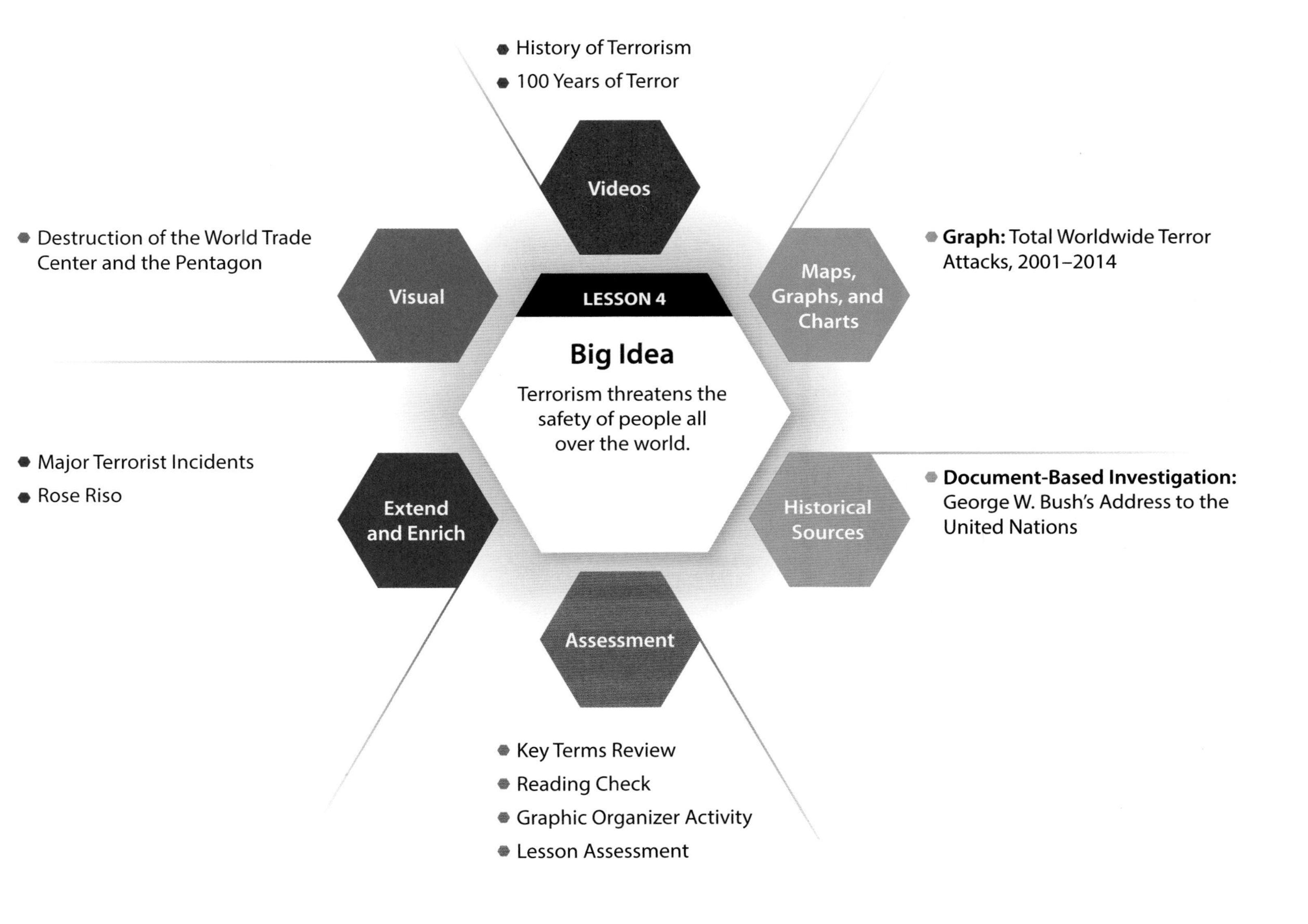

Online Lesson 4 Enrichment Activities

Major Terrorist Incidents

Timeline Activity Students create a timeline identifying major terrorist incidents since 2001. They research and annotate each timeline event with descriptions and illustrations.

Rose Riso

Biography Students read a biography about a hero of the terrorist attacks on September 11. Then they research other individuals who acted heroically during the attacks of September 11, 2001, and create a memorial video honoring the fallen heroes.

Lesson 4

Case Study

September 11, 2001

Terrorism

The Big Idea

Terrorism has threatened the safety of people all over the world.

Why It Matters Now

People and nations must work together against the dangers posed by terrorism.

Key Terms and People

terrorism
cyberterrorism
Department of Homeland Security
USA PATRIOT Act

Setting the Stage

Wars are not the only threat to international peace and security. **Terrorism**, the use of violence against noncombatants to force changes in societies or governments, strikes fear in the hearts of people everywhere. Recently, terrorist incidents have increased dramatically around the world. Because terrorists often cross national borders to commit their acts or to escape to countries friendly to their cause, most people consider terrorism an international problem.

What Is Terrorism?

Terrorism is not new. Throughout history, individuals, small groups, and governments have used terror tactics to try to achieve political or social goals, whether to bring down a government, eliminate opponents, or promote a cause. In recent times, however, terrorism has changed.

Modern Terrorism Since the late 1960s, tens of thousands of terrorist attacks have occurred worldwide. International terrorist groups have carried out increasingly destructive, high-profile attacks to call attention to their goals and to gain major media coverage. Many countries also face domestic terrorists who oppose their governments' policies or have special interests to promote.

The reasons for modern terrorism are many. The traditional motives, such as gaining independence, expelling foreigners, or changing society, still drive various terrorist groups. These groups use violence to force concessions from their enemies, usually the governments in power. But other kinds of terrorists, driven by radical religious and cultural motives, began to emerge in the late 20th century.

The goal of these terrorists is the destruction of what they consider to be evil. This evil might be located in their own countries or in other parts of the world. These terrorists are willing to die to ensure the success of their attacks.

Objectives

You may wish to discuss the following questions with students to help them frame the content as they read.

- How might globalization be a factor in the growth of terrorism? *Possible answer: Some terrorists may believe globalization undermines local or religious values.*
- Why is cyberterrorism such a threat? *Possible answer: Attacks against computers could cripple vital public or private services.*

Teach the Big Idea

1. **Whole Class Open/Introduction** Ask students to discuss what their reaction might have been if they had witnessed the September 11, 2001, terrorist attacks.
2. **Direct Teach** Read students the Big Idea: *Terrorism threatens the safety of people all over the world.* Review the following lesson objectives with students to aid in their understanding of the Big Idea.
   - Define modern terrorism.
   - Give examples of terrorism from around the world.
   - Describe the September 11, 2001, terrorist attacks on the United States.
   - Summarize U.S. response to this attack.
   - Analyze global effects of terrorism.
3. **Whole Group Close/Reflect** Have students write a one-page memo describing how life in the United States, and in other countries, changed following the September 11, 2001, attacks.

ONLINE DOCUMENT-BASED INVESTIGATION

Global Interdependence

George W. Bush's Address to the United Nations is the fourth of six document–based investigations that students will analyze in the Global Interdependence module. Two months after the 9/11 attacks, U.S. President George W. Bush addressed the United Nations General Assembly to discuss terrorism. Invite students to read the excerpt from the address and answer the associated question.

ONLINE GRAPHIC ORGANIZER

Terrorism

As students read the lesson, have them use the graphic organizer to take notes. Students can review their graphic organizer notes at the end of the lesson to answer the following question:

Summarize Describe three of the terrorist incidents that have occurred around the world. *Munich Olympics – Israeli athletes were taken hostage by terrorist group known as Black September; Tokyo Subway – sarin gas was released into the subway; act of biochemical terrorism; September 11th – Arab hijackers took over four planes; two crashed into the World Trade Center towers, one into the Pentagon; the fourth plane crashed into an empty field in Pennsylvania.*

More About . . .

Internet Security The U.S. government significantly increased spending on computer security after the attacks of September 11, 2001. Carnegie Mellon University received a multimillion-dollar, five-year grant to study cyberterrorism. One aspect of the research focused on ways to identify hackers or terrorists attempting to disrupt computer systems. Researchers also explored methods of forcing computers to shut down automatically when attacked.

Tip for English Language Learners Point out that the suffixes *-ism* (action, process or practice of) and *-ist* (one who performs an action) are added to the word *terror* (intense fear) to create new words. What *-ism* words do students recall from earlier chapters? *(communism, imperialism, Social Darwinism)*

READING CHECK

Draw Conclusions Why do terrorists tend to target crowded places? *To cause mass casualties and gain public attention so they can spread their message; it creates fear.*

ONLINE LESSON FLIP CARDS

Review Key Terms and People

Students can use the flip cards in the Lesson Review at any time to review the lesson's key terms and people: *terrorism, cyberterrorism, Department of Homeland Security,* and *USA Patriot Act.*

The sarin gas attack in the Tokyo subway in 1995 is the most notorious act of biochemical terrorism.

Terrorist Methods Terrorist acts involve violence against noncombatants. The weapons most frequently used by terrorists are the bomb and the bullet. The targets of terrorist attacks often are crowded places where people normally feel safe—subway stations, bus stops, restaurants, or shopping malls, for example. Or terrorists might target something that symbolizes what they are against, such as a government building or a religious site. Such targets are carefully chosen in order to gain the most attention and to achieve the highest level of intimidation.

Recently, some terrorist groups have used biological and chemical agents in their attacks. These actions involved the release of bacteria or poisonous gases into the atmosphere. While both biological and chemical attacks can inflict terrible casualties, they are equally powerful in generating great fear among the public. This development in terrorism is particularly worrisome, because biochemical agents are relatively easy to acquire. Laboratories all over the world use bacteria and viruses in the development of new drugs. And the raw materials needed to make some deadly chemical agents can be purchased in many stores or online.

Cyberterrorism is another recent development. This involves politically motivated attacks on information systems, such as hacking into computer networks or spreading computer viruses. Many governments and businesses now use computers and networks to store data and run operations. Cyberattacks have increased accordingly.

Responding to Terrorism Governments take various steps to stamp out terrorism. Most adopt a very aggressive approach in tracking down and punishing terrorist groups. This approach includes infiltrating the groups to gather information on membership and future plans. It also includes striking back harshly after a terrorist attack, even to the point of assassinating known terrorist leaders.

Another approach governments use is to make it more difficult for terrorists to act. This involves eliminating extremists' sources of funds, persuading governments not to protect or support terrorist groups, and tightening security measures.

Reading Check
Draw Conclusions Why do terrorists tend to target crowded places?

ENGLISH LANGUAGE LEARNERS

Understand Words in Context

1. Read aloud the paragraphs in the segment "Terrorist Methods." As you read each sentence, write down difficult or unfamiliar words or phrases on the board.
2. Ask students to look for clues as they read— such as synonyms or examples— to help them understand these terms. As students discover the clue words, write them down opposite the words in your list.
3. After you have defined all the unfamiliar terms, ask the students to summarize the paragraphs in their own words. Your list might include the following:

biological agents	living substances (point out that agents here are not people)
biochemical	biological + chemical
cyberterrorism	cyber (having to do with computers) + terrorism
information systems	computer networks
hacking	breaking into computer systems illegally
computer virus	secret computer program that spreads through a computer and causes it to break down (the way a biological virus can cause disease)

Terrorism Around the World

The problem of modern international terrorism first came to world attention in a shocking way during the 1972 Summer Olympic Games in Munich, Germany (then West Germany). Members of a Palestinian terrorist group killed two Israeli athletes and took nine others hostage, later killing them. Palestinian terrorists also used airplane hijackings and suicide bombers. Since then, few regions of the world have been spared from terrorist attacks.

Islamist Movements Some Muslims believe that society's laws should be based on what they hold is God's law as written in the Qur'an. In the mid- to late-twentieth century, some Islamic scholars turned to a strict interpretation of the Qur'an. They felt that Western influences were corrupting Muslim countries. They called for all true Muslims to join a global *jihad*, or struggle, against Western societies and governments.

Many young men radicalized by fundamentalist teachings answered that call. These men, and some women, became the foot soldiers for fundamentalist organizations such as Al-Qaeda, Hamas, Hezbollah, and the Taliban. They have been responsible for numerous acts of terrorism.

The Middle East Many terrorist organizations have roots in the Israeli-Palestinian conflict over land in the Middle East. Groups such as the Palestine Islamic Jihad, Hamas, and Hezbollah have sought to prevent a peace settlement between Israel and the Palestinians. They want a homeland for the Palestinians on their own terms, deny Israel's right to exist, and seek Israel's destruction. In a continual cycle of violence, the Israelis retaliate after most terrorist attacks, and the terrorists strike again. Moderates in the region believe that the only long-term solution is a compromise between Israel and the Palestinians over the issue of land. However, the violence has continued with only occasional breaks.

The Iran-backed Lebanese terrorist group Hezbollah formed after the 1982 Israeli invasion of Lebanon to fight the Israeli occupation of South Lebanon. One of the group's primary goals is the destruction of the state of Israel. In July 2006, Hezbollah kidnapped two Israeli soldiers and fired rockets into Israel, triggering a month-long conflict between Israel and Lebanon.

In 2002, Israel began building a security barrier to prevent Palestinian suicide bombers from entering Israel. This Palestinian protest took place in 2007.

Europe Many countries in Europe have been targets of domestic terrorists who oppose government policies. For decades the mostly Catholic Irish Republican Army (IRA) engaged in terrorist attacks against Britain because it opposed British control of Northern Ireland. Since 1998, however, the British, the IRA, and representatives of Northern Ireland's Protestants have been negotiating a peaceful solution to the situation. An agreement was reached in 2005.

Objectives

You may wish to discuss the following questions with students to help them frame the content as they read.

- How would you compare terrorism in the Middle East to terrorism in Northern Ireland? *Both involve opposing groups fighting over control of territory.*
- Why was the attack on the Tokyo subway system significant? *It focused attention on the use of chemical weapons by terrorists.*

More About . . .

Al-Qaeda Al-Qaeda was established in the late 1980s to support Muslims fighting against the Soviet Union in Afghanistan. The organization trained thousands in paramilitary skills and has groups located in 100 countries. Since the September 11, 2001, attacks on the United States, more than 3,000 suspected Al-Qaeda members have been arrested throughout the world for terrorist activities. Al-Qaeda has also claimed responsibility for recent terrorist attacks, such as the deadly siege on the Radisson Blu hotel in Mali in 2015.

Tip for Struggling Readers The word *narcoterrorism* comes from combining *narcotics* (a type of drug) and *terrorism*.

Misconception Alert Be sure to remind students that not all terrorist attacks originate in the Middle East region or from members of a single religious group. If students question this, remind them that the Oklahoma City bombing in 1995, which resulted in 168 deaths, was committed by a domestic terrorist.

ONLINE ANALYZE VIDEOS

History of Terrorism

Have students watch the video individually or as a class. You may wish to use the associated question as a discussion prompt.

Analyze Videos What are the motives of modern terrorists? *Modern terrorists are motivated by religious, cultural, and nationalistic beliefs that they believe are more important than their lives or the lives of others.*

STRUGGLING READERS

Map Terrorism Around the World

1. Pair a struggling reader with a more proficient reader. Ask students to read the segment "Terrorism Around the World," making note of every place name that is mentioned. *(Munich, Germany; Israel; Britain and Northern Ireland; Afghanistan; Saudi Arabia; Tokyo, Japan; Kenya; Tanzania; Sudan; Colombia)*
2. Have students use an atlas or a globe to help them find each of the places. Then have students place labels on the map to show each location and identify its significance.
3. Ask students how this activity affected their comprehension of the material. Encourage students to refer to an atlas whenever they are reading text that includes place names.

ONLINE INTERACTIVE GRAPHS

Total Worldwide Terror Attacks, 2001–2014

Have students explore the graph and answer the associated question.

Interpret Graphs When did the global total of terrorist incidents begin to rise above 5,000? *2010* In print edition, see graph titled Total Worldwide Terror Attacks, 1994–2014.

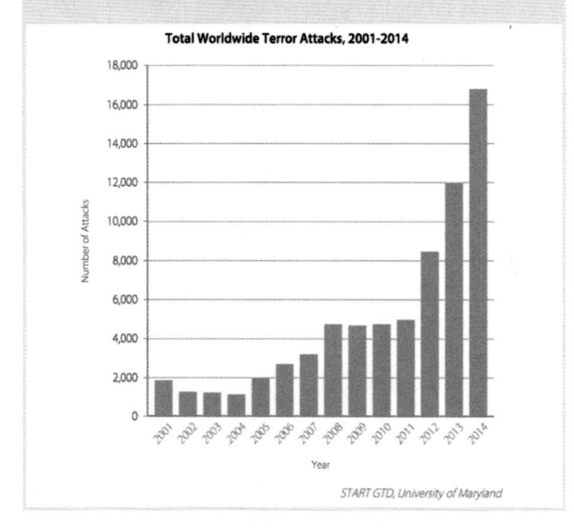

ONLINE ANALYZE VIDEOS

100 Years of Terror

Have students watch the video individually or as a class. You may wish to use the associated question as a discussion prompt.

HISTORY

Analyze Videos Why did Irish nationalists view the Truce of 1921 as a failure? *They believed that Michael Collins lost vision of the true cause and gave in to Britain.*

Other European terrorist groups include the ETA, a militant separatist group that sought independence for the Basque region of Spain, and the left-wing Red Brigades in Italy, which sought to destabilize the Italian government in the 1970s and 1980s before collapsing after many members were arrested. In 2011 the ETA announced a permanent cease-fire.

Asia Afghanistan, in Southwest Asia, became a haven for international terrorists after the Taliban came to power in 1996. In that year, Osama bin Laden, a Saudi Arabian millionaire involved in terrorist activities, moved to Afghanistan. There he began using mountain hideouts as a base of operations for his global network of Muslim terrorists known as al-Qaeda.

Terrorist groups have arisen in East Asia, as well. One, known as Aum Shinrikyo ("Supreme Truth"), is a religious cult that wants to control Japan. In 1995, cult members released sarin, a deadly nerve gas, in subway stations in Tokyo. Twelve people were killed and more than 5,700 injured. This attack brought global attention to the threat of biological and chemical agents as terrorist weapons.

In South Asia, the Tamil Tigers (LTTE) in Sri Lanka have used suicide bombings and other terrorist tactics in their fight for an independent state. In 1983, after the LTTE ambushed 13 Sinhalese soldiers, a civil war erupted. Even though a cease-fire agreement was signed with the LTTE and the government in 2002, violence continued. In 2008 the government broke the agreement to pursue and eliminate the leadership of the LTTE, which it achieved the following year.

Total Worldwide Terror Attacks, 1994–2014

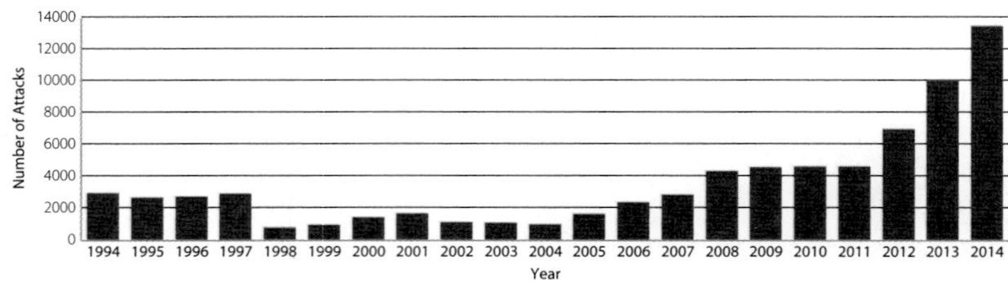

Source: START GTD

Interpret Graphs
1. **Compare** When did the global total of terrorist incidents begin to rise above 5,000?

Africa Civil unrest and regional wars were the root causes of most terrorist activity in Africa at the end of the 20th century. But al-Qaeda cells operated in many African countries, and several major attacks against U.S. personnel and facilities in Africa were linked to al-Qaeda. In 1998, for example, bombings at the U.S. embassies in Kenya and Tanzania left more than 200 people dead and more than 5,000 have injured. The United States responded to these attacks with missile strikes on suspected terrorist facilities in Afghanistan and in Sudan, where bin Laden was based from 1991 to 1996.

Latin America Narcoterrorism, or terrorism linked to drug trafficking, is a major problem in Latin America, particularly in Colombia. The powerful groups that control that country's narcotics trade have frequently turned to violence. The Revolutionary Armed Forces of Colombia (FARC) is a left-wing guerrilla group that has links with these drug traffickers. The FARC has attacked Colombian political, military, and economic targets, as well as those with American ties.

Other Latin American groups were motivated by political ideologies rather than the economics of the drug trade. Shining Path, a militant Communist group founded in 1970 in Peru, sought to overthrow the Peruvian government to replace it with a Communist government. Its 20-year campaign of violence caused tens of thousands of deaths and disrupted the country's economy.

Reading Check
Analyze Causes
What are some reasons for terrorism in various regions of the world?

History in Depth

Drug Trafficking

Drug trafficking is an illegal trade that includes producing, distributing, and selling illegal drugs. From the 1970s to the 1990s, Colombia served as the dominant location in the distribution of cocaine. Criminal organizations known as drug cartels controlled the distribution and sale of cocaine. In recent years, the United States has been working with the Colombian government as part of the Plan Colombia program. The Plan Colombia program provided hundreds of millions of dollars per year for military aid, training, and equipment to fight the FARC and other guerrilla forces involved in drug trafficking.

At the height of Colombian drug trafficking and cartel control, illegal gang and criminal activity related to drug trafficking arose. These activities, as well as economic opportunities, drove local residents to migrate to other countries, including the United States. Once working in their new countries, many of these immigrant workers sent their salaries back to family members in their home country. Once economic conditions and security improve in their home country, they often return.

READING CHECK

Analyze Causes What are some reasons for terrorism in various regions of the world? *Conflict over territory, challenging governmental control, religious beliefs, civil unrest, narcotics trafficking*

Global Interdependence 1299

Objectives

You may wish to discuss the following questions with students to help them frame the content as they read.

- Why were Americans so shocked by the attacks on September 11, 2001? *Possible answer: Americans had thought that terrorism was confined to other parts of the world.*
- How would you contrast the anthrax attacks with the attacks on September 11? *Possible answer: The anthrax attacks resulted in less loss of life than the September 11 attacks, but the widespread feelings of vulnerability was similar.*

More About . . .

Anthrax Anthrax is a very old disease, described in the Bible and by ancient Greek and Roman writers. It mostly infects animals such as cows and sheep. The form of anthrax that affects the lungs was called woolsorter's disease. Humans contracted it by inhaling spores from the wool of infected animals. Louis Pasteur developed a vaccine in 1881.

ONLINE DOCUMENT-BASED INVESTIGATION

George W. Bush's Address to the United Nations

Two months after the 9/11 attacks, U.S. President George W. Bush addressed the United Nations General Assembly to discuss terrorism. Invite students to read the excerpt from the address and answer the associated question.

Analyze Sources Describe the global security responsibilities of all United Nations members. *Member nations must work together to improve security against terrorism by sharing intelligence, coordinating law enforcement efforts, and denying aid to terrorists.*

Case Study > September 11, 2001

Attack on the United States

On the morning of September 11, 2001, nineteen Arab terrorists hijacked four airliners heading from East Coast airports to California. In a series of coordinated strikes, the hijackers crashed two of the jets into the twin towers of the World Trade Center in New York City and a third into the Pentagon outside Washington, D.C. The fourth plane crashed in an empty field in Pennsylvania.

The Destruction The planes, loaded with fuel, became destructive missiles when they crashed into the World Trade Center and the Pentagon. The explosions and fires so weakened the damaged skyscrapers that they crumbled to the ground less than two hours after impact. The fire and raining debris caused nearby buildings to collapse as well. The damage at the Pentagon, though extensive, was confined to one section of the building.

The toll in human lives was great. Nearly 3,000 people died in the attacks. All passengers on the four planes were killed, as well as workers and visitors in the World Trade Center and the Pentagon. The dead

DOCUMENT-BASED INVESTIGATION Historical Source

President George W. Bush

Two months after the 9/11 attacks, U.S. President George W. Bush addressed the United Nations General Assembly to discuss terrorism.

"The most basic obligations in this new conflict have already been defined by the United Nations.... Every United Nations member has a responsibility to crack down on terrorist financing. We must pass all necessary laws in our own countries to allow the confiscation of terrorist assets. We must apply those laws to every financial institution in every nation.

We have responsibility to share intelligence and coordinate the efforts of law enforcement. If you know something, tell us. If we know something, we'll tell you. And when we find the terrorists, we must work together to bring them to justice.... We have a responsibility to deny weapons to terrorists...."

—George W. Bush

Analyze Historical Sources
Describe the global security responsibilities of all United Nations members.

ADVANCED/GIFTED

Analyze the Damage After September 11

1. Encourage students to explore the types of damage caused by the terrorist attacks and to analyze the causes. Students may find resources on the Internet or from newspaper or magazine articles. Some possible topics include:
   - Why did the airplanes cause so much damage when they crashed into the World Trade Center?
   - How did the design of the World Trade Center lead to the collapse of the towers and nearby buildings?
   - Was the loss of life greater or less than might have been expected from this kind of attack? Why?
   - What kind of environmental damage did the attacks cause?
   - What confined the damage in the Pentagon to one area?
   - How was the Pentagon designed to withstand attack?
2. After students have done their research, ask them to present their findings in the form of a display board, model, diagram, or photo essay.
3. Have students share their findings with the class.

included more than 340 New York City firefighters and 60 police officers who rushed to the scene to help and were buried in the rubble when the skyscrapers collapsed.

The Impact of the Attack September 11 had a devastating impact on the way Americans looked at life. Many reported feeling that everything had changed—that life would never be the same. Before, Americans had viewed terrorism as something that happened in other countries. Now they felt vulnerable and afraid.

This sense of vulnerability was underscored just a few days after September 11, when terrorism struck the United States again. Letters containing spores of a bacterium that causes the disease anthrax were sent to people in the news media and to members of Congress in Washington, D.C. Anthrax bacteria, when inhaled, can damage the lungs and cause death. Five people who came in contact with spores from the tainted letters died of inhalation anthrax. Two were postal workers.

Investigators did not find a link between the September 11 attacks and the anthrax letters. Some of them believed that the letters might be the work of a lone terrorist rather than an organized group. Regardless of who was responsible for the anthrax scare, it caused incredible psychological damage. Many Americans were now fearful of an everyday part of life—the mail.

Reading Check
Make Inferences Why were the specific targets of the September 11 attacks selected by the terrorists?

History in Depth

Destruction in New York City and the Pentagon

▲ Stunned bystanders look on as smoke billows from the twin towers of the World Trade Center.

▲ The strike on the Pentagon left a charred, gaping hole in the southwest side of the building.

► A hazardous materials team prepares to enter a congressional building during the anthrax scare.

ONLINE INTERACTIVE VISUALS

Carousel: Destruction of the World Trade Center and the Pentagon

Have students navigate through the carousel and note similarities and differences among the images or identify a unifying theme. You may wish to use the associated question as a discussion prompt.

Analyze Visuals How did the attacks on September 11 affect American views on terrorism? *Americans became much more concerned about terrorism than they had been before.*

READING CHECK

Make Inferences Why were the specific targets of the September 11 attacks selected by the terrorists? *They were symbols of American power. Also, many people would be killed in the World Trade Center, heightening the level of intimidation.*

Objectives

You may wish to discuss the following questions with students to help them frame the content as they read.

- Why did the USA Patriot Act order banks to investigate large foreign accounts? *Possible answer: to find possible sources of money used to fund terrorist organizations*
- What was the psychological impact of using air marshals and National Guard troops for aviation security? *Possible answer: Doing so made people feel it was safe to fly.*

More About . . .

Homeland Security Advisory System Shortly after its establishment in 2002, the Department of Homeland Security created a five-level, color-coded alert system to keep Americans informed about the likelihood of imminent terrorist attack. The system ranged from green at the low end to red at the high end, signaling a severe risk of attack. For the first year the level was generally set at yellow, elevated. In February 2003, prior to the beginning of the war in Iraq, the alert level was raised to orange, high. Critics of the effectiveness of the system included many U.S. mayors whose cities were forced to invest extra money in emergency personnel whenever the code level was raised.

READING CHECK

Summarize Why were some people opposed to the USA Patriot Act? *They thought the government was infringing upon the civil rights of the people being detained.*

The United States Responds

Immediately after September 11, the United States called for an international effort to combat terrorist groups. President George W. Bush declared, "This battle will take time and resolve. But make no mistake about it: we will win."

The Hunt for Osama bin Laden As a first step in this battle, the U.S. government organized a massive effort to identify those responsible for the attacks. Officials concluded that Osama bin Laden directed the terrorists. The effort to bring him to justice led the United States to begin military action against Afghanistan. In spite of this military action, bin Laden managed to elude justice for nearly 10 years. But in 2011, U.S. efforts finally paid off when intelligence experts located his hideout in Abbottabad, Pakistan. On May 2, 2011, U.S. Navy commandos raided bin Laden's fortified compound and killed the terrorist leader.

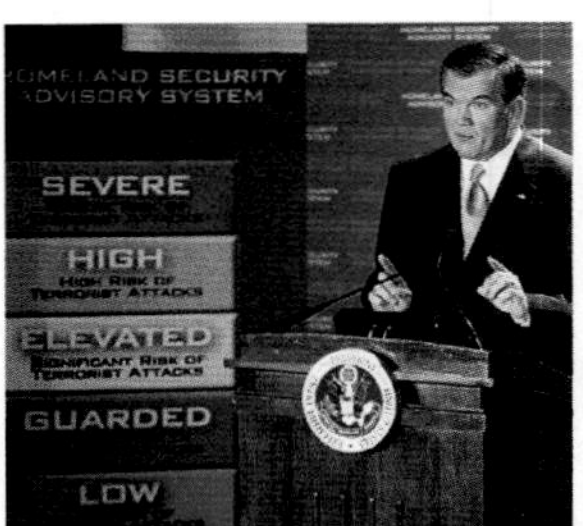

Homeland Security Alert uses a color-coded alert system to communicate effectively with the American public about terrorist threats. The colors begin with green and blue for low and guarded risk of attacks. Yellow and orange are elevated and high risk of terrorist attacks. Red signifies a severe risk of terrorist attacks.

Antiterrorism Measures The federal government warned Americans that additional terrorist attacks were likely. It then took action to prevent such attacks. The **Department of Homeland Security** was created in 2002 to coordinate national efforts against terrorism. Antiterrorism measures included a search for terrorists in the United States and the passage of antiterrorism laws. Officials began detaining and questioning other Arabs and other Muslims whose behavior was considered suspicious or who had violated immigration regulations.

Some critics charged that detaining these men was unfair to the innocent and violated their civil rights. However, the government held that the actions were justified because the hijackers had been Arabs. The government further argued that it was not unusual to curtail civil liberties during wartime in order to protect national security. This argument was also used to justify a proposal to try some terrorist suspects in military tribunals rather than in criminal courts. On October 26, 2001, President Bush signed an antiterrorism bill into law. The law, known as the **USA PATRIOT Act**, allowed the government to

- detain foreigners suspected of terrorism for seven days without charging them with a crime
- tap all phones used by suspects and monitor their e-mail and Internet use
- make search warrants valid across states
- order U.S. banks to investigate sources of large foreign accounts
- prosecute terrorist crimes without any time restrictions or limitations

Again, critics warned that these measures allowed the government to infringe on people's civil rights.

TIERED ACTIVITY

Examine Counterterrorism Controversies

Below Level Ask students to share what they know about Edward Snowden. Have them read an online article about the actions he took to expose some U.S. counterterrorism efforts and why. Then have students find reasons some people condemn Snowden's behavior while others support it. Have students make a two-column chart listing arguments of people on both sides. Finally, ask students each to write a sentence stating their own conclusion about whether what Snowden did was right or wrong.

At Level Divide the class into small groups. Tell students they will research to prepare for a debate about Edward Snowden's actions. Assign half of the groups to support his actions and the other half to oppose them. After students perform their debates in front of the class, ask the class to discuss how the research and debates affected their viewpoint on the issue.

Above Level Ask students to investigate the legality of classified programs that collect the data of Americans as part of counterterrorism efforts. Have students trace the process by which lawmakers and intelligence officials create these programs and how the Justice Department oversees them and ensures that they are in compliance with the Constitution. Have students present the results of their research in a roundtable discussion.

Aviation Security The federal government also increased its involvement in aviation security. The Federal Aviation Administration (FAA) ordered airlines to install bars on cockpit doors to prevent passengers from gaining control of planes, as the hijackers had done. Sky marshals—trained security officers—were assigned to fly on planes, and National Guard troops began patrolling airports.

The Aviation and Transportation Security Act, which became law in November 2001, made airport security the responsibility of the federal government. Previously, individual airports had been responsible. The law provided for a federal security force that would inspect passengers and carry-on bags. It also required the screening of checked baggage.

Airline and government officials debated these and other measures for making air travel more secure. Major concerns were long delays at airports and respect for passengers' privacy. It has also become clear that public debate over security measures will continue as long as the United States fights terrorism and tries to balance national security with civil rights.

Global Effects of Terrorism

For the past 15 years, terrorism has been a pressing global issue. The September 11, 2001, attacks in the United States and subsequent attacks around the world have heightened focus on the issue and its effects.

In July 2005, four suicide bombers attacked central London with backpacks full of explosives. A total of 52 people were killed and hundreds more were injured as the bombers detonated devices on the London Underground and another on a double-decker bus.

Global Security Many countries have faced security issues since 9/11. Bomb attacks on trains and buses in Madrid, London, and Jerusalem spurred Spain, Great Britain, and Israel to investigate ways to use technology to improve security for their transportation systems. Officials hoped that these measures would help to prevent future terrorist attacks.

Many countries have also increased security in other public spaces and at public events, including government buildings, tourist attractions, and public gatherings during festivals, celebrations, and holidays. Many Western countries and some Middle Eastern countries started working together to share intelligence about possible terrorists and terrorist activities. They use surveillance technology to track and record the actions of suspicious people or groups.

Impacts on Economy, Society, and Politics Terrorist attacks have ripple effects through various aspects of society. The economic effects include loss of property, loss of lives, and costs of additional security measures. The insecurity that the population feels after an attack or in anticipation of an attack affects the stock market and international investments. This was a major factor after the 9/11 attacks. Terrorist groups such as al-Qaeda want to disrupt financial institutions worldwide as this builds fear and can lead to financial and economic insecurity. In 2007, al-Qaeda developed a new strategy for attacking the United States by cutting off its energy supply. The attack failed, but had it been successful it would have crippled transportation industries globally and world economies would have been paralyzed. Militants of the terrorist group called Islamic State of Iraq and the Levant (ISIL), also known as ISIS, attacked two separate sites

Objectives

You may wish to discuss the following questions with students to help them frame the content as they read.

- What was the global response to a recent terrorist attack? *Possible answer: After the 2015 Paris attacks by ISIS, Brussels closed its subway system and American lawmakers proposed tougher counterterrorism measures.*
- What effects might the threat of global terrorism have on international travel? *Possible answers: Some people might be more reluctant to travel; airport security may become more onerous and expensive; suspicion towards citizens of foreign countries may increase.*

More About . . .

Globalization and Terrorism A connection can be made between globalization and terrorism. Computers, jets, and other technology have sped up globalization and broken down traditional ideas of sovereign nation-states. At the same time, tools of globalization can be used to spread terror.

Aviation Security In less than two years following the September 11, 2001, terrorist attack, the new Transportation Security Administration spent more than $9 billion on improvements in aviation security. The number of federal airport screeners hired topped 55,000. In spite of these efforts, areas of concern still exist. While passenger baggage was routinely being screened for explosives, the other cargo carried by planes was not being screened. With the large number of ground workers with access to aircraft—including caterers, mechanics, and baggage handlers—thorough background checks of all airport personnel is critical.

ENGLISH LANGUAGE LEARNERS

Write Synopses

1. Have students work in mixed-ability pairs to find current articles on terrorism and responses to terrorist attacks and organizations.
2. Have each student select two articles. In their pairs, have students review the articles to ensure that they understand the article completely.
3. Have partners make a list of the steps that were taken in response to each terrorist attack or organization. Then have partners discuss these steps and rank them in order of how effective they predict each will be in combatting terror. Have pairs share their predictions with the class.

READING CHECK

Compare What issues must a government address when combatting terrorism? *A government must consider how it will fund the expenses of fighting terrorism, such as which domestic programs to cut so that more money can be spent on combatting terrorism. It must also consider which countries to trust to form a coalition or agreement to work together to combat terrorism.*

Print Assessment

Review Ideas, Terms, and People

1. Complete a chart to compare and contrast world terrorist incidents and the September 11 terrorist attacks. Explain how the September 11 attacks were unique and how they were similar to other terrorist incidents. *Possible answer: World Incidents—Munich Olympics, 1972; Tokyo subway attacks, 1995; bombings in U.S. embassies, 1998. Unique—In scale; Similar—Designed to cause death and destruction and gain worldwide attention.*
2. **Key Terms and People** For each key term or person in the lesson, write a sentence explaining its significance. *Explanations of the lesson's key terms can be found on the following pages: terrorism, p. 1295; cyberterrorism, p. 1296; Department of Homeland Security, USA Patriot Act, p. 1302*
3. **Analyze Motives** What might cause individuals to use terror tactics to bring about change? *Possible answer: feel regular political activity won't cause change*
4. **Form Opinions** Is it important for the U.S. government to respect people's civil rights as it wages a war against terrorism? Why or why not? *Possible answers: yes— limiting freedoms means terrorists win; no—we must defeat terrorists, whatever the costs.*
5. **Draw Conclusions** What are the wider international consequences of terrorist attacks? *Possible answers: continued fear, limits on civil rights, the economic cost of fighting terrorism ,and the growth of terrorist attacks globally.*

Passengers wait to go through a security check at La Guardia Airport in New York.

in Tunisia in March and June 2015 and killed 60 people. These terrorist incidents affected the country's tourism industry, a mainstay of its economy. Many people who had planned to visit Tunisia canceled their plans because they feared another attack.

Political effects of terrorism include the destabilization of the government, especially when political leaders are assassinated and new leaders replace them. This could result in a change in a government's policies related to combatting terrorism. However, governments may cooperate with other governments or form military agreements in order to stop terrorism or terrorist activity. This form of global cooperation to fight terrorism has been effective. For example, coalition forces, including the United States military, launched a successful airstrike against several ISIS leaders in September 2015. Yet combatting terrorism causes financial strain. Government leaders must weigh cutting domestic programs in order to fund programs and military spending to fight terrorism.

Reading Check
Compare What issues must a government address when combatting terrorism?

Lesson 4 Assessment

1. Complete a chart to compare and contrast world terrorist incidents and the September 11 terrorist attacks. Explain how the September 11 attacks were unique and how they were similar to other terrorist incidents.

World Terrorist Incidents
September 11 Attacks

2. **Key Terms and People** For each key term or person in the lesson, write a sentence explaining its significance.
3. **Analyze Motives** What might cause individuals to use terror tactics to bring about change?
4. **Form Opinions** Is it important for the U.S. government to respect peoples' civil rights as it wages a war against terrorism? Why or why not?
5. **Draw Conclusions** What are the wider international consequences of terrorist attacks?

ADVANCED/GIFTED

Make a Multimedia Presentation

1. Have students select one terrorist event mentioned in the lesson that they would like to research.
2. Have students research the event. Students should investigate the causes, the event itself, and the consequences, both international and within the country where the attack took place.
3. Then have groups come up with a peaceful alternative by which the people responsible for the terror could have made a similar political point without violence. Groups should present two scenarios in a multimedia presentation: first, the actual scenario as it happened; second, an alternative peaceful version of the scenario. Presentations should compare the consequences of the real and imagined scenario.

Online Assessment

1. How has terrorism changed since the 1960s?
   - ● Terrorists are more influenced by radical religious convictions.
   - ○ Terrorists are more concerned that immigrants will cause social problems.
   - ○ Socialists who resort to terrorism are more likely to demand political change.
   - ○ Nationalists who resort to terrorism are more willing to attack government officials.

   Alternate Question *Select the answer choice from the drop-down list to complete the sentence correctly.*
   Modern-day terrorists spread fear among *civilians* by bombing crowded areas where many people meet, such as restaurants or shopping centers.

2. With which statement would a supporter of al-Qaeda or Hamas agree?
   - ○ Governments should be democratically elected and based on enlightened ideals.
   - ○ Governments should be inspired by the religious values contained in the Old Testament.
   - ○ Muslims who believe in a liberal interpretation of the Qur'an are the true believers of Islam.
   - ● Muslims have an obligation to oppose western influences and to call for a jihad against western nations.

   Alternate Question *Select the answer choice from the drop-down list to complete the sentence correctly.*
   Hamas and Hezbollah have refused to compromise with Israel over a political settlement in *Palestine*, preferring instead to commit terrorist acts against Israeli soldiers and civilians.

3. Who attacked the World Trade Center and the Pentagon on September 11, 2001?
   - ● Arab terrorists
   - ○ drug traffickers
   - ○ Mafia gangsters
   - ○ domestic terrorists

   Alternate Question *Drag the answer choice into the box to complete the sentence correctly.*
   In a seemingly unrelated terrorist attack, letters containing (the) *anthrax bacteria* were mailed to government officials and a news media outlet in Washington, DC, just days after September 11.

4. Which federal executive department was created to combat terrorism within the United States?
   - ○ Department of Justice
   - ○ Department of Defense
   - ○ Department of Foreign Affairs
   - ● Department of Homeland Security

   Alternate Question *Select the answer choice from the drop-down list to complete the sentence correctly.*
   Osama bin Laden was able to hide from the U.S. military for nearly 10 years before his hideout was finally discovered in *Pakistan*.

5. How have many western governments responded to possible terrorist threats to their security since 2001?
   - ○ They have restricted air travel to the Middle East.
   - ● They have shared intelligence about suspected Muslim terrorist plots.
   - ○ They have suspended foreign aid payments to Middle Eastern countries.
   - ○ They have politically isolated Muslim governments suspected of protecting terrorists.

   Alternate Question *Select the answer choice from the drop-down list to complete the sentence correctly.*
   Terrorist attacks on transportation networks in *Madrid*, London, and Jerusalem have prompted western governments to increase the use of technology to monitor main streets and subway stations.

6. **Draw Conclusions** How are many governments combating the spread of terrorism throughout the world?

   Possible answer: Modern-day terrorists often operate on a global scale and have supporters in many countries throughout the world. Often these terrorist groups are supported by governments or wealthy individuals. Governments combating terrorism try to eliminate their sources of funding by seizing international bank accounts or imposing economic sanctions on rogue governments. Since many terrorist groups operate from foreign countries, governments who have been attacked often ignore territorial boundaries and destroy their bases of operation. They try to identify terrorist networks and assassinate their leaders when possible.

7. **Draw Conclusions** How has drug trafficking caused terrorism in Latin America?

   Possible answer: Narcoterrorism is terrorism conducted by drug traffickers to control the distribution of illegal drugs. Countries where drugs are produced, such as Colombia, have been troubled by conflicts between the government, police, and private citizens who often organize themselves into private armies to protect the drug cartels. In Colombia, the left-wing FARC has organized itself into a terrorist group that engages in guerrilla attacks against the government and is funded by drug trafficking.

8. **Make Judgments** How did the September 11, 2001, attacks change the perception of Americans toward terrorism?

   Possible answer: Prior to September 11, 2001, Americans had generally believed that terrorist attacks happened in other countries and that Americans were protected from attacks by radical religious groups. The hijacking of four passenger airplanes changed that perception immediately. Americans now felt vulnerable and targeted by groups willing to resort to suicidal attacks on innocent civilians to achieve their goals.

(continued)

Online Assessment *(continued)*

9. **Make Judgments** Why have some people criticized how the federal government responded to the September 11 attacks?

   Possible answer: The United States government responded to the September 11 attacks by creating the Department of Homeland Security and passing the USA Patriot Act. The Department of Homeland Security coordinates efforts from its numerous domestic security forces and shares information on suspected terrorists that may be in the United States. Critics of the government's handling of the terrorist attac ks believe that these actions have been approved at the expense of people's civil liberties. Critics believe that the federal government has been given powers to monitor people's conversations and intrude into citizens' personal lives.

10. **Make Inferences** How have al-Qaeda's terrorist attacks affected the health of the world's economy?

    Possible answer: Terrorism creates a sense of uncertainty about the future, and uncertainty has a negative effect on stock markets. Investors are less likely to fund projects that may be disrupted by attacks on transportation networks and energy supplies. Since most of the world's oil comes from the Middle East and this is where al-Qaeda operates, its terrorist activities affect the health of the world's economy. Al-Qaeda leaders are aware of the western dependence on oil and have exploited opportunities to disrupt western economies.

ADDITIONAL LESSON CONTENT

COLLABORATIVE LEARNING

Balance Civil Liberties and National Security

1. Divide the class into small groups. Ask each group to choose a time during the Civil War, World War I, or World War II when civil liberties were restricted in the interest of national security. Or they may choose instances such as
   - the Alien and Sedition Act of 1798
   - the Red Scare of the 1920s
   - Cold War anticommunism/McCarthyism
2. Students may learn about the topic by doing research on the Internet, in encyclopedias, or in books.
3. Have students compare previous measures to increase security with the USA Patriot Act and other antiterrorism measures enacted by the United States in response to the September 11 attacks. Students may use a Venn diagram to help them compare and contrast the two examples and draw some conclusions.
4. After groups have shared their charts with the class, conduct a general class discussion about the restriction of civil liberties in the interest of national security.

Lesson 5 Planner

Environmental Challenges

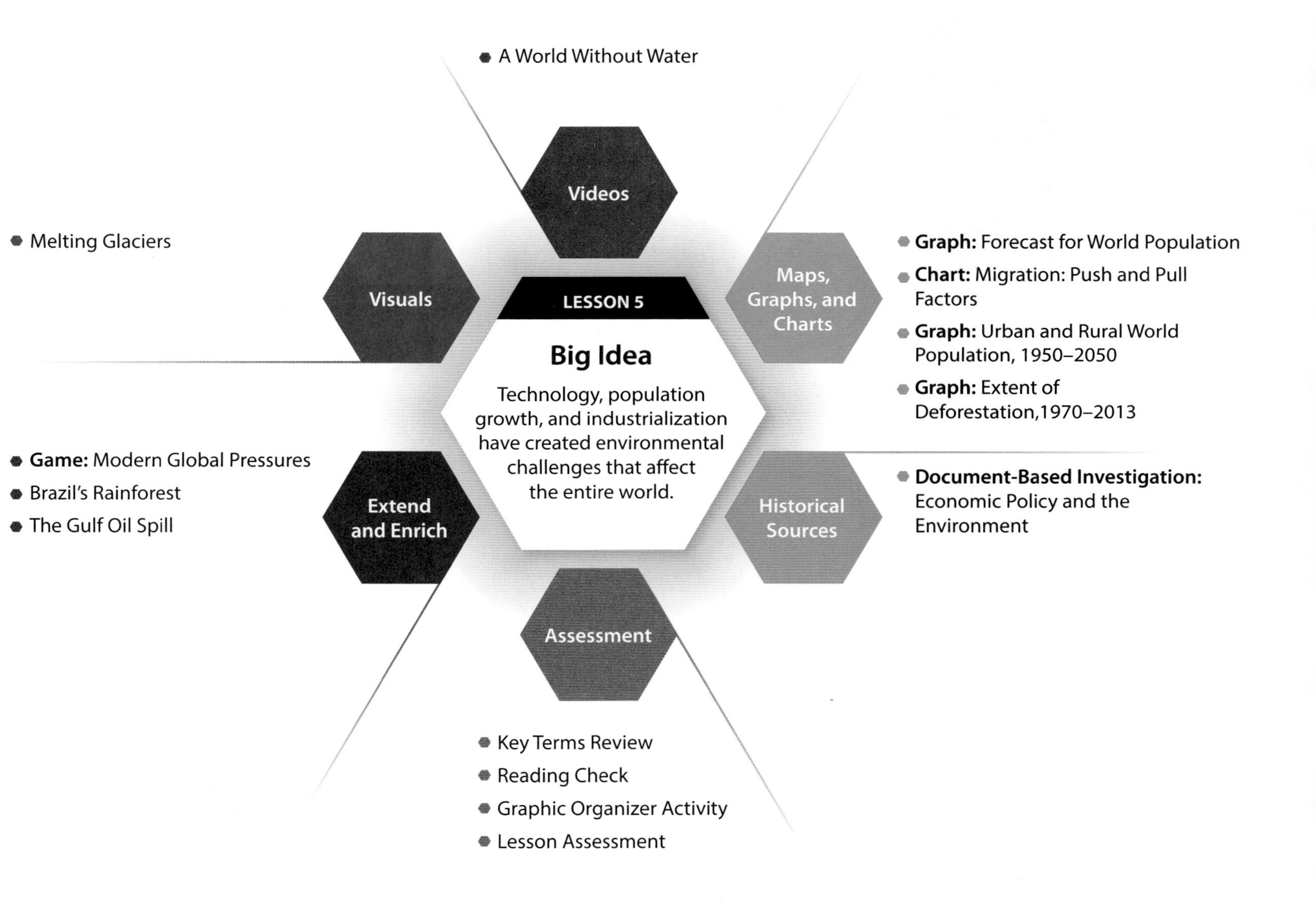

Online Lesson 5 Enrichment Activities

Brazil's Rainforest

Article Students read an article regarding deforestation in Brazil. Then they create a political cartoon that might run in a current newspaper illustrating the environmentalist opinions toward deforestation. Students may wish to research the deforestation concerns in Brazil and consult newspapers for examples of cartoons at this time.

The Gulf Oil Spill

Article Students read an article on the Gulf oil spill and its environmental impact. Then they create an infographic on the impact of the spill. Students research the statistics and data regarding the impact the oil spill has had on wildlife, habitats, communities, and people of the Gulf region. The goal of the infographic is to allow the reader to obtain information in a visually appealing way as well as to draw conclusions.

Lesson 5

Environmental Challenges

The Big Idea
Technology, population growth, and industrialization have created environmental challenges that have affected the entire world.

Why It Matters Now
Failure to solve environmental problems will threaten the health of the planet.

Key Terms and People
desertification
greenhouse effect
conservation

Setting the Stage

As the world's population increases, so do people's demands on the environment. Technology and industrialization have helped to raise standards of living for many people. But they have also affected the global environment. For two centuries, industrialization has increased the demands for energy and natural resources. In addition, industry and technology have increased the amount of pollution on the planet. Pollution and the potential shortage of natural resources have prompted everyone from world leaders to ordinary citizens to look for ways to better protect our natural surroundings.

Development and Population Pressures

The environment has been altered greatly by industrialization and human population growth. As societies have became more sophisticated and developed, populations have increased, resulting in a greater need for resources. As the global population increases, so have industrialization and technology, which have had negative effects on the environment.

Industrialization The Industrial Revolution, which began in Great Britain in the late 1700s, changed human life and greatly impacted the relationship that humans have with the environment. In the process of industrialization, the use of machines replaced human labor in Europe and later North America and other parts of the world. Industrialization affected many aspects of basic human needs, such as food, housing, and clothing. Industrialization produced products faster and in greater quantities. However, this new standard of living took a toll on the environment. Industries relied on fossil fuels for energy sources, including coal, natural gas, and oil. Because of this reliance on the burning of fossil fuels, industrialization caused pollution and many other

Global Interdependence 1305

Teach the Big Idea

1. **Whole Class Open/Introduction** In this lesson, students will read about economic and environmental issues in the developing world. Ask students why the U.S. government might take an interest in such issues. *Possible answers: out of concern for the economically less fortunate; out of interest in new markets and sources of raw materials; out of concern for the impact of the environment on the U.S. economy*
2. **Direct Teach** Read students the Big Idea: *Technology, population growth, and industrialization have created environmental challenges that affect the entire world.* Review the following lesson objectives with students to aid in their understanding of the Big Idea.
   - Identify solutions to population problems, including improving economies, limiting population growth, and improving the status of women.
   - Review concerns about effects of pollution, including the greenhouse effect and destruction of the ozone layer.
   - Describe depletion of natural resources, including rainforests and water.
   - Explore issues raised by energy usage.
3. **Whole Group Close/Reflect** Have students come up with a list of unresolved global environmental problems. Then ask them to create a corresponding list that names people and organizations that they have heard or read about who are working to solve the problems.

Objectives

You may wish to discuss the following questions with students to help them frame the content as they read.

- What conflicts exist within the issue of limiting population growth? *Possible answers: Personal freedoms can be in opposition with public health, as can the beliefs of religious organizations be in opposition with the mandates of government organizations.*
- How might improved economic conditions and improved status of women be related? *Without improved economic conditions, women will have difficulty finding alternatives to traditional child-rearing roles.*

More About . . .

Migration in China China is experiencing an unprecedented level of migration of its people from rural areas to cities. The Chinese government has a goal to move 250 million people from rural areas to cities by the year 2025. To accommodate these masses of new residents, small villages around city perimeters are being leveled to make way for towering skyscrapers. Migrants from rural areas often have better job prospects and enjoy access to modern amenities. However, many find it difficult to leave behind traditional village life—commonly characterized by tight-knit communities centered around ancient temples and shared family histories.

ONLINE DOCUMENT-BASED INVESTIGATION

Global Interdependence

Economic Policy and the Environment is the fifth of six document-based investigations that students will analyze in the Global Interdependence module. Lester R. Brown is president of the Earth Policy Institute, which researches how to attain an environmentally sustainable economy. Invite students to read the excerpt and answer the associated question.

DOCUMENT-BASED INVESTIGATION HISTORICAL SOURCE

Economic Policy and the Environment

ONLINE GRAPHIC ORGANIZER

Environmental Challenges

As students read the lesson, have them use the graphic organizer to take notes. Students can review their graphic organizer notes at the end of the lesson to answer the following question:

Summarize What are some of the environmental problems the world is facing? *The world is facing environmental problems in a variety of ways: In the atmosphere—greenhouse effect, global warming; Natural Resources—water scarcity and destruction of rainforests; Energy—nonrenewable resources, nuclear waste, oil spills*

ONLINE LESSON FLIP CARDS

Review Key Terms and People

Students can use the flip cards in the Lesson Review at any time to review the lesson's key terms and people: *desertification, greenhouse effect,* and *conservation.*

environmental problems that our world faces today. The negative effects of industrialization include global warming, air quality deterioration, oil spills, and acid rain.

Population Growth and Distribution Rapid population growth has also impacted the environment. This growth has challenged governments and societies because it is tied to the increased use of energy and other natural resources, land for agriculture and housing, and waste. In addition to increasing pollution and use of resources, rapid population growth has altered the land. Humans are modifying the environment through deforestation to meet the needs of a growing population, which sometimes leads to **desertification**, the process of land becoming desert. These conditions have caused the rapid extinction of many species.

Advancements in technology and medicine contribute to rapid population growth. The United Nations estimated in 2015 that the world population was about 7.3 billion. Because the birth rate is double the death rate, global population is projected to climb to more than 9 billion by 2050. The world's growing population is not spread evenly across the globe. Africa, for example, is one of the least developed continents. It is expected to supply more than half of the world's population growth between now and 2050.

The world's increasing population is also unevenly distributed among age brackets. About one-quarter of the world's population is under 15 years of age. This substantially large youth population provides countries, especially those that are least developed, with great economic potential.

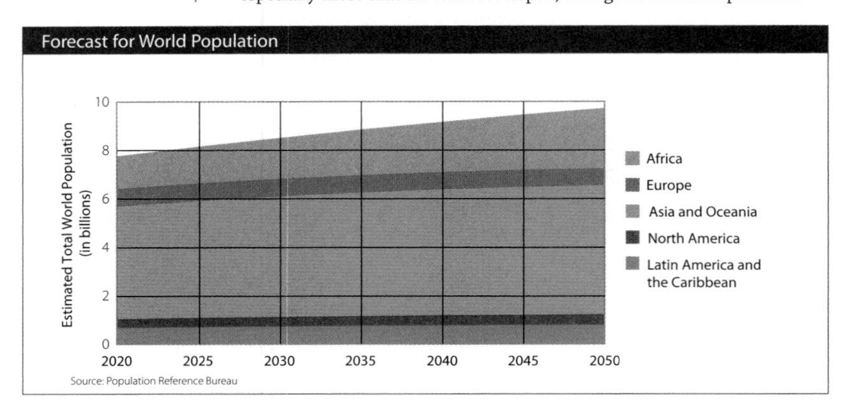

Interpret Graphs
Analyze Issues Which continent is expected to have the fastest population growth between 2020 and the year 2050?

STRUGGLING READERS

Overpopulation: Problems and Solutions

1. Ask individual students to reread the segment "Development and Population Pressures."
2. As a class, complete a chart like the one below to analyze problems and solutions related to overpopulation. Encourage students to do online research to find additional solutions for each of the issues in the chart.

Overpopulation

Definition: *Too many people, not enough food, water, or land*

Problem	Solution
Not enough food	*Green revolution = use fertilizers, weed killers, and bug killers (but can be expensive and hurt environment) Biorevolution = use seeds that scientists have experimented on (better plants, but may causes diseases if not properly tested)*
Economy is weak	
Population is growing too fast	
Women have little chance for an education or good job	

Many of the least developed countries have the largest growing youth populations. When these young people reach working age, their countries will be able to supply a large workforce and perhaps strengthen and expand their economies.

At the same time, according to the World Health Organization (WHO), people are living longer, which places a burden on a young workforce to support an aging population. In 2013, the WHO estimated that the average global life expectancy was 71 years. The causes of this longevity are better nutrition, sanitation, health care, and economic success. The effects of an aging population include social and economic challenges such as providing short- or long-term care.

Population Policies Some regions of the world have enacted population control policies to alter the population growth rate. They have put these policies in place because of concerns about global population growth and its effects on poverty, environmental degradation, and political stability. Some examples of these policies and the countries that implemented them include the following:

China: The one-child policy in China had a significant impact on its population. Beginning in the 1980s, the government imposed harsh fines and other sanctions on most Chinese couples who had more than one child. To encourage couples to follow the policy, the government made contraceptives widely available and offered financial and career incentives. The policy led to an increase in the number of girls being placed for adoption and in sex-selective abortions. As a result, China experienced a shortfall in the female population, creating a higher ratio of boys over girls. In March 2016 the government relaxed its rules to allow all couples to have two children.

India: The Indian government has tried to control its rapid population growth rate through family planning measures, such as the distribution of contraceptives. The central government develops family planning programs and helps states carry them out. The fertility rate in India has declined, but the population still has not reached a stable rate.

Nigeria: The extreme effects of overpopulation have been recognized by the Nigerian government, which has created policies to achieve a lower population growth rate. The government emphasizes contraception distribution, family planning, and fertility management.

Migration Population distribution on earth has also been affected by the migration of people. Humans migrate for a variety of reasons. They may be pushed from their home countries because of political instability or pulled to a new country to seek economic opportunities or to join family members. People can also migrate because of environmental factors. For example, severe damage to the environment, either natural or human-created, can leave people with no other choice but to relocate permanently.

ONLINE INTERACTIVE GRAPH

Forecast for World Population

Have students explore the graph and answer the associated questions.

Interpret Graphs What part of the world has the greatest population? *Asia and Oceania*

In print edition, see graph of the same title.

Analyze Issues Which continent is expected to have the fastest population growth between 2020 and the year 2050? *Africa*

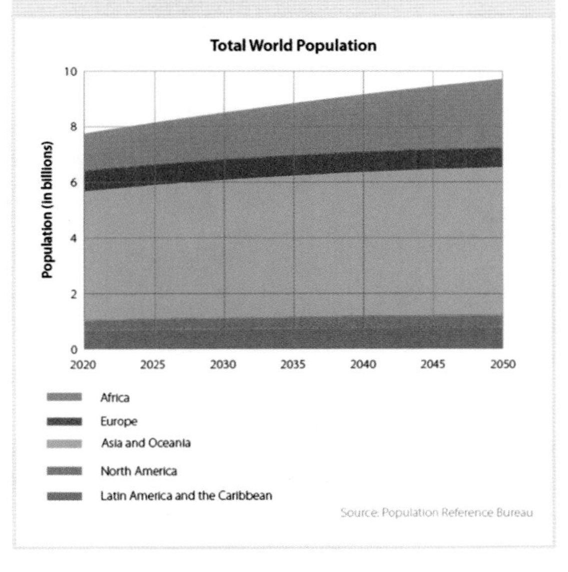

ENGLISH LANGUAGE LEARNERS

Answer Frequently Asked Questions About World Hunger

1. Pair students. Have them read the material under "Development and Population Pressures." Encourage them to consult a dictionary or glossary for help with difficult terms. Then tell students they will focus on the effects that population, climate, and governments have on food supply.
2. Assign each group one of the questions below. Pairs should use information from the lesson and from additional research if necessary to write a complete and thoughtful answer in their own words.
   - How does population affect hunger? *More people have to live on a limited supply of water, food, and land.*
   - How does climate affect hunger? *Lack of rain can limit food supplies.*
   - How do governments affect hunger? *Well-organized governments can get food to places where it is needed. Governments that are poorly organized or at war can prevent food from being farmed or from reaching people who need it.*
3. Ask volunteers to read their answers aloud. Then collect the information in a notebook or binder for classroom reference.

ONLINE INTERACTIVE CHARTS

Migration: Push and Pull Factors

Have students explore the chart and answer the associated questions.

Interpret Charts Which of the following is not a primary cause of people moving to urban areas? *seeking improved access to farmland*

In print edition, see chart of the same title.

Make Inferences Which push factors are most likely to occur in rural areas? *poverty, lack of medical facilities, lack of education, drought and famine*

Migration: Push and Pull Factors

Push Factors	Pull Factors
Poverty in rural areas	Increased job opportunities
Drought and famine	More entertainment opportunities
Poor housing	Increase in standard of living
Lack of medical facilities	Greater access to education and medical care
Lack of education	Family
Disease	

GAME

Modern Global Pressures

Have students play the game to test their knowledge of how commerce and industry impact the environment and where and how the world's population lives by placing items in the correct category.

Migration: Push and Pull Factors

Push Factors	Pull Factors
- poverty - drought and famine - war or other violent conflict - poor housing - lack of medical facilities - lack of education - disease	- increased job opportunities - increase in standard of living - greater access to education and medical care - join family members

Interpret Charts
1. **Make Inferences** Which push factors are most likely to occur in rural areas?

One historical example of this type of migration occurred in the United States. In the 1930s, people migrated from the Dust Bowl to the West because they had overfarmed the land. People could no longer cultivate crops, which was the main economic activity in the region.

In Central America, many people have migrated to cities and coastal areas to seek jobs in industry, shipping, or tourism. In Europe, people have mostly migrated from Africa, the Middle East, and South Asia to Spain, the United Kingdom, Germany, Italy, and France. They often wind up in detention centers, where living conditions can be poor. The costs for the European countries have been high, especially in places like Greece that are economically unstable. The European Commission approved a 2.4 billion euro aid package in August 2015, with much of the money going to Greece to help offset the cost of migrant rescue and support efforts.

In coming years, experts predict an increase in migration as a result of environmental degradation. Environmental changes such as global warming can affect the condition and quality of land and water resources. Food shortages, poverty, rapid urbanization, and political instability can result from such environmental changes. Developing countries suffer the most from these changes. As a result, many people in these countries are forced to migrate to new countries or regions where conditions are better or improving.

Urbanization and Its Effects In many parts of the world, people from rural areas who are in search of jobs or more opportunities are moving in large numbers to urban areas. Some urban areas also are growing due to migration from other cities and to rising birthrates. As a result, the population density in some of these cities, especially those in developing countries, is very high. The world's fastest-growing cities are located in developing countries. The sprawling urban areas of Mumbai, India, and Sao Paulo, Brazil, are examples of rapidly growing cities. Urban growth in developed countries is often much slower, but rapid urbanization is occurring worldwide.

Urban and Rural World Population, 1950–2050

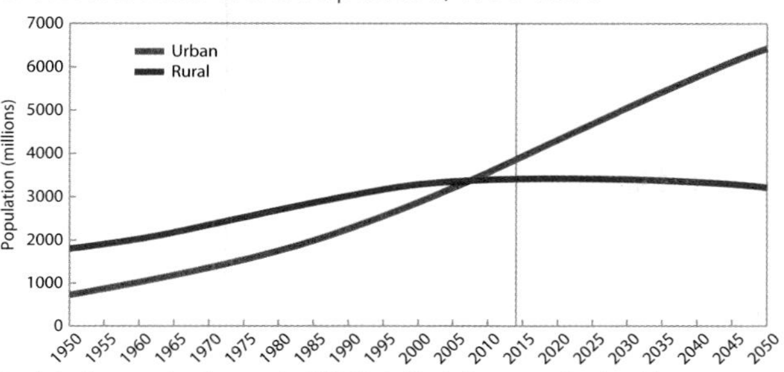

A majority of the world's population lives in urban areas. (Figures after 2014 are based on projected population data.)

Population forecasts given for years after 2014. Vertical line indicates start of projected data.

Source: United Nations

Critical Thinking

1. **Compare** Based on the data in the graph, describe the demographic changes worldwide.
2. **Evaluate** Consult two additional sources such as a world population pyramid and census data. Do you think that the population projections in this graph are accurate? Why?

Along with population growth, the redistribution of population from rural to urban areas can affect the earth's natural systems. Urban development changes the environment—for example, open land is lost when buildings, highways, and railroads are built. Urbanization leads to increased consumption of resources such as food, energy, and water because city dwellers generally have higher incomes and greater access to markets than do rural residents. People who live in urban areas also purchase more durable goods such as appliances and electronics. In the early 1990s, urban Chinese households were two times more likely than rural households to have a television and 25 times more likely to have a refrigerator.

When people alter the natural landscape to meet their needs, they directly affect the environment, including air quality, energy resources, and the local, regional, and global climates. As urban populations continue to grow, planners have to consider many factors when designing or redesigning a city's layout. One of the most important factors is transportation. Roads, mass transit, bike lanes, and other transport systems help determine a city's environmental impact as well as the mobility of its residents.

The effects of urbanization spill beyond the urban areas. In developing countries where rapid urbanization is taking place, agriculture must increase to meet food demands. When more crops are planted, land resources run the risk of being overused. In some urban areas, rapid urbanization has removed fertile land from agricultural production to increase space for housing and other buildings. Urbanization has also caused direct loss to animal habitats and vegetation biomass.

ONLINE INTERACTIVE GRAPHS

Urban and Rural World Population, 1950–2050

Have students explore the graph and answer the associated questions.

Interpret Graphs How is the world demographic forecasted to change? *Urban population is forecasted to increase and rural to decrease.*

In print edition, see graph of the same title.

Compare Based on the data in the graph, describe the demographic changes worldwide. *The world's urban population is increasing, while its rural population is decreasing.*

Evaluate Consult two additional sources such as a world population pyramid and census data. Do you think that the population projections in this graph are accurate? Why? *Yes, because the two other sources show similar data. The data is most likely accurate because the people or groups that are making projections have accurate data and tools to make such projections.*

Objectives

You may wish to discuss the following questions with students to help them frame the content as they read.

- How might economic interests affect scientific research on the greenhouse effect? *Possible answer: Industries that produce greenhouse gases might support research that questions the greenhouse effect.*
- Why might many Asian nations have been slow to pass environmental protection legislation? *Possible answer: to give industries time to develop without the encumbrance of environmental regulations*

More About . . .

Desertification The desertification in the Sahel region of West Africa began in about 1968. It has led to the deaths of more than 100,000 people. Desertification and overgrazing has also led to the deaths of more than 12 million cattle.

Pollution Pollution affects everyone to some degree. The use of polluting substances in the United States also affects relations with other nations. For example, the United States is the world's leading emitter of carbon dioxide. In March 2001, President George W. Bush announced that the United States would not sign the Kyoto Protocol. The purpose of the protocol is to commit industrialized nations to reducing emissions of greenhouse gases such as carbon dioxide.

READING CHECK

Summarize What effect have industrialization and population growth had on the environment? *They have caused changes to the natural landscape, habitat loss, and pollution.*

ONLINE INTERACTIVE VISUALS

Carousel: Melting Glaciers

Have students navigate through the carousel and note similarities and differences among the images or identify a unifying theme.

Reading Check
Summarize What effects have industrialization and population growth had on the environment?

As land is cleared for urban growth, the risks of deforestation and desertification increase. Because development and changes in land use also increase the risk of flooding, city governments need to develop systems for flood control. Officials must use stream-flow gaging stations, rainfall records, and other information to guide flood control operations and emergency action plans such as evacuations.

World Concern over the Environment

Industrial pollution has harmful effects on the earth's atmosphere. Environmentalists are especially concerned about changes in climates due to global warming caused by human activity.

Global Warming Scientists use the term **greenhouse effect** to describe the warming of Earth as a result of the buildup of gases such as carbon dioxide and methane. These gases—sometimes called greenhouse gases—absorb energy radiating from Earth's surface and slow its loss into space. By keeping this energy in Earth's atmosphere and surface longer, the greenhouse effect makes the planet warmer.

Most greenhouse gases occur naturally. But human activities such as the combustion of fossil fuels also release greenhouse gases into the atmosphere, causing additional warming. Over the past two centuries, industrialization has led to increased use of petroleum and coal for manufacturing and transportation. Globalization has also raised emissions of greenhouse gases because international trade requires products to be shipped long distances.

Since the Industrial Revolution, the amount of carbon dioxide in the atmosphere has increased by about 35 percent. Average global temperatures have increased over the same period. Many scientists fear that if

These two photos of Norway's Svartisen glacier, taken approximately 100 years apart, demonstrate how climate change has impacted Earth's geographical features. Research on glacier retreat is important to understanding the impact of global warming.

1310 Module 32

ADVANCED/GIFTED

Report on the Greenhouse Effect and the Ozone Layer

1. Divide the class into groups. After groups have read the passage in this segment about the greenhouse effect, have them do further research on the phenomenon at the library or on the Internet. In addition to researching the greenhouse effect, ask students to gather information on the depletion of the ozone layer.
2. Have students use this information in an oral report. Reports should be 10 to 15 minutes and should include a slide show or other visuals, including diagrams, images, and timelines. Among the topics students might include are the composition of Earth's atmosphere, the different greenhouse gases, ozone, chlorofluorocarbons (CFCs), ultraviolet radiation, and the Montreal and Kyoto protocols.
3. Have students prepare a brief fact sheet to hand out after their presentation. The fact sheet should include brief explanations and contact information, such as phone numbers or web addresses for environmental agencies, that people can use to learn more about the two phenomena.

SOCIAL HISTORY

Kyoto Protocol

The United Nations has attempted to reduce human effects on the environment by persuading member nations to sign treaties to reduce greenhouse gas emissions. One such effort is the Kyoto Protocol, an international agreement that is an extension of the 1992 United Nations Framework Convention on Climate Change. It was adopted in Kyoto, Japan, in 1997, and currently 192 countries have ratified it. The Protocol commits countries to reduce greenhouse gases emissions in response to global warming. The Protocol puts the responsibility to reduce current emissions on developed nations since they were the original contributors to the current levels of greenhouse gases.

global warming trends continue, deserts will expand, causing crops to fail, and polar icecaps will melt, resulting in a rise in sea levels.

To combat this problem, most industrialized nations have called for limits on the release of greenhouse gases. In the past, developed nations were the worst polluters, but future limits would also have a great effect on those countries that are trying to industrialize. So far, developing countries have resisted strict limits. They argue that they are being asked to carry too much of the burden for reducing greenhouse gases.

Air Pollution The hazardous effects of air pollution can be serious, especially when it comes to people's health. Many cities in Europe and the United States have recently taken steps to clean up the air. But air pollution is still severe in many parts of the world, especially in Asia where population growth is high. Many of the world's most polluted cities are in Asia. In countries where population growth is high, rising demand for resources often leads to an increase in pollution. For example, in China, demand for energy soared as the country industrialized. Coal, which is China's main energy resource, is a major pollutant.

Reading Check
Summarize How is industrialization related to global warming?

Meanwhile, South Korea, China, and Japan have entered talks to reduce the effects of pollution caused by China's rapid industrialization. Some cities in China are even trying to reduce air pollution on a local level. Beijing and Shanghai are among the first to implement new emissions standards with the goal of replacing old, polluting cars with new lower-emission-producing cars by 2017.

Depletion of Natural Resources

While air pollution and other environmental problems are major global concerns, so too is the growing strain on natural resources. Vital resources such as clean water, forests, and energy supplies all run the risk of becoming scarce due to industrialization and population growth.

Global Interdependence **1311**

Objectives

You may wish to discuss the following questions with students to help them frame the content as they read.

- How can governments promote the use of renewable resources? *by providing subsidies to industries developing such resources or by regulating nonrenewable resources*
- Can you think of other pollution issues not mentioned in the text? *Possible answers: nuclear waste, noise pollution*

More About . . .

Green Buildings Green buildings are designed to reduce the negative impact the building has on the environment. These buildings use less energy and water and are usually built near public transportation to reduce the need to drive cars. To promote land recycling, the green buildings are built on already developed land.

READING CHECK

Summarize How is industrialization related to global warming? *Because industries rely on burning fossil fuels, they add greenhouse gases to the atmosphere that increase global temperatures.*

ENGLISH-LANGUAGE LEARNERS

Write a Letter to the Editor

1. Have students review the information in the lesson about global warming. Guide students in a discussion about the ways in which scientists believe the problem could be alleviated or perhaps solved. Have students take notes during the discussion and then review their notes in small groups.
2. Have volunteers propose solutions that might work in their own community to solve the problems of global warming. Create a class list for all to see and have students copy the list.
3. Have students use their notes from the class discussion and the class list of solutions to write a letter to the editor describing a solution and steps the community could take to implement it.
4. Have students use proper grammar, style, and a dictionary to help them as they write their letters.

ONLINE ANALYZE VIDEOS

A World Without Water

Have students watch the video individually or as a class. You may wish to use the associated question as a discussion prompt.

Analyze Videos Why is water fundamental to our lives? *Water is necessary for survival, agriculture, and manufacturing.*

Global Patterns

Natural Resources

Natural resources are any materials, substances, or organisms that already exist in nature and are useful to people. They include sunlight, water, land, minerals, vegetation, and animals. The depletion of natural resources has become a major focus of governments worldwide and organizations such as the UN. Some of the causes of depletion of natural resources are mining, petroleum extraction, overfishing, deforestation, and population growth. The increasing consumption of nonrenewable resources, the depletion of forest areas and wetlands, the extinction of plants and animals, and pollution of air and water have caused a serious long-term problem that governments around the world are trying to address.

Natural resources are an important part of a country's wealth and often affect competition in the global market. Many governments make policies that ensure that resources contribute to long-term economic development. Yet, as some nonrenewable resources are becoming scarce, there has been heightened international competition for these resources, especially those that fuel the economy.

Human Effects on Ecosystems Humans rely on ecosystems for crop cultivation and production, clean water, and fish and game. They have depended on these resources and settled near them for millennia. For example, the earliest civilizations, which arose in Mesopotamia, settled near riverbanks to meet their needs. Populations still rely on these resources today. However, human intervention and activities affect ecosystems worldwide. Many of these activities are related to industrialization and development. For example, people who harvest timber cause soil erosion and loss of habitat. Overfishing is another human activity that can cause species to become threatened or extinct, and it can create an imbalance in the natural food web.

The agricultural industry is another example of human activity negatively affecting the environment. Agriculture removes natural vegetation, which can cause soil erosion. Soil erosion can cause rivers to become clogged with silt, and with the lack of shade and moisture in the soil, desertification can occur.

Humans also intervene with natural ecosystems by creating large dams. Dams impact the biological, chemical, and physical properties of river ecosystems. One impact of this human activity is the change upstream of a dam from a free-flowing river to a human-made reservoir. The resulting changes in temperature, chemical makeup, and dissolved oxygen levels are often not suitable for the plants and animals that rely on this river ecosystem. Large dams contribute to the extinction of aquatic species, the disappearance of birds in floodplains, and loss of lands, including forests, wetlands, and farmlands. Larger dams have also led to the erosion of deltas.

Scarcity of Clean Water In the developing world, water pollution and scarcity of clean water are serious problems. Nearly 800 million people have no access to clean water. Eighty percent of all illnesses in developing nations can be traced to inadequate supplies of clean water.

In some parts of the world, nations share the water supplies in lakes and rivers. In southwest Asia, for example, Israel and Jordan share the Jordan River—an essential source of water for farming. Any nation that pollutes shared water or stops water from flowing into a neighboring country runs the risk of starting an international conflict. Many nations try to cooperate to make sure water supplies remain clean.

In the United States, California has complex water issues. The state's large population and agricultural industry have put severe pressure on water resources. The problems worsened during a drought that lasted from 1987 to 1992. However, the state limited the negative effects of that drought by developing new ways to conserve and use water. Beginning in 2011, California entered a new period of drought. Snowmelt slowed and contributed less to reservoirs. Severe fires in drought-stricken areas have devastated California residents and wildlife. Maps, data collected from NASA and other agencies, as well as drought monitoring are tools that the state uses to try to lessen the impact of the drought, but the effects of drought have hurt the state's economy. As people migrate to populated areas, pressure mounts to provide adequate water supplies to meet the needs of a growing population.

In 2015, wildfires raged on in California as moisture levels in trees were at record lows after four years of drought.

Another drought is occurring in the Sahel region of West Africa, where people struggle with desertification. Desertification is caused partly by drought and partly by human activity. The growing population in this region clears the land and cuts down more and more trees for firewood, which is used for fuel and cooking. It also allows livestock to overgraze the land. Without plants to anchor the soil, wind blows away rich soil, making the land useless.

Since water is a vital to sustaining life, some people argue that access to clean water is a necessity that should be affordable to all. However, in places where clean water is limited, the availability and cost of clean water can make it difficult for everyone to have access to it. **Conservation**, or the act of preserving resources, is one way that people can protect clean water. For example, during periods of drought in the United States, local governments restrict the use of water by residents. In South Africa, efforts are being made to make irrigation techniques more efficient in order to save water. However, conservation is difficult to control and enforce.

Destruction of Rainforests Another critical resource issue is the destruction of tropical rainforests in Brazil's Amazon region and in areas of Africa, Asia, and Latin America. The rainforests help maintain water quality, recycle rainfall and oxygen into the atmosphere, and protect

STRUGGLING READERS

Prepare a Public Service Announcement

1. Have students review the information on environmental issues in this lesson.
2. Have students pick one environmental issue and conduct research about it using reliable online sources.
3. Have students prepare a public service announcement about their chosen issue. The announcement should inform people about the environmental problem, its consequences, and ways to help solve the problem. Students might wish to make a multimedia presentation with both video and audio components.

ONLINE DOCUMENT-BASED INVESTIGATION

Economic Policy and the Environment

Lester R. Brown is president of the Earth Policy Institute, which researches how to attain an environmentally sustainable economy and assesses current economic programs around the world. Invite students to read the excerpt and answer the associated question.

Analyze Sources Why does Brown think that the economy is a subset of the earth's ecosystem? *The economy could not exist without the ecosystem.*

DOCUMENT-BASED INVESTIGATION HISTORICAL SOURCE

Economic Policy and the Environment

Lester R. Brown is president of the Earth Policy Institute, which researches how to attain an environmentally sustainable economy and assesses current economic programs around the world.

"Most decisions taken in economic policy are made by economic advisors. You can see this in the World Bank's annual development reports where they see the environment as a sub-sector of the economy. However, if you look at it as a natural scientist or ecologist, you have to conclude that the economy is a subset of the earth's ecosystem. . . . Many of the problems that we face are the result of the incompatibility of the economy with the ecosystem. The relationship between the global economy, which has expanded sixfold over the last half century, and the earth's ecosystem is a very stressed one. The

the soil. The United Nations Food and Agriculture Organization (FAO) estimates that each decade about 500,000 square miles of forest are lost to deforestation. Deforestation results from the burning or cutting down of trees in order to dig mines or to clear land for farming or raising cattle. Loggers clear the land using a technique known as clear-cutting, where they uniformly cut down all the trees in one area. As a result, some species of animals and plants that rely on the forest ecosystem have become extinct or threatened. Experts estimate that between one-half and two-thirds of Earth's plant, animal, and insect species live in rainforests. This loss of habitat could affect all people on the planet.

In recent years, international pressure has led nations like Brazil, which is still a developing country, to make efforts to slow the destruction of the rainforests. Success has been limited, however, by Brazil's desire to develop economically and by its increasing population. The main concern of the

DOCUMENT-BASED INVESTIGATION Historical Source

Economic Policy and the Environment

Lester R. Brown is president of the Earth Policy Institute, which researches how to attain an environmentally sustainable economy and assesses current economic programs around the world.

"Most decisions taken in economic policy are made by economic advisors. You can see this in the World Bank's annual development reports where they see the environment as a sub-sector of the economy. However, if you look at it as a natural scientist or ecologist, you have to conclude that the economy is a subset of the earth's ecosystem. . . .

Many of the problems that we face are the result of the incompatibility of the economy with the ecosystem. The relationship between the global economy, which has expanded sixfold over the last half century, and the earth's ecosystem is a very stressed one. The manifestations of this stress are collapsing fisheries, falling water tables, shrinking forests, expanding deserts, rising carbon dioxide levels, rising temperatures, melting ice, dying coral reefs, and so forth. Not only is this a stressed relationship but a deteriorating one."

—Lester R. Brown
quoted from *Eco-Economy: Building an Economy for the Earth*

Analyze Historical Sources
Why does Lester think that the economy is a subset of the earth's ecosystem?

DEPLETION OF THE BRAZILIAN AMAZON RAINFOREST

Extent of Deforestation, 1970–2013

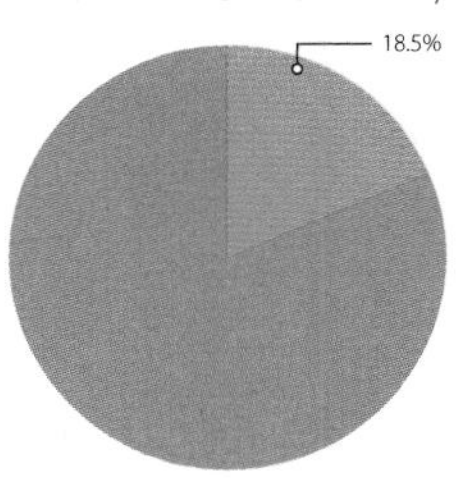

Total area: 4.1 million square miles

Sources: Mongabay.com; Brazilian National Institute of Space Research; United Nations Food and Agriculture Organization

Interpret Graphs

1. **Clarify** How many square miles of the Brazilian Amazon rainforest were deforested from 1970 to 2013?

Brazilian government is to improve the social and economic conditions of its poor population and the indigenous people who live in the rainforests of Brazil. Unlike the United States and other developed countries, Brazil does not have the financial resources or economic strength to put into place environmental policies regarding resource management. In order to diminish deforestation in the Amazon region, the government would have to use substantial financial resources. As one American diplomat explained, "Environmental concerns are a luxury of the rich, and this is not a rich country. Brazilians are not going to just preserve the Amazon. They are going to develop it. The question is, how."

Many other developing nations face the same problem as Brazil. They need to achieve sustainable development, the process of creating economic growth while preserving the environment. The United Nations Economic and Social Council (ECOSOC) has been working with other organizations and countries on sustainable development. In September 2015 the ECOSOC hosted a UN Conference on Sustainable Development to share sustainable development initiatives. In some areas, sustainable development initiatives are seeing positive results The UN estimates that over the past 25 years, the deforestation rate has slowed. It attributes this improvement to better management of forest resources.

Distribution of Natural Resources Resources are not distributed equally around the world, which gives some countries and regions economic advantages over others. Many different organizations such as the International Union for Conservation of Nature and the Hague Institute

ONLINE INTERACTIVE GRAPHS

Extent of Deforestation, 1970–2013

Have students explore the graph and answer the associated question.

Interpret Graphs About many square miles of the Brazilian Amazon rainforest were deforested from 1970 to 2013? *About 800,000 square mile*

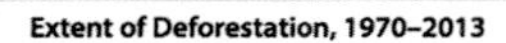

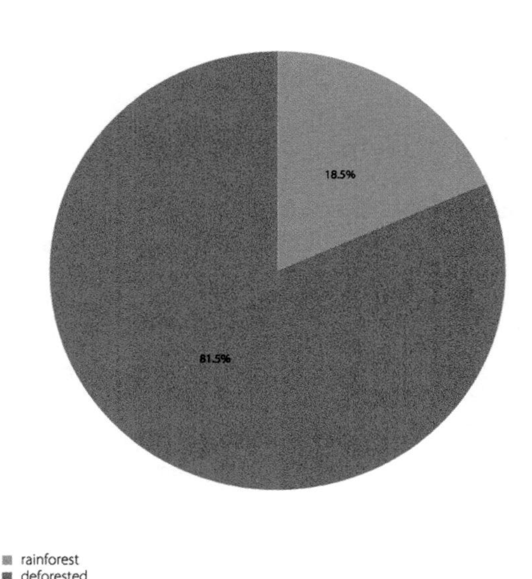

Sources: *Mongabay.com; Brazilian National Institute of Space Research; United Nations Food and Agriculture Organization*

Objectives

You may wish to discuss the following questions with students to help them frame the content as they read.

- Why might leading users of energy be reluctant to curb their consumption? *Possible answer: Cutting back is likely to be difficult and expensive.*
- Why might it be difficult to hold large energy companies responsible for their actions? *Possible answer: They have enormous financial and legal resources at their disposal.*

More About . . .

Facts About Global Warming Spring ice thaw and fall freezing happens 9 days earlier and 10 days later, respectively, than it did 150 years ago. Alaska, western Canada, and eastern Russia's average temperature has risen 5 to 7 degrees over what it was 50 years ago. In 1910, there were approximately 150 glaciers in Montana's Glacier Park; now only 25 glaciers are left. Average global sea level has risen 4 to 8 inches, and the atmosphere's carbon dioxide level has risen to about 400 parts per million.

READING CHECK

Analyze Issues What are the arguments for and against providing access to clean drinking water to everyone? *For—Access to clean water should be available to all, regardless of cost. Against—It's too expensive to provide equal access to clean drinking water.*

for Global Justice work to improve and narrow the inequitable distribution of resources. Such organizations have pointed out that conservation efforts to manage natural resources have unfairly affected indigenous peoples, who often practice and rely on subsistence agriculture.

Developed nations have other advantages that allow them to better access their natural resources. Many industrialized countries have the financial resources and the technology needed to develop their natural resources. Even though some developing countries have abundant resources, they may not have comparable technology or financial means.

As more resources become depleted, people often look to other areas where natural resources can be obtained. Sometimes this affects settlement patterns. For example, if a lake has been used for irrigation and its water is depleted, people may migrate to other areas where they can find water for irrigation, which can cause population shifts. Another example is if people clear a forested area for agriculture but experience high population growth in their village or town, they may need to migrate to new areas in search of more potential cropland. In addition, countries that have larger and increasing populations often use a higher percentage of natural resources than other countries and regions with smaller populations.

Reading Check
Analyze Issues What are the arguments for and against providing access to clean drinking water to everyone?

A Growing Appetite for Energy

Sustainable development depends on using energy sources wisely. Energy sources can be defined as renewable or nonrenewable. Renewable energy sources, such as wind, water, and solar power, can be replenished. Nonrenewable energy sources, such as oil and coal, cannot. Although nonrenewable sources are generally cheaper to use, supplies are limited. Also, their use can cause environmental damage.

U.S. Coast Guard fireboat response crews battle the blazing remnants of the off-shore oil rig Deepwater Horizon in the Gulf of Mexico on April 21, 2010, near New Orleans, Louisiana.

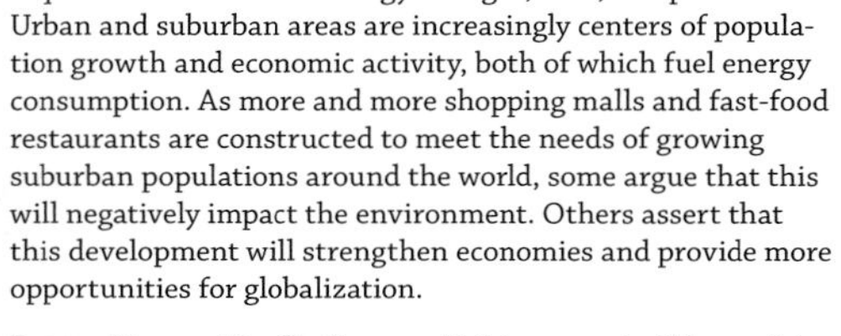

As population growth increases in urban and suburban areas, demand for energy also rises. Larger populations often require the use of more energy for light, heat, and power. Urban and suburban areas are increasingly centers of population growth and economic activity, both of which fuel energy consumption. As more and more shopping malls and fast-food restaurants are constructed to meet the needs of growing suburban populations around the world, some argue that this will negatively impact the environment. Others assert that this development will strengthen economies and provide more opportunities for globalization.

Energy Use and Its Challenges Eighty percent of the earth's energy supply now comes from nonrenewable sources. Developed countries consume most of this energy. North America, Europe, and China are the biggest consumers.

The petroleum industry has contributed greatly to industrialization, but it also contributes to the world's climate change crisis. The extraction and use of petroleum and petroleum products releases harmful toxins into

COLLABORATIVE LEARNING

Renewable and Nonrenewable Energy Sources

1. Ask pairs of students to make a two-column list and to label one side "Renewable Energy Sources" and the other "Nonrenewable Energy Sources."
2. As they read "A Growing Appetite for Energy," have pairs list different energy sources in the appropriate column. *(Renewable—Wind, water, solar; Nonrenewable—Oil, coal, wood, nuclear fuel)*
3. After they have compiled their lists, have pairs design a booklet that informs readers of these energy sources. Booklets must include a cover design, a table of contents, and a short introduction and conclusion. Booklets should feature images of the different energy sources accompanied by written explanations. The text might include information about environmental effects, economic costs, or how much of the energy consumed in the United States is produced by a specific source. Students can draw the images or gather pictures from magazines or other media. Encourage students to be creative and to express an opinion about an appropriate energy policy in their conclusions.

the environment. As much of the global community relies on petroleum to meet its energy needs, it must manage the effects on the environment and practice sustainable development. Other nonrenewable energy sources also have environmental effects. Like petroleum, the burning of coal also contributes to greenhouse gases. Cutting down trees for fuel leads to soil erosion and the expansion of deserts in some areas. Nuclear power plants produce radioactive wastes that can remain hazardous for many years.

The Gulf Oil Spill Oil spills are another example of energy-related pollution. Every year, several serious oil spills take place around the world. They foul water and shorelines and kill sea life. Although oil companies take precautions to prevent spills, spills appear to be an inevitable result of oil use.

The largest oil spill in U.S. history occurred in April 2010 when a drilling rig owned by British Petroleum (BP) exploded in the Gulf of Mexico. The accident spilled millions of gallons of oil along the Gulf coast,

Now and Then

Alternative Fuel Cars

Automobiles, most of which run on gasoline, use a great deal of the world's nonrenewable energy. But perhaps not for long. Automakers have begun creating cars fueled by alternative power, such as hydrogen—one of the most abundant natural elements on earth.

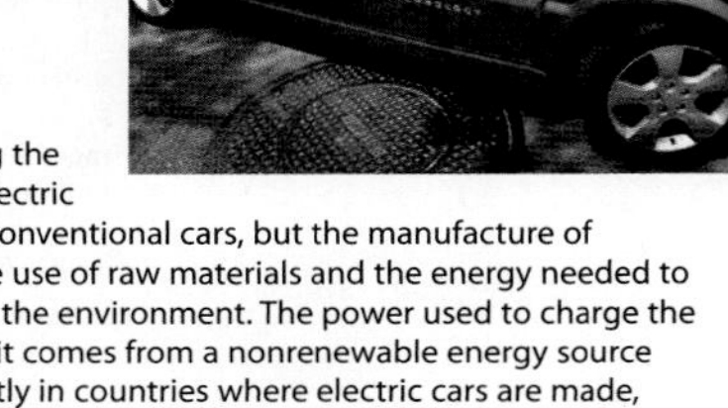

The trend toward environmentally safer vehicles is growing. California, for example, recently required the production of millions of low-emission vehicles—which use a combination of gas and electric power—over the next two decades.

However, some scientists are questioning the environmental hazards of electric cars. Electric cars do not emit hazardous gases as do conventional cars, but the manufacture of electric cars impacts global warming. The use of raw materials and the energy needed to build the lithium ion batteries also affect the environment. The power used to charge the battery contributes to global warming if it comes from a nonrenewable energy source such as coal. Energy is produced differently in countries where electric cars are made, and electricity produced from coal is the most polluting way to generate power. Even though no zero-emission vehicle currently exists, many scientists are working toward building the most environmentally friendly alternative.

NOW & THEN

Alternative Fuel Cars

The success of hydrogen-powered automobiles in limiting the use of nonrenewable sources of energy will depend on how the hydrogen is produced. The National Hydrogen Energy Roadmap indicates that "up to 90 percent of all hydrogen will be refined from oil, natural gas, and other fossil fuels—in a process using energy generated by burning oil, coal, and natural gas. The remaining 10 percent will be [taken] from water using nuclear energy." Therefore, scientists are trying to develop renewable energy sources, such as wastewater, wind, and sunlight.

READING CHECK

Identify Problems What are some problems associated with the use of nonrenewable energy? *Its supply is limited and it can pose a threat to the environment.*

Print Assessment

1. Use the web diagram below to list environmental problems. Which set of problems you consider to be the most serious? *Possible answer: Atmosphere—Greenhouse effect, air pollution; Natural Resources—Water scarcity, destruction of rainforests; Energy—Nonrenewable resources, nuclear waste, oil spills. Most serious—Atmosphere, because it affects the climate of the entire planet.*
2. **Key Terms and People** For each key term or person in the lesson, write a sentence explaining its significance. *Explanations of the lesson's key terms can be found on the following pages: desertification, p. 1306; greenhouse effect, p. 1310; conservation, p. 1313.*
3. **Analyze Issues** How are population growth and urbanization connected to global warming? *Clearing the rainforest supports a lot of Brazil's economic development, but at the same time is creating an environmental challenge for the world as it is a major factor in global warming.*
4. **Form Opinions** Should developing nations have to meet the same environmental standards as developed nations? Why or why not? *Yes—It is important to protect the environment. No—Developing nations deserve the same opportunity to make their economies grow as developed nations have had.*
5. **Compare** What are the environmental arguments for and against globalization? *Possible answer: Some argue that this will negatively impact the environment, while others assert that it will lead to improved technology to manage natural resources.*
6. **Predict** What impact will increased globalization in the 20th and 21st centuries have? *Possible answer: It will cause further stress to the environment and require governments and countries to work together to help relieve some of this stress.*

seriously damaging marine habitats and fishing and tourism industries. BP managed to contain the spill after several months and promised to pay all cleanup costs.

Solutions for the 21st Century Government action and stronger regulations may provide solutions to the world's environmental problems in the 21st century. In the long run, however, improved technology might stand as the best hope for a cleaner environment. More inexpensive ways to use renewable energy sources, such as wind and solar power, may reduce air pollution and global warming. In any event, the nations of the world will need to agree on how to achieve sustainable development in this new millennium.

Some governments have taken action against pollution and global warming by passing laws to protect Earth's air and water. Still, many nations do not have strict pollution controls in place, or even if they have enacted laws they continue to be among the world's largest polluters of the environment. The United States, for example, fits into this category. In the United States and elsewhere, politicians often have difficulty agreeing on a course of action because of differing ideologies. Some nations fear that placing strict limits on the emission of carbon dioxide and other greenhouse gases that contribute to global warming might harm economic development. Preventing and reducing pollution while protecting businesses and economies is a major political and international challenge for governments around the globe.

Reading Check
Identify Problems What are some problems associated with the use of nonrenewable energy?

Lesson 5 Assessment

1. **Organize Information** Use the web diagram below to list environmental problems. Which set of problems do you consider to be the most serious?

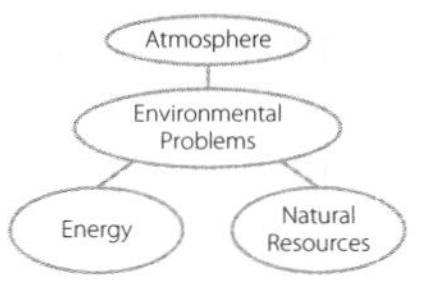

2. **Key Terms and People** For each key term or person in the lesson, write a sentence explaining its significance.
3. **Analyze Issues** How are population growth and urbanization connected to global warming?
4. **Form Opinions** Should developing nations have to meet the same environmental standards as developed nations? Why or why not?
5. **Compare** What are the environmental arguments for and against globalization?
6. **Predict** What impact will increased globalization in the 20th and 21st centuries have?

Online Assessment

1. Which statement explains the effect on a population of having better health care, sanitation, and nutrition?
   - ○ The average life expectancy will decrease.
   - ● Young workers will economically support an aging population.
   - ○ Workers will enter the workforce at a younger age than before.
   - ○ The average worker will need to have more education than before.

   Alternate Question *Select the answer choice from the drop-down list to complete the sentence correctly.*
   In order to control its growing population, *China* instituted a policy allowing a couple to raise only one child.

2. Why are emerging nations reluctant to agree to limitations of greenhouse gas emissions?
   - ○ Emerging nations have larger energy needs than industrialized nations do.
   - ● Emerging nations rely on the burning of fossil fuels to sustain industrial growth.
   - ○ Emerging nations have governments that are unconcerned by scientific predictions.
   - ○ Emerging nations are less impacted by changes in the environment than industrialized nations are.

   Alternate Question *Drag the answer choice into the box to complete the sentence correctly.*
   In 1997, government officials from many countries met in Japan to sign the *Kyoto Protocol*, pledging to reduce greenhouse gases produced by their nation.

3. Which of the following activities is an example of sustainable development?
   - ● harvesting timber from a forest and planting new trees
   - ○ constructing a dam that cuts off the spawning route of salmon
   - ○ clearing portions of a forest and replacing natural vegetation with cotton
   - ○ extracting more tilapia from a lake than the species can naturally reproduce

   Alternate Question *Select the answer choice from the drop-down list to complete the sentence correctly.*
   The United Nations provides developing nations with ideas for sustainable development through (the) *ECOSOC*, and their initiatives have significantly slowed deforestation.

4. Which of the following resources is nonrenewable?
   - ● coal
   - ○ solar
   - ○ water
   - ○ wind

   Alternate Question *Select the answer choice from the drop-down list to complete the sentence correctly.*
   Developed countries, like the United States, Germany, and *China*, use approximately 80 percent of the world's supply of nonrenewable resources of coal, oil, and natural gas.

5. **Compare and Contrast** How are the Indian and Nigerian methods of population control similar?

   Possible answer: Both India and Nigeria have growing populations that, left unchecked, will put further strain on the limited resources of each country. Indian and Nigerian government officials encourage the use of contraceptives to lower the fertility rate in each country. Family planners in each country provide services with the goal of lowering population growth. In Nigeria, the efforts of government officials and family planners have been successful in managing the growing population, but in India population growth has not leveled off.

6. **Analyze Issues** Why does Asia have some of the most-polluted cities in the world?

   Possible answer: Following World War II, Asian countries such as China, Japan, and South Korea industrialized rapidly. Asian cities are some of the most densely populated cities in the world, and this large population demands a large output of electricity. For example, China has large coal deposits and relies on coal to produce the majority of its electricity; as a result, many Chinese cities have polluted air. In fact, 13 of the 15 most-polluted cities in the world are located in Asia.

7. **Make Judgments** Which challenges do developing nations, like Brazil, face when trying to balance economic development and sustainable management?

   Possible answer: The country of Brazil is dominated by the Amazon River Basin. The Amazon rainforest is home to the majority of the world's land and plant species, and its preservation is a top priority for naturalists. Brazil is a developing nation that has used clear-cutting techniques for clearing land for pastures or mining. This has led to extensive soil erosion, damage to the fragile ecosystem, and the extinction of many species. Therefore, Brazil must balance the need for economic development with sustainable use of its land by using land management initiatives that have proven success.

8. **Evaluate** How has the use of nonrenewable resources by industrialized nations led to environmental problems?

   Possible answer: The burning of fossil fuels, such as oil, natural gas, and coal, has released tons of carbon dioxide and other greenhouse gases into the atmosphere, which has been blamed for causing a rise in global temperatures. In less-developed nations, the harvesting of trees for heating houses and for cooking has led to soil erosion and desertification. Even atomic energy, which has been praised for being a technology that does not emit carbon dioxide gases, creates a waste product that is radioactive and is difficult to store for long periods of time.

ADDITIONAL LESSON CONTENT

COLLABORATIVE LEARNING

Region Presentation

1. Point out that natural resources are an important part of a country's wealth. Many governments make policies that ensure that resources contribute to long-term economic development. Yet, as some nonrenewable resources are becoming scarce, there has been heightened international competition for these resources.
2. Have groups of students research a region's natural resources and their relationship to that region's economy.
3. Groups will create a two-part presentation about the region to share with the class. The first part should describe one of the following aspects of the region: climate, geographical features, or human modifications.
4. The second part should discuss how the region's economy is impacted both negatively and positively by that aspect.

Lesson 6 Planner

Cultures Blend in a Global Age

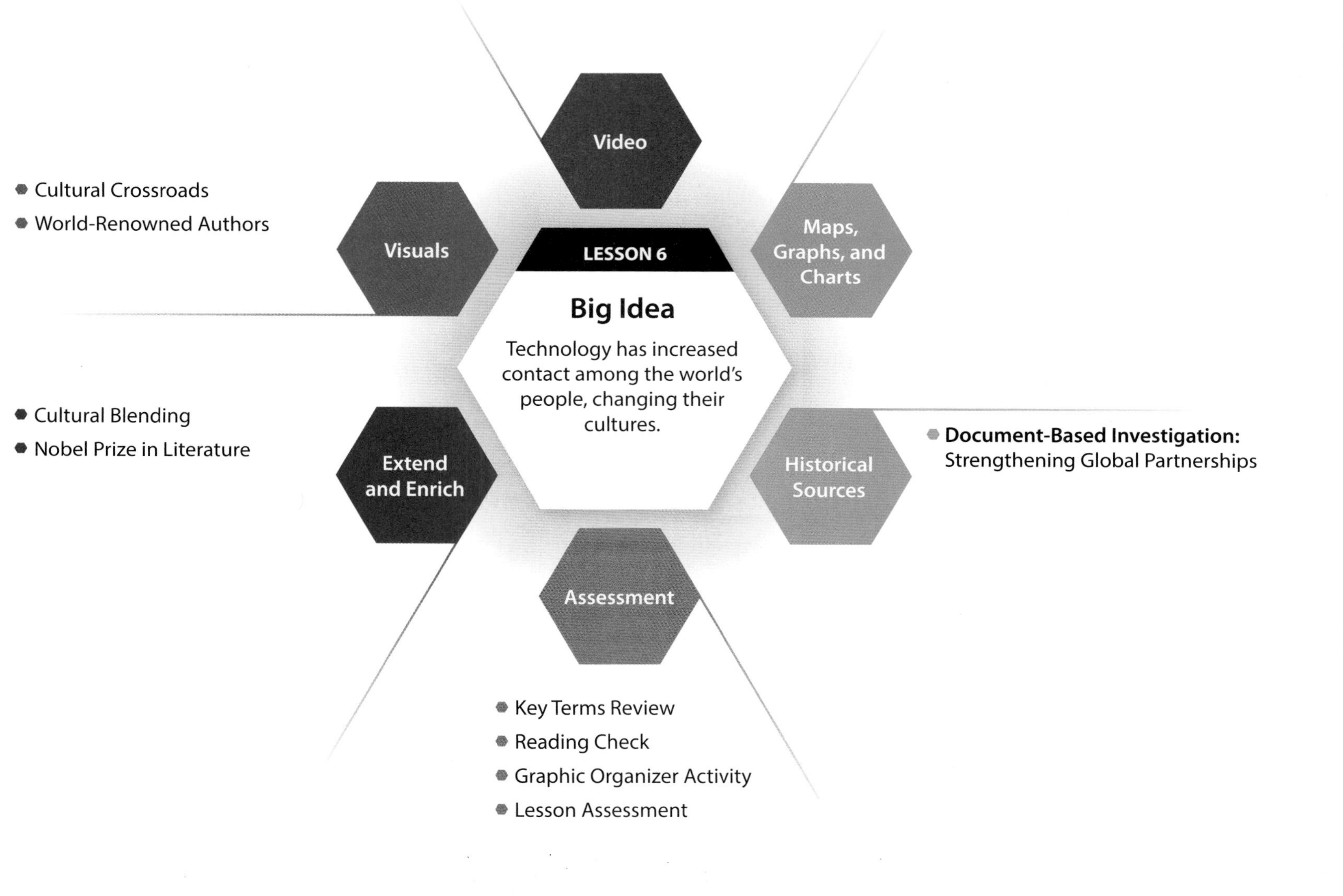

- Cultural Crossroads
- World-Renowned Authors

- Cultural Blending
- Nobel Prize in Literature

- **Document-Based Investigation:** Strengthening Global Partnerships

- Key Terms Review
- Reading Check
- Graphic Organizer Activity
- Lesson Assessment

Online Lesson 6 Enrichment Activities

Cultural Blending

Photo Collage Students create a digital photo collage highlighting cultural blending in a global economy. Focusing on religion, food, clothing, music, or television, students find photos that illustrate cultural blending and write a brief introduction summarizing their collage.

Nobel Prize in Literature

Research Presentation Students research the lives of two influential 20th-century Nobel Prize authors. Then they create a presentation that describes the effects of the authors' work.

Lesson 6

Cultures Blend in a Global Age

The Big Idea
Technology has increased contact among the world's people, changing their cultures.

Why It Matters Now
Globalization of culture has changed the ways people live, their perceptions, and their interactions.

Key Terms and People
popular culture
consumerism

Setting the Stage

Since the beginnings of civilization, people have blended ideas and ways of doing things from other cultures into their own culture. The same kind of cultural sharing and blending continues today. But, because of advances in technology, it occurs at a much more rapid pace and over much greater distances. Twenty-first-century technologies allow people from all over the world to have increasing interaction with one another. Such contacts promote widespread sharing of cultures.

Cultural Exchange Accelerates

Cultural elements that reflect a group's common background and changing interests are called **popular culture**. Popular culture involves music, sports, movies, the Internet, clothing fashions, foods, and hobbies or leisure activities. Popular culture around the world incorporates features from many different lands. Of all the technologies that contribute to such cultural sharing, television, movies, the Internet, and other mass media have been the most powerful.

Mass Media In the United States, 99 percent of American households have at least one television set. In Western Europe, too, most households have one or more televisions. Access to television is less widespread in the emerging nations, but it is growing. The speed at which television can present information helps create an up-to-the-minute shared experience of global events. Wars, natural disasters, and political drama in faraway places have become a part of everyday life.

However, no mass media does more to promote a sense of a globally shared experience than does the Internet. In a matter of minutes, a political demonstration in South America can be captured on a camera phone and uploaded

Teach the Big Idea

1. **Whole Class Open/Introduction** Discuss how international culture affects students' lives. *Possible answers: through the influence of international music, food, and films*
2. **Direct Teach** Read students the Big Idea: *Technology has increased contact among the world's people, changing their cultures.* Review the following lesson objectives with students to aid in their understanding of the Big Idea.
   - Trace the increase in worldwide cultural interaction.
   - Describe influences on world culture.
   - Explain cultural bias and explore possibilities for cultural understanding.
3. **Whole Group Close/Reflect** Have students write lyrics for a song that either describes global cultural blending or is itself an example of global cultural blending.

ONLINE DOCUMENT-BASED INVESTIGATION

Global Interdependence

Strengthening Global Partnerships is the last of six document-based investigations that students will analyze in the Global Interdependence module. Secretary of State John Kerry discussed the relationship between diversity and global interdependence at the launch of the 2015 Global Diaspora Week, an event designed to recognize the contributions made by diaspora communities. Invite students to read the excerpt and answer the associated question.

Objectives

You may wish to discuss the following questions with students to help them frame the content as they read.

- What are some conclusions about American life that people of other countries might draw from American television? *Possible answers: high standard of living; violence*
- What are some common elements that make sports a global phenomenon? *Possible answers: displaying athletic skill in competition, playing games, personal achievement*

More About . . .

Cultural Protection In 2005 the UN Educational, Scientific and Cultural Organization (UNESCO) approved the first international treaty designed to protect cultures from foreign competition. The measure was a response to increasing globalization, which threatens to diminish local cultures. U.S. officials objected to the measure, saying that it could be used to block the flow of ideas, goods, and services. The measure was supported by Canada and Britain, normally among America's closest allies. Only Israel joined the United States in voting against the measure.

ONLINE GRAPHIC ORGANIZER

Cultures Blend in a Global Age

As students read the lesson, have them use the graphic organizer to take notes. Students can review their graphic organizer notes at the end of the lesson to answer the following question:

Summarize Describe some of the popular culture elements that have become international in scope. *Television, music and movies have become international because of the streaming capabilities and the Internet.*

ONLINE LESSON FLIP CARDS

Review Key Terms and People

Students can use the flip cards in the Lesson Review at any time to review the lesson's key terms and people: *popular culture* and *consumerism.*

ONLINE INTERACTIVE VISUALS

Carousel: Cultural Crossroads

Have students navigate through the carousel and note similarities and differences among the images or identify a unifying theme.

In print edition, see Global Patterns of same title.

Make Inferences How have improvements in technology and global communications aided in the blending of musical styles? *Electronic equipment gives musicians more versatility. Modern communications technology provides easy access to music worldwide.*

Analyze Events Write a brief analysis of a major musical development that occurred in the past century.

RUBRIC Analysis should include
- *description of major music developments*
- *impacts of the developments listing musical sources*

Rock 'n' Roll

In the middle of the 1950s, a new style of music emerged on the American scene. It was called rock 'n' roll. The music explored social and political themes. Rock music, which seemed to adults to reflect a youth rebellion, soon became the dominant popular music for young people across the world. As the influence of rock music spread, international artists added their own traditions, instruments, and musical styles to the mix called rock.

▲ **U2**
U2, led by singer Bono, is one of the world's most popular and influential rock bands. Over a career spanning nearly 40 years, this Irish band has kept its music vibrant and fresh by absorbing and reworking all manner of musical styles. The band has drawn on the blues, gospel, 1950s rock 'n' roll, 1960s protest songs, and hip-hop to create a very distinctive kind of music.

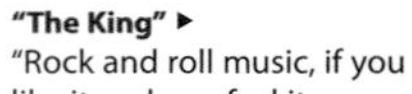

"The King" ▶
"Rock and roll music, if you like it and you feel it, you just can't help but move to it. That's what happens to me, I can't help it."—Elvis Presley, called the "King of Rock 'n' Roll" by many.

"World Pop" ▶
Youssou N'Dour, a singer from the West African country of Senegal, blends traditional African styles with American rock to create a new form that has been called "world-pop fusion."

Critical Thinking
1. **Make Inferences** How have improvements in technology and global communications aided in the blending of musical styles?
2. **Analyze Events** Write a brief analysis of a major musical development that occurred in the past century.

STRUGGLING READERS

Use a Spider Map to Summarize Text

1. Have pairs of students read the text in the "Cultural Exchange Accelerates" segment.
2. Display a concept web with a center bubble labeled *Many cultures are blending.*
3. Label secondary bubbles with the names of broad cultural elements such as *Music, Sports,* and *Mass Media.*
4. As a class, expand the concept web to include specific examples of cultural exchange in each category. For example, for *Music,* students might suggest *Rock 'n' roll, Reggae, Rap,* and *Afropop.*

to an online video community for all the world to see. Blogs, social networking sites, and real-time information networks also transmit the most current news, information, entertainment, and opinions worldwide in the blink of an eye.

Television, the Internet, and other mass media, including radio and movies, are among the world's most popular forms of entertainment. But they also show how people in other parts of the world live and what they value. Mass media is the major way popular culture spreads to all parts of the globe.

International Elements of Popular Culture The entertainment field, especially television, has a massive influence on popular culture. People from around the world are avid viewers of American TV programs. For example, in Bhutan, a tiny country high in the Himalayas, ESPN, HBO, Cartoon Network, and CNN are among the most-watched channels. CNN is a global channel, since it reaches more than 250 million households in more than 200 countries.

Television broadcasts of sporting events provide a front-row seat for sports fans all over the globe. Basketball and soccer are among the most popular televised sports. National Basketball Association (NBA) games are televised in more than 200 countries. In China, for example, broadcasts of NBA games of the week regularly attract an audience in the millions. One of the most-watched international sporting events is the soccer World Cup. Hundreds of millions of viewers worldwide watched the 2014 World Cup final.

Music is another aspect of popular culture that has become international. As the equipment for listening to music has become more portable, there are only a few places in the world that do not have access to music from other cultures. People from around the world dance to reggae bands from the Caribbean, chant rap lyrics from the United States, play air guitar to rowdy European bands, and enjoy the fast drumming of Afropop tunes. And the performers who create this music often gain international fame.

Reading Check
Analyze Effects
What effects have television and mass media had on popular culture?

Now and Then

International Baseball

The sport of baseball is an example of global popular culture. When American missionaries and teachers arrived in Japan in the 1870s, they introduced the game of baseball. Over the years the game gained popularity there. Today, some Major League teams have Japanese players and several American players play in the Japanese league.

Baseball spread to Mexico, Cuba, Puerto Rico, Panama, and the Dominican Republic in the late 19th and early 20th centuries. Today, baseball is a popular game in these and other Latin American countries. About 25 percent of the players in Major League Baseball come from Latin America.

READING CHECK

Analyze Effects What effects have television and mass media had on popular culture? *They have made certain sports, music, and entertainment programs popular internationally.*

NOW & THEN

International Baseball

Baseball gained popularity in Japan in the 1930s when American professional teams toured there. Men from Latin America who learned baseball in the United States taught the sport to local populations in their home countries. Little League baseball began in the 1930s and expanded rapidly around the world after World War II. Today, youngsters in the United States and approximately 30 other nations play the sport.

Objectives

You may wish to discuss the following questions with students to help them frame the content as they read.

- How do the mass media promote materialism? *Possible answers: portray certain lifestyles, create desires for consumer goods*
- How does the Internet promote world culture? *Possible answers: access to international media, museums, and music; e-mail allows less expensive global communication*

More About . . .

The Nobel Prize The award is named for Swedish industrialist Alfred Nobel, who endowed prizes for physics, chemistry, physiology or medicine, literature, and peace in his will in 1895. Thousands of people are involved in selecting a winner from the 100 to 250 nominees per category. Prizes include grants of money.

ONLINE INTERACTIVE VISUALS

Carousel: World-Renowned Authors

Have students navigate through the carousel and note similarities and differences among the images or identify a unifying theme.

World Culture Blends Many Influences

Greater access to the ideas and customs of different cultures often results in cultural blending. As cultural ideas move with people among cultures, some beliefs and habits seem to have a greater effect than others. In the 20th century, ideas from the West have been very dominant in shaping cultures in many parts of the globe.

Westernizing Influences on Different Cultures Western domination of the worldwide mass media helps explain the huge influence the West has on many different cultures today. However, heavy Western influence on the rest of the world's cultures is actually rooted in the 19th century. Western domination of areas all over the globe left behind a legacy of Western customs and ideas. Western languages are spoken throughout the world, mainly because of Europe's history of colonization in the Americas, Asia, and Africa.

Over the past 50 years, English has emerged as the premier international language. English is spoken by about 500 million people as their first or second language. Although more people speak Mandarin Chinese than English, English speakers are more widely distributed. English is the most common language used on the Internet and at international conferences. The language is used by scientists, diplomats, doctors, and businesspeople around the world. The widespread use of English is responsible, in part, for the emergence of a dynamic global culture.

Western influence can be seen in other aspects of popular culture. For example, blue jeans are the clothes of choice of most of the world's youth. Western business suits are standard uniforms among many people. American-style hamburgers and soft drinks can be purchased in many countries of the world. Mickey Mouse and other Disney characters are almost universally recognized.

Some people believe that these changes are largely negative. They argue that mass media and advertising impact group behavior by encouraging the growth of **consumerism**, or the preoccupation with the buying of consumer goods. For example, as individuals in developing countries gain more wealth, many begin to spend their new money on consumer goods from clothing to technological devices to automobiles. This market for consumer goods, some opponents say, is shaped by the media and advertising, rather than by actual needs. Thus, they suggest that globalization is beginning to create a common world culture and is encouraging traditional cultures to lose some of their uniqueness.

Non-Western Influences Cultural ideas are not confined to moving only from the West to other lands. Non-Western cultures also influence people in Europe and the United States. From music and clothing styles to ideas about art and architecture, to religious and ethical systems, non-Western ideas are incorporated into Western life. And cultural blending of Western and non-Western elements opens communications channels for the further exchange of ideas throughout the globe. This cross-fertilization

LINK TO LANGUAGE ARTS

Stage an International Literature Fair

1. Have students survey world literature textbooks or library and Internet sources and choose a work that interests them. They might choose a novel, short story, or poem. English learners might want to read a work in their native language. Make sure that a variety of cultures and literary genres are represented.
2. Have students write a summary and personal response to their work and present it orally in the class literature fair. Encourage students to also describe how the work is representative of the author's culture.

Global Patterns

Bollywood

Bollywood is the largest component of the Indian film industry. Bollywood films are influenced by ancient Indian epics, ancient Sanskrit dramas, traditional folk theatre of India, Parsi theatre, and Hollywood. In the 2000s, Bollywood played a key role in reviving the American musical film genre. The musical film *Moulin Rouge!* was inspired by Bollywood musicals as well as many other musical films.

As a result of globalization, Bollywood films are popular not only with Indians, but also with Nigerians, Egyptians, Senegalese, and Russians. Generations of non-Indian fans have grown up with Bollywood and have witnessed the cross-cultural appeal of Indian movies. Towards the end of the twentieth century and into the twenty-first century, Bollywood has expanded its popularity with Western audiences and music and movie producers.

between cultures can be seen in the Brazilian martial art capoeira. Capoeira combines elements of dance, acrobatics, and music. It originated in West Africa, but West Africans brought it to Brazil during the slave trade in the sixteenth century. Currently, capoeira is practiced around the world.

The Arts Become International Modern art, like popular culture, has become increasingly international. Advances in transportation and technology have facilitated the sharing of ideas about art and the sharing of actual works of art. Shows and museums throughout the world exhibit art of different styles and from different places. It became possible to see art from other cultures that had not previously been available to the public.

Literature, too, has become internationally appreciated. Well-known writers routinely have their works translated into dozens of languages, resulting in truly international audiences. The list of Nobel Prize winners in literature over the last 20 years reflects a broad variety of nationalities, including Turkish, Egyptian, Mexican, South African, West Indian, Japanese, Polish, Chinese, and Hungarian.

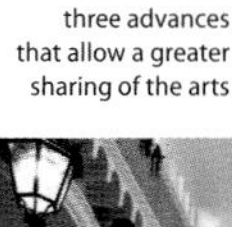

Reading Check
Summarize Name three advances that allow a greater sharing of the arts

Future Challenges and Hopes

Many people view with alarm the development of a global popular culture heavily influenced by Western, and particularly American, ways of life. They fear that this will result in the loss of their unique identity as a people or nation. As a result, many countries have adopted policies that reserve television broadcast time for national programming. For example, France requires that 40 percent of broadcast time be set aside for French-produced programs. South Korea also places significant limits on the amount of foreign programming that can be broadcast.

Inside the Villaggio shopping mall in Doha, Qatar

Objectives

You may wish to discuss the following questions with students to help them frame the content as they read.

- Why is preservation of languages important? *Possible answer: Language is a cornerstone of culture.*
- How do environmental issues bring countries together? *Possible answers: Actions have impact beyond national borders. We all have an interest in protecting Earth's resources.*

More About . . .

Fast Food and Popular Culture Although most countries still favor their own regional cuisines, fast food is now part of world popular culture. Fast food has also expanded far beyond American-style hamburgers. Asian stir-fry, Mexican tacos, Indian samosas, and French croissants are now part of many international fast-food menus.

Television and the Preservation of Culture Television can be a means of promoting traditional, local culture. In Thailand, for example, a form of comedy called *likay*, which has been performed for centuries at provincial fairs, has now been adapted for TV. Someday, these traditional comedies may be exported and become part of global popular culture.

Close Read

Strengthening Global Partnerships Have students explore the Close Read feature to aid in comprehension and understanding.

READING CHECK

Summarize Name three advances that allow a greater sharing of the arts. *Technology, improved transportation, and widespread translations*

ENGLISH LANGUAGE LEARNERS

Create Cultural Self-Portraits

1. Have students create self-portraits that depict both the influence of other cultures on them and the influence of their cultural heritage on American society. Ask students to think about the culture they have inherited from their ancestors, as well as the ways they are shaped by the current cultures within the United States and other countries. Then ask them to think of examples of how their cultural heritage is part of the United States today.
2. Have them first make life-sized outline drawings of themselves. They can either produce their own realistic or impressionistic images or ask a partner to trace their outline on a sheet of butcher paper.
3. Have them fill in their outlines with drawings, words, or objects that express the cultural interactions that make them who they are.
4. Create a class display of students' self-portraits. Use the self-portraits as the basis for a class discussion about how cultural influences can blend and affect personal style and character.

ONLINE DOCUMENT-BASED INVESTIGATION

Strengthening Global Partnerships

Secretary of State John Kerry discussed the relationship between diversity and global interdependence at the launch of the 2015 Global Diaspora Week, an event designed to recognize the contributions made by diaspora communities. Invite students to read the excerpt and answer the associated question.

Analyze Sources Explain the importance of global partnerships, as described by John Kerry. *Global partnerships give countries around the world the aid and support they need to survive and recover from natural disasters, terrorist attacks, and financial crisis.*

DOCUMENT-BASED INVESTIGATION HISTORICAL SOURCE

Strengthening Global Partnerships

Secretary of State John Kerry discussed the relationship between diversity and global interdependence at the launch of the 2015 Global Diaspora Week, an event, designed to recognize the contributions made by diaspora communities.

"[America's] diversity is a strength, not a weakness. And in today's interconnected world, let me tell you: It is also a strategic imperative. This era requires much more nimble institutions, more agile foreign policy. And part of that agility comes from engaging diaspora communities. And the reasons why are pretty simple.

First, we live in a world where the number of people living outside their country of origin has nearly tripled to more than 230 million. The United States has the largest number of diaspora members of any country. . . .

Second, diaspora communities are often the prime movers in

Kenzaburo Oe of Japan was awarded the Nobel literature prize in 1994. Oe studied Western literature in college, and he has used Western literary styles to tell stories about his personal life and the myths and history of his country.

South African writer Nadine Gordimer won the Nobel Prize for Literature in 1991. Many of her novels and stories published prior to 1991 focused on the evils of the apartheid system. As a result, much of her work was censored or banned by the South African government.

Some countries take a different approach to protecting cultural diversity in the media. Television programmers take American shows and rework them according to their own culture and traditions. As an Indian media researcher noted, "We really want to see things our own way." Other countries take more drastic steps to protect their cultural identity. They strictly censor the mass media to keep unwanted ideas from entering their nation.

Sometimes people respond to perceived threats to their culture by trying to return to traditional ways. Cultural practices and rites of passage may receive even more emphasis as a group tries to preserve its identity. In some countries, native groups take an active role in preserving the traditional ways of life. For example, the Maori in New Zealand have revived ancestral customs rather than face cultural extinction. Many Maori cultural activities are conducted in a way that preserves Maori ways of thinking and behaving. In 1987, the New Zealand government recognized the importance of this trend by making the Maori language one of the country's official languages.

1324 Module 32

ADVANCED/GIFTED

Write a Biography of Dr. Muhammed Yunus

1. Have students use the library or the Internet to find out more about the practice of microcredit. Tell them to focus their research on Dr. Muhammed Yunus, a founder of the Grameen Bank of Bangladesh, one of the world's best-known microcredit institutions.
2. Explain to students that they will be writing a short biography of Dr. Yunus to be featured in a magazine of their choosing. As they conduct their research and write their biographies, have them answer the following questions:
   - How did Dr. Yunus get involved with making small loans to poor individuals with no credit?
   - Who typically gets the small loans?
   - What percentage of the borrowers actually pay back the loans?
   - In what ways has this program benefited people in Bangladesh?
3. After they have completed their biographies, have students add a paragraph at the end that discusses how the ideas of Dr. Yunus have been used in other places around the world.

Global Interdependence Despite the fear and uncertainty accompanying global interdependence, economic, political, and environmental issues do bring all nations closer together. Nations have begun to recognize that they are dependent on other nations and deeply affected by the actions of others far away. As elements of everyday life and expressions of culture become more international in scope, people across the world gain a sense of connectedness with people in other areas of the world. For example, the response to the events of September 11, 2001, was international in scope. People from around the world expressed their concern and support for the United States. It was as if this act of terrorism had struck their own countries.

Reading Check
Analyze Effects
How do people react against greater global interdependence?

Throughout history, human beings have faced challenges to survive and to live better. In the 21st century, these challenges will be faced by people who are in increasing contact with one another. They have a greater stake in learning to live together in harmony and with the physical planet.

Lesson 6 Assessment

1. **Organize Information** Create a web listing aspects of international popular culture. Explain which of the aspects has the greatest effect on your life.

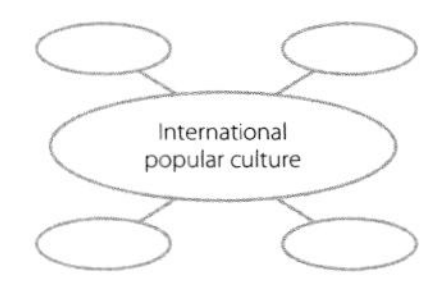

2. **Key Terms and People** For each key term or person in the lesson, write a sentence explaining its significance.
3. **Synthesize** Why are the mass media such an effective means of transmitting culture?
4. **Analyze Effects** Do you think that limiting the amount of foreign television programming is an effective way to protect cultural diversity? Why or why not?
5. **Form Opinions** "Ethnocentrism— the belief in the superiority of one's own ethnic group—has taken hold in the world." Do you agree or disagree? Explain.

READING CHECK

Analyze Effects How do people react against greater global interdependence? *Some people may try harder to stay unique by holding on to parts of their culture such as language and customs.*

Print Assessment

1. **Organize Information** Create a web listing aspects of international popular culture. Explain which of the aspects has the greatest effect on your life. *Possible answer: Television, movies, food, sports, music, art, clothing fashions. Greatest effect—Television, because of amount of time spent watching it.*
2. **Key Terms and People** For each key term or person in the lesson, write a sentence explaining its significance. *Explanations of the lesson's key terms can be found on the following pages: popular culture, p. 1319; consumerism, p. 1322*
3. **Synthesize** Why are the mass media such an effective means of transmitting culture? *Possible answer: because they can be accessed by millions of people worldwide*
4. **Analyze Effects** Do you think that limiting the amount of foreign television programming is an effective way to protect cultural diversity? Why or why not? *Possible answers: Yes—A mix of foreign and national programs supports cultural diversity. No—Limiting other cultures limits diversity.*
5. **Form Opinions** "Ethnocentrism— the belief in the superiority of one's own ethnic group—has taken hold in the world." Do you agree or disagree? Explain. *Possible answers: Yes—More people are returning to traditional ways of life. No—More people are valuing diversity.*

Online Assessment

1. Which of the following statements describes popular culture in the 21st century?
   - American sports and television shows have a limited global audience and influence.
   - The Internet plays a lesser role in spreading popular culture than books or newspapers.
   - New technologies have allowed popular culture to spread faster and farther than before.
   - The Internet has replaced television and radio as the sole technology for spreading information.

   Alternate Question *Select the answer choice from the drop-down list to complete the sentence correctly.* American sports, like *baseball*, have spread throughout the world and are wildly popular in many Latin American countries.

2. Why is English considered to be an international language?
   - English is a very precise language with few ways to misinterpret the meaning of words.
   - Scientists use English to communicate because organisms are classified in that language.
   - English was spoken throughout the British Empire as the language of commerce and government.
   - Scientists use the language at conferences because the most important scientists were American or English.

   Alternate Question *Select the answer choice from the drop-down list to complete the sentence correctly.* While English is the most widely spoken language in the world, *Mandarin* is spoken by the most people.

3. How has France responded to the challenges of preserving its national identity?
   - French cultural shows have completely replaced foreign programs.
   - Internet usage is closely monitored by censors for content and advertising.
   - Television programmers have limited the number of foreign shows aired on their channels.
   - French officials have banned the use of televisions and have heavily censored French newspapers.

   Alternate Question *Select the answer choice from the drop-down list to complete the sentence correctly.* The New Zealand government recognized the danger of losing its native culture to western influences and declared *Maori* an official state language.

4. **Evaluate** How has the Internet influenced popular culture?

   Possible answer: The Internet is the technology by which people can share music, sports information, and fashion trends. Because it is used by millions of people, trends from one country can be readily absorbed by people in other nations. Prior to the Internet, radio, television, and newspapers influenced popular culture, but the Internet allows for popular culture to be appreciated throughout the world as soon as the information can be shared.

5. **Draw Conclusions** How has the western domination of mass media influenced global consumerism?

   Possible answer: Since World War II, the United States and other western nations have produced the most widely viewed movies, television shows, newspapers, and news programs. American culture has spread throughout the world, influencing the types of clothing people wear, movies they watch, consumer products they buy, and food they eat. As the world's population has become wealthier, people become consumers of goods largely influenced by advertising rather than practicality. The spread of western popular culture has had the effect of creating a common world culture that some fear is at the expense of a country's traditional culture.

6. **Make Judgments** How has global interdependence created a global community?

   Possible answer: Despite the cultural differences of each nation, the international community shares the common bond of humanity. This interconnectedness is apparent to most people when political, economic, and environmental issues are discussed among national leaders. People understand that events on one side of the earth often have repercussions at home. As the events of September 11, 2001, demonstrate, the world shared the emotional impact of terrorist attacks on the United States as if their own countries had been attacked.

ADDITIONAL LESSON CONTENT

COLLABORATIVE LEARNING

Cultural Diffusion

1. Organize students into small groups. Have students in each group develop a list of their favorite foods, communication and music items, sports, and entertainment.
2. Have students research the origin of their favorite items.
3. Have students present their findings to the class and explain how these items came to be a part of American culture and daily life. Then guide students in a discussion about cultural diffusion and globalization.

Print Assessment

Key Terms and People

For each term or name below, write a sentence explaining its connection to global interdependence from 1960 to the present.

1. Internet
2. genetic engineering
3. global economy
4. free trade
5. political dissent
6. refugee
7. terrorism
8. USA Patriot Act
9. popular culture
10. consumerism

Explanations of the lesson's key terms can be found on the following pages: Internet, p. 1268; genetic engineering, p. 1270; global economy, p. 1276; free trade, p. 1277; political dissent, p. 1290; refugee, p. 1293; terrorism, p. 1295; USA Patriot Act, p. 1302; popular culture, 1319; consumerism, 1322.

Main Ideas

Use your notes and the information in the module to answer the following questions.

Science and Technology Transform Life

1. In what ways have science and technology changed the lives of people today? *Satellites and computers link the globe in a communications network; how and where people work have changed; diagnoses and treatment of diseases have improved; increased crop yields make more food available.*
2. What was the goal of the green revolution? *to increase food production worldwide*

Global Economic Development

3. How are a developed nation and an emerging nation different? *A developed nation has all the necessary facilities to manufacture goods; an emerging nation is in the process of becoming industrialized.*
4. What is the function of the World Trade Organization? *to ensure that trade among nations flows as freely and smoothly as possible*

Global Security Issues

5. What methods has the world community used to resolve conflicts since World War II? *military alliances, United Nations, arms agreements*
6. What efforts have been made to guarantee basic human rights? *UN Universal Declaration of Human Rights; Helsinki Accords; continued work by UN agencies and international organizations such as Amnesty International to make people aware of human rights violations*

Terrorism

7. What methods do terrorists employ? *violent attacks, biological or chemical attacks, cyberterrorism*
8. How did the United States respond to the terrorist attacks of September 11, 2001? *used military force against the Taliban government in Afghanistan, established Department of Homeland Security to coordinate efforts against terrorism, passed antiterrorism laws, improved aviation security*

Module 32 Assessment

Key Terms and People

For each term or name below, write a sentence explaining its connection to global interdependence from 1960 to the present.

1. Internet
2. genetic engineering
3. global economy
4. free trade
5. political dissent
6. refugee
7. terrorism
8. USA Patriot Act
9. popular culture
10. consumerism

Main Ideas

Science and Technology Transform Life

1. In what ways have science and technology changed the lives of people today?
2. What was the goal of the green revolution?

Global Economic Development

3. How are a developed nation and an emerging nation different?
4. What is the function of the World Trade Organization?

Global Security Issues

5. What methods has the world community used to resolve conflicts since World War II?
6. What efforts have been made to guarantee basic human rights?

Terrorism

7. What methods do terrorists employ?
8. How did the United States respond to the terrorist attacks of September 11, 2001?

Environmental Challenges

9. What natural resources does the world community fear are becoming scarce?
10. How do rain forests benefit the environment?

Cultures Blend in a Global Age

11. Which technologies have had the most powerful impact on cultural sharing?
12. Why have Western influences had a major impact all over the world?

ONLINE DOCUMENT-BASED INVESTIGATION

Global Interdependence

Have students complete and review all the DBI activities in **Part 1.**

Use this Explanatory Essay Rubric to score students' work in **Part 2.**

RUBRIC Students' essays should

- focus on the topic and support it with explanations and facts
- present information logically, clearly, and accurately
- cite at least three sources of relevant text evidence from Part 1 in support of their argument
- be organized into a distinct introduction, a main body consisting of several paragraphs, and a conclusion that sums up the main points

Write an Explanatory Essay Many issues extend beyond national boundaries. Write an essay explaining how people from different nations can work together to make the world a better place. Focus on two or three important issues that relate to globalization. Be sure to cite specific evidence from at least three sources in your response

Module 32 Assessment, continued

Critical Thinking

1. Summarize How is the UN working to address the unresolved problems of the world?
2. Analyze Issues How does globalization affect relationships and economic development among developed and developing countries?
3. Identify Solutions Imagine you are the culture minister of a small country. What steps would you take to ensure that your country's cultural identity is protected? Explain why you think these steps would be effective.
4. Recognize Effects How are individuals affected by the global economy?

Engage with History

Imagine that you are a U.S. economics analyst preparing for a group discussion on the United States' economic system and its impact on society. You may use print and electronic resources to help you gather information. Address the following topics in your discussion:

- GDP
- supply and demand
- competition
- consumer price index (CPI)
- income
- elasticity
- the role of government in the economy

Focus on Writing

Work in groups of four to create a report describing how private enterprises affect politics, the economy, and social life in countries within one of these regions: Africa, Latin America, Europe, or the United States. Each group member should research a different region. Consider the following questions as you research:

- What is a private enterprise?
- How do private enterprises interact with the government?
- Which laws affect private companies?
- Do private enterprises improve economies? How?
- In what ways do private enterprises change the lives of people who work for them or of people in the community?

Multimedia Activity

Work in groups of three to create a multimedia presentation showing how urbanization and industrialization have changed the roles of social institutions such as family, religion, education, and government in many societies. Each group should choose a region, and each person should choose one of the countries listed for that region.

- Africa: Zimbabwe, Kenya, Nigeria, Sierra Leone
- Latin America: Brazil, Argentina, Chile, Mexico
- Asia: China, India, Indonesia, South Korea

Each person should then select one social institution to research for their chosen country. Use the Internet, periodicals, and other sources to research your presentation.

Your presentation should feature historical, literary, musical, and visual materials that relate to your topic.

Global Interdependence **1327**

Essential Question ESSAY

Do the benefits of globalization outweigh the problems it causes?

RUBRIC Students' essays should

- respond to the Essential Question with a specific position
- illustrate valid reasoning supporting their position
- cite persuasive evidence supporting their position
- identify key people, events, and/or turning points that demonstrate understanding of the module content
- be organized into a distinct introduction, main body, and conclusion

Write an argument in response to this question. Your essay should discuss the benefits and problems of globalization. Identify specific economic, political, cultural, and environmental examples. Be sure to cite evidence to support your claim, and organize your essay into an introduction, body, and conclusion.

Alternative Activity Instead of writing essays, address the Essential Question through activities such as holding debates, creating multimedia presentations, or writing journal entries.

Environmental Challenges

9. What natural resources does the world community fear are becoming scarce? *clean water, forests, energy*
10. How do rainforests benefit the environment? *Rainforests maintain water quality, recycle rainfall and oxygen into the atmosphere, and protect the soil.*

Cultures Blend in a Global Age

11. Which technologies have had the most powerful impact on cultural sharing? *television, movies, radio, and other mass media*
12. Why have Western influences had a major impact all over the world? *Western colonization in the 19th century had lasting effects; English serves as an international language; Western popular culture has been widely accepted.*

Critical Thinking

1. **Summarize** How is the UN working to address the unresolved problems of the world? *The UN sends peacekeepers to resolve conflicts around the world; it defends human rights; it makes efforts to ensure that all people have healthy lives.*
2. **Analyze Issues** How does globalization affect relationships and economic development among developed and developing countries? *As a result of globalization, economic development, use of natural resources, and human rights affect countries all over the world, so new policies are needed that enforce individual countries to look out for global interests in these matters. However, these issues are a source of tension, especially in developing countries because those countries are trying to emerge economically and do not have the resources to focus on global effects.*
3. **Identify Solutions** Imagine you are the cultural minister of a small country. What steps would you take to ensure that your country's cultural identity is protected? Explain why you think these steps would be effective. *Possible answer: I would make sure that the existing cultures' traditions, language, and customs would be preserved but that any cultures that were brought in by immigrants to the country would be recognized and they would be allowed to express the cultural identity. By preserving the home culture, the country's cultural identity remains strong, but as new cultures are brought in they can be expressed but not dominant.*
4. **Recognize Effects** How are individuals affected by the global economy? *Individuals have more options for buying consumer goods and have more choices at different prices.*

Engage with History

Imagine that you are a U.S. economics analyst preparing for a group discussion on the United States economic system and its impact on society. You may use print and electronic resources to help you gather information. Address the following topics in your discussion:

(continued)

Print Assessment *(continued)*

- GDP
- consumer price index (CPI)
- supply and demand
- income
- competition
- elasticity
- the role of government in the economy

RUBRIC Discussions should
- address the full range of topics in the prompt
- include facts, statistics, and numerical data to support points
- draw on information from several reliable sources
- include all group members and be conducted respectfully

Focus on Writing

Work in groups of four to create a report describing how private enterprises affect politics, the economy, and social life in countries within one of these regions: Africa, Latin America, Europe, or the United States. Each group member should research a different region. Consider the following questions as you research:

- What is a private enterprise?
- How do private enterprises interact with the government?
- Which laws affect private companies?
- Do private enterprises improve economies? How?
- In what ways do private enterprises change the lives of people who work for them or of people in the community?

RUBRIC Reports should
- have a clear organizational structure
- be well supported by facts
- show evidence of having looked at several reliable sources
- reflect contributions from all group members

Multimedia Activity

Work in groups of three to create a multimedia presentation showing how urbanization and industrialization have changed the roles of social institutions such as family, religion, education, and government in many societies. Each group should choose a region, and each person should choose one of the countries listed for that region.

- Africa: Zimbabwe, Kenya, Nigeria, Sierra Leone
- Latin America: Brazil, Argentina, Chile, Mexico
- Asia: China, India, Indonesia, South Korea

Each person should then select one social institution to research for their chosen country. Use the Internet, periodicals, and other sources to research your presentation.

Your presentation should feature historical, literary, musical, and visual materials that relate to your topic.

RUBRIC Presentations should
- be well supported by facts from reliable sources
- include perspectives of people involved in the form of quotations, stories, or anecdotes
- consist of at least three types of media
- stay focused on the chosen topic

Online Assessment

1. Which NASA program has greatly increased our understanding of stars millions of light-years away?
   - ○ space shuttle program
   - ● Hubble Space Telescope
   - ○ robotic rovers program
   - ○ International Space Station
2. Which of the following is a development of the Information Age?
   - ● The number of Internet users has increased by billions of people.
   - ○ The use of irrigation has allowed farmers to feed millions of people.
   - ○ The use of telescopes has allowed us to better view planets in our solar system.
   - ○ The number of countries using nuclear technology has increased since World War II.
3. *Drag the name of the technology into the box next to its description.*

allows doctors to diagnose neurological issues	●	MRIs
allows doctors to view details of bacteria or viruses	●	electron microscopes
allows scientists to create an exact replica of another organism	●	cloning
allows scientists to identify genes that cause medical conditions	●	molecular medicine

4. Which of the following industries depend on "knowledge workers" to conduct business? Select the **three** correct answers.
   - ● insurance
   - ● financial services
   - ○ transportation
   - ○ textile manufacturing
   - ● market research
   - ○ agricultural production
5. How do organizations promote free trade policies among nations?
   - ● They support the elimination of tariffs.
   - ○ They settle economic disputes between nations by force.
   - ○ They encourage business practices that create monopolies.
   - ○ They endorse the exploitation of workers by multinational corporations.
6. Which organization influences the price of oil throughout the world?
   - ○ IMF
   - ○ UN
   - ● OPEC
   - ○ WTO
7. Which of the following countries have seen ethnic conflicts erupt into warfare since World War II? Select the **three** correct answers.
   - ○ Canada
   - ● Somalia
   - ○ China
   - ○ Spain
   - ● Rwanda
   - ● Sudan
8. Why did president George Bush suspect that Iraq was building weapons of mass destruction and order an invasion of that country in 2003?
   - ○ because the Iraqi government refused to join SEATO in 2000
   - ○ because Saddam Hussein was threatening to invade Kuwait in 2002
   - ○ because Saddam Hussein had ordered a gas attack on the Saudis in 1988
   - ● because the Iraqi government ordered UN inspectors to leave the country in 1998
9. Which disease infects an estimated 214 million people each year, resulting in 438,000 deaths?
   - ○ AIDS
   - ○ SARS
   - ● malaria
   - ○ tuberculosis

10. *Drag the name of the terrorist organization into the box next to its description.*

nationalist group that wants a homeland in Sri Lanka	Tamil Tigers
religious cult that released sarin gas on a Tokyo subway in 1995	Aum Shinrikyo
Basque terrorist group that fought for independence from Spain	ETA
Muslim terrorist group based in Lebanon fighting against the state of Israel	Hezbollah

11. Which of the following are powers granted to the federal government by the USA Patriot Act? Select the **three** correct answers.
    - ● detain for seven days foreign citizens suspected of being terrorists
    - ● allow U.S. banks to investigate sources of funding for suspected terrorists
    - ○ censor newspapers and media outlets critical of the U.S. war on terrorism
    - ● monitor electronic communication and Internet usage of suspected terrorists
    - ○ suspend passports of U.S. citizens who travel to countries that support terrorism
    - ○ imprison U.S. citizens suspected of being terrorists without charging them with a crime

12. How has the Aviation and Transportation Security Act changed airports and air travel?
    - ○ The federal government is now charged with air traffic control, and this has greatly increased the safety of air travel.
    - ○ Local airports are now charged with airport security, and the lack of manpower has resulted in long lines at security checkpoints.
    - ○ Individual airline companies are required to screen their employees more closely, and this has resulted in the loss of airline personnel.
    - ● The federal government is now charged with airport security, and increased security measures have resulted in a loss of personal privacy.

13. *Drag the environmental impact into the box next to its cause.*

clearing trees to create pastures	deforestation
unsustainable practice of overfishing	ecosystem collapse
dependence on coal to produce electricity	acid rain
overuse of land causing the soil to lose its nutrients	desertification

14. Which U.S. state relies on snowmelt to supply water to its extensive agricultural industry and large population?
    - ● California
    - ○ Florida
    - ○ New York
    - ○ International Space Station

15. How do electric cars impact the environment?
    - ○ They emit pollution that is harmful to animals.
    - ○ They use batteries that are inexpensive to produce.
    - ○ They emit greenhouse gases that contribute to global warming.
    - ● They require power sources that are created by burning fossil fuels.

16. *Select an answer choice for each of the drop-down lists to complete the sentence correctly.*
    The global influence of American sports is apparent in *Japan*, where baseball has been popular since American missionaries brought the sport there in the 1870s, and in *China*, where weekly televised NBA games regularly draw a viewing audience in the millions.

17. *Drag the place of origin into the box next to the cultural influence.*

reggae music	Caribbean
rock and roll music	the United States
capoeira martial art	Brazil
Bollywood film industry	India

18. Which statement accurately describes modern literature?
    - ○ The majority of popular works are nonfiction.
    - ○ Modern literature is dominated by female writers.
    - ● Modern literature reflects an appreciation of many different cultures.
    - ○ Almost all of the international literary award recipients are European.

World Religions and Ethical Systems Pages R2–R19 Print Assessment

Main Ideas

BUDDHISM

1. According to the Buddha, how does one achieve happiness and fulfillment? *by detaching one's self from all worldly goods and desires—achieved by following the Noble Eightfold Path, or the Middle Way*
2. Why do Buddhists take special care to avoid killing any living being? *Buddhists believe that all living beings possess the potential for spiritual growth and the possibility of rebirth as humans.*

CHRISTIANITY

3. Why is Jesus central to the Christian religion? *Christians believe Jesus to be the Son of God. They also believe that he died to save humanity from sin and that humans reach salvation by following Jesus's teachings.*
4. What do Christians hope to achieve by following the teachings of Jesus? *They hope to reach salvation.*

HINDUISM

5. What is the importance of the Ganges River in Hinduism? *Sacred site—Hindus believe that it has healing powers.*
6. Who are the three main gods of Hinduism? *Brahma, Vishnu, and Shiva*

ISLAM

7. What is the most important night of Ramadan? Why? *the Night of Power, because it is believed to be the night the angel Gabriel first spoke to Muhammad*
8. What are the Five Pillars of Islam? *faith, prayer, almsgiving, fasting, and pilgrimage to Mecca*

JUDAISM

9. Why do Jews consider the Western Wall to be sacred? *because it is all that remains of the Second Temple of Jerusalem, destroyed around AD 70*
10. In the Jewish tradition, how do people serve God? *People serve God by studying the Torah and living by its teachings.*

CONFUCIANISM

11. Around what five relationships did Confucius believe society should be organized? *ruler and subject, father and son, husband and wife, older brother and younger brother, friend and friend*
12. According to tradition, what does filial piety require of children? *It requires complete obedience to parents during their lifetime and the performance of rituals after their death.*

SIKHISM

13. What are the historical origins and central ideas of Sikhism? *It began in the Punjab region of India more than 500 years ago, when Guru Nanak began preaching his ideas. Central ideas: There is one God, and all people are equal in God's eyes; the path to God requires daily devotion, honest living, and charity.*
14. How has Sikhism spread beyond the Punjab region? *In the mid-1900s, Sikhs began to leave the Punjab in search of better economic opportunities. Today, there are large Sikh communities in Britain, Canada, Australia, East Asia, East Africa, and the United States.*

Critical Thinking

Answers will vary.

1. **Synthesizing** What basic principles do all of the world religions have in common? *doing good; respecting all life; participating in one's community; honoring one's elders; maintaining peace and harmony in the world*
2. **Drawing Conclusions** What role does religion play in people's everyday lives? *provides guidance on daily behavior and on relationships with family, friends, and others*
3. **Making Inferences** Why do you think ritual and celebrations are an important part of all world religions? *Rituals and celebrations enable worshipers of a single faith to come together, thus reinforcing their sense of community. They also teach worshipers about the history, symbolism, and meaning of their religion.*
4. **Forming Opinions** What do you think people hope to gain from their religion? *a sense of peace, belonging, fulfillment; a sense that life has purpose and meaning*

Engage with History

Imagine that you could meet one of the founders discussed in this section. What questions would you ask about his life and beliefs? What views of your own would you share? Take turns role-playing your conversation with a partner. Be sure to use the correct religious terminology in your conversation. Encourage students to brainstorm their question before they begin. Each partner should reread the appropriate pages about the chosen founder.

Focus on Writing

Research to learn more about one of the celebrations you read about in this section. Then write a three-paragraph essay about its origins. Discuss the celebration's history, symbolism, and meaning.

RUBRIC The essay should

- discuss the origins and meaning of the celebration
- describe the customs and symbolism